core JAVA™ 2

Volume II – Advanced Features

Cay S. Horstmann • Gary Cornell

Sun Microsystems Press
A Prentice Hall Title

The publisher offers discounts on this book when ordered in bulk quantities.
For more information, contact: Corporate Sales Department, Phone: 800-382-3419;
Fax: 201-236-7141; E-mail: corpsales@prenhall.com; or write: Prentice Hall PTR,
Corp. Sales Dept., One Lake Street, Upper Saddle River, NJ 07458.

Editorial/production supervision: *Navta Associates*
Acquisitions editor: *Gregory G. Doench*
Editorial assistant: *Mary Treacy*
Manufacturing manager: *Alexis R. Heydt*
Cover design director: *Jerry Votta*
Cover designer: *Anthony Gemmellaro*
Cover illustration: *Karen Strelecki*
Marketing manager: *Bryan Gambrel*
Project coordinator: *Anne Trowbridge*
Interior designer: *Gail Cocker-Bogusz*
Sun Microsystems Press:
Marketing manager: *Michael Llwyd Alread*
Publisher: *Rachel Borden*

10 9 8 7 6 5

ISBN 0-13-081934-4

Sun Microsystems Press
A Prentice Hall Title

Contents

Chapter 2

Chapter 5

Remote Objects, 255

Chapter 6

Advanced Swing, 319

vii

Chapter 8

JavaBeans™, 609

Chapter 9

Security, 701

ix

List of Tables, Code Examples, and Figures

Tables

Code Examples

xiii

Figures

xv

xvii

Preface

To the Reader

The book you have in your hands is the second volume of the fourth edition of *Core Java*. The first edition appeared in early 1996, the second in late 1996, and the third in 1997/1998. The first two editions appeared in a single volume, but the second edition was already 150 pages longer than the first, which was itself not a thin book. When we sat down to work on the third edition, it became clear that a one-volume treatment of all the features of the Java™ platform that a serious programmer needs to know was no longer possible. Hence, we decided to break up the third edition into two volumes. In the fourth edition, we again organized the material into two volumes. However, we rearranged the materials, moving streams into Volume 1 and collections into Volume 2.

The first volume covers the essential features of the language; this volume covers the advanced topics that a programmer will need to know for professional software development. Thus, as with the first volume and the previous editions of this book, we still *are targeting programmers who want to put Java technology to work on real projects.*

Please note: If you are an experienced developer who is comfortable with the new event model and advanced language features such as inner classes, *you need not have read the first volume* in order to benefit from this volume. (While we do refer to sections of the previous volume when appropriate and, of course, hope you will buy or have bought Volume 1, you can find the needed background material in any *comprehensive* introductory book about the Java platform.)

Finally, when any book is being written, errors and inaccuracies are inevitable. We would very much like to hear about them. Of course, we would prefer to hear about them only once. For this reason, we have put up a web site at `http://www.horstmann.com/corejava.html` with an FAQ, bug fixes, and workarounds. Strategically placed at the end of the bug report web page (to encourage you to read the previous reports) is a form that you can use to report bugs or problems and to send suggestions for improvements to future editions.

About This Book

The chapters in this book are, for the most part, independent of each other. You should be able to delve into whatever topic interests you the most and read the chapters in any order.

Chapter 1 covers *multithreading*, which enables you to program tasks to be done in parallel. (A *thread* is a flow of control within a program.) We show you how to set up threads and how to make sure none of them get stuck. We put this knowledge to practical use by example, showing you the techniques needed to build timers and animations.

The topic of Chapter 2 is the *collections* framework of the Java 2 platform. Whenever you want to collect multiple objects and retrieve them later, you will want to use a collection that is best suited for your circumstances, instead of just tossing the elements into a `Vector`. This chapter shows you how to take advantage of the standard collections that are prebuilt for your use.

Chapter 3 covers one of the most exciting APIs in the Java platform: the networking API. Java makes it phenomenally easy to do complex network programming. Not only do we cover this API in depth, we also discuss the important consequences of the applet security model for network programming.

Chapter 4 covers *JDBC™*, the Java database connectivity API. We show you how to write useful programs to handle realistic database chores, using a core subset of the JDBC API. Please note that this is not a complete treatment of everything you can do with the rich JDBC API. (A complete treatment of the JDBC API would require a book almost as long as this one.)

Chapter 5 covers *remote objects* and *Remote Method Invocation* (RMI). This API lets you work with Java objects that are distributed over multiple machines. We also show you where the rallying cry of "objects everywhere" can realistically be used.

Chapter 6 contains all the Swing material that didn't make it into Volume 1, especially the important but complex tree and table components. We show the basic uses of editor panes and the Java technology implementation of a "multiple document" interface. Again, we focus on the most useful constructs that you are likely to encounter in practical programming, since an encyclopedic coverage of the

entire Swing library would fill several volumes and would only be of interest to dedicated taxonomists.

Chapter 7 covers the Java 2D API that you can use to create realistic drawings. The chapter also covers some advanced features of the *Abstract Windowing Toolkit* (AWT) that seemed too specialized for coverage in Volume 1 but are, nonetheless, techniques that should be part of every programmer's toolkit. These features include printing and the APIs for cut-and-paste and drag-and-drop. We actually take the cut-and-paste API one step further than Sun Microsystems itself did: We show you how to cut and paste serializable Java objects between different programs in the Java programming language via the system clipboard.

Chapter 8 shows you what you need to know about the component API for the Java platform—*JavaBeans*™. You will see how to write your own beans that other programmers can manipulate in integrated builder environments. (We do not cover the various builder environments that are designed to manipulate beans, however.) The JavaBeans™ component technology is an extraordinarily important technology for the eventual success of Java technology because it can potentially bring the same ease of use to user interface programming environments that ActiveX controls give to the millions of Visual Basic programmers. Of course, since these components are written in the Java programming language, they have the advantage over ActiveX controls in that they are immediately usable across other platforms and capable of fitting into the sophisticated security model of the Java platform.

In fact, Chapter 9 takes up that security model. The Java platform was designed from the ground up to be secure, and this chapter takes you under the hood to see how this design is implemented. We show you how to write your own class loaders and security managers for special-purpose applications. Then, we take up the new security API that allows for such important features as signed classes.

Chapter 10 discusses a specialized feature that we believe can only grow in importance: internationalization. The Java programming language is one of the few languages designed from the start to handle Unicode, but the internationalization support in the Java platform goes much further. As a result, you can internationalize Java applications so that they not only cross platforms but cross country boundaries as well. For example, we show you how to write a retirement calculator applet that uses either English, German, or Chinese—depending on the locale of the browser.

Chapter 11 takes up *native methods*, which let you call methods written for a specific machine such as the Microsoft Windows API. Obviously, this feature is controversial: Use native methods, and the cross-platform nature of the Java platform vanishes. Nonetheless, every serious programmer writing Java applications for specific platforms needs to know these techniques. There will be times when you need to turn to the operating system's API for your target platform when you are writing a serious application. We illustrate this by showing you how to access the registry functions in Windows.

Conventions

As is common in many computer books, we use `courier type` to represent computer code.

NOTE: Notes are tagged with a "notepad" icon that looks like this.

TIP: Helpful tips are tagged with this icon.

CAUTION: Notes that warn of pitfalls or dangerous situations are tagged with a "Caution" icon.

C++ NOTE: There are a number of C++ notes that explain the difference between the Java programming language and C++.You can skip them if you aren't interested in C++.

The Java platform comes with a large programming library or Application Programming Interface (API). When using an API call for the first time, we add a short summary description, tagged with an API icon. These descriptions are a bit more informal but also a little more informative than those in the official on-line API documentation.

Programs whose source code is on the CD-ROM are listed as examples, for instance, **Example 5-8: WarehouseServer.java** refers to the corresponding code on the CD-ROM. You can also download these example files from the Web.

Definitions

A *Java object* is an object that is created by a program that was written in the Java programming language.

A *Java application* is a program that was written in the Java programming language and that is launched by a Java virtual machine (that is, a virtual machine for the Java platform).

Acknowledgments

Writing a book is always a monumental effort, and rewriting doesn't seem to be much easier, especially with such a rapid rate of change in Java technology. Making a book a reality takes many dedicated people, and it is my great pleasure to acknowledge the contributions of the entire Core Java team.

Our long-suffering editor Greg Doench of Prentice Hall PTR once again did a great job, coordinating all aspects of this complex project. He was ably assisted by Mary Treacy who supplied important attention to detail throughout the production process. Mary Lou Nohr copyedited the manuscript, with an excellent eye for consistency and always on the lookout for Teutonic constructions and violations of the Java trademark rules. Kathi Beste, Bert Stutz, and Marilyn Stutz at Navta Associates, Inc., came through yet one more time for a project that was again on a difficult schedule. A number of other individuals at Prentice Hall PTR and Sun Microsystems Press also provided valuable assistance, but they managed to stay behind the scenes. I'd like them all to know how much I appreciate their efforts. My thanks also to my co-author of earlier editions, Gary Cornell, who has since moved on to other ventures.

I am very grateful to Dan Gordon, Angela Gordon, and Charlie Lai of Sun Microsystems for their conscientious technical help throughout the project and to the excellent reviewing team who found many embarrassing errors and made lots of thoughtful suggestions for improvement. Those reviewers are Alec Beaton (PointBase, Inc.), Joshua Bloch (Sun Microsystems), David Brown, Dr. Nicholas J. De Lillo (Manhattan College), Rakesh Dhoopar (Oracle), David Geary, Rob Gordon, Cameron Gregory (olabs.com), Marty Hall (The Johns Hopkins University Applied Physics Lab), Vincent Hardy (Sun Microsystems), Vladimir Ivanovic (PointBase, Inc.), Jerry Jackson (ChannelPoint Software), Tim Kimmet (Preview Systems), Doug Lea (SUNY Oswego), Bob Lynch, Mark Morrissey (The Oregon Graduate Institute), Mahesh Neelakanta (Florida Atlantic University), Stuart Reges (University of Arizona), Peter Sanders (ESSI University, Nice, France), Luke Taylor (Valtech), Kim Topley, Peter van der Linden (Sun Microsystems), and Burt Walsh.

Most importantly, my love, gratitude, and apologies go to my wife Hui-Chen and my children Tommy and Nina for their continuing support of this never-ending project.

Cay Horstmann

Cupertino, December 1999

Chapter 1

Multithreading

- THREAD PROPERTIES
- THREAD PRIORITIES
- COOPERATING AND SELFISH THREADS
- SYNCHRONIZATION
- ANIMATION
- TIMERS
- THREADS AND SWING
- USING PIPES FOR COMMUNICATION BETWEEN THREADS

You are probably familiar with *multitasking:* the ability to have more than one program working at what seems like the same time. For example, you can print while editing or sending a fax. Of course, unless you have a multiple-processor machine, what is really going on is that the operating system is doling out resources to each program, giving the impression of parallel activity. This resource distribution is possible because while the user may think he or she is keeping the computer busy by, for example, entering data, most of the CPU's time will be idle. (A fast typist takes around 1/20 of a second per character typed, after all.)

Multitasking can be done in two ways, depending on whether the operating system interrupts programs without consulting with them first, or whether programs are only interrupted when they are willing to yield control. The former is called *preemptive multitasking;* the latter is called *cooperative* (or, simply, nonpreemptive) *multitasking.* Windows 3.1 is a cooperative multitasking system, and Windows NT (and Windows 95 for 32-bit programs) is preemptive. (Although

harder to implement, preemptive multitasking is much more effective. With cooperative multitasking, a badly behaved program can hog everything.)

Multithreaded programs extend the idea of multitasking by taking it one level lower: individual programs will appear to do multiple tasks at the same time. Each task is usually called a *thread*—which is short for thread of control. Programs that can run more than one thread at once are said to be *multithreaded*. Think of each thread as running in a separate context: contexts make it seem as though each thread has its own CPU—with registers, memory, and its own code.

So, what is the difference between multiple *processes* and multiple *threads?* The essential difference is that while each process has a complete set of its own variables, threads share the same data. This sounds somewhat risky, and indeed it can be, as you will see later in this chapter. But it takes much less overhead to create and destroy individual threads than it does to launch new processes, which is why all modern operating systems support multithreading. Moreover, inter-process communication is much slower and more restrictive than communication between threads.

Multithreading is extremely useful in practice: for example, a browser should be able to deal with multiple hosts or to open an e-mail window or to view another page while downloading data. The Java programming language itself uses a thread to do garbage collection in the background—thus saving you the trouble of managing memory! GUI programs have a separate thread for gathering user interface events from the host operating environment. This chapter shows you how to add multithreading capability to your Java applications and applets.

Fair warning: multithreading can get very complex. In this chapter, we present all of the tools that the Java programming language provides for thread programming. We explain their use and limitations and give some simple but typical examples. However, for more intricate situations, we suggest that you turn to a more advanced reference, such as *Concurrent Programming in Java* by Doug Lea [Addison-Wesley 1997].

NOTE: In many programming languages, you have to use an external thread package to do multithreaded programming. The Java programming language builds in multithreading, which makes your job much easier.

What Are Threads?

Let us start by looking at a program that does not use multiple threads and that, as a consequence, makes it difficult for the user to perform several tasks with that program. After we dissect it, we will then show you how easy it is to have this program run separate threads. This program animates a

bouncing ball by continually moving the ball, finding out if it bounces against a wall, and then redrawing it. (See Figure 1–1.)

As soon as you click on the "Start" button, the program launches a ball from the upper-left corner of the screen and the ball begins bouncing. The handler of the "Start" button calls the method `bounce()` of the `Ball` class, which contains a loop running through 1,000 moves. After each move, we call the static `sleep` method of the `Thread` class to pause the ball for 5 milliseconds.

```
class Ball
{  . . .
   public void bounce()
   {  draw();
      for (int i = 1; i <= 1000; i++)
      {  move();
         try
         {  Thread.sleep(5);
         }
         catch(InterruptedException e)
         {
         }
      }
   }
}
```

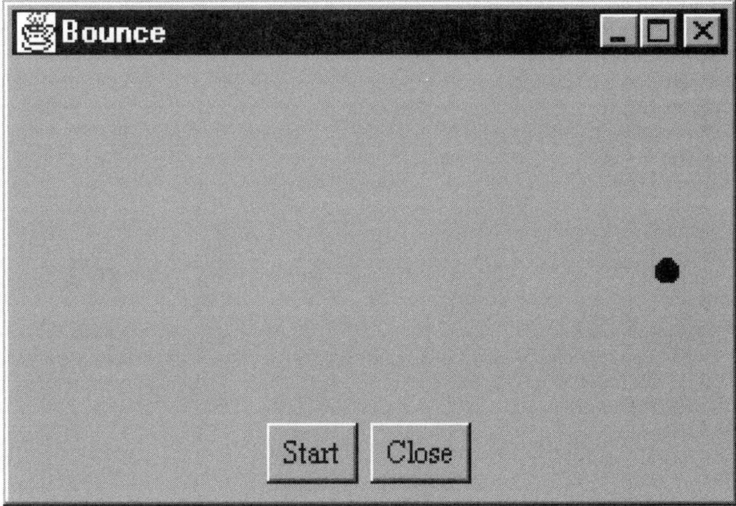

Figure 1–1: Using a thread to animate a bouncing ball

The call to `Thread.sleep` does not create a new thread—`sleep` is a static method of the `Thread` class that puts the current thread to sleep.

The `sleep` method can throw an `InterruptedException`. We will discuss this exception and its proper handling later; we just ignore it for now.

If you run the program, you can see that the ball bounces around nicely, but it completely takes over the application. If you become tired of the bouncing ball before it has finished its 1,000 bounces and click on the "Close" button, the ball continues bouncing anyway. You cannot interact with the program until the ball has finished bouncing.

This is not a good situation in theory or in practice, and it is becoming more and more of a problem as networks become more central. After all, when you are reading data over a network connection, it is all too common to be stuck in a time-consuming task that you would *really* like to interrupt. For example, suppose you download a large image and decide, after seeing a piece of it, that you do not need or want to see the rest; you certainly would like to be able to click on a "Stop" or "Back" button to interrupt the loading process. In the next section, we will show you how to keep the user in control by running crucial parts of the code in a separate *thread*.

Example 1–1 is the entire code for the program.

Example 1–1: Bounce.java

```
import java.awt.*;
import java.awt.event.*;
import javax.swing.*;

public class Bounce
{  public static void main(String[] args)
   {  JFrame frame = new BounceFrame();
      frame.show();
   }
}

class BounceFrame extends JFrame
{  public BounceFrame()
   {  setSize(300, 200);
      setTitle("Bounce");

      addWindowListener(new WindowAdapter()
         {  public void windowClosing(WindowEvent e)
            {  System.exit(0);
            }
         } );

      Container contentPane = getContentPane();
      canvas = new JPanel();
      contentPane.add(canvas, "Center");
      JPanel p = new JPanel();
      addButton(p, "Start",
         new ActionListener()
         {  public void actionPerformed(ActionEvent evt)
            {  Ball b = new Ball(canvas);
               b.bounce();
```

```
         }
      });

   addButton(p, "Close",
      new ActionListener()
      {  public void actionPerformed(ActionEvent evt)
         {  System.exit(0);
         }
      });
   contentPane.add(p, "South");
}

public void addButton(Container c, String title,
  ActionListener a)
{  JButton b = new JButton(title);
   c.add(b);
   b.addActionListener(a);
}

private JPanel canvas;
}

class Ball
{  public Ball(JPanel b) { box = b; }

   public void draw()
   {  Graphics g = box.getGraphics();
      g.fillOval(x, y, XSIZE, YSIZE);
      g.dispose();
   }

   public void move()
   {  Graphics g = box.getGraphics();
      g.setXORMode(box.getBackground());
      g.fillOval(x, y, XSIZE, YSIZE);
      x += dx;
      y += dy;
      Dimension d = box.getSize();
      if (x < 0)
      { x = 0; dx = -dx; }
      if (x + XSIZE >= d.width)
      { x = d.width - XSIZE; dx = -dx; }
      if (y < 0)
      { y = 0; dy = -dy; }
      if (y + YSIZE >= d.height)
      { y = d.height - YSIZE; dy = -dy; }
      g.fillOval(x, y, XSIZE, YSIZE);
      g.dispose();
   }

   public void bounce()
```

```
   {  draw();
      for (int i = 1; i <= 1000; i++)
      {  move();
         try { Thread.sleep(5); }
         catch(InterruptedException e) {}
      }
   }

   private JPanel box;
   private static final int XSIZE = 10;
   private static final int YSIZE = 10;
   private int x = 0;
   private int y = 0;
   private int dx = 2;
   private int dy = 2;
}
```

NOTE: In this example program, we use the XOR drawing mode to simulate the movement of the ball. This makes the program very simple so that you can focus on the thread details as we build up this example. However, the display quality is compromised with this approach since overlapping balls are not displayed correctly. A better approach would be the following: Keep a vector of all balls in a `BouncePanel`. Its `paintComponent` method should ask all balls to draw themselves. Force a `repaint` of the panel in the `move` method. However, we leave this improvement as the proverbial exercise for the reader.

Using Threads to Give Other Tasks a Chance

We will make our bouncing-ball program more responsive by running the code that moves the ball in a separate thread.

NOTE: Since most computers do not have multiple processors, the Java virtual machine uses a mechanism in which each thread gets a chance to run for a little while, then activates another thread. The virtual machine generally relies on the host operating system to provide the thread scheduling package.

In our next program, we use *two* threads: one for the bouncing ball and another for the *main thread* that takes care of the user interface. Because each thread gets a chance to run, the main thread has the opportunity to notice when you click on the "Close" button while the ball is bouncing. It can then process the "close" action.

There is a simple procedure for running code in a separate thread: place the code into the `run` method of a class derived from `Thread`.

To make our bouncing-ball program into a separate thread, we need only derive `Ball` from `Thread` and rename the `bounce` method `run`, as in the following code:

```
class Ball extends Thread
{  . . .
   public void run()
```

```
      {  try
         {  draw();
            for (int i = 1; i <= 1000; i++)
            {  move();
               sleep(5);
            }
         }
         catch(InterruptedException e) {}
      }
   }
```

You may have noticed that we are catching an exception called `InterruptedException`. Methods like `sleep` and `wait` throw this exception when your thread is interrupted because another thread has called the `interrupt` method. Interrupting a thread is a very drastic way of getting the thread's attention, even when it is not active. Typically, a thread is interrupted to terminate it. Accordingly, our `run` method exits when an `InterruptedException` occurs.

Running and Starting Threads

When you construct an object derived from `Thread`, the `run` method is not automatically called.

```
Ball b = new Ball(. . .); // won't run yet
```

You should call the `start` method in your object to actually start a thread.

```
b.start();
```

NOTE: Do *not* call the `run` method directly—`start` will call it when the thread is set up and ready to go. Calling the `run` method directly merely executes its contents in the *same* thread—no new thread is started.

In the Java programming language, a thread needs to tell the other threads when it is idle, so the other threads can grab the chance to execute the code in their `run` procedures. (See Figure 1–2.) The usual way to do this is through the static `sleep` method. The `run` method of the `Ball` class uses the call to `sleep(5)` to indicate that the thread will be idle for the next 5 milliseconds. After 5 milliseconds, it will start up again, but in the meantime, other threads have a chance to get work done.

TIP: There are a number of static methods in the `Thread` class. They all operate on the *current thread,* that is, the thread that executes the method. For example, the static `sleep` method idles the thread that is calling `sleep`.

From a design point of view, it seems strange to have the class `Ball` extend the class `Thread`. A ball is an object that moves on the screen and bounces off the corners. Does the is–a rule for inheritance apply here? Is a ball a thread? Not really. Here, we are using inheritance strictly for technical reasons. To get a thread you

can control, you need a thread object with a `run` method. We might as well add that `run` method to the class whose methods and instance fields the `run` method uses. Therefore, we make `Ball` a child class of `Thread`. Also, it makes the example easy to grasp: every `Ball` object that you construct and start executes its `run` method in its own thread. You will see later in this chapter how you can use the `Runnable` interface to avoid extending the `Thread` class.

TIP: In practice, it is a good idea to *always* implement the `Runnable` interface instead of extending the `Thread` class. However, in this chapter, we generally extend the `Thread` class to make it very clear what threads are executing.

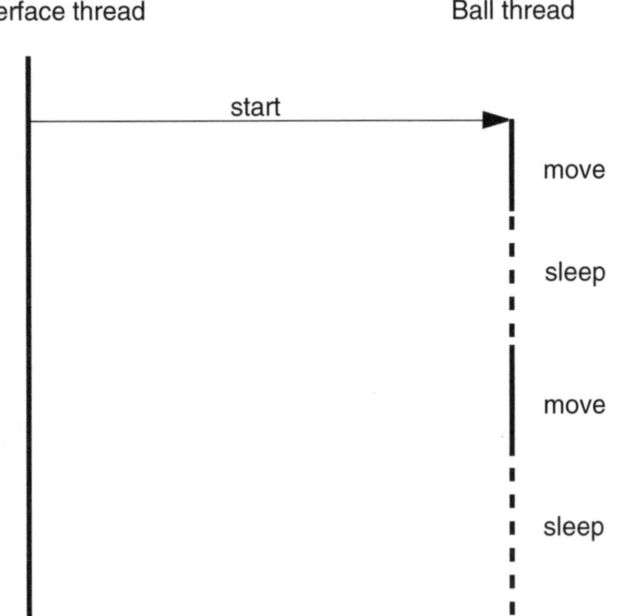

Figure 1–2: The UI and ball threads

The complete code is shown in Example 1–2.

Example 1–2: BounceThread.java

```
import java.awt.*;
import java.awt.event.*;
import javax.swing.*;

public class BounceThread
{  public static void main(String[] args)
   {  JFrame frame = new BounceThreadFrame();
      frame.show();
```

```
    }
}

class BounceThreadFrame extends JFrame
{  public BounceThreadFrame()
   {  setSize(300, 200);
      setTitle("Bounce");

      addWindowListener(new WindowAdapter()
         {  public void windowClosing(WindowEvent e)
            {  System.exit(0);
            }
         } );

      Container contentPane = getContentPane();
      canvas = new JPanel();
      contentPane.add(canvas, "Center");
      JPanel p = new JPanel();
      addButton(p, "Start",
         new ActionListener()
         {  public void actionPerformed(ActionEvent evt)
            {  Ball b = new Ball(canvas);
               b.start();
            }
         });

      addButton(p, "Close",
         new ActionListener()
         {  public void actionPerformed(ActionEvent evt)
            {  canvas.setVisible(false);
               System.exit(0);
            }
         });
      contentPane.add(p, "South");
   }

   public void addButton(Container c, String title,
      ActionListener a)
   {  JButton b = new JButton(title);
      c.add(b);
      b.addActionListener(a);
   }

   private JPanel canvas;
}

class Ball extends Thread
```

```
{  public Ball(JPanel b) { box = b; }

   public void draw()
   {  Graphics g = box.getGraphics();
      g.fillOval(x, y, XSIZE, YSIZE);
      g.dispose();
   }

   public void move()
   {  if (!box.isVisible()) return;
      Graphics g = box.getGraphics();
      g.setXORMode(box.getBackground());
      g.fillOval(x, y, XSIZE, YSIZE);
      x += dx;
      y += dy;
      Dimension d = box.getSize();
      if (x < 0)
      { x = 0; dx = -dx; }
      if (x + XSIZE >= d.width)
      { x = d.width - XSIZE; dx = -dx; }
      if (y < 0)
      { y = 0; dy = -dy; }
      if (y + YSIZE >= d.height)
      { y = d.height - YSIZE; dy = -dy; }
      g.fillOval(x, y, XSIZE, YSIZE);
      g.dispose();
   }

   public void run()
   {  try
      {  draw();
         for (int i = 1; i <= 1000; i++)
         {  move();
            sleep(5);
         }
      }
      catch(InterruptedException e) {}
   }

   private JPanel box;
   private static final int XSIZE = 10;
   private static final int YSIZE = 10;
   private int x = 0;
   private int y = 0;
   private int dx = 2;
   private int dy = 2;
}
```

`java.lang.Thread`

- `Thread()`

  constructs a new thread. You must `start` the thread to activate its `run` method.

- `void run()`

  You must override this function and add the code that you want to have executed in the thread.

- `void start()`

  starts this thread, causing the `run()` method to be called. This method will return immediately. The new thread runs concurrently.

- `static void sleep(long millis)`

  puts the currently executing thread to sleep for the specified number of milli-seconds. Note that this is a static method.

Running Multiple Threads

Run the program in the preceding section. Now, click on the "Start" button again while a ball is running. Click on it a few more times. You will see a whole bunch of balls bouncing away, as captured in Figure 1–3. Each ball will move 1,000 times until it comes to its final resting place.

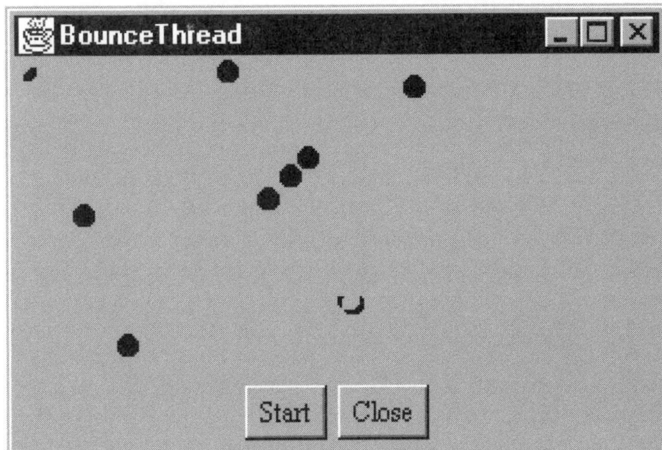

Figure 1–3: Multiple threads

This example demonstrates a great advantage of the thread architecture in the Java programming language. It is very easy to create any number of autonomous objects that appear to run in parallel.

You can enumerate the currently running threads—see the API note in the "Thread Groups" section.

Thread Properties

Thread States

Threads can be in one of four states:

- new
- runnable
- blocked
- dead

Each of these states is explained as follows.

New threads

When you create a thread with the `new` operator—for example, `new Ball()`—the thread is not yet running. This means that it is in the *new* state. When a thread is in the new state, the program has not started executing code inside of it. A certain amount of bookkeeping needs to be done before a thread can run. Doing the bookkeeping and allocating the needed resources are the tasks of the `start` method.

Runnable threads

Once you invoke the `start` method, the thread is *runnable.* A runnable thread may not yet be running. It is up to the operating system to give the thread time to run. When the code inside the thread begins executing, the thread is *running.* (The Java platform documentation does not call this a separate state, though. A running thread is still in the runnable state.)

How this happens is up to the operating system. The thread package in the Java platform needs to work with the underlying operating system. Only the operating system can provide the CPU cycles. The so-called *green threads* package that is used by the Java 1.x platform on Solaris, for example, keeps a running thread active until a higher-priority thread awakes and takes control. Other thread systems (such as Windows 95 and Windows NT) give each runnable thread a slice of time to perform its task. When that slice of time is exhausted, the operating system gives another thread an opportunity to work. This approach is more sophisticated and makes better use of the multithreading capabilities of the Java programming language. Current releases of the Java platform on Solaris can be configured to allow use of the native Solaris threads, which also perform time-slicing.

Always keep in mind that a runnable thread may or may not be running at any given time. (This is why the state is called "runnable" and not "running.") See Figure 1–4.

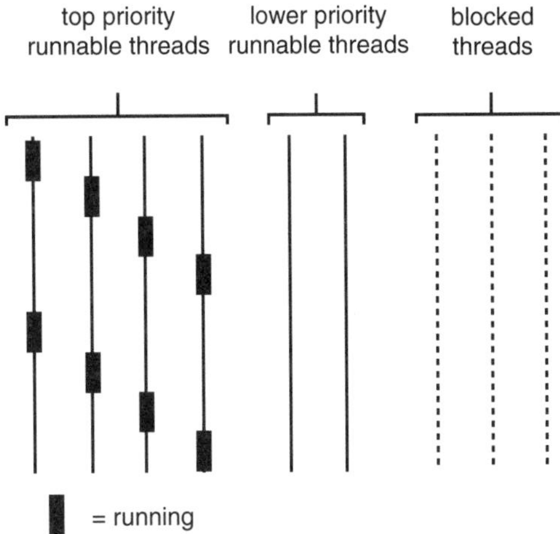

Figure 1–4: Time-slicing on a single CPU

Blocked threads

A thread enters the *blocked* state when one of the following actions occurs:

1. Someone calls the `sleep()` method of the thread.
2. The thread calls an operation that is *blocking on input/output*, that is, an operation that will not return to its caller until input and output operations are complete.
3. The thread calls the `wait()` method.
4. The thread tries to lock an object that is currently locked by another thread. We will discuss object locks later in this chapter.
5. Someone calls the `suspend()` method of the thread. However, this method is deprecated, and you should not call it in your code. We will explain the reason later in this chapter.

Figure 1–5 shows the states that a thread can have and the possible transitions from one state to another. When a thread is blocked (or, of course, when it dies), another thread is scheduled to run. When a blocked thread is reactivated (for example, because it has slept the required number of milliseconds or because the I/O it waited for is complete), the scheduler checks to see if it has a higher priority than the currently running thread. If so, it *preempts* the current thread and picks a new thread to run. (On a machine with multiple processors, each processor can run a thread, and you can have multiple threads run in parallel. On such a machine, a thread is only preempted if a higher priority thread becomes runnable and there is no available processor to run it.)

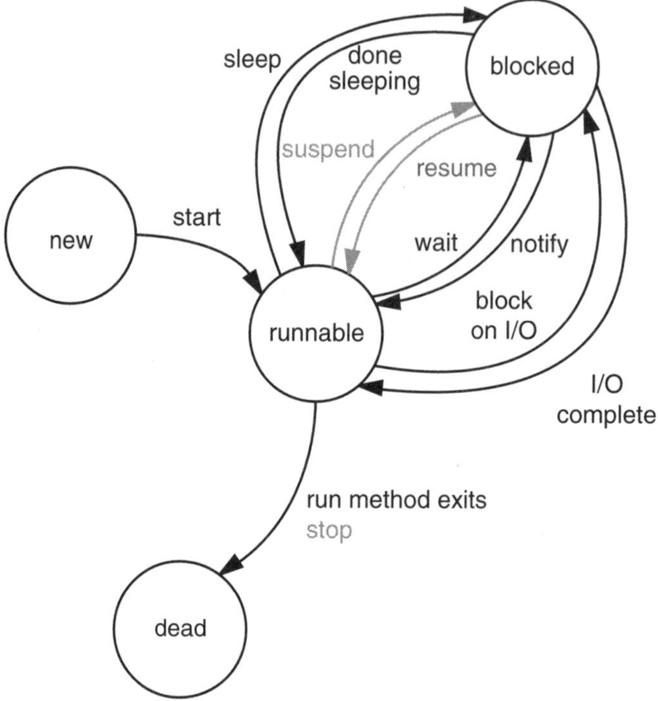

Figure 1–5: Thread states

For example, the `run` method of the `Ball` thread puts itself to sleep for 5 milliseconds after it has completed a move.

```
class Ball extends Thread
{  . . .
   public void run()
   {  try
      {  draw();
         for (int i = 1; i <= 1000; i++)
         {  move();
            sleep(5);
         }
      }
      catch(InterruptedException e) {}
   }
}
```

This gives other threads (in our case, other balls and the main thread) the chance to run. If the computer has multiple processors, then more than one thread has a chance to run at the same time.

Moving Out of a Blocked State

The thread must move out of the blocked state and back into the runnable state, using the opposite of the route that put it into the blocked state.

1. If a thread has been put to sleep, the specified number of milliseconds must expire.
2. If a thread is waiting for the completion of an input or output operation, then the operation must have finished.
3. If a thread called `wait`, then another thread must call `notify` or `notifyAll`. (We cover the `wait` and `notify`/`notifyAll` methods later in this chapter.)
4. If a thread is waiting for an object lock that was owned by another thread, then the other thread must have relinquished the lock. (You will see the details later in this chapter.)
5. If a thread has been suspended, then someone must call its `resume` method. However, since the `suspend` method has been deprecated, the `resume` method has been deprecated as well, and you should not call it in your own code.

NOTE: A blocked thread can only be activated through the same route that blocked it in the first place. For example, if a thread is blocked on input, you cannot call its `resume` method to unblock it.

If you invoke a method on a thread that is incompatible with its state, then the virtual machine throws an `IllegalThreadStateException`. For example, this happens when you call `sleep` on a thread that is currently blocked.

Dead Threads

A thread is dead for one of two reasons:

- It dies a natural death because the `run` method exits normally.
- It dies abruptly because an uncaught exception terminates the `run` method.

In particular, it is possible to kill a thread by invoking its `stop` method. That method throws a `ThreadDeath` error object which kills the thread. However, the `stop` method is deprecated, and you should not call it in your own code. We will explain later in this chapter why the `stop` method is inherently dangerous. The next section explains how to terminate a thread without using the `stop` method, by interrupting it.

To find out whether a thread is currently alive (that is, either runnable or blocked), use the `isAlive` method. This method returns `true` if the thread is runnable or blocked, `false` if the thread is still new and not yet runnable or if the thread is dead.

NOTE: You cannot find out if an alive thread is runnable or blocked, or if a runnable thread is actually running. You cannot differentiate either between a thread that has not yet become runnable and one that has already died.

java.lang.Thread

- `void interrupt()`

  sends an interrupt request to a thread. The "interrupted" status of the thread is set to `true`. If the thread is currently blocked by a call to `sleep` or `wait`, an `InterruptedException` is thrown.
- `static boolean interrupted()`

  tests whether or not the *current* thread (that is, the thread that is executing this instruction) has been interrupted. Note that this is a static method. The call has a side effect—it resets the "interrupted" status of the current thread to `false`.
- `boolean isInterrupted()`

  tests whether or not a thread has been interrupted. Unlike the `static interrupted` method, this call does not change the "interrupted" status of the thread.

Thread Priorities

In the Java programming language, every thread has a *priority*. By default, a thread inherits the priority of its parent thread. You can increase or decrease the priority of any thread with the `setPriority` method. You can set the priority to any value between `MIN_PRIORITY` (defined as 1 in the `Thread` class) and `MAX_PRIORITY` (defined as 10). `NORM_PRIORITY` is defined as 5.

Whenever the thread-scheduler has a chance to pick a new thread, it *generally* picks the *highest-priority thread that is currently runnable.*

CAUTION: We need to say right at the outset that the rules for thread priorities are highly system-dependent. When the virtual machine relies on the thread implementation of the host platform, the thread scheduling is at the mercy of that thread implementation. The virtual machine maps the thread priorities to the priority levels of the host platform (which may have more or fewer thread levels). What we describe in this section is an ideal situation that every virtual machine implementation tries to approximate to some degree.

The highest-priority runnable thread keeps running until:

- It yields by calling the `yield` method, or
- It ceases to be runnable (either by dying or by entering the blocked state), or
- A higher-priority thread has become runnable (because the higher-priority thread has slept long enough, or its I/O operation is complete, or someone called its `notify` method).

Then, the scheduler selects a new thread to run. The highest-priority remaining thread is picked among those that are runnable.

What happens if there is more than one runnable thread with the same (highest) priority? One of the highest priority threads gets picked. It is completely up to the thread scheduler how to arbitrate between threads of the same priority. The Java programming language gives no guarantee that all of the threads get treated *fairly*. Of course, it would be desirable if all threads of the same priority are served in turn, to guarantee that each of them has a chance to make progress. But it is at least theoretically possible that on some platforms a thread scheduler picks a random thread or keeps picking the first available thread. This is a weakness of the Java programming language, and it is difficult to write multithreaded programs that are guaranteed to work identically on all virtual machines.

CAUTION: Some platforms have fewer priority levels than the 10 levels that the Java platform specifies. In particular, Windows NT has only 7 priority levels. A virtual machine is free to come up with its own mapping of the JVM priority levels to those of the host system. On a virtual machine running on NT, no matter what mapping is chosen, some of the 10 JVM levels will be mapped to the same NT levels. That plainly means that you cannot rely on priority levels in your multithreaded programs.

Consider for example a call to `yield`. It may have no effect on some implementations. The levels of all runnable threads might map to the same host thread level. The host scheduler might make no effort towards fairness and might simply keep reactivating the yielding thread, even though other threads would like to get their turn. It is a good idea to call `sleep` instead—at least you know that the current thread won't be picked again right away.

As a practical matter, virtual machines have several (although not necessarily 10) priorities, and thread schedulers make some effort to rotate among equal priority threads. For example, if you watch a number of ball threads in the preceding example program, all balls progressed to the end and they appeared to get executed at approximately the same rate. Of course, that is not a guarantee. If you need to ensure a fair scheduling policy, you must implement it yourself.

Consider the following example program, which modifies the previous program to run threads of one kind of balls (displayed in red) with a higher priority than the other threads. (The bold line in the code below shows how to increase the priority of the thread.)

If you click on the "Start" button, five threads are launched at the normal priority, animating five black balls. If you click on the "Express" button, then you launch five red balls whose thread runs at a higher priority than the regular balls.

```
public BounceExpress()
{  . . .
   addButton(p, "Start",
      new ActionListener()
```

```
         {  public void actionPerformed(ActionEvent evt)
            {  for (int i = 0; i < 5; i++)
                  {  Ball b = new Ball(canvas, Color.black);
                     b.setPriority(Thread.NORM_PRIORITY);
                     b.start();
                  }
            }
         });

      addButton(p, "Express",
         new ActionListener()
         {  public void actionPerformed(ActionEvent evt)
            {  for (int i = 0; i < 5; i++)
               {  Ball b = new Ball(canvas, Color.red);
                  b.setPriority(Thread.NORM_PRIORITY + 2);
                  b.start();
               }
            }
         });
      . . .
   }
```

Try it out. Launch a set of regular balls and a set of express balls. You will notice that the express balls seem to run faster. This is solely a result of their higher priority, *not* because the red balls run at a higher speed. The code to move the express balls is the same as that of the regular balls.

Here is why this demonstration works: 5 milliseconds after an express thread goes to sleep, the scheduler wakes it. Now:

- The scheduler again evaluates the priorities of all the runnable threads.
- It finds that the express threads have the highest priority.

One of the express balls gets another turn right away. This can be the one that just woke up, or perhaps it is another express thread—you have no way of knowing. The express threads take turns, and only when they are all asleep does the scheduler give the lower-priority threads a chance to run. See Figure 1–6 and Example 1–3.

Note that the lower-priority threads would have *no* chance to run if the express threads had called `yield` instead of `sleep`.

Once again, we caution you that this program works fine on NT and Solaris, but that the Java programming language specification gives no guarantee that it works identically on other implementations.

TIP: If you find yourself tinkering with priorities to make your code work, you are on the wrong track. Instead, read the remainder of this chapter, or delve into one of the cited references, to learn more about reliable mechanisms for controlling multithreaded programs.

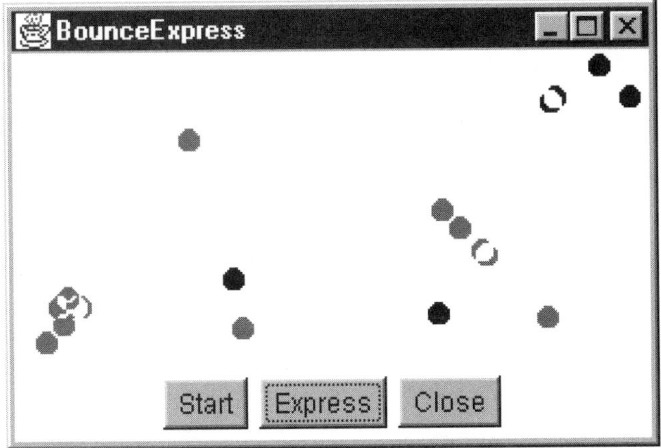

Figure 1–6: Threads with different priorities

Example 1–3: BounceExpress.java

```
import java.awt.*;
import java.awt.event.*;
import javax.swing.*;

public class BounceExpress
{  public static void main(String[] args)
   {  JFrame frame = new BounceExpressFrame();
      frame.show();
   }
}

class BounceExpressFrame extends JFrame
{  public BounceExpressFrame()
   {  setSize(300, 200);
      setTitle("Bounce");

      addWindowListener(new WindowAdapter()
         {  public void windowClosing(WindowEvent e)
            {  System.exit(0);
            }
         } );

      Container contentPane = getContentPane();
      canvas = new JPanel();
      contentPane.add(canvas, "Center");
      JPanel p = new JPanel();
      addButton(p, "Start",
         new ActionListener()
         {  public void actionPerformed(ActionEvent evt)
```

```
            {  for (int i = 0; i < 5; i++)
               {  Ball b = new Ball(canvas, Color.black);
                  b.setPriority(Thread.NORM_PRIORITY);
                  b.start();
               }
            }
         });

      addButton(p, "Express",
         new ActionListener()
         {  public void actionPerformed(ActionEvent evt)
            {  for (int i = 0; i < 5; i++)
               {  Ball b = new Ball(canvas, Color.red);
                  b.setPriority(Thread.NORM_PRIORITY + 2);
                  b.start();
               }
            }
         });

      addButton(p, "Close",
         new ActionListener()
         {  public void actionPerformed(ActionEvent evt)
            {  canvas.setVisible(false);
               System.exit(0);
            }
         });
      contentPane.add(p, "South");
   }

   public void addButton(Container c, String title,
      ActionListener a)
   {  JButton b = new JButton(title);
      c.add(b);
      b.addActionListener(a);
   }

   private JPanel canvas;
}

class Ball extends Thread
{  public Ball(JPanel b, Color c) { box = b; color = c; }

   public void draw()
   {  Graphics g = box.getGraphics();
      g.setColor(color);
      g.fillOval(x, y, XSIZE, YSIZE);
```

```
      g.dispose();
   }

   public void move()
   {  if (!box.isVisible()) return;
      Graphics g = box.getGraphics();
      g.setXORMode(box.getBackground());
      g.setColor(color);
      g.fillOval(x, y, XSIZE, YSIZE);
      x += dx;
      y += dy;
      Dimension d = box.getSize();
      if (x < 0)
      { x = 0; dx = -dx; }
      if (x + XSIZE >= d.width)
      { x = d.width - XSIZE; dx = -dx; }
      if (y < 0)
      { y = 0; dy = -dy; }
      if (y + YSIZE >= d.height)
      { y = d.height - YSIZE; dy = -dy; }
      g.fillOval(x, y, XSIZE, YSIZE);
      g.dispose();
   }

   public void run()
   {  try
      {  draw();
         for (int i = 1; i <= 1000; i++)
         {  move();
            sleep(5);
         }
      }
      catch(InterruptedException e) {}
   }

   private JPanel box;
   private static final int XSIZE = 10;
   private static final int YSIZE = 10;
   private int x = 0;
   private int y = 0;
   private int dx = 2;
   private int dy = 2;
   private Color color;
}
```

java.lang.Thread

- `void setPriority(int newPriority)`

  sets the priority of this thread. The priority must be between `Thread.MIN_PRIORITY` and `Thread.MAX_PRIORITY`. Use `Thread.NORM_PRIORITY` for normal priority.

- `static int MIN_PRIORITY`

  is the minimum priority that a `Thread` can have. The minimum priority value is 1.

- `static int NORM_PRIORITY`

  is the default priority of a `Thread`. The default priority is 5.

- `static int MAX_PRIORITY`

  is the maximum priority that a `Thread` can have. The maximum priority value is 10.

- `static void yield()`

  causes the currently executing thread to yield. If there are other runnable threads whose priority is at least as high as the priority of this thread, they will be scheduled next. Note that this is a static method.

Selfish Threads

Our ball threads were well behaved and gave each other a chance to run. They did this by calling the `sleep` method to wait their turns. The `sleep` method blocks the thread and gives the other threads an opportunity to be scheduled. Even if a thread does not want to put itself to sleep for any amount of time, it can call `yield()` whenever it does not mind being interrupted. A thread should always call `yield` or `sleep` when it is executing a long loop, to ensure that it is not monopolizing the system. A thread that does not follow this rule is called *selfish.*

The following program shows what happens when a thread contains a *tight loop,* a loop in which it carries out a lot of work without giving other threads a chance. When you click on the "Selfish" button, a blue ball is launched whose `run` method contains a tight loop.

```
class SelfishBall extends Ball
{  . . .
   public void run()
   {  draw();
      for (int i = 1; i <= 1000; i++)
      {  move();
         long t = System.currentTimeMillis();
         while (System.currentTimeMillis() < t + 5)
```

```
                ;
            }
        }
    }
```

The `run` procedure will last about 5 seconds before it returns, ending the thread. In the meantime, it never calls `yield` or `sleep`.

What actually happens when you run this program depends on your operating system and choice of thread implementation. For example, when you run this program under Solaris with the "green thread" implementation as opposed to the "native thread" implementation, you will find that the selfish ball indeed hogs the whole application. Try closing the program or launching another ball; you will have a hard time getting even a mouse-click into the application. However, when you run the same program under Windows, nothing untoward happens. The blue balls can run in parallel with other balls.

The reason for this behavioral difference is that the underlying thread package in Windows performs *time-slicing*. It periodically interrupts threads in midstream, even if they are not cooperating. When a thread (even a selfish thread) is interrupted, the scheduler activates another thread—picked among the top-priority-level runnable threads. The green threads implementation on Solaris does not perform time-slicing, but the native thread package does. (Why doesn't everyone simply use the native threads? Until recently, X11 and Motif were not thread safe, and using native threads could lock up the window manager.) If you *know* that your program will execute on a machine whose thread system performs time-slicing, then you do not need to worry about making your threads polite. But the point of Internet computing is that you generally *do not know* the environments of the people who will use your program. You should, therefore, plan for the worst and put calls to `yield` or `sleep` in every loop.

See Example 1–4 for the complete source code.

Example 1–4: BounceSelfish.java

```
import java.awt.*;
import java.awt.event.*;
import java.util.*;
import javax.swing.*;

public class BounceSelfish
{  public static void main(String[] args)
   {  JFrame frame = new BounceSelfishFrame();
      frame.show();
   }
}

class BounceSelfishFrame extends JFrame
{  public BounceSelfishFrame()
```

```
      {  setSize(300, 200);
         setTitle("Bounce");

         addWindowListener(new WindowAdapter()
            {  public void windowClosing(WindowEvent e)
               {  System.exit(0);
               }
            } );

         Container contentPane = getContentPane();
         canvas = new JPanel();
         contentPane.add(canvas, "Center");
         JPanel p = new JPanel();
         addButton(p, "Start",
            new ActionListener()
            {  public void actionPerformed(ActionEvent evt)
               {  Ball b = new Ball(canvas, Color.black);
                  b.setPriority(Thread.NORM_PRIORITY);
                  b.start();
               }
            });

         addButton(p, "Selfish",
            new ActionListener()
            {  public void actionPerformed(ActionEvent evt)
               {  Ball b = new SelfishBall(canvas, Color.blue);
                  b.setPriority(Thread.NORM_PRIORITY + 2);
                  b.start();
               }
            });

         addButton(p, "Close",
            new ActionListener()
            {  public void actionPerformed(ActionEvent evt)
               {  canvas.setVisible(false);
                  System.exit(0);
               }
            });
         contentPane.add(p, "South");
      }

   public void addButton(Container c, String title,
      ActionListener a)
   {  JButton b = new JButton(title);
      c.add(b);
      b.addActionListener(a);
   }

   private JPanel canvas;
}
```

```
class Ball extends Thread
{  public Ball(JPanel b, Color c) { box = b; color = c; }

   public void draw()
   {  Graphics g = box.getGraphics();
      g.setColor(color);
      g.fillOval(x, y, XSIZE, YSIZE);
      g.dispose();
   }

   public void move()
   {  if (!box.isVisible()) return;
      Graphics g = box.getGraphics();
      g.setColor(color);
      g.setXORMode(box.getBackground());
      g.fillOval(x, y, XSIZE, YSIZE);
      x += dx;
      y += dy;
      Dimension d = box.getSize();
      if (x < 0)
      { x = 0; dx = -dx; }
      if (x + XSIZE >= d.width)
      { x = d.width - XSIZE; dx = -dx; }
      if (y < 0)
      { y = 0; dy = -dy; }
      if (y + YSIZE >= d.height)
      { y = d.height - YSIZE; dy = -dy; }
      g.fillOval(x, y, XSIZE, YSIZE);
      g.dispose();
   }

   public void run()
   {  try
      {  draw();
         for (int i = 1; i <= 1000; i++)
         {  move();
            sleep(5);
         }
      }
      catch(InterruptedException e) {}
   }

   private JPanel box;
   private static final int XSIZE = 10;
   private static final int YSIZE = 10;
   private int x = 0;
   private int y = 0;
   private int dx = 2;
   private int dy = 2;
   private Color color;
```

```
}

class SelfishBall extends Ball
{  public SelfishBall(JPanel b, Color c) { super(b, c); }

   public void run()
   {  draw();
      for (int i = 1; i <= 1000; i++)
      {  move();
         long t = System.currentTimeMillis();
         while (System.currentTimeMillis() < t + 5)
            ;
      }
   }
}
```

Thread Groups

Some programs contain quite a few threads. It then becomes useful to categorize them by functionality. For example, consider an Internet browser. If many threads are trying to acquire images from a server and the user clicks on a "Stop" button to interrupt the loading of the current page, then it is handy to have a way of interrupting all of these threads simultaneously. The Java programming language lets you construct what it calls a *thread group* so you can simultaneously work with a group of threads.

You construct a thread group with the constructor:

```
String groupName = . . .;
ThreadGroup g = new ThreadGroup(groupName)
```

The string argument of the `ThreadGroup` constructor identifies the group and must be unique. You then add threads to the thread group by specifying the thread group in the thread constructor.

```
Thread t = new Thread(g, threadName);
```

To find out whether any threads of a particular group are still runnable, use the `activeCount` method.

```
if (g.activeCount() == 0)
{  // all threads in the group g have stopped
}
```

To interrupt all threads in a thread group, simply call `interrupt` on the group object.

```
g.interrupt(); // interrupt all threads in group g
```

Thread groups can have child subgroups. By default, a newly created thread group becomes a child of the current thread group. But you can also explicitly name the parent group in the constructor (see the API notes). Methods such as `activeCount` and `interrupt` refer to all threads in their group and all child groups.

java.lang.ThreadGroup

- `ThreadGroup(String name)`

  creates a new `ThreadGroup`. Its parent will be the thread group of the current thread.

Parameters:	`name`	the name of the new thread group

- `ThreadGroup(ThreadGroup parent, String name)`

  creates a new `ThreadGroup`.

Parameters:	`parent`	the parent thread group of the new thread group
	`name`	the name of the new thread group

- `int activeCount()`

  returns an upper bound for the number of active threads in the thread group.

- `int enumerate(Thread[] list)`

  gets references to every active thread in this thread group. You can use the `activeCount()` method to get an upper bound for the array; this method returns the number of threads put into the array.

Parameters:	`list`	an array to be filled with the thread references

- `ThreadGroup getParent()`

  gets the parent of this thread group.

- `void interrupt()`

  interrupts all threads in this thread group and all of its child groups.

java.lang.Thread

- `Thread(ThreadGroup g, String name)`

  creates a new `Thread` that belongs to a given `ThreadGroup`.

Parameters:	`g`	the thread group to which the new thread belongs
	`name`	the name of the new thread

- `ThreadGroup getThreadGroup()`

  returns the thread group of this thread.

Synchronization

In most practical multithreaded applications, two or more threads need to share access to the same objects. What happens if two threads have access to the same object and each calls a method that modifies the state of the object? As you might imagine, the threads step on each other's toes. Depending on the order in which the data was accessed, corrupted objects can result. Such a situation is often called a *race condition.*

Thread Communication Without Synchronization

To avoid simultaneous access of a shared object by multiple threads, you must learn how to *synchronize* the access. In this section, you'll see what happens if you do not use synchronization. In the next section, you'll see how to synchronize object access.

In the next test program, we simulate a bank with 10 accounts. We randomly generate transactions that move money between these accounts. There are 10 threads, one for each account. Each transaction moves a random amount of money from the account serviced by the thread to another random account.

The simulation code is straightforward. We have the class `Bank` with the method `transfer`. This method transfers some amount of money from one account to another. If the source account does not have enough money in it, then the call simply returns. Here is the code for the `transfer` method of the `Bank` class.

```
public void transfer(int from, int to, double amount)
   // CAUTION: unsafe when called from multiple threads
{  if (accounts[from] < amount) return;
   accounts[from] -= amount;
   accounts[to] += amount;
   ntransacts++;
   if (ntransacts % NTEST == 0) test();
}
```

Here is the code for the `TransferThread` class. Its `run` method keeps moving money out of a fixed bank account. In each iteration, the `run` method picks a random target account and a random amount, calls `transfer` on the bank object, and then sleeps.

```
class TransferThread extends Thread
{  public TransferThread(Bank b, int from, int max)
   {  bank = b;
      fromAccount = from;
      maxAmount = max;
   }

   public void run()
   {  try
      {  while (!interrupted())
```

```
            {  int toAccount = (int)(bank.size() * Math.random());
               int amount = (int)(maxAmount * Math.random());
               bank.transfer(fromAccount, toAccount, amount);
               sleep(1);
            }
         }
         catch(InterruptedException e) {}
      }

      private Bank bank;
      private int fromAccount;
      private int maxAmount;
   }
```

When this simulation runs, we do not know how much money is in any one bank account at any time. But we do know that the total amount of money in all the accounts should remain unchanged since all we do is move money from one account to another.

Every 10,000 transactions, the `transfer` method calls a `test` method that recomputes the total and prints it out.

This program never finishes. Just press CTRL+C to kill the program.

Here is a typical printout:

```
Transactions:10000 Sum: 100000
Transactions:20000 Sum: 100000
Transactions:30000 Sum: 100000
Transactions:40000 Sum: 100000
Transactions:50000 Sum: 100000
Transactions:60000 Sum: 100000
Transactions:70000 Sum: 100000
Transactions:80000 Sum: 100000
Transactions:90000 Sum: 100000
Transactions:100000 Sum: 100000
Transactions:110000 Sum: 100000
Transactions:120000 Sum: 100000
Transactions:130000 Sum: 94792
Transactions:140000 Sum: 94792
Transactions:150000 Sum: 94792
. . .
```

As you can see, something is very wrong. For quite a few transactions, the bank balance remains at $100,000, which is the correct total for 10 accounts of $10,000 each. But after some time, the balance changes slightly. When you run this program, you may find that errors happen quickly or it may take a long time for the balance to become corrupted. This situation does not inspire confidence, and we would probably not want to deposit our hard-earned money into this bank.

Example 1–5 provides the complete source code. See if you can spot the problem with the code. We will unravel the mystery in the next section.

Example 1–5: UnsynchBankTest.java

```
public class UnsynchBankTest
{  public static void main(String[] args)
   {  Bank b = new Bank(NACCOUNTS, INITIAL_BALANCE);
      int i;
      for (i = 0; i < NACCOUNTS; i++)
      {  TransferThread t = new TransferThread(b, i,
            INITIAL_BALANCE);
         t.setPriority(Thread.NORM_PRIORITY + i % 2);
         t.start();
      }
   }

   public static final int NACCOUNTS = 10;
   public static final int INITIAL_BALANCE = 10000;
}

class Bank
{  public Bank(int n, int initialBalance)
   {  accounts = new int[n];
      int i;
      for (i = 0; i < accounts.length; i++)
         accounts[i] = initialBalance;
      ntransacts = 0;
   }

   public void transfer(int from, int to, int amount)
   {  if (accounts[from] < amount) return;
      accounts[from] -= amount;
      accounts[to] += amount;
      ntransacts++;
      if (ntransacts % NTEST == 0) test();
   }

   public void test()
   {  int sum = 0;

      for (int i = 0; i < accounts.length; i++)
         sum += accounts[i];

      System.out.println("Transactions:" + ntransacts
         + " Sum: " + sum);
   }

   public int size()
```

```
    {  return accounts.length;
    }

    public static final int NTEST = 10000;
    private int[] accounts;
    private long ntransacts = 0;
}

class TransferThread extends Thread
{  public TransferThread(Bank b, int from, int max)
    {  bank = b;
       fromAccount = from;
       maxAmount = max;
    }

    public void run()
    {  try
       {  while (!interrupted())
          {  int toAccount = (int)(bank.size() * Math.random());
             int amount = (int)(maxAmount * Math.random());
             bank.transfer(fromAccount, toAccount, amount);
             sleep(1);
          }
       }
       catch(InterruptedException e) {}
    }

    private Bank bank;
    private int fromAccount;
    private int maxAmount;
}
```

NOTE: In this program, we tinkered with the priorities, boosting the priority of half of the transfer threads by 1. On Windows 98, this happens to make it more likely for the threads to interfere with one another, speeding up errors in the `transfer` method. On your platform, this may have no effect whatsoever.

Synchronizing Access to Shared Resources

In the previous section, we ran a program in which several threads updated bank account balances. After a while, errors crept in and some amount of money was either lost or spontaneously created. This problem occurs when two threads are simultaneously trying to update an account. Suppose two threads simultaneously carry out the instruction:

```
accounts[to] += amount;
```

The problem is that these are not *atomic* operations. The instruction might be processed as follows:

1. Load `accounts[to]` into a register.
2. Add `amount`.
3. Move the result back to `accounts[to]`.

Now, suppose the first thread executes Steps 1 and 2, and then it is interrupted. Suppose the second thread awakens and updates the same entry in the `account` array. Then, the first thread awakens and completes its Step 3.

That action wipes out the modification of the other thread. As a result, the total is no longer correct. (See Figure 1–7.)

Our test program detects this corruption. (Of course, there is a slight chance of false alarms if the thread is interrupted as it is performing the tests!)

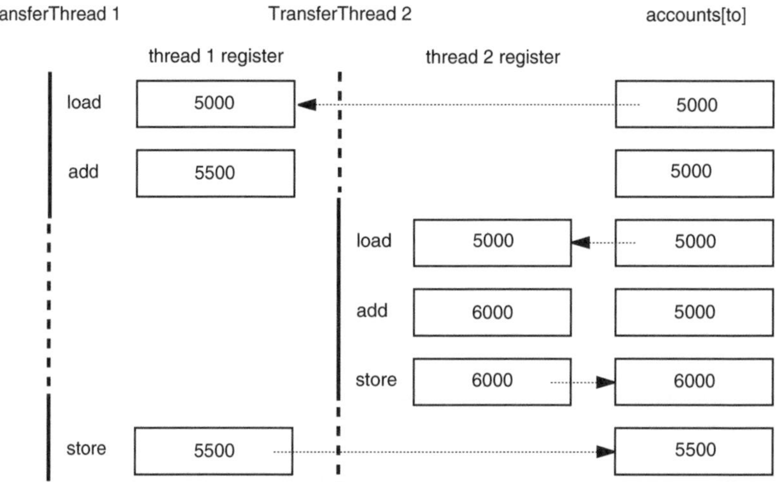

Figure 1–7: Simultaneous access by two threads

NOTE: You can actually peek at the virtual machine bytecodes that execute each statement in our class. Run the command

```
javap -c -v Bank
```

to decompile the `Bank.class` file. For example, the line

```
accounts[to] += amount;
```

is translated into the following bytecodes.

```
aload_0
getfield #16 <Field Bank.accounts [J>
iload_1
dup2
```

```
laload
iload_3
i2l
lsub
lastore
```

What these codes mean does not matter. The point is that the increment command is made up of several instructions, and the thread executing them can be interrupted at the point of any instruction.

What is the chance of this corruption occurring? If all threads are running at the same priority, it is quite low, because each thread does so little work before going to sleep again that it is unlikely that the scheduler will preempt it. We found by experimentation that we could boost the probability of corruption by assigning half of the transfer threads a higher priority than the other half. When a higher-priority transfer thread wakes up from its sleep, it will preempt a lower-priority transfer thread.

NOTE: This is exactly the kind of tinkering with priority levels that we tell you not to do in your own programs. We were in a bind—we wanted to show you a program that can demonstrate data corruption. There is no guarantee that the corruption occurs, but we found that we could increase the likelihood of corruption on some popular platforms by adjusting the priority levels. In your own programs, you presumably will not want to increase the chance of corruption, so you should not imitate this approach.

The problem is that the work of the `transfer` method can be interrupted in the middle. If we could ensure that the method runs to completion before the thread loses control, then the state of the bank account object would not be corrupted.

Many thread libraries force the programmer to fuss with so-called semaphores and critical sections to gain uninterrupted access to a resource. This is sufficient for procedural programming, but it is hardly object-oriented. The Java programming language has a nicer mechanism, inspired by the *monitors* invented by Tony Hoare.

You simply tag any operation that should not be interrupted as `synchronized`, like this:

```
public synchronized void transfer(int from, int to,
   int amount)
{  if (accounts[from] < amount) return;
   accounts[from] -= amount;
   accounts[to] += amount;
   ntransacts++;
   if (ntransacts % NTEST == 0) test();
}
```

When one thread calls a synchronized method, it is guaranteed that the method will finish before another thread can execute any synchronized method on the same object (see Figure 1–8). When one thread calls `transfer` and then another thread also calls `transfer`, the second thread cannot continue. Instead, it is deactivated and must wait for the first thread to finish executing the `transfer` method.

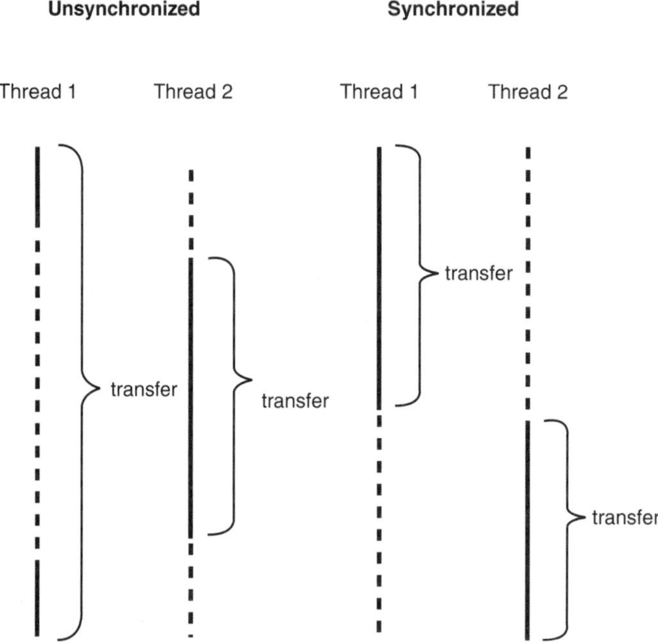

Figure 1–8: Comparison of unsynchronized and synchronized threads

Try it out. Tag the `transfer` method as `synchronized` and run the program again. You can run it forever, and the bank balance will not get corrupted.

Object Locks

When a thread calls a synchronized method, the *object* becomes "locked." Think of each object as having a key to the front door. The key initially lies on the door step. When a thread enters the synchronized method, it grabs the key, enters the object, and locks the door from the inside. When another thread tries to call a synchronized method on the same object, it can't open the door. It then looks for the key and can't find it, so it stops running. Eventually, the first thread exits its synchronized method, leaves the object and deposits the key back on the door step.

Periodically, the thread scheduler activates the threads that are waiting for the key, using its normal activation rules that we already discussed. Whenever one of

the threads that wants to use the object runs again, it checks if the object is still locked. If not, it gets to be the next one to gain exclusive access to the object.

However, other threads are still free to call unsynchronized methods on a locked object. For example, the `size` method of the `BankAccount` class does not have to be synchronized.

TIP: It is an excellent idea to declare those instance variables that do not change after construction as `final`. For example, we declared the `accounts` variable as `final`:

```
private final int[] accounts;
```

When you have a method that reports the state of `final` variables, then you can omit the `synchronized` modifier with confidence.

When a thread leaves a synchronized method by throwing an exception, it still relinquishes the object lock. That is a good thing—you wouldn't want a thread to hog the object after it has exited the synchronized method.

If a thread owns the lock of an object and it calls another synchronized method of the same object, then it is automatically granted access. The thread only relinquishes the lock when it exits the last synchronized method.

NOTE: Technically, each object has a *lock count* that counts how many synchronized methods the lock owner has called. Each time a new synchronized method is called, the lock count is increased. Each time a synchronized method terminates (either because of a normal return or because of an uncaught exception), the lock count is decremented. When the lock count reaches zero, the thread gives up the lock.

A thread can own the locks of multiple objects at the same time, simply by calling a synchronized method on an object while executing a synchronized method of another object. But, of course, an object's lock can only be owned by one thread at any given point in time.

The `wait` *and* `notify` *methods*

Let us refine our simulation of the bank. We do not want to transfer money out of an account that does not have the funds to cover it. Note that we cannot use code like:

```
if (bank.getBalance(from) >= amount)
   bank.transfer(from, to, amount);
```

It is entirely possible that the current thread will be deactivated between the successful outcome of the test and the call to `transfer`.

```
if (bank.getBalance(from) >= amount)
      // thread might be deactivated at this point
   bank.transfer(from, to, amount);
```

By the time the thread is running again, the account balance may have fallen below the withdrawal amount. You must make sure that the thread cannot be interrupted between the test and the insertion. You do so by putting the both the test and the transfer action inside the same synchronized method:

```
public synchronized void transfer(int from, int to,
    int amount)
{   while (accounts[from] < amount)
    {   // wait
    }
    // transfer funds
}
```

Now, what do we do when there is not enough money in the account? We wait until some other thread has added funds. But the `transfer` method is `synchronized`. This thread has just gained exclusive access to the bank object, so no other thread has a chance to make a deposit. A second feature of synchronized methods takes care of this situation. You use the `wait` method in the thread class if you need to wait inside a synchronized method.

When `wait` is called inside a synchronized method, the current thread is blocked and gives up the object lock. This lets in another thread that can, we hope, increase the account balance. Note that the `wait` method is a method of the class `Object`, not of the class `Thread`. When calling `wait`, the `Bank` object blocks the current thread and unlocks itself.

There is an essential difference between a thread that is waiting to get inside a synchronized method and a thread that has called `wait`. Once a thread calls the `wait` method, it enters a *wait list*. Until the thread is removed from the wait list, the scheduler ignores it and it does not have a chance to continue running.

To remove the thread from the wait list, some other thread must call the `notify` or `notifyAll` method on the *same object*. The `notify` method removes one arbitrarily chosen thread from the wait list. The `notifyAll` method removes all of them. When the threads are removed from the wait list, then the scheduler will eventually activate them again. At that time, they will attempt to reenter the object. As soon as the object lock is available, one of them will reenter the object and continue where it left off after the call to `wait`.

It is crucially important that *some* other thread calls the `notify` or `notifyAll` method periodically. When a thread calls `wait`, it has no way of unblocking itself. It puts its faith in the other threads. If none of them bother to unblock the waiting thread, it will never run again. This can lead to unpleasant *deadlock* situations. If all other threads are blocked and the last active thread calls `wait` without unblocking one of the others, then it also blocks. There is no thread left to unblock the others, and the program hangs. The waiting threads are *not* automatically reactivated when no other thread is working on the object. We will discuss deadlocks later in this chapter.

As a practical matter, it is dangerous to call `notify` because you have no control over which thread gets unblocked. If the wrong thread gets unblocked, that thread may not be able to proceed. We simply recommend that you use the `notifyAll` method and that all threads be unblocked.

When should you call `notifyAll`? The rule of thumb is to call `notifyAll` whenever the state of an object changes in a way that might be advantageous to waiting threads. For example, whenever an account balance changes, the waiting threads should be given another chance to inspect the balance. In our example, we will call `notifyAll` when we have finished with the funds transfer.

```
public synchronized void transfer(int from, int to, int
   amount)
{  . . .
   accounts[from] -= amount;
   accounts[to] += amount;
   ntransacts++;
   notifyAll();
   . . .
}
```

This notification gives the waiting threads the chance to run again. A thread that was waiting for a higher balance then gets a chance to check the balance again. If the balance is sufficient, the thread performs the transfer. If not, it calls `wait` again.

Note that the call to `notifyAll` does not immediately activate a waiting thread. It only unblocks the waiting threads so that they can compete for entry into the object after the current thread has exited the synchronized method.

TIP: If your multithreaded program gets stuck, double-check that every `wait` is matched by a `notifyAll`.

If you run the sample program with the synchronized version of the `transfer` method, you will notice that nothing ever goes wrong. The total balance stays at $100,000 forever. (Again, you need to press CTRL+C to terminate the program.)

You will also notice that the program in Example 1–6 runs a bit slower—this is the price you pay for the added bookkeeping involved in the synchronization mechanism.

Example 1–6: SynchBankTest.java

```
public class SynchBankTest
{  public static void main(String[] args)
   {  Bank b = new Bank(NACCOUNTS, INITIAL_BALANCE);
      int i;
      for (i = 0; i < NACCOUNTS; i++)
      {  TransferThread t = new TransferThread(b, i,
            INITIAL_BALANCE);
         t.setPriority(Thread.NORM_PRIORITY + i % 2);
```

```
         t.start();
      }
   }

   public static final int NACCOUNTS = 10;
   public static final int INITIAL_BALANCE = 10000;
}

class Bank
{  public Bank(int n, int initialBalance)
   {  accounts = new int[n];
      int i;
      for (i = 0; i < accounts.length; i++)
         accounts[i] = initialBalance;
      ntransacts = 0;
   }

   public synchronized void transfer(int from, int to, int amount)
   {  try
      {  while (accounts[from] < amount)
            wait();
         accounts[from] -= amount;
         accounts[to] += amount;
         ntransacts++;
         notifyAll();
         if (ntransacts % NTEST == 0) test();
      }
      catch(InterruptedException e) {}
   }

   public synchronized void test()
   {  int sum = 0;

      for (int i = 0; i < accounts.length; i++)
         sum += accounts[i];

      System.out.println("Transactions:" + ntransacts
         + " Sum: " + sum);
   }

   public int size()
   {  return accounts.length;
   }

   public static final int NTEST = 10000;
   private final int[] accounts;
   private long ntransacts = 0;
}

class TransferThread extends Thread
```

```
{  public TransferThread(Bank b, int from, int max)
   {  bank = b;
      fromAccount = from;
      maxAmount = max;
   }

   public void run()
   {  try
      {  while (!interrupted())
         {  int toAccount = (int)(bank.size() * Math.random());
            int amount = (int)(maxAmount * Math.random());
            bank.transfer(fromAccount, toAccount, amount);
            sleep(1);
         }
      }
      catch(InterruptedException e) {}
   }

   private Bank bank;
   private int fromAccount;
   private int maxAmount;
}
```

Here is a summary of how the synchronization mechanism works.

1. To call a synchronized method, the implicit parameter must not be locked. Calling the method locks the object. Returning from the call unlocks the implicit parameter object. Thus, only one thread at a time can execute synchronized methods on a particular object.
2. When a thread executes a call to `wait`, it surrenders the object lock and enters a wait list.
3. To remove a thread from the wait list, some other thread must make a call to `notifyAll` or `notify`, on the same object.

The scheduling rules are undeniably complex, but it is actually quite simple to put them into practice. Just follow these four rules:

1. If two or more threads modify an object, declare the methods that carry out the modifications as synchronized. Read-only methods that are affected by object modifications must also be synchronized.
2. If a thread must wait for the state of an object to change, it should wait inside the object, not outside, by entering a synchronized method and calling `wait`.
3. Whenever a method changes the state of an object, it should call `notifyAll`. That gives the waiting threads a chance to see if circumstances have changed.
4. Remember that `wait` and `notify`/`notifyAll` are methods of the `Object` class, not the `Thread` class. Double-check that your calls to `wait` are matched up by a notification *on the same object.*

NOTE: Occasionally, it is useful to lock an object and obtain exclusive access to it for just a few instructions without writing a new synchronized method. You use *synchronized blocks* to achieve this access. A synchronized block consists of a sequence of statements, enclosed in `{ . . . }` and prefixed with `synchronized (obj)`, where `obj` is the object to be locked. Here is an example of the syntax:

```
public void run()
{  . . .
   synchronized (bank) // lock the bank object
   {  if (bank.getBalance(from) >= amount)
         bank.transfer(from, to, amount);
   }
   . . .
}
```

In this sample code segment, the synchronized block will run to completion before any other thread can call a synchronized method on the `bank` object.

Most people find synchronized blocks confusing, and it is best to avoid them when possible. Their only advantage is that they save a method call and are therefore slightly more efficient.

`java.lang.Object`

- `void notifyAll()`

  unblocks the threads that called `wait` on this object. This method can only be called from within a synchronized method or block. The method throws an `IllegalMonitorStateException` if the current thread is not the owner of the object's lock.

- `void notify()`

  unblocks one randomly selected thread among the threads that called `wait` on this object. This method can only be called from within a synchronized method or block. The method throws an `IllegalMonitorStateException` if the current thread is not the owner of the object's lock.

- `void wait()`

  causes a thread to wait until it is notified. This method can only be called from within a synchronized method. It throws an `IllegalMonitorStateException` if the current thread is not the owner of the object's lock.

Deadlocks

The synchronization feature in the Java programming language is convenient and powerful, but it cannot solve all problems that might arise in multithreading. Consider the following situation:

Account 1: $2,000

Account 2: $3,000

Thread 1: Transfer $3,000 from Account 1 to Account 2

Thread 2: Transfer $4,000 from Account 2 to Account 1

As Figure 1–9 indicates, Threads 1 and 2 are clearly blocked. Neither can proceed since the balances in Accounts 1 and 2 are insufficient.

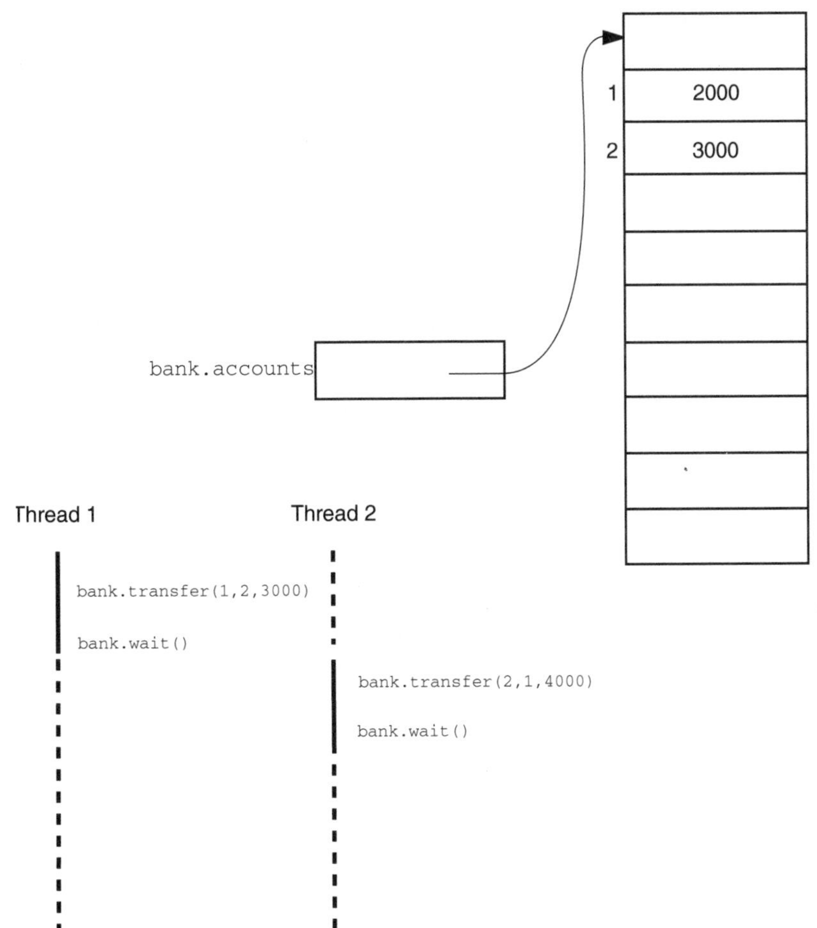

Figure 1–9: A deadlock situation

Is it possible that all 10 threads are blocked because each is waiting for more money? Such a situation is called a *deadlock*.

In our program, a deadlock could not occur for a simple reason. Each transfer amount is for, at most, $10,000. Since there are 10 accounts and a total of $100,000 in them, at least one of the accounts must have more than $10,000 at any time. The thread moving money out of that account can, therefore, proceed.

But if you change the `run` method of the threads to remove the $10,000 transaction limit, deadlocks can occur quickly. Try it out. Construct each `TransferThread` with a `maxAmount` of 14000 and run the program. The program will run for a while and then hang.

Another way to create a deadlock is to make the `i`'th thread responsible for putting money into the `i`'th account, rather than for taking it out of the `i`'th account. In this case, there is a chance that all threads will gang up on one account, each trying to remove more money from it than it contains. Try it out. In the `SynchBankTest` program, turn to the `run` method of the `TransferThread` class. In the call to `transfer`, flip `fromAccount` and `toAccount`. Run the program and see how it deadlocks almost immediately.

Here is another situation in which a deadlock can occur easily: Change the `notifyAll` method to `notify` in the `SynchBankTest` program. You will find that the program hangs quickly. Unlike `notifyAll`, which notifies all threads that are waiting for added funds, the `notify` method unblocks only one thread. If that thread can't proceed, all threads can be blocked. Consider the following sample scenario of a developing deadlock.

Account 1: $19,000

All other accounts: $9,000 each

Thread 1: Transfer $9,500 from Account 1 to Account 2

All other threads: Transfer $9,100 from their account to another account

Clearly, all threads but Thread 1 are blocked since there isn't enough money in their accounts.

Thread 1 proceeds. Afterward, we have the following situation:

Account 1: $9,500

Account 2: $18,500

All other accounts: $9,000 each

Then, Thread 1 calls `notify`. The `notify` method picks a thread at random to unblock. Suppose it picks Thread 3. That thread is awakened, finds that there isn't enough money in its account, and calls `wait` again. But Thread 1 is still running. A new random transaction is generated, say,

Thread 1: Transfer $9,600 to from Account 1 to Account 2

Now, Thread 1 also calls `wait`, and *all* threads are blocked. The system has deadlocked.

The culprit here is the call to `notify`. It only unblocks one thread, and it may not pick the thread that is essential to make progress. (In our scenario, Thread 2 must proceed to take money out of Account 2.) In contrast, `notifyAll` unblocks all threads.

Unfortunately, there is nothing in the Java programming language to avoid or break these deadlocks. You must design your threads to ensure that a deadlock situation cannot occur. You need to analyze your program and ensure that every blocked thread will eventually be notified, and that at least one of them can always proceed. Thread synchronization and deadlock avoidance are difficult subjects, and we refer the interested reader to *Programming with Threads* by Steve Kleiman, Devang Shah, and Bart Smaalders [Sunsoft Press/Prentice-Hall, 1996].

Why the `stop` and `suspend` Methods Are Deprecated

The Java 1.0 platform defined a `stop` method that simply terminates a thread, and a `suspend` method that blocks a thread until another thread calls `resume`. Both of these methods have been deprecated in the Java 2 platform. The `stop` method is inherently unsafe, and experience has shown that the `suspend` method frequently leads to deadlocks. In this section, you will see why these methods are problematic and what you can do to avoid problems.

Let us turn to the `stop` method first. When a thread is stopped, it immediately gives up the locks on all objects that it has locked. This can leave objects in an inconsistent state. For example, suppose a `TransferThread` is stopped in the middle of moving money from one account to another, after the withdrawal and before the deposit. Now the bank object is *damaged.*

CAUTION: Technically speaking, the `stop` method causes the thread to be stopped to throw an exception object of type `ThreadDeath`. This exception terminates all pending methods, including the `run` method. Whenever a synchronized method is terminated in this way, the object is unlocked.

For the same reason, *any* uncaught exception in a synchronized method can cause the method to terminate prematurely and lead to damaged objects.

When a thread wants to stop another thread, it has no way of knowing when the `stop` method is safe and when it leads to damaged objects. Therefore, the method has been deprecated.

If you need to stop a thread safely, you can have the thread periodically check a variable that indicates whether a stop has been requested.

```
public class MyThread extends Thread
{  public void run()
   {  while (!stopRequested && more work to do)
      {  do more work
      }
```

```
      }

      public void requestStop()
      {  stopRequested = true;
      }

      private boolean stopRequested;
   }
```

This code leaves the `run` method to control when to finish, and it is up to the `run` method to ensure that no objects are left in a damaged state.

Testing the `stopRequested` variable in the main loop of a thread works fine, except if the thread is currently blocked. In that case, the thread will only terminate after it is unblocked. You can force a thread out of a blocked state by interrupting it. Thus, you should define the `requestStop` method to call `interrupt`:

```
public void requestStop()
{  stopRequested = true;
   interrupt();
}
```

You can test the `stopRequested` variable in the `catch` clause for the `InterruptedException`. For example,

```
try
{  wait();
}
catch (InterruptedException e)
{  if (stopRequested)
      return; // exit the run method
}
```

Actually, many programmers take the attitude that the only reason to interrupt a thread is to stop it. Then, you don't need to test the `stopRequested` variable—simply exit the `run` method whenever you sense an interrupt.

Next, let us see what is wrong with the `suspend` method. Unlike `stop`, `suspend` won't damage objects. However, if you suspend a thread that owns a lock to an object, then the object is unavailable until the thread is resumed. If the thread that calls the `suspend` method tries to acquire the lock for the same object before calling `resume`, then the program deadlocks: the suspended thread waits to be resumed, and the suspending thread waits for the object to be unlocked.

This situation occurs frequently in graphical user interfaces. Suppose we have a graphical simulation of our bank. We have a button labeled "Pause" that suspends the transfer threads, and a button labeled "Resume" that resumes them.

```
public void actionPerformed(ActionEvent event)
{  Object source = event.getSource();
   if (source == pauseButton)
      for (int i = 0; i < threads.length; i++)
```

```
            threads[i].suspend(); // Don't do this
      else if (source == resumeButton)
         for (int i = 0; i < threads.length; i++)
            threads[i].resume(); // Don't do this
   }
```

A `paintComponent` method paints a chart of each account, calling the `bank.getAccount` method, and that method is synchronized.

As you will see in the next section, both the button actions and the repainting occur in the same thread, the *event dispatch thread.*

Now consider the following scenario:

1. One of the transfer threads acquires the lock on the `bank` object.
2. The user clicks the "Pause" button.
3. All transfer threads are suspended; one of them still holds the lock on the `bank` object.
4. For some reason, the account chart needs to be repainted.
5. The `paintComponent` method calls the synchronized method `bank.getBalance`.

Now the program is frozen.

The event dispatch thread can't proceed because the `bank` object is locked by one of the suspended threads. Thus, the user can't click the "Resume" button, and the threads won't ever resume.

If you want to safely suspend the thread, you should introduce a variable `suspendRequested` and test it in the main loop of your `run` method. When you find that the variable has been set, keep waiting until it becomes available again. However, you don't want to implement a busy wait:

```
while (suspendRequested)
   sleep(1); // NO
```

Instead, call `wait`, and define a `requestResume` method to call `notify`. Then, the thread stays blocked until it is resumed.

```
class MyThread extends Thread
{  public void requestSuspend()
   {  suspendRequested = true;
   }

   private synchronized void checkSuspended()
      throws InterruptedException
   {  while (suspendRequested)
         wait();
   }

   public synchronized void requestResume()
```

```
    {  suspendRequested = false;
       notify();
    }

    public void run()
    {  while (more work to do)
       {  checkSuspended();
          do more work
       }
    }

    private boolean suspendRequested;
}
```

Why does this approach solve the problem with frozen user interfaces? The `run` method calls `checkSuspended` in an idle moment, when it is not locking any other objects. Therefore, the thread only blocks itself when it is safe to do so.

NOTE: If you carefully look at the preceding code, you will note that the `request-Resume` and `checkSuspended` methods are synchronized. They need to be synchronized because `wait` and `notify` can only be called inside synchronized methods or blocks. But which object is being locked?

The object that is being locked is the thread itself. This is an "accidental" lock—we don't care about serializing calls to `resume` and `checkSuspended`. The only purpose of the lock object is to match up calls to `wait` and `notify`. The call to `notify` unblocks the thread waiting on the `MyThread` object, that is, the suspended thread. Some programmers prefer to use a separate dummy variable for such a matchmaking object:

```
private void checkSuspended()
   throws InterruptedException
{  synchronized (dummy)
     // synchronized necessary for calling wait
   {  while (suspendRequested)
         dummy.wait(); // block this thread
   }
}

public void requestResume()
{  suspendRequested = false;
   synchronized (dummy)
   {  dummy.notify(); // unblock the thread waiting on dummy
   }
}

private Integer dummy = new Integer(0);
   // any non-null object will work
```

Finally, you can use `notify` instead of `notifyAll` because there is only a single thread waiting on this particular object.

Of course, avoiding the `Thread.suspend` method does not automatically avoid deadlocks. If a thread calls `wait`, it might not wake up either. But there is an essential difference. A thread can control when it calls `wait`. But the `Thread.suspend` method can be invoked *externally* on a thread, at any time, without the thread's consent. The same is true for the `Thread.stop` method. For that reason, these two methods have been deprecated.

NOTE: In this section, we defined methods `requestStop`, `requestSuspend` and `requestResume`. These methods provide functionality that is similar to the deprecated `stop`, `suspend` and `resume` methods, while avoiding the risks of those deprecated methods. You will find that many programmers implement similar methods, but instead of giving them different names, they simply *override* the `stop`, `suspend` and `resume` methods. It is entirely legal to override a deprecated method with another method that is not deprecated. If you see a call to `stop`, `suspend` or `resume` in a program, you should not automatically assume that the program is wrong. First check whether the programmer overrode the deprecated methods with safer versions.

Animation

In the previous sections, you learned what is required to split a program into multiple concurrent tasks. Each task needs to be placed into a `run` method of a class that extends `Thread`. But what if we want to add the `run` method to a class that already extends another class? This occurs most often when we want to add multithreading to an applet. An applet class already inherits from `JApplet`, and we cannot inherit from two parent classes, so we need to use an interface. The necessary interface is built into the Java platform. It is called `Runnable`. We take up this important interface next.

The `Runnable` *Interface*

Whenever you need to use multithreading in a class that is already derived from a class other than `Thread`, you can make the class implement the `Runnable` interface. As though you had derived from `Thread`, put the code that needs to run in the `run` method. For example,

```
class Animation extends JApplet
   implements Runnable
{  . . .
   public void run()
   {  // thread action goes here
   }
}
```

You still need to make a thread object to launch the thread. Give that thread a reference to the `Runnable` object in its constructor. The thread then calls the `run` method of that object.

This call is commonly made in the `start` method of an applet, as in the following example:

```
class Animation extends JApplet
   implements Runnable
{  . . .
   public void start()
   {  if (runner == null)
      {  runner = new Thread(this);
         runner.start();
      }
   }
   . . .
   private Thread runner;
}
```

In this case, the `this` argument to the `Thread` constructor specifies that the object whose `run` method should be called when the thread executes is an instance of the `Animation` object.

Wouldn't it be easier if we just defined another class from `Thread` and launched it in the applet?

```
class AnimationThread extends Thread
{  public void run()
   {  // thread action goes here
   }
}

class Animation extends Applet
{  . . .
   public void start()
   {  if (runner == null)
      {  runner = new AnimationThread();
         runner.start();
      }
   }
   . . .
   private Thread runner;
}
```

Indeed, this would be clean and simple. However, if the `run` method must have access to an applet's private data, then it makes sense to keep the `run` method with the applet and use the `Runnable` interface instead.

`java.lang.Thread`

- `Thread(Runnable target)`

  constructs a new thread that calls the `run()` method of the specified target.

`java.lang.Runnable`

- `void run()`

  You must override this method and place in the thread the code that you want to have executed.

Loading and Displaying Frames

In this section, we dissect one of the most common uses for threads in applets: animation. An animation sequence displays images, giving the viewer the illusion of motion. Each of the images in the sequence is called a *frame.* If the frames are complex, they should be rendered ahead of time—the computer running the applet may not have the horsepower to compute images fast enough for real-time animation.

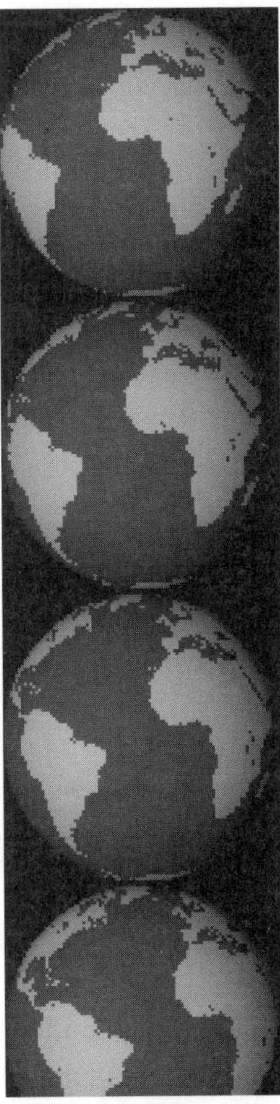

Figure 1–10: This file has 36 images of a globe

You can put each frame in a separate image file or put all frames into one file. We do the latter. It makes the process of loading the image much easier. In our example, we use a file with 36 images of a rotating globe, courtesy of Silviu Marghescu of the University of Maryland. Figure 1–10 shows the first few frames.

The animation applet must first acquire all the frames. Then, it shows each of them, in turn, for a fixed time. You use a `MediaTracker` object to load the image. Behind the scenes and transparent to the programmer, the `addImage` method fires up a new thread to acquire the image. Loading an image can be very slow, especially if the image has many frames or is located across the network. The `waitForID` call blocks until the image is fully loaded.

Once the image is loaded, we render one frame at a time. To draw the `i`'th frame, we make a method call as follows:

```
g.drawImage(image, 0, - i * imageHeight
   / imageCount, null);
```

Figure 1–11 shows the *negative* offset of the *y*-coordinate.

This offset causes the first frame to be well above the origin of the canvas. The top of the i'th frame becomes the top of the canvas.

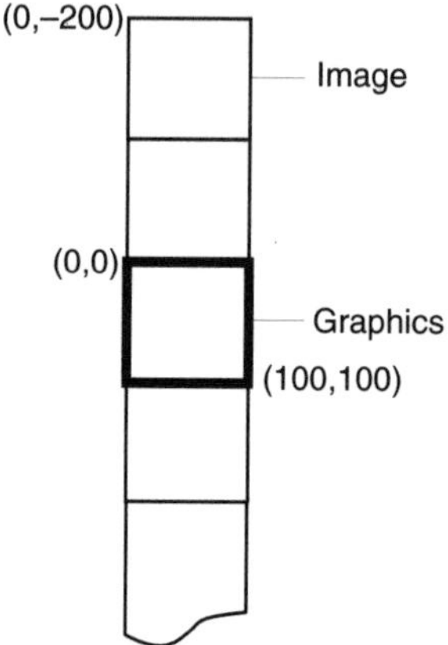

Figure 1–11: Picking a frame from a strip of frames

After a delay, we increment i and draw the next frame.

Using a Thread to Control the Animation

Our applet will have a single thread.

```
class Animation implements Runnable
{  . . .
   Thread runner = null;
}
```

You will see such a thread variable in many applets. Often, it is called kicker, and we once saw killer as the variable name. We think runner makes more sense, though.

First and foremost, we will use this thread to:

- Start the animation when the user is watching the applet.
- Stop the animation when the user has switched to a different page in the browser.

We do these tasks by creating the thread in the start method of the applet and by destroying it in the stop method. You can do this with the following code, which you will find in many applets.

```
class Animation extends JApplet
   implements Runnable
{  public void start()
   {  if (runner == null)
      {  runner = new Thread(this);
         runner.start();
```

```
      }
   }
   public void stop()
   {  runner.interrupt();
      runner = null;
   }

   . . .
}
```

Note the method call:

```
runner = new Thread(this);
```

This call creates a thread that calls the `run` method of this applet.

Here is the `run` method. It simply loops, painting the screen, advancing the frame counter, and sleeping when it can.

```
public void run()
{  try
   {  while (!Thread.interrupted())
      {  repaint();
         current = (current + 1) % imageCount;
         Thread.sleep(200);
      }
   }
   catch(InterruptedException e) {}
}
```

Finally, we implement another mechanism for stopping and restarting the animation. When you click with the mouse on the applet window, the animation stops. When you click again, it restarts. Note that we use the thread variable, `runner`, as an indication whether the thread is currently running or not. Whenever the thread is terminated, the variable is set to `null`. This is a common idiom that you will find in many multithreaded applets.

```
public void init()
{  addMouseListener(new MouseAdapter()
      {  public void mouseClicked(MouseEvent evt)
         {  if (runner == null)
               start();
            else
               stop();
         }
      });

   . . .
}
```

The applet reads the name of the image and the number of frames in the strip from the PARAM section in the HTML file (on the CD-ROM as well).

```
<applet code=Animation.class width=100 height=100>
<param name=imagename value="globe.gif">
<param name=imagecount value="36">
</applet>
```

Example 1–7 is the code of the applet. Note that the `start` and `stop` methods start and stop the applet—they are *not* methods of the thread that is generated.

This animation applet is simplified to show you what goes on behind the scenes. If you are interested only in how to put a moving image on your Web page, look instead at the `Animator` applet in the demo section of the JDK. That applet has many more options than ours, and it lets you add sound.

Example 1–7: Animation.java

```
import java.awt.*;
import java.awt.image.*;
import java.awt.event.*;
import javax.swing.*;
import java.net.*;

public class Animation extends JApplet
   implements Runnable
{  public void init()
   {  addMouseListener(new MouseAdapter()
         {  public void mousePressed(MouseEvent evt)
            {  if (runner == null)
                  start();
               else
                  stop();
            }
         });

      try
      {  imageName = getParameter("imagename");
         if (imageName == null) imageName = "";

         imageCount = 1;
         String param = getParameter("imagecount");
         if (param != null)
            imageCount = Integer.parseInt(param);
      }
      catch (Exception e)
      {  showStatus("Error: " + e);
      }

      current = 0;
```

```
      image = null;
      loadImage();
   }

   public void loadImage()
   {  try
      {  URL url = new URL(getDocumentBase(), imageName);
         image = getImage(url);
         MediaTracker tracker = new MediaTracker(this);
         tracker.addImage(image, 0);
         tracker.waitForID(0);
         imageWidth = image.getWidth(null);
         imageHeight = image.getHeight(null);
         resize(imageWidth, imageHeight / imageCount);
      }
      catch (InterruptedException e)
         // thrown by MediaTracker.waitFor
      {  showStatus("Loading interrupted");
      }
      catch(MalformedURLException e)
      {  showStatus("Bad URL");
      }
   }

   public void paintComponent(Graphics g)
   {  if (image == null) return;
      g.drawImage(image, 0, - (imageHeight / imageCount)
         * current, null);
   }

   public void start()
   {  runner = new Thread(this);
      runner.start();
      showStatus("Click to stop");
   }

   public void stop()
   {  runner.interrupt();
      runner = null;
      showStatus("Click to restart");
   }

   public void run()
   {  try
      {  while (!Thread.interrupted())
         {  repaint();
            current = (current + 1) % imageCount;
            Thread.sleep(200);
```

```
        }
      }
      catch(InterruptedException e) {}
   }

   private Image image;
   private int current;
   private int imageCount;
   private int imageWidth;
   private int imageHeight;
   private String imageName;
   private Thread runner;
}
```

Timers

In many programming environments, you can set up timers. A timer alerts your program elements at regular intervals. For example, to display a clock in a window, the clock object must be notified once every second.

Swing has a built-in timer class that is easy to use. You construct a timer by supplying an object of a class that implements the `ActionListener` interface and the delay between timer alerts, in milliseconds.

```
Timer t = new Timer(listener, 1000);
t.start();
```

Then, the `actionPerformed` method of the listener class is called whenever a timer interval has elapsed. The `actionPerformed` method is automatically called on the event dispatch thread, not the timer thread, so that you can freely invoke Swing methods in the callback.

NOTE: JDK 1.3 has an unrelated `java.util.Timer` class to schedule a `TimerTask` for later execution. The `TimerTask` class implements the `Runnable` interface and also supplies a `cancel` method to cancel the task. However, the `java.util.Timer` class has no provision for a periodic callback.

Sometimes, it is useful to bypass the Swing timer and use your own timer, for example, in an application that does not use Swing. In this section, we describe how to do that.

Our timer runs in its own thread, so it must extend `Thread`. In its `run` method, it goes to sleep for the specified interval, then notifies its target.

```
class Timer extends Thread
{  . . .
   public void run()
   {  try
```

```
        {  while (!interrupted())
           {  sleep(interval);
              target.timeElapsed(this);
           }
        }
        catch(InterruptedException e)
        {
        }
     }

     private int interval;
  }
```

We don't think that the `ActionListener` is a very appropriate interface for timer notifications, so we use a new listener interface that we call `TimerListener`.

```
  interface TimerListener
  {  void timeElapsed(Timer t);
  }
```

Thus, an object that wants to receive timer ticks must implement the `TimerListener` interface. The action to be repeated in regular intervals must be put into the `timeElapsed` method.

Figure 1–12 shows six different clocks.

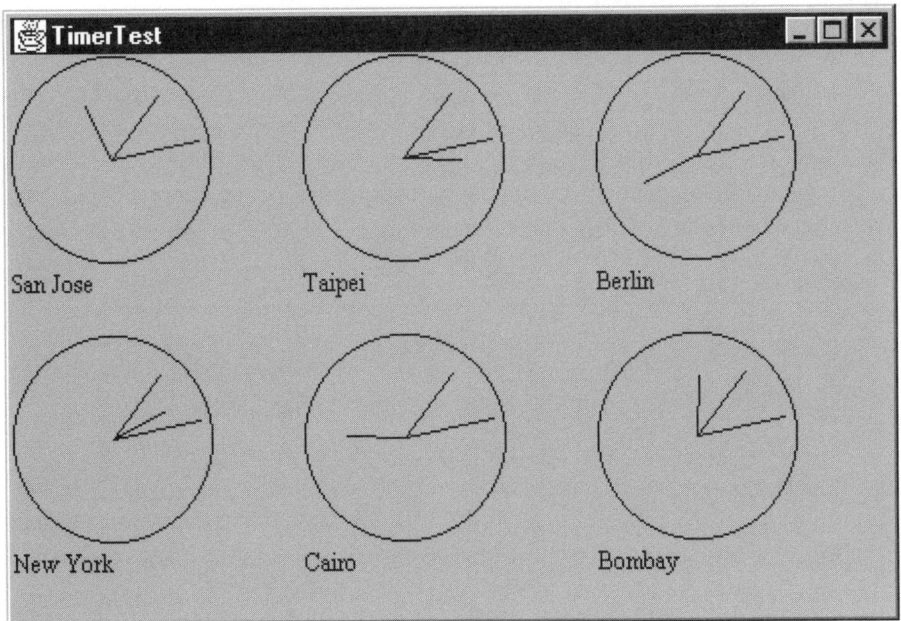

Figure 1–12: Clock threads

Each clock is an instance of the ClockCanvas class, which implements TimerListener. The timeElapsed method of the Clock class redraws the clock.

```
class ClockCanvas extends Canvas
   implements TimerListener
{  . . .
   public void timeElapsed(Timer t)
   {  calendar.setTime(new Date());
      seconds = calendar.get(Calendar.HOUR) * 60 * 60
         + calendar.get(Calendar.MINUTE) * 60
         + calendar.get(Calendar.SECOND);
      repaint();
   }
}
```

Note that the timeElapsed method does not actually get the time from the timer object t. The timer ticks come only *approximately* once a second. For an accurate clock display, we still need to get the system time.

The timeElapsed method is called from the timer thread, not the event dispatch thread. Hence, it is restricted in what Swing methods it can call. However, it only calls the repaint method, which is safe from any thread.

You will find the complete code in Example 1–8.

Example 1–8: TimerTest.java

```
import java.awt.*;
import java.awt.event.*;
import javax.swing.*;
import java.util.*;

public class TimerTest
{  public static void main(String[] args)
   {  JFrame f = new TimerTestFrame();
      f.show();
   }
}

class TimerTestFrame extends JFrame
{  public TimerTestFrame()
   {  setSize(450, 300);
      setTitle("TimerTest");

      addWindowListener(new WindowAdapter()
         {  public void windowClosing(WindowEvent e)
            {  System.exit(0);
            }
         } );

      Container c = getContentPane();
```

```
      c.setLayout(new GridLayout(2, 3));
      c.add(new ClockCanvas("San Jose", "GMT-8"));
      c.add(new ClockCanvas("Taipei", "GMT+8"));
      c.add(new ClockCanvas("Berlin", "GMT+1"));
      c.add(new ClockCanvas("New York", "GMT-5"));
      c.add(new ClockCanvas("Cairo", "GMT+2"));
      c.add(new ClockCanvas("Bombay", "GMT+5"));
   }
}

interface TimerListener
{  void timeElapsed(Timer t);
}

class Timer extends Thread
{  public Timer(int i, TimerListener t)
   {  target   = t;
      interval = i;
      setDaemon(true);
   }

   public void run()
   {  try
      {  while (!interrupted())
         {  sleep(interval);
            target.timeElapsed(this);
         }
      }
      catch(InterruptedException e) {}
   }

   private TimerListener target;
   private int interval;
}

class ClockCanvas extends JPanel
   implements TimerListener
{  public ClockCanvas(String c, String tz)
   {  city = c;
      calendar = new GregorianCalendar(TimeZone.getTimeZone(tz));
      Timer t = new Timer(1000, this);
      t.start();
      setSize(125, 125);
   }

   public void paintComponent(Graphics g)
   {  super.paintComponent(g);
      g.drawOval(0, 0, 100, 100);
      double hourAngle = 2 * Math.PI
         * (seconds - 3 * 60 * 60) / (12 * 60 * 60);
```

```
      double minuteAngle = 2 * Math.PI
         * (seconds - 15 * 60) / (60 * 60);
      double secondAngle = 2 * Math.PI
         * (seconds - 15) / 60;
      g.drawLine(50, 50, 50 + (int)(30
         * Math.cos(hourAngle)),
         50 + (int)(30 * Math.sin(hourAngle)));
      g.drawLine(50, 50, 50 + (int)(40
         * Math.cos(minuteAngle)),
         50 + (int)(40 * Math.sin(minuteAngle)));
      g.drawLine(50, 50, 50 + (int)(45
         * Math.cos(secondAngle)),
         50 + (int)(45 * Math.sin(secondAngle)));
      g.drawString(city, 0, 115);
   }

   public void timeElapsed(Timer t)
   {  calendar.setTime(new Date());
      seconds = calendar.get(Calendar.HOUR) * 60 * 60
         + calendar.get(Calendar.MINUTE) * 60
         + calendar.get(Calendar.SECOND);
      repaint();
   }

   private int seconds = 0;
   private String city;
   private int offset;
   private GregorianCalendar calendar;

   private final int LOCAL = 16;
}
```

Daemon Threads

If you look carefully into the constructor of the timer class above, you will note the method call that looks like this:

```
setDaemon(true);
```

This method call makes the timer thread a *daemon thread*. There is nothing demonic about it. A daemon is simply a thread that has no other role in life than to serve others. When only daemon threads remain, then the program exits. There is no point in keeping the program running if all remaining threads are daemons.

In a graphical application, the timer class threads do not affect when the program ends. The program stays alive until the user closes the application. (The event dispatching thread is not a daemon thread.) But when you use the timer class in a text application, you need not worry about terminating the timer threads. When the non-timer threads have finished their `run` methods, the application automatically terminates.

`javax.swing.Timer`

- `Timer(int delay, ActionListener listener)`

  Creates a new timer that sends events to a listener

Parameters:	`delay`	the delay, in milliseconds, between event notifications
	`listener`	the action listener to be notified when the delay has elapsed

- `void start()`

  Start the timer. After this call, the timer starts sending events to its action listener.

- `void stop()`

  Stop the timer. After this call, the timer stops sending events to its action listener.

`java.lang.Thread`

- `void setDaemon(boolean on)`

  marks this thread as a daemon thread or a user thread. When there are only daemon threads left running in the system, the program exits. This method must be called before the thread is started.

Threads and Swing

As we mentioned in the introduction, one of the reasons to use threads in your programs is to make your programs more responsive. When your program needs to do something time-consuming, then you should fire up another worker thread instead of blocking the user interface.

However, you have to be careful what you do in a worker thread because, perhaps surprisingly, Swing is *not thread safe*. That is, the majority of methods of Swing classes are not synchronized. If you try to manipulate user interface elements from multiple threads, then your user interface will become corrupted.

For example, run the test program whose code you will find at the end of this section. Each time you click on the "Bad" button, a new thread is started that edits a list box, adding and removing values.

```
class BadWorkerThread extends Thread
{  public BadWorderThread(DefaultListModel aModel)
   {  model = aModel;
      generator = new Random();
   }

   public void run()
   {  while (true)
```

```
        {  Integer i = new Integer(generator.nextInt(10));

           if (model.contains(i))
              model.removeElement(i);
           else
              model.addElement(i);

           yield();
        }
     }

     private DefaultListModel model;
     private Random generator;
  }
```

Try it out. Click on the "Bad" button a couple of times. If you start the program from a console window, you will see a flurry of exception reports in the console (see Figure 1–13).

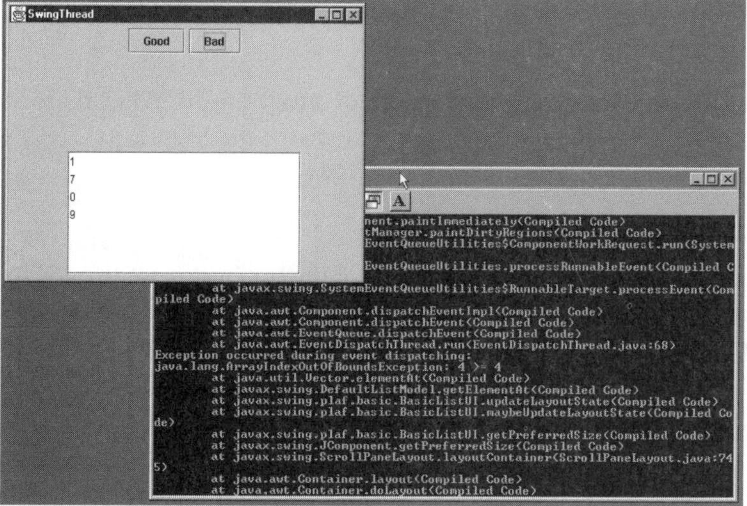

Figure 1–13: Exception reports in the console

What is going on? When an element is inserted into the list model, the model fires an event to update the display. Then, the display code springs into action, reading the current size of the model and preparing to display the model values. But the worker thread keeps on going, removing elements from the model. The display code then thinks that there are more values in the model than there actually are, asks for nonexistent values, and triggers an `ArrayIndexOutOfBounds` exception.

This situation could have been avoided by locking the model while displaying it. However, the designers of Swing decided not to expend any effort to make Swing

thread safe, for two reasons. First, synchronization takes time, and nobody wanted to slow down Swing any further. More importantly, the Swing team checked out what experience other teams had with thread-safe user interface toolkits. What they found was not encouraging. When building a user interface toolkit, you want it to be extensible so that other programmers can add their own user interface components. But user interface programmers using thread-safe toolkits turned out to be confused by the demands for synchronization and tended to create components that were prone to deadlocks.

Therefore, when you use threads together with Swing, you have to follow a few simple rules. First, however, let's see what threads are present in a Swing program.

Every Java application starts with a `main` method that runs in the *main thread*. In a Swing program, the `main` method typically does the following:

- Calls a constructor that lays out components in a frame window
- Invokes the `show` or `setVisible` method on the window

When the first window is shown, a second thread is created, the *event dispatch thread*. All event notifications, such as calls to `actionPerformed` or `paintComponent`, run in the event dispatch thread. The main thread keeps running until the `main` method exits. Usually, of course, the `main` method exits immediately after displaying the frame window (see Figure 1–14). Other threads are running behind the scenes, such as the thread that posts events into the event queue, but those threads are invisible to the application programmer.

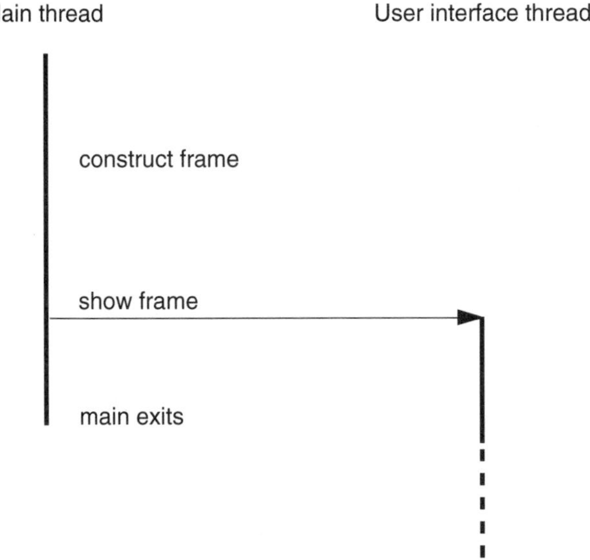

Figure 1–14: Threads in a Swing program

In a Swing application, essentially all code is contained in event handlers to respond to user interface and repaint requests. All that code runs on the event dispatching thread. Here are the rules that you need to follow.

1. If an action takes a long time, fire up a new thread to do the work. If you take a long time in the event dispatch thread, the application seems "dead" since it cannot respond to any events.
2. If an action can block on input or output, fire up a new thread to do the work. You don't want to freeze the user interface for the potentially indefinite time that a network connection is unresponsive.
3. If you need to wait for a specific amount of time, don't sleep in the event dispatch thread. Instead, use a timer.
4. The work that you do in your threads cannot touch the user interface. Read any information from the UI before you launch your threads, launch them, and then update the user interface from the event dispatching thread once the threads have completed.

The last rule is often called the *single thread rule* for Swing programming. There are a few exceptions to the single thread rule.

1. A few Swing methods are thread safe. They are specially marked in the API documentation with the sentence *"This method is thread safe, although most Swing methods are not."* The most useful among these thread-safe methods are:
   ```
   JTextComponent.setText
   JTextArea.insert
   JTextArea.append
   JTextArea.replaceRange
   ```
2. The following methods of the `JComponent` class can be called from any thread:
   ```
   repaint
   revalidate
   ```
   The `repaint` method schedules a repaint event. You use the `revalidate` method if the contents of a component have changed and the size and position of the component must be updated. The `revalidate` method marks the component's layout as invalid and schedules a layout event. (Just like paint events, layout events are *coalesced*. If there are multiple layout events in the event queue, the layout is only recomputed once.)

NOTE: The traditional AWT has `invalidate` and `validate` methods to mark a component's layout as invalid and to force the layout of a component. In Swing, you should simply call `revalidate` instead.

3. You can safely add and remove event listeners in any thread. Of course, the listener methods will be invoked in the event dispatching thread.

4. You can construct components, set their properties, and add them into containers, as long as none of the components have been *realized*. A component has been realized if it can receive paint or validation events. This is the case as soon as the `show`, `setVisible(true)`, or `pack` methods have been invoked on the component or if it has been added to a container that has been realized. Once a component has been realized, you can no longer manipulate it from another thread.

   In particular, you can create the GUI of an application in the `main` method before calling `show`, and you can create the GUI of an applet in the applet constructor or the `init` method.

These rules look complex, but they aren't actually difficult to follow. It is an easy matter to start a new thread to start a time-consuming process. Upon a user request, gather all the necessary information from the GUI, pass them to a thread, and start the thread.

```
public void actionPerformed(ActionEvent e)
{  // gather data needed by thread
   MyThread t = new MyThread(data);
   t.start();
}
```

The difficult part is to update the GUI to indicate progress within your thread and to present the result of the work when your thread is finished. Remember that you can't touch any Swing components from your thread. For example, if you want to update a progress bar or a label text, then you can't simply set its value from your thread.

To solve this problem, there are two convenient utility methods that you can use in any thread to add arbitrary actions to the event queue. For example, suppose you want to periodically update a label "x% complete" in a thread, to indicate progress. You can't call `label.setText` from your thread, but you can use the `invokeLater` and `invokeAndWait` methods of the `EventQueue` class to have that call executed in the event dispatching thread.

NOTE: These methods are also available in the `javax.swing.SwingUtilities` class. If you use Swing with JDK 1.1, you need to use that class—the methods were added to `EventQueue` in JDK 1.2.

Here is what you need to do. You place the Swing code into the `run` method of a class that implements the `Runnable` interface. Then, you create an object of that class and pass it to the static `invokeLater` or `invokeAndWait` method. For example, here is how you can update a label text. First, create the class with the `run` method.

```
public class LabelUpdater implements Runnable
{  public LabelUpdater(JLabel aLabel, int aPercentage)
```

```
    {  label = aLabel;
       percentage = aPercentage;
    }

    public void run()
    {  label.setText(percentage + "complete");
    }
}
```

Then, create an object and pass it to the invokeLater method.

```
Runnable updater = new LabelUpdater(label, percentage);
EventQueue.invokeLater(updater);
```

The invokeLater method returns immediately when the event is posted to the event queue. The run method is executed asynchronously. The invokeAndWait method waits until the run method has actually been executed. The EventQueue class handles the details of the synchronization. In the situation of updating a progress label, the invokeLater method is more appropriate. Users would rather have the worker thread make more progress than insist on the most precise display of the completed percentage.

To invoke code in the event dispatch thread, anonymous inner classes offer a useful shortcut. For example, the sample code given above can be simplified to the following, cryptic, but shorter, command:

```
EventQueue.invokeLater(new Runnable()
   {  public void run()
      {  label.setText(percentage + "% complete");
      }
   }
```

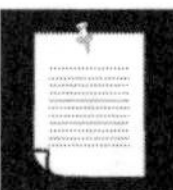

NOTE: The invokeLater and invokeAndWait methods use objects that implement the Runnable interface. You already saw how to construct new threads out of Runnable objects. However, in this case, the code of the run method executes in the event dispatching thread, not a new thread.

Example 1–9 demonstrates how to use the invokeLater method to safely modify the contents of a list box. If you click on the "Good" button, a thread inserts and removes numbers. However, the actual modification takes place in the event dispatching thread.

Example 1–9: SwingThreadTest.java

```
import java.awt.*;
import java.awt.event.*;
import java.util.*;
import javax.swing.*;

public class SwingThreadTest
```

```
{  public static void main(String[] args)
   {  JFrame frame = new SwingThreadFrame();
      frame.show();
   }
}

class SwingThreadFrame extends JFrame
{  public SwingThreadFrame()
   {  setTitle("SwingThread");
      setSize(400,300);
      addWindowListener(new WindowAdapter()
         {  public void windowClosing(WindowEvent e)
            {  System.exit(0);
            }
         } );
      model = new DefaultListModel();

      JList list = new JList(model);
      JScrollPane scrollPane = new JScrollPane(list);

      JPanel p = new JPanel();
      p.add(scrollPane);
      getContentPane().add(p, "South");

      JButton b = new JButton("Good");
      b.addActionListener(new ActionListener()
         {  public void actionPerformed(ActionEvent event)
            {  new GoodWorkerThread(model).start();
            }
         });
      p = new JPanel();
      p.add(b);
      b = new JButton("Bad");
      b.addActionListener(new ActionListener()
         {  public void actionPerformed(ActionEvent event)
            {  new BadWorkerThread(model).start();
            }
         });
      p.add(b);

      getContentPane().add(p, "North");
   }

   private DefaultListModel model;
}

class BadWorkerThread extends Thread
{  public BadWorkerThread(DefaultListModel aModel)
```

```
   {  model = aModel;
      generator = new Random();
   }

   public void run()
   {  while (true)
      {  Integer i = new Integer(generator.nextInt(10));

         if (model.contains(i))
            model.removeElement(i);
         else
            model.addElement(i);

         yield();
      }
   }

   private DefaultListModel model;
   private Random generator;
}

class GoodWorkerThread extends Thread
{  public GoodWorkerThread(DefaultListModel aModel)
   {  model = aModel;
      generator = new Random();
   }

   public void run()
   {  while (true)
      {  final Integer i = new Integer(generator.nextInt(10));
         EventQueue.invokeLater(new Runnable()
            {  public void run()
               {  if (model.contains(i))
                     model.removeElement(i);
                  else
                     model.addElement(i);
               }
            });
         yield();
      }
   }

   private DefaultListModel model;
   private Random generator;
}
```

java.awt.EventQueue

- `static void invokeLater(Runnable runnable)`

  Causes the `run` method of the `runnable` object to be executed in the event dispatch thread, after pending events have been processed.

- `static void invokeAndWait(Runnable runnable)`

  Causes the `run` method of the `runnable` object to be executed in the event dispatch thread, after pending events have been processed. This call blocks until the `run` method has terminated.

Using Pipes for Communication Between Threads

Sometimes, the communication pattern between threads is very simple. One thread, the so-called *producer,* generates a stream of bytes. Another thread, the so-called *consumer,* reads and processes that byte stream. If no bytes are available for reading, the consumer thread blocks. If the producer generates data much more quickly than the consumer can handle it, then the write operation of the producer thread blocks. The Java programming language has a convenient set of classes, `PipedInputStream` and `PipedOutputStream`, to implement this communication pattern. (There is another pair of classes, `PipedReader` and `PipedWriter`, if the producer thread generates a stream of Unicode characters instead of bytes.)

The principal reason to use pipes is to keep each thread simple. The producer thread simply sends its results to a stream and forgets about them. The consumer simply reads the data from a stream, without having to care where it comes from. By using pipes, you can connect multiple threads with each other without worrying about thread synchronization.

Example 1–10 is a program that shows off piped streams. We have a producer thread that emits random numbers at random times, a filter thread that reads the input numbers and continuously computes the average of the data, and a consumer thread that prints out the answers. (You'll need to use CTRL+C to stop this program.) Figure 1–15 shows the threads and the pipes that connect them. Unix users will recognize these pipe streams as the equivalent of pipes connecting processes in Unix.

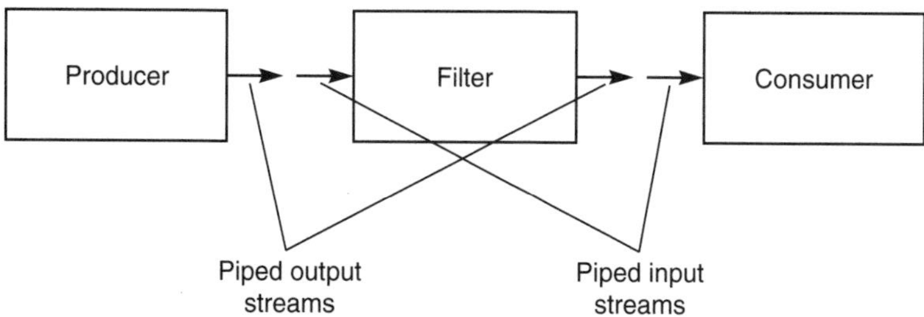

Figure 1–15: A sequence of pipes

Example 1–10: PipeTest.java

```
import java.util.*;
import java.io.*;

public class PipeTest
{  public static void main(String args[])
   {  try
      {  /* set up pipes */
         PipedOutputStream pout1 = new PipedOutputStream();
         PipedInputStream pin1 = new PipedInputStream(pout1);

         PipedOutputStream pout2 = new PipedOutputStream();
         PipedInputStream pin2 = new PipedInputStream(pout2);

         /* construct threads */

         Producer prod = new Producer(pout1);
         Filter filt = new Filter(pin1, pout2);
         Consumer cons = new Consumer(pin2);

         /* start threads */

         prod.start();
         filt.start();
         cons.start();
      }
      catch (IOException e){}
   }
}

class Producer extends Thread
{  public Producer(OutputStream os)
   {  out = new DataOutputStream(os);
   }

   public void run()
   {  while (true)
      {  try
         {  double num = rand.nextDouble();
            out.writeDouble(num);
            out.flush();
            sleep(Math.abs(rand.nextInt() % 1000));
         }
         catch(Exception e)
         {  System.out.println("Error: " + e);
         }
      }
   }

   private DataOutputStream out;
```

```
   private Random rand = new Random();
}

class Filter extends Thread
{  public Filter(InputStream is, OutputStream os)
   {  in = new DataInputStream(is);
      out = new DataOutputStream(os);
   }

   public void run()
   {  for (;;)
      {  try
         {  double x = in.readDouble();
            total += x;
            count++;
            if (count != 0) out.writeDouble(total / count);
         }
         catch(IOException e)
         {  System.out.println("Error: " + e);
         }
      }
   }

   private DataInputStream in;
   private DataOutputStream out;
   private double total = 0;
   private int count = 0;
}

class Consumer extends Thread
{  public Consumer(InputStream is)
   {   in = new DataInputStream(is);
   }

   public void run()
   {  for(;;)
      {  try
         {  double avg = in.readDouble();
            if (Math.abs(avg - old_avg) > 0.01)
            {  System.out.println("Current average is " + avg);
               old_avg = avg;
            }
         }
         catch(IOException e)
         {  System.out.println("Error: " + e);
         }
      }
   }

   private double old_avg = 0;
   private DataInputStream in;
}
```

java.io.PipedInputStream

- `PipedInputStream()`

  creates a new piped input stream that is not yet connected to a piped output stream.

- `PipedInputStream(PipedOutputStream out)`

  creates a new piped input stream that reads its data from a piped output stream.

  Parameters: `out` the source of the data

- `void connect(PipedOutputStream out)`

  attaches a piped output stream from which the data will be read.

  Parameters: `out` the source of the data

java.io.PipedOutputStream

- `PipedOutputStream()`

  creates a new piped output stream that is not yet connected to a piped input stream.

- `PipedOutputStream(PipedInputStream in)`

  creates a new piped output stream that writes its data to a piped input stream.

  Parameters: `in` the destination of the data

- `void connect(PipedInputStream in)`

  attaches a piped input stream to which the data will be written.

  Parameters: `in` the destination of the data

Chapter 2

Collections

- Collection Interfaces
- Concrete Collections
- The Collections Framework
- Algorithms
- Legacy Collections

OOP encapsulates data inside classes, but this doesn't make how you organize the data inside the classes any less important than in traditional programming languages. Of course, how you choose to structure the data depends on the problem you are trying to solve. Does your class need a way to easily search through thousands (or even millions) of items quickly? Does it need an ordered sequence of elements *and* the ability to rapidly insert and remove elements in the middle of the sequence? Does it need an arraylike structure with random-access ability that can grow at run time? The way you structure your data inside your classes can make a big difference when it comes to implementing methods in a natural style, as well as for performance.

This chapter shows how Java technology can help you accomplish the traditional data structuring needed for serious programming. In college computer science programs, there is a course called *Data Structures* that usually takes a semester to complete, so there are many, many books devoted to this important topic. Exhaustively covering all the data structures that may be useful is not our goal in this chapter; instead, we cover the fundamental ones that the standard Java library supplies. We hope that, after you finish this chapter, you will find it easy to translate any of your data structures to the Java programming language.

Collection Interfaces

Before the release of the Java 2 platform, the standard library supplied only a small set of classes for the most useful data structures: `Vector`, `Stack`, `Hashtable`, `BitSet`, and the `Enumeration` interface that provides an abstract mechanism for visiting elements in an arbitrary container. That was certainly a wise choice—it takes time and skill to come up with a comprehensive collection class library.

With the advent of the Java 2 platform, the designers felt that the time had come to roll out a full-fledged set of data structures. They faced a number of conflicting design decisions. They wanted the library to be small and easy to learn. They did not want the complexity of the "Standard Template Library" (or STL) of C++, but they wanted the benefit of "generic algorithms" that STL pioneered. They wanted the legacy classes to fit into the new framework. As all designers of collection libraries do, they had to make some hard choices, and they came up with a number of idiosyncratic design decisions along the way. In this section, we will explore the basic design of the Java collections framework, show you how to put it to work, and explain the reasoning behind some of the more controversial features.

Separating Collection Interfaces and Implementation

As is common for modern data structure libraries, the Java collection library separates *interfaces* and *implementations.* Let us look at that separation with a familiar data structure, the *queue.* The Java library does not supply a queue, but it is nevertheless a good example to introduce the basic concepts.

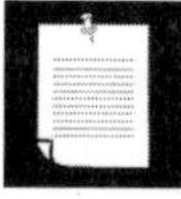

NOTE: If you need a queue, you can simply use the `LinkedList` class that we discuss later in this chapter.

A *queue interface* specifies that you can add elements at the tail end of the queue, remove them at the head, and find out how many elements are in the queue. You use a queue when you need to collect objects and retrieve them in a "first in, first out" fashion (see Figure 2–1).

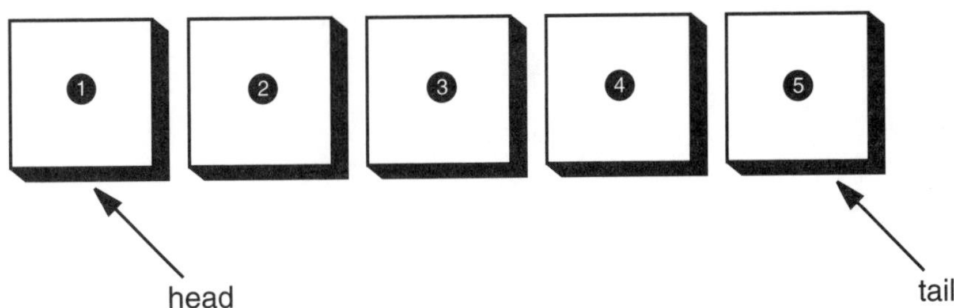

Figure 2–1: A queue

If there was a queue interface in the collections library, it might look like this:

```
interface Queue
{  void add(Object obj);
   Object remove();
   int size();
}
```

The interface tells you nothing about how the queue is implemented. There are two common implementations of a queue, one that uses a "circular array" and one that uses a linked list (see Figure 2–2).

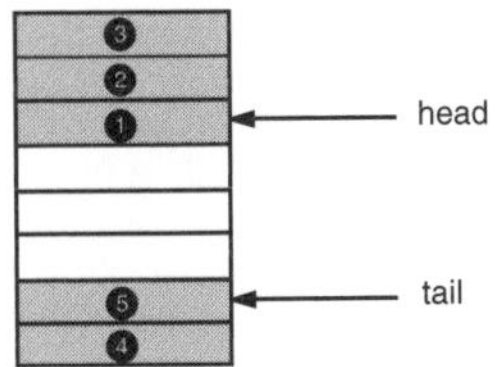

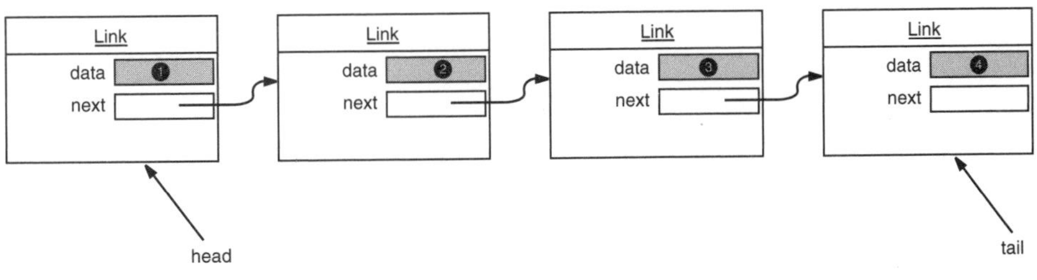

Figure 2–2: Queue implementations

Each implementation can be expressed by a class that realizes the `Queue` interface:

```
class CircularArrayQueue implements Queue
{  CircularArrayQueue(int capacity) { . . . }
   public void add(Object obj) { . . . }
   public Object remove() { . . . }
   public int size() { . . . }

   private Object[] elements;
   private int head;
   private int tail;
}

class LinkedListQueue implements Queue
{  LinkedListQueue() { . . . }
   public void add(Object obj) { . . . }
   public Object remove() { . . . }
   public int size() { . . . }

   private Link head;
   private Link tail;
}
```

When you use a queue in your program, you don't need to know which implementation is actually used once the collection has been constructed. Therefore, it makes sense to use the concrete class (such as `CircularArrayQueue`) *only* when you construct the collection object. Use the *interface type* to hold the collection reference.

```
Queue expressLane = new CircularArrayQueue(100);
expressLane.add(new Customer("Harry"));
```

This approach makes it easy to change your mind and use a different implementation. You only need to change your program in one place—the constructor. If you decide that a `LinkedListQueue` is a better choice after all, your code becomes

```
Queue expressLane = new LinkedListQueue();
expressLane.add(new Customer("Harry"));
```

Why would you choose one implementation over another? The interface says nothing about the efficiency of the implementation. A circular array is somewhat more efficient than a linked list, so it is generally preferable. However, as usual, there is a price to pay. The circular array is a *bounded* collection—it has a finite capacity. If you don't have an upper limit on the number of objects that your program will collect, you may be better off with a linked list implementation after all.

This example illustrates another issue for the designer of a collection class library. Strictly speaking, in a bounded collection, the interface of the `add` method should indicate that the method can fail:

```
class CircularArrayQueue
{  public void add(Object obj)
      throws CollectionFullException
   . . .
}
```

That's a problem—now the `CircularArrayQueue` class can't implement the `Queue` interface since you can't add exception specifiers when overriding a method. Should one have two interfaces, `BoundedQueue` and `Queue`? Or should the `add` method throw an unchecked exception? There are advantages and disadvantages to both approaches. It is these kinds of issues that make it genuinely hard to design a logically coherent collection class library.

As we already mentioned, the Java library has no separate class for queues. We just used this example to illustrate the difference between interface and implementation since a queue has a simple interface and two well-known distinct implementations. In the next section, you will see how the Java library classifies the collections that it supports.

Collection and Iterator Interfaces in the Java Library

The fundamental interface for collection classes in the Java library is the `Collection` interface. The interface has two fundamental methods:

```
boolean add(Object obj)
Iterator iterator()
```

There are several methods in addition to these two; we will discuss them later.

The `add` method adds an object to the collection. The `add` method returns `true` if adding the object actually changed the collection; `false`, if the collection is unchanged. For example, if you try to add an object to a set and the object is already present, then the `add` request is rejected since sets reject duplicates.

The `iterator` method returns an object that implements the `Iterator` interface—we will describe that interface in a moment. You can use the iterator object to visit the elements in the container one by one.

The `Iterator` interface has three fundamental methods:

```
Object next()
boolean hasNext()
void remove()
```

By repeatedly calling the `next` method, you can visit the elements from the collection one by one. However, if you reach the end of the collection, the `next` method throws a `NoSuchElementException`. Therefore, you need to call the `hasNext` method before calling `next`. That method returns `true` if the iterator object still has more elements to visit. If you want to inspect all elements in a container, you request an iterator and then keep calling the `next` method while `hasNext` returns true.

```
Iterator iter = c.iterator();
while (iter.hasNext())
{  Object obj = iter.next();
   do something with obj
}
```

NOTE: Old-timers will notice that the `next` and `hasNext` methods of the `Iterator` interface serve the same purpose as the `nextElement` and `hasMoreElements` methods of an `Enumeration`. The designers of the Java collection library could have chosen to extend the `Enumeration` interface. But they disliked the cumbersome method names and chose to introduce a new interface with shorter method names instead.

Finally, the `remove` method removes the element that was returned by the last call to `next`.

You may well wonder why the `remove` method is a part of the `Iterator` interface. It is more efficient to remove an element if you know *where* it is. The iterator knows about *positions* in the collection. Therefore, the `remove` method was added to the `Iterator` interface. If you visited an element that you didn't like, you can efficiently remove it.

There is an important conceptual difference between iterators in the Java collection library and iterators in other libraries. In traditional collection libraries such as the Standard Template Library of C++, iterators are modeled after array indexes. Given such an iterator, you can look up the element that is stored at that position, much like you can look up an array element `a[i]` if you have an array index `i`. Independently of the lookup, you can advance the iterator to the next position, just like you can advance an array index with the `i++` operation without performing a lookup. However, the Java iterators do not work like that. The lookup and position change are tightly coupled. The only way to look up an element is to call `next`, and that lookup advances the position.

Instead, you should think of Java iterators as being *between elements*. When you call `next`, the iterator *jumps over* the next element, and it returns a reference to the element that it just passed (see Figure 2–3).

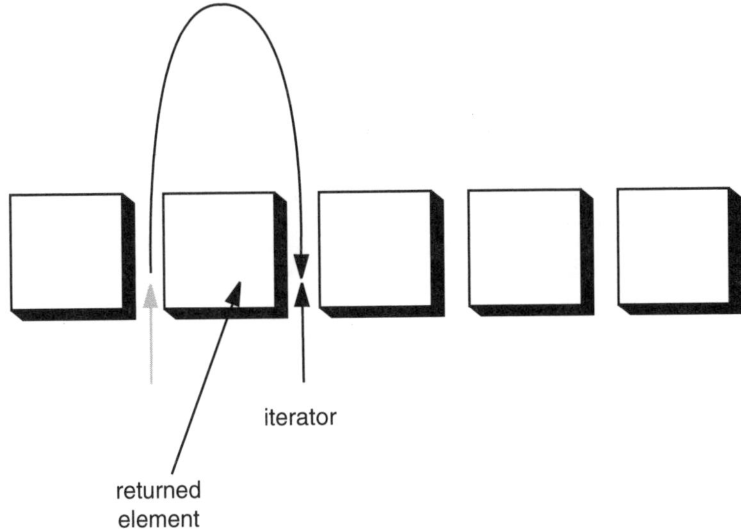

Figure 2–3: Advancing an iterator

NOTE: Here is another useful analogy. You can think of `Iterator.next` as the equivalent of `InputStream.read`. Reading a byte from a stream automatically "consumes" the byte. The next call to `read` consumes and returns the next byte from the input. Similarly, repeated calls to `next` let you read all elements in a collection.

You must be careful when using the `remove` method. Calling `remove` removes the element that was returned by the last call to `next`. That makes sense if you want to remove a particular value—you need to see the element before you can decide that it is the one that should be removed. But if you want to remove an element by position, you first need to skip past the element. For example, here is how you remove the first element in a collection.

```
Iterator it = c.iterator();
it.next(); // skip over the first element
it.remove(); // now remove it
```

More importantly, there is a dependency between calls to the `next` and `remove` methods. It is illegal to call `remove` if it wasn't preceded by a call to `next`. If you try, an `IllegalStateException` is thrown.

If you want to remove two adjacent elements, you cannot simply call

```
it.remove();
it.remove(); // Error!
```

Instead, you must first call `next` to jump over the element to be removed.

```
it.remove();
it.next();
it.remove(); // Ok
```

Because the collection and iterator interfaces are generic, you can write utility methods that operate on any kind of collection. For example, here is a generic `print` method that prints all elements in a collection.

```
public static void print(Collection c)
{  System.out.print("[ ");
   Iterator iter = c.iterator();
   while (iter.hasNext())
      System.out.print(iter.next() + " ");
   System.out.println("]");
}
```

NOTE: We give this example to illustrate how to write a generic method. If you want to print the elements in a collection, you can just call `System.out.println(c)`. This works because each collection class has a `toString` method that returns a string containing all elements in the collection.

Here is a method that adds all objects from one collection to another:

```
public static boolean addAll(Collection to, Collection from)
{  Iterator iter = from.iterator();
   boolean modified = false;
   while (iter.hasNext())
      if (to.add(iter.next()))
         modified = true;
   return modified;
}
```

Recall that the `add` method returns `true` if adding the element modified the collection. You can implement these utility methods for arbitrary collections because the `Collection` and `Iterator` interfaces supply fundamental methods such as `add` and `next`.

The designers of the Java library decided that some of these utility methods are so useful that the library should make them available. That way, users don't have to keep reinventing the wheel. The `addAll` method is one such method.

Had `Collection` been an abstract class instead of an interface, then it would have been an easy matter to supply this functionality in the class. However, you cannot supply methods in interfaces of the Java programming language. Therefore, the collection library takes a slightly different approach. The

Collection interface declares quite a few useful methods that all implementing classes must supply. Among them are:

```
int size()
boolean isEmpty()
boolean contains(Object obj)
boolean containsAll(Collection c)
boolean equals(Object other)
boolean addAll(Collection from)
boolean remove(Object obj)
boolean removeAll(Collection c)
void clear()
boolean retainAll(Collection c)
Object[] toArray()
```

Many of these methods are self-explanatory; you will find full documentation in the API notes at the end of this section.

Of course, it is a bother if every class that implements the Collection interface has to supply so many routine methods. To make life easier for implementors, the class AbstractCollection leaves the fundamental methods (such as add and iterator) abstract but implements the routine methods in terms of them. For example,

```
public class AbstractCollection
   implements Collection
{  . . .
   public abstract boolean add(Object obj);

   public boolean addAll(Collection from)
   {  Iterator iter = iterator();
      boolean modified = false;
      while (iter.hasNext())
         if (add(iter.next()))
            modified = true;
      return modified
   }
   . . .
}
```

A concrete collection class can now extend the AbstractCollection class. It is now up to the concrete collection class to supply an add method, but the addAll method has been taken care of by the AbstractCollection superclass. However, if the subclass has a more efficient way of implementing addAll, it is free to do so.

This is a good design for a class framework. The users of the collection classes have a richer set of methods available in the generic interface, but the implementors of the actual data structures do not have the burden of implementing all the routine methods.

`java.util.Collection`

- `Iterator iterator()`

  returns an iterator that can be used to visit the elements in the collection.
- `int size()`

  returns the number of elements currently stored in the collection.
- `boolean isEmpty()`

  returns `true` if this collection contains no elements.
- `boolean contains(Object obj)`

  returns `true` if this collection contains an object equal to `obj`.

  Parameters: `obj` the object to match in the collection
- `boolean containsAll(Collection other)`

  returns `true` if this collection contains all elements in the other collection.

  Parameters: `other` the collection holding the elements to match
- `boolean add(Object element)`

  adds an element to the collection. Returns `true` if the collection changed as a result of this call.

  Parameters: `element` the element to add
- `boolean addAll(Collection other)`

  adds all elements from the other collection to this collection. Returns `true` if the collection changed as a result of this call.

  Parameters: `other` the collection holding the elements to add
- `boolean remove(Object obj)`

  removes an object equal to `obj` from this collection. Returns `true` if a matching object was removed.

  Parameters: `obj` an object that equals the element to remove
- `boolean removeAll(Collection other)`

  removes all elements from the other collection from this collection. Returns `true` if the collection changed as a result of this call.

  Parameters: `other` the collection holding the elements to add
- `void clear()`

  removes all elements from this collection.
- `boolean retainAll(Collection other)`

  removes all elements from this collection that do not equal one of the

elements in the other collection. Returns `true` if the collection changed as a result of this call.

Parameters: `other` the collection holding the elements to be kept

- `Object[] toArray()`
  returns an array of the objects in the collection.

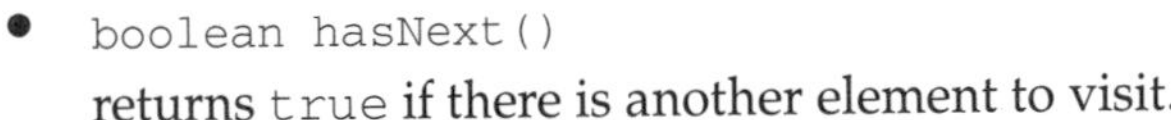

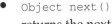

`java.util.Iterator`

- `boolean hasNext()`
  returns `true` if there is another element to visit.
- `Object next()`
  returns the next object to visit. Throws a `NoSuchElementException` if the end of the collection has been reached.
- `Object remove()`
  removes and returns the last visited object. This method must immediately follow an element visit. If the collection has been modified since the last element visit, then the method throws an `IllegalStateException`.

Concrete Collections

Rather than getting into more details about all the interfaces, we thought it would be helpful to first discuss the concrete data structures that the Java library supplies. Once you have a thorough understanding of what classes you will want to use, we will return to abstract considerations and see how the collections framework organizes these classes.

Linked Lists

We used arrays and their dynamic cousin, the `Vector` class, for many examples in Volume 1. However, arrays and vectors suffer from a major drawback. Removing an element from the middle of an array is very expensive since all array elements beyond the removed one must be moved toward the beginning of the array (see Figure 2–4). The same is true for inserting elements in the middle.

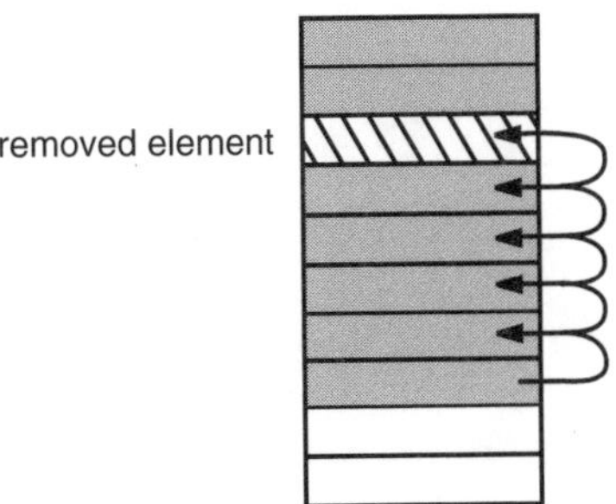

Figure 2–4: Removing an element from an array

Another well-known data structure, the *linked list*, solves this problem. Whereas an array stores object references in consecutive memory locations, a linked list stores each object in a separate *link*. Each link also stores a reference to the next link in the sequence. In the Java programming language, all linked lists are actually *doubly linked*, that is, each link also stores a reference to its predecessor (see Figure 2–5).

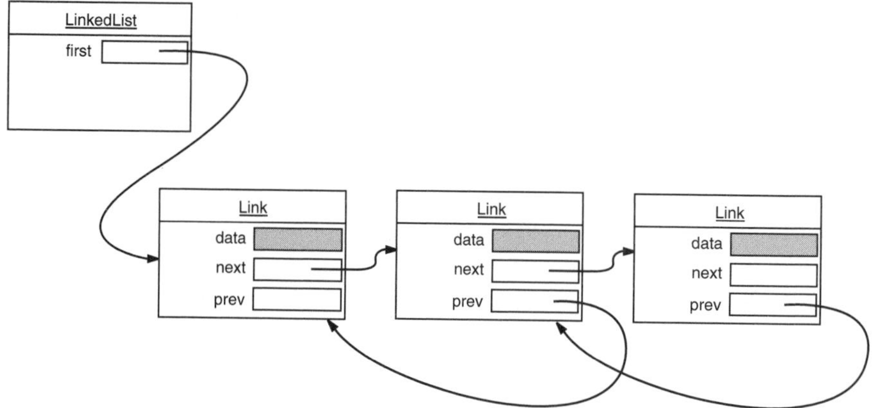

Figure 2–5: A doubly linked list

Removing an element from the middle of a linked list is an inexpensive operation—only the links around the element to be removed need to be updated (see Figure 2–6).

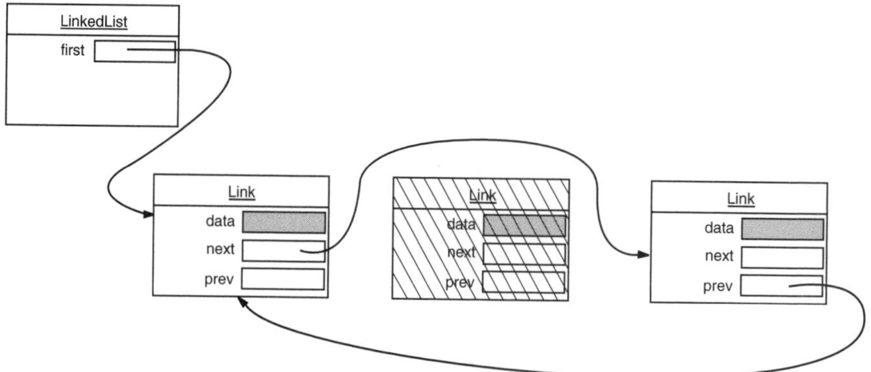

Figure 2–6: Removing an element from a linked list

Perhaps you once had a course in data structures where you learned how to implement linked lists. You may have bad memories of tangling up the links when removing or adding elements in the linked list. If so, you will be pleased to learn that the Java collections library supplies a class `LinkedList` ready for you to use.

The `LinkedList` class implements the `Collection` interface. You can use the familiar methods to traverse a list. The following code example prints the first three elements of a list, adds three elements, and then removes the third one.

```
LinkedList staff = new LinkedList();
staff.add("Angela");
staff.add("Bob");
staff.add("Carl");
Iterator iter = staff.iterator();
for (int i = 0; i < 3; i++)
   System.out.println(iter.next());
iter.remove(); // remove last visited element
```

However, there is an important difference between linked lists and generic collections. A linked list is an *ordered collection* where the position of the objects matters. The `LinkedList.add` method adds the object to the end of the list. But you often want to add objects somewhere in the middle of a list. This position-dependent `add` method is the responsibility of an iterator, since iterators describe positions in collections. Using iterators to add elements only makes sense for collections that have a natural ordering. For example, the *set* data type that we discuss in the next section does not impose any ordering on its elements. Therefore, there is no `add` method in the `Iterator` interface. Instead, the collections library supplies a subinterface `ListIterator` that contains an `add` method:

```
interface ListIterator extends Iterator
{  void add(Object);
   . . .
}
```

Unlike `Collection.add`, this method does not return a `boolean`—it is assumed that the `add` operation always succeeds.

In addition, the `ListIterator` interface has two methods—

```
Object previous()
boolean hasPrevious()
```

—that you can use for traversing a list backwards. Like the `next` method, the `previous` method returns the object that it skipped over.

The `listIterator` method of the `LinkedList` class returns an iterator object that implements the `ListIterator` interface.

```
ListIterator iter = staff.listIterator();
```

The `add` method adds the new element *before* the iterator position. For example, the code

```
ListIterator iter = staff.listIterator();
iter.next();
iter.add("Juliet");
```

skips past the first element in the linked list and adds "Juliet" before the second element (see Figure 2–7).

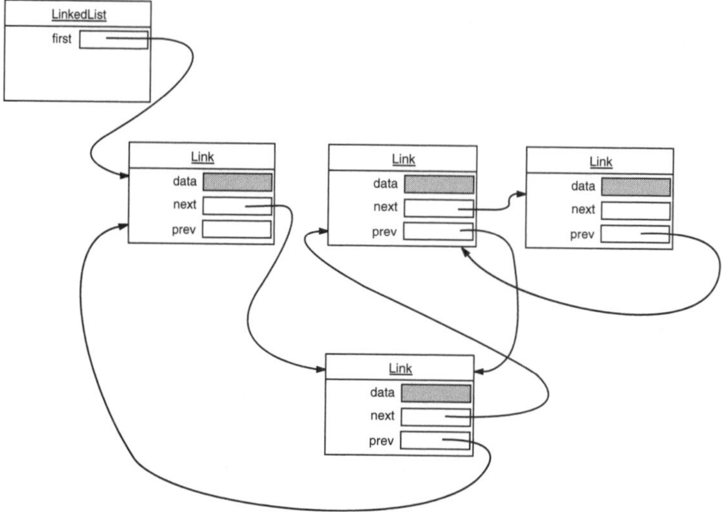

Figure 2–7: Adding an element to a linked list

If you call the `add` method multiple times, the elements are simply added in the order in which you supplied them. They all get added in turn before the current iterator position.

When you use the `add` operation with an iterator that was freshly returned from the `listIterator` method and that points to the beginning of the linked list, the newly added element becomes the new head of the list. When the iterator has passed the last element of the list (that is, when `hasNext` returns `false`), the added element becomes the new tail of the list. If the linked list has n elements, there are $n + 1$ spots for adding a new element. These spots correspond to the $n + 1$ possible positions of the iterator. For example, if a linked list contains three elements A, B, and C, then the four possible positions (marked as |) for inserting a new element are:

```
|ABC
A|BC
AB|C
ABC|
```

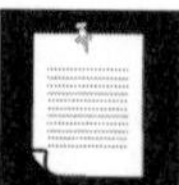

NOTE: You have to be careful with the "cursor" analogy. The `remove` operation does not quite work like the BACKSPACE key. Immediately after a call to `next`, the `remove` method indeed removes the element to the left of the iterator, just like the BACKSPACE key would. However, if you just called `previous`, the element to the right is removed. And you can't call `remove` twice in a row.

Unlike the `add` method, which only depends on the iterator position, the `remove` method depends on the iterator state.

Finally, there is a `set` method that replaces the last element returned by a call to `next` or `previous` with a new element. For example, the following code replaces the first element of a list with a new value:

```
ListIterator iter = list.listIterator();
Object oldValue = iter.next(); // returns first element
iter.set(newValue); // sets first element to newValue
```

As you might imagine, if an iterator traverses a collection while another iterator is modifying it, confusing situations can occur. For example, suppose an iterator points before an element that another iterator has just removed. The iterator is now invalid and should no longer be used. The linked list iterators have been designed to detect such modifications. If an iterator finds that its collection has been modified by another iterator or by a method of the collection itself, then it throws a `ConcurrentModificationException`. For example, consider the following code:

```
LinkedList list = . . .;
ListIterator iter1 = list.listIterator();
ListIterator iter2 = list.listIterator();
iter1.next();
iter1.remove();
iter2.next(); // throws ConcurrentModificationException
```

The call to `iter2.next` throws a `ConcurrentModificationException` since `iter2` detects that the list was modified externally.

To avoid concurrent modification exceptions, follow this simple rule: You can attach as many iterators to a container as you like, provided that all of them are only readers. Alternatively, you can attach a single iterator that can both read and write.

Concurrent modification detection is achieved in a simple way. The container keeps track of the number of mutating operations (such as adding and removing elements). Each iterator keeps a separate count of the number of mutating operations that *it* was responsible for. At the beginning of each iterator method, the iterator simply checks whether its own mutation count equals that of the container. If not, it throws a `ConcurrentModificationException`.

This is an excellent check and a great improvement over the fundamentally unsafe iterators in the C++ STL framework. Note, however, that it does not automatically make collections safe for multithreading. We discuss thread safety issues later in this chapter.

NOTE: There is, however, a curious exception to the detection of concurrent modifications. The linked list only keeps track of *structural* modifications to the list, such as adding and removing links. The `set` method does *not* count as a structural modification. You can attach multiple iterators to a linked list, all of which call `set` to change the contents of existing links. This capability is required for a number of algorithms in the `Collections` class that we discuss later in this chapter.

Now you have seen the fundamental methods of the `LinkedList` class. You use a `ListIterator` to traverse the elements of the linked list in either direction and to add and remove elements.

As you saw in the preceding section, there are many other useful methods for operating on linked lists that are declared in the `Collection` interface. These are, for the most part, implemented in the `AbstractCollection` superclass of the `LinkedList` class. For example, the `toString` method invokes `toString` on all elements and produces one long string of the format `[A, B, C]`. This is handy for debugging. Use the `contains` method to check whether an element is present in a linked list. For example, the call `staff.contains("Harry")` returns `true` if the linked list already contains a string that is equal to the String `"Harry"`. However, there is no method that returns an iterator to that position. If you want to do something with the element beyond knowing that it exists, you have to program an iteration loop by hand.

CAUTION: The Java platform documentation points out that you should not add a reference of a collection to itself. Otherwise, it is easy to generate a stack overflow in the virtual machine. For example, the following call is fatal:

```
LinkedList list = new LinkedList();
list.add(list); // add list to itself
String contents = list.toString(); // dies with infinite recursion
```

Naturally, this is not a situation that comes up in everyday programming.

The library also supplies a number of methods that are, from a theoretical perspective, somewhat dubious. Linked lists do not support fast random access. If you want to see the *n*th element of a linked list, you have to start at the beginning and skip past the first $n - 1$ elements first. There is no shortcut. For that reason, programmers don't usually use linked lists in programming situations where elements need to be accessed by an integer index.

Nevertheless, the `LinkedList` class supplies a `get` method that lets you access a particular element:

```
Object obj = list.get(n);
```

Of course, this method is not very efficient. If you find yourself using it, you are probably using the wrong data structure for your problem.

You should *never* use this illusory random access method to step through a linked list. The code

```
for (int i = 0; i < list.size(); i++)
   do something with list.get(i);
```

is staggeringly inefficient. Each time you look up another element, the search starts again from the beginning of the list. The `LinkedList` object makes no effort to cache the position information.

NOTE: The `get` method has one slight optimization: if the index is at least `size() / 2`, then the search for the element starts at the end of the list.

The list iterator interface also has a method to tell you the index of the current position. In fact, because Java iterators conceptually point between elements, it has two of them: the `nextIndex` method returns the integer index of the element that would be returned by the next call to `next`; the `previousIndex` method returns the index of the element that would be returned by the next call to `previous`. Of course, that is simply one less than `nextIndex`. These methods are efficient—the iterators keep a count of the current position. Finally, if you have an integer index `n`, then `list.listIterator(n)` returns an iterator that points just before the element with index `n`. That is, calling `next` yields the same element as `list.get(n)`. Of course, obtaining that iterator is inefficient.

If you have a linked list with only a handful of elements, then you don't have to be overly paranoid about the cost of the `get` and `set` methods. But then why use a linked list in the first place? The only reason to use a linked list is to minimize the cost of insertion and removal in the middle of the list. If you only have a few elements, you can just use an array or a collection such as `ArrayList`.

We recommend that you simply stay away from all methods that use an integer index to denote a position in a linked list. If you want random access into a collection, use an array or `ArrayList`, not a linked list.

The program in Example 2–1 puts linked lists to work. It simply creates two lists, merges them, then removes every second element from the second list, and finally tests the `removeAll` method. We recommend that you trace the program flow and pay special attention to the iterators. You may find it helpful to draw diagrams of the iterator positions, like this:

```
|ACE   |BDFG
A|CE   |BDFG
AB|CE  B|DFG
. . .
```

Note that the call

```
System.out.println(a);
```

prints all elements in the linked list `a`.

Example 2–1: LinkedListTest.java

```
import java.util.*;

public class LinkedListTest
{  public static void main(String[] args)
```

```
    {  List a = new LinkedList();
       a.add("Angela");
       a.add("Carl");
       a.add("Erica");

       List b = new LinkedList();
       b.add("Bob");
       b.add("Doug");
       b.add("Frances");
       b.add("Gloria");

       // merge the words from b into a

       ListIterator aIter = a.listIterator();
       Iterator bIter = b.iterator();

       while (bIter.hasNext())
       {  if (aIter.hasNext()) aIter.next();
          aIter.add(bIter.next());
       }

       System.out.println(a);

       // remove every second word from b

       bIter = b.iterator();
       while (bIter.hasNext())
       {  bIter.next(); // skip one element
          if (bIter.hasNext())
          {  bIter.next(); // skip next element
             bIter.remove(); // remove that element
          }
       }

       System.out.println(b);

       // bulk operation: remove all words in b from a

       a.removeAll(b);

       System.out.println(a);

    }
}
```

`java.util.List`

- `ListIterator listIterator()`
  returns a list iterator for visiting the elements of the list.
- `ListIterator listIterator(int index)`
  returns a list iterator for visiting the elements of the list whose first call to `next` will return the element with the given index.

  Parameters: `index` the position of the next visited element
- `void add(int i, Object element)`
  adds an element at the specified position.

  Parameters: `index` the position of the new element
  `element` the element to add
- `void addAll(int i, Collection elements)`
  adds all elements from a collection to the specified position.

  Parameters: `index` the position of the first new element
  `elements` the elements to add
- `Object remove(int i)`
  removes and returns an element at the specified position.

  Parameters: `index` the position of the element to remove
- `Object set(int i, Object element)`
  replaces the element at the specified position with a new element and returns the old element.

  Parameters: `index` the replacement position
  `element` the new element
- `int indexOf(Object element)`
  returns the position of the first occurrence of an element equal to the specified element, or –1 if no matching element is found.

  Parameters: `element` the element to match
- `int lastIndexOf(Object element)`
  returns the position of the last occurrence of an element equal to the specified element, or –1 if no matching element is found.

  Parameters: `element` the element to match

java.util.ListIterator

- `void add(Object element)`

  adds an element before the current position.

  Parameters: `element` the element to add

- `void set(Object element)`

  replaces the last element visited by `next` or `previous` with a new element. Throws an `IllegalStateException` if the list structure was modified since the last call to `next` or `previous`.

  Parameters: `element` the new element

- `boolean hasPrevious()`

  returns `true` if there is another element to visit when iterating backwards through the list.

- `Object previous()`

  returns the previous object. Throws a `NoSuchElementException` if the beginning of the list has been reached.

- `int nextIndex()`

  returns the index of the element that would be returned by the next call to `next`.

- `int previousIndex()`

  returns the index of the element that would be returned by the next call to `previous`.

java.util.LinkedList

- `LinkedList()`

  constructs an empty linked list.

- `LinkedList(Collection elements)`

  constructs a linked list and adds all elements from a collection.

  Parameters: `elements` the elements to add

- `void addFirst(Object element)`
- `void addLast(Object element)`

  add an element to the beginning or the end of the list.

  Parameters: `element` the element to add

- `Object getFirst()`
- `Object getLast()`

  return the element at the beginning or the end of the list.

- `Object removeFirst()`
- `Object removeLast()`

  remove and return the element at the beginning or the end of the list.

Array Lists

In the preceding section, you saw the `List` interface and the `LinkedList` class that implements it. The `List` interface describes an ordered collection in which the position of elements matters. There are two protocols for visiting the elements: through an iterator and by random access with methods `get` and `set`. The latter are not appropriate for linked lists, but of course they make a lot of sense for arrays. The collections library supplies an `ArrayList` class that implements the `List` interface. An `ArrayList` is similar to a `Vector`: it encapsulates a dynamically reallocated `Object[]` array.

Why use an `ArrayList` instead of a `Vector`? There is one simple reason. All methods of the `Vector` class are *synchronized*. It is safe to access a `Vector` object from two threads. But if you only access a vector from a single thread—by far the more common case—your code wastes quite a bit of time with synchronization. In contrast, the `ArrayList` methods are not synchronized. We recommend that you use an `ArrayList` instead of a `Vector` whenever you don't need synchronization.

Using an `ArrayList` is as simple as using a `Vector`. Just keep in mind that you need to use the short method names `get` and `set` instead of the `elementAt` and `setElementAt` methods.

Hash Sets

Linked lists and arrays let you specify in which order you want to arrange the elements. However, if you are looking for a particular element and you don't remember its position, then you need to visit all elements until you find a match. That can be time-consuming if the collection contains many elements. If you don't care about the ordering of the elements, then there are data structures that let you find elements much faster. The drawback is that those data structures give you no control over the order in which the elements appear. The data structures organize the elements in an order that is convenient for their own purposes.

A well-known data structure for finding objects quickly is the *hash table*. A hash table computes an integer, called the *hash code*, for each object. We see in the next section how these hash codes are computed. What's important for now is that hash codes can be computed quickly and that the computation only depends on the state of the object that needs to be hashed, and not on the other objects in the hash table.

A hash table is an array of linked lists. Each list is called a *bucket* (see Figure 2–8). To find the place of an object in the table, compute its hash code and reduce it modulo the total number of buckets. The resulting number is the index of the bucket that holds the element. For example, if an object has hash code 345 and there are 101 buckets, then the object is placed in bucket 42 (because the remainder of the integer division 345/101 is 42). Perhaps you are lucky and there is no other element in that bucket. Then, you simply insert the element into that bucket. Of course, it is inevitable that you sometimes hit a bucket that is already filled. This is called a *hash collision*. Then, you need to compare the new object with all objects in that bucket to see if it is already present. Provided that the hash codes are reasonably randomly distributed and the number of buckets is large enough, only a few comparisons should be necessary.

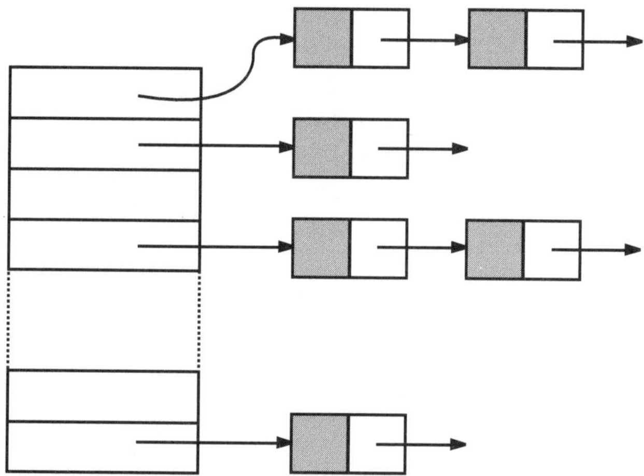

Figure 2–8: A hash table

If you want more control over the performance of the hash table, you can specify the initial bucket count. The bucket count gives the number of buckets that are used to collect objects with identical hash values. If too many elements are inserted into a hash table, the number of collisions increases and retrieval performance suffers.

If you know approximately how many elements will eventually be in the table, then you should set the initial bucket count to about 150 percent of the expected element count. Some researchers believe that it is a good idea to make the size of the hash table a prime number to prevent a clustering of keys. The evidence for this isn't conclusive, but it certainly can't hurt. For example, if you need to store about 100 entries, set the initial bucket size to 151.

Of course, you do not always know how many elements you need to store, or your initial guess may be too low. If the hash table gets too full, it needs to be

rehashed. To rehash the table, a table with more buckets is created, all elements are inserted into the new table, and the original table is discarded. In the Java programming language, the *load factor* determines when a hash table is rehashed. For example, if the load factor is 0.75 (which is the default) and the hash table becomes more than 75 percent full, then the table is automatically rehashed, using twice as many buckets. For most applications, it is reasonable to leave the load factor at 0.75.

Hash tables can be used to implement several important data structures. The simplest among them is the *set* type. A set is a collection of elements without duplicates. The `add` method of a set first tries to find the object to be added and only adds it if it is not yet present.

The Java collections library supplies a `HashSet` class that implements a set based on a hash table. At the time of this writing, the default constructor `HashSet` constructs a hash table with 101 buckets and a load factor of 0.75. These values may change in future releases. If you at all care about these values, you should specify your own, with the constructors

```
HashSet(int initialCapacity)
HashSet(int initialCapacity, float loadFactor)
```

You add elements with the `add` method. The `contains` method is redefined to make a quick lookup to find if an element is already present in the set. It only checks the elements in one bucket and not all elements in the collection. The hash set iterator visits all buckets in turn. Since the hashing scatters the elements around in the table, they are visited in seemingly random order. You would only use a hash set if you don't care about the ordering of the elements in the collection.

The sample program at the end of this section (Example 2–2) reads words from `System.in`, adds them to a set and finally prints out all words in the set. For example, you can feed the program the text from *Alice in Wonderland* (which you can obtain from `www.gutenberg.net`) by launching it from a command shell as

```
java SetTest < alice30.txt
```

The program reads all words from the input and adds them to the hash set. It then iterates through the unique words in the set and finally prints out a count. (*Alice in Wonderland* has 5,909 unique words, including the copyright notice at the beginning.) The words appear in random order.

Example 2–2: SetTest.java

```
import java.util.*;
import java.io.*;

public class SetTest
{  public static void main(String[] args)
```

```
   {  Set words = new HashSet(59999);
         // set to HashSet or TreeSet
      long totalTime = 0;

      try
      {  BufferedReader in = new
            BufferedReader(new InputStreamReader(System.in));
         String line;
         while ((line = in.readLine()) != null)
         {  StringTokenizer tokenizer = new StringTokenizer(line);
            while (tokenizer.hasMoreTokens())
            {  String word = tokenizer.nextToken();
               long callTime = System.currentTimeMillis();
               words.add(word);
               callTime = System.currentTimeMillis() - callTime;
               totalTime += callTime;
            }
         }
      }
      catch (IOException e)
      {  System.out.println("Error " + e);
      }

      Iterator iter = words.iterator();
      while (iter.hasNext())
         System.out.println(iter.next());
      System.out.println(words.size()
         + " distinct words. " + totalTime + " milliseconds.");
   }
}
```

`java.util.HashSet`

- `HashSet()`
  constructs an empty hash set.
- `HashSet(Collection elements)`
  constructs a hash set and adds all elements from a collection.

  Parameters: `elements` the elements to add
- `HashSet(int initialCapacity)`
  constructs an empty hash set with the specified capacity.

  Parameters: `initialCapacity` the initial number of buckets
- `HashSet(int initialCapacity, float loadFactor)`
  constructs an empty hash set with the specified capacity and load factor.

Parameters:	`initialCapacity`	the initial number of buckets
	`loadFactor`	a number between 0.0 and 1.0 that determines at what percentage of fullness the hash table will be rehashed into a larger one

Hash functions

You can insert strings into a hash set because the `String` class has a `hashCode` method that computes a *hash code* for a string. A hash code is an integer that is somehow derived from the characters in the string. Table 2–1 lists a few examples of hash codes that result from the `hashCode` function of the `String` class.

Table 2–1: Hash codes resulting from the `hashCode` function

String	Hash code
Hello	140207504
Harry	140013338
Hacker	884756206

The `hashCode` method is defined in the `Object` class. Therefore, every object has a default hash code. That hash code is derived from the object's memory address. In general, the default hash function is not very useful because objects with identical contents may yield different hash codes. Consider this example.

```
String s = "Ok";
StringBuffer sb = new StringBuffer(s);
System.out.println(s.hashCode() + " " + sb.hashCode());
String t = "Ok";
StringBuffer tb = new StringBuffer(t);
System.out.println(t.hashCode() + " " + tb.hashCode());
```

Table 2–2 shows the result.

Table 2–2: Hash codes of objects with identical contents

`"Ok" String` hash code	`"Ok" StringBuffer` hash code
`3030`	`20526976`
`3030`	`20527144`

Note that the strings `s` and `t` have the same hash value because, for strings, the hash values are derived from their *contents*. The string buffers `sb` and `tb` have different hash values because no special hash function has been defined for the `StringBuffer` class and the default hash code function in the `Object` class derives the hash code from the object's memory address.

You should always define the hashCode method for objects that you insert into a hash table. This method should return an integer (which can be negative). The hash table code will later reduce the integer by dividing by the bucket count and taking the remainder. Just scramble up the hash codes of the data fields in some way that will give the hash codes for different objects a good chance of being widely scattered.

For example, suppose you have the class Item for inventory items. An item consists of a description string and a part number.

```
anItem = new Item("Toaster", 49954);
```

If you want to construct a hash set of items, you need to define a hash code. For example,

```
class Item
{   . . .
   public int hashCode()
   {   return 13 * description.hashCode() + 17 * partNumber;
   }
   . . .
   private String description;
   private int partNumber;
}
```

As a practical matter, if the part number uniquely identifies the item, you don't need to incorporate the hash code of the description.

Furthermore, you *also* need to make sure that the equals method is well defined. The Object class defines equals, but that method only tests whether or not two objects are *identical*. If you don't redefine equals, then every new object that you insert into the table will be considered a *different* object.

You need to redefine equals to check for equal contents.

```
class Item
{  . . .
     public boolean equals(Object other)
     {  if (other != null && getClass() == other.getClass())
        {  Item otherItem = (Item)other;
           return description.equals(otherItem.description)
               && partNumber == otherItem.partNumber;
        }
        else
           return false;
     }
     . . .
}
```

CAUTION: Your definitions of `equals` and `hashCode` must be *compatible:* if `x.equals(y)` is `true`, then `x.hashCode()` must be the same value as `y.hashCode()`.

`java.lang.Object`

- `boolean equals(Object obj)`

  compares two objects for equality; returns `true` if both objects are equal; `false` otherwise.

  Parameters: `obj` the object to compare with the first object (may be `null`, in which case the method should return `false`)

- `int hashCode()`

  returns a hash code for this object. A hash code can be any integer, positive or negative. Equal objects need to return identical hash codes.

Tree Sets

The `TreeSet` class is similar to the hash set, with one added improvement. A tree set is a *sorted collection*. You insert elements into the collection in any order. When you iterate through the collection, the values are automatically presented in sorted order. For example, suppose you insert three strings and then visit all elements that you added.

```
TreeSet sorter = new TreeSet();
sorter.add("Bob");
sorter.add("Angela");
sorter.add("Carl");
Iterator iter = sorter.iterator();
while (iter.hasNext()) System.println(iter.next());
```

Then, the values are printed in sorted order: `Angela Bob Carl`. As the name of the class suggests, the sorting is accomplished by a tree data structure. (The current implementation uses a *red-black tree*. For a detailed description of red-black trees, see, for example, *Introduction to Algorithms* by Thomas Cormen, Charles Leiserson, and Ronald Rivest [The MIT Press 1990].) Every time an element is added to a tree, it is placed into its proper sorting position. Therefore, the iterator always visits the elements in sorted order.

Adding an element to a tree is slower than adding it to a hash table, but it is still much faster than adding it into the right place in an array or linked list. If the tree contains n elements, then an average of $\log_2 n$ comparisons are required to find the correct position for the new element. For example, if the tree already contains 1,000 elements, then adding a new element requires about 10 comparisons.

Thus, adding elements into a `TreeSet` is somewhat slower than adding into a `HashSet` —see Table 2–3 for a comparison—but the `TreeSet` automatically sorts the elements.

Table 2–3: Adding elements into hash and tree sets

Document	Total number of words	Number of distinct words	`HashSet`	`TreeSet`
Alice in Wonderland	28195	5909	5 sec	7 sec
The Count of Monte Cristo	466300	37545	75 sec	98 sec

`java.util.TreeSet`

- `TreeSet()`
  constructs an empty tree set.
- `TreeSet(Collection elements)`
  constructs a tree set and adds all elements from a collection.
  Parameters: `elements` the elements to add

Object comparison

How does the `TreeSet` know how you want the elements sorted? By default, the tree set assumes that you insert elements that implement the `Comparable` interface. That interface defines a single method:

```
int compareTo(Object other)
```

The call `a.compareTo(b)` must return 0 if `a` and `b` are equal, a negative integer if `a` comes before `b` in the sort order, and a positive integer if `a` comes after `b`. The exact value does not matter; only its sign (>0, 0, or < 0) matters. Several standard Java platform classes implement the `Comparable` interface. One example is the `String` class. Its `compareTo` method compares strings in dictionary order (sometimes called *lexicographic order*).

If you insert your own objects, you need to define a sort order yourself by implementing the `Comparable` interface. There is no default implementation of `compareTo` in the `Object` class.

For example, here is how you can sort `Item` objects by part number.

```
class Item implements Comparable
{  public int compareTo(Object other)
   {  Item otherItem = (Item)other;
      return partNumber - otherItem.partNumber;
   }
   . . .
}
```

Note that the explicit argument of the `compareTo` method has type `Object`, not `Comparable`. If the object is not of the correct type, then this `compareTo` method simply throws a `ClassCastException`. (The `compareTo` methods in the standard library behave in the same way when presented with illegal argument types.)

If you compare two *positive* integers, such as part numbers in our example, then you can simply return their difference—it will be negative if the first item should come before the second item, zero if the part numbers are identical, and positive otherwise.

CAUTION: This trick does *not* work if the integers can be negative. If `x` is a large positive integer and `y` is a large negative integer, then the difference `x - y` can overflow.

However, using the `Comparable` interface for defining the sort order has obvious limitations. You can only implement the interface once. But what can you do if you need to sort a bunch of items by part number in one collection and by description in another? Furthermore, what can you do if you need to sort objects of a class whose creator didn't bother to implement the `Comparable` interface?

In those situations, you tell the tree set to use a different comparison method, by passing a `Comparator` object into the `TreeSet` constructor. The `Comparator` interface has a single method, with two explicit parameters:

```
int compare(Object a, Object b)
```

Just like the `compareTo` method, the `compare` method returns a negative integer if `a` comes before `b`, zero if they are identical, or a positive integer otherwise.

To sort items by their description, simply define a class that implements the `Comparator` interface:

```
class ItemComparator implements Comparator
{  public int compare(Object a, Object b)
   {  Item itemA = (Item)a;
      Item itemB = (Item)b;
      String descrA = itemA.getDescription();
      String descrB = itemB.getDescription();
      return descrA.compareTo(descrB);
   }
}
```

You then pass an object of this class to the tree set constructor:

```
ItemComparator comp = new ItemComparator();
TreeSet sortByDescription = new TreeSet(comp);
```

If you construct a tree with a comparator, it uses this object whenever it needs to compare two elements.

Note that the item comparator has no data. It is just a holder for the comparison method. Such an object is sometimes called a *function object*.

Function objects are commonly defined "on the fly," as instances of anonymous inner classes:

```
TreeSet sortByDescription = new TreeSet(
   new Comparator()
   {  public int compare(Object a, Object b)
      {  Item itemA = (Item)a;
         Item itemB = (Item)b;
         String descrA = itemA.getDescription();
         String descrB = itemB.getDescription();
         return descrA.compareTo(descrB);
      }
   });
```

Using comparators, you can sort elements in any way you wish.

If you look back at Table 2–3, you may well wonder if you should always use a tree set instead of a hash set. After all, adding elements does not seem to take much longer, and the elements are automatically sorted. The answer depends on the data that you are collecting. If you don't need the data sorted, there is no reason to pay for the sorting overhead. More importantly, with some data it is very difficult to come up with a sort order. Suppose you collect a bunch of rectangles. How do you sort them? By area? You can have two different rectangles with different positions but the same area. If you sort by area, the second one is not inserted into the set. The sort order for a tree must be a *total ordering:* Any two elements must be comparable, and the comparison can only be zero if the elements are equal. There is such a sort order for rectangles (the lexicographic ordering on its coordinates), but it is unnatural and cumbersome to compute. In contrast, hash functions are usually easier to define. They only need to do a reasonably good job of scrambling the objects, whereas comparison functions must tell objects apart with complete precision.

The program in Example 2–3 builds two tree sets of `Item` objects. The first one is sorted by part number, the default sort order of item objects. The second set is sorted by description, using a custom comparator.

Example 2–3: TreeSetTest.java

```
import java.util.*;

public class TreeSetTest
{  public static void main(String[] args)
```

```
    {  SortedSet parts = new TreeSet();
       parts.add(new Item("Toaster", 1234));
       parts.add(new Item("Widget", 4562));
       parts.add(new Item("Modem", 9912));
       System.out.println(parts);

       SortedSet sortByDescription = new TreeSet(
          new Comparator()
          {  public int compare(Object a, Object b)
             {  Item itemA = (Item)a;
                Item itemB = (Item)b;
                String descrA = itemA.getDescription();
                String descrB = itemB.getDescription();
                return descrA.compareTo(descrB);
             }
          });

       sortByDescription.addAll(parts);
       System.out.println(sortByDescription);
    }
}

class Item implements Comparable
{  public Item(String aDescription, int aPartNumber)
   {  description = aDescription;
      partNumber = aPartNumber;
   }

   public String getDescription()
   {  return description;
   }

   public String toString()
   {  return "[description=" + description
         + ", partNumber=" + partNumber + "]";
   }

   public boolean equals(Object other)
   {  if (getClass() == other.getClass())
      {  Item otherItem = (Item)other;
         return description.equals(otherItem.description)
            && partNumber == otherItem.partNumber;
      }
      else
         return false;
   }

   public int hashCode()
```

```
    {   return 13 * description.hashCode() + 17 * partNumber;
    }

    public int compareTo(Object other)
    {   Item otherItem = (Item)other;
        return partNumber - otherItem.partNumber;
    }

    private String description;
    private int partNumber;
}
```

java.lang.Comparable

- `int compareTo(Object other)`
  compares this object with another object and returns a negative value if `this` comes before `other`, zero if they are considered identical in the sort order, and a positive value if `this` comes after `other`.

Parameters:	`other`	the object to compare

java.util.Comparator

- `int compare(Object a, Object b)`
  compares two objects and returns a negative value if `a` comes before `b`, zero if they are considered identical in the sort order, and a positive value if `a` comes after `b`.

Parameters:	`a, b`	the objects to compare

java.util.SortedSet

- `Comparator comparator()`
  returns the comparator used for sorting the elements, or `null` if the elements are compared with the `compareTo` method of the `Comparable` interface.
- `Object first()`
- `Object last()`
  return the smallest or largest element in the sorted set.

java.util.TreeSet

- `TreeSet(Comparator c)`
  constructs a tree set and uses the specified comparator for sorting its elements.

Parameters:	`c`	the comparator to use for sorting

- `TreeSet(SortedSet elements)`
  constructs a tree set, adds all elements from a sorted set, and uses the same element comparator as the given sorted set.

Parameters: `elements` the sorted set with the elements to add and the comparator to use

Maps

A set is a collection that lets you quickly find an existing element. However, to look up an element, you need to have an exact copy of the element to find. That isn't a very common lookup—usually, you have some key information, and you want to look up the associated element. The *map* data structure serves that purpose. A map stores key/value pairs. You can find a value if you provide the key. For example, you may store a table of employee records, where the keys are the employee IDs and the values are `Employee` objects.

The Java library supplies two general purpose implementations for maps: `HashMap` and `TreeMap`. A hash map hashes the keys, and a tree map uses a total ordering on the keys to organize them in a search tree. The hash or comparison function is applied *only to the keys*. The values associated with the keys are not hashed or compared.

Should you choose a hash map or a tree map? As with sets, hashing is a bit faster, and it is the preferred choice if you don't need to visit the keys in sorted order.

Here is how you set up a hash map for storing employees.

```
HashMap staff = new HashMap();
Employee harry = new Employee("Harry Hacker");
staff.put("987-98-9996", harry);
. . .
```

Whenever you add an object to a map, you must supply a key as well. In our case, the key is a string, and the corresponding value is an `Employee` object.

To retrieve an object, you must use (and, therefore, remember) the key.

```
String s = "1411-16-2536";
e = (Employee)staff.get(s); // gets harry
```

If no information is stored in the map with the particular key specified, then `get` returns `null`.

Keys must be unique. You cannot store two values with the same key. If you call the `put` method twice with the same key, then the second value replaces the first one. In fact, `put` returns the previous value stored with the key parameter. (This feature is useful; if `put` returns a non-`null` value, then you know you replaced a previous entry.)

The `remove()` method removes an element from the map. The `size()` method returns the number of entries in the map.

The collections framework does not consider a map itself as a collection. (Other frameworks for data structures consider a map as a collection of *pairs*, or as a collection of values that is indexed by the keys.) However, you can obtain *views* of the map, objects that implement the `Collection` interface or one of its subinterfaces.

There are three views: the set of keys, the collection of values (which is not a set), and the set of key/value pairs. The keys and key/value pairs form a set because there can be only one copy of a key in a map. The methods

```
Set keySet()
Collection values()
Set entrySet()
```

return these three views. (The elements of the entry set are objects of the inner class `Map.Entry`.)

Note that the `keySet` is *not* a `HashSet` or `TreeSet`, but it is an object of some other class that implements the `Set` interface. We discuss the `Set` interface and its purpose in detail in the next section. The `Set` interface extends the `Collection` interface. In fact, as you will see, it does not add any new methods. Therefore, you can use it exactly as you use the `Collection` interface.

For example, you can enumerate all keys of a map:

```
Set keys = map.keySet();
Iterator iter = keys.iterator();
while (iter.hasNext())
{  Object key = iter.next();
   do something with key
}
```

TIP: If you want to look at both keys and values, then you can avoid value lookups by enumerating the *entries*. Use the following code skeleton:

```
Set entries = staff.entrySet();
Iterator iter = entries.iterator();
while (iter.hasNext())
{  Map.Entry entry = (Map.Entry)iter.next();
   Object key = entry.getKey();
   Object value = entry.getValue();
   do something with key, value
}
```

If you invoke the `remove` method of the iterator, you actually remove the key *and its associated value* from the map. However, you cannot *add* an element to the key set view. It makes no sense to add a key without also adding a value. If you try to invoke the `add` method, it throws an `UnsupportedOperationException`. The key/value set view has the same restriction, even though it would make conceptual sense to add a new key/value pair.

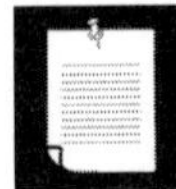

NOTE: The legacy `Hashtable` class (which we cover later in this chapter) has methods that return enumeration objects—the classical analog to iterators—that traverse keys and values. However, having collection views is more powerful since they let you operate on all keys or values at once.

Example 2–4 illustrates a map at work. We first add key/value pairs to a map. Then, we remove one key from the map, which removes its associated value as well. Next, we change the value that is associated with a key and call the `get` method to look up a value. Finally, we iterate through the entry set.

Example 2–4: MapTest.java

```
import java.util.*;

public class MapTest
{  public static void main(String[] args)
   {  Map staff = new HashMap();
      staff.put("144-25-5464", new Employee("Angela Hung"));
      staff.put("567-24-2546", new Employee("Harry Hacker"));
      staff.put("157-62-7935", new Employee("Gary Cooper"));
      staff.put("456-62-5527", new Employee("Francesca Cruz"));

      // print all entries

      System.out.println(staff);

      // remove an entry

      staff.remove("567-24-2546");

      // replace an entry

      staff.put("456-62-5527", new Employee("Francesca Miller"));

      // look up a value

      System.out.println(staff.get("157-62-7935"));

      // iterate through all entries

      Set entries = staff.entrySet();
      Iterator iter = entries.iterator();
      while (iter.hasNext())
      {  Map.Entry entry = (Map.Entry)iter.next();
```

```
            Object key = entry.getKey();
            Object value = entry.getValue();
            System.out.println("key=" + key + ", value=" + value);
         }
      }
   }

class Employee
{  public Employee(String n)
   {  name = n;
      salary = 0;
   }

   public String toString()
   {  return "[name=" + name + ", salary=" + salary + "]";
   }

   public void setSalary(double s)
   {  salary = s;
   }

   private String name;
   private double salary;
}
```

Weak Hash Maps

The `WeakHashMap` class was designed to solve an interesting problem. What happens with a value whose key is no longer used anywhere in your program? Suppose the last reference to a key has gone away. Then, there is no longer any way to refer to the value object. But since no part of the program has the key any more, the key/value pair cannot be removed from the map. Why can't the garbage collector remove it? Isn't it the job of the garbage collector to remove unused objects?

Unfortunately, it isn't quite so simple. The garbage collector traces *live* objects. As long as the map object is live, then *all* buckets in it are live and they won't be reclaimed. Thus, your program should take care to remove unused values from long-lived maps. Or, you can use a `WeakHashMap` instead. This data structure cooperates with the garbage collector to remove key/value pairs when the only reference to the key is the one from the hash table entry.

Here are the inner workings of this mechanism. The `WeakHashMap` uses *weak references* to hold keys. A `WeakReference` object holds a reference to another object, in our case, a hash table key. Objects of this type are treated in a special way by the garbage collector. Normally, if the garbage collector finds that a particular object

has no references to it, it simply reclaims the object. However, if the object is reachable *only* by a `WeakReference`, the garbage collector still reclaims the object, but it places the weak reference that led to it onto a queue. The operations of the `WeakHashMap` periodically check that queue for newly arrived weak references. When a weak reference arrives in the queue, this is an indication that the key was no longer used by anyone and that it has been collected. The `WeakHashMap` then removes the associated entry.

java.util.Map

- `Object get(Object key)`
  gets the value associated with the key; returns the object associated with the key, or `null` if the key is not found in the map.
  Parameters: `key` the key to use for retrieval (may be `null`)
- `Object put(Object key, Object value)`
  puts the association of a key and a value into the map. If the key is already present, the new object replaces the old one previously associated with the key. This method returns the old value of the key, or `null` if the key was not previously present.
  Parameters: `key` the key to use for retrieval (may be `null`)
  `value` the associated object (may not be `null`)
- `void putAll(Map entries)`
  adds all entries from the specified map to this map.
  Parameters: `entries` the map with the entries to be added
- `boolean containsKey(Object key)`
  returns `true` if the key is present in the map.
  Parameters: `key` the key to find
- `boolean containsValue(Object value)`
  returns `true` if the value is present in the map.
  Parameters: `value` the value to find
- `Set entrySet()`
  returns a set view of `Map.Entry` objects, the key/value pairs in the map. You can remove elements from this set, and they are removed from the map, but you cannot add any elements.

- `Set keySet()`
  returns a set view of all keys in the map. You can remove elements from this set, and the key and associated values are removed from the map, but you cannot add any elements.
- `Collection values()`
  returns a collection view of all values in the map. You can remove elements from this set, and the removed value and its key are removed from the map, but you cannot add any elements.

`java.util.Map.Entry`

- `Object getKey()`
- `Object getValue()`
  return the key or value of this entry.
- `Object setValue(Object value)`
  changes the value *in the associated map* to the new value and returns the old value.

Parameters:	`value`	the new value to associate with the key

`java.util.HashMap`

- `HashMap()`
  constructs an empty hash map.
- `HashMap(Map entries)`
  constructs a hash map and adds all entries from a map.

Parameters:	`entries`	the entries to add

- `HashMap(int initialCapacity)`
- `HashMap(int initialCapacity, float loadFactor)`
  construct an empty hash map with the specified capacity and load factor.

Parameters:	`initialCapacity`	the initial number of buckets
	`loadFactor`	a number between 0.0 and 1.0 that determines at what percentage of fullness the hash table will be rehashed into a larger one. The default is 0.75

`java.util.WeakHashMap`

- `WeakHashMap()`
  constructs an empty weak hash map.
- `WeakHashMap(int initialCapacity)`
- `WeakHashMap(int initialCapacity, float loadFactor)`
  construct an empty hash map with the specified capacity and load factor.

Parameters:	`initialCapacity`	the initial number of buckets
	`loadFactor`	a number between 0.0 and 1.0 that determines at what percentage of fullness the hash table will be rehashed into a larger one. The default is 0.75

`java.util.SortedMap`

- `Comparator comparator()`
  returns the comparator used for sorting the keys, or `null` if the keys are compared with the `compareTo` method of the `Comparable` interface.
- `Object firstKey()`
- `Object lastKey()`
  return the smallest or largest key in the map.

`java.util.TreeMap`

- `TreeMap(Comparator c)`
  constructs a tree set and uses the specified comparator for sorting its keys.

Parameters:	`c`	the comparator to use for sorting

- `TreeMap(Map entries)`
  constructs a tree map and adds all entries from a map.

Parameters:	`entries`	the entries to add

- `TreeMap(SortedMap entries)`
  constructs a tree set, adds all entries from a sorted map, and uses the same element comparator as the given sorted map.

Parameters:	`entries`	the sorted set with the entries to add and the comparator to use

The Collections Framework

A *framework* is a set of classes that form the basis for building advanced functionality. A framework contains superclasses with useful functionality, policies, and mechanisms. The user of a framework forms sublasses to extend the functionality without having to reinvent the basic mechanisms. For example, Swing is a framework for user interfaces.

The Java collections library forms a framework for collection classes. It defines a number of interfaces and abstract classes for implementors of collections (see Figure 2–9), and it prescribes certain mechanisms, such as the iteration protocol. You can use the collection classes without having to know much about the framework—we did just that in the preceding sections. However, if you want to implement generic algorithms that work for multiple collection types, or if you want to add a new collection type, then it is helpful to understand the framework.

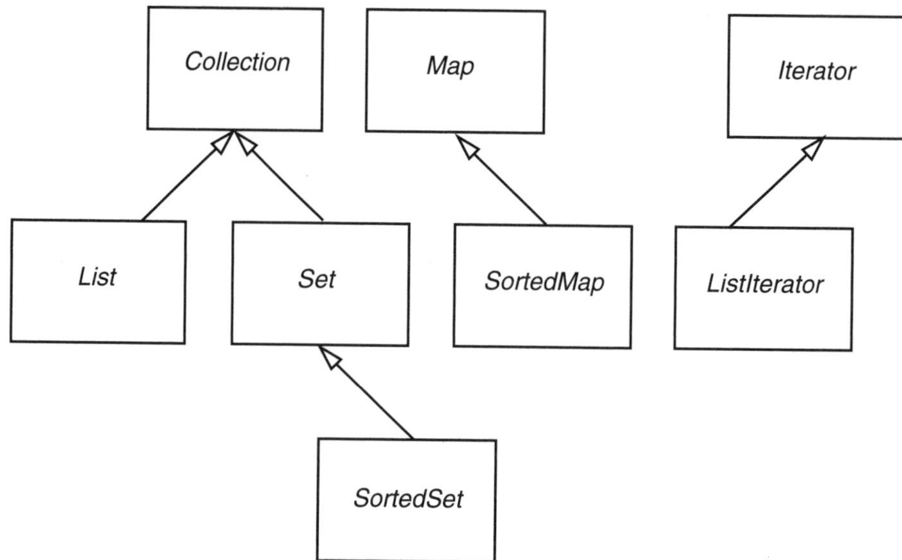

Figure 2–9: The interfaces of the collections framework

There are two fundamental interfaces for containers: `Collection` and `Map`. You insert elements into a collection with a method:

```
boolean add(Object element)
```

However, maps hold key/value pairs, and you use the `put` method to insert them.

```
boolean put(Object key, Object value)
```

To read elements from a collection, you visit them with an iterator. However, you can read values from a map with the `get` method:

```
Object get(Object key)
```

A `List` is an *ordered collection*. Elements are added into a particular position in the container. An object can be placed into its position in two ways: by an integer index and by a list iterator. The `List` interface defines methods for random access:

```
void add(int index, Object element)
Object get(int index)
void remove(int index)
```

The `ListIterator` interface defines a method for adding an element before the iterator position:

```
void add(Object element)
```

To get and remove elements at a particular position, you simply use the `next` and `remove` methods of the `Iterator` interface.

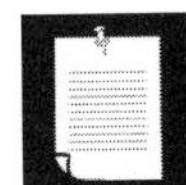

NOTE: From a theoretical point of view, it would have made sense to have a separate `Array` interface that extends the `List` interface and declares the random access methods. If there was a separate `Array` interface, then those algorithms that require random access would use `Array` parameters and you could not accidentally apply them to collections with slow random access. However, the designers of the collections framework chose not to define a separate interface. They wanted to keep the number of interfaces in the library small. Also, they did not want to take a paternalistic attitude toward programmers. You are free to pass a linked list to algorithms that use random access—you just need to be aware of the performance costs.

The `Set` interface is identical to the `Collection` interface, but the behavior of the methods is more tightly defined. The `add` method of a set should reject duplicates. The `equals` method of a set should be defined so that two sets are identical if they have the same elements, but not necessarily in the same order. The `hashCode` method should be defined such that two sets with the same elements yield the same hash code.

NOTE: For sets and lists, there is a well-defined notion of equality. Two sets are equal if they contain the same elements in some order. Two lists are equal if they contain the same elements in the same order. However, there is no well-defined notion of equality for collections. You should therefore not use the `equals` method on `Collection` references.

Why make a separate interface if the method signatures are the same? Conceptually, not all collections are sets. Making a `Set` interface enables programmers to write methods that only accept sets.

Finally, the `SortedSet` and `SortedMap` interfaces expose the comparison object used for sorting, and they define methods to obtain views of subsets of the containers. We discuss these views in the next section.

Now, let us turn from the interfaces to the classes that implement them. We already discussed that the collection interfaces have quite a few methods that can be trivially implemented from more fundamental methods. There are five abstract classes that supply many of these routine implementations:

```
AbstractCollection
AbstractList
AbstractSequentialList
AbstractSet
AbstractMap
```

If you implement your own collection class, then you probably want to extend one of these classes so that you can pick up the implementations of the routine operations.

The Java library supplies six concrete classes:

```
LinkedList
ArrayList
HashSet
TreeSet
HashMap
TreeMap
```

Figure 2–10 shows the relationships between these classes.

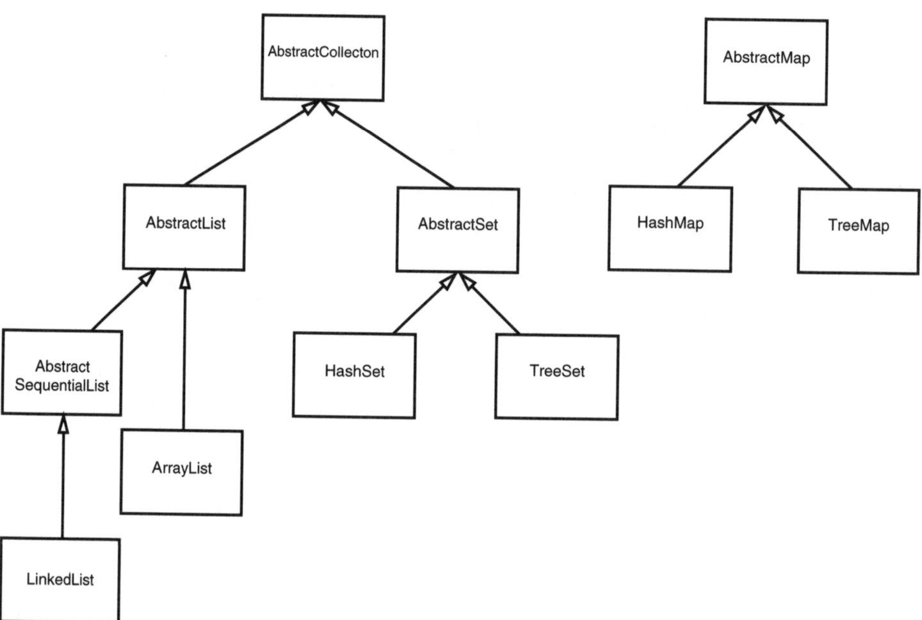

Figure 2–10: Classes in the collections framework

Finally, there are a number of "legacy" container classes that have been present since the beginning, before there was a collections framework:

```
Vector
Stack
Hashtable
Properties
```

They have been integrated into the collections framework—see Figure 2–11. We discuss these classes later in this chapter.

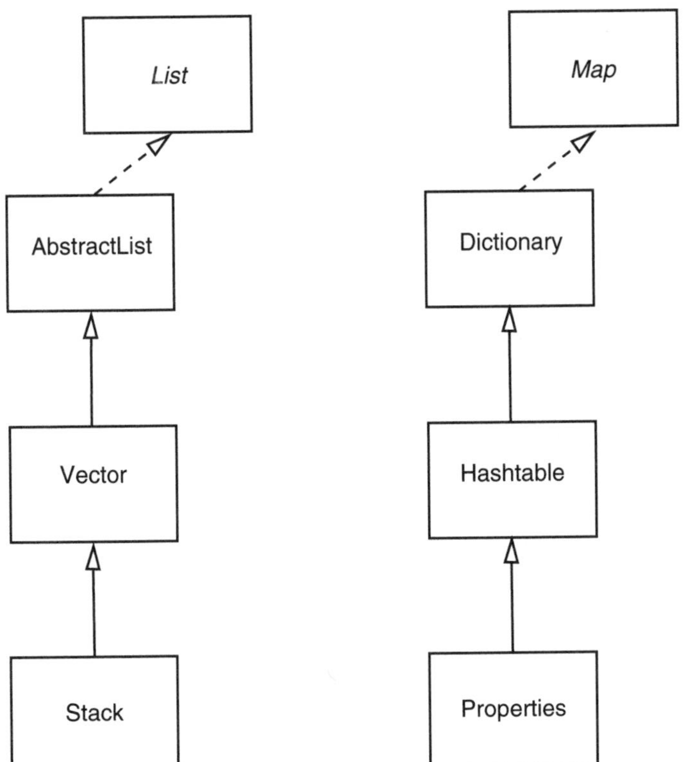

Figure 2–11: Legacy classes in the collections framework

Views and Wrappers

If you look at Figure 2–9 and Figure 2–10, you might think it is overkill to have six interfaces and five abstract classes to implement six concrete collection classes. However, these figures don't tell the whole story. By using *views,* you can obtain other objects that implement the `Collection` or `Map` interfaces. You saw one

example of this with the `keySet` method of the map classes. At first glance, it appears as if the method creates a new set, fills it with all keys of the map, and returns it. However, that is not the case. Instead, the `keySet` method returns an object of a class that implements the `Set` interface and whose methods manipulate the original map. Such a collection is called a *view*. You have no way of knowing, and you need not know, exactly what class the library uses to implement the view.

The technique of views has a number of useful applications in the collections framework. Here is the most compelling one. Recall that the methods of the `Vector` class are synchronized, which is unnecessarily slow if the vector is only accessed from a single thread. For that reason, we recommended the use of the `ArrayList` instead of the `Vector` class. However, if you do access a collection from multiple threads, it is very important that the methods are synchronized. For example, it would be disastrous if one thread tried to add to a hash table while another thread is rehashing the elements. The library designers could have implemented companion classes with synchronized methods for all data structures. But they did something more useful. They supplied a mechanism that produces synchronized views for all *interfaces*. For example, the static `synchronizedMap` class in the `Collections` class can turn any `Map` into a `Map` with synchronized access methods:

```
HashMap hashMap = new HashMap();
map = Collections.synchronizedMap(hashMap);
```

Now, you can access the `map` object from multiple threads. The methods such as `get` and `put` are synchronized—each method call must be finished completely before another thread can call another method.

There are six methods to obtain synchronized collections:

```
Collections.synchronizedCollection
Collections.synchronizedList
Collections.synchronizedSet
Collections.synchronizedSortedSet
Collections.synchronizedMap
Collections.synchronizedSortedMap
```

The views that are returned by these methods are sometimes called *wrappers*.

You should make sure that no thread accesses the data structure through the original unsynchronized methods. The easiest way to ensure this is not to save any reference to the original object, but to simply pass the constructed collection to the wrapper method:

```
map = Collections.synchronizedMap(new HashMap());
```

There is one caveat when accessing a collection from multiple threads. Recall that you can either have multiple iterators that read from a collection or have a single thread that modifies the collection. For that reason, you will want to make sure that any iteration—

```
Iterator iter = collection.iterator();
while (iter.hasNext())
   do something with iter.next();
```

—does not occur at a time when another thread modifies the collection. If it did, then the `next` method would throw a `ConcurrentModificationException`. One way to ensure exclusive access is to place the iteration inside a block that locks the container:

```
synchronized (container)
{  Iterator iter = collection.iterator();
   while (iter.hasNext())
      do something with iter.next();
}
```

Since the wrappers wrap the *interface* and not the actual collection object, you only have access to those methods that are defined in the interface. For example, the `LinkedList` class has convenience methods, `addFirst` and `addLast`, that are not part of the `List` interface. These methods are not accessible through the synchronization wrapper.

CAUTION: The `synchronizedCollection` method (as well as the `unmodifiableCollection` method discussed later in this section) returns a collection whose `equals` method does *not* invoke the `equals` method of the underlying collection. Instead, it inherits the `equals` method of the `Object` class, which just tests whether the objects are identical. If you turn a set or list into just a collection, you can no longer test for equal contents. The wrapper acts in this way because equality testing is not well defined at this level of the hierarchy.

However, the `synchronizedSet` and `synchronizedList` class do not hide the `equals` methods of the underlying collections.

The wrappers treat the `hashCode` method in the same way.

The `Collections` class has another potentially useful set of wrappers to produce unmodifiable views of collections. These wrappers add a runtime check to an existing collection. If an attempt to modify the collection is detected, then an exception is thrown and the collection remains untouched.

For example, suppose you want to let some part of your code look at, but not touch, the contents of a collection. Here is what you could do.

```
List staff = new LinkedList();
. . .
lookAt(new Collections.unmodifiableList(staff));
```

The `Collections.unmodifiableList` method returns an object of a class implementing the `List` interface. Its accessor methods retrieve values from the staff collection. Of course, the lookAt method can call all methods of the List interface, not just the accessors. But all mutator methods (such as add) have been redefined to throw an UnsupportedOperationException instead of forwarding the call to the underlying collection. There are similar methods to obtain unmodifiable wrappers to the other collection interfaces.

NOTE: In the API documentation, certain methods of the collection interfaces, such as add, are described as "optional operations." This is curious—isn't the purpose of an interface to lay out the methods that a class *must* implement? Indeed, it would have made sense to separate the read-only interfaces from the interfaces that allow full access. But that would have doubled the number of interfaces, which the designers of the library found unacceptable.

The Arrays class has a static asList method that returns a List wrapper around a plain Java array. This method lets you pass the array to a method that expects a list or collection argument. For example,

```
Card[] cardDeck = new Card[52];
. . .
List cardList = Arrays.asList(cardDeck);
```

The returned object is *not* an ArrayList. It is a view object whose get and set methods access the underlying array. All methods that would change the size of the array (such as add and the remove method of the associated iterator) throw an UnsupportedOperationException.

Subranges

You can form subrange views for a number of collections. For example, suppose you have a list staff and want to extract elements 10 to 19. You use the subList method to obtain a view into the subrange of the list.

```
List group2 = staff.subList(10, 20);
```

The first index is inclusive, the second exclusive—just like the parameters for the substring operation of the String class.

You can apply any operations to the subrange, and they automatically reflect the entire list. For example, you can erase the entire subrange:

```
group2.clear(); // staff reduction
```

The elements are now automatically cleared from the staff list.

For sorted sets and maps, you use the sort order, not the element position, to form subranges. The SortedSet interface declares three methods:

```
subSet(from, to)
headSet(to)
tailSet(from)
```

These return the subsets of all elements that are larger than or equal to `from` and strictly smaller than `to`. For sorted maps, there are similar methods

```
subMap(from, to)
headMap(to)
tailMap(from)
```

that return views into the maps consisting of all entries where the *keys* fall into the specified ranges.

Lightweight collection wrappers

The method call

```
Collections.nCopies(n, anObject)
```

returns an immutable object that implements the `List` interface and gives the illusion of having `n` elements, each of which appears as `anObject`. There is very little storage cost—the object is only stored once. This is a cute application of the wrapper technique. You can use such a list to initialize a concrete container. For example, the following call creates an `ArrayList` containing 100 strings, all set to `"DEFAULT"`:

```
ArrayList settings
    = new ArrayList(Collections.nCopies(100, "DEFAULT"));
```

The method call

```
Collections.singleton(anObject)
```

returns a wrapper object that implements the `Set` interface (unlike `ncopies` which produces a `List`). The returned object implements an immutable single-element set without the overhead of a hash table or tree. The constants `Collections.EMPTY_LIST` and `Collections.EMPTY_SET` return objects that implement the `List` and `Set` interfaces and contain no elements. The advantage is similar to that of the `singleton` method: the returned objects do not have the overhead of a data structure. Singletons and empty objects are potentially useful as parameters to methods that expect a list, set, or container.

NOTE: JDK 1.3 adds methods `singletonList` and `singletonMap` and a constant `EMPTY_MAP`.

A final note on optional operations

We'd like to end this section with a few words about the "optional" or unsupported operations in the collection and iterator interfaces. This is undoubtedly the most controversial design decision in the collections framework. The problem is caused by the undeniably powerful and convenient views. Views are good because they lead to efficient code, and their "plug and play" nature means you only need to learn a few basic concepts. A view usually has some restriction—it may be read-only, it may not be able to change the size, or it may support removal, but not insertion, as is the case for the key view of a map. The restriction is different for each view. Making a separate interface for each restricted view would lead to a bewildering tangle of interfaces that would be unusable in practice.

Should you extend the technique of "optional" methods to your own interfaces? We think not. Even though collections are used very frequently, the coding style for implementing them is not typical for other problem domains. The designers of a collection class library have to resolve a particularly brutal set of conflicting requirements. Users want the library to be easy to learn, convenient to use, completely generic, idiot-proof, and at the same time as efficient as hand-coded algorithms. It is plainly impossible to achieve all these goals simultaneously, or even to come close. Look at a few other libraries, such as the JGL library from ObjectSpace (`www.objectspace.com`), to see a different set of trade-offs. Or, even better, try your hand at designing your own library of collections and algorithms. You will soon run into the inevitable conflicts and feel much more sympathy with the folks from Sun. But in your own programming problems, you will rarely encounter such an extreme set of constraints. You should be able to find solutions that do not rely on the extreme measure of "optional" interface operations.

`java.util.Collections`

- `static Collection synchronizedCollection(Collection c)`
- `static List synchronizedList(List c)`
- `static Set synchronizedSet(Set c)`
- `static SortedSet synchronizedSortedSet(SortedSet c)`
- `static Map synchronizedMap(Map c)`
- `static SortedMap synchronizedSortedMap(SortedMap c)`

  construct a view of the collection whose methods are synchronized.

  Parameters: `c` the collection to wrap

- `static Collection unmodifiableCollection(Collection c)`
- `static List unmodifiableList(List c)`
- `static Set unmodifiableSet(Set c)`
- `static SortedSet unmodifiableSortedSet(SortedSet c)`
- `static Map unmodifiableMap(Map c)`
- `static SortedMap unmodifiableSortedMap(SortedMap c)`

  construct a view of the collection whose mutator methods throw an `UnsupportedOperationException`.

  Parameters: `c` the collection to wrap

- `static List nCopies(int n, Object value)`
- `static Set singleton(Object value)`

  construct a view of the object as either an unmodifiable list with `n` identical elements or a set with a single element.

Parameters:	`n`	the number of times to repeat the value in the list
	`value`	the element value in the collection

- `static final List EMPTY_LIST`
- `static final Set EMPTY_SET`

  An unmodifiable wrapper for an empty list or set.

`java.util.Arrays`

- `static List asList(Object[] array)`

  returns a list view of the elements in an array that is modifiable but not resizable.

Parameters:	`array`	the array to wrap

`java.util.List`

- `List subList(int from, int to)`

  returns a list view of the elements within a range of positions.

Parameters:	`from`	the first position to include in the view
	`to`	the first position to exclude in the view

`java.util.SortedSet`

- `SortedSet subSet(Object from, Object to)`
- `SortedSet headSet(Object to)`
- `SortedSet tailSet(Object from)`

  return a view of the elements within a range.

Parameters:	`from`	the first element to include in the view
	`to`	the first element to exclude in the view

`java.util.SortedMap`

- `SortedMap subMap(Object from, Object to)`
- `SortedMap headMap(Object to)`
- `SortedMap tailMap(Object from)`

  return a map view of the entries whose keys are within a range.

Parameters:	`from`	the first key to include in the view
	`to`	the first key to exclude in the view

Bulk Operations

So far, most of our examples used an iterator to traverse a collection, one element at a time. However, you can often avoid iteration by using one of the *bulk operations* in the library.

Suppose you want to find the *intersection* of two sets, the elements that two sets have in common. First, make a new set to hold the result.

```
Set result = new HashSet(a);
```

Here, you use the fact that every collection has a constructor whose parameter is another collection that holds the initialization values.

Now, use the `retainAll` method:

```
result.retainAll(b);
```

It retains all elements that also happen to be in `b`. You have formed the intersection without programming a loop.

You can carry this idea further and apply a bulk operation to a *view*. For example, suppose you have a map that maps employee IDs to employee objects, and you have a set of the IDs of all employees that are to be terminated.

```
Map staffMap = . . .;
Set terminatedIDs = . . .;
```

Simply form the key set and remove all IDs of terminated employees.

```
staffMap.keySet().removeAll(terminatedIDs);
```

Because the key set is a view into the map, the keys and associated employee names are automatically removed from the map.

By using a subrange view, you can restrict bulk operations to sublists and subsets. For example, suppose you want to add the first ten elements of a list to another container. Form a sublist to pick out the first ten:

```
relocated.addAll(staff.subList(0, 10));
```

The subrange can also be a target of a mutating operation.

```
staff.subList(0, 10).clear();
```

Interfacing with Legacy APIs

Since large portions of the Java platform API were designed before the collections framework was created, you occasionally need to translate between traditional arrays and vectors and the more modern collections.

First, consider the case where you have values in an array or vector and you want to put them into a collection. If the values are inside a `Vector`, simply construct your collection from the vector:

```
Vector values = . . .;
HashSet staff = new HashSet(values);
```

All collection classes have a constructor that can take an arbitrary collection object. Since the Java 2 platform, the `Vector` class implements the `List` interface.

If you have an array, you need to turn it into a collection. The `Arrays.asList` wrapper serves this purpose:

```
String[] values = . . .;
HashSet staff = new HashSet(Arrays.asList(values));
```

Conversely, if you need to call a method that requires a vector, you can construct a vector from any collection:

```
Vector values = new Vector(staff);
```

Obtaining an array is a bit trickier. Of course, you can use the `toArray` method:

```
Object[] values = staff.toArray();
```

But the result is an array of *objects*. Even if you know that your collection contained objects of a specific type, you cannot use a cast:

```
String[] values = (String[])staff.toArray(); // Error!
```

The array returned by the `toArray` method was created as an `Object[]` array, and you cannot change its type. Instead, you need to use a variant of the `toArray` method. Give it an array of length 0 of the type that you'd like. Then, the returned array is created as the same array type, and you can cast it:

```
String[] values = (String[])staff.toArray(new String[0]);
```

NOTE: You may wonder why you don't simply pass a `Class` object (such as `String.class`) to the `toArray` method. However, as you can see from the API notes, this method does "double duty," both to fill an existing array (provided it is long enough) and to create a new array.

java.util.Collection

- `Object[] toArray(Object[] array)`

  checks if the array parameter is larger than the size of the collection. If so, it adds all elements of the collection into the array, followed by a `null` terminator, and it returns the array. If the length of `array` equals the size of the collection, then the method adds all elements of the collection to the array but does not add a `null` terminator. If there isn't enough room, then the method creates a new array, *of the same type as the incoming array*, and fills it with the elements of the collection.

Parameters:	`array`	the array that holds the collection elements, or whose element type is used to create a new array to hold the collection elements

Algorithms

Generic collection interfaces have a great advantage—you only need to implement your algorithms once. For example, consider a simple algorithm to compute the maximum element in a collection. Traditionally, programmers would implement such an algorithm as a loop. Here is how you find the largest element of an array.

```
if (a.length == 0) throw new NoSuchElementException();
Comparable largest = a[0];
for (int i = 1; i < a.length; i++)
   if (largest.compareTo(a[i]) < 0) largest = a[i];
```

Of course, to find the maximum of a vector, the code would be slightly different.

```
if (v.size() == 0) throw new NoSuchElementException();
Comparable largest = (Comparable)v.get(0);
for (int i = 1; i < v.size(); i++)
   if (largest.compareTo((Comparable)v.get(i)) < 0)
      largest = v.get(i);
```

What about a linked list? You don't have random access in a linked list. But you can use an iterator.

```
if (l.isEmpty()) throw new NoSuchElementException();
Iterator iter = l.iterator();
Comparable largest = (Comparable)iter.next();
while (iter.hasNext())
{  Comparable next = (Comparable)iter.next();
   if (largest.compareTo(next) < 0) largest = next;
}
```

These loops are tedious to write, and they are just a bit error-prone. Is there an off-by-one error? Do the loops work correctly for empty containers? For containers with only one element? You don't want to test and debug this code every time, but you also don't want to implement a whole slew of methods such as these:

```
Object max(Comparable[] a)
Object max(Vector v)
Object max(LinkedList l)
```

That's where the collection interfaces come in. Think of the *minimal* collection interface that you need to efficiently carry out the algorithm. Random access with `get` and `set` comes higher in the food chain than simple iteration. As you have seen in the computation of the maximum element in a linked list, random access is not required for this task. Computing the maximum can be done simply by iterating through the elements. Therefore, you can implement the `max` method to take *any* object that implements the `Collection` interface.

```
public static Object max(Collection c)
{  if (c.isEmpty()) throw new NoSuchElementException();
   Iterator iter = c.iterator();
```

```
      Comparable largest = (Comparable)iter.next();
      while (iter.hasNext())
      {  Comparable next = (Comparable)iter.next();
         if (largest.compareTo(next) < 0) largest = next;
      }
      return largest;
   }
```

Now you can compute the maximum of a linked list, a vector, or an array, with a single method.

```
LinkedList l;
Vector v;
Employee[] a;
. . .
largest = max(l);
largest = max(v);
largest = max(Arrays.asList(a));
```

That's a powerful concept. In fact, the standard C++ library has dozens of useful algorithms, each of which operates on a generic collection. The Java library is not quite so rich, but it does contain the basics: sorting, binary search, and some utility algorithms.

Sorting and Shuffling

Computer old-timers will sometimes reminisce about how they had to use punched cards and how they actually had to program sorting algorithms by hand. Nowadays, of course, sorting algorithms are part of the standard library for most programming languages, and the Java programming language is no exception.

The `sort` method in the `Collections` class sorts a collection that implements the `List` interface.

```
List staff = new LinkedList();
// fill collection . . .;
Collections.sort(staff);
```

This method assumes that the list elements implement the `Comparable` interface. If you want to sort the list in some other way, you can pass a `Comparator` object as a second parameter. (We discussed comparators in the section on sorted sets.) Here is how you can sort a list of employees by increasing salary.

```
Collections.sort(staff,
   new Comparator()
   {  public compare(Object a, Object b)
      {  double salaryDifference = (Employee)a.getSalary()
            - (Employee)b.getSalary();
         if (salaryDifference < 0) return -1;
         if (salaryDifference > 0) return 1;
         return 0;
```

```
    }
  });
```

If you want to sort a list in *descending* order, then use the static convenience method `Collections.reverseOrder()`. It returns a comparator that returns `b.compareTo(a)`. (The objects must implement the `Comparable` interface.) For example,

```
Collections.sort(staff, Collections.reverseOrder())
```

sorts the elements in the list `staff` in reverse order, according to the ordering given by the `compareTo` method of the element type.

You may wonder how the `sort` method sorts a list. Typically, when you look at a sorting algorithm in a book on algorithms, it is presented for arrays and uses random element access. But random access in a list can be inefficient. You can actually sort lists efficiently by using a form of merge sort (see, for example, *Algorithms in C++, Parts 1–4,* by Robert Sedgwick [Addison-Wesley 1998, p. 366–369]). However, the implementation in the Java programming language does not do that. It simply dumps all elements into an array, sorts the array, using a different variant of merge sort, and then copies the sorted sequence back into the list.

The merge sort algorithm used in the collections library is a bit slower than *quick sort,* the traditional choice for a general-purpose sorting algorithm. However, it has one major advantage: it is *stable,* that is, it doesn't switch equal elements. Why do you care about the order of equal elements? Here is a common scenario. Suppose you have an employee list that you already sorted by name. Now you sort by salary. What happens to employees with equal salary? With a stable sort, the ordering by name is preserved. In other words, the outcome is a list that is sorted first by salary, then by name.

Because collections need not implement all of their "optional" methods, all methods that receive collection parameters need to describe when it is safe to pass a collection to an algorithm. For example, you clearly cannot pass an `unmodifiableList` list to the `sort` algorithm. What kind of list *can* you pass? According to the documentation, the list must be modifiable but need not be resizable.

These terms are defined as follows:

- A list is *modifiable* if it supports the `set` method.
- A list is *resizable* if it supports the `add` and `remove` operations.

The `Collections` class has an algorithm `shuffle` that does the opposite of sorting—it randomly permutes the order of the elements in a list. You supply the list to be shuffled and a random number generator. For example,

```
ArrayList cards = . . .;
Collections.shuffle(cards);
```

The current implementation of the `shuffle` algorithm requires random access to the list elements, so it won't work too well with a large linked list.

The program in Example 2–5 fills an array list with 49 `Integer` objects containing the numbers 1 through 49. It then randomly shuffles the list and selects the first 6 values from the shuffled list. Finally, it sorts the selected values and prints them out.

Example 2–5: ShuffleTest.java

```
import java.util.*;

public class ShuffleTest
{  public static void main(String[] args)
   {  List numbers = new ArrayList(49);
      for (int i = 1; i <= 49; i++)
         numbers.add(new Integer(i));
      Collections.shuffle(numbers);
      List winningCombination = numbers.subList(0, 6);
      Collections.sort(winningCombination);
      System.out.println(winningCombination);
   }
}
```

`java.util.Collections`

- `static void sort(List elements)`
- `static void sort(List elements, Comparator c)`

  sort the elements in the list, using a stable sort algorithm. The algorithm is guaranteed to run in $O(n \log n)$ time, where n is the length of the list.

Parameters:	`elements`	the list to sort
	`c`	the comparator to use for sorting

- `static void shuffle(List elements)`
- `static void shuffle(List elements, Random r)`

  randomly shuffles the elements in the list. This algorithm runs in $O(n\ a(n))$ time, where n is the length of the list and $a(n)$ is the average time to access an element.

Parameters:	`elements`	the list to shuffle
	`r`	the source of randomness for shuffling

- `static Comparator reverseOrder()`

  returns a comparator that sorts elements in the reverse order of the one given by the `compareTo` method of the `Comparable` interface.

Binary Search

To find an object in an array, you normally need to visit all elements until you find a match. However, if the array is sorted, then you can look at the middle element and check if it is larger than the element that you are trying to find. If so, you keep looking in the first half of the array; otherwise, you look in the second half. That cuts the problem in half. You keep going in the same way. For example, if the array has 1024 elements, you will locate the match (or confirm that there is none) after 10 steps, whereas a linear search would have taken you an average of 512 steps if the element is present and 1024 steps to confirm that it is not.

The `binarySearch` of the `Collections` class implements this algorithm. Note that the collection must already be sorted or the algorithm will return the wrong answer. To find an element, supply the collection (which must implement the `List` interface—more on that in the note below) and the element to be located. If the collection is not sorted by the `compareTo` element of the `Comparable` interface, then you need to supply a comparator object as well.

```
i = Collections.binarySearch(c, element);
i = Collections.binarySearch(c, element, comparator);
```

If the return value of the `binarySearch` method is ≥ 0, it denotes the index of the matching object. That is, `c.get(i)` is equal to `element` under the comparison order. If the value is negative, then there is no matching element. However, you can use the return value to compute the location where you *should* insert `element` into the collection to keep it sorted. The insertion location is

```
insertionPoint = -i - 1;
```

It isn't simply `-i` because then the value of 0 would be ambiguous. In other words, the operation

```
if (i < 0)
   c.add(-i - 1, element);
```

adds the element in the correct place.

To be worthwhile, binary search requires random access. If you have to iterate one by one through half of a linked list to find the middle element, you have lost all advantage of the binary search. Therefore, the `binarySearch` algorithm reverts to a linear search if you give it a linked list.

NOTE: Unfortunately, since there is no separate interface for an ordered collection with efficient random access, the `binarySearch` method employs a very crude device to find out whether to carry out a binary or a linear search. It checks whether the list parameter implements the `AbstractSequentialList` class. If it does, then the parameter is certainly a linked list, because the abstract sequential list is a skeleton implementation of a linked list. In all other cases, the `binarySearch` algorithm makes the assumption that the collection supports efficient random access and proceeds with a binary search.

`java.util.Collections`

- `static int binarySearch(List elements, Object key)`
- `static int binarySearch(List elements, Object key, Comparator c)`

  search for a key in a sorted list, using a linear search if `elements` extends the `AbstractSequentialList` class, a binary search in all other cases. The methods are guaranteed to run in O($a(n)$ log n) time, where n is the length of the list and $a(n)$ is the average time to access an element. The methods return either the index of the key in the list, or a negative value `i` if the key is not present in the list. In that case, the key should be inserted at index `-i - 1` for the list to stay sorted.

Parameters:	`elements`	the list to search
	`key`	the object to find
	`c`	the comparator used for sorting the list elements

Simple Algorithms

The `Collections` class contains several simple but useful algorithms. Among them is the example from the beginning of this section, finding the maximum value of a collection. Others include copying elements from one list to another, filling a container with a constant value, and reversing a list. Why supply such simple algorithms in the standard library? Surely most programmers could easily implement them with simple loops. We like the algorithms because they make life easier for the programmer *reading* the code. When you read a loop that was implemented by someone else, you have to decipher the original programmer's intentions. When you see a call to a method such as `Collections.max`, you know right away what the code does.

The following API notes describe the simple algorithms in the `Collections` class.

`java.util.Collections`

- `static Object min(Collection elements)`
- `static Object max(Collection elements)`
- `static Object min(Collection elements, Comparator c)`
- `static Object max(Collection elements, Comparator c)`

  return the smallest or largest element in the collection.

Parameters:	`elements`	the collection to search
	`c`	the comparator used for sorting the elements

- `static void copy(List to, List from)`
  copies all elements from a source list to the same positions in the target list. The target list must be at least as long as the source list.

Parameters:	`to`	the target list
	`from`	the source list

- `static void fill(List l, Object value)`
  sets all positions of a list to the same value.

Parameters:	`l`	the list to fill
	`value`	the value with which to fill the list

- `static void reverse(List l)`
  reverses the order of the elements in a list. This method runs in O(n) time, where n is the length of the list.

Parameters:	`l`	the list to reverse

Writing Your Own Algorithms

If you write your own algorithm (or in fact, any method that has a collection as a parameter), you should work with *interfaces,* not concrete implementations, whenever possible. For example, suppose you want to fill a `JComboBox` with a set of strings. Traditionally, such a method might have been implemented like this:

```
void fillComboBox(JComboBox comboBox, Vector choices)
{  for (int i = 0; i < choices.size(); i++)
      comboBox.addItem(choices.get(i));
}
```

However, you now constrained the caller of your method—the caller must supply the choices in a vector. If the choices happened to be in another container, they need to first be repackaged. It is much better to accept a more general collection.

You should ask yourself what is the most general collection interface that can do the job. In this case, you just need to visit all elements, a capability of the basic `Collection` interface. Here is how you can rewrite the `fillComboBox` method to accept collections of any kind.

```
void fillComboBox(JComboBox comboBox, Collection choices)
{  Iterator iter = choices.iterator();
   while (iter.hasNext())
      comboBox.addItem(iter.next());
}
```

Now, anyone can call this method with a vector or even with an array, wrapped with the `Arrays.asList` wrapper.

NOTE: If it is such a good idea to use collection interfaces as method parameters, why doesn't the Java library follow this rule more often? For example, the `JComboBox` class has two constructors:

```
JComboBox(Object[] items)
JComboBox(Vector items)
```

The reason is simply timing. The Swing library was created before the collections library. You should expect future APIs to rely more heavily on the collections library. In particular, vectors should be "on their way out" because of the synchronization overhead.

If you write a method that *returns* a collection, you don't have to change the return type to a collection interface. The user of your method might in fact have a slight preference to receive the most concrete class possible. However, for your own convenience, you may want to return an interface instead of a class, because you can then change your mind and reimplement the method later with a different collection.

For example, let's write a method `getAllItems` that returns all items of a combo box. You could simply return the collection that you used to gather the items, say, an `ArrayList`.

```
ArrayList getAllItems(JComboBox comboBox)
{  ArrayList items = new ArrayList(comboBox.getItemCount());
   for (int i = 0; i < comboBox.getItemCount(); i++)
      items.set(i, comboBox.getItemAt(i));
   return items;
}
```

Or, you could change the return type to `List`.

```
List getAllItems(JComboBox comboBox)
```

Then, you are free to change the implementation later. For example, you may decide that you don't want to *copy* the elements of the combo box but simply provide a view into them. You achieve this by returning an anonymous subclass of `AbstractList`.

```
List getAllItems(final JComboBox comboBox)
{  return new
      AbstractList()
      {  public Object get(int i)
         {  return comboBox.getItemAt(i);
         }
         public int size()
```

```
            {   return comboBox.getItemCount();
            }
        };
    }
```

Of course, this is an advanced technique. If you employ it, be careful to document exactly which "optional" operations are supported. In this case, you must advise the caller that the returned object is an unmodifiable list.

Legacy Collections

In this section, we discuss the collection classes that existed in the Java programming language since the beginning: the `Hashtable` class and its useful `Properties` subclass, the `Stack` subclass of `Vector`, and the `BitSet` class.

The `Hashtable` *Class*

The classic `Hashtable` class serves the same purpose as the `HashMap` and has essentially the same interface. Just like methods of the `Vector` class, the `Hashtable` methods are synchronized. If you do not require synchronization or compatibility with legacy code, you should use the `HashMap` instead.

NOTE: The name of the class is `Hashtable`, with a lowercase `t`. Under Windows, you'll get strange error messages if you use `HashTable`, because the Windows file system is not case sensitive but the Java compiler is.

Enumerations

The legacy collections use the `Enumeration` interface for traversing sequences of elements. The `Enumeration` interface has two methods, `hasMoreElements` and `nextElement`. These are entirely analogous to the `hasNext` and `next` methods of the `Iterator` interface.

For example, the `elements` method of the `Hashtable` class yields an object for enumerating the values in the table:

```
Enumeration e = staff.elements();
while (e.hasMoreElements())
{   Employee e = (Employee)e.nextElement();
    . . .
}
```

You will occasionally encounter a legacy method that expects an enumeration parameter. The static method `Collections.enumeration` yields an enumeration object that enumerates the elements in the collection. For example,

```
ArraySet streams = . . .; // a sequence of input streams
SequenceInputStream in
   = new SequenceInputStream(Collections.enumeration(streams));
   // the SequenceInputStream constructor expects an enumeration
```

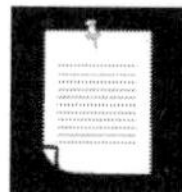

NOTE: In C++, it is quite common to use iterators as parameters. Fortunately, in programming for the Java platform, very few programmers use this idiom. It is much smarter to pass around the collection than to pass an iterator. The collection object is more useful. The recipients can always obtain the iterator from it when they need it, plus they have all the collection methods at their disposal. However, you will find enumerations in some legacy code since they were the only available mechanism for generic collections until the collections framework appeared in the Java 2 platform.

`java.util.Enumeration`

- `boolean hasMoreElements()`
  returns `true` if there are more elements yet to be inspected.
- `Object nextElement()`
  returns the next element to be inspected. Do not call this method if `hasMoreElements()` returned `false`.

`java.util.Hashtable`

- `Enumeration keys()`
  returns an enumeration object that traverses the keys of the hash table.
- `Enumeration elements()`
  returns an enumeration object that traverses the elements of the hash table.

`java.util.Vector`

- `Enumeration elements()`
  returns an enumeration object that traverses the elements of the vector.

Property Sets

A *property set* is a map structure of a very special type. It has three particular characteristics.

- The keys and values are strings.
- The table can be saved to a file and loaded from a file.
- There is a secondary table for defaults.

The Java platform class that implements a property set is called `Properties`.

Property sets are useful in specifying configuration options for programs. The environment variables in UNIX and DOS are good examples. On a PC, your `AUTOEXEC.BAT` file might contain the settings:

```
SET PROMPT=$p$g
SET TEMP=C:\Windows\Temp
SET CLASSPATH=c:\jdk\lib;.
```

Here is how you would model those settings as a property set in the Java programming language.

```
Properties settings = new Properties();
settings.put("PROMPT", "$p$g");
settings.put("TEMP", "C:\\Windows\\Temp");
settings.put("CLASSPATH", "c:\\jdk\\lib;.");
```

Use the `store` method to save this list of properties to a file. Here, we just print the property set to the standard output. The second argument is a comment that is included in the file.

```
settings.store(System.out, "Environment settings");
```

The sample table gives the following output.

```
#Environment settings
#Sun Jan 21 07:22:52  1996
CLASSPATH=c:\\jdk\\lib;.
TEMP=C:\\Windows\\Temp
PROMPT=$p$g
```

System information

Here's another example of the ubiquity of the `Properties` set: information about your system is stored in a `Properties` object that is returned by a method of the `System` class. Applications have complete access to this information, but applets that are loaded from a Web page do not—a security exception is thrown if they try to access certain keys. The following code prints out the key/value pairs in the `Properties` object that stores the system properties.

```
import java.util.*;

public class SystemInfo
{  public static void main(String args[])
   {  Properties systemProperties = System.getProperties();
      Enumeration enum = systemProperties.propertyNames();
      while (enum.hasMoreElements())
      {  String key = (String)enum.nextElement();
         System.out.println(key + "=" +
            systemProperties.getProperty(key));
      }
   }
}
```

Here is an example of what you would see when you run the program. You can see all the values stored in this `Properties` object. (What you would get will, of course, reflect your machine's settings):

```
java.specification.name=Java Platform API Specification
awt.toolkit=sun.awt.windows.WToolkit
java.version=1.2.1
java.awt.graphicsenv=sun.awt.Win32GraphicsEnvironment
user.timezone=America/Los_Angeles
java.specification.version=1.2
java.vm.vendor=Sun Microsystems Inc.
user.home=C:\WINDOWS
java.vm.specification.version=1.0
os.arch=x86
java.awt.fonts=
java.vendor.url=http://java.sun.com/
user.region=US
file.encoding.pkg=sun.io
java.home=C:\JDK1.2.1\JRE
java.class.path=.
line.separator=

java.ext.dirs=C:\JDK1.2.1\JRE\lib\ext
java.io.tmpdir=C:\WINDOWS\TEMP\
os.name=Windows 95
java.vendor=Sun Microsystems Inc.
java.awt.printerjob=sun.awt.windows.WPrinterJob
java.vm.specification.vendor=Sun Microsystems Inc.
sun.io.unicode.encoding=UnicodeLittle
file.encoding=Cp1252
java.specification.vendor=Sun Microsystems Inc.
user.language=en
user.name=Cay
java.vendor.url.bug=http://java.sun.com/cgi-bin/bugreport.cgi
java.vm.name=Classic VM
java.class.version=46.0
java.vm.specification.name=Java Virtual Machine Specification
sun.boot.library.path=C:\JDK1.2.1\JRE\bin
os.version=4.10
java.vm.version=1.2.1
java.vm.info=build JDK-1.2.1-A, native threads, symcjit
java.compiler=symcjit
path.separator=;
file.separator=\
user.dir=C:\temp
```

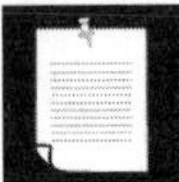

NOTE: For security reasons, applets can only access a small subset of these properties.

Property defaults

A property set is also a useful gadget whenever you want to allow the user to customize an application. Here is how your users can customize the `NotHelloWorld` program to their hearts' content. We'll allow them to specify the following in the configuration file `CustomWorld.ini`:

- window size
- font
- point size
- background color
- message string

If the user doesn't specify some of the settings, we will provide defaults.

The `Properties` class has two mechanisms for providing defaults. First, whenever you look up the value of a string, you can specify a default that should be used automatically when the key is not present.

```
String font = settings.getProperty("FONT", "Courier");
```

If there is a `"FONT"` property in the property table, then `font` is set to that string. Otherwise, `font` is set to `"Courier"`.

If you find it too tedious to specify the default in every call to `getProperty`, then you can pack all the defaults into a secondary property set and supply that in the constructor of your lookup table.

```
Properties defaultSettings = new Properties();
defaultSettings.put("FONT", "Courier");
defaultSettings.put("SIZE", "10");
defaultSettings.put("MESSAGE", "Hello, World");
. . .
Properties settings = new Properties(defaultSettings);
FileInputStream sf = new FileInputStream("CustomWorld.ini");
settings.load(sf);
. . .
```

Yes, you can even specify defaults to defaults if you give another property set parameter to the `defaultSettings` constructor, but it is not something one would normally do.

Figure 2–12 is the customizable `"Hello World"` program. Just edit the `.ini` file to change the program's appearance to the way *you* want (see Figure 2–12).

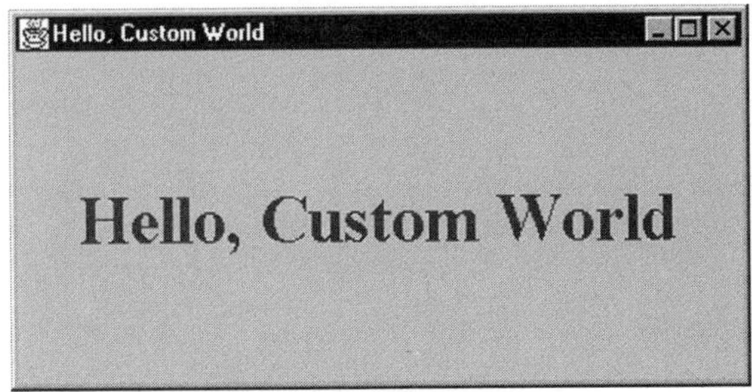

Figure 2–12: The customized Hello World program

Here are the current property settings.

```
#Environment settings
#Sun Jan 21 07:22:52  1996
FONT=Times New Roman
SIZE=400 200
MESSAGE=Hello, Custom World
COLOR=0 50 100
PTSIZE=36
```

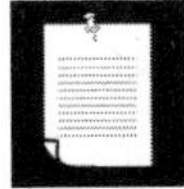

NOTE: The `Properties` class *extends* the `Hashtable` class. That means, all methods of `Hashtable` are available to `Properties` objects. Some functions are useful. For example, `size` returns the number of possible properties (well, it isn't *that* nice—it doesn't count the defaults). Similarly, `keys` returns an enumeration of all keys, except for the defaults. There is also a second function, called `propertyNames`, that returns all keys. The `put` function is downright dangerous. It doesn't check that you put strings into the table.

Does the *is-a* rule for using inheritance apply here? Is every property set a hash table? Not really. That these are true is really just an implementation detail. Maybe it is better to think of a property set as having a hash table. But then the hash table should be a private data field. Actually, in this case, a property set uses two hash tables, one for the defaults and one for the nondefault values.

We think a better design would be the following:

```
class Properties
{  public String getProperty(String) { . . . }
   public void put(String, String) { . . . }
   . . .
   private Hashtable nonDefaults;
   private Hashtable defaults;
}
```

We don't want to tell you to avoid the `Properties` class in the Java library. Provided you are careful to put nothing but strings in it, it works just fine. But think twice before using "quick and dirty" inheritance in your own programs.

Example 2–6: CustomWorld.java

```
import java.awt.*;
import java.awt.event.*;
import java.util.*;
import java.io.*;
import javax.swing.*;

public class CustomWorld
{  public static void main(String[] args)
   {  JFrame frame = new CustomWorldFrame();
      frame.show();
   }
}

class CustomWorldFrame extends JFrame
{  public CustomWorldFrame()
   {  addWindowListener(new WindowAdapter()
         {  public void windowClosing(WindowEvent e)
            {  System.exit(0);
            }
         } );

      Properties defaultSettings = new Properties();
      defaultSettings.put("FONT", "Monospaced");
      defaultSettings.put("SIZE", "300 200");
      defaultSettings.put("MESSAGE", "Hello, World");
      defaultSettings.put("COLOR", "0 50 50");
      defaultSettings.put("PTSIZE", "12");

      Properties settings = new Properties(defaultSettings);
      try
      {  FileInputStream sf
            = new FileInputStream("CustomWorld.ini");
         settings.load(sf);
      }
      catch (FileNotFoundException e) {}
      catch (IOException e) {}

      StringTokenizer st = new StringTokenizer
         (settings.getProperty("COLOR"));
      int red = Integer.parseInt(st.nextToken());
      int green = Integer.parseInt(st.nextToken());
      int blue = Integer.parseInt(st.nextToken());
```

```
      Color foreground = new Color(red, green, blue);

      String name = settings.getProperty("FONT");
      int size = Integer.parseInt(settings.getProperty("PTSIZE"));
      Font f = new Font(name, Font.BOLD, size);

      st = new StringTokenizer(settings.getProperty("SIZE"));
      int hsize = Integer.parseInt(st.nextToken());
      int vsize = Integer.parseInt(st.nextToken());
      setSize(hsize, vsize);
      setTitle(settings.getProperty("MESSAGE"));

      getContentPane().add(new HelloWorldPanel(getTitle(),
         foreground, f), "Center");
   }
}

class HelloWorldPanel extends JPanel
{  public HelloWorldPanel(String aMessage, Color aForeground,
      Font aFont)
   {  message = aMessage;
      foreground = aForeground;
      font = aFont;
   }

   public void paintComponent(Graphics g)
   {  super.paintComponent(g);
      g.setColor(foreground);
      g.setFont(font);

      FontMetrics fm = g.getFontMetrics(font);
      int w = fm.stringWidth(message);

      Dimension d = getSize();
      int cx = (d.width - w) / 2;
      int cy = (d.height + fm.getHeight()) / 2 - fm.getDescent();

      g.drawString(message, cx, cy);
   }

   private Color foreground;
   private Font font;
   private String message;
}
```

java.util.Properties

- `Properties()`

  creates an empty property list.

- `Properties(Properties defaults)`

  creates an empty property list with a set of defaults.

  Parameters: `defaults` the defaults to use for lookups

- `String getProperty(String key)`

  gets a property association; returns the string associated with the key, or the string associated with the key in the default table if it wasn't present in the table.

  Parameters: `key` the key whose associated string to get

- `String getProperty(String key, String defaultValue)`

  gets a property with a default value if the key is not found; returns the string associated with the key, or the default string if it wasn't present in the table.

  Parameters: `key` the key whose associated string to get

  `defaultValue` the string to return if the key is not present

- `void load(InputStream in) throws IOException`

  loads a property set from an `InputStream`.

  Parameters: `in` the input stream

java.util.Stack

- `void push(Object item)`

  pushes an item onto the stack.

  Parameters: `item` the item to be added

- `Object pop()`

  pops and returns the top item of the stack. Don't call this method if the stack is empty.

- `Object peek()`

  returns the top of the stack without popping it. Don't call this method if the stack is empty.

Bit Sets

The Java platform `BitSet` class stores a sequence of bits. (It is not a *set* in the mathematical sense—bit *vector* or bit *array* would have been more appropriate terms.) Use a bit set if you need to store a sequence of bits (for example, flags)

efficiently. Because a bit set packs the bits into bytes, it is far more efficient to use a bit set than to use an `ArrayList` of `Boolean` objects.

The `BitSet` class gives you a convenient interface for reading, setting, or resetting individual bits. Use of this interface avoids the masking and other bit-fiddling operations that would be necessary if you stored bits in `int` or `long` variables.

For example, for a `BitSet` named `bucketOfBits`,

```
bucketOfBits.get(i)
```

returns `true` if the `i`'th bit is on, and `false` otherwise. Similarly,

```
bucketOfBits.set(i)
```

turns the `i`'th bit on. Finally,

```
bucketOfBits.clear(i)
```

turns the `i`'th bit off.

C++ NOTE: The C++ `bitset` template has the same functionality as the Java platform `BitSet`.

`java.util.BitSet`

- `BitSet(int nbits)`
  constructs a bit set.

  Parameters: `nbits` the initial number of bits

- `int length()`
  returns the "logical length" of the bit set: one plus the index of the highest set bit.

- `boolean get(int bit)`
  gets a bit.

  Parameters: `bit` the position of the requested bit

- `void set(int bit)`
  sets a bit.

  Parameters: `bit` the position of the bit to be set

- `void clear(int bit)`
  clears a bit.

  Parameters: `bit` the position of the bit to be cleared

- `void and(BitSet set)`
  logically ANDs this bit set with another.

Parameters: set the bit set to be combined with this bit set

- `void or(BitSet set)`
  logically ORs this bit set with another.
  Parameters: set the bit set to be combined with this bit set
- `void xor(BitSet set)`
  logically XORs this bit set with another.
  Parameters: set the bit set to be combined with this bit set
- `void andNot(BitSet set)`
  clears all bits in this bitset that are set in the other bit set..
  Parameters: set the bit set to be combined with this bit set

The sieve of Eratosthenes benchmark

As an example of using bit sets, we want to show you an implementation of the "sieve of Eratosthenes" algorithm for finding prime numbers. (A prime number is a number like 2, 3, or 5 that is divisible only by itself and 1, and the sieve of Eratosthenes was one of the first methods discovered to enumerate these fundamental building blocks.) This isn't a terribly good algorithm for finding the number of primes, but for some reason it has become a popular benchmark for compiler performance. (It isn't a good benchmark either, since it mainly tests bit operations.)

Oh well, we bow to tradition and include an implementation. This program counts all prime numbers between 2 and 1,000,000. (There are 78,498 primes, so you probably don't want to print them all out.) You will find that the program takes a little while to get going, but eventually it picks up speed.

Without going into too many details of this program, the key is to march through a bit set with one million bits. We first turn on all the bits. After that, we turn off the bits that are multiples of numbers known to be prime. The positions of the bits that remain after this process are, themselves, the prime numbers. Example 2–7 illustrates this program in the Java programming language, and Example 2–8 is the C++ code.

NOTE: Even though the sieve isn't a good benchmark, we couldn't resist timing the two implementations of the algorithm. Here are the timing results on a Pentium-166 with 96 megabytes of RAM, running Windows 98.

Borland C++ 5.4: 3750 milliseconds

JDK 1.2.1: 1640 milliseconds

We have run this test for four editions of Core Java, and this is the first time that the Java programming language beat C++. However, in all fairness, we should point out that the culprit for the bad C++ result is the lousy implementation of the standard `bitset` tem-

plate in the Borland compiler. When we reimplemented `bitset`, the time for C++ went down to 1090 milliseconds.

Of course, these are perfect benchmark results because they allow you to put on any spin that you like. If you want to "prove" that the Java programming language is 50 percent slower than C++, make use of the latter results. Or you can "prove" that it has now overtaken C++. Point out that it is only fair to compare the language implementation as a whole, including standard class libraries, and quote the first set of numbers.

Example 2–7: Sieve.java

```
import java.util.*;

public class Sieve
{  public static final boolean PRINT = false;

   public static void main(String[] s)
   {  int n = 1000000;
      long start = System.currentTimeMillis();
      BitSet b = new BitSet(n);
      int count = 0;
      int i;
      for (i = 2; i <= n; i++)
         b.set(i);
      i = 2;
      while (i * i <= n)
      {  if (b.get(i))
         {  if (PRINT) System.out.println(i);
            count++;
            int k = 2 * i;
            while (k <= n)
            {  b.clear(k);
               k += i;
            }
         }
         i++;
      }
      while (i <= n)
      {  if (b.get(i))
         {  if (PRINT) System.out.println(i);
            count++;
         }
         i++;
      }
      long end =  System.currentTimeMillis();
      System.out.println(count + " primes");
      System.out.println((end - start) + " milliseconds");
   }
}
```

Example 2–8: Sieve.cpp

```
#ifndef AVOID_STANDARD_BITSET

#include <bitset>

#else

template<int N>
class bitset
{
public:
   bitset() : bits(new char[(N - 1) / 8 + 1]) {}

   bool test(int n)
   {  return (bits[n >> 3] & (1 << (n & 7))) != 0;
   }

   void set(int n)
   {  bits[n >> 3] |= 1 << (n & 7);
   }

   void reset(int n)
   {  bits[n >> 3] &= ~(1 << (n & 7));
   }

private:
   char* bits;
};

#endif

#include <iostream>
#include <ctime>

using namespace std;

int main()
{  const int N = 1000000;
   clock_t cstart = clock();

   bitset<N + 1> b;
   int count = 0;
   int i;
   for (i = 2; i <= N; i++)
      b.set(i);
   i = 2;
   while (i * i <= N)
   {  if (b.test(i))
```

```
      {  int k = 2 * i;
         while (k <= N)
         {  b.reset(k);
            k += i;
         }
      }
      i++;
   }
   for (i = 2; i <= N; i++)
   {  if (b.test(i))
      {
#ifdef PRINT
         cout << i << "\n";
#endif
         count++;
      }
   }

   clock_t cend = clock();
   double millis = 1000.0
      * (cend - cstart) / CLOCKS_PER_SEC;

   cout << count << " primes\n"
      << millis << " milliseconds\n";

   return 0;
}
```

Chapter 3

Networking

- Connecting to a Server
- Implementing Servers
- Sending E-mail
- URL Connections
- Posting Form Data
- Harvesting Information from the Web

The Java programming language is supposed to become the premier tool for connecting computers over the Internet and corporate Intranets and, in this realm, Java mostly lives up to the hype. If you are accustomed to programming network connections in C or C++, you will be pleasantly surprised at how easy it is to program them in the Java programming language. For example, as you saw in the applet chapter in Volume 1, it is easy to open a URL (uniform resource locator) on the Net: simply pass the URL to the `showDocument` method in the `AppletContext` class.

We begin this chapter by talking a little bit about basic networking. Then, we move on to reviewing and extending the information that was briefly presented in the applet chapter in Volume 1. The rest of the chapter moves on to the intricacies of doing sophisticated work on the Net with the Java programming language. For example, we show you how to do common gateway interface (CGI) programming on the server, using a Java application. In particular, we show you how to use a combination of an applet and a servlet to harvest information on the Internet.

In the first part of this chapter, we assume that you have no network programming experience. If you have written TCP/IP programs before and ports and sockets are no mystery to you, you should breeze through the sample code. Toward the end of this chapter, the code becomes complex and is geared more toward those with some experience in network programming.

Connecting to a Server

Before writing our first network program, let's learn about a great debugging tool for network programming that you already have, namely, telnet. Unix systems always come with telnet; Windows 95 and NT also come with a simple telnet program. However, it is optional, and you may not have installed it when you installed the operating system. Just look for `TELNET.EXE` in the `\Windows` directory. If you don't find it, run Setup again.

You may have used telnet to connect to a remote computer and to check your e-mail, but you can use it to communicate with other services provided by Net hosts as well. Here is an example of what you can do:

1. Start telnet.
2. In the host field, type `time-A.timefreq.bldrdoc.gov`.
3. In the port field, type `13`. (It doesn't matter what terminal type you choose.)

See Figure 3–1.

If you have a command-line version of telnet, type

```
telnet time-A.timefreq.bldrdoc.gov 13
```

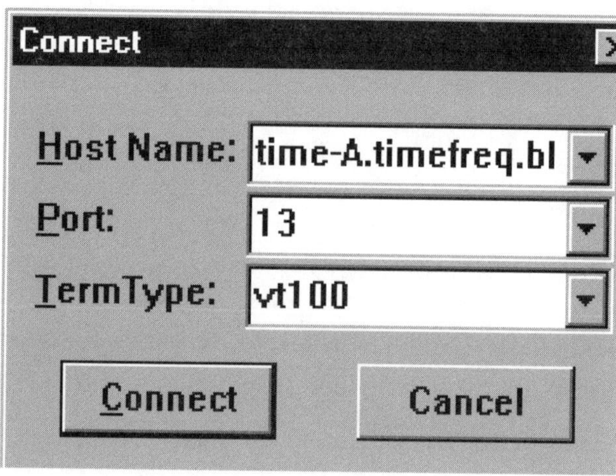

Figure 3–1: The Telnet Connect dialog box

As Figure 3–2 shows, you should get back a line like this:

```
50692 97-09-01 21:43:15 50 0 0  50.0 UTC(NIST) *
```

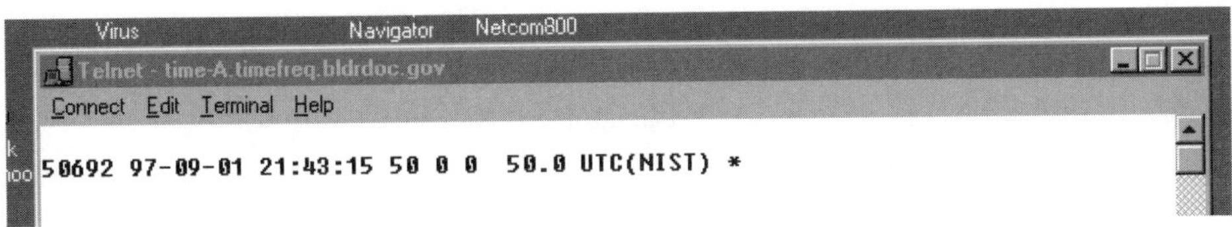

Figure 3–2: Output of the "time of day" service

What is going on? You have connected to the "time of day" service that most Unix machines constantly run. The particular server that you connected to is operated by the National Institute of Standards and Technology in Boulder, Colorado, and gives the measurement of a Cesium atomic clock. (Of course, the reported time is not completely accurate due to network delays.) By convention, the "time of day" service is always attached to "port" number 13.

NOTE: In network parlance, a port is not a physical device, but an abstraction to facilitate communication between a server and a client (see Figure 3–3).

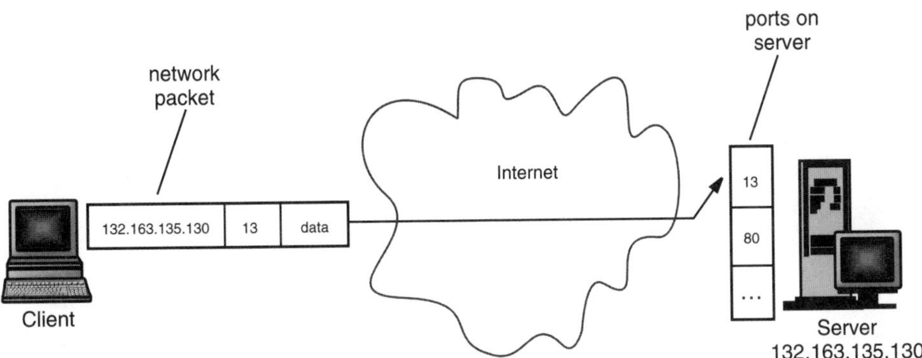

Figure 3–3: A client connecting to a server port

What is happening is that the server software is continuously running on the remote machine, waiting for any network traffic that wants to chat with port 13. When the operating system on the remote computer gets a network package that contains a request to connect to port number 13, it wakes up the listening server process and establishes the connection. The connection stays up until it is terminated by one of the parties.

When you began the telnet session with `time-A.timefreq.bldrdoc.gov` at port 13, an unrelated piece of network software knew enough to convert the string `"time-A.timefreq.bldrdoc.gov"` to its correct Internet Protocol address, 132.163.135.130. The software then sent a connection request to that computer, asking for a connection to port 13. Once the connection was established, the remote program sent back a line of data and then closed the connection. In general, of course, clients and servers engage in a more extensive dialog before one or the other closes the connection.

Here is another experiment, along the same lines, that is a bit more interesting. First, turn on the local key echo. (In Windows 95, this is done from the Terminal Preferences dialog box in the Windows telnet program.) Then, do the following:

1. Connect to `java.sun.com` on port 80.
2. Type the following, *exactly as it appears, without pressing backspace.*
   `GET / HTTP/1.0`
3. Now, press the ENTER key *two times.*

Figure 3–4 shows the response. It should look eerily familiar—you got a page of HTML-formatted text, namely, the main web page for Java technology.

This is *exactly* the same process that your web browser goes through to get a web page.

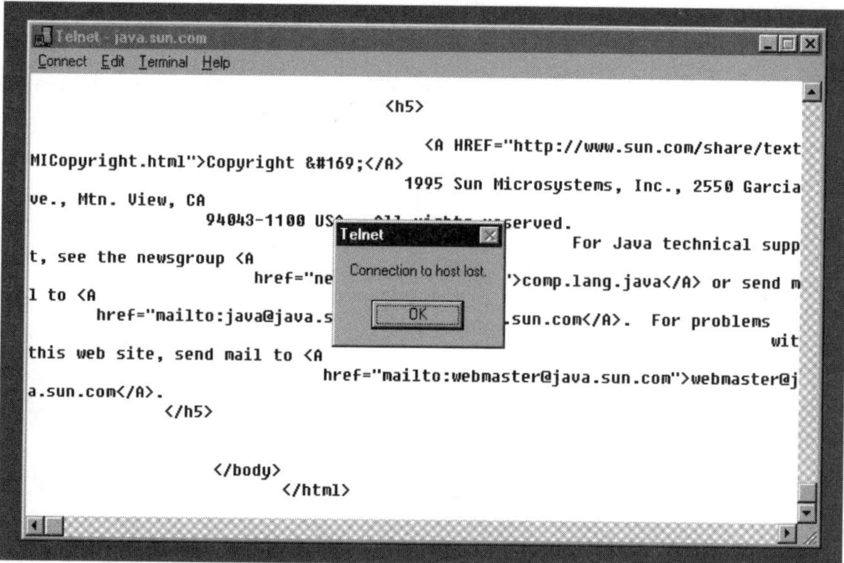

Figure 3–4: Using telnet to access an HTTP port

Our first network program in Example 3–1 will do the same thing we did using telnet—connect to a port and print out what it finds.

Example 3–1: SocketTest.java

```
import java.io.*;
import java.net.*;

public class SocketTest
{  public static void main(String[] args)
   {  try
```

```
      {  Socket s = new Socket("time-A.timefreq.bldrdoc.gov",
            13);

         BufferedReader in = new BufferedReader
            (new InputStreamReader(s.getInputStream()));
         boolean more = true;
         while (more)
         {  String line = in.readLine();
            if (line == null) more = false;
            else
               System.out.println(line);
         }

      }
      catch (IOException e)
      {  System.out.println("Error" + e);
      }
   }
}
```

This program is extremely simple, but before we analyze the two key lines, note that we are importing the `java.net` class and catching any input/output errors because the code is encased in a `try/catch` block. (Since many things can go wrong with a network connection, most of the network-related methods threaten to throw I/O errors. You must catch them for the code to compile.)

As for the code itself, the key lines are as follows:

```
Socket s = new Socket("time-A.timefreq.bldrdoc.gov", 13);
BufferedReader in = new BufferedReader
   new InputStreamReader(s.getInputStream()));
```

The first line opens a *socket*, which is an abstraction for the network software that enables communication out of and into this program. We pass the remote address and the port number to the socket constructor. If the connection fails, then an `UnknownHostException` is thrown. If there is another problem, then an `IOException` occurs. Since `UnknownHostException` is derived from `IOException` and this is a sample program, we just catch the base class.

Once the socket is open, the `getInputStream` method in `java.net.Socket` returns an `InputStream` object that you can use just like any other file. (See Chapter 12 of Volume 1.) Once you have grabbed the stream, this program simply

1. Reads all characters sent by the server using `readLine`
2. Prints each line out to standard output

This process continues until the stream is finished and the server disconnects. You know this happens when the `readLine` method returns a `null` string.

Plainly, the `Socket` class is pleasant and easy to use because Java technology hides the complexities of establishing a networking connection and sending data across. The `java.net` package essentially gives you the same programming interface you would use to work with a file.

Socket timeouts

In real-life programs, you don't just want to read from a socket, because the read methods will block until data is available. If the host is unreachable, then your application waits for a long time, and you are at the mercy of the underlying operating system to time out eventually.

Instead, you should decide what timeout value is reasonable for your particular application. Then, call the `setSoTimeout` method to set a timeout value (in milliseconds).

```
Socket s = new Socket(. . .);
s.setSoTimeout(10000); // time out after 10 seconds
```

If the timeout value has been set for a socket, then all subsequent read operations throw an `InterruptedIOException` when the timeout has been reached before input is available. You can catch that exception and react to the timeout.

```
try
{  String line
   while ((String line = in.readLine()) != null)
   {  process line
   }
}
catch (InterruptedIOException exception)
{  react to timeout
}
```

There is only one problem. You need to have a socket object to call the `setSoTimeout` method, but the `Socket` constructor itself can block indefinitely until an initial connection to the host is established. Today, the Java platform does not offer a convenient solution to this problem. If it is a concern, you will need to construct the socket in a separate thread and wait for that thread to either complete or time out.

The next example program shows how to achieve that. You use the static method `SocketOpener.openSocket` to open a socket with a given timeout:

```
Socket s = SocketOpener.openSocket(host, port, timeout);
```

That method starts a new thread whose run method simply tries to construct the socket.

```
public void run()
{  try
   {  socket = new Socket(host, port);
   }
   catch (IOException exception)
   {
   }
}
```

The `openSocket` method then starts the thread and calls the `join` method with a timeout parameter. The `join` method returns when the thread has died or when the timeout has expired, whichever happens first.

```
t.start();
try
{  t.join(timeout);
}
catch (InterruptedException exception)
{
}
```

Example 3–2 shows the complete program. You can simply use the `SocketOpener` class in your own programs if you want to be able to time out a socket construction.

Example 3–2: SocketOpenerTest.java

```
import java.io.*;
import java.net.*;

public class SocketOpenerTest
{  public static void main(String[] args)
   {  String host;
      if (args.length > 0) host = args[0];
      else host = "www.yourcompany.com";

      int port;
      if (args.length > 1) port = Integer.parseInt(args[1]);
      else port = 80;

      int timeout = 5000;
      Socket s = SocketOpener.openSocket(host, port, timeout);

      if (s == null)
         System.out.println("The socket could not be opened.");
      else
         System.out.println(s);
   }
}

class SocketOpener implements Runnable
{  public static Socket openSocket(String aHost, int aPort,
      int timeout)
   {  SocketOpener opener = new SocketOpener(aHost, aPort);
      Thread t = new Thread(opener);
      t.start();
      try
      {  t.join(timeout);
      }
      catch (InterruptedException exception)
      {
      }
      return opener.getSocket();
```

```
    }

    public SocketOpener(String aHost, int aPort)
    {  socket = null;
       host = aHost;
       port = aPort;
    }

    public void run()
    {  try
       {  socket = new Socket(host, port);
       }
       catch (IOException exception)
       {
       }
    }

    public Socket getSocket()
    {  return socket;
    }

    private String host;
    private int port;
    private Socket socket;
};
```

Internet addresses

Usually, you don't have to worry too much about Internet addresses—the numerical host addresses that consist of four (or perhaps, at some future time, six) bytes such as 132.163.135.130. However, you can use the `InetAddress` class if you need to convert between host names and internet addresses.

The static `getByName` method returns an `InetAddress` object of a host. For example,

```
InetAddress address
   = InetAddress.getByName("time-A.timefreq.bldrdoc.gov");
```

returns an `InetAddress` object that encapsulates the sequence of four bytes 132.163.135.130. You can access the bytes with the `getBytes` method.

```
byte[] addressBytes = address.getBytes();
```

Some host names with a lot of traffic correspond to multiple internet addresses, to facilitate load balancing. For example, at the time of this writing, the host name `java.sun.com` corresponds to three different Internet addresses. One of them is picked at random when the host is accessed. You can get all hosts with the `getAllByName` method.

```
InetAddress[] addresses = InetAddress.getAllByName(host);
```

Finally, you sometimes need the address of the local host. If you simply ask for the address of `localhost`, you always get the address 127.0.0.1, which isn't very

useful. Instead, use the static `getLocalHost` method to get the address of your local host.

```
InetAddress address
   = InetAddress.getLocalHost();
```

Example 3–3 is a simple program that prints the Internet address of your local host if you do not specify any command-line parameters, or all Internet addresses of another host if you specify the host name on the command line, such as

```
java InetAddressTest java.sun.com
```

Example 3–3: InetAddressTest.java

```
import java.net.*;

public class InetAddressTest
{  public static void main(String[] args)
   {  try
      {
         if (args.length > 0)
         {  String host = args[0];
            InetAddress[] addresses
               = InetAddress.getAllByName(host);
            for (int i = 0; i < addresses.length; i++)
               System.out.println(addresses[i]);
         }
         else
         {  InetAddress localHostAddress
               = InetAddress.getLocalHost();
            System.out.println(localHostAddress);
         }
      }
      catch (Exception e)
      {  System.out.println("Error: " + e);
      }
   }
}
```

NOTE: In this book, we cover only the TCP (Transmission Control Protocol) networking protocol. TCP establishes a reliable connection between two computers. The Java platform also supports the so-called UDP (User Datagram Protocol) protocol, which can be used to send packets (also called *datagrams*) with much less overhead than that for TCP. The drawback is that the packets can be delivered in random order, or even dropped altogether. It is up to the recipient to put the packets in order and to request retransmission of missing packets. UDP is most suited for applications where missing packets can be tolerated, for example, in audio or video streams, or for continuous measurements. To learn more about UDP programming for the Java platform, see, for example, *Java Network Programming* by Elliotte Harold (O'Reilly, 1997).

`java.net.Socket`

- `Socket(String host, int port)`
  creates a socket and connects it to a port on a remote host.

  Parameters: `host` the host name
  `port` the port number

- `void close()`
  closes the socket.
- `InputStream getInputStream()`
  gets the input stream to read from the socket.
- `OutputStream getOutputStream()`
  gets an output stream to write to this socket.
- `void setSoTimeout(int timeout)`
  sets the blocking time for read requests on this `Socket`. If the timeout is reached, then an `InterruptedIOException` is raised.

  Parameters: `timeout` the timeout in milliseconds (0 for infinite timeout)

`java.net.InetAddress`

- `static InetAddress getByName(String host)`
- `static InetAddress[] getAllByName(String host)`

  These methods construct an `InetAddress`, or an array of all Internet addresses, for the given host name.
- `static InetAddress getLocalHost()`
  constructs an `InetAddress` for the local host.
- `byte[] getAddress()`
  returns an array of bytes that contains the numerical address.
- `String getHostAddress()`
  returns a string with decimal numbers, separated by periods, for example `"132.163.135.130"`.
- `String getHostName()`
  returns the host name.

Implementing Servers

Now that we have implemented a basic network client that receives data from the Net, let's implement a simple server that can send information out to the Net. Once you start the server program, it waits for some client to attach to its port. We chose port number 8189, which is not used by any of the standard services. The `ServerSocket` class is used to establish a socket. In our case, the command

```
ServerSocket s = new ServerSocket(8189);
```

establishes a server that monitors port 8189. The command

```
Socket incoming = s.accept();
```

tells the program to wait indefinitely until a client connects to that port. Once someone connects to this port by sending the correct request over the network, this method returns a `Socket` object that represents the connection that was made. You can use this object to get an input reader and an output writer from that socket, as is shown in the following code:

```
BufferedReader in = new BufferedReader
   (new InputStreamReader(incoming.getInputStream()));
PrintWriter out = new PrintWriter
   (incoming.getOutputStream(), true /* autoFlush */);
```

Everything that the server sends to the server output stream becomes the input of the client program, and all the output from the client program ends up in the server input stream.

In all of the examples in this chapter, we will transmit text through sockets. We, therefore, turn the streams into readers and writers. Then, we can use the `readLine` method (defined in `BufferedReader`, but not in `InputStream`) and the `print` method (defined in `PrintWriter`, but not in `OutputStream`). If we wanted to transmit *binary data,* we would turn the streams into `DataInputStream` and `DataOutputStreams`. To transmit *serialized objects,* we would use `ObjectInputStream` and `ObjectOutputStreams` instead.

Let's send the client a greeting:

```
out.println("Hello! Enter BYE to exit.");
```

When you use telnet to connect to this server program at port 8189, you will see the above greeting on the terminal screen.

In this simple server, we just read the client input, a line at a time, and echo it. This demonstrates that the program gets the client's input. An actual server would obviously compute and return an answer that depended on the input.

```
String line = in.readLine();
if (line != null)
{  out.println("Echo: " + line);
   if (line.trim().equals("BYE")) done = true;
}
else done = true;
```

In the end, we close the incoming socket.

```
incoming.close();
```

That is all there is to it. Every server program, such as an http web server, continues performing this loop:

1. It gets a command from the client ("get me this information") through an incoming data stream.
2. It somehow fetches the information.

3. It sends the information to the client through the outgoing data stream.

Example 3–4 is the complete program.

Example 3–4: EchoServer.java

```
import java.io.*;
import java.net.*;

public class EchoServer
{  public static void main(String[] args )
   {  try
      {  ServerSocket s = new ServerSocket(8189);
         Socket incoming = s.accept( );
         BufferedReader in = new BufferedReader
            (new InputStreamReader(incoming.getInputStream()));
         PrintWriter out = new PrintWriter
            (incoming.getOutputStream(), true /* autoFlush */);

         out.println( "Hello! Enter BYE to exit." );

         boolean done = false;
         while (!done)
         {  String line = in.readLine();
            if (line == null) done = true;
            else
            {  out.println("Echo: " + line);

               if (line.trim().equals("BYE"))
                  done = true;
            }
         }
         incoming.close();
      }
      catch (Exception e)
      {  System.out.println(e);
      }
   }
}
```

To try it out, you need to compile and run the program. Then, use telnet to connect to the following server and port:

Server: 127.0.0.1

Port: 8189

The IP address 127.0.0.1 is a special address, called the *local loopback address*, that denotes the local machine. Since you are running the echo server locally, that is where you want to connect.

NOTE: If you are using a dial-up connection, you need to have it running for this experiment. Even though you are only talking to your local machine, the network software must be loaded.

Actually, anyone in the world can access your echo server, provided it is running and they know your IP address and the magic port number.

When you connect to the port, you will get the message shown in Figure 3–5:

```
Hello! Enter BYE to exit.
```

Type anything and watch the input echo on your screen. Type `BYE` (all uppercase letters) to disconnect. The server program will terminate as well.

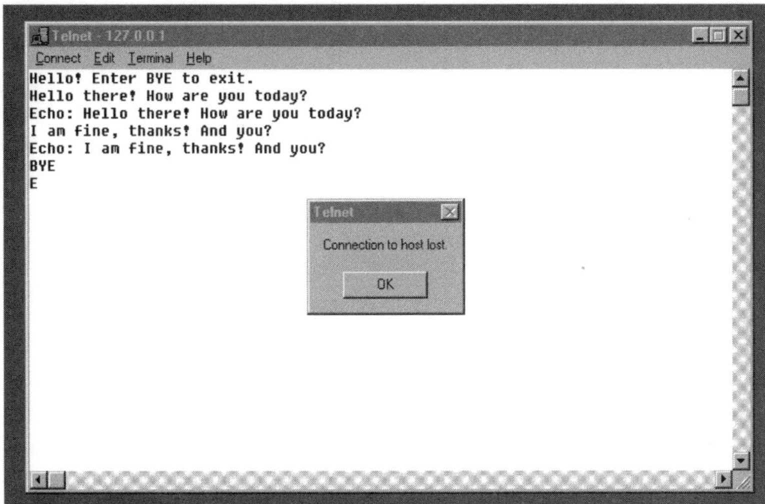

Figure 3–5: Accessing an echo server

Serving Multiple Clients

There is one problem with the simple server in the preceding example. Suppose we want to allow multiple clients to connect to our server at the same time. Typically, a server runs constantly on a server computer, and clients from all over the Internet may want to use the server at the same time. Rejecting multiple connections allows any one client to monopolize the service by connecting to it for a long time. We can do much better through the magic of threads.

Every time we know the program has established a new socket connection, that is, when the call to accept was successful, we will launch a new thread to take care of the connection between the server and *that* client. The main program will just go back and wait for the next connection. For this to happen, the main loop of the server should look like this:

```
while (true)
{  Socket incoming = s.accept();
   Thread t = new ThreadedEchoHandler(incoming);
   t.start();
}
```

The `ThreadedEchoHandler` class derives from `Thread` and contains the communication loop with the client in its `run` method.

```
class ThreadedEchoHandler extends Thread
{  . . .
   public void run()
   {  try
      {  BufferedReader in = new BufferedReader
              (new InputStreamReader(incoming.getInputStream()));
         PrintWriter out = new PrintWriter
            (incoming.getOutputStream(), true /* autoFlush */);

         String line;
         while ((line = in.readLine()) != null)
         {  process line
         }
         incoming.close();
      }
      catch(Exception e)
      {  handle exception
      }
   }
}
```

Because each connection starts a new thread, multiple clients can connect to the server at the same time. You can easily check out this fact. Compile and run the server program (Example 3–5). Open several telnet windows as we have in Figure 3–6. You can communicate through all of them simultaneously. The server program never dies. Use CTRL+C to kill it.

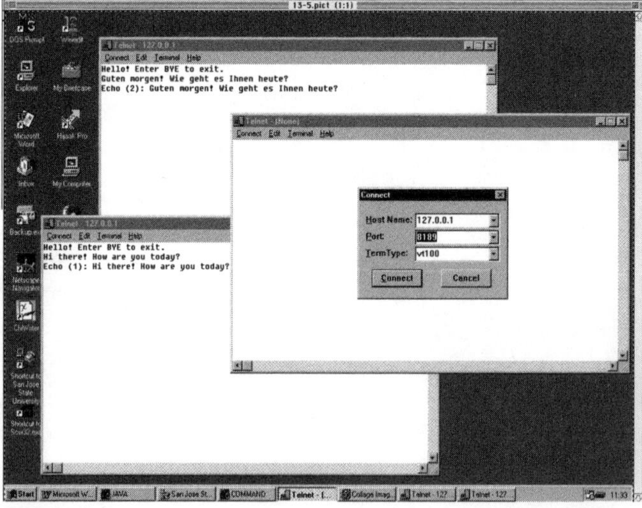

Figure 3–6: Simultaneous access to the threaded echo server

Example 3–5: ThreadedEchoServer.java

```
import java.io.*;
import java.net.*;

public class ThreadedEchoServer
{  public static void main(String[] args )
   {  int i = 1;
      try
      {  ServerSocket s = new ServerSocket(8189);

         for (;;)
         {  Socket incoming = s.accept( );
            System.out.println("Spawning " + i);
            new ThreadedEchoHandler(incoming, i).start();
            i++;
         }
      }
      catch (Exception e)
      {  System.out.println(e);
      }
   }
}

class ThreadedEchoHandler extends Thread
{  public ThreadedEchoHandler(Socket i, int c)
   { incoming = i; counter = c; }

   public void run()
   {  try
      {  BufferedReader in = new BufferedReader
            (new InputStreamReader(incoming.getInputStream()));
         PrintWriter out = new PrintWriter
            (incoming.getOutputStream(), true /* autoFlush */);

         out.println( "Hello! Enter BYE to exit." );

         boolean done = false;
         while (!done)
         {  String str = in.readLine();
            if (str == null) done = true;
            else
            {  out.println("Echo (" + counter + "): " + str);

               if (str.trim().equals("BYE"))
                  done = true;
            }
         }
         incoming.close();
      }
      catch (Exception e)
      {  System.out.println(e);
      }
```

```
    }

    private Socket incoming;
    private int counter;
}
```

`java.net.ServerSocket`

- `ServerSocket(int port) throws IOException`
  creates a server socket that monitors a port.
  Parameters: `port` the port number
- `Socket accept() throws IOException`
  waits for a connection. This method will block (that is, idle) the current thread until the connection is made. The method returns a `Socket` object through which the program can communicate with the connecting client.
- `void close() throws IOException`
  closes the server socket.

Sending E-mail

In this section, we show you a practical example of socket programming: a program that sends e-mail to a remote site.

To send e-mail, you make a socket connection to port 25, the SMTP port. SMTP is the Simple Mail Transport Protocol that describes the format for e-mail messages. You can connect to any server that runs an SMTP service. On Unix machines, that service is typically implemented by the `sendmail` daemon. However, the server must be willing to accept your request. It used to be that sendmail servers were routinely willing to route e-mail from anyone, but in these days of spam floods, most servers now have built-in checks and only accept requests from users, domains, or IP address ranges that they trust.

Once you are connected to the server, send a mail header (in the SMTP format, which is easy to generate), followed by the mail message.

Here are the details:

1. Open a socket to your host.

   ```
   Socket s = new Socket("mail.yourserver.com", 25); // 25 is SMTP
   PrintWriter out = new PrintWriter(s.getOutputStream());
   ```

2. Send the following information to the print stream:

   ```
   HELO sending host
   MAIL FROM: sender email address
   RCPT TO: recipient email address
   DATA
   mail message
   (any number of lines)
   .
   QUIT
   ```

Most SMTP servers do not check this information—you may be able to supply any sender you like. (Keep this in mind the next time you get an e-mail message from `president@whitehouse.gov` inviting you to a black-tie affair on the front lawn. Anyone could have connected to an SMTP server and created a fake message.)

The program in Example 3–6 is a very simple e-mail program. As you can see in Figure 3–7, you type in the sender, recipient, mail message, and SMTP server. Then, click on the "Send" button, and your message is sent.

The program simply sends the sequence of commands that we just discussed. It displays the commands that it sends to the SMTP server and the responses that it receives. Note that the communication with the mail server occurs in a separate thread so that the user interface thread is not blocked when the program tries to connect to the mail server. (See Chapter 1 for more details on threads in Swing applications.)

Figure 3–7: The `MailTest` program

Example 3–6: MailTest.java

```
import java.awt.*;
import java.awt.event.*;
import java.util.*;
import java.net.*;
import java.io.*;
import javax.swing.*;

public class MailTest
{  public static void main(String[] args)
   {  JFrame frame = new MailTestFrame();
      frame.show();
   }
}

class MailTestFrame extends JFrame
   implements ActionListener
{  public MailTestFrame()
   {  setTitle("MailTest");
      setSize(300, 300);
```

```
      addWindowListener(new WindowAdapter()
         {  public void windowClosing(WindowEvent e)
            {  System.exit(0);
            }
         } );

      getContentPane().setLayout(new GridBagLayout());

      GridBagConstraints gbc = new GridBagConstraints();
      gbc.fill = GridBagConstraints.HORIZONTAL;
      gbc.weightx = 0;
      gbc.weighty = 0;

      gbc.weightx = 0;
      add(new JLabel("From:"), gbc, 0, 0, 1, 1);
      gbc.weightx = 100;
      from = new JTextField(20);
      add(from, gbc, 1, 0, 1, 1);

      gbc.weightx = 0;
      add(new JLabel("To:"), gbc, 0, 1, 1, 1);
      gbc.weightx = 100;
      to = new JTextField(20);
      add(to, gbc, 1, 1, 1, 1);

      gbc.weightx = 0;
      add(new JLabel("SMTP server:"), gbc, 0, 2, 1, 1);
      gbc.weightx = 100;
      smtpServer = new JTextField(20);
      add(smtpServer, gbc, 1, 2, 1, 1);

      gbc.fill = GridBagConstraints.BOTH;
      gbc.weighty = 100;
      message = new JTextArea();
      add(new JScrollPane(message), gbc, 0, 3, 2, 1);

      response = new JTextArea();
      add(new JScrollPane(response), gbc, 0, 4, 2, 1);

      gbc.weighty = 0;
      JButton sendButton = new JButton("Send");
      sendButton.addActionListener(this);
      JPanel buttonPanel = new JPanel();
      buttonPanel.add(sendButton);
      add(buttonPanel, gbc, 0, 5, 2, 1);
   }

   private void add(Component c, GridBagConstraints gbc,
      int x, int y, int w, int h)
   {  gbc.gridx = x;
      gbc.gridy = y;
      gbc.gridwidth = w;
      gbc.gridheight = h;
      getContentPane().add(c, gbc);
```

```
   }

   public void actionPerformed(ActionEvent evt)
   {  SwingUtilities.invokeLater(new Runnable()
         {  public void run()
            {   sendMail();
            }
         });
   }

   public void sendMail()
   {  try
      {  Socket s = new Socket(smtpServer.getText(), 25);

         out = new PrintWriter(s.getOutputStream());
         in = new BufferedReader(new
            InputStreamReader(s.getInputStream()));

         String hostName
            = InetAddress.getLocalHost().getHostName();

         send(null);
         send("HELO " + hostName);
         send("MAIL FROM: " + from.getText());
         send("RCPT TO: " + to.getText());
         send("DATA");
         out.println(message.getText());
         send(".");
         s.close();
      }
      catch (IOException exception)
      {  response.append("Error: " + exception);
      }
   }

   public void send(String s) throws IOException
   {  if (s != null)
      {  response.append(s + "\n");
         out.println(s);
         out.flush();
      }
      String line;
      if ((line = in.readLine()) != null)
         response.append(line + "\n");
   }

   private BufferedReader in;
   private PrintWriter out;
   private JTextField from;
   private JTextField to;
   private JTextField smtpServer;
   private JTextArea message;
   private JTextArea response;
}
```

URL Connections

In the last section, you saw how to use socket-level programming to connect to an SMTP server and send an e-mail message. It is nice to know that this can be done, and to get a glimpse what goes on "under the hood" of an Internet service such as e-mail. However, if you are planning an application that incorporates e-mail, you will probably want to work at a higher level and use a library that encapsulates the protocol details. For example, Sun Microsystems has developed the JavaMail API as a standard extension of the Java platform. In the JavaMail API, you simply issue a call such as

```
Transport.send(message);
```

to send a message. The library takes care of message protocols, multiple recipients, handling attachment, and so on.

For the remainder of this chapter, we will concentrate on higher-level services that the standard edition of the Java platform provides. Of course, the runtime library uses sockets to implement these services. But you don't have to worry about the protocol details when you use the higher-level services.

Retrieving Information from a Remote Site

The `URL` and `URLConnection` classes encapsulate much of the complexity of retrieving information from a remote site. Here is how you specify a URL.

```
URL url = new URL(protocol:resource);
```

The Java 2 platform supports both HTTP and FTP resources.

If you simply want to fetch the contents of the resource, then you can use the `openStream` method of the `URL` class. This method yields an `InputStream` object. Using this stream object, you can easily read the contents of the resource.

```
InputStream uin = url.openStream();
BufferedReader in
   = new BufferedReader(new InputStreamReader(uin));
String line;
while ((line = in.readLine()) != null)
{  process line;
}
```

However, if you want additional information about the resource, then you should use the `URLConnection` class, which gives you much more control over accessing web resources.

When working with a `URLConnection` object, you must carefully schedule your steps, as follows:

1. Call the `openConnection` method of the `URL` class to obtain the `URLConnection` object:

   ```
   URLConnection connection = url.openConnection();
   ```

2. Set any properties, using the methods

   ```
   setDoInput
   setDoOutput
   setIfModifiedSince
   setUseCaches
   setAllowUserInteraction
   setRequestProperty
   ```

   We discuss these methods later in this section and in the API notes.

3. Connect to the remote resource by calling the `connect` method.

   ```
   connection.connect();
   ```

   Besides making a socket connection to the server, this method also queries the server for *header information.*

4. After connecting to the server, you can query the header information. There are two methods, `getHeaderFieldKey` and `getHeaderField`, to enumerate all fields of the header. For your convenience, the following methods query standard fields.

   ```
   getContentType
   getContentLength
   getContentEncoding
   getDate
   getExpiration
   getLastModified
   ```

5. Finally, you can access the resource data. Use the `getInputStream` method to obtain an input stream for reading the information. (This is the same input stream that the `openStream` method of the `URL` class returns.) There is also a method `getObject`; however, in practice, it isn't very useful. The objects that are returned by standard content types such as `text/plain` and `image/gif` require classes in the `com.sun` hierarchy for processing. It is possible to register your own content handlers, but we will not discuss that technique in this book.

Let us now look at some of these methods in detail. There are several methods to set properties of the connection before connecting to the server. The most important ones are `setDoInput` and `setDoOutput`. By default, the connection yields an input stream for reading from the server but no output stream for writing. If you want an output stream (for example, for posting data to a web server—see the next section), then you need to call

```
connection.setDoOutput(true);
```

The `setIfModifiedSince` method tells the connection that you are only interested in data that has been modified since a certain date. The `setUseCaches` and `setAllowUserInteraction` are only used inside applets. The `setUseCaches` method directs the ambient browser to first check the browser cache. The `setAllowUserInteraction` method allows an application to pop up a dialog for querying the user name and password for password-protected resources (see Figure 3–8). These settings have no effect outside applets.

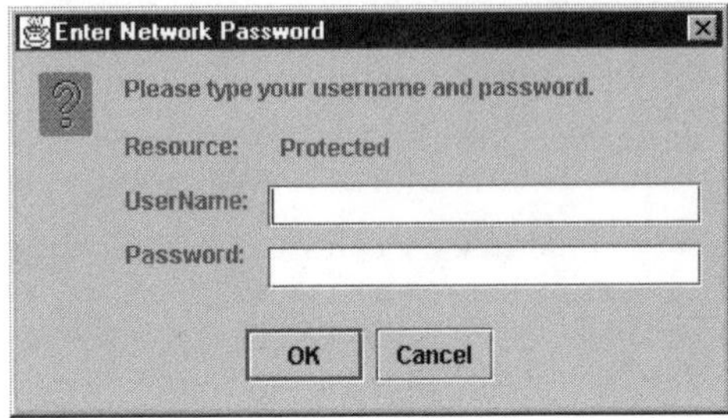

Figure 3–8: A network password dialog

Finally, there is a catch-all `setRequestProperty` method that you can use to set any name/value pair that is meaningful for the particular protocol. These parameters are not well documented and are passed around by word of mouth from one programmer to the next. For example, if you want to access a password-protected web page, you must do the following:

1. Concatenate the user name, a colon, and the password.
   ```
   String input = username + ":" + password;
   ```
2. Compute the Base 64 encoding of the resulting string. (The Base64 encoding encodes a sequence of bytes into a sequence of printable ASCII characters.)
   ```
   String encoding = base64Encode(input);
   ```
3. Call the `setRequestProperty` method with a name of `"Authorization"` and value `"Basic " + encoding`:
   ```
   connection.setRequestProperty("Authorization",
      "Basic " + encoding);
   ```

TIP: You just saw how to access a password-protected web page. To access a password-protected file by FTP, you use an entirely different method. You simply construct a URL of the form

```
ftp://username:password@ftp.yourserver.com/pub/file.txt
```

This, too, does not seem to be documented anywhere. We found out by looking inside `rt.jar`, locating the promising-looking class `sun.net.www.protocol.ftp.FtpURLConnection`, and decompiling that class with `javap`.

Once you call the `connect` method, you can query the header information. First, let us see how to enumerate all header fields. The implementors of this class felt a need to express their individuality by introducing yet another iteration protocol. The call

```
String key = connection.getHeaderFieldKey(n);
```

gets the nth key from the header, where n starts from 1! It returns null if n is zero or larger than the total number of header fields. There is no method to return the number of fields; you simply keep calling getHeaderFieldKey until you get null. Similarly, the call

```
String value = connection.getHeaderField(n);
```

returns the nth value.

Here is a set of header fields from a typical HTTP request.

```
Date: Sun, 29 Aug 1999 00:15:48 GMT
Server: Apache/1.3.3 (Unix)
Last-Modified: Thu, 24 Jun 1999 20:53:38 GMT
ETag: "28094e-12cd-37729ad2"
Accept-Ranges: bytes
Content-Length: 4813
Connection: close
Content-Type: text/html
```

As a convenience, six methods query the values of the most common header types and convert them to numeric types when appropriate. Table 3–1 shows these convenience methods. The methods with return type long return the number of seconds since January 1, 1970 GMT.

Table 3–1: Convenience methods for connection header values

Key name	Method name	Return type
Date	getDate	long
Expires	getExpiration	long
Last-Modified	getLastModified	long
Content-Length	getContentLength	int
Content-Type	getContentType	String
Content-Encoding	getContentEncoding	String

The program in Example 3–7 lets you experiment with URL connections. Supply a URL and an optional user name and password on the command line when running the program, for example:

```
java URLConnectionTest http://www.yourserver.com user pw
```

The program prints out

- All keys and values of the header
- The return values of the six convenience methods in Table 3–1
- The first ten lines of the requested resource

The program is straightforward, except for the computation of the Base 64 encoding. There is an undocumented class, sun.misc.Base64Encoder, that you can use instead of the one that we provide in the example program. Simply replace the call to `base64Encode` with

```
String encoding
   = new sun.misc.BASE64Encoder().encode(input.getBytes());
```

However, we supplied our own class because we do not like to rely on the classes in the `sun` or `com.sun` packages.

NOTE: The `javax.mail.internet.MimeUtility` class in the JavaMail standard extension package also has a method for Base64 encoding.

Example 3–7: URLConnectionTest.java

```
import java.io.*;
import java.net.*;
import java.util.*;

public class URLConnectionTest
{  public static void main(String[] args)
   {  try
      {  String urlName;
         if (args.length > 0)
            urlName = args[0];
         else
            urlName = "http://java.sun.com";

         URL url = new URL(urlName);
         URLConnection connection = url.openConnection();

         // set username, password if specified on command line

         if (args.length > 2)
         {  String username = args[1];
            String password = args[2];
            String input = username + ":" + password;
            String encoding = base64Encode(input);
            connection.setRequestProperty("Authorization",
               "Basic " + encoding);
         }

         connection.connect();

         // print header fields

         int n = 1;
         String key;
         while ((key = connection.getHeaderFieldKey(n)) != null)
         {  String value = connection.getHeaderField(n);
            System.out.println(key + ": " + value);
            n++;
```

```
        }

        // print convenience functions

        System.out.println("----------");
        System.out.println("getContentType: "
           + connection.getContentType());
        System.out.println("getContentLength: "
           + connection.getContentLength());
        System.out.println("getContentEncoding: "
           + connection.getContentEncoding());
        System.out.println("getDate: "
           + connection.getDate());
        System.out.println("getExpiration: "
           + connection.getExpiration());
        System.out.println("getLastModifed: "
           + connection.getLastModified());
        System.out.println("----------");

        BufferedReader in = new BufferedReader(new
           InputStreamReader(connection.getInputStream()));

        // print first ten lines of contents

        String line;
        n = 1;
        while ((line = in.readLine()) != null && n <= 10)
        {  System.out.println(line);
           n++;
        }
        if (line != null) System.out.println(". . .");
     }
     catch (IOException exception)
     {  System.out.println("Error: " + exception);
     }
  }

  public static String base64Encode(String s)
  {  ByteArrayOutputStream bOut
        = new ByteArrayOutputStream();
     Base64OutputStream out = new Base64OutputStream(bOut);
     try
     {  out.write(s.getBytes());
        out.flush();
     }
     catch (IOException exception)
     {
     }
     return bOut.toString();
  }
}
```

```
/* BASE64 encoding encodes 3 bytes into 4 characters.
   |11111122|22223333|33444444|
   Each set of 6 bits is encoded according to the
   toBase64 map. If the number of input bytes is not
   a multiple of 3, then the last group of 4 characters
   is padded with one or two = signs. Each output line
   is at most 76 characters.
*/

class Base64OutputStream extends FilterOutputStream
{  public Base64OutputStream(OutputStream out)
   {  super(out);
   }

   public void write(int c) throws IOException
   {  inbuf[i] = c;
      i++;
      if (i == 3)
      {  super.write(toBase64[(inbuf[0] & 0xFC) >> 2]);
         super.write(toBase64[((inbuf[0] & 0x03) << 4) |
            ((inbuf[1] & 0xF0) >> 4)]);
         super.write(toBase64[((inbuf[1] & 0x0F) << 2) |
            ((inbuf[2] & 0xC0) >> 6)]);
         super.write(toBase64[inbuf[2] & 0x3F]);
         col += 4;
         i = 0;
         if (col >= 76)
         {  super.write('\n');
            col = 0;
         }
      }
   }

   public void flush() throws IOException
   {  if (i == 1)
      {  super.write(toBase64[(inbuf[0] & 0xFC) >> 2]);
         super.write(toBase64[(inbuf[0] & 0x03) << 4]);
         super.write('=');
         super.write('=');
      }
      else if (i == 2)
      {  super.write(toBase64[(inbuf[0] & 0xFC) >> 2]);
         super.write(toBase64[((inbuf[0] & 0x03) << 4) |
            ((inbuf[1] & 0xF0) >> 4)]);
         super.write(toBase64[(inbuf[1] & 0x0F) << 2]);
         super.write('=');
      }
   }

   private static char[] toBase64 =
   {  'A', 'B', 'C', 'D', 'E', 'F', 'G', 'H',
      'I', 'J', 'K', 'L', 'M', 'N', 'O', 'P',
      'Q', 'R', 'S', 'T', 'U', 'V', 'W', 'X',
```

```
        'Y', 'Z', 'a', 'b', 'c', 'd', 'e', 'f',
        'g', 'h', 'i', 'j', 'k', 'l', 'm', 'n',
        'o', 'p', 'q', 'r', 's', 't', 'u', 'v',
        'w', 'x', 'y', 'z', '0', '1', '2', '3',
        '4', '5', '6', '7', '8', '9', '+', '/'
    };

    private int col = 0;
    private int i = 0;
    private int[] inbuf = new int[3];
}
```

NOTE: A commonly asked question is whether the Java platform supports access of secure web pages. If you open a connection to an `https` URL inside an applet, then the applet will indeed access the page, by taking advantage of the SSL implementation of the browser. However, in a standalone application, there is no support for `https` URLs. If you need SSL support in your application, you can install the SSL standard extension library and a cryptographic service provider for the RSA algorithm. You need the RSA algorithm because it is by far the most common algorithm for session key exchange in SSL connections. In the United States, you need to obtain government approval if you want to export your product, and you need to pay a patent royalty to RSA. (The RSA patent expires in October 2000.) However, if you deploy your product inside a browser, then the browser manufacturer has already made the export control and patent licensing arrangements. See `http://java.sun.com/products/plugin/1.2/docs/https.html` for more information on SSL support in the Java Plug-in.

`java.net.URL`

- `InputStream openStream()`

  opens an input stream for reading the resource data.

- `URLConnection openConnection();`

  returns a `URLConnection` object that manages the connection to the resource.

`java.net.URLConnection`

- `void setDoInput(boolean doInput)`

  If `doInput` is `true`, then the user can receive input from this `URLConnection`.

- `void setDoOutput(boolean doOutput)`

  If `doOutput` is `true`, then the user can receive output from this `URLConnection`.

- `void setIfModifiedSince(long time)`

  configures this `URLConnection` to only fetch data that has been modified since a given time. The time is given in seconds from midnight, GMT, January 1, 1970.

- `void setUseCaches(boolean useCaches)`

  If `useCaches` is `true`, then data can be retrieved from a local cache. Note that the `URLConnection` itself does not maintain such a cache. The cache must be supplied by an external program such as a browser.
- `void setAllowUserInteraction(boolean allowUserInteraction)`

  If `allowUserInteraction` is `true`, then the user can be queried for passwords. Note that the `URLConnection` itself has no facilities for executing such a query. The query must be carried out by an external program such as a browser or browser plugin.
- `void setRequestProperty(String key, String value)`

  sets a request property. The `key/value` pair must be meaningful for the request type.
- `void connect()`

  connects to the remote resource and retrieves header information.
- `String getHeaderFieldKey(int n)`

  gets the `n`th header field key, or `null` if `n` is ≤ 0 or larger than the number of header fields.
- `String getHeaderField(int n)`

  gets the `n`th header field value, or `null` if `n` is ≤ 0 or larger than the number of header fields.
- `int getContentLength()`

  gets the content length, if available, or `-1` if unknown.
- `String getContentType`

  gets the content type, such as `text/plain` or `image/gif`.
- `String getContentEncoding()`

  gets the content encoding, such as `gzip`. This value is not commonly used, as the default `identity` encoding is not supposed to be specified with a `Content-Encoding` header.
- `long getDate()`
- `long getExpiration()`
- `long getLastModifed()`

  These methods get the date of creation, expiration, and last modification of the resource. The dates are specified as seconds from midnight, GMT, January 1, 1970.
- `InputStream openInputStream()`
- `OutputStream openOutputStream()`

  These methods return a stream for reading from the resource or writing to the resource.

- `Object getObject()`

  selects the appropriate content handler to read the resource data and convert it into an object. This method is not useful for reading standard types such as `text/plain` or `image/gif` unless you install your own content handler.

Posting Form Data

In the preceding section, you saw how to read data from a web server. Now we will show you how your programs can send data back to a web server and to programs that the web server invokes, using the CGI and servlet mechanisms.

CGI Scripts and Servlets

Even before Java technology came along, there was a mechanism for writing interactive web applications. To send information from a web browser to the web server, a user would fill out a *form,* like the one in Figure 3–9.

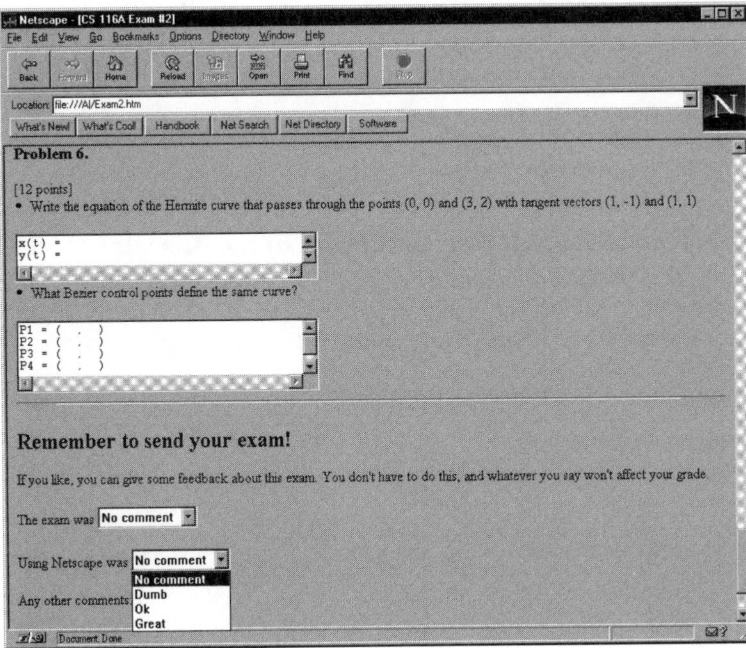

Figure 3–9: An HTML form

When the user clicks on the "Submit" button, the text in the text fields and the settings of the check boxes and radio buttons are sent back to the server to be processed by a so-called CGI script. (CGI stands for *Common Gateway Interface*). The CGI script to use is specified in the `ACTION` attribute of the `FORM` tag.

The CGI script is a program that resides on the server computer. There are usually many CGI scripts on a server, conventionally residing in the `cgi-bin` directory. The

web server launches the CGI script and feeds it the form data. The CGI script processes the form data and produces another HTML page that the web server sends back to the browser. This sequence is illustrated in Figure 3–10. The response page can contain new information (for example, in an information-search program) or just an acknowledgment. The Web browser then displays the response page.

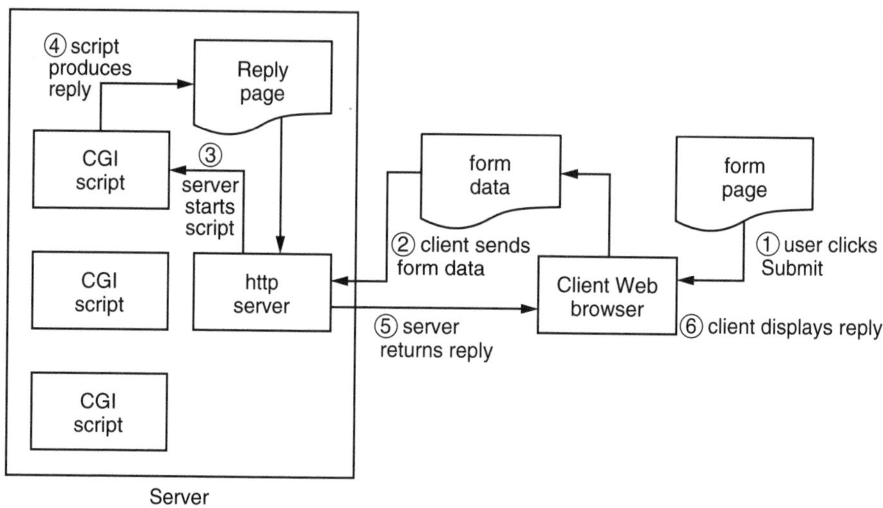

Figure 3–10: Data flow during execution of a CGI script

CGI programs are commonly written in Perl, but they can be written in any language that can read from standard input and write to standard output.

NOTE: We will not discuss how to design HTML forms that interact with CGI. A good reference for that topic is *HTML: The Definitive Guide* (2nd edition) by Musciano and Kennedy (O'Reilly, 1997). Our interest lies in the interface between CGI and Java applets, not in HTML forms.

CGI is often a good mechanism to use because it is well established and system administrators are familiar with it. It does have a major disadvantage. Each request forks a new process and not just a new thread. Furthermore, it is difficult to control the security of those scripts. The newer *servlet* technology overcomes both of these disadvantages. Servlet engines use Java technology to start each servlet in a separate thread and to control the security privileges of servlets. You will see an example servlet later in this chapter. For more information on servlets, we recommend the book *Core Java Web Server* by Chris Taylor and Tim Kimmet [Prentice-Hall 1998].

Sending Data to a Web Server

When data is sent to a web server, it does not matter whether the data is interpreted by a CGI script or a servlet. The client sends the data to the web server in a

standard format, and the web server takes care of passing it on to the program that generates the response.

There are two methods with which to send information to a web server: the GET method and the POST method.

In the GET method, you simply attach parameters to the end of the URL. The URL has the form

```
http://host/script?parameters
```

For example, at the time of this writing, the Yahoo web site has a script py/maps.py at the host maps.yahoo.com. The script requires two parameters, addr and csz. You need to separate the parameters by an & and encode the parameters, using the following scheme.

Replace all spaces with a +. Replace all nonalphanumeric characters by a %, followed by a two-digit hexadecimal number. For example, to transmit the book title *Mastering C++*, you use Mastering+C%2b%2b, since the hexadecimal number 2b (or decimal 43) is the ASCII code of the + character. This encoding keeps any intermediate programs from messing with spaces and interpreting other special characters. This encoding scheme is called URL *encoding*.

For example, to get a map of 1 Infinite Loop, Cupertino, CA, simply request the following URL:

```
http://maps.yahoo.com/py/maps.py?addr=1+Infinite+Loop&csz=
   Cupertino+CA
```

The GET method is simple, but it has a major limitation that makes it relatively unpopular. Most browsers have a limit on the number of characters that you can include in a GET request.

In the POST method, you do not attach parameters to a URL. Instead, you get an output stream from the URLConnection and write name/value pairs to the output stream. You still have to URL-encode the values and separate them with & characters.

Let us look at this process in more detail. To post data to a script, you first establish a URLConnection.

```
URL url = new URL("http:/host/script");
URLConnection connection = url.openConnection();
```

Then, you call the setDoOutput method to set up the connection for output.

```
connection.setDoOutput(true);
```

Next, you call getOutputStream to get a stream through which you can send data to the server. If you are sending text to the server, it is convenient to wrap that stream into a PrintWriter.

```
PrintWriter out
   = new PrintWriter(connection.getOutputStream());
```

Now you are ready to send data to the server:

```
out.print(name1 + "=" + URLEncoder.encode(value1) + "&");
out.print(name2 + "=" + URLEncoder.encode(value2) + "\n");
```

Finally, close the output stream.

```
out.close();
```

You read the server response in the usual way.

```
BufferedReader in = new BufferedReader(new
   InputStreamReader(connection.getInputStream()));
String line;
while ((line = in.readLine()) != null)
{  process line
}
```

Let us run through a practical example. The web site at `http://www.census.gov/ipc/www/idbprint.html` contains a form to request population data (see Figure 3–11). If you look at the HTML source, you will see the following HTML tag:

```
<FORM METHOD=POST ACTION="/cgi-bin/ipc/idbsprd">
```

This tag indicates that the name of the script that is executed when the user clicks the "Submit" button is `/cgi-bin/ipc/idbsprd`, and that you need to use the `POST` method to send data to the script.

Next, you need to find out the field names that the script expects. Look at the user interface components. Each of them has a `NAME` attribute, for example,

```
<SELECT NAME="tbl" SIZE=8>
<OPTION VALUE="001">001 Total Midyear Population
more options . . .
</SELECT>
```

This tells you that the name of the field is `tbl`. This field specifies the population table type. If you specify the table type `001`, you will get a table of the total midyear population. If you look further, you will also find a country field name `cty` with values such as `US` for the United States and `CH` (!) for China. (Sadly, the census bureau seems to be unaware of the ISO-3166 standard for country codes.)

Finally, there is a field named `optyr` for the year range selection. For this example, we will just set it to `latest checked`. Then, the remaining fields will not be filled and the latest available data will be displayed.

For example, to get the latest data for the total midyear population of China, you construct this string:

```
tbl=1&cty=CH&optyr=latest+checked
```

Send the string to the URL

```
http://www.census.gov/cgi-bin/ipc/idbsprd:
```

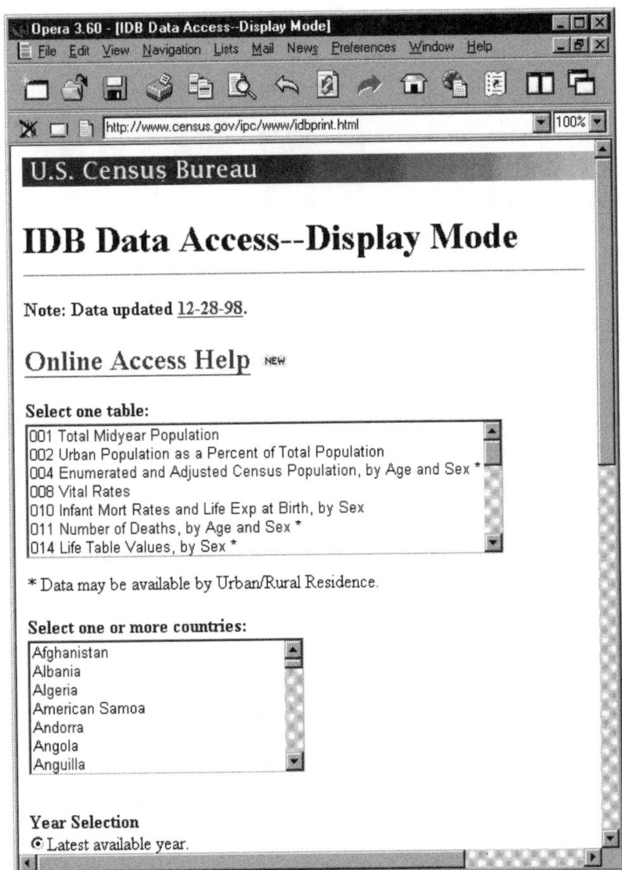

Figure 3–11: A web form to request census data

The script sends back the following reply:

```
<PRE>
U.S. Bureau of the Census, International Data Base

Table 001. Total Midyear Population
--------------------------
CtYear          Population
--------------------------



CH1999          1246871951
--------------------------
Source: U.S. Bureau of the Census, International
        Data Base.
</PRE>
```

As you can see, the script formats the reply as a minimally acceptable HTML page, by placing `<PRE>` and `</PRE>` tags around the data. This particular script doesn't bother with constructing a pretty table, though. That is the reason we picked it as an example—it is easy to see what happens with this script, whereas it can be confusing to decipher a complex set of HTML tags that other scripts produce.

The program in Example 3–8 sends `POST` data to an arbitrary URL. You can use it to send data to the Census Bureau script that we just discussed or to any other URL. You specify the data in a properties file (by default `PostTest.properties`), for example,

```
URL=http://www.census.gov/cgi-bin/ipc/idbsprd
tbl=001
cty=CH
optyr=latest checked
```

Here is how the program works. First, we check if the user supplied a command-line argument to override the default property file. Then, we read the property file.

```
Properties props = new Properties();
FileInputStream in = new FileInputStream(fileName);
props.load(in);
```

Next, we use the `URL` property to construct the URL object, and we remove that property so that it isn't sent to the web server.

```
URL url = new URL(props.getProperty("URL"));
props.remove("URL");
```

In the `doPost` method, we first open the connection, call `doOutput(true)`, and open the output stream. Then, we enumerate the names and values in the `Properties` object. For each of them, we send the string

```
name + "=" + URLEncoder.encode(value) + ch
```

to the server, where `ch` is a `'&'` until the last name/value pair has been sent, in which case it becomes a `'\n'`. Finally, we read the response from the server.

There is one twist with reading the response. If a script error occurs, then the call to `connection.getInputStream()` throws a `FileNotFoundException`. However, the server still sends an error page back to the browser (such as the ubiquitous "Error 404 -page not found"). To capture this error page, you cast the `URLConnection` object to the `HttpURLConnection` class and call its `getErrorStream` method:

```
InputStream err
   = ((HttpURLConnection)connection).getErrorStream();
```

Then, you can read the error page from the stream `err`.

If you run the program with the supplied properties file, then you will see the result from the Census Bureau script. We supply a second file, `Zip.properties`, that performs a zip code lookup, using a script provided by the United States Postal Service. The query result contains a list of city names for a given zip code.

The technique that this program displays is useful whenever you need to query information from an existing web site. Simply find out the parameters that you

need to send (usually by inspecting the HTML source of a web page that carries out the same query), and then strip out the HTML tags and other unnecessary information from the reply.

Example 3–8: PostTest.java

```
import java.io.*;
import java.net.*;
import java.util.*;

public class PostTest
{  public static void main(String[] args)
   {  try
      {  String fileName;
         if (args.length > 0)
            fileName = args[0];
         else
            fileName = "PostTest.properties";
         Properties props = new Properties();
         FileInputStream in = new FileInputStream(fileName);
         props.load(in);

         URL url = new URL(props.getProperty("URL"));
         props.remove("URL");
         String r = doPost(url, props);
         System.out.println(r);
      }
      catch (IOException exception)
      {  System.out.println("Error: " + exception);
      }
   }

   public static String doPost(URL url,
      Properties nameValuePairs) throws IOException
   {  URLConnection connection = url.openConnection();
      connection.setDoOutput(true);

      PrintWriter out
         = new PrintWriter(connection.getOutputStream());

      Enumeration enum = nameValuePairs.keys();

      while (enum.hasMoreElements())
      {  String name = (String)enum.nextElement();
         String value = nameValuePairs.getProperty(name);
         char ch;
         if (enum.hasMoreElements()) ch = '&'; else ch = '\n';
         out.print(name + "="
            + URLEncoder.encode(value) + ch);
      }

      out.close();

      BufferedReader in;
```

```
      try
      {  in = new BufferedReader(new
            InputStreamReader(connection.getInputStream()));
      }
      catch (FileNotFoundException exception)
      {  InputStream err
            = ((HttpURLConnection)connection).getErrorStream();
         if (err == null) throw exception;
         in = new BufferedReader(new InputStreamReader(err));
      }
      StringBuffer response = new StringBuffer();
      String line;

      while ((line = in.readLine()) != null)
         response.append(line + "\n");

      in.close();
      return response.toString();
   }
}
```

Our example program uses the `URLConnection` class to post data to a web site. More for curiosity's sake than for practical usage, you may like to know exactly what information the `URLConnection` sends to the server in addition to the data that you supply.

The `URLConnection` object first sends a request header to the server. The first line of the header must be

```
Content-Type: type
```

where *type* is usually one of the following:

```
text/plain
text/html
application/octet-stream
application/x-www-form-urlencoded
```

The content type must be followed by the line

```
Content-Length: length
```

for example,

```
Content-Length: 1024
```

The end of the header is indicated by a blank line. Then, the data portion follows. The web server strips off the header and routes the data portion to the server script.

Note that the `URLConnection` object buffers all data that you send to the output stream since it must first determine the total content length.

java.net.HttpURLConnection

- `InputStream getErrorStream()`

  returns a stream from which you can read web server error messages.

`java.net.URLEncoder`

- `static String encode(String s)`

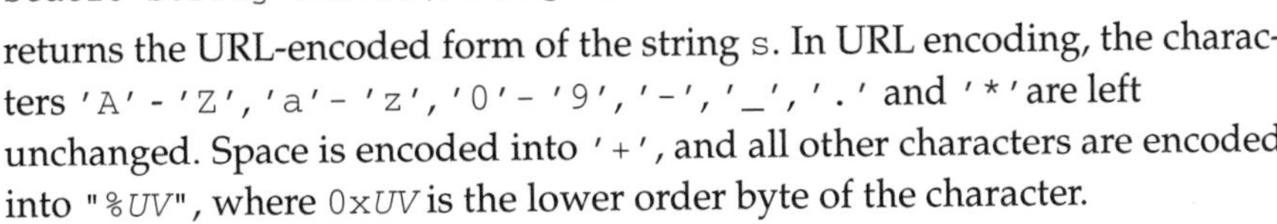
returns the URL-encoded form of the string `s`. In URL encoding, the characters `'A'` - `'Z'`, `'a'` - `'z'`, `'0'` - `'9'`, `'-'`, `'_'`, `'.'` and `'*'` are left unchanged. Space is encoded into `'+'`, and all other characters are encoded into `"%UV"`, where `0xUV` is the lower order byte of the character.

`java.net.URLDecoder`

- `static string decode(String s)`

  returns the decoding of the URL encoded string `s`.

Harvesting Information from the Web

The last example showed you how to read data from a web server. The Internet contains a wealth of information both interesting and not: it is the lack of guidance through this mass of information that is the major complaint of most web users. One promise of the Java technology is that it may help to bring order to this chaos: you can use Java applets to retrieve information and present it to the user in an appealing format.

There are many possible uses. Here are a few that come to mind:

- An applet can look at all the web pages the user has specified as interesting and find which have recently changed.
- An applet can visit the web pages of all scheduled airlines to find out which is running a special.
- Applets can gather and display recent stock quotes, monetary exchange rates, and other financial information.
- Applets can search FAQs, press releases, articles, and so on, and return text that contains certain keywords.

We give a simple example of such an applet. The National Weather Service stores weather reports in various files on the server `http://iwin.nws.noaa.gov`. For example, an hourly forecast for California is stored at

```
http://iwin.nws.noaa.gov/iwin/ca/hourly.html
```

Other directories contain similar reports.

Our applet presents the user with two lists, one with states and another with report types. If you click on Get report, the applet fetches the report and places it into a text area (see Figure 3–12). You will find the code for the applet in Example 3–9.

The applet code itself is straightforward. The only interesting action occurs in the `getWeather` method. That method first builds up the query string. It obtains the base URL (`http://iwin.nws.noaa.gov/iwin/`) from the `queryBase` parameter of the applet tag. Then, it adds the state and report name and the extension `.html`:

```
String queryBase = getParameter("queryBase");
String query = queryBase + state + "/" + report + ".html";
```

Next, we create an `URL` object and call `openStream`.

```
URL url = new URL(query);
BufferedReader in = new BufferedReader(new
   InputStreamReader(url.openStream()));
```

The remainder of the method simply reads the file, removes HTML tags, and places the file in the text area.

```
String line;
while ((line = in.readLine()) != null)
   weather.append(removeTags(line) + "\n");
```

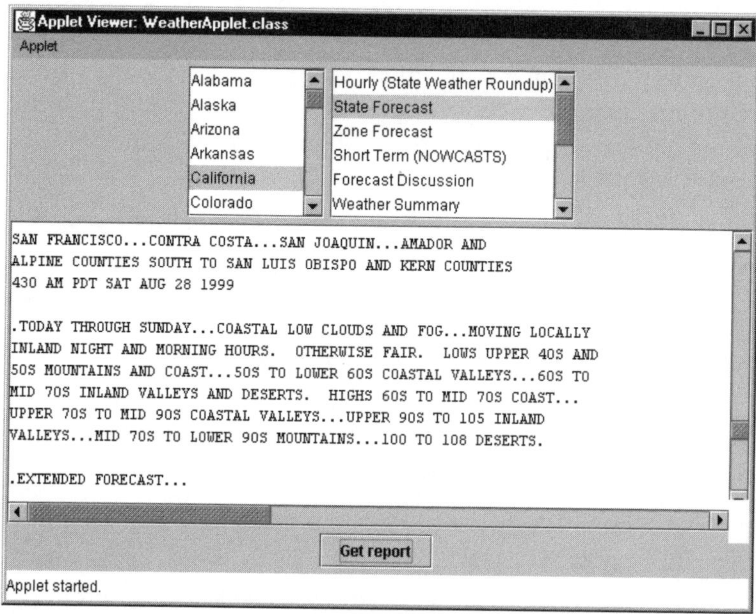

Figure 3–12: The `WeatherReport` applet

Example 3–9: WeatherApplet.java

```
import java.net.*;
import java.io.*;
import java.util.*;
import java.awt.*;
import java.awt.event.*;
import java.applet.*;
import javax.swing.*;

public class WeatherApplet extends JApplet
```

```
   implements ActionListener
{  public void init()
   {  Container contentPane = getContentPane();
      contentPane.setLayout(new BorderLayout());

      // Set up the lists of choices for states and reports
      JPanel listPanel = new JPanel();
      state = makeList(states, 6, listPanel);
      report = makeList(reports, 6, listPanel);
      contentPane.add(listPanel, "North");

      // Add the text area
      weather = new JTextArea(20, 80);
      weather.setFont(new Font("Courier", Font.PLAIN, 12));

      // Add the report button
      contentPane.add(new JScrollPane(weather), "Center");
      JPanel buttonPanel = new JPanel();
      JButton reportButton = new JButton("Get report");
      reportButton.addActionListener(this);
      buttonPanel.add(reportButton);
      contentPane.add(buttonPanel, "South");
   }

   public JList makeList(final String[][] items, int visibleRows,
      Container parent)
   {  JList list = new JList(new AbstractListModel()
         {  public Object getElementAt(int i)
            {  return items[i][0];
            }

            public int getSize()
            {  return items.length;
            }
         });
      list.setSelectionMode(ListSelectionModel.SINGLE_SELECTION);
      list.setVisibleRowCount(visibleRows);
      parent.add(new JScrollPane(list));
      return list;
   }


   public String getItem(JList list, String[][] items)
   {  return items[list.getSelectedIndex()][1];
   }

   public void actionPerformed(ActionEvent evt)
   {  weather.setText("");
      getWeather(getItem(state, states), getItem(report, reports));
   }

   // Put together the URL query and go get the data from it
   public void getWeather(String state, String report)
   {  String r = new String();
```

```
    try
    {  String queryBase = getParameter("queryBase");
       String query
          = queryBase + state + "/" + report + ".html";
       URL url = new URL(query);
       BufferedReader in = new BufferedReader(new
          InputStreamReader(url.openStream()));

       String line;
       while ((line = in.readLine()) != null)
          weather.append(removeTags(line) + "\n");
    }
    catch(IOException e)
    {  showStatus("Error " + e);
    }
 }

 public static String removeTags(String s)
 {  while (true)
    {  int lb = s.indexOf('<');
       if (lb < 0) return s;
       int rb = s.indexOf('>', lb);
       if (rb < 0) return s;
       s = s.substring(0, lb) + " " + s.substring(rb + 1);
    }
 }

 private JTextArea weather;
 private JList state;
 private JList report;

 private String[][] states =
    {  { "Alabama", "al" },
       { "Alaska", "ak" },
       { "Arizona", "az" },
       { "Arkansas", "ar" },
       { "California", "ca" },
       { "Colorado", "co" },
       { "Connecticut", "ct" },
       { "Delaware", "de" },
       { "Florida", "fl" },
       { "Georgia", "ga" },
       { "Hawaii", "hi" },
       { "Idaho", "id" },
       { "Illinois", "il" },
       { "Indiana", "in" },
       { "Iowa", "ia" },
       { "Kansas", "ks" },
       { "Kentucky", "ky" },
       { "Lousisiana", "la" },
       { "Maine", "me" },
       { "Maryland", "md" },
       { "Massachusetts", "ma" },
```

```
            { "Michigan", "mi" },
            { "Minnesota", "mn" },
            { "Mississippi", "ms" },
            { "Missouri", "mo" },
            { "Montana", "mt" },
            { "Nebraska", "ne" },
            { "Nevada", "nv" },
            { "New Hampshire", "nh" },
            { "New Jersey", "nj" },
            { "New Mexico", "nm" },
            { "New York", "ny" },
            { "North Carolina", "nc" },
            { "North Dakota", "nd" },
            { "Ohio", "oh" },
            { "Oklahoma", "ok" },
            { "Oregon", "or" },
            { "Pennsylvania", "pa" },
            { "Rhode Island", "ri" },
            { "South Carolina", "sc" },
            { "South Dakota", "sd" },
            { "Tennessee", "tn" },
            { "Texas", "tx" },
            { "Utah", "ut" },
            { "Vermont", "vt" },
            { "Virginia", "va" },
            { "Washington", "wa" },
            { "West Virginia", "wv" },
            { "Wisconsin", "wi" },
            { "Wyoming", "wy" }
         };

   private String[][] reports =
         {  { "Hourly (State Weather Roundup)", "hourly" },
            { "State Forecast", "state" },
            { "Zone Forecast", "zone" },
            { "Short Term (NOWCASTS)", "shortterm" },
            { "Forecast Discussion", "discussion" },
            { "Weather Summary", "summary" },
            { "Public Information", "public" },
            { "Climate Data", "climate" },
            { "Hydrological Data", "hydro" },
            { "Watches", "watches" },
            { "Special Weather Statements", "special" },
            { "Warnings and Advisories", "allwarnings" }
         };
}
```

Unfortunately, when you try running this applet, you will be disappointed. Both the applet viewer and the browser refuse to run it. Whenever you click on Get report, a security violation is generated. We discuss the reason for this violation, and how to overcome this problem, in the next section. Right now, we'll just show you how to force the applet viewer to run the applet anyway.

First, create a text file with the following contents:

```
grant
{  permission java.net.SocketPermission
      "iwin.nws.noaa.gov:80", "connect";
};
```

Call it `WeatherApplet.policy`. We will discuss policy files in detail in Chapter 9. However, this particular policy file is easy to understand. It simply grants the applet the permission to connect to the host `iwin.nws.noaa.gov` on port 80, the HTTP port. Why the applet needs such a permission is the topic of the next section.

Now start the applet viewer with the following command line:

```
appletviewer -J-Djava.security.policy=WeatherApplet.policy
   WeatherApplet.html
```

The `-J` option of the applet viewer passes command-line arguments to the Java bytecode interpreter. The `-D` option of the Java bytecode interpreter sets the value of a system property. Here, we set the system property `java.security.policy` to the name of a policy file that contains the security permissions for this program.

If you want to run the applet in a browser, you first have to sign it. Then, you and, more importantly, anyone else who wants to run it, must tell the browser:

- To verify the signature (unless it was guaranteed by a trusted certificate authority);
- To agree with the requested privileges.

We discuss applet signing in detail in Chapter 9.

Applet Security

As you just saw, your applet was forbidden from doing a very simple operation, namely, connecting to port 80 of a web server. In this section, we discuss the reason for this prohibition and describe how to deploy the applet without making your users fuss with certificates.

Web browsers allow an applet to read and write data only on the host that serves the applet. Applets can connect only to sockets on the computer from which the applet came. This rule is often described as "applets can only phone home."

At first, this restriction seems to make no sense. Why should the applet be denied an operation that the ambient browser carries out all the time, namely, to get data from a web host? To understand the rationale, it helps to visualize the three hosts involved, as shown in Figure 3–13:

- The originating host — your computer that delivers the Web page and Java applet to clients;
- The local host — the user's machine that runs your applet;
- The third-party data repository that your applet would like to see.

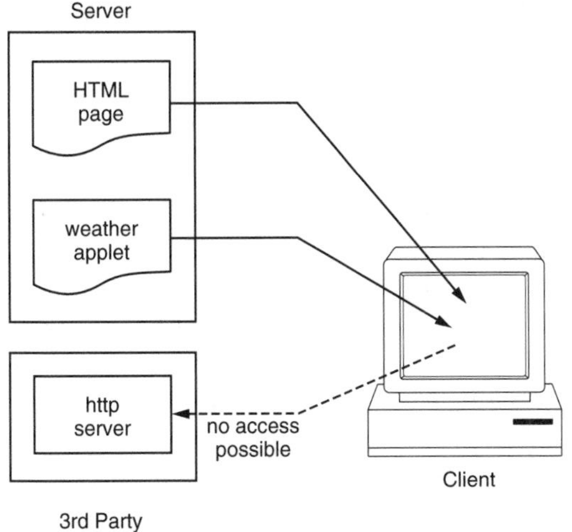

Figure 3–13: Applet security disallows connection to third party

The applet security rule says that the applet can read and write data only on the originating host. Certainly it makes sense that the applet cannot write to the local host. If it could, it might be able to plant viruses or alter important files. After all, the applet starts running immediately when the user stumbles upon our web page, and the user must be protected from damage by malicious or incompetent applets.

It also makes sense that the applet cannot read from the local host. Otherwise, it might browse the files on the local computer for sensitive information, such as credit card numbers, open a socket connection to the applet host, and write the information back. You might open a great-looking web page, interact with an applet that does something fun or useful, and be completely unaware of what that applet does in other threads. The browser denies your applet all access to the files on your computer.

DILBERT reprinted by permission of United Feature Syndicate, Inc.

But why can't the applet read other files from the Web? Isn't the Web a wealth of publicly available information, made available for everyone to read? If you browse the Web from home, through a service provider, this is indeed the situation. But it is quite different when you do your Web surfing in your office (searching only for work-relevant information, of course). Many companies have their computer sitting behind a firewall.

A firewall is a computer that filters traffic going into and out of the corporate network. This computer will deny attempts to access services with less than stellar security histories. For example, there are known security holes in many FTP implementations. The firewall might simply disallow anonymous ftp requests or shunt them off to an isolated FTP server. It might also deny a request to access the mail port on all machines except the mail server. Depending on the security philosophy, the firewall (shown in Figure 3–14) can also apply filtering rules to the traffic between the corporate network and the Internet.

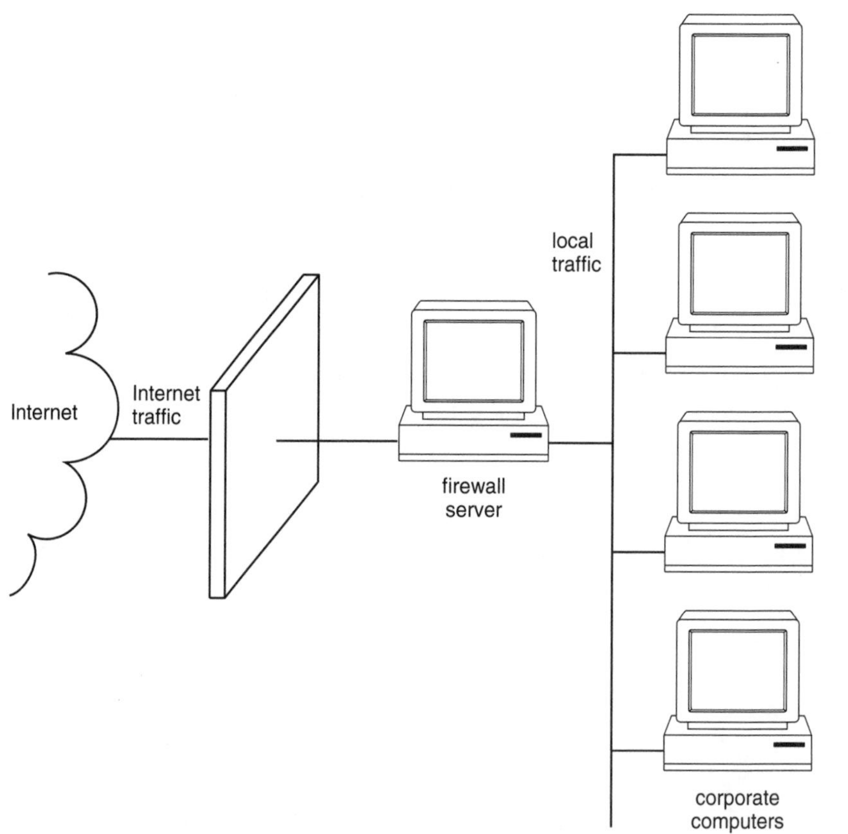

Figure 3–14: A firewall provides security

(If you are interested in this topic, turn to *Firewalls and Internet Security* by William R. Cheswick and Steven M. Bellovin [Addison-Wesley, 1994].)

Having a firewall allows a company to use the Web to distribute internal information that is of interest to employees but should not be accessible outside the

company. The company simply sets up a web server, tells the address only to its employees, and programs the firewall to deny any access requests to that server from the outside. The employees can then browse the internal information with the same web tools they already know and use.

If an employee visits your web page, the applet is downloaded into the computer behind the firewall and starts running there. If it were able to read all the web pages that the ambient browser can read, it would have access to the corporate information. Then, it could open a connection to the host from which it came and send all that private information back. That is obviously insecure. Since the browser has no idea which web pages are public and which are confidential, it disallows access to all of them.

That is too bad—you simply cannot write an applet that goes out on the Web, grabs information, processes and formats it, and presents it to the applet user. For example, our weather report applet does not want to write any information back to its host. Why doesn't the browser let the applet strike a deal? If the applet promises not to write anywhere, it ought to be able to read from everywhere. That way, it would just be a harvester and processor, showing an ephemeral result on the user's screen.

The trouble is that a browser cannot distinguish *read* from *write* requests. When you ask to open a stream on a URL, this is obviously a read request. Well, maybe not. The URL might be of the form

```
http://www.rogue.com/cgi-bin/cracker.pl?Garys+password+is+Sicily
```

Here, the culprit is the CGI mechanism. It is designed to take arbitrary arguments and process them. The script that handles the CGI request can, and often does, store the request data. It is easy to hide information in a CGI query text. (A data stream that contains hidden information is called a *covert channel* in security circles.)

So, should the browser disallow all CGI queries and allow access only to plain web pages? The solution is not that simple. The browser has no way of knowing that the server to which it connects on port 80 (the http port) is actually a standard http server. It might be just a shell that saves all requests to a file and returns an HTML page: "Sorry, the information you requested is not available." Then, the applet could transmit information by pretending to read from the URL

```
http://www.rogue.com/Garys/password/is/Sicily
```

Since the browser cannot distinguish read from write requests, it must disallow them both.

To summarize: Applets run on the computer browsing your web page, but they can connect *only* to the computer serving the web page. That is the "applets can only phone home" rule.

Proxy Servers

How, then, can you distribute an applet that harvests information for your users? You could make a web page that shows the applet in action with fake data, stored on your server. (This is exactly the approach that Sun takes with their stock-ticker sample applet.) You could then provide a button with which the user downloads the applet and a policy file. Users could then run it from the applet viewer.

That approach will probably greatly limit the attractiveness of your applet. Many people will be too lazy to download and install the applet locally if they did not first get to use it a few times with real data on your web page.

Fortunately, there is a way to feed the applet real data: install a proxy server on your HTML server. That proxy server is a service that grabs requested information from the Web and sends it to whoever requested it. For example, suppose your applet makes a `GET` request

```
http://www.yourserver.com/proxysvr?URL=http://iwin.nws.noaa.gov
   /iwin/CA/hourly.html
```

to the proxy server that resides on the same host as the applet code. Then the proxy server fetches the web page for the applet and sends it as the result of the `GET` request (see Figure 3–15).

Proxy servers for this purpose must exist, but we could not find one, so we wrote our own. You can see the code in Example 3–10. We implemented the proxy as a *servlet*, a program that is started by a servlet engine. Most web servers can either run servlets directly or can be extended to do so.

Servlets are not a part of the standard edition of the Java platform, and a detailed discussion of servlets is beyond the scope of this book. For details, please turn to *Core Java Web Server* by Chris Taylor and Tim Kimmet [Prentice-Hall 1998]. However, the servlet in Example 3–10 is quite simple. Here is a brief explanation of how it works.

When the web server receives a `GET` request for the servlet, it calls its `doGet` method. The `HttpServletRequest` parameter contains the request parameters. The servlet uses the `getParameter` method to get the value of the `URL` parameter. In any servlet, you send your response to the `PrintStream` that the `getWriter` method of the `HttpServletResponse` class returns. This servlet simply connects to the resource given in the `URL` parameter, reads the data a line at a time, and sends it to the response stream. Finally, you can see how the `sendError` method is used for error reporting.

The next section tells you how to configure the servlet if you use the Java Servlet Development Kit. That development kit contains a small web server that you can run locally to test the weather report applet.

You don't have to use servlets to implement a proxy server. The sidebar tells you how you can implement the proxy server in C or Perl.

Example 3–10: ProxySvr.java

```
import java.io.*;
import java.net.*;
import javax.servlet.*;
import javax.servlet.http.*;

public class ProxySvr extends HttpServlet
{  public void doGet(HttpServletRequest request,
      HttpServletResponse response)
      throws ServletException, IOException
   {  String query = null;

      response.setContentType("text/html");
      PrintWriter out = response.getWriter();

      query = request.getParameter("URL");
      if (query == null)
      {  response.sendError(HttpServletResponse.SC_BAD_REQUEST,
            "Missing URL parameter");
         return;
      }

      try
      {  query = URLDecoder.decode(query);
      }
      catch(Exception exception)
      {  response.sendError(HttpServletResponse.SC_BAD_REQUEST,
            "URL decode error " + exception);
         return;
      }

      try
      {  URL url = new URL(query);
         BufferedReader in = new BufferedReader(new
            InputStreamReader(url.openStream()));

         String line;
         while ((line = in.readLine()) != null)
            out.println(line);
         out.flush();
      }
      catch(IOException exception)
      {  response.sendError(HttpServletResponse.SC_NOT_FOUND,
            "Exception: " + exception);
      }
   }
}
```

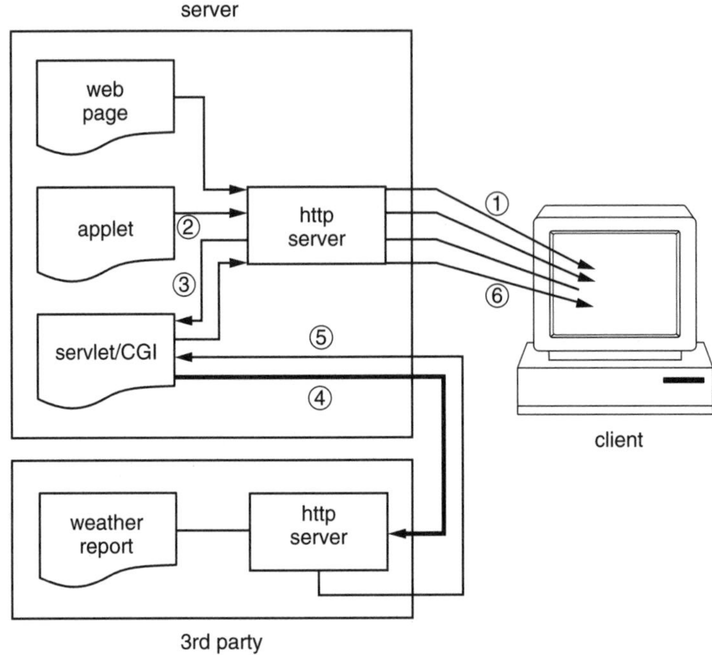

Figure 3–15: Data flow in the weather report applet

Comparing Servlets, Perl, and C for Server-side Processing

CGI scripts can be written in any language that can read from standard input and write to standard output. The "traditional" choice for CGI scripts is Perl. However, we actually wrote our first proxy server script in C because we did not realize that Perl can connect to sockets.

The Perl and C codes are listed in Example 3–11 and 3–12. As you can see, the C code is quite long. Even the most elementary operations (for example, reading a line of input) must be programmed in gory detail in C. Networking code is even worse. We didn't come up with the networking code ourselves. We modified a sample program from *Unix Network Programming,* by W. Richard Stevens (Prentice-Hall, 1990). Have a look at the code, and you will really appreciate the simplicity and elegance of the `java.net` package.

The Perl code is much shorter but, as you can see by glancing at it, is completely unreadable to the uninitiated. There are charming variable names like `$!` and `$|` and inscrutable statements such as

```
$url =~ s/%([a-fA-F0-9][a-fA-F0-9])/pack("C", hex($1))/eg;
```

This means "replace all strings of the form '% followed by two hex digits' by the corresponding hex value." (No, we didn't figure that out ourselves. Like everybody else, we copied it from another script.) The remainder of the program is a

modification of an example from *Programming Perl,* by Larry Wall and Randal L. Schwarz (O'Reilly, 1991). We don't pretend to understand the details, but it works.

As a result of this experiment, we can heartily recommend servlets as a great mechanism for server-side processing. The network programming and string handling in the Java platform beat the daylights out of C, and the Java programming language code is far more readable and maintainable than the Perl equivalent.

Example 3–11: proxysvr.c

```
#include <netdb.h>
#include <sys/types.h>
#include <sys/socket.h>
#include <netinet/in.h>
#include <arpa/inet.h>
#include <stdio.h>
#include <string.h>
#include <stdlib.h>

#define MAXLINE 512
#define MAXNAME 128
#define HTTP 80

unsigned writen(fd, vptr, n)
int fd;
char* vptr;
unsigned n;
{  unsigned nleft;
   unsigned nwritten;
   char* ptr;

   ptr = (char*)vptr;
   nleft = n;
   while (nleft > 0)
   {  if ((nwritten = write(fd, ptr, nleft)) <= 0)
         return nwritten;
      nleft -= nwritten;
      ptr += nwritten;
   }
   return n - nleft;
}

unsigned readline(fd, vptr, maxlen)
int fd;
char* vptr;
int maxlen;
{  unsigned n;
   unsigned rc;
```

```
   char* ptr;
   char c;

   ptr = vptr;
   for (n = 1; n < maxlen; n++)
   {  if ((rc = read(fd, &c, 1)) == 1)
      {  *ptr++ = c;
         if (c == '\n')
         {  *ptr = 0;
            return n;
         }
      }
      else if (rc == 0)
      {  if (n == 1) return 0;
         else
         {  *ptr = 0;
            return n;
         }
      }
      else
         return -1;
   }
   *ptr = 0;
   return n;
}

void error(msg)
char* msg;
{  fputs(msg, stderr);
   fputc('\n', stderr);
   exit(1);
}

void url_decode(in, out, outlen)
char* in;
char* out;
int outlen;
{  int i = 0;
   int j = 0;
   while (in[i] != '\0' && j < outlen - 1)
   {  if (in[i] == '+') out[j] = ' ';
      else if (in[i] == '%')
      {  int ch;
         sscanf(in + i + 1, "%x", &ch);
         out[j] = ch;
         i += 2;
      }
      else out[j] = in[i];
      i++;
      j++;
   }
```

```
   out[j] = 0;
}

int main(argc, argv)
int argc;
char** argv;
{  int sockfd;
   struct sockaddr_in serv_addr;
   int n;
   char* name;
   struct hostent* hostptr;
   char url[MAXLINE + 1];
   char sendline[MAXLINE + 1];
   char recvline[MAXLINE + 1];
   char server_name[MAXNAME];
   char file_name[MAXLINE];
   int port;
   int service = 0;
   char* p;
   char* q;

   url_decode(argv[1], url, sizeof(url));

   p = strstr(url, "URL=http://");
   if (p != url)
      error("Sorry--can only recognize URL=service://server/file");
   service = HTTP;
   p += strlen("URL=http://");
   q = strchr(p, '/');
   if (q == NULL)
      error("Sorry--can only recognize //server/file");
   strncpy(server_name, p, q - p);
   server_name[q - p] = '\0';
   strncpy(file_name, q, sizeof(file_name) - 1);
   file_name[sizeof(file_name) - 1] = '\0';
   port = service;

   if ((sockfd = socket(PF_INET, SOCK_STREAM, 0)) < 0)
      error("Can't open stream socket");

   bzero((char*)&serv_addr, sizeof(serv_addr));
   serv_addr.sin_family = AF_INET;
   hostptr = gethostbyname(server_name);
   if (hostptr == 0) error("Can't find host");
   name = inet_ntoa(*(struct in_addr*)*hostptr->h_addr_list);
   serv_addr.sin_addr.s_addr = inet_addr(name);
   serv_addr.sin_port = htons(port);

   if (connect(sockfd, (struct sockaddr*)&serv_addr,
         sizeof(serv_addr)) < 0)
```

```
      error("Can't connect to server");

   sendline[sizeof(sendline) - 1] = 0;
   if (service == HTTP)
   {  strcpy(sendline, "GET ");
      strncat(sendline, file_name, sizeof(sendline) - 1
         - strlen(sendline));
   }
   strncat(sendline, "\r\n", sizeof(sendline) - 1
      - strlen(sendline));

   n = strlen(sendline);
   if (writen(sockfd, sendline, n) != n)
      error("Write error on socket");

   fputs("Content-type: text/html\n\n", stdout);

   do
   {  n = readline(sockfd, recvline, MAXLINE);
      if (n < 0)
         error("Read error on socket");
      else if (n > 0)
      {  recvline[n] = 0;
         fputs(recvline, stdout);
      }
   } while (n > 0);

   return 0;
}
```

Example 3–12: proxysvr.pl

```
($url) = @ARGV;

$url =~ tr/+/ /;
$url =~ s/%([a-fA-F0-9][a-fA-F0-9])/pack("C", hex($1))/eg;

$pos = index($url, "URL=http://");

if ($pos != 0)
{  die "Sorry--can only recognize URL=http://server/file";
}

$port = 80;

$pos = 11;
$pos2 = index($url, "/", $pos);
if ($pos2 < 0)
{  die "Sorry--can only recognize //server/file";
```

```
}

$server_name = substr($url, $pos, $pos2 - $pos);
$file_name = substr($url, $pos2);
$AF_INET = 2;
$SOCK_STREAM =1;

$sockaddr = 'S n a4 x8';

($name, $aliases, $proto) = getprotobyname ('tcp');
($name,$aliases,$type,$len,$thataddr)
   = gethostbyname($server_name);
$that = pack($sockaddr, $AF_INET, $port, $thataddr);

if (!socket (S, $AF_INET, $SOCK_STREAM, $proto))
{  die $!;
}

if (!connect (S, $that))
{  die $!;
}

select(S); $|=1; select(STDOUT);

$command = "GET ".$file_name;

print S $command."\r\n";

print "Content-type: text/html\n\n";
while (<S>)
{  print;
}
```

Testing the `WeatherReport` *Applet*

In this section, we show you how to test the weather report applet. You need a web server that can execute either servlets or CGI scripts. We give you detailed instructions for the web server that comes with the Java Servlet Development Kit. If you use another web server, you will need to make the appropriate adjustments.

Here are the steps.

1. Download the Java Web Server Development Kit from `http://java.sun.com/products/jsp/download.html`.
2. Install the kit. To keep the instructions uncluttered, let's assume you installed it onto the `\jswdk` directory. If you use another directory, modify the instructions accordingly. If you use Unix or Linux, change the path separator to a `/`.
3. Change the server port from the default 8080 to port 80. Edit the file `\jswdk\webserver.xml` and change the `port` property to
   `port NMTOKEN "80"`

4. Compile the servlet code:

```
javac -classpath \jswdk\lib\servlet.jar;. proxySvr.java
```

5. Copy the class file `ProxySvr.class` to the `\jswdk\webpages\WEB-INF\servlets` directory.
6. Edit the `\jswdk\webpages\WEB-INF\mappings.properties` file by adding the line:

```
/proxysvr=proxysvr
```

7. Edit the `\jswdk\webpages\WEB-INF\servlets.properties` file by adding the line:

```
proxysvr.code=ProxySvr
```

8. Copy the files

```
WeatherApplet.html
WeatherApplet.class
WeatherApplet$1.class
```

to the `\jswdk\webpages` directory
9. Edit the `WeatherApplet.html` file and change the `PARAM` tag to

```
<PARAM NAME="queryBase" VALUE=
"http://localhost/proxysvr?URL=http://iwin.nws.noaa.gov/iwin/">
```

10. Start the web server by running

```
\jswdk\startserver
```

11. Run the applet by running

```
appletviewer http://localhost/WeatherApplet.html
```

Alternatively, use your browser to view that URL. Your browser needs a Java 2 plugin. Note that no security policy file is required!

Now that you have seen the applet in action, let us review why the proxy server solves the applet security problem. When the user selects a state and report type, the weather applet requests the information from the proxy server on its local host. The proxy server then goes out to the National Weather Service, gets the data, and feeds it back to the applet.

This looks like a lot of trouble, but we have avoided the security risk. The applet only talks to the proxy server. The proxy server cannot peek at documents that may be accessible from the machine that is running the applet.

You can use this technique whenever you want to deploy an applet that harvests information from other web sites. In effect, you have offloaded the harvesting to the server, and you use the applet for presenting the results.

Now the security monkey is on *your* back. By installing the proxy server on your web server, you enable anyone to access it and download any files that are visible

from your server. It is then up to you to configure your network so that the proxy server cannot pick up any of your confidential files.

Does it make sense to have the server merely grab the information and reflect it to the applet? In this case, it does, but in general, it often makes sense for the server to cache it, thus improving performance when there are multiple requests, or to preprocess the information. In this example, we used server-side processing to avoid a security issue. In many other situations, it is best to process as much information as possible on the server because the server software is easier to control and maintain. Applets still have their place—interacting with the user and presenting results. In a typical 3-tier (or *n*-tier) application, the applet is paired with a servlet that does the "heavy lifting."

Chapter 4

Database Connectivity: JDBC

- Structured Query Language
- Installing JDBC
- Basic JDBC Programming Concepts
- Populating a Database
- Executing Queries
- Metadata
- Scrollable and Updatable Result Sets

In the summer of 1996, Sun released the first version of the JDBC (Java database connectivity) kit. This package lets programmers connect to a database, query it, or update it, using the Structured Query Language or SQL. (SQL, usually pronounced like "sequel," is an industry standard for database access.) We think this was one of the most important developments in programming for the Java platform. It is not just that databases are among the most common use of hardware and software today. After all, there are a lot of products running after this market; so why do we think the Java programming language has the potential to make a big splash? The reason that Java and JDBC have an essential advantage over other database programming environments is this:

- Programs developed with the Java programming language and JDBC are platform independent and vendor independent.

The same database program written in the Java programming language can run on an NT box, a Solaris server, or a database appliance powered by the Java platform. You can move your data from one database to another, for example, from Microsoft SQL Server to Oracle, or even to a tiny database embedded in a device, and the same program can still read your data. This is in sharp contrast to traditional database programming. It is all too common that one writes database applications in a proprietary database language, using a database management system that is available only from a single vendor. The result is that you can run the resulting application only on one or two platforms. We believe that *because of their universality,* the Java programming language and JDBC will eventually replace proprietary database languages and call level interfaces used by vendors such as Oracle, Informix, and Microsoft for accessing databases.

NOTE: Some database vendors now build a JVM into the database itself so that you can write stored procedures in Java. This technology is a part of the SQLJ specification. For more information on SQLJ, see `http://www.sqlj.org`.

As part of the release of Java 2 in 1998, a second version of JDBC was issued as well. At the time of this writing, support for JDBC2 is still sporadic, but we expect that JDBC2 drivers will become the norm in the near future. In this chapter, we introduce the major JDBC2 features (such as scrollable cursors) and alert you when you need to be aware of the version differences.

We still must caution you that the JDK offers no tools for database programming with the Java programming language. For form designers, query builders, and report generators, you need to turn to third-party packages. "Corporate" or "professional" versions of development environments for the Java platform, such as Visual Café and JBuilder ship with database integration tools.

In this chapter:

- We explain some of the ideas behind JDBC—the "Java database connectivity API."
- We provide enough details and examples so that you can get started in actually using JDBC.

The first part of this chapter gives you an overview of how JDBC is put together. The last part gives you example code that illustrates the major JDBC features.

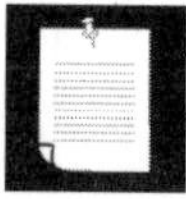

NOTE: Over the years, many technologies were invented to make database access more efficient and fail-safe. Standard databases support indexes, triggers, stored procedures, and transaction management. JDBC supports all these features, but we do not discuss them in this chapter. One could write an entire book on advanced database programming for the Java platform, and many such books have been written. The material in this chapter will give you enough information to effectively use JDBC with a departmental database. To go further with JDBC, we suggest *JDBC API Tutorial and Reference* by Seth White, Maydene Fisher, Rick Cattell, Graham Hamilton, and Mark Hapner (Addison-Wesley 1999).

The Design of JDBC

From the start, the developers of the Java technology at Sun were aware of the potential Java showed for working with databases. Starting in 1995, they began working on extending the standard Java library to deal with SQL access to databases. What they first hoped to do was to extend Java so that it could talk to any random database, using only "pure" Java. It didn't take them very long to realize that this is an impossible task: there are simply too many databases out there, using too many protocols. Moreover, while database vendors were all in favor of Sun providing a standard network protocol for database access, they were only in favor of it if Sun decided to use *their* network protocol.

What all the database vendors and tool vendors *did* agree on was that it would be useful if Sun provided a pure Java API for SQL access *along* with a driver manager to allow third-party drivers to connect to specific databases. Database vendors could provide their own drivers to plug into the driver manager. There would then be a simple mechanism for registering third-party drivers with the driver manager—the point being that all the drivers needed to do was follow the requirements laid out in the driver manager API.

After a fairly long period of public discussion, the API for database access became the JDBC API, and the rules for writing drivers were encapsulated in the JDBC driver API. (The JDBC driver API is of interest only to database vendors and database tool providers; we don't cover it here.)

This protocol follows the very successful model of Microsoft's ODBC, which provided a C programming language interface for database access. Both JDBC and ODBC are based on the same idea: Programs written according to the JDBC API would talk to the JDBC driver manager, which, in turn, would use the drivers that were plugged into it at that moment to talk to the actual database.

NOTE: A list of JDBC drivers currently available can be found at the web site `java.sun.com/products/jdbc/drivers.html`

More precisely, the JDBC consists of two layers. The top layer is the JDBC API. This API communicates with the JDBC manager driver API, sending it the various SQL statements. The manager should (transparently to the programmer) communicate with the various third-party drivers that actually connect to the database and return the information from the query or perform the action specified by the query.

NOTE: The JDBC specification will actually allow you to pass any string to the underlying driver. The driver can pass this string to the database. This feature allows you to use specialized versions of SQL that may be supported by the driver and its associated database.

All this means the Java/JDBC layer is all that most programmers will ever have to deal with. Figure 4–1 illustrates what happens.

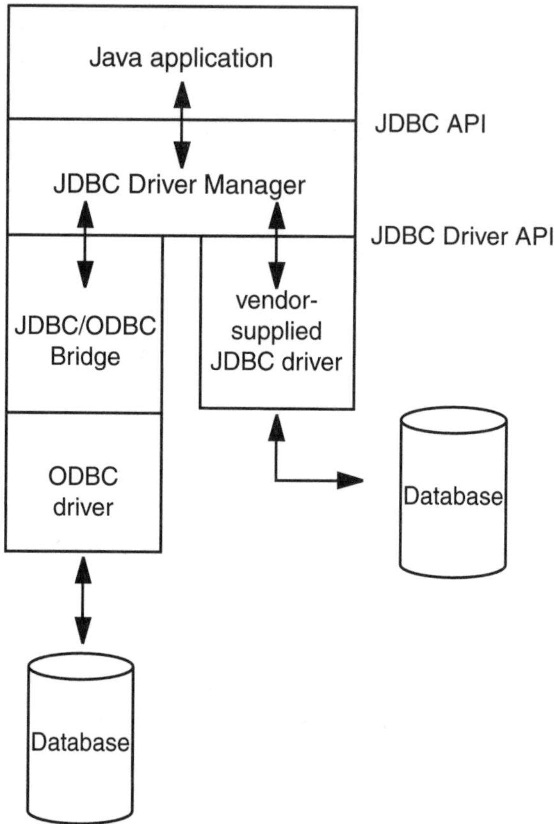

Figure 4–1 : JDBC-to-database communication path

JDBC drivers are classified into the following *types:*

- A *type 1 driver* translates JDBC to ODBC and relies on an ODBC driver to communicate with the database. Sun includes one such driver, the *JDBC/ODBC bridge,* with the JDK. However, the bridge does not support JDBC2, and it requires deployment and proper configuration of an ODBC driver. The bridge is handy for testing, but we don't recommend it for production use.
- A *type 2 driver* is a driver, written partly in the Java programming language and partly in native code, that communicates with the client API of a database. When you use such a driver, you must install some platform-specific code in addition to a Java library.

- A *type 3 driver* is a pure Java client library that uses a database-independent protocol to communicate database requests to a server component, which then translates the requests into a database-specific protocol. The client library is independent of the actual database, thus simplifying deployment.
- A *type 4 driver* is a pure Java library that translates JDBC requests directly to a database-specific protocol.

Most database vendors supply either a type 3 or type 4 driver with their database. Furthermore, a number of third-party companies specialize in producing drivers with better standards conformance, support for more platforms, or, in some cases, simply better reliability than the drivers that are provided by the database vendors.

In summary, the ultimate goal of the JDBC is to make possible the following:

- Programmers can write applications in the Java programming language to access any database, using standard SQL statements—or even specialized extensions of SQL—while still following Java language conventions. (All JDBC drivers must support at least the entry-level version of SQL 92.)
- Database vendors and database tool vendors can supply the low-level drivers. Thus, they can optimize their drivers for their specific products.

NOTE: If you are curious as to why Sun just didn't adopt the ODBC model, their response, as given at the JavaOne conference in May 1996, was:

- ODBC is hard to learn.
- ODBC has a few commands with lots of complex options. The preferred style in the Java programming language is to have simple and intuitive methods, but to have lots of them.
- ODBC relies on the use of `void*` pointers and other C features that are not natural in the Java programming language.
- An ODBC-based solution is inherently less safe and harder to deploy than a pure Java solution.

Typical Uses of JDBC

You can use JDBC in both applications and applets. In an applet, all the normal security restrictions apply. By default, the security manager assumes that all applets written in the Java programming language are untrusted.

In particular, applets that use JDBC are only able to open a database connection to the server from which they are downloaded. That means the Web server and the database server must be the same machine, which is not a typical setup. Of course, the Web server can have a proxy service that routes database traffic to another machine. With signed applets, this restriction can be loosened.

Applications, on the other hand, have complete freedom to access remote database servers. If you implement a traditional client/server program (see Figure 4–2), it probably makes more sense to use an application, not an applet, for database access.

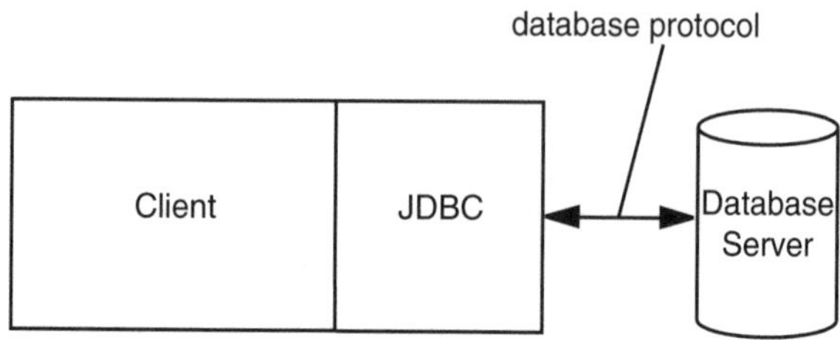

Figure 4–2: A client/server application

However, the world is moving away from client/server and toward a "three tier model" or even more advanced "*n* tier models." In the three-tier model, the client does not make database calls. Instead, it calls on a middleware layer on the server that in turn makes the database queries. The three-tier model has a couple of advantages. It separates *visual presentation* (on the client) from the *business logic* (in the middle tier) and the raw data (in the database). Therefore, it becomes possible to access the same data and the same business rules from multiple clients, such as a Java application or applet or a web form.

Communication between the client and middle tier can occur through HTTP (when you use a web browser as the client), RMI (when you use an application or applet—see Chapter 5), or another mechanism. JDBC is used to manage the communication between the middle tier and the back-end database. Figure 4–3 shows the basic architecture. There are, of course, many variations of this model. In particular, the Java 2 Enterprise Edition defines a structure for *application servers* that manage code modules called *Enterprise JavaBeans*, and provide valuable services such as load balancing, request caching, security, and simple database access. In that architecture, JDBC still plays an important role for issuing complex database queries. (For more information on the Enterprise Edition, see `http://java.sun.com/j2ee`.)

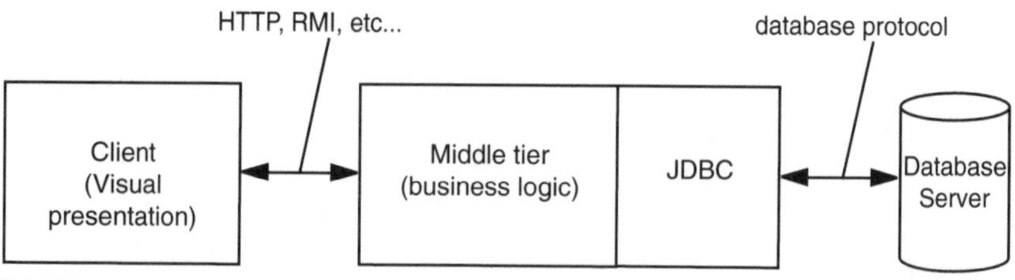

Figure 4–3: A three-tier application

The Structured Query Language

JDBC is an interface to SQL, which is the interface to essentially all modern relational databases. Desktop databases usually have a graphical user interfaces that lets users manipulate the data directly, but server-based databases are accessed purely through SQL. Most desktop databases have a SQL interface as well, but it often does not support the full range of ANSI SQL92 features, the current standard for SQL.

The JDBC package can be thought of as nothing more than an application programming interface (API) for communicating SQL statements to databases. We will give a short introduction to SQL in this section. If you have never seen SQL before, you may not find this material sufficient. If so, you should turn to one of the many books on the topic. We recommend *Client/Server Databases* by James Martin and Joe Leben [Prentice-Hall 1995] or the venerable and opinionated book *A Guide to the SQL Standard* by C. J. Date [Addison-Wesley 1996].

You can think of a database as a bunch of named tables with rows and columns. Each column has a *column name*. The rows contain the actual data. These are sometimes called *records*.

As the example database for this book, we use a set of tables that describe a collection of books on HTML. (Thanks to Cye H. Waldman at `http://wwwiz.com/books` for supplying the sample data.)

Table 4–1: The `Authors` table

Author_ID	Name	URL
ARON	Aronson, Larry	http://...
ARPA	Arpajian, Scott	http://...
...	...	...

Table 4–2: The `Books` table

Title	ISBN	Publisher_ID	URL	Price
Beyond HTML	0-07-882198-3	00788	http://...	27.95
10 Minute Guide to HTML	0-78970541-9	07897	http://...	15.00
...	...	...	...	...

Table 4–3: The `BooksAuthors` table

ISBN	Author_ID	Seq_No
1-56-884454-9	TAYL	1
1-56884645-2	SMIT	1
1-56884645-2	BEBA	2
...	...	...

Table 4–4: The `Publishers` table

Publisher_ID	Name	URL
01262	Academic Press	www.apnet.com/
18835	Coriolis	www.coriolis.com/
...	...	...

Figure 4–4 shows a view of the `Books` table. Figure 4–5 shows the result of *joining* this table with a table of publishers. Both the `Books` and the `Publishers` table contain a numerical code for the publisher. When we join both tables on the publisher code, we obtain a *query result* made up of values from the joined tables. Each row in the result contains the information about a book, together with the publisher name and Web page URL. Note that the publisher names and URLs are duplicated across several rows since we have several rows with the same publisher.

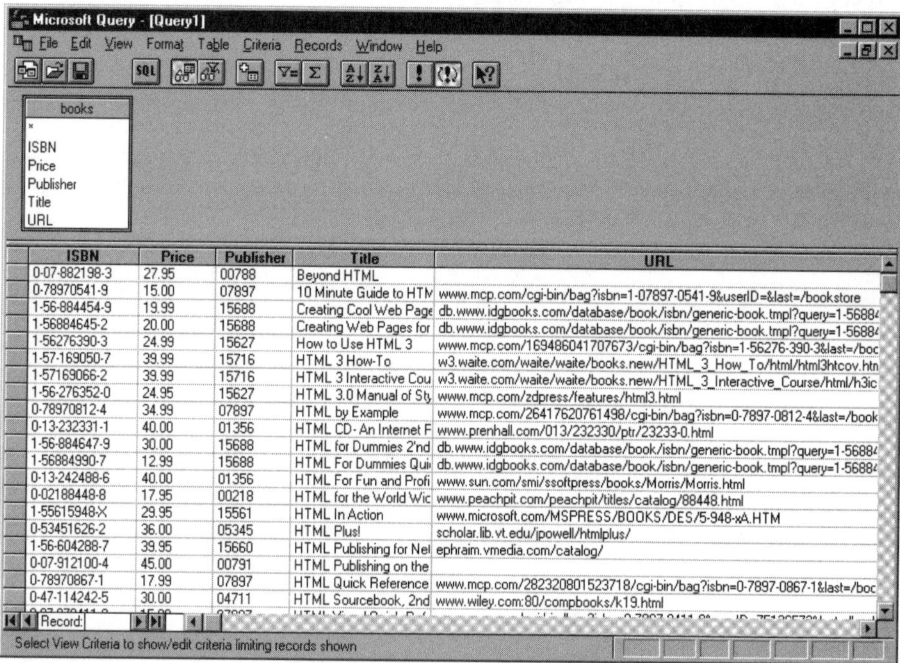

ISBN	Price	Publisher	Title	URL
0-07-882198-3	27.95	00788	Beyond HTML	
0-78970541-9	15.00	07897	10 Minute Guide to HTM	www.mcp.com/cgi-bin/bag?isbn=1-07897-0541-9&userID=&last=/bookstore
1-56-884454-9	19.99	15688	Creating Cool Web Page	db.www.idgbooks.com/database/book/isbn/generic-book.tmpl?query=1-5688
1-56884645-2	20.00	15688	Creating Web Pages for	db.www.idgbooks.com/database/book/isbn/generic-book.tmpl?query=1-5688
1-56276390-3	24.99	15627	How to Use HTML 3	www.mcp.com/169486041707673/cgi-bin/bag?isbn=1-56276-390-3&last=/boc
1-57-169050-7	39.99	15716	HTML 3 How-To	w3.waite.com/waite/waite/books.new/HTML_3_How_To/html/html3htcov.htn
1-57169066-2	39.99	15716	HTML 3 Interactive Cou	w3.waite.com/waite/waite/books.new/HTML_3_Interactive_Course/html/h3ic
1-56-276352-0	24.95	15627	HTML 3.0 Manual of Sty	www.mcp.com/zdpress/features/html3.html
0-78970812-4	34.99	07897	HTML by Example	www.mcp.com/26417620761498/cgi-bin/bag?isbn=0-7897-0812-4&last=/book
0-13-232331-1	40.00	01356	HTML CD- An Internet F	www.prenhall.com/013/232330/ptr/23233-0.html
1-56-884647-9	30.00	15688	HTML for Dummies 2'nd	db.www.idgbooks.com/database/book/isbn/generic-book.tmpl?query=1-5688
1-56884990-7	12.99	15688	HTML For Dummies Qui	db.www.idgbooks.com/database/book/isbn/generic-book.tmpl?query=1-5688
0-13-242488-6	40.00	01356	HTML For Fun and Profi	www.sun.com/smi/ssoftpress/books/Morris/Morris.html
0-02188448-8	17.95	00218	HTML for the World Wic	www.peachpit.com/peachpit/titles/catalog/88448.html
1-55615948-X	29.95	15561	HTML In Action	www.microsoft.com/MSPRESS/BOOKS/DES/5-948-xA.HTM
0-53451626-2	36.00	05345	HTML Plus!	scholar.lib.vt.edu/jpowell/htmlplus/
1-56-604288-7	39.95	15660	HTML Publishing for Nel	ephraim.vmedia.com/catalog/
0-07-912100-4	45.00	00791	HTML Publishing on the	
0-78970867-1	17.99	07897	HTML Quick Reference	www.mcp.com/282320801523718/cgi-bin/bag?isbn=0-7897-0867-1&last=/boc
0-47-114242-5	30.00	04711	HTML Sourcebook, 2nd	www.wiley.com:80/compbooks/k19.html

Figure 4–4: Sample table containing the HTML books

Microsoft Query - [Query1]

File Edit View Format Table Criteria Records Window Help

books: * ISBN Price Publisher Title URL

Publishers: * Name Publisher URL

ISBN	Price	Publisher	Name	URL	Title
0-07-882198-3	27.95	00788	Osborne/McGraw-Hill	www.osborne.com	Beyond HTML
0-78970541-9	15.00	07897	Que	www.mcp.com/que/	10 Minute Guide to HTML
1-56-884454-9	19.99	15688	IDG Books	www.idgbooks.com/	Creating Cool Web Pages with HTML
1-56884645-2	20.00	15688	IDG Books	www.idgbooks.com/	Creating Web Pages for Dummies
1-56276390-3	24.99	15627	Ziff-Davis	www.mcp.com/zdpress/	How to Use HTML 3
1-57-169050-7	39.99	15716	Waite	www.waite.com/waite/	HTML 3 How-To
1-57169066-2	39.99	15716	Waite	www.waite.com/waite/	HTML 3 Interactive Course
1-56-276352-0	24.95	15627	Ziff-Davis	www.mcp.com/zdpress/	HTML 3.0 Manual of Style (2nd Ed.)
0-78970812-4	34.99	07897	Que	www.mcp.com/que/	HTML by Example
0-13-232331-1	40.00	01356	Prentice Hall	www.prenhall.com/	HTML CD- An Internet Publishing Toolkit - Windows V
1-56-884647-9	30.00	15688	IDG Books	www.idgbooks.com/	HTML for Dummies 2'nd Edition
1-56884990-7	12.99	15688	IDG Books	www.idgbooks.com/	HTML For Dummies Quick Reference
0-13-242488-6	40.00	01356	Prentice Hall	www.prenhall.com/	HTML For Fun and Profit: Gold Signature Edition
0-02188448-8	17.95	00218	Peachpit Press	www.peachpit.com/	HTML for the World Wide Web: Visual Quick Start Gu
1-55615948-X	29.95	15561	Microsoft Press	www.microsoft.com/msp	HTML In Action
0-53451626-2	36.00	05345	Integrated Media Group	www.thomson.com/rcer	HTML Plus!
1-56-604288-7	39.95	15660	Netscape Press	www.netscapepress.cor	HTML Publishing for Netscape, Windows Edition
0-07-912100-4	45.00	00791	McGraw-Hill	www.mcgraw-hill.com/	HTML Publishing on the Internet
0-78970867-1	17.99	07897	Que	www.mcp.com/que/	HTML Quick Reference
0-47-114242-5	30.00	04711	Wiley	www.wiley.com/	HTML Sourcebook, 2nd Ed.

Record:

Select View Criteria to show/edit criteria limiting records shown

Figure 4–5: Two tables joined together

The benefit of joining tables is to avoid unnecessary duplication of data in the database tables. For example, a naive database design might have had columns for the publisher name and URL right in the `Books` table. But then the database itself, and not just the query result, would have many duplicates of these entries. If a publisher's Web address changed, *all* entries would need to be updated. Clearly, this is somewhat error prone. In the relational model, we distribute data into multiple tables such that no information is ever unnecessarily duplicated. For example, each publisher URL is contained only once in the publisher table. If the information needs to be combined, then the tables are joined.

In this example, we used the Microsoft Query tool to inspect and link the tables. Microsoft Query is a part of Microsoft Office, so if you have Office, you already have a copy. Many other vendors have similar tools. Microsoft Query is a graphical tool that lets us express queries in a simple form by connecting column names and filling information into forms. Such tools are often called *query by example* (QBE) tools. In contrast, a query that uses SQL is written out in text, using the SQL syntax. For example:

```
SELECT Books.ISBN, Books.Price, Books.Title,
   Books.Publisher_Id, Publishers.Name, Publishers.URL
FROM Books, Publishers
WHERE Books.Publisher_Id = Publishers.Publisher_Id
```

In the remainder of this section, you will learn how to write such queries. If you are already familiar with SQL, just skip this section.

By convention, SQL keywords are written in all caps, although this is not necessary.

The `SELECT` operation is quite flexible. You can simply select all elements in the `Books` table with the following query:

```
SELECT * FROM Books
```

The `FROM` statement is required in every SQL `SELECT` statement. The `FROM` clause tells the database which tables to examine to find the data.

You can choose the columns that you want.

```
SELECT ISBN, Price, Title
FROM Books
```

You can restrict the rows in the answer with the `WHERE` clause.

```
SELECT ISBN, Price, Title
FROM Books
WHERE Price <= 29.95
```

Be careful with the "equals" comparison. SQL uses `=` and `<>`, not `==` or `!=`, as in the Java programming language, for equality testing.

NOTE: Some database vendors support the use of `!=` for inequality testing. This is not standard SQL, so we recommend against using it.

The `WHERE` clause can also use pattern matching, using the `LIKE` operator. The wildcard characters are not the usual `*` and `?`, however. Use a `%` for zero or more characters and an underscore for a single character. For example:

```
SELECT ISBN, Price, Title
FROM Books
WHERE Title NOT LIKE '%H_M%'
```

Note that strings are enclosed in single quotes, not double quotes. A single quote inside a string is denoted as a pair of single quotes. For example,

```
SELECT Title
FROM Books
WHERE Books.Title LIKE '%''%'
```

reports all titles that contain a single quote.

You can select data from multiple tables.

```
SELECT * FROM Books, Publishers
```

Without a `WHERE` clause, this query is not very interesting. It lists *all combinations* of rows from both tables. In our case, where Books has 37 rows and Publishers has 18 rows, the result is a table with 37×18 entries and lots of duplications. We really

want to constrain the query to say that we are only interested in *matching* books with their publishers.

```
SELECT * FROM Books, Publishers
WHERE Books.Publisher_Id = Publishers.Publisher_Id
```

This query result has 37 rows, one for each book, since each book has a publisher in the `Publisher` table.

Whenever you have multiple tables in a query, the same column name can occur in two different places. That happened in our example. There is a publisher code column called `Publisher_Id` in both the Books and the Publishers table. When an ambiguity would otherwise result, you must prefix each column name with the name of the table to which it belongs, such as `Books.Publisher_Id`.

Now you have seen all SQL constructs that were used in the query at the beginning of this section:

```
SELECT Books.ISBN, Books.Price, Books.Title,
   Books.Publisher_Id,  Publishers.Name, Publishers.URL
FROM Books, Publishers
WHERE Books.Publisher_Id = Publishers.Publisher_Id
```

You can use SQL to change the data inside a database as well, by using so-called *action queries* (i.e., queries that move or change data). For example, suppose you want to reduce by $5.00 the current price of all books that do not have HTML 3 in their title.

```
UPDATE Books
SET Price = Price - 5.00
WHERE Title NOT LIKE '%HTML 3%'
```

Similarly, you can change several fields at the same time by separating the `SET` clauses with commas. There are many other SQL keywords you can use in an action query. Probably the most important besides `UPDATE` is `DELETE`, which allows the query to delete those records that satisfy certain criteria. Finally, SQL comes with built-in functions for taking averages, finding maximums and minimums in a column, and a lot more. Consult a book on SQL for more information.

Typically, to insert values into a table, you use the `INSERT` statement:

```
INSERT INTO Books
VALUES ('Beyond HTML', '0-07-882198-3', '00788', '', 27.95)
```

You need a separate `INSERT` statement for every row being inserted in the table.

Of course, before you can query, modify, and insert data, you must have a place to store data. Use the `CREATE TABLE` command to make a new table. You specify the name and data type for each column. For example,

```
CREATE TABLE Books
(  Title CHAR(60),
   ISBN CHAR(13),
```

```
    Publisher_Id CHAR(5),
    URL CHAR(80),
    Price DECIMAL(6,2)
)
```

Table 4–5 shows the most common SQL data types.

Table 4–5 : SQL Data Types

Data Types	Description
`INTEGER` or `INT`	Typically, a 32-bit integer
`SMALLINT`	Typically, a 16-bit integer
`NUMERIC(m,n)`, `DECIMAL(m,n)` or `DEC(m,n)`	Fixed-point decimal number with *m* total digits and *n* digits after the decimal point
`FLOAT(n)`	A floating-point number with *n* binary digits of precision
`REAL`	Typically, a 32-bit floating-point number
`DOUBLE`	Typically, a 64-bit floating-point number
`CHARACTER(n)` or `CHAR(n)`	Fixed-length string of length *n*
`VARCHAR(n)`	Variable-length strings of maximum length *n*
`BOOLEAN`	A boolean value
`DATE`	Calendar date, implementation dependent
`TIME`	Time of day, implementation dependent
`TIMESTAMP`	Date and time of day, implementation dependent
`BLOB`	A binary large object
`CLOB`	A character large object

In this book, we are not discussing the additional clauses, such as keys and constraints, that you can use with the `CREATE TABLE` command.

Installing JDBC

If you install the software from the CD-ROM, you will already have the JDBC package installed. You can also obtain the newest JDBC version from Sun and combine it with your existing development environment. Be sure that the version numbers are compatible, and carefully follow the installation directions.

Of course, you need a database program that is compatible with JDBC. You will also need to create a database for your experimental use. We assume you will call this database `COREJAVA`. Create a new database, or have your database administrator create one with the appropriate permissions. You need to be able to create, update, and drop tables.

Some database vendors already have JDBC drivers, so you may be able to install one, following your vendor's directions. For those databases that do not have a JDBC driver, you need to go a different route. Since most databases have ODBC drivers, Sun supplies a JDBC/ODBC bridge driver. To make a connection between such a database and your program, you need to install the database's ODBC driver and the JDBC/ODBC bridge.

As of this writing, the JDBC/ODBC bridge works only with the Solaris Operating Environment and Windows. The bridge does not work with Microsoft J++—the Microsoft virtual machine uses a nonstandard native calling convention that is not compatible with the native bridge code. The bridge also does not support JDBC2. Nevertheless, we describe the bridge because many readers have ready access to databases with ODBC drivers. For production work, we suggest you use a native JDBC driver. But for experimentation, the bridge works just fine.

In this chapter, we developed the examples by using the following configurations:

- Microsoft SQL Server running on NT Workstation 4.0 with the JDBC/ODBC bridge
- Microsoft Access running on Windows 95 with the JDBC/ODBC bridge
- Interbase running on Windows 98
- The pure Java PointBase Mobile Edition database. See the CD-ROM for a demo version.

In addition, we did limited testing with JDBC 2.0 drivers. However, at the time of this writing, fully functional JDBC 2.0 drivers were not widely available. For that reason, the sample programs in this chapter do not use JDBC 2.0 features. We show you separately how they can be enhanced for JDBC 2.0.

If your database doesn't have direct JDBC support, you need to install the ODBC driver for your database. Directions for installation vary widely, so consult your database administrator or, if all else fails, the vendor documentation.

You then need to make your experimental database into an ODBC data source. In Windows, you use the ODBC control in the control panel.

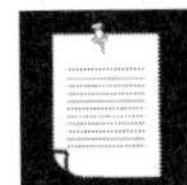

NOTE: Some desktop databases support SQL through a proprietary mechanism, not JDBC or ODBC. For example, Borland has a BDE engine and Microsoft has a Jet engine that give somewhat better performance than ODBC for local database access. These mechanisms are not compatible with the Java platform. If you are looking in vain for JDBC or ODBC drivers, you may not have installed or purchased the correct driver.

If you have never installed a client/server database before, you may find that setting up the database and the ODBC driver is somewhat complex and that it can be difficult to diagnose the cause for failure. It may be best to seek expert help if your setup is not working correctly. When working with Microsoft SQL Server, we found it to be a real lifesaver to have a book on server and database administration such as *Microsoft BackOffice Administrator Survival Guide* by Arthur Knowles [Sams Publications 1996]. The same is undoubtedly true on other platforms as well.

TIP: If you are interested in databases for embedded systems or if you just want to experiment with the programs in this chapter, install the demo version of the PointBase Mobile Edition from the CD-ROM. It is easier to set up than traditional databases.

Basic JDBC Programming Concepts

Programming with the JDBC classes is, by design, not very different from programming with the usual Java platform classes: you build objects from the JDBC core classes, extending them by inheritance if need be. This section takes you through the details.

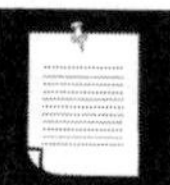

NOTE: The classes that you use for JDBC programming are contained in the `java.sql` package.

Database URLs

When connecting to a database, you must specify the data source and you may need to specify additional parameters. For example, network protocol drivers may need a port, and ODBC drivers may need various attributes.

As you might expect, JDBC uses a syntax similar to ordinary Net URLs to describe data sources. Here are examples of the syntax:

```
jdbc:odbc:COREJAVA
jdbc:pointbase:CATS
```

This command would access an ODBC data source named `COREJAVA`, using the JDBC/ODBC bridge. The general syntax is

```
jdbc:subprotocol name:other_stuff
```

where a subprotocol is used to select the specific driver for connecting to the database.

The format for the *`other_stuff`* parameter depends on the subprotocol used. Sun recommends that if you are using a network address as part of the *`other_stuff`* parameter, you use the standard URL naming convention of *`//hostname:port/other`*. For example:

```
jdbc:odbc://whitehouse.gov:5000/CATS;PWD=Hillary
```

would connect to the `CATS` database on port 5000 of `whitehouse.gov`, using the ODBC attribute value of PWD set to "Hillary."

Making the Connection

The `DriverManager` is the class responsible for selecting database drivers and creating a new database connection. However, before the driver manager can activate a driver, the driver must be registered.

There are two methods for registering drivers. Your program can set the system property `jdbc.drivers` to a list of drivers. For example, your application can add a properties file with the line

```
jdbc.drivers=com.pointbase.jdbc.jdbcDriver:com.foo.aDriver
```

to the system properties. This approach allows users of your application to install appropriate drivers simply by modifying a property file.

The `jdbc.drivers` property contains a list of class names for the drivers that the driver manager can use. The names are separated by colons.

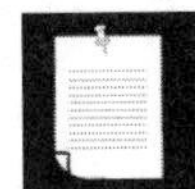

NOTE: The `MakeDB` sample program reads the driver name as well as the database URL, user name, and password from a file `MakeDB.properties`. You can also specify system properties on the command line, for example

```
java -classpath classpath -Djdbc.drivers=drivers MakeDB
```

You need to find out the names of the driver classes used by your vendor, such as `com.pointbase.jdbc.jdbcDriver` for the PointBase driver or `sun.jdbc.odbc.JdbcOdbcDriver` for the JDBC/ODBC bridge. You also need to place the driver code somewhere on the class path to ensure that the application can load the class.

Alternatively, you can manually register a driver by loading its class. For example, to load the JDBC/ODBC bridge driver, you use the command

```
Class.forName("com.pointbase.jdbc.jdbcDriver");
   // force registration of driver
```

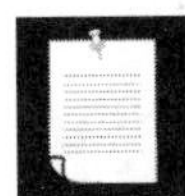

NOTE: In a real application, you will want to give your users some way of installing drivers. However, in our sample programs, we simply load the drivers and leave it to you to change the driver name (as well as the user name and password) in the property files associated with the programs.

After registering drivers, you open a database connection with code that is similar to the following example:

```
String url = "jdbc:pointbase:COREJAVA";
String username = "Cay";
String password = "wombat";
Connection con = DriverManager.getConnection(url,
    username, password);
```

The driver manager will try to find a driver that can use the protocol specified in the database URL by iterating through the available drivers currently registered with the driver manager.

For our example program, we find it convenient to use a properties file to specify the URL, user name, and password in addition to the database driver. A typical properties file has the following contents:

```
jdbc.drivers=com.pointbase.jdbc.jdbcDriver:com.foo.aDriver
jdbc.url=jdbc:pointbase:COREJAVA
jdbc.username=Cay
jdbc.password=wombat
```

Here is the code for reading a properties file and opening the database connection.

```
Properties props = new Properties();
FileInputStream in = new FileInputStream(fileName);
props.load(in);

String drivers = props.getProperty("jdbc.drivers");
if (drivers != null)
   System.setProperty("jdbc.drivers", drivers);
String url = props.getProperty("jdbc.url");
String username = props.getProperty("jdbc.username");
String password = props.getProperty("jdbc.password");
return DriverManager.getConnection(url, username, password);
```

Note that we do *not* simply add the loaded properties to the system properties:

```
System.setProperties(props); // we do not do that
```

That call might inadvertently overwrite other system properties. Therefore, we only transfer the `jdbc.drivers` property.

The `getConnection` method returns a `Connection` object. You use the connection object to execute queries and action statements and commit or roll back transactions.

TIP: A good way to debug JDBC-related problems is to enable JDBC tracing. Call the `DriverManager.setLogWriter` method to send trace messages to a `PrintWriter`. The trace output contains a detailed listing of the JDBC activity.

When deploying a JDBC 2 application in an enterprise environment, the management of database connections can be integrated with the Java Naming and Directory Interface (JNDI). A directory manages the location of data sources

across the enterprise. In such an environment, you use the following code to establish a database connection:

```
Context jndiContext = . . .;
DataSource source
   = (DataSource)jndiContext.lookup("jdbc/corejava");
Connection con = source.getConnection(username, password);
```

As you can see, the code is similar. However, the `DriverManager` is no longer involved. Instead, the JNDI service locates a *data source*. A data source is an interface that allows for simple JDBC connections as well as more advanced services, such as connection pooling and executing distributed transactions that involve multiple databases. The `DataSource` interface is defined in the `javax.sql` standard extension package.

The trend in enterprise JDBC deployment is to support an increasing array of services such as directories and connection pooling but to have them decoupled from database programming. In this chapter, you learn how to make JDBC calls, and that knowledge applies whether you access a desktop database or a distributed and scalable set of enterprise databases. Moreover, you can be assured that scalability and performance enhancements are available in the enterprise platform when you need them.

Executing Action Commands

To execute a SQL command, you first create a `Statement` object. The `Connection` object that you obtained from the call to `DriverManager.getConnection` can be used to create statement objects.

```
Statement stmt = con.createStatement();
```

Next, you place the statement that you want to execute into a string, for example,

```
String command = "UPDATE Books "
   + "SET Price = Price - 5.00"
   + "WHERE Title NOT LIKE '%HTML 3%'";
```

Then you call the `executeUpdate` method of the `Statement` class:

```
stmt.executeUpdate(command);
```

The commands can be actions such as `INSERT`, `UPDATE`, and `DELETE` as well as data definition commands such as `CREATE TABLE`, and `DROP TABLE`. However, you cannot use the `executeUpdate` method to execute `SELECT` queries. Executing queries is the topic of the next section.

The `executeUpdate` method returns a count of the rows that were affected by the SQL command. For example, the call to `executeUpdate` in the preceding example returns the number of book records whose price was lowered by $5.00.

NOTE: You can also use the `execute` method of the `Statement` interface to execute an arbitrary SQL statement. However, we like the expressiveness of calling `executeUpdate` for updates and `executeQuery` for queries.

While we do not want to go deep into transaction support, we do want to show you how to group a set of statements to form a transaction that can be committed when all has gone well, or rolled back as if none of the commands had been issued if an error has occurred in one of them.

The major reason for grouping commands into transactions is *database integrity*. For example, suppose we want to add a new book to our book database. Then, it is important that we simultaneously update the `Books`, `Authors`, and `BooksAuthors` table. If the update were to add new rows into the first two tables but not into the third, then the books and authors would not be properly matched up.

If you group updates to a transaction, then the transaction either succeeds in its entirety and it can be *committed*, or it fails somewhere in the middle. In that case, you can carry out a *rollback* and the database automatically undoes the effect of all updates that occurred since the last committed transaction. Furthermore, queries are guaranteed to report only on the committed state of the database.

By default, a database connection is in *autocommit mode*, and each SQL command is committed to the database as soon as it is executed. Once a command is committed, you cannot roll it back.

To check the current autocommit mode setting, call the `getAutoCommit` method of the `Connection` class.

You turn off autocommit mode with the command

```
con.setAutoCommit(false);
```

Now you create a statement object in the normal way:

```
Statement stmt = con.createStatement();
```

Call `executeUpdate` any number of times:

```
stmt.executeUpdate(command1);
stmt.executeUpdate(command2);
stmt.executeUpdate(command3);
. . .
```

When all commands have been executed, call the `commit` method:

```
con.commit();
```

However, if an error occurred, call

```
con.rollback();
```

Then, all commands until the last commit are automatically reversed. You typically issue a rollback when your transaction was interrupted by a `SQLException`.

Querying with JDBC

To make a query, you first create a `Statement` object as described in the preceding section. You can then execute a query simply by using the `executeQuery` object of the `Statement` class and supplying the SQL command for the query as a string. Note that you can use the same `Statement` object for multiple, unrelated queries.

Of course, you are interested in the result of the query. The `executeQuery` object returns an object of type `ResultSet` that you use to walk through the result a row at a time.

```
ResultSet rs = stmt.executeQuery("SELECT * FROM Books")
```

The basic loop for analyzing a result set looks like this:

```
while (rs.next())
{  look at a row of the result set
}
```

CAUTION: The iteration protocol of the `ResultSet` class is slightly different from the protocol of the `Iterator` and `Enumeration` interfaces that we discussed in Chapter 2. Here, the iterator is initialized to a position *before* the first row. You must call the `next` method once to move it to the first row.

When inspecting an individual row, you will want to know the contents of each column. A large number of accessor methods give you this information.

```
String isbn = rs.getString(1);
float price = rs.getDouble("Price");
```

There are accessors for every Java programming language *type*, such as `getString` and `getDouble`. Each accessor has two forms, one that takes a numeric argument and one that takes a string argument. When you supply a numeric argument, you refer to the column with that number. For example, `rs.getString(1)` returns the value of the first column in the current row.

CAUTION: Unlike array indexes, database column numbers start at 1.

When you supply a string argument, you refer to the column in the result set with that name. For example, `rs.getDouble("Price")` returns the value of the column with name `Price`. Using the numeric argument is a bit more efficient, but the string arguments make the code easier to read and maintain.

Each `get` method will make reasonable type conversions when the type of the method doesn't match the type of the column. For example, the call `rs.getString("Price")` converts the floating-point value of the `Price` column to a string.

NOTE: SQL data types and Java data types are not exactly the same. SeeTable 4–6 for a listing of the basic SQL data types and their equivalents in the Java programming language.

Table 4–6 : SQL data types and their corresponding Java language types

SQL data type	Java data type
`INTEGER` or `INT`	`int`
`SMALLINT`	`short`
`NUMERIC(m,n)`, `DECIMAL(m,n)` or `DEC(m,n)`	`java.sql.Numeric`
`FLOAT(n)`	`double`
`REAL`	`float`
`DOUBLE`	`double`
`CHARACTER(n)` or `CHAR(n)`	`String`
`VARCHAR(n)`	`String`
`BOOLEAN`	`boolean`
`DATE`	`java.sql.Date`
`TIME`	`java.sql.Time`
`TIMESTAMP`	`java.sql.Timestamp`
`BLOB`	`java.sql.Blob`
`CLOB`	`java.sql.Clob`
`ARRAY`	`java.sql.Array`

Advanced SQL Types (JDBC 2)

In addition to numbers, strings, and dates, many databases can store *large objects* such as images or other data. In SQL, binary large objects are called BLOBs, and character large objects are called CLOBs. The `getBlob` and `getClob` methods return objects of type `Blob` and `Clob`. These classes have methods to fetch the bytes or characters in the large objects.

A SQL `ARRAY` is a sequence of values. For example, in a `Student` table, you can have a `Scores` column that is an `ARRAY OF INTEGER`. The `getArray` method returns an object of type `java.sql.Array` (which is different from the `java.lang.reflect.Array` class that we discussed in Volume 1). The `java.sql.Array` interface has methods to fetch the array values.

NOTE: The `BLOB`, `CLOB`, and `ARRAY` types are features of SQL3. Java platform support for `BLOB` and `CLOB` has been greatly enhanced in JDBC 2, and support for `ARRAY` is a new feature in JDBC 2.

When you get a blob or an array from a database, the actual contents are only fetched from the database when you request individual values. This is a useful performance enhancement, since the data can be quite voluminous.

Some databases are able to store user-defined structured types. JDBC 2 supports a mechanism for automatically mapping structured SQL types to Java objects.

However, in this introductory chapter, we do not discuss blobs, arrays, and user-defined types any further.

`java.sql.DriverManager`

- `static Connection getConnection(String url, String user, String password)`

  establishes a connection to the given database and returns a `Connection` object.

Parameters:	`url`	the URL for the database
	`user`	the database logon ID
	`password`	the database logon password

`java.sql.Connection`

- `Statement createStatement()`

  creates a statement object that can be used to execute SQL queries and updates without parameters.
- `void close()`

  immediately closes the current connection.
- `void setAutoCommit(boolean b)`

  sets the autocommit mode of this connection to `b`. If autocommit is true, all statements are committed as soon as their execution is completed.
- `boolean getAutoCommit()`

  gets the autocommit mode of this connection.
- `void commit()`

  commits all statements that were issued since the last commit.
- `void rollback()`

  undoes the effect of all statements that were issued since the last commit.

`java.sql.Statement`

- `ResultSet executeQuery(String sql)`

  executes the SQL statement given in the string and returns a `ResultSet` to view the query result.

Parameters: `sql` the SQL query

- `int executeUpdate(String sql)`

  executes the SQL `INSERT`, `UPDATE`, or `DELETE` statement specified by the string. Also used to execute DDL (Data Definition Language) statements such as `CREATE TABLE`. Returns the number of records affected.

  Parameters: `sql` the SQL statement

- `void cancel()`

  creates a thread to cancel a JDBC statement that is being executed.

`java.sql.ResultSet`

- `boolean next()`

  makes the current row in the result set move forward by one. Returns `false` after the last row. Note that you must call this method to advance to the first row.

- `Xxx getXxx(int columnNumber)`
- `Xxx getXxx(String columnName)`

  (*Xxx* is a type such as `int`, `double`, `String`, `Date`, etc.)
  return the value of the column with column index `columnNumber` or with column names, converted to the specified type. Not all type conversions are legal. See documentation for details.

- `int findColumn(String columnName)`

  gives the column index associated with a column name.

- `void close()`

  immediately closes the current result set.

`java.sql.SQLException`

Most JDBC methods throw this exception, and you must be prepared to catch it. The following methods give more information about the exceptions.

- `String getSQLState()`

  gets the SQLState formatted, using the X/Open standard.

- `int getErrorCode()`

  gets the vendor-specific exception code.

- `SQLException getNextException()`

  gets the exception chained to this one. It may contain more information about the error.

Populating a Database

We now want to write our first, real, JDBC program. Of course, it would be nice if we could execute some of the fancy queries that we discussed earlier. Unfortunately, we have a problem: right now, there is no data in the database. And you won't find a database file on the CD-ROM that you can simply copy onto your hard disk for the database program to read, because no database file format lets you interchange SQL relational databases from one vendor to another. SQL does not have anything to do with files. It is a language to issue queries and updates to a database. How the database executes these statements most efficiently and what file formats it uses toward that goal are entirely up to the *implementation* of the database. Database vendors try very hard to come up with clever strategies for query optimization and data storage, and different vendors arrive at different mechanisms. Thus, while SQL statements are portable, the underlying data representation is not.

To get around our problem, we provide you with a small set of data in a series of text files. The first program reads such a text file and creates a table. The first line of the file contains the column names and types. The remaining lines of the input file are the data, and we insert the lines into the table. Of course, we use SQL statements and JDBC to create the table and insert the data.

Specifically, the program reads data from a text file in a format such as

```
Publisher_Id char(5), Name char(30), URL char(80)
'01262', 'Academic Press', 'www.apnet.com'
'18835', 'Coriolis', 'www.coriolis.com/'
. . .
```

The first line of the text file lists the names and types of the columns. The following lines list the data to be inserted, in comma-delimited format.

The `MakeDB` program reads the first line and turns it into a `CREATE TABLE` statement such as

```
CREATE TABLE Publishers (Publisher_Id char(5), Name char(30),
   URL char(80))
```

All other input lines become `INSERT` statements such as

```
INSERT INTO Publishers VALUES ('01262', 'Academic Press',
   'www.apnet.com')
```

At the end of this section, you can see the code for the program that reads a text file and populates a database table. Even if you are not interested in looking at the implementation, you must run this program if you want to execute the more interesting examples in the next two sections. Run the program as follows:

```
java MakeDB Books
java MakeDB Authors
```

```
java MakeDB Publishers
java MakeDB BooksAuthors
```

Before running the program, check the file `MakeDB.properties`. It looks like this:

```
jdbc.drivers=com.pointbase.jdbc.jdbcDriver
jdbc.url=jdbc:pointbase:COREJAVA
jdbc.username=PUBLIC
jdbc.password=PUBLIC
```

These values work for the PointBase database; change them if you use another database.

CAUTION: Make sure that both the database driver and the current directory are on the class path. Alternatively, start up the program as

```
java -classpath paths MakeDB tableName
```

The following steps provide an overview of the `MakeDB` program.

1. Connect to the database. The `getConnection` method reads the properties in the file `MakeDB.properties` and adds the `jdbc.drivers` property to the system properties. The driver manager uses the `jdbc.drivers` property to load the appropriate database driver. The `getConnection` method uses the `jdbc.url`, `jdbc.username`, and `jdbc.password` properties to open the database connection.
2. Obtain the file name from the table name by appending the extension `dat` (e.g., the data for the `Books` table is stored in the file `Books.dat`).
3. Read in the column names and types and construct a `CREATE TABLE` command. Then execute that command:

   ```
   String line = in.readLine();
   String command = "CREATE TABLE " + tableName
      + "(" + line + ")";
   stmt.executeUpdate(command);
   ```

   Here, we use `executeUpdate`, not `executeQuery`, because this statement has no result.
4. For each line in the input file, execute an `INSERT` statement:

   ```
   command = "INSERT INTO " + tableName
      + " VALUES (" + line + ")";
   stmt.executeUpdate(command);
   ```

5. After all elements have been inserted, run a `SELECT * FROM tableName` query, using the `showTable` method to show the result. This method shows that the data has been successfully inserted. To find the number of columns in the result set, we need the `getColumnCount` method of the `ResultSet-MetaData` class. We discuss metadata in detail later in this chapter.

Example 4–1 provides the code for these steps.

Example 4–1: MakeDB.java

```
import java.net.*;
import java.sql.*;
import java.io.*;
import java.util.*;

class MakeDB
{  public static void main (String args[])
   {  try
      {  Connection con = getConnection();
         Statement stmt = con.createStatement();

         String tableName = "";
         if (args.length > 0)
            tableName = args[0];
         else
         {  System.out.println("Usage: MakeDB TableName");
            System.exit(0);
         }

         BufferedReader in = new BufferedReader(new
            FileReader(tableName + ".dat"));

         createTable(tableName, in, stmt);
         showTable(tableName, stmt);

         in.close();
         stmt.close();
         con.close();
      }
      catch (SQLException ex)
      {  System.out.println ("SQLException:");
         while (ex != null)
         {  System.out.println ("SQLState: "
               + ex.getSQLState());
            System.out.println ("Message:  "
               + ex.getMessage());
            System.out.println ("Vendor:   "
               + ex.getErrorCode());
            ex = ex.getNextException();
            System.out.println ("");
          }
      }
      catch (IOException ex)
      {  System.out.println("Exception: " + ex);
         ex.printStackTrace ();
      }
```

```
   }

   public static Connection getConnection()
      throws SQLException, IOException
   {  Properties props = new Properties();
      String fileName = "MakeDB.properties";
      FileInputStream in = new FileInputStream(fileName);
      props.load(in);

      String drivers = props.getProperty("jdbc.drivers");
      if (drivers != null)
         System.setProperty("jdbc.drivers", drivers);
      String url = props.getProperty("jdbc.url");
      String username = props.getProperty("jdbc.username");
      String password = props.getProperty("jdbc.password");

      return
         DriverManager.getConnection(url, username, password);
   }

   public static void createTable(String tableName,
      BufferedReader in, Statement stmt)
      throws SQLException, IOException
   {  String line = in.readLine();
      String command = "CREATE TABLE " + tableName
         + "(" + line + ")";
      stmt.executeUpdate(command);

      while ((line = in.readLine()) != null)
      {  command = "INSERT INTO " + tableName
            + " VALUES (" + line + ")";
         stmt.executeUpdate(command);
      }
   }

   public static void showTable(String tableName,
      Statement stmt) throws SQLException
   {  String query = "SELECT * FROM " + tableName;
      ResultSet rs = stmt.executeQuery(query);
      ResultSetMetaData rsmd = rs.getMetaData();
      int columnCount = rsmd.getColumnCount();
      while (rs.next())
      {  for (int i = 1; i <= columnCount; i++)
         {  if (i > 1) System.out.print(", ");
            System.out.print(rs.getString(i));
         }
         System.out.println();
      }
      rs.close();
   }
}
```

Batch Updates (JDBC 2)

In JDBC 2, you can improve the performance of the program in the preceding example by using a *batch update.* In a batch update, a sequence of commands is collected and submitted as a batch.

The commands in a batch can be actions such as `INSERT`, `UPDATE`, and `DELETE` as well as data definition commands such as `CREATE TABLE` and `DROP TABLE`. However, you cannot add `SELECT` commands to a batch since executing a `SELECT` statement returns a result set.

To execute a batch, you first create a new `Statement` object:

```
Statement stmt = con.createStatement();
```

Now, instead of calling `executeUpdate`, you call the `addBatch` method:

```
String line = in.readLine();
String command = "CREATE TABLE " + tableName
   + "(" + line + ")";
stmt.addBatch(command);

while ((line = in.readLine()) != null)
{  command = "INSERT INTO " + tableName
      + " VALUES (" + line + ")";
   stmt.addBatch(command);
}
```

Finally, you submit the entire batch.

```
int[] counts = stmt.executeBatch();
```

The call to `executeBatch` returns an array of the row counts for all submitted commands. (Recall that an individual call to `executeUpdate` returns an integer, namely, the count of the rows that are affected by the command.) In our example, the `executeBatch` method returns an array with first element equal to 0 (because the `CREATE TABLE` command yields a row count of 0) and all other elements equal to 1 (because each `INSERT` command affects one row).

For proper error handling in batch mode, you want to treat the batch execution as a single transaction. If a batch fails in the middle, you want to roll back to the state before the beginning of the batch.

First, turn autocommit mode off, then collect the batch, execute it, commit it, and finally restore the original autocommit mode:

```
boolean autoCommit = con.getAutoCommit();
con.setAutoCommit(false);
Statement stmt = con.getStatement();
. . .
// keep calling stmt.addBatch(. . .);
. . .
```

```
stmt.executeBatch();
stmt.commit();
con.setAutoCommit(autoCommit);
```

`java.sql.Statement`

- `void addBatch(String command)`

  (JDBC 2) adds the command to the current batch of commands for this statement.

- `int[] executeBatch()`

  (JDBC 2) executes all commands in the current batch. Returns an array of row counts, containing an element for each command in the batch that denotes the number of rows affected by that command.

Executing Queries

In this section, we will write a program that executes queries against the `COREJAVA` database. For this program to work, you must have populated the `COREJAVA` database with tables, as described in the preceding section. Figure 4–6 shows the query application.

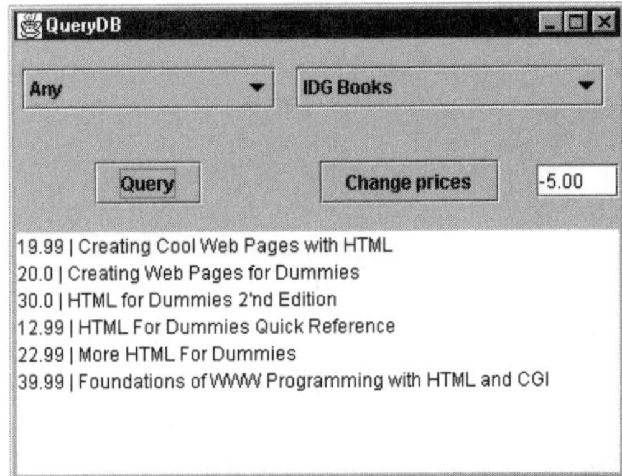

Figure 4–6: The QueryDB application

You can select the author and the publisher or leave either of them as "Any." Click on "Query"; all books matching your selection will be displayed in the text box.

You can also change the data in the database. Select a publisher and type an amount into the text box next to the "Change prices" button. When you click on the button, all prices of that publisher are adjusted by the amount you entered, and the text area contains a message indicating how many records were changed. However, to minimize unintended changes to the database, you can't change all prices at once. The author field is ignored when you change prices. After a price change, you may want to run a query to verify the new prices.

In this program, we use one new feature, *prepared statements*. Consider the query for all books by a particular publisher, independent of the author. The SQL query is

```
SELECT Books.Price, Books.Title
FROM Books, Publishers
WHERE Books.Publisher_Id = Publishers.Publisher_Id
AND Publishers.Name = the name from the list box
```

Rather than build a separate query command every time the user launches such a query, we can *prepare* a query with a host variable and use it many times, each time filling in a different string for the variable. That technique gives us a performance benefit. Whenever the database executes a query, it first computes a strategy of how to efficiently execute the query. By preparing the query and reusing it, you ensure that the planning step is done only once. (The reason you do not *always* want to prepare a query is that the optimal strategy may change as your data changes. You have to balance the expense of optimization versus the expense of querying your data less efficiently.)

Each host variable in a prepared query is indicated with a `?`. If there is more than one variable, then you must keep track of the positions of the `?` when setting the values. For example, our prepared query becomes

```
String publisherQuery =
   "SELECT Books.Price, Books.Title " +
   "FROM Books, Publishers " +
   "WHERE Books.Publisher_Id = Publishers.Publisher_Id " +
   "AND Publishers.Name = ?";
PreparedStatement publisherQueryStmt
   = con.prepareStatement(publisherQuery);
```

Before executing the prepared statement, you must bind the host variables to actual values with a `set` method. As with the `ResultSet get` methods, there are different `set` methods for the various types. Here, we want to set a string to a publisher name.

```
publisherQueryStmt.setString(1, publisher);
```

The first argument is the host variable that we want to set. The position 1 denotes the first `?`. The second argument is the value that we want to assign to the host variable.

If you reuse a prepared query that you have already executed and the query has more than one host variable, all host variables stay bound as you set them unless you change them with a `set` method. That means you only need to call `set` on those host variables that change from one query to the next.

Once all variables have been bound to values, you can execute the query

```
ResultSet rs = publisherQueryStmt.executeQuery();
```

You process the result set in the usual way. Here, we add the information to the text area `result`.

```
result.setText("");
while (rs.next())
   result.appendText(rs.getString(1) + " | " +
      rs.getString(2) + "\n");
rs.close();
```

There are a total of four prepared queries in this program, one each for the cases shown in Table 4–7.

Table 4–7: Selected queries

Author	Publisher
any	any
any	specified
specified	any
specified	specified

The price update feature is implemented as a simple `UPDATE` statement. For variety, we did not choose to make a prepared statement in this case. Note that we call `executeUpdate`, not `executeQuery`, since the `UPDATE` statement does not return a result set and we don't need one. The return value of `executeUpdate` is the count of changed rows. We display the count in the text area.

```
String updateStatement = "UPDATE Books ...";
int r = stmt.executeUpdate(updateStatement);
result.setText(r + " records updated");
```

The following steps provide an overview of the program.

1. Arrange the components in the frame, using a grid bag layout (see Chapter 9 in Volume 1).
2. Populate the author and publisher text boxes by running two queries that return all author and publisher names in the database.
3. When the user selects "Query," find which of the four query types needs to be executed. If this is the first time this query type is executed, then the prepared statement variable is `null`, and the prepared statement is constructed. Then, the values are bound to the query and the query is executed.

   The queries involving authors are more complex. Because a book can have multiple authors, the `BooksAuthors` table gives the correspondence between authors and books. For example, the book with ISBN number 1-56-604288-7 has two authors with codes `HARR` and `KIDD`. The `BooksAuthors` table has the rows

   ```
   1-56-604288-7 | HARR | 1
   1-56-604288-7 | KIDD | 2
   ```

to indicate this fact. The third column lists the order of the authors. (We can't just use the position of the records in the table. There is no fixed row ordering in a relational table.) Thus, the query has to snake (join) itself from the `Books` table to the `BooksAuthors` table, then to the `Authors` table to compare the author name with the one selected by the user.

```
SELECT Books.Price, Books.Title
FROM Books, Publishers, BooksAuthors, Authors
WHERE Books.Publisher_Id = Publishers.Publisher_Id
AND Publishers.Name = ?
AND Books.ISBN = BooksAuthors.ISBN
AND BooksAuthors.Author = Authors.Author
AND Authors.Name = ?
```

4. The results of the query are displayed in the results text box.
5. When the user selects "Change price," then the update query is constructed and executed. The query is quite complex because the `WHERE` clause of the `UPDATE` statement needs the publisher *code* and we know only the publisher *name*. This problem is solved with a nested subquery.

```
UPDATE Books
SET Price = Price + price change
WHERE Books.Publisher_Id =
   (SELECT Publisher_Id
   FROM Publishers
   WHERE Name = publisher name)
```

NOTE: Nested subqueries are explained in most books on SQL, including the book by Martin and Leben mentioned earlier.

6. We initialize the connection and statement objects in the constructor. We hang on to them for the life of the program. Just before the program exits, we call the `dispose` method, and these objects are closed.

```
class QueryDB extends Frame
{  QueryDB()
   {  con = DriverManager.getConnection(url, user,
      password);
      stmt = con.createStatement();
      . . .
   }
   . . .
   void dispose()
   {  stmt.close();
      con.close();
   }
   . . .
```

```
      Connection con;
      Statement stmt;
   }
```

Example 4–2 is the complete program code.

Example 4–2: QueryDB.java

```
import java.net.*;
import java.sql.*;
import java.awt.*;
import java.awt.event.*;
import java.io.*;
import java.util.*;
import javax.swing.*;

public class QueryDB
{  public static void main(String[] args)
   {  JFrame frame = new QueryDBFrame();
      frame.show();
   }
}

class QueryDBFrame extends JFrame
   implements ActionListener
{  public QueryDBFrame()
   {  setTitle("QueryDB");
      setSize(400, 300);
      addWindowListener(new WindowAdapter()
         {  public void windowClosing(WindowEvent e)
            {  System.exit(0);
            }
         } );

      getContentPane().setLayout(new GridBagLayout());
      GridBagConstraints gbc = new GridBagConstraints();

      authors = new JComboBox();
      authors.setEditable(false);
      authors.addItem("Any");

      publishers = new JComboBox();
      publishers.setEditable(false);
      publishers.addItem("Any");

      result = new JTextArea(4, 50);
      result.setEditable(false);

      priceChange = new JTextField(8);
      priceChange.setText("-5.00");

      try
```

```
   {  con = getConnection();
      stmt = con.createStatement();

      String query = "SELECT Name FROM Authors";
      ResultSet rs = stmt.executeQuery(query);
      while (rs.next())
         authors.addItem(rs.getString(1));

      query = "SELECT Name FROM Publishers";
      rs = stmt.executeQuery(query);
      while (rs.next())
         publishers.addItem(rs.getString(1));
   }
   catch(Exception e)
   {  result.setText("Error " + e);
   }

   gbc.fill = GridBagConstraints.NONE;
   gbc.weightx = 100;
   gbc.weighty = 100;
   add(authors, gbc, 0, 0, 2, 1);

   add(publishers, gbc, 2, 0, 2, 1);

   gbc.fill = GridBagConstraints.NONE;
   JButton queryButton = new JButton("Query");
   queryButton.addActionListener(this);
   add(queryButton, gbc, 0, 1, 1, 1);

   JButton changeButton = new JButton("Change prices");
   changeButton.addActionListener(this);
   add(changeButton, gbc, 2, 1, 1, 1);

   gbc.fill = GridBagConstraints.HORIZONTAL;
   add(priceChange, gbc, 3, 1, 1, 1);

   gbc.fill = GridBagConstraints.BOTH;
   add(result, gbc, 0, 2, 4, 1);
}

public static Connection getConnection()
   throws SQLException, IOException
{  Properties props = new Properties();
   String fileName = "QueryDB.properties";
   FileInputStream in = new FileInputStream(fileName);
   props.load(in);

   String drivers = props.getProperty("jdbc.drivers");
   if (drivers != null)
      System.setProperty("jdbc.drivers", drivers);
   String url = props.getProperty("jdbc.url");
```

```
      String username = props.getProperty("jdbc.username");
      String password = props.getProperty("jdbc.password");

      return
         DriverManager.getConnection(url, username, password);
   }

   private void add(Component c, GridBagConstraints gbc,
      int x, int y, int w, int h)
   {  gbc.gridx = x;
      gbc.gridy = y;
      gbc.gridwidth = w;
      gbc.gridheight = h;
      getContentPane().add(c, gbc);
   }

   public void actionPerformed(ActionEvent evt)
   {  String arg = evt.getActionCommand();
      if (arg.equals("Query"))
      {  ResultSet rs = null;
         try
         {  String author
               = (String)authors.getSelectedItem();
            String publisher
               = (String)publishers.getSelectedItem();
            if (!author.equals("Any")
               && !publisher.equals("Any"))
            {  if (authorPublisherQueryStmt == null)
               {  String authorPublisherQuery =
"SELECT Books.Price, Books.Title " +
"FROM Books, BooksAuthors, Authors, Publishers " +
"WHERE Authors.Author_Id = BooksAuthors.Author_Id AND " +
"BooksAuthors.ISBN = Books.ISBN AND " +
"Books.Publisher_Id = Publishers.Publisher_Id AND " +
"Authors.Name = ? AND " +
"Publishers.Name = ?";
                  authorPublisherQueryStmt
                  = con.prepareStatement(authorPublisherQuery);
               }
               authorPublisherQueryStmt.setString(1, author);
               authorPublisherQueryStmt.setString(2,
                  publisher);
               rs = authorPublisherQueryStmt.executeQuery();
            }
            else if (!author.equals("Any")
               && publisher.equals("Any"))
            {  if (authorQueryStmt == null)
               {  String authorQuery =
"SELECT Books.Price, Books.Title " +
"FROM Books, BooksAuthors, Authors " +
"WHERE Authors.Author_Id = BooksAuthors.Author_Id AND " +
```

```
"BooksAuthors.ISBN = Books.ISBN AND " +
"Authors.Name = ?";
                  authorQueryStmt
                     = con.prepareStatement(authorQuery);
               }
               authorQueryStmt.setString(1, author);
               rs = authorQueryStmt.executeQuery();
            }
            else if (author.equals("Any")
               && !publisher.equals("Any"))
            {  if (publisherQueryStmt == null)
               {  String publisherQuery =
"SELECT Books.Price, Books.Title " +
"FROM Books, Publishers " +
"WHERE Books.Publisher_Id = Publishers.Publisher_Id AND " +
"Publishers.Name = ?";
                  publisherQueryStmt
                     = con.prepareStatement(publisherQuery);
               }
               publisherQueryStmt.setString(1, publisher);
               rs = publisherQueryStmt.executeQuery();
            }
            else
            {  if (allQueryStmt == null)
               {  String allQuery =
"SELECT Books.Price, Books.Title FROM Books";
                  allQueryStmt
                     = con.prepareStatement(allQuery);
               }
               rs = allQueryStmt.executeQuery();
            }

            result.setText("");
            while (rs.next())
               result.append(rs.getString(1)
                  + " | " + rs.getString(2) + "\n");
            rs.close();
         }
         catch(Exception e)
         {  result.setText("Error " + e);
         }
      }
      else if (arg.equals("Change prices"))
      {  String publisher
            = (String)publishers.getSelectedItem();
         if (publisher.equals("Any"))
            result.setText
               ("I am sorry, but I cannot do that.");
         else
            try
            {  String updateStatement =
```

```
"UPDATE Books " +
"SET Price = Price + " + priceChange.getText() +
" WHERE Books.Publisher_Id = " +
"(SELECT Publisher_Id FROM Publishers WHERE Name = '" +
   publisher + "')";
                  int r = stmt.executeUpdate(updateStatement);
                  result.setText(r + " records updated.");
               }
               catch(Exception e)
               {  result.setText("Error " + e);
               }
         }
   }

   public void dispose()
   {  try
      {  stmt.close();
         con.close();
      }
      catch(SQLException e) {}
   }

   private JComboBox authors;
   private JComboBox publishers;
   private JTextField priceChange;
   private JTextArea result;
   private Connection con;
   private Statement stmt;
   private PreparedStatement authorQueryStmt;
   private PreparedStatement authorPublisherQueryStmt;
   private PreparedStatement publisherQueryStmt;
   private PreparedStatement allQueryStmt;
}
```

java.sql.Connection

- `PreparedStatement prepareStatement(String sql)`

  returns a `PreparedStatement` object containing the precompiled statement. The string `sql` contains a SQL statement that can contain one or more parameter placeholders denoted by `?` characters.

java.sql.PreparedStatement

- `void set`*`Xxx`*`(int n, `*`Xxx`*` x)`

  (*Xxx* is a type such as `int`, `double`, `String`, `Date`, etc.)
  sets the value of the `n`th parameter to `x`.

- `void clearParameters()`

  clears all current parameters in the prepared statement.

- `ResultSet executeQuery()`

  executes a prepared SQL query and returns a `ResultSet` object.

- `int executeUpdate()`

  executes the prepared SQL `INSERT`, `UPDATE`, or `DELETE` statement represented by the `PreparedStatement` object. Returns the number of rows affected, or 0 for DDL statements.

Metadata

In the last two sections, you saw how to populate, query, and update database tables. However, JDBC can give you additional information about the *structure* of a database and its tables. For example, you can get a list of the tables in a particular database or the column names and types of a table. This information is not useful when you are implementing a particular database. After all, if you design the tables, you know the tables and their structure. Structural information is, however, extremely useful for programmers who write tools that work with any database.

In this section, we will show you how to write such a simple tool. This tool lets you browse all tables in a database.

The combo box on top displays all tables in the database. Select one of them, and the center of the frame is filled with the field names of that table and the values of the first record, as shown in Figure 4–7. Click on "Next" to scroll through the records in the table.

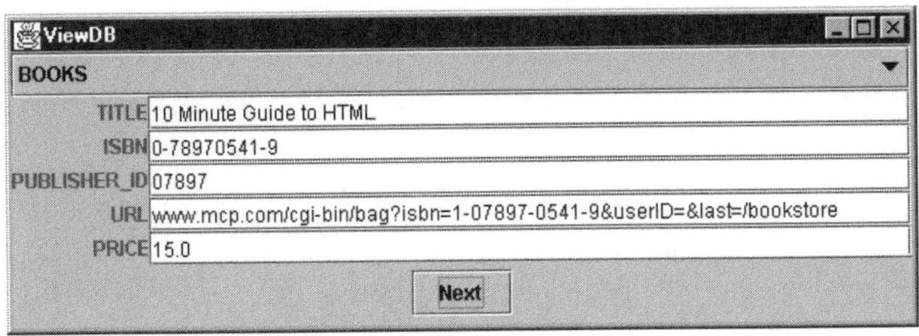

Figure 4–7: The ViewDB application

We fully expect tool vendors to develop much more sophisticated versions of programs like this one. For example, it would be possible to let the user edit the values or add new ones, and then update the database. We developed this program mostly to show you how such tools can be built.

In SQL, data that describes the database or one of its parts is called *metadata* (to distinguish it from the actual data that is stored in the database). You can get two kinds of metadata: about a database and about a result set.

To find out more about the database, you need to request an object of type `DatabaseMetaData` from the database connection.

```
DatabaseMetaData md = con.getMetaData();
```

Databases are complex, and the SQL standard leaves plenty of room for variability. There are well over a hundred methods in the `DatabaseMetaData` class to inquire about the database, including calls with exotic names such as

```
md.supportsCatalogsInPrivilegeDefinitions()
```

and

```
md.nullPlusNonNullIsNull()
```

Clearly, these are geared toward advanced users with special needs, in particular, those who need to write highly portable code. In this section, we study only one method that lets you list all tables in a database, and we won't even look at all *its* options. The call

```
ResultSet rs = md.getTables(null, null, null, new String[]
   { "TABLE" })
```

returns a result set that contains information about all tables in the database. (See the API note for other parameters to this method.)

Each row in the result set contains information about the table. We only care about the third entry, the name of the table. (Again, see the API note for the other columns.) Thus, `rs.getString(3)` is the table name. Here is the code that populates the combo box.

```
while (rs.next())
   tableNames.addItem(rs.getString(3));
rs.close();
```

The more interesting metadata is reported about result sets. Whenever you have a result set from a query, you can inquire about the number of columns and each column's name, type, and field width.

We will make use of this information to make a label for each name and a text field of sufficient size for each value.

```
ResultSet rs = stmt.executeQuery("SELECT * FROM " + tableName);
ResultSetMetaData rsmd = rs.getMetaData();
for (int i = 1; i <= rsmd.getColumnCount(); i++)
{  String columnName = rsmd.getColumnLabel(i);
   int columnWidth = rsmd.getColumnDisplaySize(i);
   Label l = new Label(columnName);
   TextField tf = new TextField(columnWidth);
   . . .
}
```

The following steps provide a brief overview of the program.

1. Have the border layout put the table name combo box on the top, the table values in the center, and the "Next" button on the bottom.
2. Connect to the database. Get the table names and fill them into the choice component.

3. When the user selects a table, make a query to see all its values. Get the metadata. Throw out the old components from the center panel. Create a gridbag layout of labels and text boxes. Store the text boxes in a vector. Call the `pack` method to have the window resize itself to exactly hold the newly added components. Then, call `showNextRow` to show the first row.
4. The `showNextRow` method is called to show the first record and is also called whenever the "Next" button is clicked. It gets the next row from the table and fills the column values into the text boxes. When the end of the table is reached, the result set is closed.

Example 4–3 is the program.

Example 4–3: ViewDB.java

```
import java.net.*;
import java.sql.*;
import java.awt.*;
import java.awt.event.*;
import java.io.*;
import java.util.*;
import javax.swing.*;

public class ViewDB
{  public static void main(String[] args)
   {  JFrame frame = new ViewDBFrame();
      frame.show();
   }
}

class ViewDBFrame extends JFrame
   implements ActionListener
{  public ViewDBFrame()
   {  setTitle("ViewDB");
      setSize(300, 200);
      addWindowListener(new WindowAdapter()
         {  public void windowClosing(WindowEvent e)
            {  System.exit(0);
            }
         } );

      Container contentPane = getContentPane();

      tableNames = new JComboBox();
      tableNames.addActionListener(this);

      dataPanel = new JPanel();
      contentPane.add(dataPanel, "Center");

      nextButton = new JButton("Next");
      nextButton.addActionListener(this);
      JPanel p = new JPanel();
```

```
      p.add(nextButton);
      contentPane.add(p, "South");

      fields = new ArrayList();

      try
      {  con = getConnection();
         stmt = con.createStatement();
         md = con.getMetaData();
         ResultSet mrs = md.getTables(null, null, null,
            new String[] { "TABLE" });
         while (mrs.next())
            tableNames.addItem(mrs.getString(3));
         mrs.close();
      }
      catch(Exception e)
      {  JOptionPane.showMessageDialog(this, e);
      }

      contentPane.add(tableNames, "North");
   }

   public static Connection getConnection()
      throws SQLException, IOException
   {  Properties props = new Properties();
      String fileName = "ViewDB.properties";
      FileInputStream in = new FileInputStream(fileName);
      props.load(in);

      String drivers = props.getProperty("jdbc.drivers");
      if (drivers != null)
         System.setProperty("jdbc.drivers", drivers);
      String url = props.getProperty("jdbc.url");
      String username = props.getProperty("jdbc.username");
      String password = props.getProperty("jdbc.password");

      return
         DriverManager.getConnection(url, username, password);
   }

   private void add(Container p, Component c,
      GridBagConstraints gbc, int x, int y, int w, int h)
   {  gbc.gridx = x;
      gbc.gridy = y;
      gbc.gridwidth = w;
      gbc.gridheight = h;
      p.add(c, gbc);
   }

   public void actionPerformed(ActionEvent evt)
   {  if (evt.getSource() == nextButton)
      {  showNextRow();
```

```
   }
   else if (evt.getSource() == tableNames)
   {  remove(dataPanel);
      dataPanel = new JPanel();
      fields.clear();
      dataPanel.setLayout(new GridBagLayout());
      GridBagConstraints gbc = new GridBagConstraints();
      gbc.weighty = 100;

      try
      {  String tableName
            = (String)tableNames.getSelectedItem();
         if (rs != null) rs.close();
         rs = stmt.executeQuery("SELECT * FROM "
            + tableName);
         ResultSetMetaData rsmd = rs.getMetaData();
         for (int i = 1; i <= rsmd.getColumnCount(); i++)
         {  String columnName = rsmd.getColumnLabel(i);
            int columnWidth = rsmd.getColumnDisplaySize(i);
            JTextField tb = new JTextField(columnWidth);
            fields.add(tb);

            gbc.weightx = 0;
            gbc.anchor = GridBagConstraints.EAST;
            gbc.fill = GridBagConstraints.NONE;
            add(dataPanel, new JLabel(columnName),
               gbc, 0, i - 1, 1, 1);

            gbc.weightx = 100;
            gbc.anchor = GridBagConstraints.WEST;
            gbc.fill = GridBagConstraints.HORIZONTAL;
            add(dataPanel, tb, gbc, 1, i - 1, 1, 1);
         }
      }
      catch(Exception e)
      {  JOptionPane.showMessageDialog(this, e);
      }
      getContentPane().add(dataPanel, "Center");
      doLayout();
      pack();

      showNextRow();
   }
}

public void showNextRow()
{  if (rs == null) return;
   {  try
      {  if (rs.next())
         {  for (int i = 1; i <= fields.size(); i++)
            {  String field = rs.getString(i);
               JTextField tb
```

```
                  = (JTextField)fields.get(i - 1);
               tb.setText(field);
            }
         }
         else
         {  rs.close();
            rs = null;
         }
      }
      catch(Exception e)
      {  System.out.println("Error " + e);
      }
   }
}

private JButton nextButton;
private JPanel dataPanel;
private JComboBox tableNames;
private ArrayList fields;

private Connection con;
private Statement stmt;
private DatabaseMetaData md;
private ResultSet rs;
}
```

java.sql.Connection

- `DatabaseMetaData getMetaData()`

  returns the metadata for the connection as a `DataBaseMetaData` object.

java.sql.DatabaseMetaData

- `ResultSet getTables(String catalog, String schemaPattern, String tableNamePattern, String types[])`

  gets a description of all tables in a catalog that match the schema and table name patterns and the type criteria. (A *schema* describes a group of related tables and access permissions. A *catalog* describes a related group of schemas. These concepts are important for structuring large databases.)

  The `catalog` and `schema` parameters can be `""` to retrieve those tables without a catalog or schema, or `null` to return tables regardless of catalog or schema.

  The `types` array contains the names of the table types to include. Typical types are `TABLE`, `VIEW`, `SYSTEM TABLE`, `GLOBAL TEMPORARY`, `LOCAL TEMPORARY`, `ALIAS`, and `SYNONYM`. If `types` is `null`, then tables of all types are returned.

The result set has five columns, all of which are of type `String`, as shown in Table 4–8.

Table 4–8: Five columns of the result set

1	`TABLE_CAT`	Table catalog (may be `null`)
2	`TABLE_SCHEM`	Table schema (may be `null`)
3	`TABLE_NAME`	Table name
4	`TABLE_TYPE`	Table type
5	`REMARKS`	Comment on the table

`java.sql.ResultSet`

- `ResultSetMetaData getMetaData()`

  gives you the metadata associated with the current `ResultSet` columns.

`java.sql.ResultSetMetaData`

- `int getColumnCount()`

  returns the number of columns in the current `ResultSet` object.

- `int getColumnDisplaySize(int column)`

  tells you the maximum width of the column specified by the index parameter.

  Parameters: `column` the column number

- `String getColumnLabel(int column)`

  gives you the suggested title for the column.

  Parameters: `column` the column number

- `String getColumnName(int column)`

  gives the column name associated with the column index specified.

  Parameters: `column` the column number

Scrollable and Updatable Result Sets

The most useful improvements in JDBC 2 are in the `ResultSet` class. As you have seen, the `next` method of the `ResultSet` class iterates over the rows in a result set. That is certainly adequate for a program that needs to analyze the data. However, consider a visual data display such as the one in the preceding example (see Figure 4–7 on page 239). You usually want the user to be able to move both forward and backward in the result set. But in JDBC 1, there was no `previous` method. Programmers who wanted to implement backwards iteration had to manually cache the result set data. The *scrolling* result set in JDBC 2 lets you move forward and backward through a result set and jump to any position in the result set.

Furthermore, once you display the contents of a result set to users, they may be tempted to edit it. If you supply an editable view to your users, you have to make sure that the user edits are posted back to the database. In JDBC 1, you had to program `UPDATE` statements. In JDBC 2, you can simply update the result set entries, and the database is automatically updated.

These two enhancements are the topic of this section. JDBC 2 delivers additional enhancements to result sets, such as the capability of updating a result set with the most recent data. However, these advanced features are outside the scope of this introductory chapter. We refer you to the *JDBC API Tutorial and Reference* by Seth White, Maydene Fisher, Rick Cattell, *et al.*, Addison-Wesley 1999 for more information.

Scrollable Result Sets (JDBC 2)

To obtain scrolling result sets from your queries, you must obtain a different `Statement` object with the method

```
Statement stmt = con.createStatement(type, concurrency);
```

For a prepared statement, use the call

```
PreparedStatement stmt = con.prepareStatement(command,
   type, concurrency);
```

The possible values of `type` and `concurrency` are listed in Table 4–9 and Table 4–10. You have the following choices:

- Do you want the result set to be scrollable or not? If not, use `ResultSet.TYPE_FORWARD_ONLY`.
- If the result set is scrollable, do you want it to be able to reflect changes in the database that occurred after the query that yielded it? (In our discussion, we will assume the `ResultSet.TYPE_SCROLL_INSENSITIVE` setting for scrolling result sets. This assumes that the result set does not "sense" database changes that occurred after the query.)
- Do you want to be able to update the database by editing the result set? (See the next section for details.)

For example, if you simply want to be able to scroll through a result set but you don't want to edit its data, you use:

```
Statement stmt
   = con.createStatement(ResultSet.TYPE_SCROLL_INSENSITIVE,
     ResultSet.CONCUR_READ_ONLY);
```

Table 4–9: `ResultSet` type values

`TYPE_FORWARD_ONLY`	The result set is not scrollable.
`TYPE_SCROLL_INSENSITIVE`	The result set is scrollable but not sensitive to database changes.
`TYPE_SCROLL_SENSITIVE`	The result set is scrollable and sensitive to database changes.

Table 4–10: `ResultSet` concurrency values

`CONCUR_READ_ONLY`	The result set cannot be used to update the database.
`CONCUR_UPDATABLE`	The result set can be used to update the database.

All result sets that are returned by method calls

```
ResultSet rs = stmt.executeQuery(query)
```

are now scrollable. A scrolling result set has a *cursor* that indicates the current position.

NOTE: Actually, a database driver might not be able to honor your request for a scrolling or updatable cursor. (The `supportsResultSetType` and `supportsResultSetConcurrency` methods of the `DatabaseMetaData` class tell you which types and concurrency modes are supported by a particular database.) But even if a database supports all result set modes, a particular query might not be able to yield a result set with all the properties that you requested. (For example, the result set of a complex query may not be updatable.) In that case, the `executeQuery` method returns a `ResultSet` of lesser capabilities and adds a *warning* to the connection object. You can retrieve warnings with the `getWarnings` method of the `Connection` class. Alternatively, you can use the `getType` and `getConcurrency` methods of the `ResultSet` class to find out what mode a result set actually has. If you do not check the result set capabilities and issue an unsupported operation, such as `previous` on a result set that is not scrollable, then the operation throws a `SQLException`.

CAUTION: In JDBC 1 drivers, the `Connection` class does not have a method

```
Statement createStatement(int type, int concurrency);
```

If a program that you compiled for JDBC 2 inadvertently loads a JDBC 1 driver and then call this nonexistent method, the program will crash. Unfortunately, there is no JDBC mechanism for querying a driver whether it is JDBC 2 compliant.

Scrolling is very simple. You use

```
if (rs.previous()) . . .
```

to scroll backward. The method returns `true` if the cursor is positioned on an actual row; `false` if it now is positioned before the first row.

You can move the cursor backward or forward by a number of rows with the command

```
rs.relative(n);
```

If *n* is positive, the cursor moves forward. If *n* is negative, it moves backwards. If *n* is zero, the call has no effect. If you attempt to move the cursor outside the current set of rows, it is set to point either after the last row or before the first row, depending on the sign of *n*. Then, the method returns `false` and the cursor does not move. The method returns `true` if the cursor landed on an actual row.

Alternatively, you can set the cursor to a particular row number:

```
rs.absolute(n);
```

You get the current row number with the call

```
int n = rs.getRow();
```

The first row in the result set has number 1. If the return value is 0, the cursor is not currently on a row—it is either before the first or after the last row.

NOTE: The order of the rows in a result set is completely arbitrary. You should never attach any significance to the row numbers.

There are convenience methods

```
first
last
beforeFirst
afterLast
```

to move the cursor to the first, to the last, before the first, or after the last position.

Finally, the methods

```
isFirst
isLast
isBeforeFirst
isAfterLast
```

test whether the cursor is at one of these special positions.

Using a scrolling cursor is very straightforward. For example, if you want to enhance the `ViewDB` program of the preceding section to scroll backward as well as forward, simply add the following method as the handler of a "Previous" button:

```
public void showPreviousRow()
{  . . .
   if (rs.previous())
   {  for (int i = 1; i <= fields.size(); i++)
      {  String field = rs.getString(i);
         JTextField tf
            = (JTextField)fields.get(i - 1);
```

```
            tf.setText(field);
         }
      }
      . . .
   }
```

The method looks exactly like the `showNextMethod` in Example 4–3, with the `previous` method replacing the `next` method. (For simplicity, we omitted the error handling from the code fragment.)

The hard work of caching the query data is carried out behind the scenes by the database driver.

Updatable Result Sets (JDBC 2)

If you want to be able to edit result set data and have the changes automatically reflected in the database, you need to create an updatable result set. Updatable result sets don't have to be scrollable, but if you present data to a user for editing, you usually want to allow scrolling as well.

To obtain updatable result sets, you create a statement as follows.

```
Statement stmt
   = con.createStatement(ResultSet.TYPE_SCROLL_INSENSITIVE,
      ResultSet.CONCUR_UPDATABLE);
```

Then, the result sets returned by a call to `executeQuery` are updatable.

NOTE: Not all queries return updatable result sets. If your query is a join that involves multiple tables, the result may not be updatable. If your query involves only a single table or if it joins multiple tables by their primary keys, you should expect the result set to be updatable. Call the `getConcurrency` method of the `ResultSet` class to find out for sure.

For example, suppose you want to raise the prices of some books, but you don't have a simple criterion for issuing an `UPDATE` command. Then, you can iterate through all books and update prices, based on arbitrary conditions.

```
String query = "SELECT * FROM Books";
ResultSet rs = stmt.executeQuery(query);
while (rs.next())
{  if (. . .)
   {  double increase = . . .
      double price = rs.getDouble("Price");
      rs.updateDouble("Price", price + increase);
      rs.updateRow();
   }
}
```

There are `updateXxx` methods for all data types that correspond to SQL types, such as `updateDouble`, `updateString`, and so on. As with the `getXxx` methods, you specify the name or the number of the column. Then, you specify the new value for the field.

NOTE: If you use the `updateXxx` method whose first parameter is the column number, be aware that this is the column number in the *result set*. It may well be different from the column number in the database.

The `updateXxx` method only changes the row values, not the database. When you are done with the field updates in a row, you must call the `updateRow` method. That method sends all updates in the current row to the database. If you move the cursor to another row without calling `updateRow`, all updates are discarded from the row set and they are never communicated to the database. You can also call the `cancelRowUpdates` method to cancel the updates to the current row.

The preceding example shows how you modify an existing row. If you want to add a new row to the database, you first use the `moveToInsertRow` method to move the cursor to a special position, called the *insert row*. You build up a new row in the insert row position by issuing `updateXxx` instructions. Finally, when you are done, call the `insertRow` method to deliver the new row to the database. When you are done inserting, call `moveToCurrentRow` to move the cursor back to the position before the call to `moveToInsertRow`. Here is an example.

```
rs.moveToInsertRow();
rs.updateString("Title", title);
rs.updateString("ISBN", isbn);
rs.updateString("Publisher_Id", pubid);
rs.updateString("URL", url);
rs.updateDouble("Price", price);
rs.insertRow();
rs.moveToCurrentRow();
```

Note that you have no influence *where* the new data is added in the result set or the database.

Finally, you can delete the row under the cursor.

```
rs.deleteRow();
```

The `deleteRow` method immediately removes the row from both the result set and the database.

The `updateRow`, `insertRow`, and `deleteRow` methods of the `ResultSet` class give you the same power as executing `UPDATE`, `INSERT`, and `DELETE` SQL commands. However, programmers who are used to the Java programming language will find it more natural to manipulate the database contents through result sets than by constructing SQL statements. Once JDBC 2 drivers are widely available, we expect this programming style to become very popular.

`javax.sql.Connection`

- `Statement createStatement(int type, int concurrency)`
- `PreparedStatement prepareStatement(String command, int type, int concurrency)`

  (JDBC 2) create a statement or prepared statement that yields result sets with the given type and concurrency.

Parameters:	`command`	the command to prepare
	`type`	one of the constants `TYPE_FORWARD_ONLY`, `TYPE_SCROLL_INSENSITIVE`, or `TYPE_SCROLL_SENSITIVE` of the `ResultSet` interface.
	`concurrency`	one of the constants `CONCUR_READ_ONLY` or `CONCUR_UPDATABLE` of the `ResultSet` interface.

- `SQLWarning getWarnings()`

  returns the first of the pending warnings on this connection, or `null` if no warnings are pending. The warnings are chained together—keep calling `getNextWarning` on the returned `SQLWarning` object until that method returns `null`. This call does not consume the warnings. The `SQLWarning` class extends `SQLException`. Use the inherited `getErrorCode` and `getSQLState` to analyze the warnings.

- `void clearWarnings()`

  clears all warnings that have been reported on this connection.

`java.sql.ResultSet`

- `int getType()`

  (JDBC 2) returns the type of this result set, one of `TYPE_FORWARD_ONLY`, `TYPE_SCROLL_INSENSITIVE`, or `TYPE_SCROLL_SENSITIVE`.

- `int getConcurrency()`

  (JDBC 2) returns the concurrency setting of this result set, one of `CONCUR_READ_ONLY` or `CONCUR_UPDATABLE`.

- `boolean previous()`

  (JDBC 2) moves the cursor to the preceding row. Returns `true` if the cursor is positioned on a row.

- `int getRow()`

  (JDBC 2) gets the number of the current row. Rows are numbered starting with 1.

- `boolean absolute(int r)`

  (JDBC 2) moves the cursor to row `r`. Returns `true` if the cursor is positioned on a row.

- `boolean relative(int d)`

  (JDBC 2) moves the cursor by `d` rows. If `d` is negative, the cursor is moved backward. Returns `true` if the cursor is positioned on a row.

- `boolean first()`
- `boolean last()`

  (JDBC 2) move the cursor to the first or last row. Return `true` if the cursor is positioned on a row.

- `void beforeFirst()`
- `void afterLast()`

  (JDBC 2) move the cursor before the first or after the last row.

- `boolean isFirst()`
- `boolean isLast()`

  (JDBC 2) test if the cursor is at the first or last row.

- `boolean isBeforeFirst()`
- `boolean isAfterLast()`

  (JDBC 2) test if the cursor is before the first or after the last row.

- `void moveToInsertRow()`

  (JDBC 2) moves the cursor to the *insert row.* The insert row is a special row that is used for inserting new data with the `updateXxx` and `insertRow` methods.

- `void moveToCurrentRow()`

  (JDBC 2) moves the cursor back from the insert row to the row that it occupied when the `moveToInsertRow` method was called.

- `void insertRow()`

  (JDBC 2) inserts the contents of the insert row into the database and the result set.

- `void deleteRow()`

  (JDBC 2) deletes the current row from the database and the result set.

- `void updateXxx(int column, Xxx data)`
- `void updateXxx(String columnName, Xxx data)`

  (*Xxx* is a type such as `int`, `double`, `String`, `Date`, etc.)
  (JDBC 2) update a field in the current row of the result set.

- `void updateRow()`

  (JDBC 2) sends the current row updates to the database.

- `void cancelRowUpdates()`

  (JDBC 2) cancels the current row updates.

java.sql.DatabaseMetaData

- `boolean supportsResultSetType(int type)`

  (JDBC 2) returns `true` if the database can support result sets of the given type.

Parameters:	`command`	the command to prepare
	`type`	one of the constants `TYPE_FORWARD_ONLY`, `TYPE_SCROLL_INSENSITIVE`, or `TYPE_SCROLL_SENSITIVE` of the `ResultSet` interface.

- `boolean supportsResultSetConcurrency(int type, int concurrency)`

  (JDBC 2) Returns `true` if the database can support result sets of the given combination of type and concurrency.

Parameters:	`command`	the command to prepare
	`type`	one of the constants `TYPE_FORWARD_ONLY`, `TYPE_SCROLL_INSENSITIVE`, or `TYPE_SCROLL_SENSITIVE` of the `Result-Set` interface.
	`concurrency`	one of the constants `CONCUR_READ_ONLY` or `CONCUR_UPDATABLE` of the `ResultSet` interface.

Chapter 5

Remote Objects

- ▼ Remote Method Invocations
- ▼ Setting Up Remote Method Invocation
- ▼ Parameter Passing in Remote Methods
- ▼ Using RMI with Applets
- ▼ Java IDL and CORBA

Periodically, the programming community starts thinking of "objects everywhere" as the solution to all its problems. The idea is to have a happy family of collaborating objects that can be located anywhere. These objects are, of course, supposed to communicate through standard protocols across a network. For example, you'll have an object on the client where the user can fill in a request for data. The client object sends a message to an object on the server that contains the details of the request. The server object gathers the requested information, perhaps by accessing a database or by communicating with additional objects. Once the server object has the answer to the client request, it sends the answer back to the client. Like most bandwagons in programming, this plan contains a fair amount of hype that can obscure the utility of the concept. This chapter:

- Explains the models that make interobject communication possible;
- Explains situations where distributed objects can be useful;
- Shows you how to use remote objects and the associated *remote method invocation* (RMI) for communicating between two Java virtual machines (which may run on different computers);

- Introduces you to CORBA, the Common Object Request Broker Architecture that allows communication between objects that are written in different programming languages (such as the Java programming language, C++, and so on).

Introduction to Remote Objects: The Roles of Client and Server

Let's go back to that idea of locally collecting information on a client computer and sending the information across the Net to a server. We are supposing that a user on a local machine will fill out an information request form. The form data gets sent to the vendor's server, and the server processes the request and will, in turn, want to send back product information the client can view, as shown in Figure 5–1.

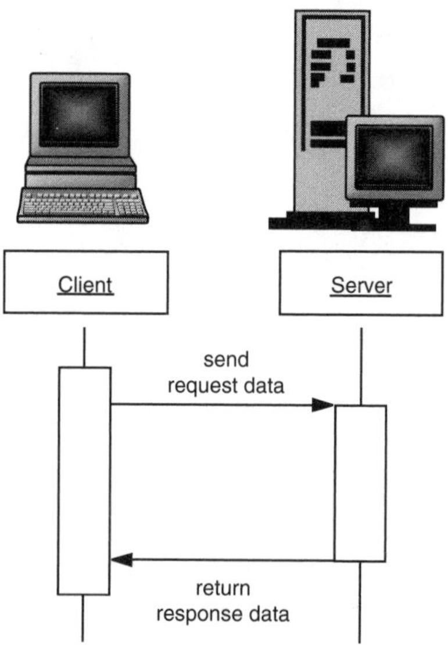

Figure 5–1: Transmitting objects between client and server

In the traditional client/server model, the request is translated to an intermediary format (such as name/value pairs or XML data). The server parses the request format, computes the response, and formats the response for transmission to the client. The client then parses the response and displays it to the user.

But if your data is structured, then there is a significant coding hassle: you have to come up with appropriate ways of translating the data to and from the transmission format.

NOTE: Another method for sending a request for data to a server is with HTML forms. Then, the client is simply the browser, and the server needs to gather the requested information and format it as HTML. Even in that model, it makes sense to separate the form processing from the data gathering. Typically, the form processing happens on the web

server, and the data gathering happens on a different server, called an *application server.* You again have two communicating objects, the client object on the web server and the server object on the application server. This is a very common model in practice. In this chapter, we stick to a more traditional client/server example because it makes the roles of the client and server more intuitive.

What would go into a possible solution? Well, keeping in mind that objects sending requests to one another is the central tenet of OOP, we could put objects on different machines and have them send messages *directly* to each other. Let's assume that the client object was written in the Java programming language so that it can theoretically run anywhere. For the server objects, there are two obvious possibilities:

- The server object was *not* written in the Java programming language (either because it is a legacy object or because somebody hasn't joined the appropriate bandwagon).
- The server object *was* written in the Java programming language.

The first situation requires us to have a way for objects to talk to each other *regardless* of what language they were originally written in. If you think about it, you will agree with us that even the theoretical possibility of this is an amazing achievement. How can what is ultimately a sequence of bytes written in an arbitrary language, that we may have no knowledge of, tell us what services it offers, what messages it responds to? Of course, getting this to work in practice isn't easy, but the idea is elegant. The "common object request broker architecture," or CORBA standard, by the Object Management Group or OMG (`www.omg.org`) defines a common mechanism for interchanging data and discovering services.

The fundamental idea is that we delegate the task of finding out this information and activating any requested services to a so-called *Object Request Broker* (or ORB). You can think of an ORB as a kind of universal translator for interobject communication. Objects don't talk directly to each other. They always use an object broker to bargain between them. ORBs are located across the network, and it is important that they can communicate with each other. Most ORBs follow the specification set up by the OMG for inter-ORB communication. This specification is called the Internet Inter-ORB Protocol or IIOP.

NOTE: Microsoft uses a different, lower-level protocol (called COM+ at the time of this writing) for interobject communication. ORB-like services are bundled into the Windows operating system. Although some vendors offer some level of interoperability on some Unix platforms, COM+ is mainly a Windows solution. CORBA, on the other hand, is truly a cross-language and cross-platform architecture for interobject communication.

CORBA is completely language neutral. Client and server programs can be written in C++, the Java programming language, or any other language with a

CORBA binding. You use an *Interface Definition Language* (or IDL) to specify the signatures of the messages and the types of the data your objects can send and understand. (IDL specifications look a lot like interfaces in the Java programming language; in fact, you can think of them as defining interfaces that the communicating objects must support. One nice feature of this model is that you can supply an IDL specification for an existing legacy object and then access its services through the ORB even if it was written long before the first ORB arrived.) There are quite a few people who believe that CORBA will become very important very soon and that the Java programming language is an excellent choice for implementing CORBA clients and servers. However, frankly speaking, CORBA has had a reputation—sometimes deserved—for slow performance, complex implementations, and interoperability problems.

If both communicating objects are written in the Java programming language, then the full generality and complexity of CORBA is not required. Sun developed a simpler mechanism, called Remote Method Invocation (RMI), specifically for communication between Java applications.

NOTE: CORBA supporters initially did not like RMI because it completely ignored the CORBA standard. However, there are efforts to make CORBA and RMI more interoperable. In particular, future versions of RMI will use the IIOP protocol instead of the proprietary RMI protocol for object communication.

While CORBA may be interesting tomorrow, RMI is easier to understand and more convenient to use. For that reason, we will start out this chapter with RMI. Of course, RMI is useful only for communication between Java objects. In the last section of this chapter, we briefly introduce CORBA programming and show you how to hook up a C++ client with a server implemented in the Java programming language and a client implemented in the Java programming language with a C++ server.

Remote Method Invocations

The Remote Method Invocation mechanism lets you do something that sounds simple. If you have access to an object on a different machine, you can call methods of the remote object. Of course, the method parameters must somehow be shipped to the other machine, the object must be informed to execute the method, and the return value must be shipped back. RMI handles these details.

For example, the client seeking product information can query a `Warehouse` object on the server. It calls a remote method, `find`, which has one parameter: a `Customer` object. The `find` method returns an object to the client: the product information object. (See Figure 5–2.)

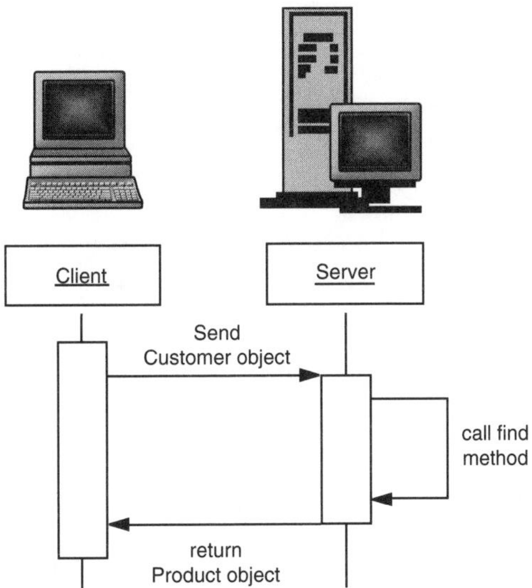

Figure 5–2: Invoking a remote method on a server object

In RMI terminology, the object whose method makes the remote call is called the *client object*. The remote object is called the *server object*. It is important to remember that the client/server terminology applies only to a single method call. The computer running the code in the Java programming language, that calls the remote method is the client for *that* call, and the computer hosting the object that processes the call is the server for *that* call. It is entirely possible that the roles are reversed somewhere down the road. The server of a previous call can itself become the client when it invokes a remote method on an object residing on another computer.

Stubs and Parameter Marshalling

When client code wants to invoke a remote method on a remote object, it actually calls an ordinary method of the Java programming language that is encapsulated in a surrogate object called a *stub*. The stub resides on the client machine, not on the server. The stub packages as a block of bytes the parameters used in the remote method. This packaging uses a device-independent encoding for each parameter. For example, numbers are always sent in big-endian byte ordering. Objects are encoded with the serialization mechanism that is described in Chapter 12 of Volume 1. The process of encoding the parameters is called *parameter marshalling*. The purpose of parameter marshalling is to convert the parameters into a format suitable for transport from one virtual machine to another.

To sum up: the stub method on the client builds an information block that consists of:

- An identifier of the remote object to be used;
- A description of the method to be called;
- The marshalled parameters.

The stub then sends this information to the server. On the server side, a receiver object performs the following actions for every remote method call:

- It unmarshals the parameters.
- It locates the object to be called.
- It calls the desired method.
- It captures and marshals the return value or exception of the call.
- It sends a package consisting of the marshalled return data back to the stub on the client.

The client stub unmarshals the return value or exception from the server. This value becomes the return value of the stub call. Or, if the remote method threw an exception, the stub rethrows it in the process space of the caller. Figure 5–3 shows the information flow of a remote method invocation.

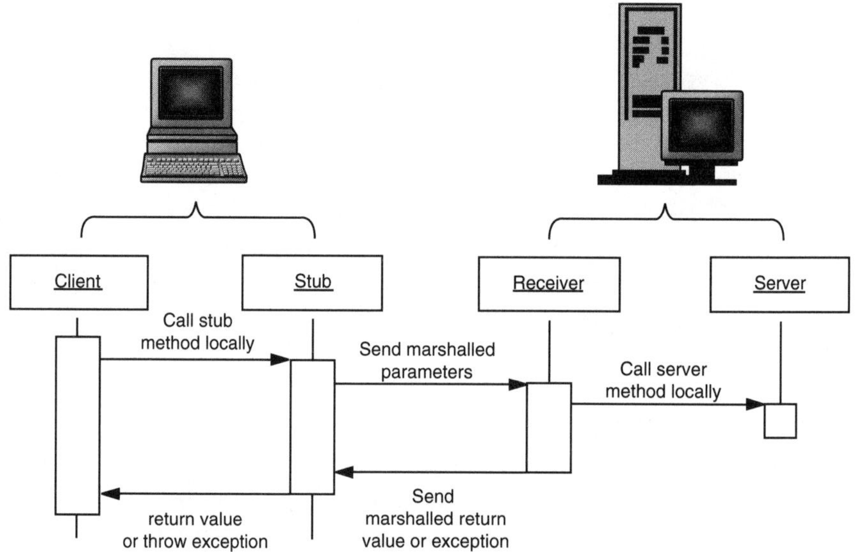

Figure 5–3: Parameter marshalling

This process is obviously complex, but the good news is that it is completely automatic and, to a large extent, transparent for the programmer. Moreover, the designers of the remote Java object tried hard to give remote objects the same "look and feel" as local objects.

The syntax for a remote method call is the same as for a local call. If `centralWarehouse` is a stub object for a central warehouse object on a remote machine and `getQuantity` is the method you want to invoke on it, then a typical call looks like this:

```
centralWarehouse.getQuantity("SuperSucker 100 Vacuum Cleaner");
```

The client code always uses object variables whose type is an `interface` to access remote objects. For example, associated to this call would be an interface:

```
interface Warehouse
{  public int getQuantity(String description)
      throws RemoteException;
   . . .
}
```

An object declaration for a variable that will implement the interface is:

```
Warehouse centralWarehouse = . . .;
```

Of course, interfaces are abstract entities that only spell out what methods can be called along with their signatures. Variables whose type is an interface must always be bound to an actual object of some type. When calling remote methods, the object variable refers to a *stub object*. The client program does not actually know the type of those objects. The stub classes and the associated objects are created automatically.

While the designers did a good job of hiding many details of remote method invocation from the programmer, a number of techniques and caveats still must be mastered. Those programming tasks are the topic of the rest of this chapter.

NOTE: Remote objects are garbage collected automatically, just as local objects are. However, the current distributed collector uses reference counting and cannot detect cycles of unreferenced objects. Cycles must be explicitly broken by the programmer.

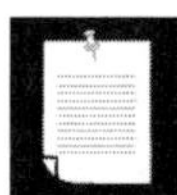

Dynamic Class Loading

When you pass a remote object to another program, either as a parameter or return value of a remote method, then that program must be able to deal with the associated stub object. That is, it must have the code for the stub class. The stub methods don't do a lot of interesting work. They just marshal and unmarshal the parameters and then contact the server for method calls. Of course, they do all this work transparently to the programmer.

Furthermore, the classes for parameters, return values, and exception objects may need to be loaded as well. This loading can be more complex than you might think. For example, you may declare a remote method with a certain return type that is known to the client, but the method actually returns an object of a subclass that is not known to the client. The class loader will then load that derived class.

While unglamorous, the stub classes must be available to the running client program. One obvious way to make these classes available is to put them on the local file system. However, if the server program is extended and new classes for return types and exceptions are added, then it would be a hassle to keep updating the client.

For that reason, RMI clients can automatically load stub classes from another place. The process is similar to the class loading process of applets that run in a browser.

Whenever a program loads new code from another network location, there is a security issue. For that reason, you need to use a *security manager* in RMI client applications. This is a safety mechanism that protects the program from viruses in stub code. For specialized applications, programmers can substitute their own class loaders and security managers, but those provided by the RMI system suffice for normal usage. (See Chapter 9 for more information on class loaders and security managers.)

Setting Up Remote Method Invocation

Running even the simplest remote object example requires quite a bit more setup than does running a standalone program or applet. You must run programs on both the server and client computers. The necessary object information must be separated into client-side interfaces and server-side implementations. There is also a special lookup mechanism that allows the client to locate objects on the server.

To get started with the actual coding, we walk through each of these requirements, using a simple example. In our first example, we generate a couple of objects of a type `Product` on the server computer. We then run a program on a client computer that locates and queries these objects.

NOTE: You can try out this example on a single computer or on a pair of networked computers. We give you instructions for both scenarios.

Even if you run this code on a single computer, you must have network services available. In particular, be sure that you have TCP/IP running. If your computer doesn't have a network card, then you can activate TCP/IP by establishing a dialup networking connection.

Interfaces and Implementations

Your client program needs to manipulate server objects, but it doesn't actually have copies of them. The objects themselves reside on the server. The client code must still know what it can do with those objects. Their capabilities are expressed in an interface that is shared between the client and server and so resides simultaneously on both machines.

```
interface Product // shared by client and server
   extends Remote
{  public String getDescription() throws RemoteException;
}
```

Just as in this example, *all* interfaces for remote objects must extend the `Remote` interface defined in the `java.rmi` package. All the methods in those interfaces must also declare that they will throw a `RemoteException`. The reason for the

declaration is that remote method calls are inherently less reliable than local calls—it is always possible that a remote call will fail. For example, the server or the network connection may be temporarily unavailable, or there may be a network problem. Your client code must be prepared to deal with these possibilities. For these reasons, the Java programming language forces you to catch the `RemoteException` with *every* remote method call and to specify the appropriate action to take when the call does not succeed.

The client accesses the server object through a stub that implements this interface.

```
Product p = ...;
   // see below how the client gets a stub
   // reference to a remote object
String d = p.getDescription();
System.out.println(d);
```

In the next section, you will see how the client can obtain a reference to this kind of remote object.

Next, on the server side, you must implement the class that actually carries out the methods advertised in the remote interface.

```
public class ProductImpl // server
   extends UnicastRemoteObject
   implements Product
{  public ProductImpl(String d)
      throws RemoteException
   {  descr = d;
   }

   public String getDescription()
      throws RemoteException
   {  return "I am a " + descr + ". Buy me!";
   }

   private String descr;
}
```

This class has a single method, `getDescription`, that can be called from the remote client.

You can tell that the class is a server for remote methods because it extends `UnicastRemoteObject`, which is a concrete Java platform class that makes objects remotely accessible.

NOTE: The `ProductImpl` class is *not* a typical server class because it does so little work. Normally, you only want to have server classes that do some heavy-duty work that a client could not carry out locally. We just use the `Product` example to walk you through the mechanics of calling remote methods.

All server classes must extend the class `RemoteServer` from the `java.rmi.server` package, but `RemoteServer` is an abstract class that defines only the basic mechanisms for the communication between server objects and their remote stubs. The `UnicastRemoteObject` class that comes with RMI extends the `RemoteServer` abstract class and is concrete—so you can use it without writing any code. The "path of least resistance" for a server class is to derive from `UnicastRemoteObject`, and all server classes in this chapter will do so. Figure 5–4 shows the inheritance relationship between these classes.

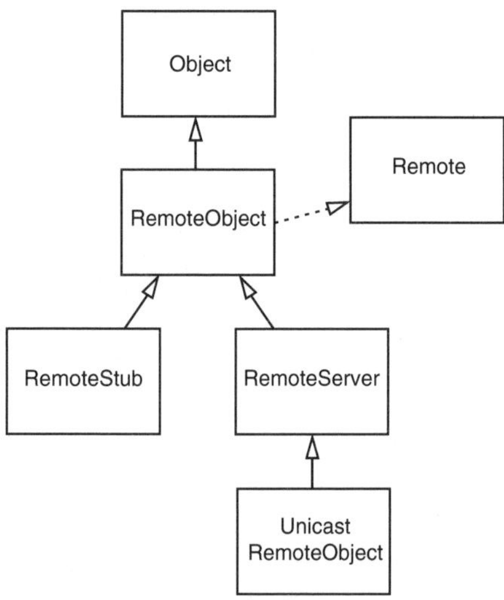

Figure 5–4: Inheritance diagram

A `UnicastRemoteObject` object resides on a server. It must be alive when a service is requested and must be reachable through the TCP/IP protocol. This is the class that we will be extending for all the server classes in this book and is the only server class available in the current version of the RMI package. Sun or third-party vendors may, in the future, design other classes for use by servers for RMI. For example, Sun is talking about a `MulticastRemoteObject` class for objects that are replicated over multiple servers. Other possibilities are for objects that are activated on demand or ones that can use other communications protocols, such as UDP.

NOTE: When you use RMI (or any distributed object mechanism, for that matter), there is a somewhat bewildering set of classes to master. In this chapter, we use a uniform naming convention for all of our examples that, hopefully, makes it easier to recognize the purpose of each class. (See Table 5–1.)

Table 5–1: Naming conventions for RMI classes

no suffix (e.g., `Product`)	A remote interface
`Impl` suffix (e.g., `ProductImpl`)	A server class implementing that interface
`Server` suffix (e.g., `ProductServer`)	A server program that creates server objects
`Client` suffix (e.g., `ProductClient`)	A client program that calls remote methods
`_Stub` suffix (e.g., `ProductImpl_Stub`)	A stub class that is automatically generated by the `rmic` program
`_Skel` suffix (e.g., `ProductImpl_Skel`)	A skeleton class that is automatically generated by the `rmic` program; needed for JDK 1.1.

You need to generate stubs for the `ProductImpl` class. Recall that stubs are the classes that marshal (encode and send) the parameters and marshal the results of method calls across the network. The programmer never uses those classes directly. Moreover, they need *not* be written by hand. The `rmic` tool generates them automatically, as in the following example.

```
rmic -v1.2 ProductImpl
```

This call to the `rmic` tool generates a class file `ProductImpl_Stub.class`. If your class is in a package, you must call `rmic` with the full package name.

If your client uses JDK 1.1, you should instead call

```
rmic ProductImpl
```

Then, two files are generated: the stub file and a second class file named `ProductImpl_Skel.class`. This "skeleton" file is no longer necessary with the Java 2 platform.

NOTE: Remember to first compile the source file with `javac` before running `rmic`. If you are generating stubs for a class in a package, you must give `rmic` the full package name.

Locating Server Objects

To access a remote object that exists on the server, the client needs a local stub object. How can the client request such a stub? The most common method is to call a remote method of another server object and to get a stub object as a return value. There is, however, a chicken-and-egg problem here. The *first* server object needs to be located some other way. The Sun RMI library provides a *bootstrap registry service* to locate the first server object.

A server program registers objects with the bootstrap registry service, and the client retrieves stubs to those objects. You register a server object by giving the

bootstrap registry service a reference to the object and a *name*. The name is a string that is (hopefully) unique.

```
// server
ProductImpl p1 = new ProductImpl("Blackwell Toaster");
Naming.bind("toaster", p1);
```

The client code gets a stub to access that server object by specifying the server name and the object name in the following way:

```
// client
Product p
   = (Product)Naming.lookup("rmi://yourserver.com/toaster");
```

RMI URLs start with `rmi:/` and are followed by a server, an optional port number, another slash, and the name of the remote object. Another example is:

```
rmi://localhost:99/central_warehouse
```

By default, the port number is 1099.

NOTE: Because it is notoriously difficult to keep names unique in a global registry, you should not use this technique as the general method for locating objects on the server. Instead, there should be relatively few named server objects registered with the bootstrap service. These should be objects that can locate other objects for you. In our example, we temporarily violate this rule and register relatively trivial objects to show you the mechanics for registering and locating objects.

For security reasons, an application can bind, unbind, or rebind registry objects references only if it runs on the same host as the registry. This prevents hostile clients from changing the registry information. However, any client can look up objects.

Example 5–1 shows a complete server program that registers two `Product` objects under the names `toaster` and `microwave`.

TIP: If you compare our server with the server examples in the tutorial documentation, you will note that we do not install a security manager in the server. Contrary to the statements in the tutorial, a security manager is neither necessary nor particularly beneficial for RMI servers. Since adding a security manager yields yet another fertile source for configuration errors, we suggest that you only install a security manager if you want to constrain the actions in the server implementation or if the server is itself an RMI client of another server.

Example 5–1: ProductServer.java

```
import java.rmi.*;
import java.rmi.server.*;
import sun.applet.*;

public class ProductServer
```

```
{  public static void main(String args[])
   {  try
      {  System.out.println
            ("Constructing server implementations...");

         ProductImpl p1
            = new ProductImpl("Blackwell Toaster");
         ProductImpl p2
            = new ProductImpl("ZapXpress Microwave Oven");

         System.out.println
            ("Binding server implementations to registry...");

         Naming.rebind("toaster", p1);
         Naming.rebind("microwave", p2);

         System.out.println
            ("Waiting for invocations from clients...");
      }
      catch(Exception e)
      {  System.out.println("Error: " + e);
      }
   }
}
```

Example 5–2: ProductImpl.java

```
import java.rmi.*;
import java.rmi.server.*;

public class ProductImpl
   extends UnicastRemoteObject
   implements Product
{  public ProductImpl(String n)
      throws RemoteException
   {  name = n;
   }

   public String getDescription()
      throws RemoteException
   {  return "I am a " + name + ". Buy me!";
   }

   private String name;
}
```

Example 5–3: Product.java

```
import java.rmi.*;

public interface Product extends Remote
{  String getDescription()
```

```
        throws RemoteException;
}
```

Starting the Server

Our server program isn't quite ready to run, yet. Because it uses the bootstrap RMI registry, that service must be available. To start the RMI registry under Windows 95 or NT, you execute the statement

```
start rmiregistry
```

at a DOS prompt or from the Run dialog box. (The `start` command is a Windows command that starts a program in a new window.)

Under Unix, use:

```
rmiregistry &
```

Now you are ready to start the server. Under Windows, use the command:

```
start java ProductServer
```

Under Unix, use the command:

```
java ProductServer &
```

If you run the server program as

```
java ProductServer
```

then the program will never exit normally. This seems strange—after all, the program just creates two objects and registers them. Actually, the `main` function does exit immediately after registration, as you would expect. But, when you create an object of a class that extends `UnicastRemoteObject`, a separate thread is started that keeps the program alive indefinitely. Thus, the program stays around in order to allow clients to connect to it.

TIP: The Windows version of the JDK contains a command, `javaw`, that starts the bytecode interpreter as a separate Windows process and keeps it running. Some sources recommend that you use `javaw`, not `start java`, to run a Java session in the background in Windows for RMI. Doing so is not a good idea, for two reasons. Windows has no tool to kill a `javaw` background process—it does not show up in the task list. It turns out that you need to kill and restart the bootstrap registry service when you change the stub of a registered class. To kill a process that you started with the `start` command, all you have to do is click on the window and press CTRL+C.

There is another important reason to use the `start` command. When you run a server process by using `javaw`, messages sent to the output or error streams are discarded. In particular, they *are not* displayed *anywhere*. If you want to see output or error messages, use `start` instead. Then, error messages at least show up on the console. And trust us, you will want to see these messages. There are lots of things that can go wrong when you experiment with RMI. The most common error is probably that you forget to run `rmic`. Then, the server complains about missing stubs. If you use `javaw`, you won't see that error message, and you'll scratch your head wondering why the client can't find the server objects.

Before writing the client program, let's verify that we succeeded in registering the remote objects. The `Naming` class has a method `list` that returns a list of all currently registered names. Example 5–4 shows a simple program that lists the names in the registry.

In our case, its output is

```
rmi:/toaster
rmi:/microwave
```

Example 5–4: ShowBindings.java

```
import java.rmi.*;
import java.rmi.server.*;

public class ShowBindings
{  public static void main(String[] args)
   {  try
      {  String[] bindings = Naming.list("");
         for (int i = 0; i < bindings.length; i++)
            System.out.println(bindings[i]);
      }
      catch(Exception e)
      {  System.out.println("Error: " + e);
      }
   }
}
```

The Client Side

Now, we can write the client program that asks each newly registered product object to print its description.

Client programs that use RMI should install a security manager to control the activities of the dynamically loaded stubs. The `RMISecurityManager` is such a security manager. You install it with the instruction

```
System.setSecurityManager(new RMISecurityManager());
```

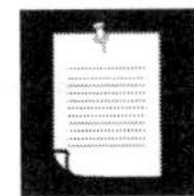

NOTE: If all classes (including stubs) are available locally, then you do not actually need a security manager. If you know all class files of your program at deployment time, you can deploy them all locally. However, it often happens that the server program evolves and new classes are added over time. Then you benefit from dynamic class loading. Any time you load code from another source, you need a security manager.

Applets already have a security manager which is able to control the stub classes. When using RMI from an applet, you do not install another security manager. However, for applications that are RMI clients, you should use the `RMISecurityManager`.

Example 5–5 shows the complete client program. The client simply obtains references to two `Product` objects in the RMI registry and invokes the `getDescription` method on both objects.

Example 5–5: ProductClient.java

```
import java.rmi.*;
import java.rmi.server.*;

public class ProductClient
{  public static void main(String[] args)
   {  System.setSecurityManager(new RMISecurityManager());
      String url = "rmi://localhost/";
         // change to "rmi://yourserver.com/"
         // when server runs on remote machine
         // yourserver.com
      try
      {  Product c1 = (Product)Naming.lookup(url + "toaster");
         Product c2 = (Product)Naming.lookup(url + "microwave");
         System.out.println(c1.getDescription());
         System.out.println(c2.getDescription());
      }
      catch(Exception e)
      {  System.out.println("Error " + e);
      }
      System.exit(0);
   }
}
```

Running the Client

By default, the `RMISecurityManager` restricts all code in the program from establishing network connections. But the program needs to make network connections

- to reach the RMI registry
- to contact the server objects

NOTE: Once the client program is deployed, it also needs permission to load its stub classes. We address this issue later when we discuss deployment.

To allow the client to connect to the RMI registry and the server object, you need to supply a *policy file*. We discuss policy files in greater detail in Chapter 9. For now, just use and modify the samples that we supply. Here is a policy file that allows an application to make any network connection to a port with port number

at least 1024. (The RMI port is 1099 by default, and the server objects also use ports ≥ 1024.)

```
grant
{  permission java.net.SocketPermission
      "*:1024-65535", "connect";
};
```

When you run the client program, you must specify the policy file.

```
java ProductClient -Djava.security.policy=client.policy
```

NOTE: In JDK 1.1, a policy file was not required for RMI clients.

If the RMI registry and server are still running, you can proceed to run the client. Or, if you want to start from scratch, kill the RMI registry and the server. Then follow these steps:

1. Compile the source files for the interface, implementation, client and server classes.
   `javac Product*.java`
2. Run `rmic` on the implementation class.
   `rmic -v1.2 ProductImpl`
3. Start the RMI registry:
   `start rmiregistry`
   or
   `rmiregistry &`
4. Start the server:
   `start java ProductServer`
   or
   `java ProductServer &`
5. Run the client:
   `java -Djava.security.policy=client.policy ProductClient`

The program simply prints

```
I am a Blackwell Toaster. Buy me!
I am a ZapXpress Microwave Oven. Buy me!
```

This output doesn't seem all that impressive, but consider what goes on behind the scenes when Java executes the call to the `getDescription` method. The client program has a reference to a stub object that it obtained from the `lookup` method. It calls the `getDescription` method, which sends a network message to a receiver object on the server side. The receiver object invokes the `getDescription` method on the `ProductImpl` object located on the server. That method computes a string. The receiver sends that string across the network. The stub receives it and returns it as the result. See Figure 5–5.

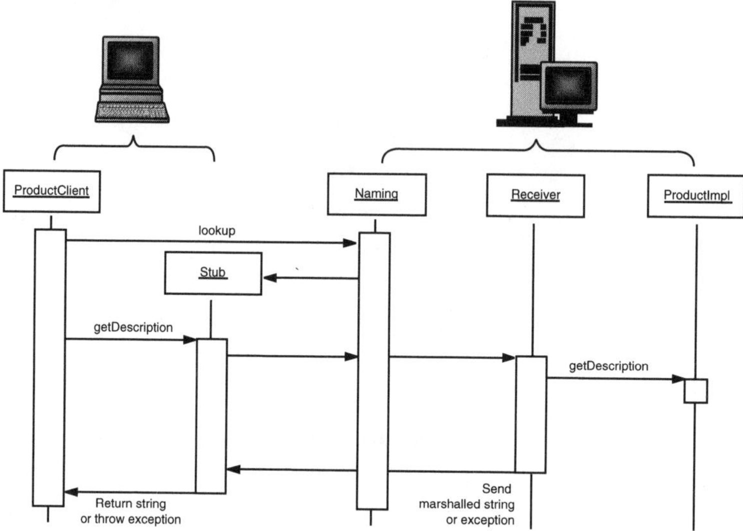

Figure 5–5: Calling the remote `getDescription` method

`java.rmi.server.Naming`

- `static Remote lookup(String url)`
  returns the remote object for the URL. Throws the `NotBound` exception if the name is not currently bound.
- `static void bind(String name, Remote obj)`
  binds `name` to the remote object `obj`. Throws an `AlreadyBoundException` if the object is already bound.
- `static void unbind(String name)`
  unbinds the name. Throws the `NotBound` exception if the name is not currently bound.
- `static void rebind(String name, Remote obj)`
  binds `name` to the remote object `obj`. Replaces any existing binding.
- `static String[] list(String url)`
  returns an array of strings of the URLs in the registry located at the given URL. The array contains a snapshot of the names present in the registry.

Preparing for Deployment

Deploying an application that uses RMI can be tricky because so many things can go wrong and because the error messages that you get when something does go wrong are so poor. We have found that it really pays off to stage the deployment locally. In this preparatory step, separate the class files into three subdirectories:

```
server
download
client
```

The `server` directory contains all files that are needed to *run the server.* You will later move these files to the machine running the server process. In our example, the `server` directory contains the following files:

```
server:
    ProductServer.class
    ProductImpl.class
    Product.class
    ProductImpl_Stub.class
```

CAUTION: Add the stub classes to the `server` directory. They are needed when the server registers the implementation object. Contrary to popular belief, the server will not locate them in the download directory, even if you set the codebase.

The `download` directory contains those class files that will be loaded into the client, *as well as the classes they depend on.* In our example, you must add the following classes to the download directory:

```
download:
    ProductImpl_Stub.class
    Product.class
```

If your program was written with JDK 1.1, then you also need to supply the skeleton classes (such as `ProductImpl_Skel.class`). You will later place these files on a web server.

CAUTION: In addition to the interface stubs, you must include the class files for the remote interfaces (such as `Product`) in the download directory. If you don't, then the server will mysteriously die when trying to register the server class.

Finally, the `client` directory contains the files that are needed to *start the client.* These are:

```
client:
    ProductClient.class
    Product.class
    client.policy
```

You will deploy these files on the client computer.

CAUTION: You must deploy the class files for the remote interfaces (such as `Product`) to the client. If you don't, then the client will not load. It does not download these classes.

Now you have all class files partitioned correctly, and you can test that they can all be loaded.

We assume that you can start a web server on your computer. Alternatively, you can get a lightweight server from `ftp://java.sun.com/pub/jdk1.1/rmi/class-server.zip`. That server is not a full-blown web server, but it is easier to install and has enough functionality to serve class files.

First, move the download directory into the web documents directory of the web server.

Next, edit the `client.policy` file. It must give the client these permissions:

- To connect to ports 1024 and above to reach the RMI registry and the server implementations
- To connect to the HTTP port (usually 80) to load the stub class files

Change the file to look like this:

```
grant
{  permission java.net.SocketPermission
      "*:1024-65535", "connect";
   permission java.net.SocketPermission
      "*:80", "connect";
};
```

Finally, you are ready to test your setup.

1. Start the web server.
2. Start a new shell. Make sure that the class path is not set to anything. Change to a directory that contains no class files. Then start the RMI registry.

CAUTION: If you just want to test out your program and have client, server, and stub class files in a single directory, then you can start the RMI registry in that directory. However, for deployment, make sure to start the registry in a shell with *no class path* and in a directory with *no class files*. Otherwise, the RMI registry may find spurious class files which will confuse it when trying to download stub classes from a different directory. (There is a reason for this behavior; see `http://java.sun.com/products/jdk/1.2/docs/guide/rmi/codebase.html`). RMI registry flakiness is a major source of grief for RMI deployment. The easiest way of protecting yourself is to make sure that the RMI registry cannot find any classes.

3. Start a new shell. Change to the `server` directory. Start the server, giving a URL to the download directory as the value of the `java.rmi.server.codebase` property:

```
start java
   -Djava.rmi.server.codebase=http://localhost/download/
   ProductServer
```

CAUTION: It is very important that you make sure that *the URL ends with a slash (/)*.

4. Change to the `client` directory. Start the client, giving the policy file as the value of the `java.security.policy` property:

```
java -Djava.security.policy=client.policy ProductClient
```

If both the server and the client started up without a hitch, then you are ready to go to the next step and deploy the classes on a separate client and server. If not, you need to do some more tweaking.

TIP: If you do not want to install a web server locally, you can use a file URL to test class loading. However, the setup is a bit trickier. Add the line

```
permission java.io.FilePermission
    "downloadDirectory", "read";
```

to your client policy file. Here, the download directory is the full path name to the download directory, enclosed in quotes, and ending in a minus sign (to denote all files in that directory and its subdirectories). In Windows file names, you have to double each backslash. For example,

```
permission java.io.FilePermission
   "c:\\home\\test\\download\\-", "read";
```

or (under Unix)

```
permission java.io.FilePermission
   "/home/test/download/-", "read";
```

Start the RMI registry, then the server with

```
start java
    -Djava.rmi.server.codebase=file:/c:\home\test\download/
    ProductServer
```

or

```
java -Djava.rmi.server.codebase=file://home/test/download/
    ProductServer &
```

(Remember to add a slash at the end of the URL.) Then start the client.

Deploying the Program

Now that you have tested the deployment of your program, you are ready to distribute it onto the actual clients and servers.

Move the classes in the `download` directory to the web server. Make sure to use that URL when starting the server. Move the classes in the `server` directory onto your server and start the RMI registry and the server.

Your server setup is now finalized. But you need to make two changes in the client. First, edit the policy file and replace * with your server name:

```
grant
{  permission java.net.SocketPermission
      "yourserver.com:1024-65535", "connect";
   permission java.net.SocketPermission
      "yourserver.com:80", "connect";
};
```

Finally, replace `localhost` in the RMI URL of the client program with the actual server.

```
String url = "rmi://yourserver.com/";
Product c1 = (Product)Naming.lookup(url + "toaster");
. . .
```

Then, recompile the client and try it. If everything works, then congratulations are in order. If not, you may find the following sidebar helpful. It contains a checklist of a number of problems that can commonly arise when trying to get RMI to work.

TIP: In practice, you would not want to hardcode the RMI URLs into your program. Instead, you can store them in a property file. We will use that technique in Example 5–13.

RMI Deployment Checklist

Deploying RMI is tough because it either works, or it fails with a very cryptic error message. Judging from the traffic on the RMI discussion list at `http://archives.java.sun.com/archives/rmi-users.html`, many programmers initially run into grief. If you do too, you may find it helpful to check out the following issues. We managed to get every one of them wrong at least once during testing.

- Did you put the stub class files into the server directory?
- Did you put the interface class files into the download and client directory?
- When starting `rmiregistry`, was the `CLASSPATH` unset? Was the current directory free from class files?
- Do you use a policy file when starting the client? Does the policy file contain the correct server names (or * to connect to any host)?
- If you use a `file:` URL for testing, do you specify the correct file name in the policy file? Does it end in a `/-` or `\\-`? Did you remember to use `\\` for Windows file names?
- Does your codebase URL end in a slash?

Finally, note that the RMI registry remembers all class files that it found. If you keep removing various class files to test which files are really necessary, make sure to restart `rmiregistry` each time.

Parameter Passing in Remote Methods

You often want to pass parameters to remote objects. This section explains some of the techniques for doing so—along with some of the pitfalls.

Passing Nonremote Objects

When a remote object is passed from the server to the client, the client receives a stub. Using the stub, it can manipulate the server object by invoking remote methods. The object, however, stays on the server. It is also possible to pass and return

any objects via a remote method call, not just those that implement the `Remote` interface. For example, the `getDescription` method of the preceding section returned a `String` object. That string was created on the server and had to be transported to the client. Since `String` does not implement the `Remote` interface, the client cannot return a string stub object. Instead, the client gets a *copy* of the string. Then, after the call, the client has its own `String` object to work with. This means that there is no need for any further connection to any object on the server to deal with that string.

Whenever an object that is not a remote object needs to be transported from one Java virtual machine to another, the Java virtual machine makes a copy and sends that copy across the network connection. This technique is very different from parameter passing in a local method. When you pass objects into a local method or return them as method results, only object *references* are passed. However, object references are memory addresses of objects in the local Java virtual machine. This information is meaningless to a different Java virtual machine.

It is not difficult to imagine how a copy of a string can be transported across a network. The RMI mechanism can also make copies of more complex objects, provided they are *serializable.* RMI uses the serialization mechanism described in Chapter 12 of Volume 1 to send objects across a network connection. This means that only the information in any classes that implement the `Serializable` interface can be copied. The following program shows the copying of parameters and return values in action. This program is a simple application that lets a user shop for a gift. On the client, the user runs a program that gathers information about the gift recipient, in this case, age, sex, and hobbies (see Figure 5–6).

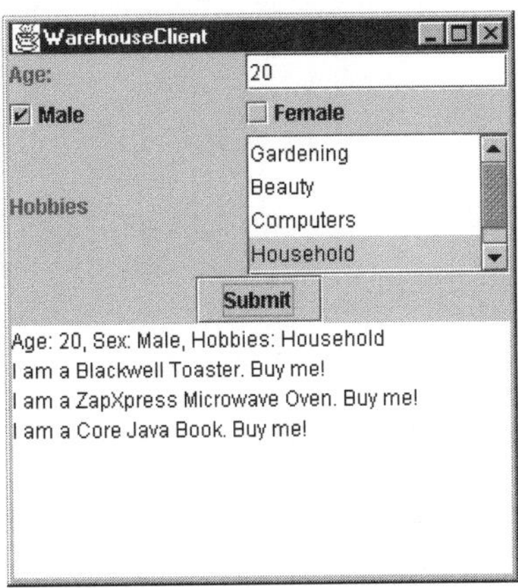

Figure 5–6: Obtaining product suggestions from the server

An object of type `Customer` is then sent to the server. Since `Customer` is not a remote object, a copy of the object is made on the server. The server program sends back a vector of products. The vector contains those products that match the customer profile, and it always contains that one item that will delight anyone, namely, a copy of the book *Core Java*. Again, `Vector` is not a remote class, so the vector is copied from the server back to its client. As described in Chapter 12 of Volume 1, the serialization mechanism makes copies of all objects that are referenced inside a copied object. In our case, it makes a copy of all vector entries as well. We added an extra complexity: the entries are actually remote `Product` objects. Thus, the recipient gets a copy of the vector, filled with stub objects to the products on the server (see Figure 5–7).

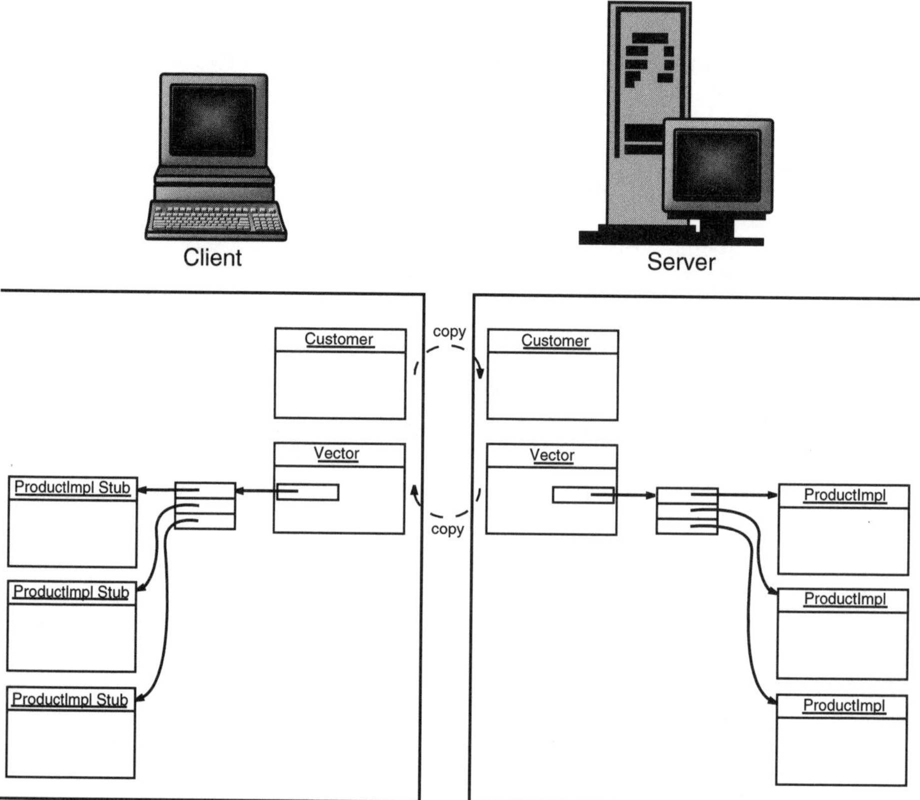

Figure 5–7: Copying local parameter and result objects

To summarize, remote objects are passed across the network as stubs. Nonremote objects are copied. All of this is automatic and requires no programmer intervention.

Whenever code calls a remote method, the stub makes a package that contains copies of all parameter values and sends it to the server, using the object serialization

mechanism to marshal the parameters. The server unmarshals them. Naturally, the process can be quite slow—especially when the parameter objects are large.

Let's look at the complete program. First, we have the interfaces for the product and warehouse services, as shown in Example 5–6 and Example 5–7.

Example 5–6: Product.java

```
import java.rmi.*;
import java.awt.*;

public interface Product
   extends Remote
{  String getDescription()
      throws RemoteException;

   static final int MALE = 1;
   static final int FEMALE = 2;
   static final int BOTH = MALE + FEMALE;
}
```

Example 5–7: Warehouse.java

```
import java.rmi.*;
import java.util.*;

public interface Warehouse
   extends Remote
{  public Vector find(Customer c)
      throws RemoteException;
}
```

Example 5–8 shows the implementation for the product service. Products store a description, an age range, the gender targeted (male, female, or both), and the matching hobby. Note that this class implements the `getDescription` method advertised in the `Product` interface, and it also implements another method, `match`, which is not a part of that interface. The `match` method is an example of a *local method*, a method that can be called only from the local program, not remotely. Since the `match` method is local, it need not be prepared to throw a `RemoteException`.

Example 5–9 contains the code for the `Customer` class. Note once again that `Customer` is not a remote class—none of its methods can be executed remotely. However, the class is serializable. Therefore, objects of this class can be transported from one virtual machine to another.

Example 5–11 shows the implementation for the warehouse service. Like the `ProductImpl` class, the `WarehouseImpl` class has local and remote methods. The `add` method is local; it is used by the server to add products to the warehouse. The `find` method is remote; it is used to find items in the warehouse.

To illustrate that the `Customer` object is actually copied, the `find` method of the `WarehouseImpl` class clears the customer object it receives. When the remote method returns, the `WarehouseClient` displays the customer object that it sent to the server. As you will see, that object has not changed. The server cleared only *its copy*. In this case, the `clear` operation serves no useful purpose except to demonstrate that local objects are copied when they are passed as parameters.

In general, the methods of server classes such as `ProductImpl` and `WarehouseImpl` should be synchronized. Then, it is possible for multiple client stubs to make simultaneous calls to a server object, even if some of the methods change the state of the server. (See Chapter 2 for more details on synchronized methods.) In Example 5–11, we synchronize the methods of the `WarehouseImpl` class because it is conceivable that the local `add` and the remote `find` methods are called simultaneously. We don't synchronize the methods of the `ProductImpl` class because the product server objects don't change their state. Example 5–12 shows the server program that creates a warehouse object and registers it with the bootstrap registry service.

NOTE: Remember that you must start the registry and the server program and keep both running before you start the client.

Example 5–13 shows the code for the client. When the user clicks on the "Submit" button, a new customer object is generated and passed to the remote `find` method. Then, the customer record is displayed in the text area (to prove that the `clear` call in the server did not affect it). Finally, the product descriptions of the returned products in the vector are added to the text area. Note that each `getDescription` call is again a remote method invocation.

TIP: If you start the server with

```
java -Djava.rmi.server.logCalls=true WarehouseServer
```

then the server logs all remote method calls on its console. Try it—you'll get a good impression of the RMI traffic.

Example 5–8: ProductImpl.java

```
import java.rmi.*;
import java.rmi.server.*;
import java.awt.*;

public class ProductImpl
   extends UnicastRemoteObject
   implements Product
{  public ProductImpl(String n, int s, int age1, int age2,
```

```
      String h, String i)
      throws RemoteException
   {  name = n;
      ageLow = age1;
      ageHigh = age2;
      sex = s;
      hobby = h;
      imageFile = i;
   }

   public boolean match(Customer c) // local method
   {  if (c.getAge() < ageLow || c.getAge() > ageHigh)
      return false;
      if (!c.hasHobby(hobby)) return false;
      if ((sex & c.getSex()) == 0) return false;
      return true;
   }

   public String getDescription() throws RemoteException
   {  return "I am a " + name + ". Buy me!";
   }

   public String getImageFile() throws RemoteException
   {  return imageFile;
   }

   private String name;
   private int ageLow;
   private int ageHigh;
   private int sex;
   private String hobby;
   private String imageFile;
}
```

Example 5–9: Customer.java

```
import java.io.*;

public class Customer implements Serializable
{  public Customer(int theAge, int theSex, String[] theHobbies)
   {  age = theAge;
      sex = theSex;
      hobbies = theHobbies;
   }

   public int getAge() { return age; }

   public int getSex() { return sex; }

   public boolean hasHobby(String aHobby)
   {  if (aHobby == "") return true;
      for (int i = 0; i < hobbies.length; i++)
```

```
         if (hobbies[i].equals(aHobby)) return true;

      return false;
   }

   public void reset()
   {  age = 0;
      sex = 0;
      hobbies = null;
   }

   public String toString()
   {  String result = "Age: " + age + ", Sex: ";
      if (sex == Product.MALE) result += "Male";
      else if (sex == Product.FEMALE) result += "Female";
      else result += "Male or Female";
      result += ", Hobbies:";
      for (int i = 0; i < hobbies.length; i++)
         result += " " + hobbies[i];
      return result;
   }

   private int age;
   private int sex;
   private String[] hobbies;
}
```

Example 5–10: Warehouse.java

```
import java.rmi.*;
import java.util.*;

public interface Warehouse
   extends Remote
{  public Vector find(Customer c)
      throws RemoteException;
}
```

Example 5–11: WarehouseImpl.java

```
import java.rmi.*;
import java.util.*;
import java.rmi.server.*;


public class WarehouseImpl
   extends UnicastRemoteObject
   implements Warehouse
{  public WarehouseImpl()
      throws RemoteException
   {  products = new Vector();
```

```
   }

   public synchronized void add(ProductImpl p)
   // local method
   {  products.add(p);
   }

   public synchronized Vector find(Customer c)
      throws RemoteException
   {  Vector result = new Vector();
      for (int i = 0; i < products.size(); i++)
      {  ProductImpl p = (ProductImpl)products.get(i);
         if (p.match(c)) result.add(p);
      }
      result.add(new ProductImpl("Core Java Book",
         0, 200, Product.BOTH, "", "corejava.jpg"));
      c.reset();
      return result;
   }

   private Vector products;
}
```

Example 5–12: WarehouseServer.java

```
import java.rmi.*;
import java.rmi.server.*;

public class WarehouseServer
{  public static void main(String[] args)
   {  try
      {  System.out.println
            ("Constructing server implementations...");

         WarehouseImpl w = new WarehouseImpl();
         fillWarehouse(w);

         System.out.println
            ("Binding server implementations to registry...");

         Naming.rebind("central_warehouse", w);

         System.out.println
            ("Waiting for invocations from clients...");
      }
      catch(Exception e)
      {  System.out.println("Error: " + e);
      }
   }

   public static void fillWarehouse(WarehouseImpl w)
```

```
         throws RemoteException
      {  w.add(new ProductImpl("Blackwell Toaster",
            Product.BOTH, 18, 200, "Household"));
         w.add(new ProductImpl("ZapXpress Microwave Oven",
            Product.BOTH, 18, 200, "Household"));
         w.add(new ProductImpl("Jimbo After Shave",
            Product.MALE, 18, 200, "Beauty"));
         w.add(new ProductImpl("Handy Hand Grenade",
            Product.MALE, 20, 60, "Gardening"));
         w.add(new ProductImpl("DirtDigger Steam Shovel",
            Product.MALE, 20, 60, "Gardening"));
         w.add(new ProductImpl("U238 Weed Killer",
            Product.BOTH, 20, 200, "Gardening"));
         w.add(new ProductImpl("Van Hope Cosmetic Set",
            Product.FEMALE, 15, 45, "Beauty"));
         w.add(new ProductImpl("Persistent Java Fragrance",
            Product.FEMALE, 15, 45, "Beauty"));
         w.add(new ProductImpl("Rabid Rodent Computer Mouse",
            Product.BOTH, 6, 40, "Computers"));
         w.add(new ProductImpl
            ("Learn Bad Java Habits in 21 Days Book",
            Product.BOTH, 20, 200, "Computers"));
         w.add(new ProductImpl("My first Espresso Maker",
            Product.FEMALE, 6, 10, "Household"));
         w.add(new ProductImpl("JavaJungle Eau de Cologne",
            Product.FEMALE, 20, 200, "Beauty"));
         w.add(new ProductImpl("Fast/Wide SCSI Coffee Maker",
            Product.MALE, 20, 50, "Computers"));
         w.add(new ProductImpl("ClueLess Network Computer",
            Product.BOTH,6, 200, "Computers"));
      }
}
```

Example 5–13: WarehouseClient.java

```
import java.awt.*;
import java.awt.event.*;
import java.io.*;
import java.rmi.*;
import java.rmi.server.*;
import java.util.*;
import javax.swing.*;

public class WarehouseClient
{  public static void main(String[] args)
   {  JFrame frame = new WarehouseClientFrame();
      frame.show();
   }
}

class WarehouseClientFrame extends JFrame
```

```
   implements ActionListener
{  public WarehouseClientFrame()
   {  initUI();

      System.setSecurityManager(new RMISecurityManager());
      try
      {  Properties props = new Properties();
         String fileName = "WarehouseClient.properties";
         FileInputStream in = new FileInputStream(fileName);
         props.load(in);
         String url = props.getProperty("warehouse.url");
         if (url == null)
            url = "rmi://localhost/central_warehouse";

         centralWarehouse = (Warehouse)Naming.lookup(url);
      }
      catch(Exception e)
      {  System.out.println("Error: Can't connect to warehouse. " + e);
      }
   }

   private void callWarehouse(Customer c)
   {  try
      {  Vector recommendations = centralWarehouse.find(c);
         result.setText(c + "\n");
         for (int i = 0; i < recommendations.size(); i++)
         {  Product p = (Product)recommendations.get(i);
            String t = p.getDescription() + "\n";
            result.append(t);
         }
      }
      catch(Exception e)
      {  result.setText("Error: " + e);
      }
   }


   public void actionPerformed(ActionEvent evt)
   {  Object[] hobbyObjects = hobbies.getSelectedValues();
      String[] hobbyStrings = new String[hobbyObjects.length];
      System.arraycopy(hobbyObjects, 0, hobbyStrings, 0,
         hobbyObjects.length);
      Customer c = new Customer(Integer.parseInt(age.getText()),
         (male.isSelected() ? Product.MALE : 0)
            + (female.isSelected() ? Product.FEMALE : 0),
         hobbyStrings);
      callWarehouse(c);
   }

   private void initUI()
   {  setTitle("WarehouseClient");
```

```
      setSize(300, 300);
      addWindowListener(new WindowAdapter()
         {  public void windowClosing(WindowEvent e)
            {  System.exit(0);
            }
         } );

      getContentPane().setLayout(new GridBagLayout());

      GridBagConstraints gbc = new GridBagConstraints();
      gbc.fill = GridBagConstraints.HORIZONTAL;
      gbc.weightx = 100;
      gbc.weighty = 0;

      add(new JLabel("Age:"), gbc, 0, 0, 1, 1);
      age = new JTextField(4);
      age.setText("20");
      add(age, gbc, 1, 0, 1, 1);

      male = new JCheckBox("Male", true);
      female = new JCheckBox("Female", true);
      add(male, gbc, 0, 1, 1, 1);
      add(female, gbc, 1, 1, 1, 1);

      gbc.weighty = 100;
      add(new JLabel("Hobbies"), gbc, 0, 2, 1, 1);
      String[] choices = { "Gardening", "Beauty",
         "Computers", "Household", "Sports" };
      gbc.fill = GridBagConstraints.BOTH;
      hobbies = new JList(choices);
      add(new JScrollPane(hobbies), gbc, 1, 2, 1, 1);

      gbc.weighty = 0;
      gbc.fill = GridBagConstraints.NONE;
      JButton submitButton = new JButton("Submit");
      add(submitButton, gbc, 0, 3, 2, 1);
      submitButton.addActionListener(this);

      gbc.weighty = 100;
      gbc.fill = GridBagConstraints.BOTH;
      result = new JTextArea(4, 40);
      result.setEditable(false);
      add(result, gbc, 0, 4, 2, 1);
   }

   private void add(Component c, GridBagConstraints gbc,
      int x, int y, int w, int h)
   {  gbc.gridx = x;
      gbc.gridy = y;
```

```
        gbc.gridwidth = w;
        gbc.gridheight = h;
        getContentPane().add(c, gbc);
    }

    private Warehouse centralWarehouse;
    private JTextField age;
    private JCheckBox male;
    private JCheckBox female;
    private JList hobbies;
    private JTextArea result;
}
```

Passing Remote Objects

Passing remote objects from the server to the client is simple. The client receives a stub object, then saves it in an object variable whose type is the same as the remote interface. The client can now access the actual object on the server through the variable. The client can copy this variable in its own local machine—all those copies are simply references to the same stub. It is important to note that only the *remote interfaces* can be accessed through the stub. A remote interface is any interface extending `Remote`. All local methods are inaccessible through the stub. (A local method is any method that is not defined in a remote interface.) Local methods can run only on the virtual machine containing the actual object.

Next, stubs are generated only from classes that implement a remote interface, and only the methods specified in the interfaces are provided in the stub classes. If a subclass doesn't implement a remote interface but a superclass does and an object of the subclass is passed to a remote method, only the superclass methods are accessible. To understand this better, consider the following example. We derive a class `BookImpl` from `ProductImpl`.

```
class BookImpl extends ProductImpl
{  public BookImpl(String title, String theISBN,
      int sex, int age1, int age2, String hobby)
   {  super(title + " Book", sex, age1, age2, hobby);
      ISBN = theISBN;
   }
   public String getStockCode() { return ISBN; }
   private String ISBN;
}
```

Now, suppose we pass a book object to a remote method, either as a parameter or as a return value. The recipient obtains a stub object. But that stub is not a book stub. Instead, it is a stub to the superclass `ProductImpl` since only that class implements a remote interface (see Figure 5–8). Thus, in this case, the `getStockCode` method isn't available remotely.

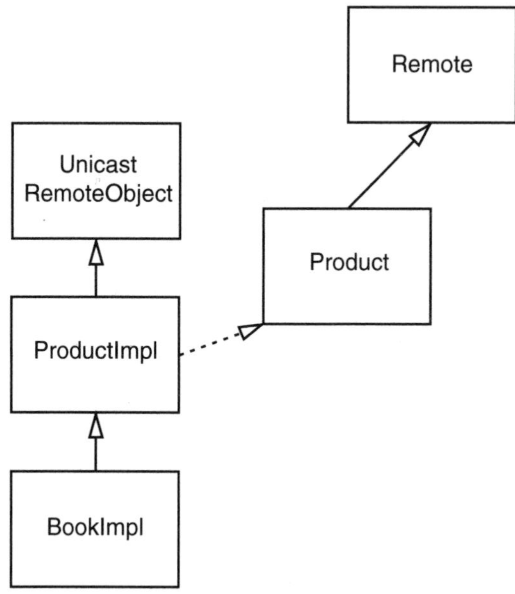

Figure 5–8: Only the `ProductImpl` methods are remote

A remote class can implement multiple interfaces. For example, the `BookImpl` class can implement a second interface in addition to `Product`. Here, we define a remote interface `StockUnit` and have the `BookImpl` class implement it.

```
interface StockUnit extends Remote
{  public String getStockCode() throws RemoteException;
}

class BookImpl extends ProductImpl implements StockUnit
{  public BookImpl(String title, String theISBN,
      int sex, int age1, int age2, String hobby)
      throws RemoteException
   {  super(title + " Book", sex, age1, age2, hobby);
      ISBN = theISBN;
   }
   public String getStockCode() throws RemoteException
   { return ISBN; }

   private String ISBN;
}
```

Figure 5–9 shows the inheritance diagram.

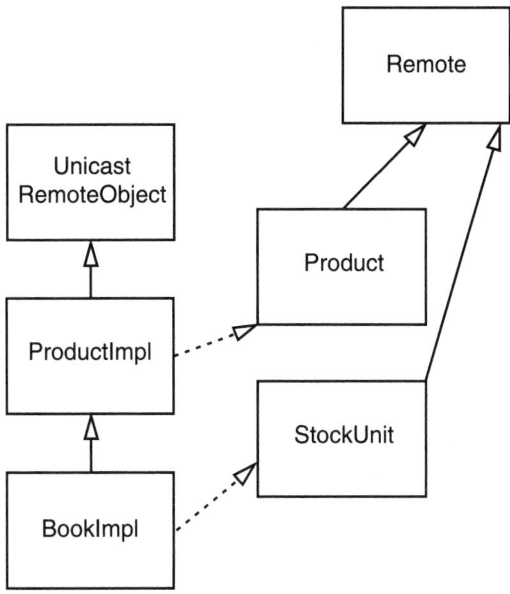

Figure 5–9: `BookImpl` has additional remote methods

Now, when a book object is passed to a remote method, the recipient obtains a stub that has access to the remote methods in both the `Product` and the `StockUnit` class. In fact, you can use the `instanceof` operator to find out whether a particular remote object implements an interface. Here is a typical situation where you will use this feature. Suppose you receive a remote object through a variable of type `Product`.

```
Vector result = centralWarehouse.find(c);
for (int i = 0; i < result.size(); i++)
{  Product p = (Product)result.elementAt(i);
   . . .
}
```

Now, the remote object may or may not be a book. We'd like to use `instanceof` to find out whether it is or not. But we can't test

```
if (p instanceof BookImpl) // wrong
{  BookImpl b = (BookImpl)p;
   . . .
}
```

The object `p` refers to a stub object, and `BookImpl` is the class of the server object. We could cast the stub object to a `BookImpl_Stub`,

```
if (p instanceof BookImpl_Stub)
{  BookImpl_Stub b = (BookImpl_Stub)p; // not useful
   . . .
}
```

but that would not do us much good. The stubs are generated mechanically by the `rmic` program for internal use by the RMI mechanism, and clients should not have to think about them. Instead, we cast to the second interface:

```
if (p instanceof StockUnit)
{  StockUnit s = (StockUnit)p;
   String c = s.getStockCode();
   . . .
}
```

This code tests whether the stub object to which `p` refers implements the `StockUnit` interface. If so, it calls the `getStockCode` remote method of that interface.

To summarize:

- If an object belonging to a class that implements a remote interface is passed to a remote method, the remote method receives a stub object.
- You can cast that stub object to any of the remote interfaces that the implementation class implements.
- You can call all remote methods defined in those interfaces, but you cannot call any local methods through the stub.

Using Remote Objects in Sets

As we saw in Chapter 2, objects inserted in sets must override the `equals` method. In the case of a hash set or hash table, the `hashCode` method must be defined as well. However, there is a problem when trying to compare remote objects. To find out if two remote objects have the same contents, the call to `equals` would need to contact the servers containing the objects and compare their contents. And that call could fail. But the `equals` method in the class `Object` is not declared to throw a `RemoteException`, whereas all methods in a remote interface must throw that exception. Since a subclass method cannot throw more exceptions than the superclass method it replaces, you cannot define an `equals` method in a remote interface. The same holds for `hashCode`.

Instead, you must rely on the redefinitions of the `equals` and `hashCode` methods in the `RemoteObject` class that is the superclass for all stub and server objects. These methods do not look at the object contents, just at the location of the server objects. The `equals` method of the `RemoteObject` class deems two stubs equal if they refer to the same server object. Two stubs that refer to different server objects are never equal, even if those objects have identical contents. Similarly, the hash code is computed only from the object identifier. Stubs that refer to different server objects will likely have different hash codes, even if the server objects have identical contents.

This limitation refers only to stubs. You can redefine `equals` or `hashCode` for the server object classes. Those methods are called when you are inserting server

objects in a collection on the server, but they are never called when you are comparing or hashing stubs. To clarify the difference between client and server behavior, look at the inheritance diagram in Figure 5–10.

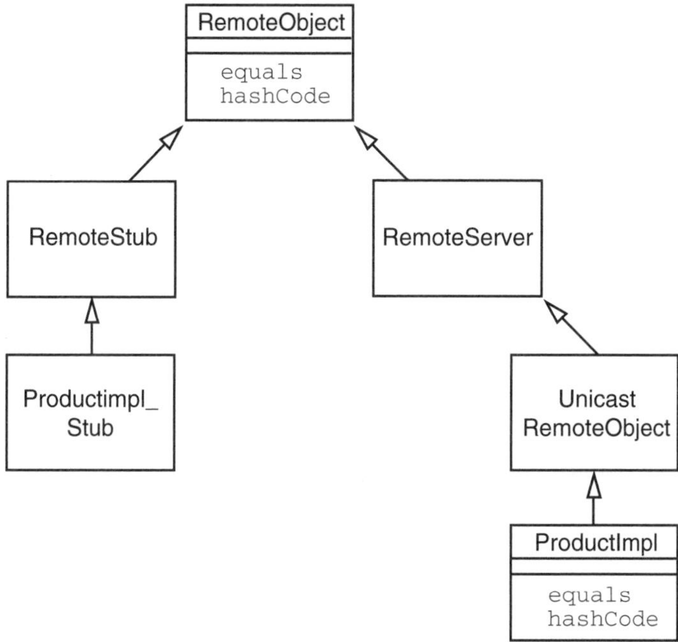

Figure 5–10: Inheritance of `equals` and `hashCode` methods

The `RemoteObject` class is the base for *both* stub and server classes. On the stub side, you cannot override the `equals` and `hashCode` methods because the stubs are mechanically generated. On the server side, you can override the methods for the implementation classes, but they are only used locally on the server. If you do override these methods, implementation and stub objects are no longer considered identical.

To summarize: You can use stub objects in hash tables, but you must remember that equality testing and hashing do not take the contents of the remote objects into account.

Cloning Remote Objects

Stubs do not have a `clone` method, so you cannot clone a remote object by invoking `clone` on the stub. The reason is again somewhat technical. If `clone` were to make a remote call to tell the server to clone the implementation object, then the `clone` method would need to throw a `RemoteException`. But the `clone` method in the `Object` superclass promised never to throw any exception except `CloneNotSupportedException`. That is the same limitation that you encountered in the previous section, when you saw that `equals` and `hashCode` don't look up the remote object value at all but just compare stub references. But it makes no sense for `clone` to make another clone of a stub—if you wanted to have another reference to the remote object, you could just copy the stub variable. Therefore, `clone` is simply not defined for stubs.

If you want to clone a remote object, you must write another method, say, `remoteClone`. Place it into the interface that defines the remote object services. Of course, that method may throw a `RemoteException`. In the implementation class, simply define `remoteClone` to call `clone` and return the cloned implementation object.

```
interface Product extends Remote
{  public Object remoteClone()
      throws RemoteException, CloneNotSupportedException;
   . . .
}

class ProductImpl extends UnicastRemoteObject
   implements Product
{  public Object remoteClone()
      throws CloneNotSupportedException
   { return clone(); }
   . . .
}
```

Inappropriate Remote Parameters

Suppose we enhance our shopping application by having the application show a picture of each gift. Can we simply add the remote method

```
void paint(Graphics g) throws RemoteException
```

to the `Product` interface? Unfortunately, this code cannot work, and it is important to understand why. The problem is that the `Graphics` class does not implement remote interfaces. Therefore, a copy of an object of type `Graphics` would need to be passed to the remote object, and you can't do this. Why? Well, `Graphics` is an abstract class, and `Graphics` objects are returned via a call to the `getGraphics` method of the `Component` class. This call, in turn, can happen only when you have some subclass that implements a graphics context on a particular platform. Those objects, in turn, need to interact with the native graphics code, and to do so, they must store pointers to the memory blocks that are needed by the native graphics methods. The Java programming language, of course, has no pointers, so this information is stored as integers in the graphics object and is only cast back to pointers in the native peer methods. Now, first of all, the target machine may be a different platform. For example, if the client runs Windows and the server runs X11, then the server does not

have the native methods available to render Windows graphics. But even if the server and the client have the same graphics system, the pointer values would not be valid on the server. Therefore, it makes no sense to copy a graphics object. For that reason, the `Graphics` class is not serializable and so cannot be sent via RMI.

Instead, if the server wants to send an image to the client, it has to come up with some other mechanism for transporting the data across the network. As it turns out, this data transport is actually difficult to do for images. The `Image` class is just as device dependent as the `Graphics` class. We could send the image data as a sequence of bytes in JPEG format, but there is no method in the AWT package to turn a block of JPEG data into an image. (Currently, this can be done only by using unpublished classes in the `sun.awt.image` package.) Another alternative is to send an array of integers representing the pixels. In the next section, we show how to solve this problem in a more mundane way: by sending a URL to the client and using a method of the `Applet` class that can read an image from a URL.

Using RMI with Applets

There are a number of special concerns when running RMI with applets. Applets have their own security manager since they run inside a browser. Thus, we do not use the `RMISecurityManager` on the client side.

We must take care where to place the stub and server files. Consider a browser that opens a web page with an `APPLET` tag. The browser loads the class file referenced in that tag and all other class files as they are needed during execution. The class files are loaded from the same host that contains the web page. Because of applet security restrictions, the applet can make network connections only to its originating host. Therefore, the server objects must reside on the same host as the web page. That is, the same server must store

- Web pages
- Applet code
- Stub classes
- Server objects
- The RMI registry

Here is a sample applet that further extends our shopping program. Just like the preceding application, the applet gets the customer information and then selects matching products. However, this applet sends images of the recommended items. As we mentioned previously, it is not easy to send an image from the server to the client because images are stored in a format that depends on the local graphics system. Instead, the server simply sends the client a string with the

image file name, and we use the getImage method of the Applet class to obtain the image (see Figure 5–11).

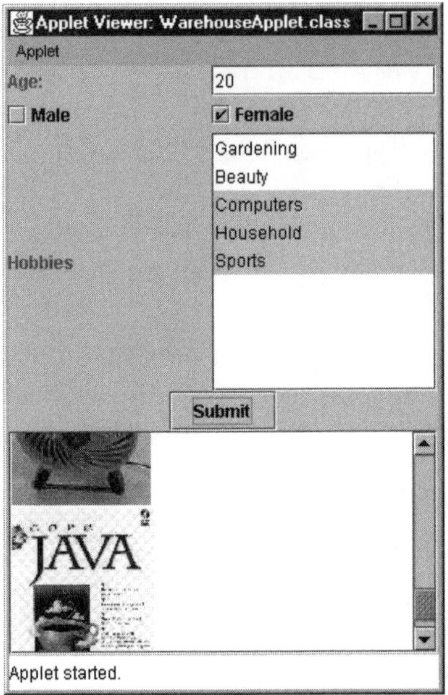

Figure 5–11: The warehouse applet

Here is how you must distribute the code for this kind of situation:

- java.rmi.registry.RegistryImpl—Anywhere on the host; the registry must be running before the applet starts
- WarehouseServer—Anywhere on the host; must be running before the applet starts
- WarehouseImpl—Can be anywhere on the host as long as WarehouseServer can find it
- WarehouseApplet—Directory referenced in APPLET tag
- Stubs—Must be in the same directory as WarehouseApplet

The applet looks for the RMI registry on the same host that contains the applet. To find out its host, it uses the getCodeBase and getHost methods:

```
String url = getCodeBase().getHost();
url = "rmi://" + url;
centralWarehouse
   = (Warehouse)Naming.lookup(url + "/central_warehouse");
```

Example 5–14 shows the code for the applet. Note that the applet does not install a security manager. Example 5–15 shows the code for the server.

Example 5–14: WarehouseApplet.java

```
import java.awt.*;
import java.awt.event.*;
import java.applet.*;
import java.rmi.*;
import java.rmi.server.*;
import java.util.*;
import javax.swing.*;

public class WarehouseApplet extends JApplet
   implements ActionListener
{  public void init()
   {  initUI();
      String url = getCodeBase().getHost();
      url = "rmi://" + url;
      try
      {  centralWarehouse = (Warehouse)Naming.lookup(url
            + "/central_warehouse");
      }
      catch(Exception e)
      {  showStatus("Error: Can't connect to warehouse. " + e);
      }
   }

   private void callWarehouse(Customer c)
   {  try
      {  products = centralWarehouse.find(c);
         descriptionListModel.clear();
         for (int i = 0; i < products.size(); i++)
         {  Product p = (Product)products.get(i);
            Image productImage
               = getImage(getCodeBase(), p.getImageFile());
            Icon productIcon = new ImageIcon(productImage);
            descriptionListModel.addElement(productIcon);
         }
      }
      catch(Exception e)
      {  showStatus("Error: " + e);
      }
   }

   private void initUI()
   {  getContentPane().setLayout(new GridBagLayout());

      GridBagConstraints gbc = new GridBagConstraints();
      gbc.fill = GridBagConstraints.HORIZONTAL;
      gbc.weightx = 100;
      gbc.weighty = 0;

      add(new JLabel("Age:"), gbc, 0, 0, 1, 1);
```

```
      age = new JTextField(4);
      age.setText("20");
      add(age, gbc, 1, 0, 1, 1);

      male = new JCheckBox("Male", true);
      female = new JCheckBox("Female", true);
      add(male, gbc, 0, 1, 1, 1);
      add(female, gbc, 1, 1, 1, 1);

      gbc.weighty = 100;
      add(new JLabel("Hobbies"), gbc, 0, 2, 1, 1);
      String[] choices = { "Gardening", "Beauty",
         "Computers", "Household", "Sports" };
      gbc.fill = GridBagConstraints.BOTH;
      hobbies = new JList(choices);
      add(new JScrollPane(hobbies), gbc, 1, 2, 1, 1);

      gbc.weighty = 0;
      gbc.fill = GridBagConstraints.NONE;
      submitButton = new JButton("Submit");
      add(submitButton, gbc, 0, 3, 2, 1);
      submitButton.addActionListener(this);


      gbc.weighty = 100;
      gbc.fill = GridBagConstraints.BOTH;
      descriptionListModel = new DefaultListModel();
      descriptions = new JList(descriptionListModel);
      add(new JScrollPane(descriptions), gbc, 0, 4, 2, 1);
   }

   private void add(Component c, GridBagConstraints gbc,
      int x, int y, int w, int h)
   {  gbc.gridx = x;
      gbc.gridy = y;
      gbc.gridwidth = w;
      gbc.gridheight = h;
      getContentPane().add(c, gbc);
   }

   public void actionPerformed(ActionEvent event)
   {  Object[] hobbyObjects = hobbies.getSelectedValues();
      String[] hobbyStrings = new String[hobbyObjects.length];
      System.arraycopy(hobbyObjects, 0, hobbyStrings, 0,
         hobbyObjects.length);
      Customer c = new Customer(Integer.parseInt(age.getText()),
         (male.isSelected() ? Product.MALE : 0)
         + (female.isSelected() ? Product.FEMALE : 0),
         hobbyStrings);
      callWarehouse(c);
```

```
   }

   private Warehouse centralWarehouse;
   private JTextField age;
   private JCheckBox male;
   private JCheckBox female;
   private JList hobbies;
   private JButton submitButton;
   private JList descriptions;
   private DefaultListModel descriptionListModel;
   private Vector products;
}
```

Example 5–15: WarehouseServer.java

```
import java.rmi.*;
import java.rmi.server.*;

public class WarehouseServer
{  public static void main(String args[])
   {  try
      {  System.out.println
            ("Constructing server implementations...");

         WarehouseImpl w = new WarehouseImpl();
         fillWarehouse(w);

         System.out.println
            ("Binding server implementations to registry...");

         Naming.rebind("central_warehouse", w);

         System.out.println
            ("Waiting for invocations from clients...");
      }
      catch(Exception e)
      {  System.out.println("Error: " + e);
      }
   }

   public static void fillWarehouse(WarehouseImpl w)
      throws RemoteException
   {  w.add(new ProductImpl("Blackwell Toaster",
         Product.BOTH, 18, 200, "Household", "toaster.jpg"));
      w.add(new ProductImpl("Jimbo After Shave",
         Product.MALE, 18, 200, "Beauty", "shave.jpg"));
      w.add(new ProductImpl("U238 Weed Killer",
         Product.BOTH, 20, 200, "Gardening", "weed.jpg"));
      w.add(new ProductImpl("Rabid Rodent Computer Mouse",
         Product.BOTH, 6, 40, "Computers", "rodent.jpg"));
      w.add(new ProductImpl
```

```
            ("Learn Bad Java Habits in 21 Days Book",
            Product.BOTH, 20, 200, "Computers", "book.jpg"));
         w.add(new ProductImpl("JavaJungle Eau de Cologne",
            Product.FEMALE, 20, 200, "Beauty", "cologne.jpg"));
         w.add(new ProductImpl("Fast/Wide SCSI Coffee Maker",
            Product.MALE, 20, 50, "Computers", "coffee.jpg"));
         w.add(new ProductImpl("ClueLess Network Computer",
            Product.BOTH, 6, 200, "Computers", "computer.jpg"));
         w.add(new ProductImpl("Digging Dinosaur",
            Product.BOTH, 6, 200, "Gardening", "dino.jpg"));
         w.add(new ProductImpl("Fantastic Fan",
            Product.BOTH, 6, 200, "Household", "fan.jpg"));
         w.add(new ProductImpl("Japanese Cat",
            Product.BOTH, 6, 200, "Gardening", "cat.jpg"));
         w.add(new ProductImpl("Ms. Frizzle Curling Iron",
            Product.FEMALE, 6, 200, "Beauty", "curl.jpg"));
   }
}
```

Java IDL and CORBA

Unlike RMI, CORBA lets you make calls between Java objects and objects written in other languages. CORBA depends on having an ORB (Object Request Broker) available on both client and server. You can think of an ORB as a kind of universal translator for interobject CORBA communication. The CORBA 2 specification defines more than a dozen "services" that the ORB can use for various kinds of housekeeping tasks. These range from a "startup service" to get the process going, to a "life cycle service" that you use to create, copy, move or destroy objects to a "naming service" that allows you to search for objects if you know their name.

The Java 2 platform contains a full implementation of a CORBA 2 compliant ORB. Thus, all applications and applets that you deploy for the Java 2 platform have the ability to connect to remote CORBA objects.

NOTE: Sun refers to the CORBA support in the Java 2 platform as "Java IDL." That term is really a misnomer. IDL refers to the interface definition language, a language for describing class interfaces. The important aspect of the technology is connectivity with CORBA, not just support for IDL.

Here are the steps for implementing CORBA objects:

1. Write the interface that specifies how the object works, using IDL, the *interface definition language* for defining CORBA interfaces. IDL is a special language to specify interfaces in a language-neutral form.

2. Using the IDL compiler(s) for the target language(s), generate the needed stub and helper classes.
3. Add the implementation code for the server objects, using the language of your choice. (The skeleton created by the IDL compiler is only glue code. You still need to provide the actual implementation code for the server methods.) Compile the implementation code.
4. Write a server program that creates and registers the server objects. The most convenient method for registration is to use the CORBA *naming service,* a service that is similar to the `rmiregistry`.
5. Write a client program that locates the server objects and invokes services on them.
6. Start the naming service and the server program on the server and the client program on the client.

These steps are quite similar to the steps that you use to build distributed applications with RMI. There are two important differences:

- You can use any language with a CORBA binding to implement clients and servers.
- You use IDL to specify interfaces.

In the following sections, you will see how to use IDL to define CORBA interfaces, and how to connect clients implemented in the Java programming language with C++ servers and C++ clients with servers implemented in the Java programming language.

However, CORBA is a complex subject, and we only give you a couple of basic examples to show you how to get started. For more information, we recommend *Client/Server Programming with Java and CORBA* by Robert Orfali and Dan Harkey [John Wiley & Sons 1998]. More advanced, and definitely not for the faint of heart, is *Advanced CORBA Programming with C++* by Michi Henning and Steve Vinoski [Addison-Wesley 1999].

The Interface Definition Language

To introduce the IDL syntax, let us quickly run through the same example that we used for RMI. In RMI, you started out with an interface in the Java programming language. With CORBA, the starting point is an interface in IDL syntax:

```
interface Product
{  string getDescription();
};
```

There are a few subtle differences between IDL and the Java programming language. In IDL, the interface definition ends with a semicolon. Note that `string` is written in lower case. In fact, the `string` class refers to the CORBA notion of a

string, which is different from a Java string. In the Java programming language, strings contain 16-bit Unicode characters. In CORBA, strings only contain 8-bit characters. If you send the 16-bit string through the ORB and the string has characters with nonzero high byte, an exception is thrown. This kind of type mismatch problem is the price you pay for interoperability between programming languages.

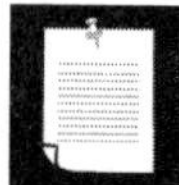

NOTE: CORBA also has a `wchar` type for "wide" characters. However, there is no guarantee that wide character strings use the Unicode encoding.

The "IDL to Java" compiler (Java IDL compiler) translates IDL definitions to definitions for interfaces in the Java programming language. For example, if you place the IDL `Product` definition into a file `Product.idl` and run `idltojava`, the result is a file `Product.java` with the following contents.

```
interface Product
{  String getDescription();
}
```

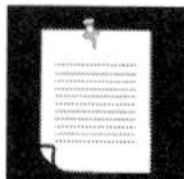

NOTE: In JDK1.3, the `idlj` program replaces the `idltojava` program.

The IDL compiler also generates a number of other source files—the stub class for communicating with the ORB and three helper classes that you will encounter later in this section and the next.

NOTE: You cannot do any programming in IDL. IDL can only express interfaces. The CORBA objects that IDL describes must still be implemented, for example, in C++ or the Java programming language.

The rules that govern the translation from IDL to the Java programming language are collectively called the *Java programming language binding*. Language bindings are standardized by the OMG; all CORBA vendors are required to use the same rules for mapping IDL constructs to a particular programming language.

We will not discuss all aspects of IDL or the Java programming language binding—see the CORBA documentation at the web site of the Object Management Group (`www.omg.org`) for a full description. However, there are a number of important concepts that every IDL user needs to know.

When defining a method, you have more choices for parameter passing than the Java programming language offers. Every parameter can be declared as `in`, `out`, or `inout`. An `in` parameter is simply passed to the method—this is the same parameter passing mechanism as in the Java programming language. However, the Java programming language has no analog to an `out` parameter. A method

stores a value in each `out` parameter before it returns. The caller can retrieve the values stored in `out` parameters.

For example, a `find` method might store the product object that it has found:

```
interface Warehouse
{  boolean locate(in String descr, out Product p);
   . . .
};
```

If the parameter is declared as `out` only, then the method should not expect the parameter to be initialized. However, if it is declared as `inout`, then the caller needs to supply a value for the method, and the method can change that value so that the caller can retrieve the changed value. In the Java programming language, these parameters are simulated with special *holder classes* that are generated by the Java IDL compiler.

The IDL compiler generates a class with suffix `Holder` for every interface. For example, when compiling the `Product` interface, it automatically generates a `ProductHolder` class. Every holder class has a public instance variable called `value`.

When a method has an `out` parameter, the IDL compiler changes the method signature to use a holder, for example

```
interface Warehouse
{  boolean locate(String descr, ProductHolder p);
   . . .
};
```

When calling the method, you need to pass in a holder object. After the method returns, you retrieve the value of the `out` parameter from the holder object. Here is how you call the `locate` method.

```
Warehouse w = . . .;
String descr = . . .;
Product p;
ProductHolder pHolder = new ProductHolder();
if (w.locate(descr, pHolder))
   p = pHolder.value;
```

There are predefined holder classes for fundamental types (such as `IntHolder`, `DoubleHolder` and so on).

NOTE: IDL does not support overloaded methods. You need to come up with a different name for each method.

In IDL, you use the `sequence` construct to define arrays of variable size. You must first define a type before you can declare sequence parameters or return values. For example, here is the definition of a "sequence of products" type.

```
typedef sequence<Product> ProductSeq;
```

Then you can use that type in method declarations:

```
interface Warehouse
{  ProductSeq find(in Customer c);
   . . .
};
```

In the Java programming language, sequences correspond to arrays. For example, the `find` method is mapped to

```
Product[] find(Customer c)
```

If a method can throw an exception, you first define the exception type and then use a `raises` declaration. In the following example, the `find` method can raise a `BadCustomer` exception.

```
interface Warehouse
{  exception BadCustomer { string reason; };
   ProductSeq find(in Customer c) raises BadCustomer;
   . . .
};
```

The IDL compiler translates the exception type into a class.

```
final public class BadCustomer
   extends org.omg.CORBA.UserException
{  public BadCustomer() {}
   public BadCustomer(String __reason) { reason = __reason; }
   public String reason;
}
```

If you catch such an exception, you can look into its public instance variables.

The `raises` specifier becomes a `throws` specifier of the Java method

```
ProductSeq find(Customer c) throws BadCustomer
```

Interfaces can contain constants, for example,

```
interface Warehouse
{  const int SOLD_OUT = 404;
   . . .
};
```

Interfaces can also contain attributes. Attributes look like instance variables, but they are actually a shorthand for a pair of accessor and mutator methods. For example, here is a `Book` interface with an `isbn` attribute.

```
interface Book
{  attribute string isbn;
   . . .
};
```

The equivalent in the Java programming language is a pair of methods, both with the name `isbn`:

```
String isbn() // accessor
void isbn(String __isbn) // mutator
```

If the attribute is declared as `readonly`, then no mutator method is generated.

You cannot specify variables in CORBA interfaces—the data representation for objects is part of the implementation strategy, and IDL does not address implementation at all.

CORBA supports interface inheritance, for example,

```
interface Book : Product { /* . . . */ };
```

You use the colon (`:`) to denote inheritance. An interface can inherit multiple interfaces.

In IDL, you can group definitions of interfaces, types, constants, and exceptions into *modules*.

```
module corejava
{  interface Product
   {  . . .
   };

   interface Warehouse
   {  . . .
   };
};
```

Modules are translated to packages in the Java programming language.

Once you have the IDL file, you run the IDL compiler that your ORB vendor supplies, to get stubs and helper classes for your target language (such as the Java programming language or the C++ language).

For example, to convert IDL files to the Java programming language, you run the `idltojava` program. Supply the name of the IDL file on the command line:

```
idltojava Product.idl
```

The program creates five source files:

- `Product.java`, the interface definition
- `ProductHolder.java`, the holder class for `out` parameters
- `ProductHelper.java`, a helper class, which you will see used in the next section
- `_ProductImplBase.java`, the superclass for the implementation class
- `_ProductStub.java`, the stub class for communicating with the ORB.

The same IDL file can be compiled to C++. We will use a freely available ORB called omniORB for our examples. The omniORB package contains an IDL-to-C++ compiler called `omniidl2`. When you run that compiler on `Product.idl`, you get two C++ files:

- `Product.hh`, a header file that defines classes `Product`, `ProductHelper`, and `_sk_Product` (the base class for the server implementation class).
- `ProductSK.cpp`, a C++ file that contains the source code for these classes.

NOTE: While the language binding is standardized, it is up to each vendor to decide how to generate and package the code that realizes the binding. IDL-to-C++ compilers of other vendors will generate a different set of files.

A CORBA example

In our first example, we show you how to call a C++ server object from a client implemented in the Java programming language, using the CORBA support that is built into the Java 2 platform. On the server side, we will use omniORB, a freely available ORB that works very well with the Java 2 platform. You can download omniORB from `http://www.uk.research.att.com/omniORB/index.html`.

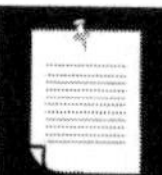

NOTE: The omniORB product is free, but on Windows, it requires the Microsoft C++ compiler. On Linux, you can use omniORB with the GNU C++ compiler.

NOTE: In principle, of course, you can use any CORBA 2 compliant ORB on the server. However, you will need to make some changes to the C++ code if you use a different ORB. Also, if our experience is any guide, you may run into bootstrapping issues. At the end of this section, we give you a couple of tips on connecting to other ORBs.

Our example C++ server object simply reports the value of an environment variable on the server. The interface is

```
interface Env
{  string getenv(in string name);
};
```

For example, the following program fragment in the Java programming language obtains the value of the `PATH` environment variable of the process in which the server object runs.

```
Env env = . . .;
String value = env.getenv("PATH")
```

The C++ implementation code for this interface is straightforward. We simply call the `getenv` method in the standard C library.

```
class EnvImpl : public virtual _sk_Env
{
public:
  virtual char* getenv(const char *name)
  {  char* value = ::getenv(name);
     return CORBA::string_dup(value);
  }
};
```

You don't need to understand the C++ code to follow this section—just treat it as a bit of legacy code that you want to encapsulate in a CORBA object so that you can call it from programs written in the Java programming language.

On the server side, you now need to write a C++ program that does the following:

1. Starts the ORB;
2. Creates an object of the `EnvImpl` class and registers it with the ORB;
3. Uses the name server to bind the object to a name;
4. Waits for invocations from a client.

You can find that program in Example 5–17 at the end of this section. We will not discuss the C++ code in detail. If you are interested, consult the omniORB documentation for more information. The documentation contains a very nice tutorial that explains each step in detail.

Let us now turn to the client code. You already saw how to invoke a method on the server object once you have a reference to the remote object. However, to get to that reference, you have to go through a different set of mumbo-jumbo than in RMI.

First, you initialize the ORB. The ORB is simply a code library that knows how to talk to other ORBs and how to marshal and unmarshal parameters.

```
ORB orb = ORB.init(args, null);
```

Next, you need to locate the naming service that helps you locate other objects. However, in CORBA, the naming service is just another CORBA object. To call the naming service, you first need to locate it. In the days of CORBA 1, this was a major problem, since there was no standard way of getting a reference to it. However, a CORBA 2 ORB lets you locate certain standard services by name. The call

```
String[] services = orb.list_initial_services();
```

lists the names of the standard services that the ORB can connect to. The naming service has the standard name `NameService`. Some ORBs have additional initial services; others—such as the ORB for the Java 2 platform—only list the naming service itself.

To obtain an object reference to the service, you use the `resolve_initial_references` method. It returns a generic CORBA object, an instance of the class `org.omg.corba.Object`. You need to use the full package prefix; if you just use `Object`, then the compiler assumes that you mean `java.lang.Object`.

```
org.omg.CORBA.Object object
   = orb.resolve_initial_references("NameService");
```

Next, you need to convert this reference into a `NamingContext` reference so that you can invoke the methods of the `NamingContext` interface. In RMI, you would simply cast the reference to a different type. However, in CORBA, you cannot simply cast references.

```
NamingContext namingContext
   = (NamingContext)object; // ERROR
```

Instead, you have to use the `narrow` method of the helper class of the target interface.

```
NamingContext namingContext
   = NamingContextHelper.narrow(object);
```

CAUTION: Casting a CORBA object reference to a subtype will *sometimes* succeed. Many `org.omg.CORBA.Object` references already point to objects that implement the appropriate interface. But an object reference can also hold a delegate to another object that actually implements the interface. Since you don't have any way of knowing how the stub objects were generated, you should always use the `narrow` method to convert a CORBA object reference to a subtype.

Now that you have the naming context, you can use it to locate the object that the server placed into it. The naming context associates names with server objects. Names are nested sequences of *name components*. You can use the nesting levels to organize hierarchies of names, much like you use directories in a file system.

A name component consists of an *ID* and a *kind*. The ID is a name for the component that is unique among all names with the same parent component. The kind is some indication of the type of the component. These kinds are not standardized; we use `"Context"` for name components that have nested names, and `"Object"` for object names.

In our example, the server program has placed the `EnvImpl` object into the name expressed by the sequence

```
(id="corejava", kind="Context"), (id="Env", kind="Object")
```

We retrieve a remote reference to it by building up an array of name components and passing it to the `resolve` method of the `NamingContext` interface.

```
NameComponent[] path =
   {  new NameComponent("corejava", "Context"),
      new NameComponent("Env", "Object")
   };
org.omg.CORBA.Object envObj = namingContext.resolve(path);
```

Once again, we must narrow the resulting object reference:

```
Env env = EnvHelper.narrow(envObj);
```

Now we are ready to call the remote method:

```
String value = env.getenv("PATH");
```

You will find the complete code in Example 5–16.

This example shows the steps to follow in a typical client program:

1. Start the ORB.
2. Locate the naming service by retrieving an initial reference to `"NameService"` and narrowing it to a `NamingContext` reference.
3. Locate the object whose methods you want to call by assembling its name and calling the `resolve` method of the `NamingContext`.
4. Narrow the returned object to the correct type and invoke your methods.

To actually test this program, do the following.

1. Compile the IDL file, using both the C++ and Java IDL compilers.
2. Compile the C++ server program. (A make file is provided on the CD-ROM.)
3. Compile the client program.
4. Start the naming service on the server (for example, `omniNames` if you use omniORB). The naming service runs until you kill it.
5. Start the server (`EnvServer`). The server also runs until you kill it.
6. Run the client (`java EnvClient`). It should report the `PATH` of the server process.

If the server is on a remote machine or the initial port of the server ORB is not the same as the Java IDL default of 900, then you need to set the `ORBInitialHost` and `ORBInitialPort` properties. There are two methods for setting these properties. You can set the system properties

```
org.omg.CORBA.ORBInitialHost
org.omg.CORBA.ORBInitialPort
```

for example, by starting the bytecode interpreter with the `-D` option. Or, you can specify the values on the command line:

```
java EnvClient -ORBInitialHost warthog -ORBInitialPort 1050
```

The command line parameters are passed to the ORB by the call

```
ORB orb = ORB.init(args, null);
```

In principle, your ORB vendor should tell you with great clarity how its bootstrap process works. In practice, we have found that vendors blithely assume that you would never dream of mixing their precious ORB with another, and they tend to be less than forthcoming with this information. If your client won't find the naming service, try forcing the initial ports for both the server and the client to the same value.

TIP: If you have trouble connecting to the naming service, print out a list of initial services that your ORB can locate.

```
public class ListServices
{  public static void main(String args[]) throws Exception
   {  ORB orb = ORB.init(args, null);
      String[] services = orb.list_initial_services();
      for (int i = 0; i < services.length; i++)
         System.out.println(services[i]);
   }
}
```

With some ORBs, `NameService` isn't among the listed services, no matter how much you tweak the configuration. Then, you should switch to plan B and locate the server object by its Interoperable Object Reference, or IOR. See the sidebar for more information.

Locating Objects Through IORs

If you can't configure your server ORB and name service so that your client can invoke it, you can still locate CORBA objects by using an *Interoperable Object Reference*, or IOR. An IOR is a long string starting with `IOR:` and followed by many hexadecimal digits, for example:

```
IOR:012020201000000049444c3a4163636f756e743a312e30000100000
000000004e000000010100200f000000323136 2e31352e3131322e313739
0020350420202e000000001504d43000000000100000049444c3a4163636f
756e743a312e30000e0000004a61636b20422e20517569636b00
```

An IOR describes an object uniquely. By convention, many server classes print out the IORs of all objects they register, to enable clients to locate them. You can then paste the server IOR into the client program. Specifically, use the following code:

```
String ref = "IOR:012020201000000049444c3a4163636f...";
   // paste IOR from server
org.omg.CORBA.Object object = orb.string_to_object(ref);
```

Then, narrow the returned object to the appropriate type, for example

```
Env env = EnvHelper.narrow(object);
```

When testing the code for this book, we successfully used this method to connect clients with Visibroker.

In this section, you saw how to connect to a server that was implemented in C++. We believe that is a particularly useful scenario. You can wrap legacy services into CORBA objects and access them from any program for the Java 2 platform, without having to deploy additional system software on the client. In the next section, you will see the opposite scenario, where the server is implemented in the Java programming language and the client in C++.

Example 5–16: EnvClient.java

```
import org.omg.CosNaming.*;
import org.omg.CORBA.*;

public class EnvClient
{  public static void main(String args[])
   {  try
      {  ORB orb = ORB.init(args, null);
         org.omg.CORBA.Object namingContextObj
            = orb.resolve_initial_references("NameService");
         NamingContext namingContext
            = NamingContextHelper.narrow(namingContextObj);

         NameComponent[] path = { new NameComponent
            ("corejava", "Context"),
            new NameComponent("Env", "Object") };
         org.omg.CORBA.Object envObj = namingContext.resolve(path);
         Env env = EnvHelper.narrow(envObj);
         System.out.println(env.getenv("PATH"));
      }
      catch(Exception e)
      {   System.out.println("Error: " + e);
          e.printStackTrace(System.out);
      }
   }
}
```

Example 5–17: EnvServer.cpp

```
#include <iostream.h>
#include "omnithread.h"

#include "Env.hh"

class EnvImpl : public virtual _sk_Env
{
public:
  virtual ~EnvImpl() {}
  virtual char* getenv(const char *name);
};

char* EnvImpl::getenv(const char *name)
{  char* value = ::getenv(name);
   return CORBA::string_dup(value);
}

void bindObjectToName(CORBA::ORB_ptr orb,
   const char name[], CORBA::Object_ptr obj)
{  CosNaming::NamingContext_var rootContext;

   try
```

```
{  // Obtain a reference to the root context of the Name service:
   CORBA::Object_var initServ
      = orb->resolve_initial_references("NameService");

   rootContext = CosNaming::NamingContext::_narrow(initServ);

   if (CORBA::is_nil(rootContext))
   {  cerr << "Failed to narrow naming context." << endl;
      return;
   }
}
catch(CORBA::ORB::InvalidName& ex)
{  cerr << "Service does not exist." << endl;
   return;
}

try
{  // Bind a context called "corejava" to the root context:

   CosNaming::Name contextName;
   contextName.length(1);
   contextName[0].id   = "corejava";
   contextName[0].kind = "Context";

   CosNaming::NamingContext_var corejavaContext;
   try
   {  // Bind the context to root, and assign testContext to it:
      corejavaContext = rootContext->bind_new_context(contextName);
   }
   catch(CosNaming::NamingContext::AlreadyBound&)
   {  // If the context already exists, this exception will be raised.
      // In this case, just resolve the name and assign testContext
      // to the object returned:
      CORBA::Object_var contextObj
         = rootContext->resolve(contextName);
      corejavaContext = CosNaming::NamingContext::_narrow(contextObj);
      if (CORBA::is_nil(corejavaContext))
      {  cerr << "Failed to narrow corejava context." << endl;
         return;
      }
   }

   // Bind obj to name in the corejava context
   CosNaming::Name objectName;
   objectName.length(1);
   objectName[0].id   = name;
   objectName[0].kind = "Object";

   corejavaContext->rebind(objectName, obj);
}
catch (CORBA::COMM_FAILURE&)
```

```
    {  cerr << "COMM_FAILURE" << endl;
    }
}

int main(int argc, char *argv[])
{  cout << "Creating and initializing the ORB..." << endl;

   CORBA::ORB_ptr orb = CORBA::ORB_init(argc, argv, "omniORB2");
   CORBA::BOA_ptr boa = orb->BOA_init(argc,argv,"omniORB2_BOA");

   cout << "Registering server implementation with the ORB..." <<
      endl;

   EnvImpl* impl = new EnvImpl();
   impl->_obj_is_ready(boa);

   CORBA::String_var s = orb->object_to_string(impl);
   cout << s << endl;

   cout << "Binding server implementation to name service..." <<
      endl;

   Env_var env = impl->_this();
   bindObjectToName(orb, "Env", env);

   cout << "Waiting for invocations from clients..." << endl;

   boa->impl_is_ready();

   return 0;
}
```

`org.omg.CORBA.ORB`

- `static ORB init(String[] args, Properties props)`

  creates a new ORB and initializes it.

  Parameters: `args` command-line arguments for configuring the ORB

  `props` a table with properties for configuring the ORB

- `String[] list_initial_services()`

  returns a list of the initially available services such as `"NameService"`.

- `org.omg.CORBA.Object resolve_initial_references(String name)`

  returns an object that carries out one of the initial services.

  Parameters: `name` the name of the initial service

- `org.omg.CORBA.Object string_to_object(String ior)`

  locates the object with a given IOR (interoperable object reference).

`org.omg.CosNaming.NamingContext`

- `org.omg.CORBA.Object resolve(NameComponent[] name)`

  returns the object that is bound to the given name

`org.omg.CosNaming.NameComponent`

- `NameComponent(String id, String kind)`

  constructs a new name component.

  Parameters: `id` A string describing the identity of this component

  `kind` A string describing the type of this component

Implementing CORBA Servers

If you are deploying a CORBA infrastructure, you will find that the Java programming language is a good implementation language for CORBA server objects. The language binding is natural, and it is easier to build robust server software than with C++. This section describes how to implement a CORBA server in the Java programming language.

The example program in this section is similar to that of the preceding section. We supply a service to look up a system property of a Java virtual machine. Here is the IDL description:

```
interface SysProp
{  string getProperty(in string name);
};
```

For example, our client test program calls the server as follows:

```
CORBA::String_var key = "java.vendor";
CORBA::String_var value = sysProp->getProperty(key);
```

The result is a string describing the vendor of the Java virtual machine that is executing the server program. We won't look into the details of the C++ client program. You will find the code in Example Example 5–19.

To implement the server, you extend the `_SysPropImplBase` class that the `idltojava` compiler generated from the IDL file. Here is the implementation:

```
class SysPropImpl extends _SysPropImplBase
{  public String getProperty(String key)
   {  return System.getProperty(key);
   }
}
```

NOTE: You can choose any name you like for the implementation class. In this book, we follow the RMI convention and use the suffix `Impl` for the implementation class name. Other programmers use a suffix `Servant` or `_i`.

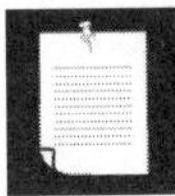

NOTE: If your implementation class already extends another class, you cannot simultaneously extend the implementation base class. In that case, you can instruct the `idl-tojava` compiler to create an *operations* interface and a *tie* class. Your server class then implements the operations interface instead of extending the implementation base class. However, any server objects must be created by means of the tie class. For details, check out the tutorial for the Java IDL product at `http://java.sun.com/products/jdk/1.2/docs/guide/idl/`.

Next, you need write a server program that carries out the following tasks:

1. Start the ORB.
2. Create the server implementation and register it with the ORB.
3. Print out its IOR (for name-service-challenged clients—see the Sidebar on page 308).
4. Bind the server implementation to the naming service.
5. Wait for invocations from clients.

You will find the complete code in Example 5–18. Here are the highlights.

You start the ORB as you would for a client program:

```
ORB orb = ORB.init(args, null);
```

To register an object with the ORB, use the `connect` method:

```
SysPropImpl impl = new SysPropImpl();
orb.connect(impl);
```

Next, obtain the IOR with the `object_to_string` method and print it out:

```
System.out.println(orb.object_to_string(impl));
```

You obtain a reference to the naming service in exactly the same way as with a client program:

```
org.omg.CORBA.Object namingContextObj =
   orb.resolve_initial_references("NameService");
NamingContext namingContext
   = NamingContextHelper.narrow(namingContextObj);
```

You then build up the desired name for the object. Here, we call the object `SysProp`:

```
NameComponent[] path =
   {  new NameComponent("SysProp", "Object")
   };
```

CAUTION: We don't use a nested name because at the time of this writing, the `tnameserv` name service that is included in the JDK does not support nested names.

You use the `rebind` method to bind the object to the name:

```
namingContext.rebind(path, impl);
```

Finally, you wait forever. To avoid a busy wait, simply call `wait` on an object that is never notified.

```
java.lang.Object sync = new java.lang.Object();
synchronized (sync)
{  sync.wait();
}
```

To test this program, do the following.

1. Compile the IDL file, using both the C++ and Java IDL compilers.
2. Compile the server program.
3. Compile the C++ client program. (There is a make file provided on the CD-ROM.)
4. Start the `tnameserv` naming service on the server. This program is a part of the JDK. The naming service runs until you kill it. If necessary, you can use the `-ORBInitialPort` parameter to set the initial port to a different value than the default 900.
5. Start the server (`java SysPropServer`). The server also runs until you kill it.
6. Run the client (`java EnvClient`). It should print out the JVM vendor of the server.

You have now seen how to use CORBA to connect clients and servers that were written in different programming languages. This concludes our discussion of CORBA. CORBA has a number of other interesting features, such as dynamic method invocation and a number of standard services such as transaction handling and persistence. We refer you to *Client/Server Programming with Java and CORBA* by Robert Orfali and Dan Harkey [John Wiley & Sons 1998] for an in-depth discussion of advanced CORBA issues.

Example 5–18: SysPropServer.java

```
import org.omg.CosNaming.*;
import org.omg.CORBA.*;

class SysPropImpl extends _SysPropImplBase
{  public String getProperty(String key)
   {  return System.getProperty(key);
   }
}

public class SysPropServer
{  public static void main(String args[])
   {  try
      {  System.out.println("Creating and initializing the ORB...");

         ORB orb = ORB.init(args, null);

         System.out.println
```

```
            ("Registering server implementation with the ORB...");

         SysPropImpl impl = new SysPropImpl();
         orb.connect(impl);
         System.out.println(orb.object_to_string(impl));

         org.omg.CORBA.Object namingContextObj =
             orb.resolve_initial_references("NameService");
         NamingContext namingContext
            = NamingContextHelper.narrow(namingContextObj);

         NameComponent[] path =
            {  new NameComponent("SysProp", "Object")
            };

         System.out.println
            ("Binding server implementation to name service...");

         namingContext.rebind(path, impl);

         System.out.println
            ("Waiting for invocations from clients...");

         java.lang.Object sync = new java.lang.Object();
         synchronized (sync)
         {  sync.wait();
         }
      }
      catch (Exception e)
      {  System.err.println("Error: " + e);
         e.printStackTrace(System.out);
      }
   }
}
```

Example 5–19: SysPropClient.cpp

```
#include <iostream.h>
#include "SysProp.hh"

CORBA::Object_ptr getObjectReference(CORBA::ORB_ptr orb,
   const char serviceName[])
{  CosNaming::NamingContext_var rootContext;

   try
   {  // Obtain a reference to the root context of the Name service:
      CORBA::Object_var initServ;
      initServ = orb->resolve_initial_references("NameService");

      // Narrow the object returned by resolve_initial_references()
      // to a CosNaming::NamingContext object:
      rootContext = CosNaming::NamingContext::_narrow(initServ);
```

```
        if (CORBA::is_nil(rootContext))
        {  cerr << "Failed to narrow naming context." << endl;
           return CORBA::Object::_nil();
        }
     }
     catch(CORBA::ORB::InvalidName&)
     {  cerr << "Name service does not exist." << endl;
        return CORBA::Object::_nil();
     }

     // Create a name object, containing the name corejava/SysProp:
     CosNaming::Name name;
     name.length(1);

     name[0].id   = serviceName;
     name[0].kind = "Object";

     CORBA::Object_ptr obj;
     try
     {  // Resolve the name to an object reference, and assign the reference
        // returned to a CORBA::Object:
        obj = rootContext->resolve(name);
     }
     catch(CosNaming::NamingContext::NotFound&)
     {  // This exception is thrown if any of the components of the
        // path [contexts or the object] aren't found:
        cerr << "Context not found." << endl;
        return CORBA::Object::_nil();
     }
     return obj;
}

void callServer(CORBA::Object_ptr obj)
{  SysProp_var sysProp = SysProp::_narrow(obj);

   if (CORBA::is_nil(sysProp))
   {  cerr << "hello: cannot invoke on a nil object reference.\n" << endl;
      return;
   }

   CORBA::String_var key = "java.vendor";
   CORBA::String_var value = sysProp->getProperty(key);

   cerr << key << "=" << value << endl;
}

int main (int argc, char *argv[])
{  CORBA::ORB_ptr orb = CORBA::ORB_init(argc, argv, "omniORB2");
   CORBA::BOA_ptr boa = orb->BOA_init(argc, argv, "omniORB2_BOA");

   try
```

```
    {  CORBA::Object_var obj = getObjectReference(orb, "SysProp");
       callServer(obj);
    }
    catch (CORBA::COMM_FAILURE&)
    {  cerr << "COMM_FAILURE" << endl;
    }

    return 0;
}
```

`org.omg.CORBA.ORB`

- `void connect(org.omg.CORBA.Object obj)`

  connects the given implementation object to this ORB, enabling the ORB to forward calls to the object's methods.

- `String object_to_string(org.omg.CORBA.Object obj)`

  returns the IOR (interoperable object reference) string of the given object.

`org.omg.CosNaming.NamingContext`

API

- `void bind(NameComponent[] name, org.omg.CORBA.Object obj)`
- `void rebind(NameComponent[] name, org.omg.CORBA.Object obj)`

  bind an object to a name. The `bind` method throws an `AlreadyBound` exception if the object has been previously bound. The `rebind` method replaces any previously bound objects.

Parameters:	`name`	the name to which the object is bound
	`obj`	the object to store in the naming context

Chapter 6

Advanced Swing

- Trees
- Tables
- Styled Text Components
- Sliders and Progress Meters
- Tool Bars and Tool Tips
- Component Organizers

In this chapter, we continue our discussion of the Swing user interface toolkit from Volume 1. Swing is a very large and complex toolkit, and Volume 1 only covered the most important components. Since there is no consensus which components are important, we put those components that had an equivalent in the original AWT into Volume 1. That leaves us with two very complex components for trees and tables, whose exploration will occupy the bulk of this chapter. We finish the chapter by covering the remaining Swing components such as progress monitors, sliders, and tool bars.

Trees

Every computer user who uses a hierarchical file system has encountered *tree* displays such as the one in Figure 6–1. Of course, directories and files form only one of the many examples of treelike organizations. Programmers are familiar with inheritance trees for classes. There are many tree structures that arise in everyday life, such as the hierarchy of countries, states, and cities shown in Figure 6–2.

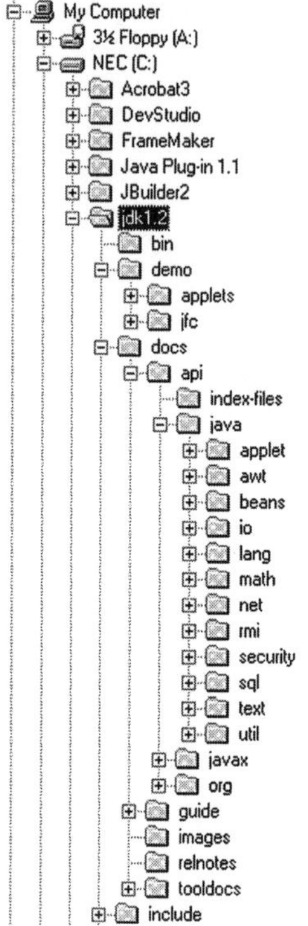

Figure 6–1: A directory tree

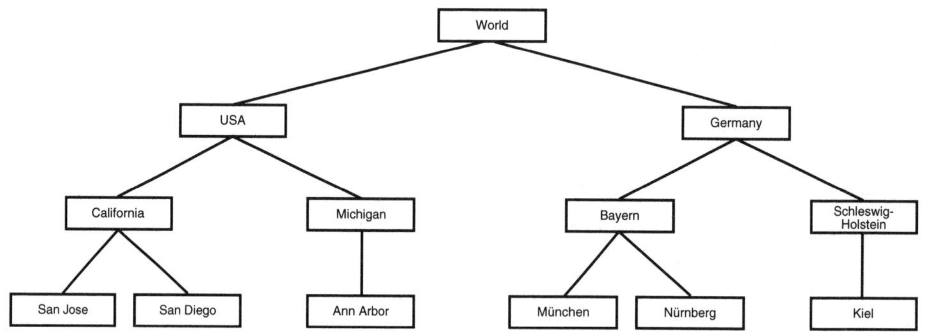

Figure 6–2: A hierarchy of countries, states, and cities

As programmers, we often have to display these tree structures. Fortunately, the Swing library has a `JTree` class for this purpose. The `JTree` class (together with its helper classes) takes care of laying out the tree and of processing user requests for expanding and collapsing nodes. In this section, you will learn how to put the

JTree class to use. As with the other complex Swing components, we must focus on the common and useful cases and cannot cover every nuance—we recommend that you consult *Core Java Foundation Classes* by Kim Topley [Prentice-Hall 1998] or *Graphic Java 2* by David M. Geary [Prentice-Hall 1999] if you want to achieve an unusual effect.

Before going any further, let's settle on some terminology (see Figure 6–3). A tree is composed of *nodes*. Every node is either a *leaf* or it has *child nodes*. Every node, with the exception of the root node, has exactly one *parent*. A tree has exactly one root node. Sometimes you have a collection of trees, each of which has its own root node. Such a collection is called a *forest*.

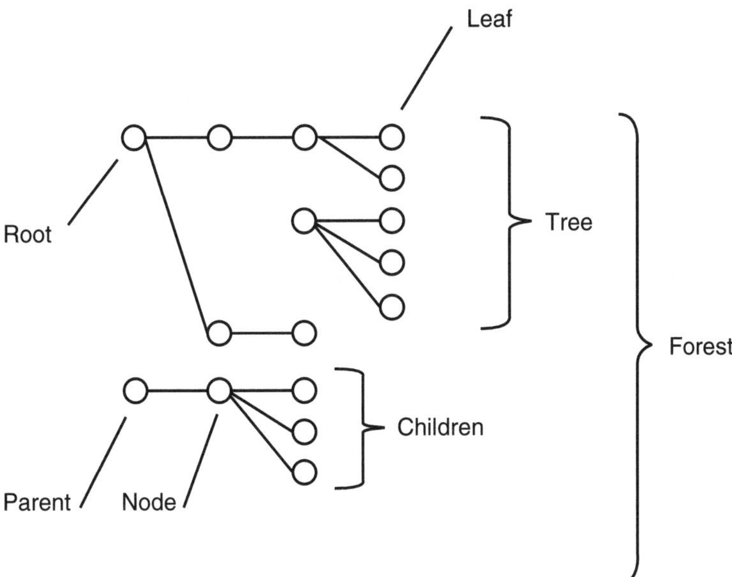

Figure 6–3: Tree terminology

Simple trees

In our first example program, we simply display a tree with a few nodes (see Figure 6–5 on page 323). As with most other Swing components, the JTree component follows the model/view/controller pattern. You provide a model of the hierarchical data, and the component displays it for you. To construct a JTree, you supply the tree model in the constructor:

```
TreeModel model = . . .;
JTree tree = new JTree(model);
```

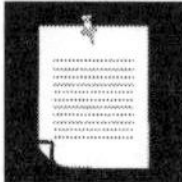

NOTE: There are also constructors that construct trees out of a collection of elements

```
JTree(Object[] nodes)
JTree(Vector nodes)
JTree(Hashtable nodes) // the values become the nodes
```

These constructors are not very useful. They merely build a forest of trees, each with a single node. The third constructor seems particularly useless since the nodes appear in the essentially random order given by the hash codes of the keys.

How do you obtain a tree model? You can construct your own model by creating a class that implements the `TreeModel` interface. You will see later in this chapter how to do that. For now, we'll stick with the `DefaultTreeModel` that the Swing library supplies.

To construct a default tree model, you must supply a root node.

```
TreeNode root = . . .;
DefaultTreeModel model = new DefaultTreeModel(root);
```

`TreeNode` is another interface. You populate the default tree model with objects of any class that implements the interface. For now, we will use the concrete node class that Swing supplies, namely `DefaultMutableTreeNode`. This class implements the `MutableTreeNode` interface, a subinterface of `TreeNode` (see Figure 6–4).

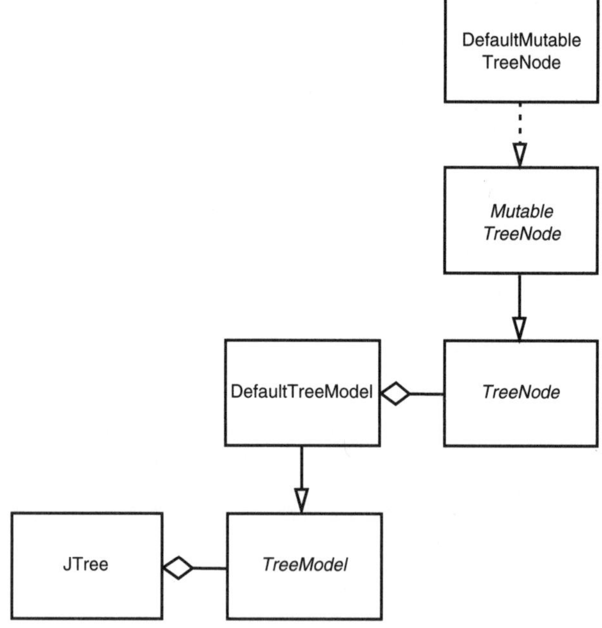

Figure 6–4: Tree classes

A default mutable tree node holds an object, the *user object*. The tree renders the user objects for all nodes. Unless you specify a renderer, the tree simply displays the string that is the result of the `toString` method.

In our first example, we use strings as user objects. In practice, you would usually populate a tree with more expressive user objects. For example, when displaying a directory tree, it makes sense to use `File` objects for the nodes.

You can specify the user object in the constructor, or you can set it later with the `setUserObject` method.

```
DefaultMutableTreeNode node
   = new DefaultMutableTreeNode("Texas");
node.setUserObject("California");
```

Next, you establish the parent/child relationships between the nodes. Start with the root node, and use the `add` method to add the children:

```
DefaultMutableTreeNode root
   = new DefaultMutableTreeNode("World");
DefaultMutableTreeNode country
   = new DefaultMutableTreeNode("USA");
root.add(country);
DefaultMutableTreeNode state
   = new DefaultMutableTreeNode("California");
country.add(state);
```

Figure 6–5 illustrates how the tree will look.

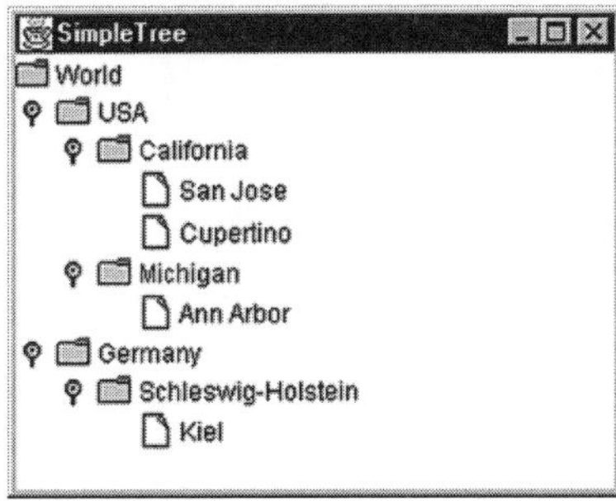

Figure 6–5: A simple tree

Link up all nodes in this fashion. Then, construct a `DefaultTreeModel` with the root node. Finally, construct a `JTree` with the tree model.

```
DefaultTreeModel treeModel = new DefaultTreeModel(root);
JTree tree = new JTree(treeModel);
```

Or, as a shortcut, you can simply pass the root node to the `JTree` constructor. Then the tree automatically constructs a default tree model:

```
JTree tree = new JTree(root);
```

Example 6–1 contains the complete code.

Example 6–1: SimpleTree.java

```
import java.awt.*;
import java.awt.event.*;
import javax.swing.*;
import javax.swing.tree.*;

public class SimpleTree
{  public static void main(String[] args)
   {  JFrame frame = new SimpleTreeFrame();
      frame.show();
   }
}

class SimpleTreeFrame extends JFrame
{  public SimpleTreeFrame()
   {  setTitle("SimpleTree");
      setSize(300, 200);
      addWindowListener(new WindowAdapter()
         {  public void windowClosing(WindowEvent e)
            {  System.exit(0);
            }
         } );

      // set up tree model data

      DefaultMutableTreeNode root
         = new DefaultMutableTreeNode("World");
      DefaultMutableTreeNode country
         = new DefaultMutableTreeNode("USA");
      root.add(country);
      DefaultMutableTreeNode state
         = new DefaultMutableTreeNode("California");
      country.add(state);
      DefaultMutableTreeNode city
         = new DefaultMutableTreeNode("San Jose");
      state.add(city);
      city = new DefaultMutableTreeNode("Cupertino");
      state.add(city);
      state = new DefaultMutableTreeNode("Michigan");
      country.add(state);
      city = new DefaultMutableTreeNode("Ann Arbor");
      state.add(city);
      country = new DefaultMutableTreeNode("Germany");
      root.add(country);
      state = new DefaultMutableTreeNode("Schleswig-Holstein");
      country.add(state);
      city = new DefaultMutableTreeNode("Kiel");
```

```
        state.add(city);

        // construct tree and put it in a scroll pane

        JTree tree = new JTree(root);
        Container contentPane = getContentPane();
        contentPane.add(new JScrollPane(tree));
    }
}
```

When you run the program, the tree first looks as in Figure 6–6. Only the root node and its children are visible. Click on the circle icons (the *handles*) to open up the subtrees. The line sticking out from the handle icon points to the right when the subtree is collapsed, and it points down when the subtree is expanded (see Figure 6–7). We don't know what the designers of the Metal look and feel had in mind, but we think of the icon as a door handle. You push down on the handle to open the subtree.

NOTE: Of course, the display of the tree depends on the selected look and feel. We just described the Java look and feel (a.k.a. "Metal"). In the Windows and Motif look and feel, the handles have the more familiar look—a "+" or "–" in a box (see Figure 6–8).

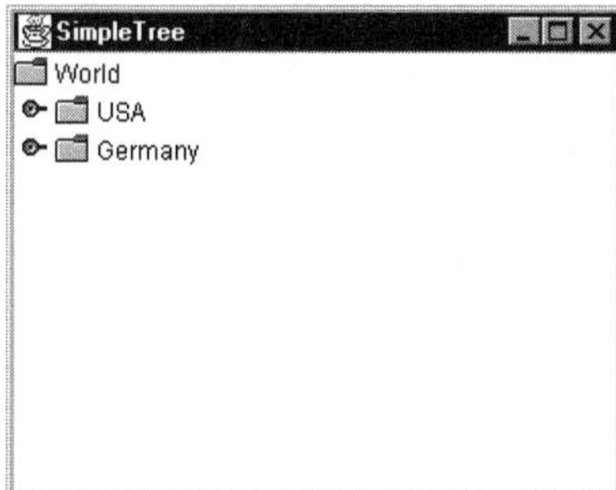

Figure 6–6: The initial tree display

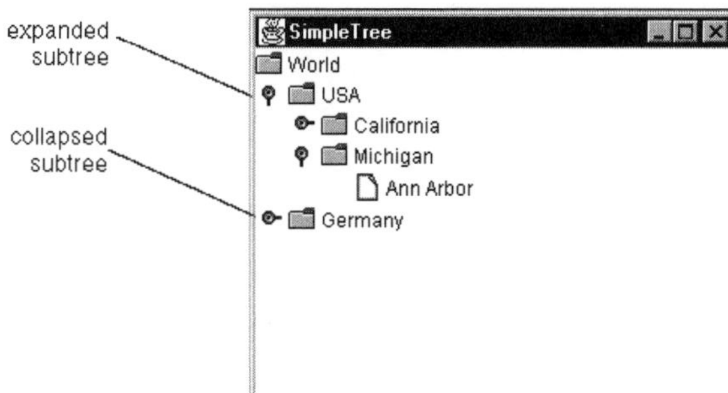

Figure 6–7: Collapsed and expanded subtrees

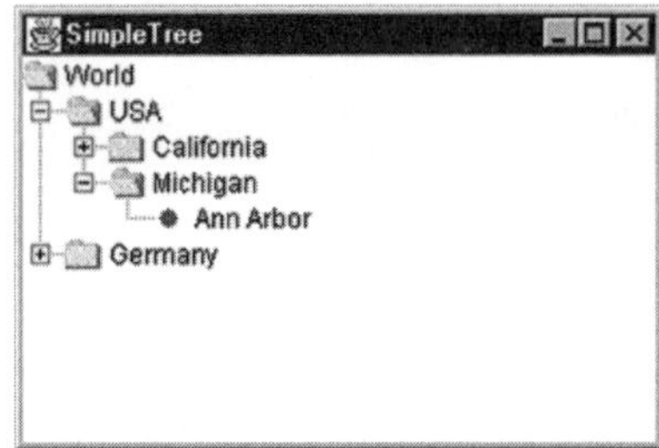

Figure 6–8: A tree with the Windows look and feel

The Java look and feel does not display the tree outline by default. Use the following magic incantation to show lines joining parents and children:

```
tree.putClientProperty("JTree.lineStyle", "Angled");
```

Figure 6–9 shows the result.

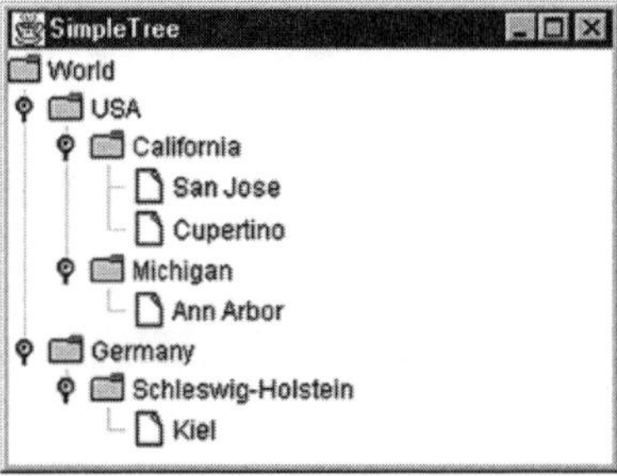

Figure 6–9: A tree with the angled line style

There is also another line style `"Horizontal"` that is shown in Figure 6–10. The tree is displayed with horizontal lines separating only the children of the root. We aren't quite sure what it is good for.

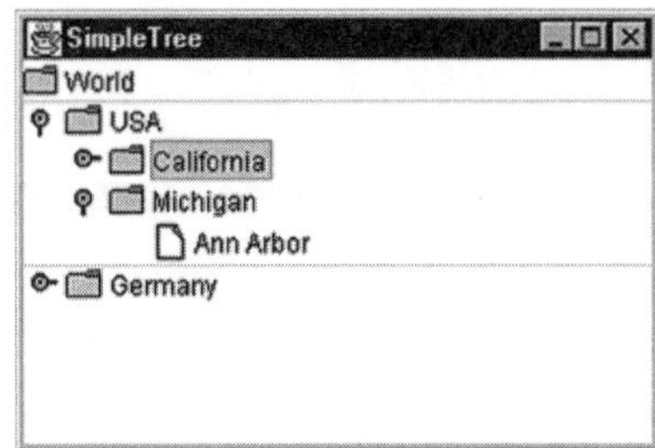

Figure 6–10: A tree with the horizontal line style

By default, there is no handle for collapsing the root of the tree. If you like, you can add one with the call

```
tree.setShowsRootHandles(true);
```

Figure 6–11 shows the result. Now you can collapse the entire tree into the root node.

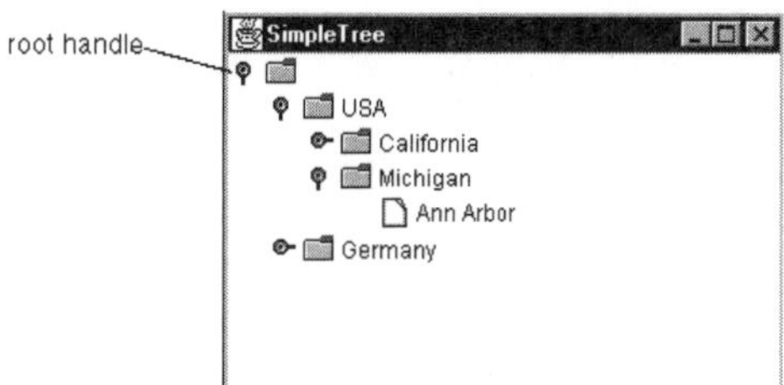

Figure 6–11: A tree with a root handle

Conversely, you can hide the root altogether. You do that to display a *forest*, a set of trees, each of which has its own root. You still must join all trees in the forest to a common root. Then, you hide the root with the instruction

```
tree.setRootVisible(false);
```

Look at Figure 6–12. There appear to be two roots, labeled "USA" and "Germany." The actual root that joins the two is made invisible.

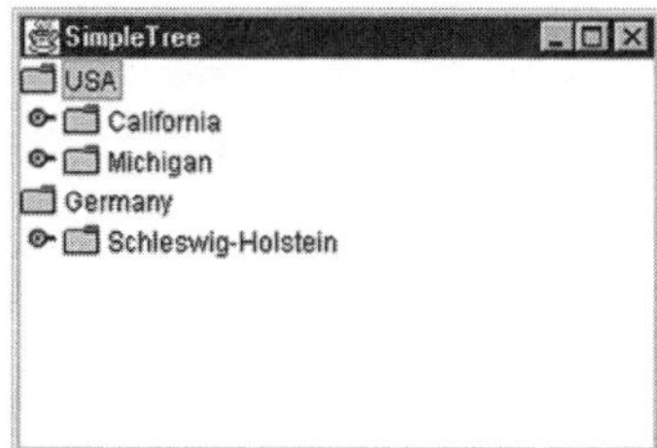

Figure 6–12: A forest

Let's turn from the root to the leaves of the tree. Note that the leaves have a different icon than the other nodes (see Figure 6–13).

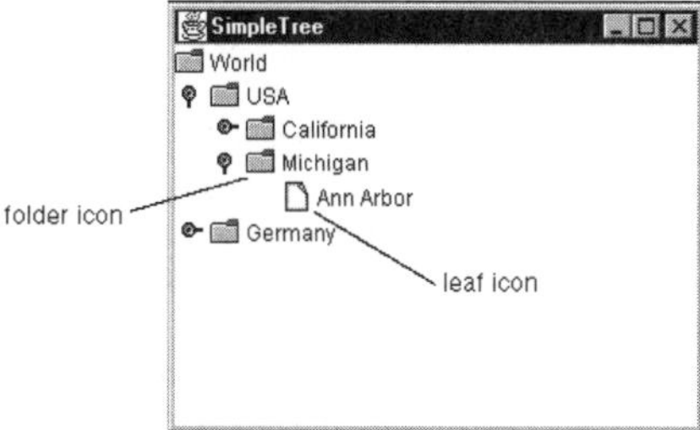

Figure 6–13: Leaf icons

When displaying the tree, each node is drawn with an icon. There are actually three kinds of icons: a leaf icon, an opened non-leaf icon and a closed non-leaf icon. For simplicity, we'll refer to the last two as folder icons.

The node renderer needs to know which icon to use for each node. By default, the decision process works like this: If the `isLeaf` method of a node returns `true`, then the leaf icon is used. Otherwise, a folder icon is used.

The `isLeaf` method of the `DefaultMutableTreeNode` class returns `true` if the node has no children. Thus, nodes with children get folder icons, and nodes without children get leaf icons.

Sometimes, that behavior is not appropriate. Suppose we added a node "Montana" to our sample tree, but we're at a loss as to what cities to add. We would not want the state node to get a leaf icon since conceptually only the cities are leaves.

The `JTree` class has no idea which nodes should be leaves. It asks the tree model. If a childless node isn't automatically a conceptual leaf, you can ask the tree model to use a different criterion for leafiness, namely to query the "allows children" node property.

For those nodes that should not have children, call

```
node.setAllowsChildren(false);
```

Then, tell the tree model to ask the value of the "allows children" property to determine whether a node should be displayed with a leaf icon. You use the `setAsksAllowsChildren` method of the `DefaultTreeModel` class to set this behavior:

```
model.setAsksAllowsChildren(true);
```

With this decision criterion, nodes that allow children get folder icons, and nodes that don't allow children get leaf icons.

Alternatively, if you construct the tree by supplying the root node, supply the setting for the "asks allows children" property in the constructor.

```
JTree tree = new JTree(root, true);
   // nodes that don't allow children get leaf icons
```

`javax.swing.JTree`

- `JTree(TreeModel model)`

  constructs a tree from a tree model.

- `JTree(TreeNode root)`
- `JTree(TreeNode root, boolean asksAllowChildren)`

  construct a tree with a default tree model that displays the root and its children.

Parameters:	`root`	The root node
	`asksAllowsChildren`	`true` to use the "allows children" node property for determining whether a node is a leaf

- `void setShowsRootHandles(boolean b)`

  If `b` is `true`, then the root node has a handle for collapsing or expanding its children.

- `void setRootVisible(boolean b)`

  If `b` is true, then the root node is displayed. Otherwise, it is hidden.

javax.swing.tree.TreeNode

- `boolean isLeaf()`

  returns `true` if this node is conceptually a leaf.

- `boolean getAllowsChildren()`

  returns `true` if this node can have child nodes.

javax.swing.tree.MutableTreeNode

- `void setUserObject(Object userObject)`

  sets the "user object" that the tree node uses for rendering.

javax.swing.tree.TreeModel

- `boolean isLeaf(TreeNode node)`

  returns `true` if `node` should be displayed as a leaf node.

javax.swing.tree.DefaultTreeModel

- `void setAsksAllowsChildren(boolean b)`

  If `b` is `true`, then nodes are displayed as leaves when their `getAllowsChildren` method returns `false`. Otherwise, they are displayed as leaves when their `isLeaf` method returns `true`.

javax.swing.tree.DefaultMutableTreeNode

- `DefaultMutableTreeNode(Object userObject)`

  constructs a mutable tree node with the given user object.

- `void add(MutableTreeNode child)`

  adds a node as the last child of this node.

- `void setAllowsChildren(boolean b)`

  If `b` is `true`, then children can be added to this node.

javax.swing.JComponent

- `void putClientProperty(Object key, Object value)`

  adds a key/value pair to a small table that each component manages. This is an "escape hatch" mechanism that some Swing components use for storing look-and-feel specific properties.

Editing trees and tree paths

In the next example program, you will see how to edit a tree. Figure 6–14 shows the user interface. If you click on the "Add Sibling" or "Add Child" button, the program adds a new node (with title New) to the tree. If you click on the "Delete" button, the program deletes the currently selected node.

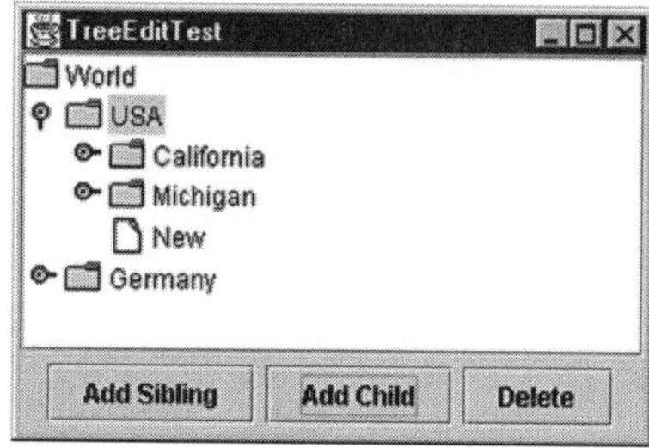

Figure 6–14: Editing a tree

To implement this behavior, you need to find out which tree node is currently selected. The `JTree` class has a surprising way of identifying nodes in a tree. It does not deal with tree nodes, but with *paths of objects,* called *tree paths.* A tree path starts at the root and consists of a sequence of child nodes—see Figure 6–15.

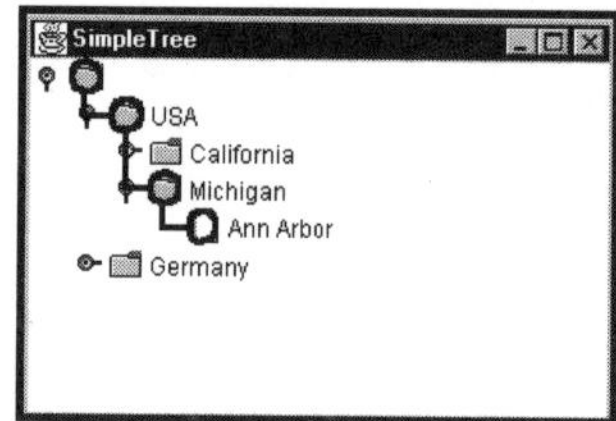

Figure 6–15: A tree path

You may wonder why the `JTree` class needs the whole path. Couldn't it just get a `TreeNode` and keep calling the `getParent` method? In fact, the `JTree` class knows nothing about the `TreeNode` interface. That interface is never used by the `TreeModel` interface; it is only used by the `DefaultTreeModel` implementation. You can have other tree models in which the nodes do not implement the `TreeNode` interface at all. If you use a tree model that manages other types of objects, then those objects may not have `getParent` and `getChild` methods. They would of course need to have some other connection to each other. It is the job of the tree model to link nodes together. The `JTree` class itself has no clue about the nature of their linkage. For that reason, the `JTree` class always needs to work with complete paths.

The `TreePath` class manages a sequence of `Object` (not `TreeNode`!) references. A number of `JTree` methods return `TreePath` objects. When you have a tree path, you usually just need to know the terminal node, which you get with the getLastPathComponent method. For example, to find out the currently selected node in a tree, you use the getSelectionPath method of the JTree class. You get a TreePath object back, from which you can retrieve the actual node.

```
TreePath selectionPath = tree.getSelectionPath();
DefaultMutableTreeNode selectedNode = (DefaultMutableTreeNode)
   selectionPath.getLastPathComponent();
```

Actually, because this particular query is so common, there is a convenience method that gives the selected node immediately.

```
DefaultMutableTreeNode selectedNode = (DefaultMutableTreeNode)
   tree.getLastSelectedPathComponent();
```

This method is not called getSelectedNode because the tree does not know that it contains nodes—its tree model only deals with paths of objects.

NOTE: Tree paths are one of two ways that the JTree class uses to describe nodes. There are also quite a few JTree methods that take or return an integer index, the *row position*. A row position is simply the row number (starting with 0) of the node in the tree display. Only visible nodes have row numbers, and the row number of a node changes if other nodes before it are expanded, collapsed, or modified. For that reason, you should avoid row positions. All JTree methods that use rows have equivalents that use tree paths instead.

Once you have the selected node, you can edit it. However, do not simply add children to a tree node:

```
selectedNode.add(newNode); // NO!
```

If you change the structure of the nodes, you change the model but the associated view is not notified. You could send out a notification yourself, but if you use the insertNodeInto method of the DefaultTreeModel class, the model class takes care of that. For example, the following call appends a new node as the last child of the selected node and notifies the tree view.

```
model.insertNodeInto(newNode, selectedNode,
   selectedNode.getChildCount());
```

The analogous call removeNodeFromParent removes a node and notifies the view:

```
model.removeNodeFromParent(selectedNode);
```

If you keep the node structure in place but you changed the user object, you should call the following method:

```
model.nodeChanged(changedNode);
```

The automatic notification is a major advantage of using the DefaultTree-Model. If you supply your own tree model, you have to implement it by hand. (See *Core Java Foundation Classes* by Kim Topley for details.)

CAUTION: The DefaultTreeModel class has a reload method that reloads the entire model. However, don't call reload simply to update the tree after making a few changes. When the tree is regenerated, all nodes beyond the root's children are collapsed again. It is quite disconcerting to your users if they have to keep expanding the tree after every change.

When the view is notified of a change in the node structure, it updates the display but it does not automatically expand a node to show newly added children. In particular, if a user in our sample program adds a new child node to a node whose children are currently collapsed, then the new node is silently added to the collapsed subtree. This gives the user no feedback that the command was actually carried out. In such a case, you should make a special effort to expand all parent nodes so that the newly added node becomes visible. You use the `makeVisible` method of the `JTree` class for this purpose. The `makeVisible` method expects a tree path leading to the node that should become visible.

Thus, you need to construct a tree path from the root to the newly inserted node. To get a tree path, you first call the `getPathToRoot` method of the `DefaultTreeModel` class. It returns a `TreeNode[]` array of all nodes from a node to the root node. You pass that array to a `TreePath` constructor.

For example, here is how you make the new node visible:

```
TreeNode[] nodes = model.getPathToRoot(newNode);
TreePath path = new TreePath(nodes);
tree.makeVisible(path);
```

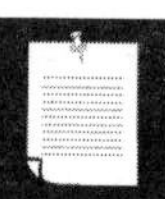

NOTE: It is curious that the DefaultTreeModel class feigns almost complete ignorance about the TreePath class, even though its job is to communicate with a JTree. The JTree class uses tree paths a lot, and it never uses arrays of node objects.

But now suppose your tree is contained inside a scroll pane. After the tree node expansion, the new node may still not be visible because it falls outside the viewport. To overcome that problem, call

```
tree.scrollPathToVisible(path);
```

instead of calling `makeVisible`. This call expands all nodes along the path, and it tells the ambient scroll pane to scroll the node at the end of the path into view (see Figure 6–16).

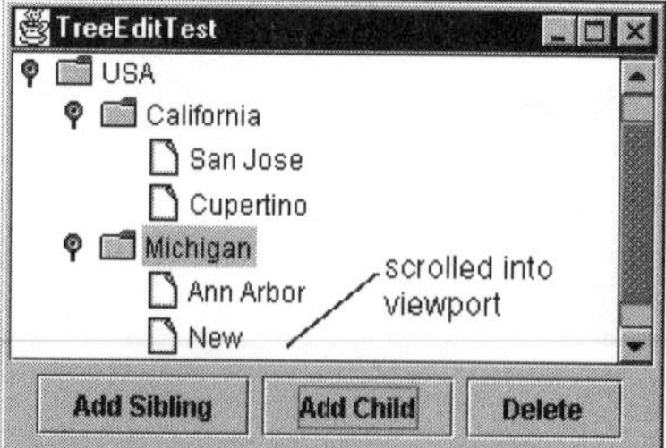

Figure 6–16: The scroll pane scrolls to display a new node

By default, tree nodes cannot be edited. However, if you call

```
tree.setEditable(true);
```

then the user can edit a node simply by double-clicking. This invokes the *default cell editor*, which is implemented by the `DefaultCellEditor` class. It is possible to install other cell editors, but we will defer our discussion of cell editors until the section on tables, where cell editors are more commonly used.

Example 6–2 shows the complete source code of the tree editing program. Run the program, add a few nodes, and edit them by double-clicking them. Observe how collapsed nodes expand to show added children and how the scroll pane keeps added nodes in the viewport.

Example 6–2: TreeEditTest.java

```
import java.awt.*;
import java.awt.event.*;
import javax.swing.*;
import javax.swing.tree.*;

public class TreeEditTest
{  public static void main(String[] args)
   {  JFrame frame = new TreeEditFrame();
      frame.show();
   }
}

class TreeEditFrame extends JFrame
   implements ActionListener
{  public TreeEditFrame()
   {  setTitle("TreeEditTest");
      setSize(300, 200);
      addWindowListener(new WindowAdapter()
         {  public void windowClosing(WindowEvent e)
            {  System.exit(0);
            }
         } );

      // construct tree

      TreeNode root = makeSampleTree();
      model = new DefaultTreeModel(root);
      tree = new JTree(model);
      tree.setEditable(true);

      // add scroll pane with tree to content pane

      Container contentPane = getContentPane();
      JScrollPane scrollPane = new JScrollPane(tree);
      contentPane.add(scrollPane, "Center");
```

```
      // make button panel

      JPanel panel = new JPanel();
      addSiblingButton = new JButton("Add Sibling");
      addSiblingButton.addActionListener(this);
      panel.add(addSiblingButton);
      addChildButton = new JButton("Add Child");
      addChildButton.addActionListener(this);
      panel.add(addChildButton);
      deleteButton = new JButton("Delete");
      deleteButton.addActionListener(this);
      panel.add(deleteButton);
      contentPane.add(panel, "South");
   }

   public TreeNode makeSampleTree()
   {  DefaultMutableTreeNode root
         = new DefaultMutableTreeNode("World");
      DefaultMutableTreeNode country
         = new DefaultMutableTreeNode("USA");
      root.add(country);
      DefaultMutableTreeNode state
         = new DefaultMutableTreeNode("California");
      country.add(state);
      DefaultMutableTreeNode city
         = new DefaultMutableTreeNode("San Jose");
      state.add(city);
      city = new DefaultMutableTreeNode("Cupertino");
      state.add(city);
      state = new DefaultMutableTreeNode("Michigan");
      country.add(state);
      city = new DefaultMutableTreeNode("Ann Arbor");
      state.add(city);
      country = new DefaultMutableTreeNode("Germany");
      root.add(country);
      state = new DefaultMutableTreeNode("Schleswig-Holstein");
      country.add(state);
      city = new DefaultMutableTreeNode("Kiel");
      state.add(city);
      return root;
   }

   public void actionPerformed(ActionEvent event)
   {  DefaultMutableTreeNode selectedNode
         = (DefaultMutableTreeNode)
            tree.getLastSelectedPathComponent();

      if (selectedNode == null) return;

      if (event.getSource().equals(deleteButton))
      {  if (selectedNode.getParent() != null)
            model.removeNodeFromParent(selectedNode);
         return;
```

```
      }

      // add new node as sibling or child

      DefaultMutableTreeNode newNode
         = new DefaultMutableTreeNode("New");

      if (event.getSource().equals(addSiblingButton))
      {  DefaultMutableTreeNode parent
            = (DefaultMutableTreeNode)selectedNode.getParent();

         if (parent != null)
         {  int selectedIndex = parent.getIndex(selectedNode);
            model.insertNodeInto(newNode, parent,
               selectedIndex + 1);
         }
      }
      else if (event.getSource().equals(addChildButton))
      {  model.insertNodeInto(newNode, selectedNode,
            selectedNode.getChildCount());
      }

      // now display new node

      TreeNode[] nodes = model.getPathToRoot(newNode);
      TreePath path = new TreePath(nodes);
      tree.scrollPathToVisible(path);
   }

   private DefaultTreeModel model;
   private JTree tree;
   private JButton addSiblingButton;
   private JButton addChildButton;
   private JButton deleteButton;
   private JButton editButton;
}
```

javax.swing.JTree API

- `TreePath getSelectionPath()`

  gets the path to the currently selected node (or the path to the first selected node if multiple nodes are selected). Returns `null` if no node is selected.

- `Object getLastSelectedPathComponent()`

  gets the node object that represents the currently selected node (or the first node if multiple nodes are selected). Returns `null` if no node is selected.

- `void makeVisible(TreePath path)`

  expands all nodes along the path.

- `void scrollPathToVisible(TreePath path)`

  expands all nodes along the path and, if the tree is contained in a scroll pane, scrolls to ensure that the last node on the path is visible.

`javax.swing.tree.TreePath`

- `Object getLastPathComponent()`

  gets the last object on this path, i.e., the node object that the path represents.

`javax.swing.tree.TreeNode`

- `TreeNode getParent()`

  returns the parent node of this node.

- `TreeNode getChildAt(int index)`

  looks up the child node at the given index. The index must be between 0 and `getChildCount() - 1`.

- `int getChildCount()`

  returns the number of children of this node.

- `Enumeration children()`

  returns an enumeration object that iterates through all children of this node.

`javax.swing.DefaultTreeModel`

- `void insertNodeInto(MutableTreeNode newChild, MutableTreeNode parent, int index)`

  inserts `newChild` as a new child node of `parent` at the given index.

- `void removeNodeFromParent(MutableTreeNode node)`

  removes `node` from this model.

- `void nodeChanged(TreeNode node)`

  notifies the tree model listeners that `node` has changed.

- `void nodesChanged(TreeNode parent, int[] changedChildIndexes)`

  notifies the tree model listeners that all child nodes of `parent` with the given indexes have changed.

- `void reload()`

  reloads all nodes into the model. This is a drastic operation that you should only use if the nodes have changed completely due to some outside influence.

Node enumeration

Sometimes you need to find a node in a tree, by starting at the root and visiting all children until you have found a match. The `DefaultMutableTreeNode` class has several convenience methods for iterating through nodes.

The `breadthFirstEnumeration` and `depthFirstEnumeration` methods return enumeration objects whose `nextElement` method visits all children of the current node, using either a breadth-first or depth-first traversal. Figure 6–17 shows the traversals for a sample tree—the node labels indicate the order in which the nodes are traversed.

Breadth-first enumeration is the easiest to visualize. The tree is traversed in layers. The root is visited first, followed by all of its children, then followed by the grandchildren, and so on.

To visualize depth-first enumeration, imagine a rat trapped in a tree-shaped maze. It first rushes along the first path until it comes to a leaf. Then, it backtracks and turns around to the next path, and so on.

Computer science types also call this *postorder traversal,* because the search process first visits the children before visiting the parents. The `postOrderTraversal` method is a synonym for `depthFirstTraversal`. For completeness, there is also a `preOrderTraversal`, a depth-first search that enumerates parents before the children.

Here is the typical usage pattern:

```
Enumeration breadthFirst = node.breadthFirstEnumeration();
while (breadthFirst.hasMoreElements())
   do something with breadthFirst.nextElement();
```

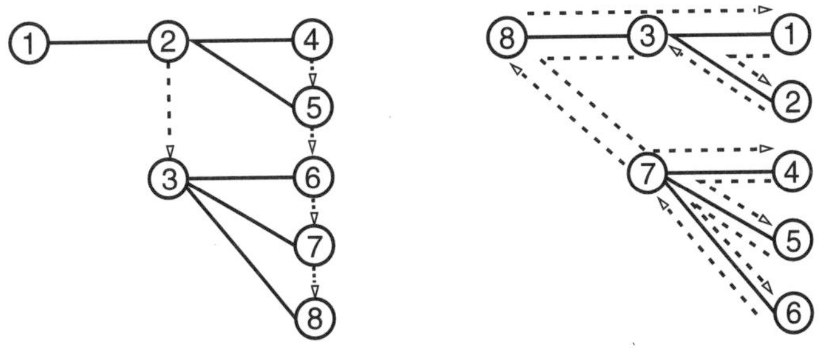

Figure 6–17: Tree traversal orders

Finally, there is a related method `pathFromAncestorEnumeration` that finds a path from an ancestor to a given node and then enumerates the nodes along that path. That's no big deal—it just keeps calling `getParent` until the ancestor is found and then presents the path in reverse order.

In our next example program, we put node enumeration to work. The program displays inheritance trees of classes. Type the name of a class into the text field on the bottom of the frame. The class and all of its superclasses are added to the tree (see Figure 6–18).

In this example, we take advantage of the fact that the user objects of the tree nodes can be objects of any type. Since our nodes describe classes, we will store `Class` objects in the nodes.

Of course, we don't want to add the same class object twice, so we need to check whether a class already exists in the tree. The following method finds the node with a given user object if it exists in the tree.

```
public DefaultMutableTreeNode findUserObject(Object obj)
{  Enumeration e = root.breadthFirstEnumeration();
   while (e.hasMoreElements())
   {  DefaultMutableTreeNode node
         = (DefaultMutableTreeNode)e.nextElement();
      if (node.getUserObject().equals(obj))
         return node;
   }
   return null;
}
```

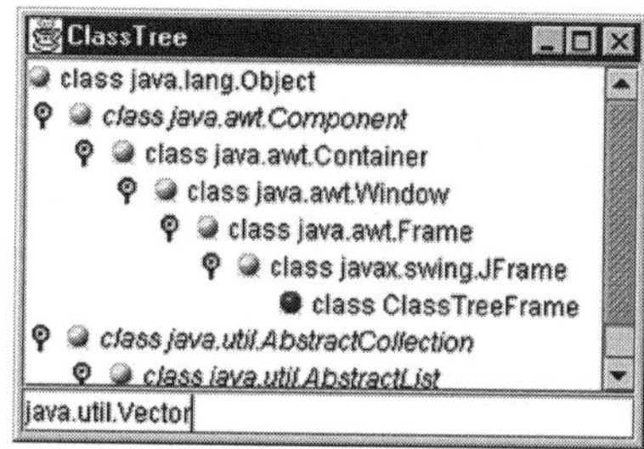

Figure 6–18: An inheritance tree

Rendering nodes

In your applications, you will often need to change the way in which a tree component draws the nodes. The most common change is, of course, to choose different icons for nodes and leaves. Other changes might involve changing the font of the node labels or drawing images at the nodes. All these changes are made possible by installing a new *tree cell renderer* into the tree. By default, the `JTree` class uses `DefaultTreeCellRenderer` objects to draw each node. The `DefaultTreeCellRenderer` class extends the `JLabel` class. The label contains the node icon and the node label.

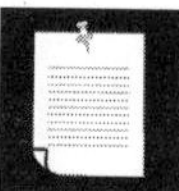

NOTE: The cell renderer does not draw the "handles" for expanding and collapsing subtrees. The handles are part of the look and feel, and it is recommended that you not change them.

You can customize the display in three ways.

1. You can change the icons, font, and background color used by a `DefaultTreeCellRenderer`. These settings are used for all nodes in the tree.
2. You can install a renderer that extends the `DefaultTreeCellRenderer` class and vary the icons, fonts, and background color for each node.
3. You can install a renderer that implements the `TreeCellRenderer` interface, to draw a custom image for each node.

Let us look at these possibilities one by one. The easiest customization is to construct a `DefaultTreeCellRenderer` object, change the icons, and install it into the tree:

```
DefaultTreeCellRenderer renderer
   = new DefaultTreeCellRenderer();
renderer.setLeafIcon(new ImageIcon("blue-ball.gif"));
   // used for leaf nodes
renderer.setClosedIcon(new ImageIcon("red-ball.gif"));
   // used for collapsed nodes
renderer.setOpenIcon(new ImageIcon("yellow-ball.gif"));
   // used for expanded nodes
tree.setCellRenderer(renderer);
```

You can see the effect in Figure 6–18 on page 338. We just use the "ball" icons as placeholders—presumably your user interface designer would supply you with appropriate icons to use for your applications.

We don't recommend that you change the font or background color for an entire tree—that is really the job of the look and feel.

However, it can be useful to change the font for individual nodes in a tree to highlight some of them. If you look carefully at Figure 6–18, you will notice that the *abstract* classes are set in italics.

To change the appearance of individual nodes, you install a tree cell renderer. Tree cell renderers are very similar to the list cell renderers we discussed in Chapter 9 of Volume 1. The `TreeCellRenderer` interface has a single method

```
Component getTreeCellRendererComponent(JTree tree,
   Object value, boolean selected, boolean expanded,
   boolean leaf, int row, boolean hasFocus)
```

This method is called for each node. It returns a *component* whose `paint` method renders the node in the tree display. The `paint` method is invoked with an appropriate `Graphics` object, with coordinates and clip rectangle set so that the drawing appears at the correct location.

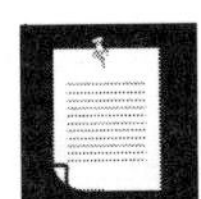

NOTE: You may wonder why you don't simply get to place a `paint` method into the class that implements the tree cell renderer interface. There is a very good reason. It is usually easier for you to tweak existing components than to program the actual drawing code. For example, the default tree cell renderer simply extends `JLabel` and lets the label worry about the correct spacing between the icon and the label text.

The `getTreeCellRendererComponent` method of the `DefaultTreeCell-Renderer` class returns `this`—in other words, a label. (Recall that the `DefaultTreeCellRenderer` class extends the `JLabel` class.) To customize the component, extend the `DefaultTreeCellRenderer` class. Override the `getTreeCellRendererComponent` method as follows: Call the superclass method, so that it can prepare the label data. Customize the label properties, and finally return `this`.

```
class MyTreeCellRenderer extends DefaultTreeCellRenderer
{  public Component getTreeCellRendererComponent(JTree tree,
      Object value, boolean selected, boolean expanded,
      boolean leaf, int row, boolean hasFocus)
   {  super.getTreeCellRendererComponent(tree, value,
         selected, expanded, leaf, row, hasFocus);
      DefaultMutableTreeNode node
         = (DefaultMutableTreeNode)value;
      look at node.getUserObject();
      Font font = appropriate font;
      setFont(font);
      return this;
   }
};
```

CAUTION: The `value` parameter of the `getTreeCellRendererComponent` method is the *node* object, *not* the user object! Recall that the user object is a feature of the `DefaultMutableTreeNode`, and that a `JTree` can contain nodes of an arbitrary type. If your tree uses `DefaultMutableTreeNode` nodes, then you must retrieve the user object in a second step, as we did in the preceding code sample.

CAUTION: The `DefaultTreeCellRenderer` uses the *same* label object for all nodes, only changing the label text for each node. If you change the font for a particular node, you must set it back to its default value when the method is called again. Otherwise, all subsequent nodes will be drawn in the changed font! Look at the code in Example 6–3 to see how to restore the font to the default.

We will not show an example for a tree cell renderer that draws arbitrary graphics. You can look at the list cell renderer in Chapter 9 of Volume 1—the technique is entirely analogous.

Let's put tree cell renderers to work. Example 6–3 shows the complete source code for the class tree program. The program displays inheritance hierarchies, and it customizes the display to show abstract classes in italics. You can type the name of any class into the text field at the bottom of the frame. Press the ENTER key to add the class and its superclasses to the tree. (This is not a stellar user interface, but it was easy to program since pressing ENTER in a text field generates an action event.) You must enter the full package name, such as `java.util.Vector`.

This program is a bit tricky because it uses reflection to construct the class tree. This work is contained inside the `addClass` method. (The details are not that important. We use the class tree in this example because inheritance trees yield a nice supply of trees without laborious coding. If you display trees in your own

applications, you will have your own source of hierarchical data.) The method first uses breadth-first search to find whether the current class is already in the tree by calling the `findUserObject` method that we implemented in the preceding section. If the class is not already in the tree, we add the superclass to the tree, then make the new class node a child and make that node visible.

The `ClassNameTreeCellRenderer` sets the class name in either the normal or italic font, depending on the `ABSTRACT` modifier of the `Class` object. We don't want to set a particular font since we don't want to change whatever font the look and feel normally uses for labels. For that reason, we use the font from the label and *derive* an italic font from it. Recall that there is only a single shared `JLabel` object that is returned by all calls. We need to hang on to the original font and restore it in the next call to the `getTreeCellRendererComponent` method.

Finally, note how we change the node icons in the `ClassTreeFrame` constructor.

Example 6–3: ClassTree.java

```
import java.awt.*;
import java.awt.event.*;
import java.lang.reflect.*;
import java.util.*;
import javax.swing.*;
import javax.swing.event.*;
import javax.swing.tree.*;

public class ClassTree
{  public static void main(String[] args)
   {  JFrame frame = new ClassTreeFrame();
      frame.show();
   }
}

class ClassTreeFrame extends JFrame
   implements ActionListener
{  public ClassTreeFrame()
   {  setTitle("ClassTree");
      setSize(300, 200);
      addWindowListener(new WindowAdapter()
         {  public void windowClosing(WindowEvent e)
            {  System.exit(0);
            }
         } );

      // the root of the class tree is Object
      root = new DefaultMutableTreeNode(java.lang.Object.class);
      model = new DefaultTreeModel(root);
      tree = new JTree(model);

      // add this class to populate the tree with some data
```

```
        addClass(getClass());

        // set up node icons
        ClassNameTreeCellRenderer renderer
           = new ClassNameTreeCellRenderer();
        renderer.setClosedIcon(new ImageIcon("red-ball.gif"));
        renderer.setOpenIcon(new ImageIcon("yellow-ball.gif"));
        renderer.setLeafIcon(new ImageIcon("blue-ball.gif"));
        tree.setCellRenderer(renderer);

        Container contentPane = getContentPane();
        contentPane.add(new JScrollPane(tree), "Center");

        // new class names are typed into this text field
        textField = new JTextField();
        textField.addActionListener(this);
        contentPane.add(textField, "South");
     }

     public void actionPerformed(ActionEvent event)
     {  // add the class whose name is in the text field
        try
        {  String text = textField.getText();
           addClass(Class.forName(text));
           // clear text field to indicate success
           textField.setText("");
        }
        catch (ClassNotFoundException e)
        {  Toolkit.getDefaultToolkit().beep();
        }
     }

     public DefaultMutableTreeNode findUserObject(Object obj)
     {  // find the node containing a user object
        Enumeration e = root.breadthFirstEnumeration();
        while (e.hasMoreElements())
        {  DefaultMutableTreeNode node
              = (DefaultMutableTreeNode)e.nextElement();
           if (node.getUserObject().equals(obj))
              return node;
        }
        return null;
     }

     public DefaultMutableTreeNode addClass(Class c)
     {  // add a new class to the tree

        // skip non-class types
        if (c.isInterface() || c.isPrimitive()) return null;

        // if the class is already in the tree, return its node
        DefaultMutableTreeNode node = findUserObject(c);
```

```
      if (node != null) return node;

      // class isn't present--first add class parent recursively

      Class s = c.getSuperclass();

      DefaultMutableTreeNode parent;
      if (s == null)
         parent = root;
      else
         parent = addClass(s);

      // add the class as a child to the parent
      DefaultMutableTreeNode newNode = new DefaultMutableTreeNode(c);
      model.insertNodeInto(newNode, parent, parent.getChildCount());

      // make node visible
      TreePath path = new TreePath(model.getPathToRoot(newNode));
      tree.makeVisible(path);

      return newNode;
   }

   private DefaultMutableTreeNode root;
   private DefaultTreeModel model;
   private JTree tree;
   private JTextField textField;
}

class ClassNameTreeCellRenderer extends DefaultTreeCellRenderer
{  public Component getTreeCellRendererComponent(JTree tree,
      Object value, boolean selected, boolean expanded,
      boolean leaf, int row, boolean hasFocus)
   {  super.getTreeCellRendererComponent(tree, value,
         selected, expanded, leaf, row, hasFocus);
      // get the user object
      DefaultMutableTreeNode node = (DefaultMutableTreeNode)value;
      Class c = (Class)node.getUserObject();

      // the first time, derive italic font from plain font
      if (plainFont == null)
      {  plainFont = getFont();
         /* the tree cell renderer is sometimes called with a
            label that has a null font
         */
         if (plainFont != null)
            italicFont = plainFont.deriveFont(Font.ITALIC);
      }

      // set font to italic if the class is abstract
      if ((c.getModifiers() & Modifier.ABSTRACT) == 0)
         setFont(plainFont);
```

```
      else
         setFont(italicFont);
      return this;
   }

   private Font plainFont = null;
   private Font italicFont = null;
}
```

javax.swing.tree.DefaultMutableTreeNode

- `Enumeration breadthFirstEnumeration()`
- `Enumeration depthFirstEnumeration()`
- `Enumeration preOrderTraversal()`
- `Enumeration postOrderTraversal()`

  return enumeration objects for visiting all nodes of the tree model in a particular order. In breadth-first traversal, children that are closer to the root are visited before those that are farther away. In depth-first traversal, all children of a node are completely enumerated before its siblings are visited. The `postOrderTraversal` method is a synonym for `depthFirstEnumeration`. The `preOrderTraversal` is identical to the postorder traversal except that parents are enumerated before their children.

javax.swing.tree.TreeCellRenderer

- `Component getTreeCellRendererComponent(JTree tree, Object value, boolean selected, boolean expanded, boolean leaf, int row, boolean hasFocus)`

  returns a component whose `paint` method is invoked to render a tree cell.

Parameters:	`tree`	the tree containing the node to be rendered
	`value`	the node to be rendered
	`selected`	`true` if the node is currently selected
	`expanded`	`true` if the children of the node are visible
	`leaf`	`true` if the node needs to be displayed as a tree
	`row`	the display row containing the node
	`hasFocus`	`true` if the node currently has input focus

javax.swing.tree.DefaultTreeCellRenderer

- `void setLeafIcon(Icon icon)`
- `void setOpenIcon(Icon icon)`
- `void setClosedIcon(Icon icon)`

  set the icon to show for a leaf node, an expanded node, and a collapsed node.

Listening to tree events

Most commonly, a tree component is paired with some other component. When the user selects tree nodes, some information shows up in another window. Look at Figure 6–19 for an example. When the user selects a class, the instance and static variables of that class are displayed in the text area to the right.

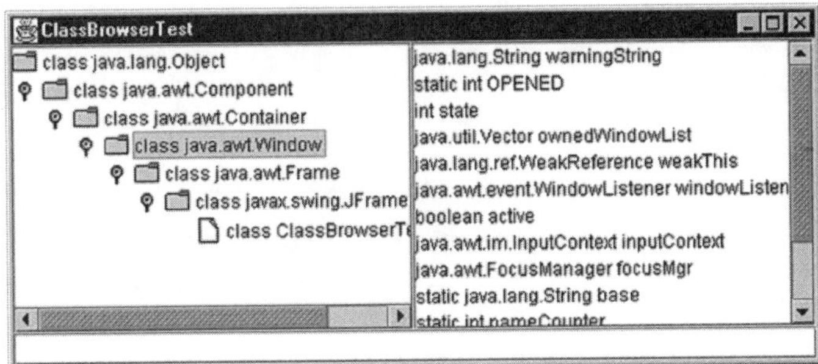

Figure 6–19: A class browser

To obtain this behavior, you install a *tree selection listener*. The listener must implement the `TreeSelectionListener` interface, an interface with a single method

```
void valueChanged(TreeSelectionEvent event)
```

That method is called whenever the user selects or deselects tree nodes.

You add the listener to the tree in the normal way:

```
tree.addTreeSelectionListener(listener);
```

You can specify whether the user is allowed to select a single node, a contiguous range of nodes, or an arbitrary, potentially discontiguous, set of nodes. The `JTree` class uses a `TreeSelectionModel` to manage node selection. You need to retrieve the model to set the selection state to one of `SINGLE_TREE_SELECTION`, `CONTIGUOUS_TREE_SELECTION`, or `DISCONTIGUOUS_TREE_SELECTION`. (Discontiguous selection mode is the default.) For example, in our class browser, we only want to allow selection of a single class:

```
int mode = TreeSelectionModel.SINGLE_TREE_SELECTION;
tree.getSelectionModel().setSelectionMode(mode);
```

Apart from setting the selection mode, you need not worry about the tree selection model.

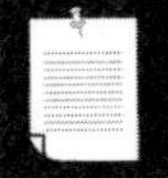

NOTE: How the user selects multiple items depends on the look and feel. In the Metal look and feel, hold down the CTRL key while clicking on an item to add the item to the selection, or to remove it if it was currently selected. Hold down the SHIFT key while clicking on an item to select a *range* of items, extending from the previously selected item to the new item.

To find out the current selection, you query the tree with the `getSelectionPaths` method:

```
TreePath[] selectedPaths = tree.getSelectionPaths();
```

If you restricted the user to a single selection, you can use the convenience method `getSelectionPath`, which returns the first selected path, or `null` if no path was selected.

CAUTION: The `TreeSelectionEvent` class has a `getPaths` method that returns an array of `TreePath` objects, but that array describes *selection changes*, not the current selection.

Example 6–4 puts tree selection to work. This program builds upon Example 6–3; however, to keep the program short, we did not use a custom tree cell renderer. In the frame constructor, we restrict the user to single item selection and add a tree selection listener. When the `valueChanged` method is called, we ignore its event parameter and simply ask the tree for the current selection path. As always, we need to get the last node of the path and look up its user object. We then call the `getFieldDescription` method, which uses reflection to assemble a string with all fields of the selected class. Finally, that string is displayed in the text area.

Example 6–4: ClassBrowserTree.java

```
import java.awt.*;
import java.awt.event.*;
import java.lang.reflect.*;
import java.util.*;
import javax.swing.*;
import javax.swing.event.*;
import javax.swing.tree.*;

public class ClassBrowserTest
{  public static void main(String[] args)
   {  JFrame frame = new ClassBrowserTestFrame();
      frame.show();
   }
}

class ClassBrowserTestFrame extends JFrame
   implements ActionListener, TreeSelectionListener
{  public ClassBrowserTestFrame()
   {  setTitle("ClassBrowserTest");
      setSize(300, 200);
      addWindowListener(new WindowAdapter()
         {  public void windowClosing(WindowEvent e)
            {  System.exit(0);
```

```
         }
      } );

   // the root of the class tree is Object
   root = new DefaultMutableTreeNode(java.lang.Object.class);
   model = new DefaultTreeModel(root);
   tree = new JTree(model);

   // add this class to populate the tree with some data
   addClass(getClass());

   // set up selection mode
   tree.addTreeSelectionListener(this);
   int mode = TreeSelectionModel.SINGLE_TREE_SELECTION;
   tree.getSelectionModel().setSelectionMode(mode);

   // this text area holds the class description
   textArea = new JTextArea();

   // add tree and text area to the content pane
   JPanel panel = new JPanel();
   panel.setLayout(new GridLayout(1, 2));
   panel.add(new JScrollPane(tree));
   panel.add(new JScrollPane(textArea));

   Container contentPane = getContentPane();
   contentPane.add(panel, "Center");

   // new class names are typed into this text
   textField = new JTextField();
   textField.addActionListener(this);
   contentPane.add(textField, "South");
}

public void actionPerformed(ActionEvent event)
{  // add the class whose name is in the text field
   try
   {  String text = textField.getText();
      addClass(Class.forName(text));
      // clear text field to indicate success
      textField.setText("");
   }
   catch (ClassNotFoundException e)
   {  Toolkit.getDefaultToolkit().beep();
   }
}

public void valueChanged(TreeSelectionEvent event)
{  // the user selected a different node--update description
```

```
      TreePath path = tree.getSelectionPath();
      if (path == null) return;
      DefaultMutableTreeNode selectedNode
         = (DefaultMutableTreeNode)path.getLastPathComponent();
      Class c = (Class)selectedNode.getUserObject();
      String description = getFieldDescription(c);
      textArea.setText(description);
   }

   public DefaultMutableTreeNode findUserObject(Object obj)
   {  // find the node containing a user object
      Enumeration e = root.breadthFirstEnumeration();
      while (e.hasMoreElements())
      {  DefaultMutableTreeNode node
            = (DefaultMutableTreeNode)e.nextElement();
         if (node.getUserObject().equals(obj))
            return node;
      }
      return null;
   }

   public DefaultMutableTreeNode addClass(Class c)
   {  // add a new class to the tree

      // skip non-class types
      if (c.isInterface() || c.isPrimitive()) return null;

      // if the class is already in the tree, return its node
      DefaultMutableTreeNode node = findUserObject(c);
      if (node != null) return node;

      // class isn't present--first add class parent recursively

      Class s = c.getSuperclass();

      DefaultMutableTreeNode parent;
      if (s == null)
         parent = root;
      else
         parent = addClass(s);

      parent = addClass(s);

      // add the class as a child to the parent
      DefaultMutableTreeNode newNode = new DefaultMutableTreeNode(c);
      model.insertNodeInto(newNode, parent, parent.getChildCount());

      // make node visible
      TreePath path = new TreePath(model.getPathToRoot(newNode));
```

```
      tree.makeVisible(path);

      return newNode;
   }

   public static String getFieldDescription(Class c)
   {  // use reflection to find types and names of fields
      String r = "";
      Field[] fields = c.getDeclaredFields();
      for (int i = 0; i < fields.length; i++)
      {  Field f = fields[i];
         if ((f.getModifiers() & Modifier.STATIC) != 0)
            r += "static ";
         r += f.getType().getName() + " ";
         r += f.getName() + "\n";
      }
      return r;
   }

   private DefaultMutableTreeNode root;
   private DefaultTreeModel model;
   private JTree tree;
   private JTextField textField;
   private JTextArea textArea;
}
```

`javax.swing.JTree`

- `Path getSelectionPath()`
- `Path[] getSelectionPaths()`

  returns the first selected path, or an array of paths to all selected nodes. If no paths are selected, both methods return `null`.

`javax.swing.event.TreeSelectionListener`

- `void valueChanged(TreeSelectionEvent event)`

  is called whenever nodes are selected or deselected.

`javax.swing.event.TreeSelectionEvent`

- `TreePath getPath()`
- `TreePath[] getPaths()`

  get the first path, or all paths, that have *changed* in this selection event. If you want to know the current selection, not the selection change, you should call `JTree.getSelectionPaths` instead.

Custom tree models

In the final example, we implement a program that inspects the contents of a variable, just like a debugger does (see Figure 6–20).

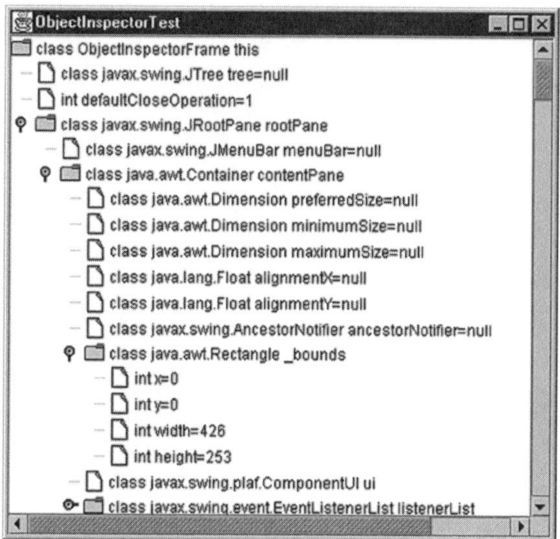

Figure 6–20: An object inspection tree

Before going further, compile and run the example program! Each node corresponds to an instance variable. If the variable is an object, expand it to see *its* instance variables. The program inspects the contents of the frame window. If you poke around a few of the instance variables, you should be able to find some familiar classes. You'll also gain some respect for how complex the Swing user interface components are under the hood.

What's remarkable about the program is that the tree does not use the `DefaultTreeModel`. If you already have data that is hierarchically organized, you may not want to build a duplicate tree and worry about keeping both trees synchronized. That is the situation in our case—the inspected objects are already linked to each other through the object references, so there is no need to replicate the linking structure.

The `TreeModel` interface has only a handful of methods. The first group of methods enables the `JTree` to find the tree nodes by first getting the root, then the children. The `JTree` class only calls these methods when the user actually expands a node.

```
Object getRoot()
int getChildCount(Object parent)
Object getChild(Object parent, int index)
```

Note that the `TreeModel` interface, like the `JTree` class itself, has no notion of nodes! The root and its children can be any objects. The `TreeModel` is responsible for telling the `JTree` how they are connected.

The next method of the `TreeModel` interface is the reverse of `getChild`:

```
int getIndexOfChild(Object parent, Object child)
```

Actually, this method can be implemented in terms of the first three—see the code in Example 6–5.

The tree model tells the `JTree` which nodes should be displayed as leaves:

```
boolean isLeaf(Object node)
```

If your code changes the tree model, then the tree needs to be notified so that it can redraw itself. The tree adds itself as a `TreeModelListener` to the model. Thus, the model must support the usual listener management methods:

```
void addTreeModelListener(TreeModelListener l)
void removeTreeModelListener(TreeModelListener l)
```

You can see implementations for these methods in Example 6–5.

When the model modifies the tree contents, it calls one of the four methods of the `TreeModelListener` interface:

```
void treeNodesChanged(TreeModelEvent e)
void treeNodesInserted(TreeModelEvent e)
void treeNodesRemoved(TreeModelEvent e)
void treeStructureChanged(TreeModelEvent e)
```

The `TreeModelEvent` object describes the location of the change. The details of assembling a tree model event that describes an insertion or removal event are quite technical. You only need to worry about firing these events if your tree can actually have nodes added and removed. In Example 6–5, we show you how to fire one event: replacing the root with a new object.

TIP: The Swing programmers evidently got tired enough of event firing that they provide a convenience class `javax.swing.EventListenerList` that collects listeners. The API notes describe how to use the class.

Finally, if the user edits a tree node, your model gets called with the change:

```
void valueForPathChanged(TreePath path, Object newValue)
```

If you don't allow editing, this method is never called.

If you don't need to support editing, then it is very easy to construct a tree model. Implement the three methods

```
Object getRoot()
int getChildCount(Object parent)
Object getChild(Object parent, int index)
```

These methods describe the structure of the tree. Supply routine implementations of the other five methods, as in Example 6–5. Then, you are ready to display your tree.

Now let's turn to the implementation of the example program. Our tree will contain objects of type `Variable`.

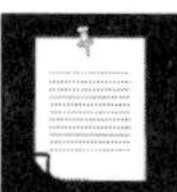

NOTE: Had we used the `DefaultTreeModel`, our nodes would have been objects of type `DefaultMutableTreeNode` with *user objects* of type `Variable`.

For example, suppose you inspect the variable

```
Employee joe;
```

That variable has a *type* `Employee.class`, a *name* `"joe"`, and a *value*, the value of the object reference `joe`. We define a class `Variable` that describes a variable in a program:

```
Variable v = new Variable(Employee.class, "joe", joe);
```

If the type of the variable is a primitive type, you must use an object wrapper for the value.

```
new Variable(double.class, "salary", new Double(salary));
```

If the type of the variable is a class, then the variable has *fields*. Using reflection, we enumerate all fields and collect them in an `ArrayList`. Since the `getFields` method of the `Class` class does not return fields of the superclass, we need to call `getFields` on all superclasses as well. You will find the code in the `Variable` constructor. The `getFields` method of our `Variable` class returns the array of fields. Finally, the `toString` method of the `Variable` class formats the node label. The label always contains the variable type and name. If the variable is not a class, the label also contains the value.

NOTE: If the type is an array, then we do not display the elements of the array. This would not be difficult to do; we leave it as the proverbial "exercise for the reader."

Let's move on to the tree model. The first two methods are very simple.

```
public Object getRoot()
{  return root;
}

public int getChildCount(Object parent)
{  return ((Variable)parent).getFields().size();
}
```

The `getChild` method returns a new `Variable` object that describes a particular field. The `getType` and `getName` method of the `Field` class yield the field type and name. By using reflection, you can read the field value as `f.get(parentValue)`.

That method can throw an `IllegalAccessException`. However, we made all fields accessible in the `Variable` constructor, so this won't happen in practice.

Here is the complete code of the `getChild` method.

```
public Object getChild(Object parent, int index)
{  ArrayList fields = ((Variable)parent).getFields();
   Field f = (Field)fields.get(index);
   Object parentValue = ((Variable)parent).getValue();
   try
   {  return new Variable(f.getType(), f.getName(),
         f.get(parentValue));
   }
   catch(IllegalAccessException e)
   {  return null;
   }
}
```

These three methods reveal the structure of the object tree to the `JTree` component. The remaining methods are routine—see the source code in Example 6–5.

There is one remarkable fact about this tree model: it actually describes an *infinite* tree. You can verify this by following one of the `WeakReference` objects. Click on the variable named `referent`. It leads you right back to the original object. You get an identical subtree, and you can open its `WeakReference` object again, ad infinitum. Of course, you cannot *store* an infinite set of nodes. The tree model simply generates the nodes on demand, as the user expands the parents.

This example concludes our discussion on trees. We move on to the table component, another complex Swing component. Superficially, trees and tables don't seem to have much in common, but you will find that they both use the same concepts for data models and cell rendering.

Example 6–5: ObjectInspectorTest.java

```
import java.awt.*;
import java.awt.event.*;
import java.lang.reflect.*;
import java.util.*;
import javax.swing.*;
import javax.swing.event.*;
import javax.swing.tree.*;

public class ObjectInspectorTest
{  public static void main(String[] args)
   {  JFrame frame = new ObjectInspectorFrame();
      frame.show();
   }
}

class ObjectInspectorFrame extends JFrame
```

```
{  public ObjectInspectorFrame()
   {  setTitle("ObjectInspectorTest");
      setSize(300, 200);
      addWindowListener(new WindowAdapter()
         {  public void windowClosing(WindowEvent e)
            {  System.exit(0);
            }
         } );

      // we inspect this frame object

      Variable v = new Variable(getClass(), "this", this);
      ObjectTreeModel model = new ObjectTreeModel();
      model.setRoot(v);

      // construct and show tree

      tree = new JTree(model);
      JScrollPane scrollPane = new JScrollPane(tree);
      Container contentPane = getContentPane();
      contentPane.add(scrollPane, "Center");
   }

   private JTree tree;
}

class ObjectTreeModel implements TreeModel
{  public ObjectTreeModel()
   {  root = null;
   }

   public void setRoot(Variable v)
   {  Variable oldRoot = v;
      root = v;
      fireTreeStructureChanged(oldRoot);
   }

   public Object getRoot()
   {  return root;
   }

   public int getChildCount(Object parent)
   {  return ((Variable)parent).getFields().size();
   }

   public Object getChild(Object parent, int index)
   {  ArrayList fields = ((Variable)parent).getFields();
      Field f = (Field)fields.get(index);
      Object parentValue = ((Variable)parent).getValue();
      try
      {  return new Variable(f.getType(), f.getName(),
            f.get(parentValue));
```

```
      }
      catch(IllegalAccessException e)
      {  return null;
      }
   }

   public int getIndexOfChild(Object parent, Object child)
   {  int n = getChildCount(parent);
      for (int i = 0; i < n; i++)
         if (getChild(parent, i).equals(child))
            return i;
      return -1;
   }

   public boolean isLeaf(Object node)
   {  return getChildCount(node) == 0;
   }

   public void valueForPathChanged(TreePath path, Object newValue)
   {}

   public void addTreeModelListener(TreeModelListener l)
   {  listenerList.add(TreeModelListener.class, l);
   }

   public void removeTreeModelListener(TreeModelListener l)
   {  listenerList.remove(TreeModelListener.class, l);
   }

   protected void fireTreeStructureChanged(Object oldRoot)
   {  TreeModelEvent event
         = new TreeModelEvent(this, new Object[] {oldRoot});
      Object[] listeners = listenerList.getListenerList();
      for (int i = listeners.length - 2; i >= 0; i -= 2)
         ((TreeModelListener)listeners[i+1]).
               treeStructureChanged(event);
   }

   private Variable root;
   private EventListenerList listenerList
      = new EventListenerList();
}

class Variable
{  public Variable(Class aType, String aName, Object aValue)
   {  type = aType;
      name = aName;
      value = aValue;
      fields = new ArrayList();

      /* find all fields if we have a class type
         except we don't expand strings and null values
```

```
      */

      if (!type.isPrimitive() && !type.isArray() &&
         !type.equals(String.class) && value != null)
      {  // get fields from the class and all superclasses
         for (Class c = value.getClass(); c != null;
            c = c.getSuperclass())
         {  Field[] f = c.getDeclaredFields();
            AccessibleObject.setAccessible(f, true);

            // get all nonstatic fields
            for (int i = 0; i < f.length; i++)
               if ((f[i].getModifiers() & Modifier.STATIC) == 0)
                  fields.add(f[i]);
         }
      }
   }

   public Object getValue()
   {  return value;
   }

   public ArrayList getFields()
   {  return fields;
   }

   public String toString()
   {  String r = type + " " + name;
      if (type.isPrimitive())
         r += "=" + value;
      else if (type.equals(String.class))
         r += "=" + value;
      else if (value == null)
         r += "=null";
      return r;
   }

   private Class type;
   private String name;
   private Object value;
   private ArrayList fields;
}
```

javax.swing.tree.TreeModel

- `Object getRoot()`

  returns the root node.
- `int getChildCount(Object parent)`

  gets the number of children of the `parent` node.
- `Object getChild(Object parent, int index)`

  gets the child node of the `parent` node at the given index.

- `int getIndexOfChild(Object parent, Object child)`

  gets the index of the `child` node. It must be a child of the `parent` node.

- `boolean isLeaf(Object node)`

  returns `true` if `node` is conceptually a leaf of the tree.

- `void addTreeModelListener(TreeModelListener l)`
- `void removeTreeModelListener(TreeModelListener l)`

  add and remove listeners that are notified when the information in the tree model changes.

- `void valueForPathChanged(TreePath path, Object newValue)`

  is called when a cell editor has modified the value of a node.

  Parameters: `path` the path to the node that has been edited

  `object` the replacement value returned by the editor

javax.swing.event.TreeModelListener

- `void treeNodesChanged(TreeModelEvent e)`
- `void treeNodesInserted(TreeModelEvent e)`
- `void treeNodesRemoved(TreeModelEvent e)`
- `void treeStructureChanged(TreeModelEvent e)`

  are called by the tree model when the tree has been modified.

javax.swing.event.TreeModelEvent

- `TreeModelEvent(Object eventSource, TreePath node)`

  constructs a tree model event.

  Parameters: `eventSource` the tree model generating this event

  `node` the path to the node that is being changed

javax.swing.EventListenerList

- `void add(Class t, EventListener l)`

  adds an event listener and its class to the list. The class is stored so that event firing methods can selectively call events. Typical usage is in an `addXxxListener` method:

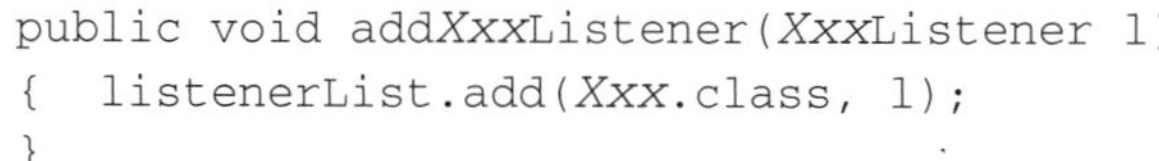

```
public void addXxxListener(XxxListener l)
{  listenerList.add(Xxx.class, l);
}
```

  Parameters: `c` the listener type

  `l` the listener

- `void remove(Class t, EventListener l)`

  removes an event listener and its class from the list. Typical usage is in a `removeXxxListener` method:

```
public void removeXxxListener(XxxListener l)
{  listenerList.remove(XxxListener.class, l);
}
```

Parameters:	c	the listener type
	l	the listener

- `Object[] getListenerList()`

  returns an array whose elements with even-numbered index are listener classes and whose elements with odd-numbered index are listener objects. The array is guaranteed to be non-`null`. Typical usage is in an event firing method:

```
protected void fireEventOccurred(EventParameters p)
{  XxxEvent event = new XxxEvent(this, p);
   Object[] listeners = listenerList.getListenerList();
   for (int i = listeners.length - 2; i >= 0; i -= 2)
      if (listeners[i] instanceof XxxListener.class)
         ((XxxListener)listeners[i+1]).
               eventOccurred(event);
}
```

Tables

The `JTable` component displays a two-dimensional grid of objects. Of course, tables are very common in user interfaces. The Swing team has put a lot of effort into the table control. Tables are inherently complex, but—perhaps more successfully than with other Swing classes—the `JTable` component hides much of that complexity. You can produce fully functional tables with rich behavior by writing a few lines of code. Of course, you can write more code and customize the display and behavior for your specific applications.

In this section, we explain how to make simple tables, how the user interacts with them, and how to make some of the most common adjustments. As with the other complex Swing controls, it is impossible to cover all aspects in complete detail. If you need more information, you can find it in *Core Java Foundation Classes* by Kim Topley or *Graphic Java 2* by David Geary.

A Simple Table

As with the tree control, a `JTable` does not store its own data, but it obtains its data from a *table model*. Furthermore, you can construct a table from a two-dimensional array of objects, and it automatically wraps the array into a default model. That is the strategy that we will use in our first example. Later in this chapter, we will turn to table models.

Figure 6–21 shows a typical table, describing properties of the planets of the solar system. (A planet is *gaseous* if it consists mostly of hydrogen and helium. You should take the "Color" entries with a grain of salt—that column was added because it will be useful in a later code example.)

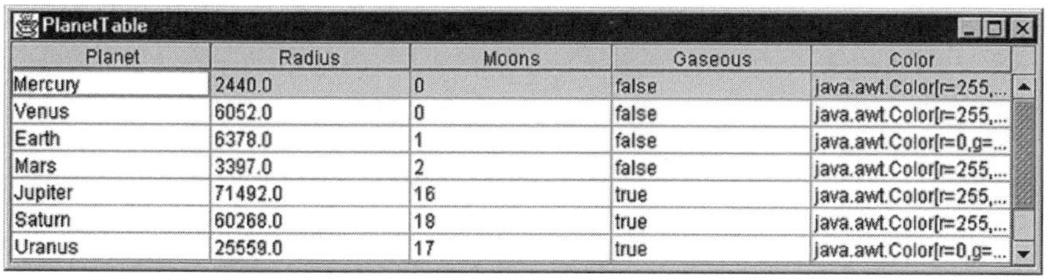

PlanetTable

Planet	Radius	Moons	Gaseous	Color
Mercury	2440.0	0	false	java.awt.Color[r=255,...
Venus	6052.0	0	false	java.awt.Color[r=255,...
Earth	6378.0	1	false	java.awt.Color[r=0,g=...
Mars	3397.0	2	false	java.awt.Color[r=255,...
Jupiter	71492.0	16	true	java.awt.Color[r=255,...
Saturn	60268.0	18	true	java.awt.Color[r=255,...
Uranus	25559.0	17	true	java.awt.Color[r=0,g=...

Figure 6–21: A simple table

As you can see from the code in Example 6–6, the data of the table is stored as a two-dimensional array of `Object` values:

```
Object[][] cells =
{  { "Mercury", new Double(2440),  new Integer(0),
      Boolean.FALSE, Color.yellow
   },
   { "Venus", new Double(6052), new Integer(0),
      Boolean.FALSE, Color.yellow
   },
   . . .
}
```

The table simply invokes the `toString` method on each object to display it. That's why the colors show up as `java.awt.Color[r=...,g=...,b=...]`.

You supply the column names in a separate array of strings:

```
String[] columnNames =
   {  "Planet", "Radius", "Moons", "Gaseous", "Color"
   };
```

Then, you construct a table from the cell and column name arrays. Finally, add scroll bars in the usual way, by wrapping the table in a `JScrollPane`.

```
JTable table = new JTable(cells, columnNames);
JScrollPane pane = new JScrollPane(table);
```

The resulting table already has surprisingly rich behavior. Resize the table vertically until the scroll bar shows up. Then, scroll the table. Note that the column headers don't scroll out of view!

Next, click on one of the column headers and drag it to the left or right. See how the entire column becomes detached (see Figure 6–22). You can drop it to a different location. This rearranges the columns *in the view only.* The data model is not affected.

PlanetTable

Planet		Moons	adius	Gaseous	Color
Mercury		0	0.0	false	java.aw...
Venus		0	2.0	false	java.aw...
Earth		1	8.0	false	java.aw...
Mars		2	7.0	false	java.aw...
Jupiter		16	92.0	true	java.aw...
Saturn		18	68.0	true	java.aw...
Uranus		17	59.0	true	java.aw...
Neptune		8	66.0	true	java.aw...
Pluto		1	7.0	false	java.aw...

Figure 6–22: Moving a column

To *resize* columns, simply place the cursor between two columns until the cursor shape changes to an arrow. Then, drag the column boundary to the desired place (see Figure 6–23).

PlanetTable

Planet	Radius	Moons	Gaseous	Color
Mercury	2440.0	0	false	java.awt.Color[r=255,g=...
Venus	6052.0	0	false	java.awt.Color[r=255,g=...
Earth	6378.0	1	false	java.awt.Color[r=0,g=0,...
Mars	3397.0	2	false	java.awt.Color[r=255,g=...
Jupiter	71492.0	16	true	java.awt.Color[r=255,g=...
Saturn	60268.0	18	true	java.awt.Color[r=255,g=...
Uranus	25559.0	17	true	java.awt.Color[r=0,g=0,...
Neptune	24766.0	8	true	java.awt.Color[r=0,g=0,...
Pluto	1137.0	1	false	java.awt.Color[r=0,g=0,...

Figure 6–23: Resizing columns

Users can select rows by clicking anywhere in a row. The selected rows are highlighted; you will see later how to get selection events. Users can also edit the table entries by clicking on a cell and typing into it. However, in this code example, the edits do not change the underlying data. In your programs, you should either make cells uneditable or handle cell editing events and update your model. We will discuss those topics later in this section.

Example 6–6: PlanetTable.java

```
import java.awt.*;
import java.awt.event.*;
import javax.swing.*;
import javax.swing.table.*;

public class PlanetTable
{  public static void main(String[] args)
   {  JFrame frame = new PlanetTableFrame();
      frame.show();
   }
}

class PlanetTableFrame extends JFrame
```

```
{  public PlanetTableFrame()
   {  setTitle("PlanetTable");
      setSize(300, 200);
      addWindowListener(new WindowAdapter()
         {  public void windowClosing(WindowEvent e)
            {  System.exit(0);
            }
         } );

      JTable table = new JTable(cells, columnNames);

      Container contentPane = getContentPane();
      contentPane.add(new JScrollPane(table), "Center");
   }

   private Object[][] cells =
      {  { "Mercury", new Double(2440),  new Integer(0),
            Boolean.FALSE, Color.yellow
         },
         { "Venus", new Double(6052), new Integer(0),
            Boolean.FALSE, Color.yellow
         },
         { "Earth", new Double(6378), new Integer(1),
            Boolean.FALSE, Color.blue
         },
         { "Mars", new Double(3397), new Integer(2),
            Boolean.FALSE, Color.red
         },
         { "Jupiter", new Double(71492), new Integer(16),
            Boolean.TRUE, Color.orange
         },
         { "Saturn", new Double(60268), new Integer(18),
            Boolean.TRUE, Color.orange
         },
         { "Uranus", new Double(25559), new Integer(17),
            Boolean.TRUE, Color.blue
         },
         { "Neptune", new Double(24766), new Integer(8),
            Boolean.TRUE, Color.blue
         },
         { "Pluto", new Double(1137), new Integer(1),
            Boolean.FALSE, Color.black
         }
      };

   private String[] columnNames =
      {  "Planet", "Radius", "Moons", "Gaseous", "Color"
      };
}
```

`javax.swing.JTable`

- `JTable(Object[][] entries, Object[] columnNames)`
  constructs a table with a default table model.

  Parameters:

`entries`	the cells in the table
`colummNames`	the titles for the columns

Table Models

In the preceding example, the table rendered objects were stored in a two-dimensional array. However, you should generally not use that strategy in your own code. If you find yourself dumping data into an array in order to display it as a table, you should instead think about implementing your own table model.

Table models are particularly simple to implement because you can take advantage of the `AbstractTableModel` class that implements most of the required methods. You only need to supply three methods:

```
public int getRowCount();
public int getColumnCount();
public Object getValueAt(int row, int column);
```

There are many ways for implementing the `getValueAt` method. You can simply compute the answer. Or you can look up the value from a database or from some other repository. Let us look at a couple of examples.

In the first example, we construct a table that simply shows some computed values, namely, the growth of an investment under different interest rate scenarios (see Figure 6–24).

InvestmentTable

5%	6%	7%	8%	9%	10%
$100,000.00	$100,000.00	$100,000.00	$100,000.00	$100,000.00	$100,000.00
$105,000.00	$106,000.00	$107,000.00	$108,000.00	$109,000.00	$110,000.00
$110,250.00	$112,360.00	$114,490.00	$116,640.00	$118,810.00	$121,000.00
$115,762.50	$119,101.60	$122,504.30	$125,971.20	$129,502.90	$133,100.00
$121,550.62	$126,247.70	$131,079.60	$136,048.90	$141,158.16	$146,410.00
$127,628.16	$133,822.56	$140,255.17	$146,932.81	$153,862.40	$161,051.00
$134,009.56	$141,851.91	$150,073.04	$158,687.43	$167,710.01	$177,156.10
$140,710.04	$150,363.03	$160,578.15	$171,382.43	$182,803.91	$194,871.71
$147,745.54	$159,384.81	$171,818.62	$185,093.02	$199,256.26	$214,358.88

Figure 6–24: Growth of an investment

The `getValueAt` method computes the appropriate value and formats it:

```
public Object getValueAt(int r, int c)
{  double rate = (c + minRate) / 100.0;
   int nperiods = r;

   double futureBalance = INITIAL_BALANCE
      * Math.pow(1 + rate, nperiods);

  return
```

```
         NumberFormat.getCurrencyInstance().format(futureBalance);
   }
```

The getRowCount and getColumnCount methods simply return the number of rows and columns.

```
public int getRowCount()
{  return years;
}

public int getColumnCount()
{  return maxRate - minRate + 1;
}
```

If you don't supply column names, the getColumnName method of the AbstractTableModel names the columns A, B, C, and so on.To change column names, override the getColumnName method. You will usually want to override that default behavior. In this example, we simply label each column with the interest rate.

```
public String getColumnName(int c)
{  double rate = (c + minRate) / 100.0;
   return
      NumberFormat.getPercentInstance().format(rate);
}
```

You can find the complete source code in Example 6–7.

Example 6–7: InvestmentTable.java

```
import java.awt.*;
import java.awt.event.*;
import java.text.*;
import javax.swing.*;
import javax.swing.table.*;

public class InvestmentTable
{  public static void main(String[] args)
   {  JFrame frame = new InvestmentTableFrame();
      frame.show();
   }
}

/* this data model computes the cell entries each time they
   are requested
*/

class InvestmentTableModel extends AbstractTableModel
{  public InvestmentTableModel(int y, int r1, int r2)
   {  years = y;
      minRate = r1;
      maxRate = r2;
   }
```

```
   public int getRowCount()
   {  return years;
   }

   public int getColumnCount()
   {  return maxRate - minRate + 1;
   }

   public Object getValueAt(int r, int c)
   {  double rate = (c + minRate) / 100.0;
      int nperiods = r;

      double futureBalance = INITIAL_BALANCE
         * Math.pow(1 + rate, nperiods);

      return
         NumberFormat.getCurrencyInstance().format(futureBalance);
   }

   public String getColumnName(int c)
   {  double rate = (c + minRate) / 100.0;
      return
         NumberFormat.getPercentInstance().format(rate);
   }

   private int years;
   private int minRate;
   private int maxRate;

   private static double INITIAL_BALANCE = 100000.0;
}

class InvestmentTableFrame extends JFrame
{  public InvestmentTableFrame()
   {  setTitle("InvestmentTable");
      setSize(300, 200);
      addWindowListener(new WindowAdapter()
         {  public void windowClosing(WindowEvent e)
            {  System.exit(0);
            }
         } );


      TableModel model = new InvestmentTableModel(30, 5, 10);
      JTable table = new JTable(model);
      Container contentPane = getContentPane();
      contentPane.add(new JScrollPane(table), "Center");
   }
}
```

Displaying database records

Probably the most common information to be displayed in a table is a set of records from a database. If you use a professional development environment, it almost certainly includes convenient Java beans for accessing database information. However, if you don't have database beans or if you are simply curious what goes on under the hood, you will find the next example interesting. Figure 6–25 shows the output—the result of a query for all rows in a database table.

ResultSet

AUTHORS

AUTHOR_ID	NAME	URL
ARON	Aronson, Larry	www.interport.net/~laron...
ARPA	Arpajian, Scott	...
BEBA	Bebak, Arthur	db.www.idgbooks.com/d...
BRAN	Brandon, Bill	...
BROW	Brown, Mark	...
CAST	Castro, Elizabeth	www.peachpit.com/peac...
CEAR	Cearly, Kent	...
CHIN	Chin, Francis	...
CHU1	Chu, Kenny	...
DOWN	Downing, Troy	found.cs.nyu.edu/downin...
DUNT	Duntemann, Jeff	...
EWRI	Erwin, Mike	...
EVAN	Evans, Tim	...
FOUS	Foust, Jeff	...
FOX1	Fox, David	found.cs.nyu.edu/dfox/in...
GAIT	Gaither, Mark	...
GRAH	Graham, Ian	www.utirc.utoronto.ca/pe...
GROV	Groves, Dawn	www.skycat.com/~dawn...
HARR	Harris, Stuart	www.esnet.com/~sirrah/...
HASS	Hassinger, Sebastian	...
JAME	James, Steve	www.lanw.com/sjbio.ht...
JUNG	Jung, John	...
KARP	Karpinski, Richard	...

Figure 6–25: Displaying a query result in a table

In the example program, we define a `ResultSetTableModel` that fetches data from the result set of a database query. (See Chapter 4 for more information on Java database access and result sets.)

You can obtain the column count and the column names from the *result set metadata* object `rsmd`:

```
public String getColumnName(int c)
{  try
   {  return rsmd.getColumnName(c + 1);
   }
   catch(SQLException e)
   {  . . .
   }
}

public int getColumnCount()
```

```
{  try
   {  return rsmd.getColumnCount();
   }
   catch(SQLException e)
   {  . . .
   }
}
```

If the database supports scrolling cursors, then it is particularly easy to get a cell value: just move the cursor to the requested row and fetch the column value.

```
public Object getValueAt(int r, int c)
{  try
   {  ResultSet rs = getResultSet();
      rs.absolute(r + 1);
      return rs.getObject(c + 1);
   }
   catch(SQLException e)
   {  System.out.println("Error " + e);
      return null;
   }
}
```

It makes a lot of sense to use this data model instead of the `DefaultTableModel`. If you created an array of values, then you would duplicate the cache that the database driver is already managing.

If the database does not support scrolling cursors or if you are using a JDBC 1 driver, then the query data must be cached manually. The example program contains such a manual cache. We factored out the common behavior in a base class `ResultSetTableModel`. The subclass `ScrollingResultSetTableModel` uses a scrolling cursor, and the subclass `CachingResultSetTableModel` caches the result set.

Example 6–8: ResultSetTable.java

```
import java.awt.*;
import java.awt.event.*;
import java.sql.*;
import java.util.*;
import javax.swing.*;
import javax.swing.table.*;

public class ResultSetTable
{  public static void main(String[] args)
   {  JFrame frame = new ResultSetFrame();
      frame.show();
   }
}

/* this class is the base class for the scrolling and the
   caching result set table model. It stores the result set
   and its metadata.
```

```
*/

abstract class ResultSetTableModel extends AbstractTableModel
{  public ResultSetTableModel(ResultSet aResultSet)
   {  rs = aResultSet;
      try
      {  rsmd = rs.getMetaData();
      }
      catch(SQLException e)
      {  System.out.println("Error " + e);
      }
   }

   public String getColumnName(int c)
   {  try
      {  return rsmd.getColumnName(c + 1);
      }
      catch(SQLException e)
      {  System.out.println("Error " + e);
         return "";
      }
   }

   public int getColumnCount()
   {  try
      {  return rsmd.getColumnCount();
      }
      catch(SQLException e)
      {  System.out.println("Error " + e);
         return 0;
      }
   }

   protected ResultSet getResultSet()
   {  return rs;
   }

   private ResultSet rs;
   private ResultSetMetaData rsmd;
}

/* this class uses a scrolling cursor, a JDBC 2 feature
*/

class ScrollingResultSetTableModel extends ResultSetTableModel
{  public ScrollingResultSetTableModel(ResultSet aResultSet)
   {  super(aResultSet);
   }

   public Object getValueAt(int r, int c)
   {  try
      {  ResultSet rs = getResultSet();
```

```
            rs.absolute(r + 1);
            return rs.getObject(c + 1);
         }
         catch(SQLException e)
         {  System.out.println("Error " + e);
            return null;
         }
      }

      public int getRowCount()
      {  try
         {  ResultSet rs = getResultSet();
            rs.last();
            return rs.getRow();
         }
         catch(SQLException e)
         {  System.out.println("Error " + e);
            return 0;
         }
      }
   }

   /* this class caches the result set data; it can be used
      if scrolling cursors are not supported
   */

   class CachingResultSetTableModel extends ResultSetTableModel
   {  public CachingResultSetTableModel(ResultSet aResultSet)
      {  super(aResultSet);
         try
         {  cache = new ArrayList();
            int cols = getColumnCount();
            ResultSet rs = getResultSet();

            /* place all data in an array list of Object[] arrays
               We don't use an Object[][] because we don't know
               how many rows are in the result set
            */

            while (rs.next())
            {  Object[] row = new Object[cols];
               for (int j = 0; j < row.length; j++)
                  row[j] = rs.getObject(j + 1);
               cache.add(row);
            }
         }
         catch(SQLException e)
         {  System.out.println("Error " + e);
         }
      }

      public Object getValueAt(int r, int c)
```

```
   {  if (r < cache.size())
         return ((Object[])cache.get(r))[c];
      else
         return null;
   }

   public int getRowCount()
   {  return cache.size();
   }

   private ArrayList cache;
}

class ResultSetFrame extends JFrame
   implements ActionListener
{  public ResultSetFrame()
   {  setTitle("ResultSet");
      setSize(300, 200);
      addWindowListener(new WindowAdapter()
         {  public void windowClosing(WindowEvent e)
            {  System.exit(0);
            }
         } );

      /* find all tables in the database and add them to
         a combo box
      */

      Container contentPane = getContentPane();
      tableNames = new JComboBox();
      tableNames.addActionListener(this);
      JPanel p = new JPanel();
      p.add(tableNames);
      contentPane.add(p, "North");

      try
      {  Class.forName("com.pointbase.jdbc.jdbcDriver");
            // force loading of driver
         String url = "jdbc:pointbase:corejava";
         String user = "PUBLIC";
         String password = "PUBLIC";
         con = DriverManager.getConnection(url, user,
            password);
         if (SCROLLABLE)
            stmt = con.createStatement(
               ResultSet.TYPE_SCROLL_INSENSITIVE,
               ResultSet.CONCUR_READ_ONLY);
         else
            stmt = con.createStatement();
         DatabaseMetaData md = con.getMetaData();
         ResultSet mrs = md.getTables(null, null, null,
            new String[] { "TABLE" });
```

```
         while (mrs.next())
            tableNames.addItem(mrs.getString(3));
         mrs.close();
      }
      catch(ClassNotFoundException e)
      {  System.out.println("Error " + e);
      }
      catch(SQLException e)
      {  System.out.println("Error " + e);
      }
   }

   public void actionPerformed(ActionEvent evt)
   {  if (evt.getSource() == tableNames)
      {  // show the selected table from the combo box

         if (scrollPane != null)
            getContentPane().remove(scrollPane);
         try
         {  String tableName
               = (String)tableNames.getSelectedItem();
            if (rs != null) rs.close();
            String query = "SELECT * FROM " + tableName;
            rs = stmt.executeQuery(query);
            if (SCROLLABLE)
               model = new ScrollingResultSetTableModel(rs);
            else
               model = new CachingResultSetTableModel(rs);

            JTable table = new JTable(model);
            scrollPane = new JScrollPane(table);
            getContentPane().add(scrollPane, "Center");
            pack();
            doLayout();
         }
         catch(SQLException e)
         {  System.out.println("Error " + e);
         }
      }
   }

   private JScrollPane scrollPane;
   private ResultSetTableModel model;
   private JComboBox tableNames;
   private JButton nextButton;
   private JButton previousButton;
   private ResultSet rs;
   private Connection con;
   private Statement stmt;

   private static boolean SCROLLABLE = false;
      // set to true if your database supports scrolling cursors
}
```

A sort filter

The last two examples drove home the point that tables don't store the cell data; they get them from a model. The model need not store the data either. It can compute the cell values or fetch them from somewhere else.

In this section, we introduce another useful technique, a *filter model* that presents information from another table in a different form. In our example, we will *sort* the rows in a table. Run the program in Example 6–9 and *double-click* on one of the column headers. You will see how the rows are rearranged so that the column entries are sorted (see Figure 6–26).

TableSortTest

Planet	Radius	Moons	Gaseous	Color
Mercury	2440.0	0	false	java.aw...
Venus	6052.0	0	false	java.aw...
Earth	6378.0	1	false	java.aw...
Pluto	1137.0	1	false	java.aw...
Mars	3397.0	2	false	java.aw...
Neptune	24766.0	8	true	java.aw...
Jupiter	71492.0	16	true	java.aw...
Uranus	25559.0	17	true	java.aw...
Saturn	60268.0	18	true	java.aw...

Figure 6–26: Sorting the rows of a table

However, we won't physically rearrange the rows in the data model. Instead, we will use a *filter model* that keeps an array with the permuted row indexes.

The filter model stores a reference to the actual table model. When the `JTable` needs to look up a value, the filter model computes the actual row index and gets the value from the model. For example,

```
public Object getValueAt(int r, int c)
{  return model.getValueAt(actual row index, c);
}
```

All other methods are simply passed on to the original model.

```
public String getColumnName(int c)
{  return model.getColumnName(c);
}
```

Figure 6–27 shows how the filter sits between the `JTable` object and the actual table model.

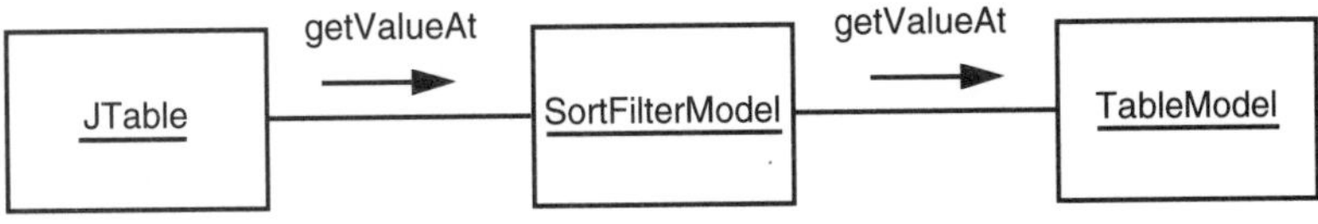

Figure 6–27: A table model filter

There are two complexities when you implement such a sort filter. First, you need to be notified when the user double-clicks on one of the column headers. We don't want to go into too much detail on this technical point. You can find the code in the `addMouseListener` method of the `SortFilterModel` in Example 6–9. Here is the idea behind the code. First, get the table header component and attach a mouse listener. When a double click is detected, you need to find out in which table column the mouse click fell. Then, you need to translate the table column to the model column—they can be different if the user moved the table columns around. Once you know the model column, you can start sorting the table rows.

There is a problem with sorting the table rows. We don't want to physically rearrange the rows. What we want is a sequence of row indexes that tell us how we would rearrange them if they were being sorted. However, the sort algorithms in the `Arrays` and `Collections` classes don't tell us how they rearrange the elements. Of course, you could reimplement a sorting algorithm and keep track of the object rearrangements. But there is a much smarter way. The trick is to come up with custom objects and a custom comparison method so that the library sorting algorithm can be pressed into service.

We will sort objects of a type `Row`. A `Row` object contains the index `r` of a row in the model. Compare two such objects as follows: find the elements in the model and compare them. In other words, the `compareTo` method for `Row` objects computes

```
model.getValueAt(r1, c).compareTo(model.getValueAt(r2, c))
```

Here r_1 and r_2 are the row indexes of the `Row` objects, and `c` is the column whose elements should be sorted.

We make the `Row` class into an inner class of the `SortFilterModel` because the `compareTo` method needs to access the current model and column. Here is the code:

```
class SortFilterModel extends AbstractTableModel
{  . . .
   private class Row implements Comparable
   {  public int index;
      public int compareTo(Object other)
      {  Row otherRow = (Row)other;
         Object a = model.getValueAt(index, sortColumn);
         Object b = model.getValueAt(otherRow.index, sortColumn);
         if (a instanceof Comparable)
            return ((Comparable)a).compareTo(b);
         else
            /* compare index with otherRow.index and
               return < 0, 0 or > 0 value
            */
            return index - otherRow.index;
      }
   }
```

```
      private TableModel model;
      private int sortColumn;
      private Row[] rows;
   }
```

In the constructor, we build an array `rows`, initialized such that `rows[i]` is set to `i`:

```
   public SortFilterModel(TableModel m)
   {  model = m;
      rows = new Row[model.getRowCount()];
      for (int i = 0; i < rows.length; i++)
      {  rows[i] = new Row();
         rows[i].index = i;
      }
   }
```

In the `sort` method, we invoke the `Arrays.sort` algorithm. It sorts the `Row` objects. Because the comparison criterion looks at the model elements in the appropriate column, the elements are arranged so that afterwards `row[0]` contains the index of the smallest element in the column, `row[1]` contains the index of the next-smallest element, and so on.

When the array is sorted, we notify all table model listeners (in particular, the `JTable`) that the table contents have changed and must be redrawn.

```
   public void sort(int c)
   {  sortColumn = c;
      Arrays.sort(rows);
      fireTableDataChanged();
   }
```

Finally, we can show you the exact computation of the `getValueAt` method of the filter class. It simply translates a row index `r` to the model row index `rows[r].index`:

```
      public Object getValueAt(int r, int c)
      {  return model.getValueAt(rows[r].index, c);
      }
```

The sort model filter shows again the power of the model-view pattern. Because the data and the display are separated, we are able to change the mapping between the two.

Example 6–9: TableSortTest.java

```
import java.awt.*;
import java.awt.event.*;
import java.util.*;
import javax.swing.*;
import javax.swing.event.*;
import javax.swing.table.*;

public class TableSortTest
{  public static void main(String[] args)
```

```
   {  JFrame frame = new TableSortFrame();
      frame.show();
   }
}

class SortFilterModel extends AbstractTableModel
{  public SortFilterModel(TableModel m)
   {  model = m;
      rows = new Row[model.getRowCount()];
      for (int i = 0; i < rows.length; i++)
      {  rows[i] = new Row();
         rows[i].index = i;
      }
   }

   public void sort(int c)
   {  sortColumn = c;
      Arrays.sort(rows);
      fireTableDataChanged();
   }

   public void addMouseListener(final JTable table)
   {  table.getTableHeader().addMouseListener(new MouseAdapter()
         {  public void mouseClicked(MouseEvent event)
            {  // check for double click
               if (event.getClickCount() < 2) return;

               // find column of click and
               int tableColumn
                  = table.columnAtPoint(event.getPoint());

               // translate to table model index and sort
               int modelColumn
                  = table.convertColumnIndexToModel(tableColumn);
               sort(modelColumn);
            }
         });
   }

   /* compute the moved row for the three methods that access
      model elements
   */

   public Object getValueAt(int r, int c)
   {  return model.getValueAt(rows[r].index, c);
   }

   public boolean isCellEditable(int r, int c)
   {  return model.isCellEditable(rows[r].index, c);
   }

   public void setValueAt(Object aValue, int r, int c)
```

```
   {  model.setValueAt(aValue, rows[r].index, c);
   }

   /* delegate all remaining methods to the model
   */

   public int getRowCount()
   {  return model.getRowCount();
   }

   public int getColumnCount()
   {  return model.getColumnCount();
   }

   public String getColumnName(int c)
   {  return model.getColumnName(c);
   }

   public Class getColumnClass(int c)
   {  return model.getColumnClass(c);
   }

   /* this inner class holds the index of the model row
      Rows are compared by looking at the model row entries
      in the sort column
   */

   private class Row implements Comparable
   {  public int index;
      public int compareTo(Object other)
      {  Row otherRow = (Row)other;
         Object a = model.getValueAt(index, sortColumn);
         Object b = model.getValueAt(otherRow.index, sortColumn);
         if (a instanceof Comparable)
            return ((Comparable)a).compareTo(b);
         else
            return index - otherRow.index;
      }
   }

   private TableModel model;
   private int sortColumn;
   private Row[] rows;
}

class TableSortFrame extends JFrame
{  public TableSortFrame()
   {  setTitle("TableSortTest");
      setSize(300, 200);
      addWindowListener(new WindowAdapter()
         {  public void windowClosing(WindowEvent e)
            {  System.exit(0);
            }
```

```
         } );

      // set up table model and interpose sorter

      DefaultTableModel model
         = new DefaultTableModel(cells, columnNames);
      SortFilterModel sorter = new SortFilterModel(model);

      // show table

      JTable table = new JTable(sorter);
      Container contentPane = getContentPane();
      contentPane.add(new JScrollPane(table), "Center");

      // set up double click handler for column headers

      sorter.addMouseListener(table);
   }

   private Object[][] cells =
      {  { "Mercury", new Double(2440),  new Integer(0),
            Boolean.FALSE, Color.yellow
         },
         { "Venus", new Double(6052), new Integer(0),
            Boolean.FALSE, Color.yellow
         },
         { "Earth", new Double(6378), new Integer(1),
            Boolean.FALSE, Color.blue
         },
         { "Mars", new Double(3397), new Integer(2),
            Boolean.FALSE, Color.red
         },
         { "Jupiter", new Double(71492), new Integer(16),
            Boolean.TRUE, Color.orange
         },
         { "Saturn", new Double(60268), new Integer(18),
            Boolean.TRUE, Color.orange
         },
         { "Uranus", new Double(25559), new Integer(17),
            Boolean.TRUE, Color.blue
         },
         { "Neptune", new Double(24766), new Integer(8),
            Boolean.TRUE, Color.blue
         },
         { "Pluto", new Double(1137), new Integer(1),
            Boolean.FALSE, Color.black
         }
      };

   private String[] columnNames =
      {  "Planet", "Radius", "Moons", "Gaseous", "Color"
      };
}
```

`javax.swing.table.TableModel`

- `int getRowCount()`
- `int getColumnCount()`

  get the number of rows and columns in the table model.
- `Object getValueAt(int row, int column)`

  gets the value at the given row and column.
- `void setValueAt(Object newValue, int row, int column)`

  sets a new value at the given row and column.
- `boolean isCellEditable(int row, int column)`

  returns `true` if the cell at the given row and column is editable.
- `String getColumnName(int column)`

  gets the column title.

`javax.swing.table.AbstractTableModel`

- `void fireTableDataChanged()`

  notifies all table model listeners that the table data has changed.

`javax.swing.JTable`

- `JTableHeader getTableHeader()`

  returns the table header component of this table.
- `int columnAtPoint(Point p)`

  returns the number of the table column that falls under the pixel position `p`.
- `int convertColumnIndexToModel(int tableColumn)`

  returns the model index of the column with the given index. This value is different from `tableColumn` if some of the table columns are moved or hidden.

Cell Rendering and Editing

In the next example, we again display our planet data, but this time, we want to give the table more information about the *column types*. If you define the method

```
Class getColumnClass(int columnIndex)
```

of your table model to return the class that describes the column type, then the `JTable` class picks an appropriate *renderer* for the class. Table 6–1 shows the renderers that the `JTable` class provides by default.

Table 6–1: Default renderers

Type	Rendered as
`ImageIcon`	image
`Boolean`	check box
`Object`	string

You can see the check boxes and images in Figure 6–28. (Thanks to Jim Evins, `http://www.clark.net/pub/evins/Main/`, for providing the planet images!)

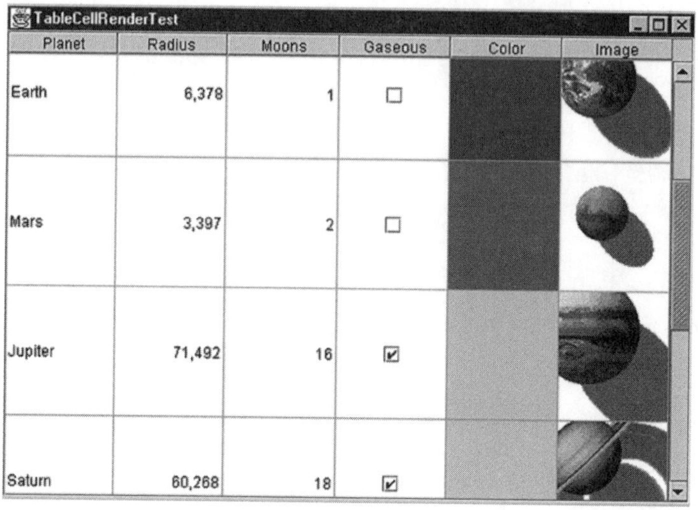

TableCellRenderTest

Planet	Radius	Moons	Gaseous	Color	Image
Earth	6,378	1	☐		
Mars	3,397	2	☐		
Jupiter	71,492	16	☑		
Saturn	60,268	18	☑		

Figure 6–28: A table with cell renderers

For other types, you can supply your own cell renderers. Table cell renderers are similar to the tree cell renderers that you saw earlier. They implement the `TableCellRenderer` interface, which has a single method

```
Component getTableCellRendererComponent(JTable table,
   Object value, boolean isSelected, boolean hasFocus,
   int row, int column)
```

That method is called when the tree needs to draw a cell. You return a component whose `paint` method is then invoked to fill the cell area.

To display a cell of type `Color`, you can simply return a panel whose background color you set to the color object stored in the cell. The color is passed as the `value` parameter.

```
class ColorTableCellRenderer implements TableCellRenderer
{  public Component getTableCellRendererComponent(JTable table,
      Object value, boolean isSelected, boolean hasFocus,
      int row, int column)
   {  panel.setBackground((Color)value);
      return panel;
   }

   private JPanel panel = new JPanel();
}
```

You need to tell the table to use this renderer with all objects of type `Color`. The `setDefaultRenderer` method of the `JTable` class lets you establish this association. You supply a `Class` object and the renderer:

```
table.setDefaultRenderer(Color.class,
   new ColorTableCellRenderer());
```

That renderer is now used for all objects of the given type.

NOTE: For a more realistic cell renderer, you would want to give visual clues when the cell is *selected* and when it has *editing focus*. To do that, you need the cell dimensions and the color schemes for selection and focus. In the Java look and feel, selection is indicated by a pale blue background.

To get the cell dimensions, call the `getCellRect` method of the `JTable` class. For the selection colors, call `getSelectionBackground` and `getSelectionForeground`.

However, there does not seem to be a uniform standard for focus. If you run the sample program and click on cells in the three editable columns, you will find that the text field, combo box and check box each use a *different* color scheme to indicate focus.

TIP: If your renderer simply draws a text string or an icon, you can extend the `DefaultTableCellRenderer` class. It takes care of selection handling and focus for you.

Cell editing

To enable cell editing, the table model must indicate which cells are editable by defining the `isCellEditable` method. Most commonly, you will want to make certain columns editable. In the example program, we allow editing in four columns.

```
public boolean isCellEditable(int r, int c)
{  return c == NAME_COLUMN
      || c == MOON_COLUMN
      || c == GASEOUS_COLUMN
      || c == COLOR_COLUMN;
}

private static final int NAME_COLUMN = 0;
private static final int MOON_COLUMN = 2;
private static final int GASEOUS_COLUMN = 3;
private static final int COLOR_COLUMN = 4;
```

NOTE: The `AbstractTableModel` defines the `isCellEditable` method to always return `false`. The `DefaultTableModel` overrides the method to always return `true`.

If you run the program in Example 6–10, note that you can click on the check boxes in the Gaseous column and turn the check marks on and off. If you click on the Moons column, a combo box appears (see Figure 6–29). You will see in a minute how to install such a combo box as cell editor.

Finally, click on a cell in the first column. The cell gains focus. You can start typing and the cell contents changes.

Figure 6–29: A cell editor

What you just saw in action are the three variations of the `DefaultCellEditor` class. A `DefaultCellEditor` can be constructed with a `JTextField`, a `JCheckBox`, or a `JComboBox`. The `JTable` class automatically installs a check box editor for Boolean cells and a text field editor for all editable cells that don't supply their own renderer. The text fields let the user edit the strings that result from applying `toString` to the return value of the `getValueAt` method of the table model.

When the edit is complete, the cell editor passes the result back to the model by calling its `setValueAt` method. It is up to you to define the `setValueAt` method of your model to turn the edited result back into an appropriate value.

CAUTION: It is easy for the default text field editor to turn your cell value into a string, simply by calling `getValueAt` and applying `toString`. However, for the reverse conversion, the monkey is on your back. When the editing is finished, the cell editor calls `setValueAt` with the resulting `String` object. Your `setValueAt` method needs to know how to parse that string. For example, if your cell stores integers, you need to call `Integer.parseInt`.

To get a combo box editor, you set a cell editor manually—the `JTable` component has no idea what values might be appropriate for a particular type. For the Moons column, we wanted to enable the user to pick any value between 0 and 20. Here is the code for initializing the combo box.

```
JComboBox moonCombo = new JComboBox();
for (int i = 0; i <= 20; i++)
   moonCombo.addItem(new Integer(i));
```

To construct a `DefaultCellEditor`, supply the combo box in the constructor:

```
TableCellEditor moonEditor = new DefaultCellEditor(moonCombo);
```

Next, we need to install the editor. Unlike the color cell renderer, this editor does not depend on the object *type*—we don't necessarily want to use it for all objects of type `Integer`. Instead, we need to install it into a particular column.

The `JTable` class stores information about table columns in objects of type `TableColumn`. A `TableColumnModel` class manages the columns. (Figure 6–30 shows the relationships among the most important table classes.) If you don't want to insert or remove columns dynamically, you won't use the table column model much. However, to get a particular `TableColumn` object, you need to get the column model to ask it for the column object:

```
TableColumnModel columnModel = table.getColumnModel()
TableColumn moonColumn
   = columnModel.getColumn(PlanetTableModel.MOON_COLUMN);
```

Finally, you can install the cell editor:

```
moonColumn.setCellEditor(moonEditor);
```

If your cells are taller than the default, you also want to set the row height.

```
table.setRowHeight(100);
```

All rows of the table have the same height.

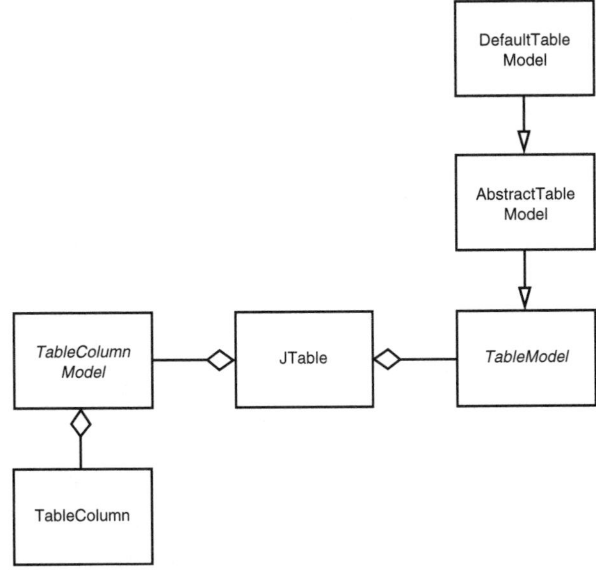

Figure 6–30: Relationship between Table classes

Custom editors

Run the example program again and click on a color. A *color chooser* pops up to let you pick a new color for the planet. Select a color and click OK. The cell color is updated (see Figure 6–31).

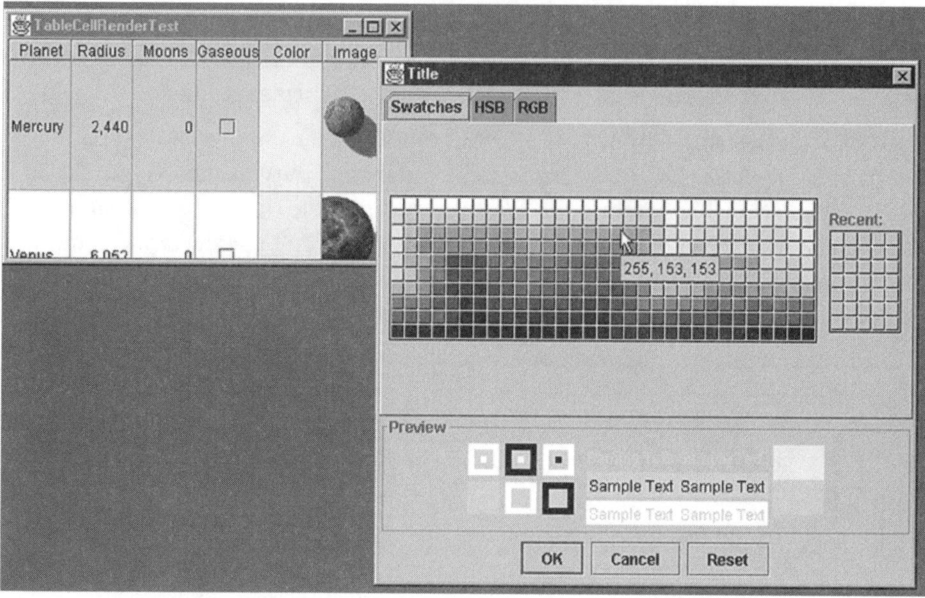

Figure 6–31: Editing the cell color with a color chooser

The color cell editor is not a standard table cell editor but a custom implementation. To create a custom cell editor, you implement the `TableCellEditor` interface. That interface is a bit tedious. If you aren't interested in custom editors, you may want to skip to the end of this section where we tell you how to update the model once editing is completed.

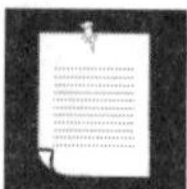

NOTE: The Java Swing tutorial at `http://java.sun.com/docs/books/tutorial/uiswing/components/table.html` shows how you can extend the `DefaultCellEditor` to implement a custom cell editor. That technique is a bit dubious because you have to feed the `DefaultCellEditor` superclass a bogus component—it must be constructed with a text field, check box, or combo box.

The `getTableCellEditorComponent` method of the `TableCellEditor` interface requests a component to render the cell. It is exactly the same as the `getTableCellRenderer` method of the `TableCellRenderer` interface, except that there is no `focus` parameter. Since the cell is being edited, it is presumed to have focus. In the case of the combo box, the editor component temporarily

replaces the renderer. However, if you have a pop-up editor, you can simply have the editor class extend the renderer class and call the `getTableCellRenderer-Component` with a parameter of `true` for the focus.

```
class ColorTableCellEditor
   extends ColorTableCellRenderer
   implements TableCellEditor
{   public Component getTableCellEditorComponent(JTable table,
      Object value, boolean isSelected, int row, int column)
   {  return getTableCellRendererComponent(table, value,
         isSelected, true, row, column);
   }
}
```

Next, you want to have your editor pop up when the user clicks on the cell.

The `JTable` class calls your editor with an event (such as a mouse click) to find out if that event is acceptable to initiate the editing process. Our editor isn't picky, and it accepts all events.

```
public boolean isCellEditable(EventObject anEvent)
{  return true;
}
```

However, if this method returned `false`, then the table would not go through the trouble of inserting the editor component.

Once the editor component is installed, the `shouldSelectCell` method is called, presumably with the same event. You should initiate editing in this method, for example, by popping up an external edit dialog.

```
public boolean shouldSelectCell(EventObject anEvent)
{  colorDialog.setVisible(true);
   return true;
}
```

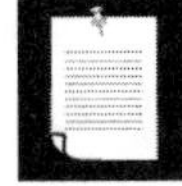

NOTE: In this example, we use the `JColorChooser` Swing dialog. We did not discuss that dialog in the section on dialog boxes in Chapter 9 of Volume 1. However, the dialog is easy to use. If you simply want to obtain a color value, then you can use the static `showDialog` method. It shows a modal color dialog. The method returns when the user has selected a color value or canceled the dialog. The return value is the selected color or `null` if the user canceled the dialog.

```
Color selected = JColorChooser.showDialog(parent,
   "Title", defaultColor);
```

In our example, we use the more complex, modeless dialog. We manually show and hide the dialog with the `setVisible` method, and we supply action listeners that are notified when the user makes a selection or cancels the dialog.

If the table wants to cancel or stop the edit (because the user has clicked on another table cell), it calls the `cancelCellEditing` or `stopCellEditing` method. You should then hide the dialog. When your `stopCellEditing` method is called, the table would like to use the partially edited value. You should return `true` if the current value is valid. In the color chooser, any value is valid. But if you edit other data, you can ensure that only valid data is retrieved from the editor.

The table will install a `CellEditorListener` into your editor. You need to supply the usual methods for adding and removing a listener and for firing events. You can find this routine code in Example 6–10.

When your dialog is finished, your editor should fire either an "editing stopped" or an "editing canceled" event, depending on whether the user accepted or canceled the dialog. When constructing the color dialog, we install accept and cancel callbacks that fire these events.

```
colorDialog = JColorChooser.createDialog(null,
   "Planet Color", false, colorChooser,
   new ActionListener() // OK button listener
   {  public void actionPerformed(ActionEvent event)
      {  fireEditingStopped();
      }
   },
   new ActionListener() // Cancel button listener
   {  public void actionPerformed(ActionEvent event)
      {  fireEditingCanceled();
      }
   });
```

The editing is completed either because the user dismissed the dialog and the tree received the fired event or because the tree stopped the editing process. If the tree wants to use the value that resulted from the editing process, it calls the `getCellEditorValue` method. We simply return the color that the user chose.

```
public Object getCellEditorValue()
{  return colorChooser.getColor();
}
```

This completes the implementation of the custom editor.

You now know how to make a cell editable and how to install an editor. There is one remaining issue—how to update the model with the value that the user edited. When editing is complete, the `JTable` class calls the following method of the table model:

```
void setValueAt(Object value, int r, int c)
```

You need to override the method to store the new value. The `value` parameter is the object that was returned by the cell editor. It is a `Boolean` if the cell editor is a check box, a string if it is a text field. If the value comes from a combo box, then it is the object that the user selected.

If the `value` object does not have the appropriate type, then you need to convert it. That happens most commonly when a number is edited in a text field. In our example, we populated the combo box with `Integer` objects so that no conversion is necessary.

Example 6–10: TableCellRenderTest.java

```
import java.awt.*;
import java.awt.event.*;
import java.util.*;
import javax.swing.*;
import javax.swing.event.*;
import javax.swing.table.*;

public class TableCellRenderTest
{  public static void main(String[] args)
   {  JFrame frame = new TableCellRenderFrame();
      frame.show();
   }
}

/* the planet table model specifies the values, rendering
   and editing properties for the planet data
*/

class PlanetTableModel extends AbstractTableModel
{  public String getColumnName(int c)
   {  return columnNames[c];
   }

   public Class getColumnClass(int c)
   {  return cells[0][c].getClass();
   }

   public int getColumnCount()
   {  return cells[0].length;
   }

   public int getRowCount()
   {  return cells.length;
   }

   public Object getValueAt(int r, int c)
   {  return cells[r][c];
   }

   public void setValueAt(Object obj, int r, int c)
   {  cells[r][c] = obj;
   }

   public boolean isCellEditable(int r, int c)
   {  return c == NAME_COLUMN
         || c == MOON_COLUMN
         || c == GASEOUS_COLUMN
         || c == COLOR_COLUMN;
   }

   public static final int NAME_COLUMN = 0;
```

```
   public static final int MOON_COLUMN = 2;
   public static final int GASEOUS_COLUMN = 3;
   public static final int COLOR_COLUMN = 4;

   private Object[][] cells =
      {  { "Mercury", new Double(2440),  new Integer(0),
            Boolean.FALSE, Color.yellow,
            new ImageIcon("Mercury.gif")
         },
         { "Venus", new Double(6052), new Integer(0),
            Boolean.FALSE, Color.yellow,
            new ImageIcon("Venus.gif")
         },
         { "Earth", new Double(6378), new Integer(1),
            Boolean.FALSE, Color.blue,
            new ImageIcon("Earth.gif")
         },
         { "Mars", new Double(3397), new Integer(2),
            Boolean.FALSE, Color.red,
            new ImageIcon("Mars.gif")
         },
         { "Jupiter", new Double(71492), new Integer(16),
            Boolean.TRUE, Color.orange,
            new ImageIcon("Jupiter.gif")
         },
         { "Saturn", new Double(60268), new Integer(18),
            Boolean.TRUE, Color.orange,
            new ImageIcon("Saturn.gif")
         },
         { "Uranus", new Double(25559), new Integer(17),
            Boolean.TRUE, Color.blue,
            new ImageIcon("Uranus.gif")
         },
         { "Neptune", new Double(24766), new Integer(8),
            Boolean.TRUE, Color.blue,
            new ImageIcon("Neptune.gif")
         },
         { "Pluto", new Double(1137), new Integer(1),
            Boolean.FALSE, Color.black,
            new ImageIcon("Pluto.gif")
         }
      };

   private String[] columnNames =
      {  "Planet", "Radius", "Moons", "Gaseous", "Color", "Image"
      };
}

class TableCellRenderFrame extends JFrame
{  public TableCellRenderFrame()
   {  setTitle("TableCellRenderTest");
      setSize(300, 200);
```

```
      addWindowListener(new WindowAdapter()
         {  public void windowClosing(WindowEvent e)
            {  System.exit(0);
            }
         } );

      TableModel model = new PlanetTableModel();
      JTable table = new JTable(model);

      // set up renderers and editors

      table.setDefaultRenderer(Color.class,
         new ColorTableCellRenderer());
      table.setDefaultEditor(Color.class,
         new ColorTableCellEditor());

      JComboBox moonCombo = new JComboBox();
      for (int i = 0; i <= 20; i++)
         moonCombo.addItem(new Integer(i));
      TableColumnModel columnModel = table.getColumnModel();
      TableColumn moonColumn
         = columnModel.getColumn(PlanetTableModel.MOON_COLUMN);
      moonColumn.setCellEditor(new DefaultCellEditor(moonCombo));

      // show table

      table.setRowHeight(100);
      Container contentPane = getContentPane();
      contentPane.add(new JScrollPane(table), "Center");
   }
}

class ColorTableCellRenderer implements TableCellRenderer
{  public Component getTableCellRendererComponent(JTable table,
      Object value, boolean isSelected, boolean hasFocus,
      int row, int column)
   {  panel.setBackground((Color)value);
      return panel;
   }

   /* the following panel is returned for all cells, with
      the background color set to the Color value of the cell
   */

   private JPanel panel = new JPanel();
}

class ColorTableCellEditor extends ColorTableCellRenderer
   implements TableCellEditor
{  ColorTableCellEditor()
   {  // prepare color dialog

      colorChooser = new JColorChooser();
```

```
      colorDialog = JColorChooser.createDialog(null,
         "Planet Color", false, colorChooser,
         new ActionListener() // OK button listener
         {  public void actionPerformed(ActionEvent event)
            {  fireEditingStopped();
            }
         },
         new ActionListener() // Cancel button listener
         {  public void actionPerformed(ActionEvent event)
            {  fireEditingCanceled();
            }
         });
   }

   public Component getTableCellEditorComponent(JTable table,
      Object value, boolean isSelected, int row, int column)
   {  /* this is where we get the current Color value
         We store it in the dialog in case the user starts editing
      */
      colorChooser.setColor((Color)value);
      return getTableCellRendererComponent(table, value,
         isSelected, true, row, column);
   }

   public boolean isCellEditable(EventObject anEvent)
   {  return true;
   }

   public boolean shouldSelectCell(EventObject anEvent)
   {  // start editing
      colorDialog.setVisible(true);

      // tell caller it is ok to select this cell
      return true;
   }

   public void cancelCellEditing()
   {  // editing is canceled--hide dialog
      colorDialog.setVisible(false);
   }

   public boolean stopCellEditing()
   {  // editing is complete--hide dialog
      colorDialog.setVisible(false);

      // tell caller it is ok to use color value
      return true;
   }

   public Object getCellEditorValue()
   {  return colorChooser.getColor();
```

```
   }

   public void addCellEditorListener(CellEditorListener l)
   {  listenerList.add(CellEditorListener.class, l);
   }

   public void removeCellEditorListener(CellEditorListener l)
   {  listenerList.remove(CellEditorListener.class, l);
   }

   protected void fireEditingStopped()
   {  Object[] listeners = listenerList.getListenerList();
      for (int i = listeners.length - 2; i >= 0; i -= 2)
         ((CellEditorListener)listeners[i+1]).
               editingStopped(event);
   }

   protected void fireEditingCanceled()
   {  Object[] listeners = listenerList.getListenerList();
      for (int i = listeners.length - 2; i >= 0; i -= 2)
         ((CellEditorListener)listeners[i+1]).
               editingCanceled(event);
   }

   private Color color;
   private JColorChooser colorChooser;
   private JDialog colorDialog;
   private EventListenerList listenerList
      = new EventListenerList();
   private ChangeEvent event
      = new ChangeEvent(this);
}
```

`javax.swing.JTable`

- `void setRowHeight(int height)`

  sets the height of all rows of the table to `height` pixels.

- `Rectangle getCellRect(int row, int column, boolean includeSpacing)`

  returns the bounding rectangle of a table cell.

Parameters:	`row, column`	the row and column of the cell
	`includeSpacing`	`true` if the space around the cell should be included

- `Color getSelectionBackground()`
- `Color getSelectionForeground()`

  return the background and foreground colors to use for selected cells.

javax.swing.table.TableModel

- `Class getColumnClass(int columnIndex)`

  gets the class for the values in this column. This information is used by the cell renderer and editor.

javax.swing.table.TableCellRenderer

- `Component getTableCellRendererComponent(JTable table, Object value, boolean selected, boolean hasFocus, int row, int column)`

  returns a component whose `paint` method is invoked to render a table cell.

Parameters:	`table`	the table containing the cell to be rendered
	`value`	the cell to be rendered
	`selected`	`true` if the cell is currently selected
	`hasFocus`	`true` if the cell currently has focus
	`row, column`	the row and column of the cell

javax.swing.table.TableColumnModel

- `TableColumn getColumn(int index)`

  gets the table column object that describes the column with the given index.

`javax.swing.table.TableColumn`

- `void setCellEditor(TableCellEditor editor)`
- `void setCellRenderer(TableCellRenderer renderer)`

  set the cell editor or renderer for all cells in this column.

`javax.swing.table.DefaultCellEditor`

- `DefaultCellEditor(JComboBox comboBox)`

  constructs a cell editor that presents the combo box for selecting cell values.

javax.swing.CellEditor

- `boolean isCellEditable(EventObject event)`

  returns `true` if the event is suitable for initiating the editing process for this cell.
- `boolean shouldSelectCell(EventObject anEvent)`

  starts the editing process. Returns `true` if the edited cell should be *selected.* Normally, you want to return `true`, but you can return `false` if you don't want the editing process to change the cell selection.

- `void cancelCellEditing()`
  cancels the editing process. You can abandon partial edits.
- `boolean stopCellEditing()`
  stops the editing process, with the intent of using the result. Returns `true` if the edited value is in a proper state for retrieval.
- `Object getCellEditorValue()`
  returns the edited result.
- `void addCellEditorListener(CellEditorListener l)`
- `void removeCellEditorListener(CellEditorListener l)`
  add and remove the obligatory cell editor listener.

`javax.swing.table.TableCellEditor`

- `Component getTableCellEditorComponent(JTable table, Object value, boolean selected, int row, int column)`
  returns a component whose `paint` method renders a table cell.

Parameters:	`table`	the table containing the cell to be rendered
	`value`	the cell to be rendered
	`selected`	`true` if the cell is currently selected
	`row, column`	the row and column of the cell

`javax.swing.JColorChooser`

- `JColorChooser()`
  constructs a color chooser with an initial color of white.
- `Color getColor()`
- `void setColor(Color c)`
  get and set the current color of this color chooser.
- `static JDialog createDialog(Component parent, String title, boolean modal, JColorChooser chooser, ActionListener okListener, ActionListener cancelListener)`
  creates a dialog box that contains a color chooser.

Parameters:	`parent`	the component over which to pop up the dialog
	`title`	the title for the dialog box frame
	`modal`	`true` if this call should block until the dialog is closed
	`chooser`	the color chooser to add to the dialog
	`okListener, cancelListener`	the listeners of the OK and Cancel buttons

- `static Color showDialog(Component component, String title, Color initialColor)`

  creates and shows a modal dialog box that contains a color chooser.

Parameters:	`parent`	the component over which to pop up the dialog
	`title`	the title for the dialog box frame
	`initialColor`	the initial selected color

Working with Rows and Columns

In this subsection, you will see how to manipulate the rows and columns in a table. As you read through this material, you should keep in mind that a Swing table is quite asymmetric—there are different operations that you can carry out on rows and columns. The table component was optimized to display rows of information with the same structure, such as the result of a database query, not an arbitrary two-dimensional grid of objects. You will see this asymmetry throughout this subsection.

Resizing columns

The `TableColumn` class gives you control over the resizing behavior of columns. You can set the preferred, minimum, and maximum width with the methods

```
void setPreferredWidth(int width)
void setMinimumWidth(int width)
void setMaximumWidth(int width)
```

This information is used by the table component to lay out the columns.

Use the method

```
void setResizable(boolean resizable)
```

to control whether the user is allowed to resize the column.

You can programmatically resize a column with the method

```
void setWidth(int width)
```

When a column is resized, the default is to leave the total size of the table unchanged. Of course, the width increase or decrease of the resized column must then be distributed over other columns. The default behavior is to change the size of all columns to the right of the resized column. That's a good default because it allows a user to adjust all columns to a desired width, moving from left to right.

You can set another behavior from Table 6–2 by using the method

```
void setAutoResizeMode(int mode)
```

of the `JTable` class.

Table 6–2: Resize modes

Mode	Behavior
`AUTO_RESIZE_OFF`	Don't resize other columns; change the table size
`AUTO_RESIZE_NEXT_COLUMN`	Resize the next column only
`AUTO_RESIZE_SUBSEQUENT_COLUMNS`	Resize all subsequent columns equally; this is the default behavior
`AUTO_RESIZE_LAST_COLUMN`	Resize the last column only
`AUTO_RESIZE_ALL_COLUMNS`	Resize all columns in the table; this is not a good choice because it makes it challenging for the user to adjust multiple columns to a desired size

Selecting rows, columns, and cells

Depending on the selection mode, the user can select rows, columns, or individual cells in the table. By default, row selection is enabled. Clicking inside a cell selects the entire row. Call

```
table.setRowSelectionAllowed(false)
```

to disable row selection.

When row selection is enabled, you can control whether the user is allowed to select a single row, a contiguous set of rows, or any set of rows. You need to retrieve the *selection model* and use its `setSelectionMode` method:

```
table.getSelectionModel().setSelectionMode(mode);
```

Here, `mode` is one of the three values:

```
ListSelectionModel.SINGLE_SELECTION
ListSelectionModel.SINGLE_INTERVAL_SELECTION
ListSelectionModel.MULTIPLE_INTERVAL_SELECTION
```

Column selection is disabled by default. You turn it on with the call

```
table.setColumnSelectionAllowed(true)
```

If both row and column selection are enabled, then every mouse click selects a "+" shaped area (see Figure 6–32).

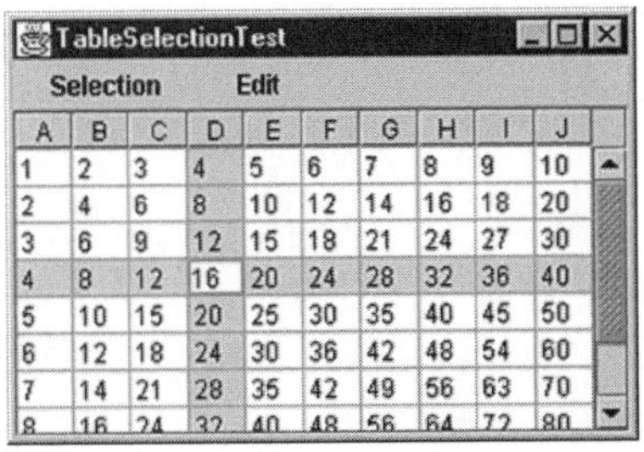

Figure 6–32: Selecting a row and column

You can find out which rows and columns are selected by calling the `getSelectedRows` and `getSelectedColumns` methods. Both return an `int[]` array of the indexes of the selected items.

You can let your users select individual cells instead of selecting rows or columns, by calling

```
table.setCellSelectionEnabled(true)
```

Once cell selection is enabled, the settings for row and column selection are ignored. Figure 6–33 shows a table with cell selection enabled.

Figure 6–33: Selecting a range of cells

You can run the program in Example 6–11 to watch cell selection in action. Enable row, column, or cell selection in the Selection menu and watch how the selection behavior changes.

Hiding and displaying columns

The `removeColumn` method of the `JTable` class removes a column from the table view. The column data is not actually removed from the model—it is just hidden from the view. The `removeColumn` method takes a `TableColumn` argument. If you have the column number (for example, from a call to `getSelectedColumns`), you need to ask the table model for the actual table column object:

```
TableColumnModel columnModel = table.getColumnModel();
TableColumn column = columnModel.getColumn(i);
table.removeColumn(column);
```

If you remember the column, you can later add it back in:

```
table.addColumn(column);
```

This method adds the column to the end. If you want it to appear elsewhere, you have to call the `moveColumn` method.

You can also add a new column that corresponds to a column index in the table model, by adding a new `TableColumn` object:

```
table.addColumn(new TableColumn(modelColumnIndex));
```

You can have multiple table columns that view the same column of the model.

However, there is no `JTable` method to actually insert a new column into the model or to remove a column from the model. There are also no `JTable` methods for hiding or showing rows. If you want to hide rows, you can create a filter model similar to the sort filter that you saw earlier.

Adding and removing rows in the default table model

The `DefaultTableModel` class is a concrete class that implements the `TableModel` interface. It stores a two-dimensional grid of objects. If you already have your data in a tabular arrangement, then there is no point in copying all the data into a default table model, but it is handy if you quickly need to make a table from a small data set. The `DefaultTableModel` class has methods for adding rows and columns and for removing rows.

The `addRow` and `addColumn` methods add a row or column of new data. You supply an `Object[]` array or a vector that holds the new data. With the `addColumn` method, you also need to supply a name for the new column. These methods add the new data to the end of the grid. To insert a row in the middle, use the `insertRow` method. There is no method for inserting a column in the middle of the grid.

Conversely, the `removeRow` method removes a row from the model. There is no method for removing a column.

Since the `JTable` object registers itself as a table model listener, the model notifies the table when data is inserted or removed. At that time, the table refreshes the display.

The program in Example 6–11 shows both selection and editing at work. A default table model contains a simple data set (a multiplication table). The Edit menu contains these commands

- Hide all selected columns.
- Show all columns that you've ever hidden.
- Remove selected rows from the model.
- Add a row of data to the end of the model.

This example concludes the discussion of Swing tables. Tables are conceptually a bit easier to grasp than trees because the underlying data model—a grid of objects—is easy to visualize. However, under the hood, the table component is actually quite a bit more complex than the tree component. Column headers, resizable columns, and column-specific renderers and editors all add to the complexity. In this section, we focused on those topics that you are most likely to encounter in practice: displaying database information, sorting, and custom cell rendering and editing. If you have special advanced needs, we once again refer you to *Core Java Foundation Classes* by Kim Topley and *Graphic Java 2* by David Geary.

Example 6–11: TableSelectionTest.java

```
import java.awt.*;
import java.awt.event.*;
import java.util.*;
```

```
import java.text.*;
import javax.swing.*;
import javax.swing.table.*;

public class TableSelectionTest
{  public static void main(String[] args)
   {  JFrame frame = new TableSelectionFrame();
      frame.show();
   }
}

class TableSelectionFrame extends JFrame
   implements ActionListener
{  public TableSelectionFrame()
   {  setTitle("TableSelectionTest");
      setSize(300, 200);
      addWindowListener(new WindowAdapter()
         {  public void windowClosing(WindowEvent e)
            {  System.exit(0);
            }
         } );

      // set up multiplication table

      model = new DefaultTableModel(10, 10);

      for (int i = 0; i < model.getRowCount(); i++)
         for (int j = 0; j < model.getColumnCount(); j++)
            model.setValueAt(
               new Integer((i + 1) * (j + 1)), i, j);

      table = new JTable(model);

      Container contentPane = getContentPane();
      contentPane.add(new JScrollPane(table), "Center");

      // create menu

      JMenuBar menuBar = new JMenuBar();
      setJMenuBar(menuBar);

      JMenu selectionMenu = new JMenu("Selection");
      menuBar.add(selectionMenu);

      rowsItem = new JCheckBoxMenuItem("Rows");
      rowsItem.setSelected(table.getRowSelectionAllowed());
      rowsItem.addActionListener(this);
      selectionMenu.add(rowsItem);

      columnsItem = new JCheckBoxMenuItem("Columns");
      columnsItem.setSelected(table.getColumnSelectionAllowed());
```

```
      columnsItem.addActionListener(this);
      selectionMenu.add(columnsItem);

      cellsItem = new JCheckBoxMenuItem("Cells");
      cellsItem.setSelected(table.getCellSelectionEnabled());
      cellsItem.addActionListener(this);
      selectionMenu.add(cellsItem);

      JMenu tableMenu = new JMenu("Edit");
      menuBar.add(tableMenu);

      showColumnsItem = new JMenuItem("Show Columns");
      showColumnsItem.addActionListener(this);
      tableMenu.add(showColumnsItem);

      hideColumnsItem = new  JMenuItem("Hide Columns");
      hideColumnsItem.addActionListener(this);
      tableMenu.add(hideColumnsItem);

      addRowItem = new JMenuItem("Add Row");
      addRowItem.addActionListener(this);
      tableMenu.add(addRowItem);

      removeRowsItem = new  JMenuItem("Remove Rows");
      removeRowsItem.addActionListener(this);
      tableMenu.add(removeRowsItem);

      clearCellsItem = new  JMenuItem("Clear Cells");
      clearCellsItem.addActionListener(this);
      tableMenu.add(clearCellsItem);
   }

   public void actionPerformed(ActionEvent event)
   {  Object source = event.getSource();
      if (source == rowsItem)
      {  table.setRowSelectionAllowed(rowsItem.isSelected());
         table.clearSelection();
      }
      else if (source == columnsItem)
      {  table.setColumnSelectionAllowed(columnsItem.isSelected());
         table.clearSelection();
      }
      else if (source == cellsItem)
      {  table.setCellSelectionEnabled(cellsItem.isSelected());
         table.clearSelection();
      }
      else if (source == hideColumnsItem)
      {  int[] selected = table.getSelectedColumns();
         TableColumnModel columnModel = table.getColumnModel();

         /* remove columns from view, starting at the last
```

```
            index so that the column numbers aren't affected
         */

         for (int i = selected.length - 1; i >= 0; i--)
         {  TableColumn column
               = columnModel.getColumn(selected[i]);
            table.removeColumn(column);

            // store removed columns for "show columns" command

            removedColumns.add(column);
         }
      }
      else if (source == showColumnsItem)
      {  // restore all removed columns
         for (int i = 0; i < removedColumns.size(); i++)
            table.addColumn((TableColumn)removedColumns.get(i));
         removedColumns.clear();
      }
      else if (source == removeRowsItem)
      {  int[] selected = table.getSelectedRows();

         /* remove rows from model, starting at the last
            index so that the row numbers aren't affected
         */

         for (int i = selected.length - 1; i >= 0; i--)
            model.removeRow(selected[i]);
      }
      else if (source == addRowItem)
      {  // add a new row to the multiplication table in the model

         Integer[] newCells = new Integer[model.getColumnCount()];
         for (int i = 0; i < newCells.length; i++)
            newCells[i]
               = new Integer((i + 1) * (model.getRowCount() + 1));
         model.addRow(newCells);
      }
      else if (source == clearCellsItem)
      {  // set all selected cells to 0

         for (int i = 0; i < table.getRowCount(); i++)
            for (int j = 0; j < table.getColumnCount(); j++)
               if (table.isCellSelected(i, j))
                  table.setValueAt(new Integer(0), i, j);
      }
   }

   private DefaultTableModel model;
   private JTable table;
```

```
   private JMenuItem showColumnsItem;
   private JMenuItem hideColumnsItem;

   private JMenuItem addRowItem;
   private JMenuItem removeRowsItem;

   private JMenuItem clearCellsItem;

   private JCheckBoxMenuItem rowsItem;
   private JCheckBoxMenuItem columnsItem;
   private JCheckBoxMenuItem cellsItem;

   private ArrayList removedColumns = new ArrayList();
}
```

`javax.swing.JTable`

- `void setAutoResizeMode(int mode)`

  sets the mode for automatic resizing of table columns.

  Parameters: `mode` one of `AUTO_RESIZE_OFF`, `AUTO_RESIZE_NEXT_COLUMN`, `AUTO_RESIZE_SUBSEQUENT_COLUMNS`, `AUTO_RESIZE_LAST_COLUMN`, `AUTO_RESIZE_ALL_COLUMNS`

- `ListSelectionModel getSelectionModel()`

  returns the list selection model. You need that model to choose between row, column, and cell selection.

- `void setCellSelectionEnabled(boolean b)`

  If `b` is `true`, then individual cells are selected. If it is `false`, then rows and columns can be selected.

- `void setRowSelectionAllowed(boolean b)`

  If `b` is `true`, then rows can be selected when the user clicks on cells.

- `void setColumnSelectionAllowed(boolean b)`

  If `b` is `true`, then columns can be selected when the user clicks on cells.

- `void addColumn(TableColumn column)`

  adds a column to the table view.

- `void moveColumn(int from, int to)`

  moves the column at table index `from` so that its index becomes `to`. Only the view is affected.

- `void removeColumn(TableColumn column)`

  removes the given column from the view.

`javax.swing.table.TableColumn`

- `TableColumn(int modelColumnIndex)`

  constructs a table column for viewing the model column with the given index.
- `void setPreferredWidth(int width)`
- `void setMinimumWidth(int width)`
- `void setMaximumWidth(int width)`

  set the preferred, minimum, and maximum width of this table column to `width`.
- `void setWidth(int width)`

  sets the actual width of this column to `width`.
- `void setResizable(boolean b)`

  If `b` is `true`, this column is resizable.

`javax.swing.ListSelectionModel`

- `void setSelectionMode(int mode)`

Parameters:	`mode`	one of `SINGLE_SELECTION`, `SINGLE_INTERVAL_SELECTION`, and `MULTIPLE_INTERVAL_SELECTION`

`javax.swing.DefaultTableModel`

- `void addRow(Object[] rowData)`
- `void addColumn(Object columnName, Object[] columnData)`

  add a row or column of data to the end of the table model.
- `void insertRow(int row, Object[] rowData)`

  adds a row of data at index `row`.
- `removeRow(int row)`

  removes the given row from the model.
- `void moveRow(int start, int end, int to)`

  moves all rows with indexes between `start` and `end` to a new location starting at `to`.

Styled Text Components

In Volume 1, we discussed the basic text component classes `JTextField` and `JTextArea`. Of course, these classes are very useful for obtaining text input from the user. There is another useful class, `JEditorPane`, that displays and edits text in HTML and RTF format. (RTF is the "rich text format" that is used by a number of Microsoft applications for document interchange. It is a poorly documented format that doesn't work well even between Microsoft's own applications. We do not cover the RTF capabilities in this book; Sun claims only "limited" support for it. We

wouldn't be surprised to see this feature dropped in the future since it would make more sense for Sun to spend its resources on improving the HTML support.)

Frankly, at this point, the `JEditorPane` is pretty limited. The HTML renderer can display simple files, but it chokes at many complex pages that you typically find on the Web. The HTML editor is quite poor and unstable. Of course, except for HTML editors, few applications require users to edit HTML text, so this is not a major restriction.

We think that the perfect application for the `JEditorPane` is to display program help in HTML format. Since you have control over the help files that you provide, you can stay away from features that the `JEditorPane` does not display well.

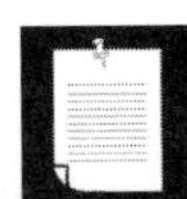

NOTE: For more information on an industrial-strength help system, check out JavaHelp at `http://java.sun.com/products/javahelp/index.html`.

NOTE: The subclass `JTextPane` of `JEditorPane` can hold styled text with special fonts and text formats, as well as embedded components. We will not cover that component in this book. If you need to implement a component that allows users of your program to enter styled text, have a look at the implementation of the StylePad demo that is included in the JDK.

The program in Example 6–12 contains an editor pane that shows the contents of an HTML page. Type a URL into the text field. The URL must start with "`http:`" or "`file:`". Then, click the Load button. The selected HTML page is displayed in the editor pane (see Figure 6–34).

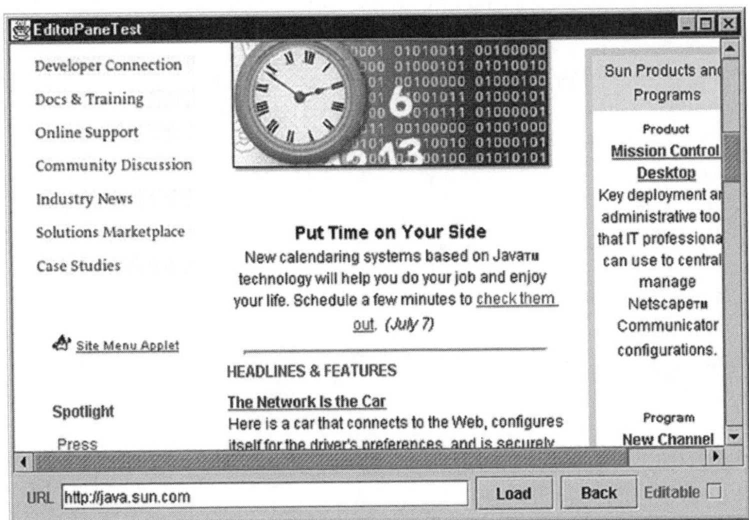

Figure 6–34: The editor pane displaying an HTML page

The hyperlinks are active: if you click on a link, the application loads it. The Back button returns to the previous page.

This program is in fact a very simple browser. Of course, it does not have any of the comfort features, such as page caching or bookmark lists, that you expect from a commercial browser. Also, the editor pane does not yet display applets.

If you click on the Editable check box, then the editor pane becomes editable. You can type in text and use the BACKSPACE key to delete text. The component also understands the CTRL+X, CTRL+C, and CTRL+V shortcuts for cut, copy, and paste. However, even with those simple commands, it is easy to cause the editor to malfunction. Watch the window from which you launched the application for occasional exception stack traces.

When the component is editable, then hyperlinks are not active. Also, with some web pages you can see JavaScript commands, comments, and other tags when edit mode is turned on (see Figure 6–35). The example program lets you investigate the editing feature, but we recommend that you omit that feature in your programs.

TIP: By default, the `JEditorPane` is in edit mode. You should call `editorPane.setEditable(false)` to turn it off.

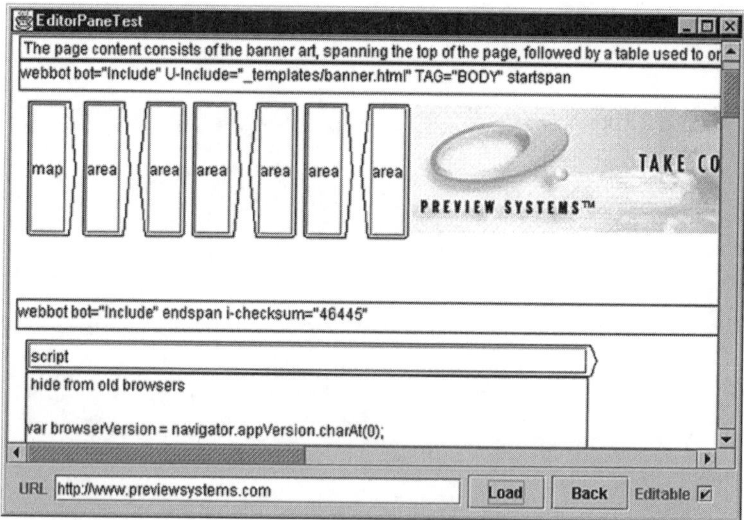

Figure 6–35: The editor pane in edit mode

The features of the editor pane that you saw in the example program are very easy to use. You use the `setPage` method to load a new document. The parameter is either a string or a `URL` object. The `JEditorPane` class extends the `JTextComponent` class. Therefore, you can call the `setText` method as well—it simply displays plain text.

To listen to hyperlink clicks, you add a `HyperlinkListener`. The `HyperlinkListener` interface has a single method, `hyperlinkUpdate`, that is called when the user moves over or clicks on a link. The method has a parameter of type `HyperlinkEvent`.

You need to call the `getEventType` method to find out what kind of event occurred. There are three possible return values:

```
HyperlinkEvent.EventType.ACTIVATED
HyperlinkEvent.EventType.ENTERED
HyperlinkEvent.EventType.EXITED
```

The first value indicates that the user clicked on the hyperlink. In that case, you typically want to open the new link. You can use the second and third values to give some visual feedback, such as a tooltip, when the mouse hovers over the link.

NOTE: It is a complete mystery why there aren't three separate methods to handle activation, entry, and exit in the `HyperlinkListener` interface.

The `getURL` method of the `HyperlinkEvent` class returns the URL of the hyperlink. For example, here is how you can install a hyperlink listener that follows the links that a user activates:

```
editorPane.addHyperlinkListener(new HyperlinkListener()
   {  public void hyperlinkUpdate(HyperlinkEvent event)
      {  if (event.getEventType()
            == HyperlinkEvent.EventType.ACTIVATED)
         {  try
            {  editorPane.setPage(event.getURL());
            }
            catch(IOException e)
            {  editorPane.setText("Error: " + e);
            }
         }
      }
   });
```

The event handler simply gets the URL and updates the editor pane. The `setPage` method can throw an `IOException`. In that case, we display an error message as plain text.

The program in Example 6–12 shows all the features that you need to put together an HTML help system. Under the hood, the `JEditorPane` is even more complex than the tree and table components. However, if you don't need to write a text editor or a renderer of a custom text format, that complexity is hidden from you.

Example 6–12: EditorPaneTest.java

```
import java.awt.*;
import java.awt.event.*;
import java.io.*;
import java.util.*;
import javax.swing.*;
import javax.swing.event.*;

public class EditorPaneTest
{  public static void main(String[] args)
   {  JFrame frame = new EditorPaneFrame();
      frame.show();
   }
}

class EditorPaneFrame extends JFrame
{  public EditorPaneFrame()
   {  setTitle("EditorPaneTest");
      setSize(600, 400);
      addWindowListener(new WindowAdapter()
         {  public void windowClosing(WindowEvent e)
            {  System.exit(0);
            }
         } );

      // set up text field and load button for typing in URL

      url = new JTextField(30);

      loadButton = new JButton("Load");
      loadButton.addActionListener(new ActionListener()
         {  public void actionPerformed(ActionEvent event)
            {  try
               {  // remember URL for back button
                  urlStack.push(url.getText());

                  editorPane.setPage(url.getText());
               }
               catch(IOException e)
               {  editorPane.setText("Error: " + e);
               }
            }
```

```
   });

// set up back button and button action

backButton = new JButton("Back");
backButton.addActionListener(new ActionListener()
   {  public void actionPerformed(ActionEvent event)
      {  if (urlStack.size() <= 1) return;
         try
         {  // get URL from back button
            urlStack.pop();
            // show URL in text field
            String urlString = (String)urlStack.peek();
            url.setText(urlString);

            editorPane.setPage(urlString);
         }
         catch(IOException e)
         {  editorPane.setText("Error: " + e);
         }
      }
   });

// set up editor pane and hyperlink listener

editorPane = new JEditorPane();
editorPane.setEditable(false);
editorPane.addHyperlinkListener(new HyperlinkListener()
   {  public void hyperlinkUpdate(HyperlinkEvent event)
      {  if (event.getEventType()
            == HyperlinkEvent.EventType.ACTIVATED)
         {  try
            {  // remember URL for back button
               urlStack.push(event.getURL().toString());
               // show URL in text field
               url.setText(event.getURL().toString());

               editorPane.setPage(event.getURL());
            }
            catch(IOException e)
            {  editorPane.setText("Error: " + e);
            }
         }
      }
   });

// set up checkbox for toggling edit mode

editable = new JCheckBox();
editable.addActionListener(new ActionListener()
```

```
         {  public void actionPerformed(ActionEvent event)
            {  editorPane.setEditable(editable.isSelected());
            }
         });

      Container contentPane = getContentPane();
      contentPane.add(new JScrollPane(editorPane), "Center");

      // put all control components in a panel

      JPanel panel = new JPanel();
      panel.add(new JLabel("URL"));
      panel.add(url);
      panel.add(loadButton);
      panel.add(backButton);
      panel.add(new JLabel("Editable"));
      panel.add(editable);

      contentPane.add(panel, "South");
   }

   private JTextField url;
   private JCheckBox editable;
   private JButton loadButton;
   private JButton backButton;
   private JEditorPane editorPane;
   private Stack urlStack = new Stack();
}
```

`javax.swing.JEditorPane`

- `void setPage(URL url)`

  loads the page from `url` into the editor pane.
- `void addHyperlinkListener(HyperLinkListener listener)`

  adds a hyperlink listener to this editor pane.

`javax.swing.event.HyperlinkListener`

- `void hyperlinkUpdate(HyperlinkEvent event)`

  is called whenever a hyperlink was selected.

`javax.swing.HyperlinkEvent`

- `URL getURL()`

  returns the URL of the selected hyperlink.

Sliders and Progress Meters

In this section, we discuss two Swing controls that look superficially similar: a slider that lets a user input a quantity on a linear scale, and a progress meter that allows a program to output a linear quantity.

Sliders

Sliders are similar to scroll bars. However, scroll bars are usually intended to move a viewport, whereas sliders are used to supply values. Despite their similarity in behavior, the APIs are charmingly different. Scroll bars implement the `Adjustable` interface and emit adjustment events. Sliders do not implement the `Adjustable` interface, even though it would appear to be a good interface for expressing the commonality between the two; instead, they notify their listeners by sending `ChangeEvent` objects.

The most common way of constructing a slider is as follows:

```
JSlider slider = new JSlider(min, max, initialValue);
```

If you omit the minimum, maximum, and initial values, they are initialized with 0, 100, and 50, respectively.

Or, if you want the slider to be vertical, then use the following constructor call:

```
JSlider slider = new JSlider(SwingConstants.VERTICAL,
   min, max, initialValue);
```

These constructors create a plain slider, such as the top slider in Figure 6–36. You will see presently how to add decorations to a slider.

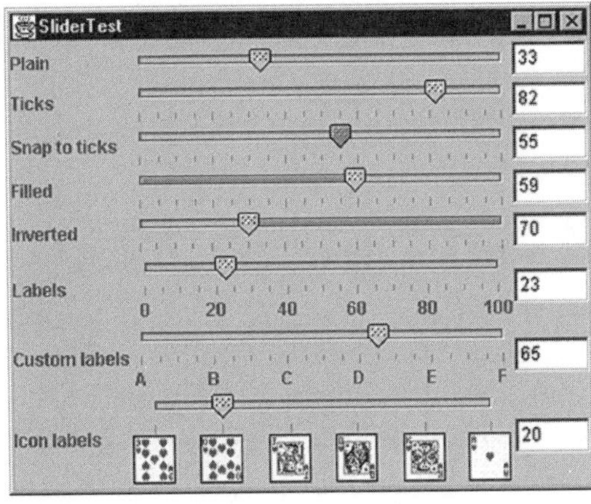

Figure 6–36: Sliders

As the user slides the slider bar, the *value* of the slider moves between the minimum and the maximum values. When the value changes, a `ChangeEvent` is sent to all change listeners. To be notified of the change, you need to call the `addChangeListener` method and install an object that implements the `ChangeListener` interface. That interface has a single method, `stateChanged`. In that method, you should retrieve the slider value:

```
public void stateChanged(ChangeEvent event)
{  JSlider slider = (JSlider)event.getSource();
   int value = slider.getValue();
   . . .
}
```

You can embellish the slider by showing *ticks*. For example, in the sample program, the second slider uses the following settings:

```
slider.setMajorTickSpacing(20);
slider.setMinorTickSpacing(5);
```

The slider is decorated with large tick marks every 20 units and small tick marks every 5 units. The units refer to slider values, not pixels.

These instructions only set the units for the tick marks. To actually have the tick marks appear, you also need to call

```
slider.setPaintTicks(true);
```

The major and minor tick marks are independent. For example, you can set major tick marks every 20 units and minor tick marks every 7 units, but you'll get a very messy scale.

You can force the slider to *snap to ticks*. Whenever the user has finished dragging a slider in snap mode, it is immediately moved to the closest tick. You activate this mode with the call

```
slider.setSnapToTicks(true);
```

You can ask for *tick mark labels* for the major tick marks, by calling

```
slider.setPaintLabels(true);
```

For example, with a slider ranging from 0 to 100 and major tick spacing of 20, the ticks are labeled 0, 20, 40, 60, 80, and 100.

You can also supply other tick marks, such as strings or icons (see Figure 6–36). The process is a bit convoluted. You need to fill a hash table with keys `new Integer(tickValue)` and values of type `Component`. Then you call the `setLabelTable` method. The components are placed under the tick marks. Usually, you use `JLabel` objects. Here is how you can label ticks as A, B, C, D, E, F.

```
Hashtable labelTable = new Hashtable();
labelTable.put(new Integer(0), new JLabel("A"));
labelTable.put(new Integer(20), new JLabel("B"));
. . .
labelTable.put(new Integer(100), new JLabel("F"));
slider.setLabelTable(labelTable);
```

Example 6–13 also shows a slider with icons as tick labels.

TIP: If your tick marks or labels don't show, double-check that you called `setPaintTicks(true)` and `setPaintLabels(true)`.

Finally, if you use the Metal look and feel, you can add a visual enhancement to your sliders and have the portion from the minimum value to the current value "filled in." The fourth and fifth sliders in Figure 6–36 are filled. You fill a slider by setting a client property as follows:

```
slider.putClientProperty("JSlider.isFilled", Boolean.TRUE);
```

The fifth slider has its direction reversed by calling

```
slider.setInverted(true);
```

The example program shows all these visual effects with a collection of sliders. Each slider has a change event listener installed that places the current slider value into the text field to the right of the slider.

Example 6–13: SliderTest.java

```
import java.awt.*;
import java.awt.event.*;
import java.util.*;
import javax.swing.*;
import javax.swing.event.*;

public class SliderTest
{  public static void main(String[] args)
   {  JFrame frame = new SliderTestFrame();
      frame.show();
   }
}

class SliderTestFrame extends JFrame
{  public SliderTestFrame()
   {  setTitle("SliderTest");
      setSize(400, 300);
      addWindowListener(new WindowAdapter()
         {  public void windowClosing(WindowEvent e)
            {  System.exit(0);
            }
         } );

      // set up grid bag layout and constraints

      getContentPane().setLayout(new GridBagLayout());
      constraints = new GridBagConstraints();
      constraints.weighty = 100;
      constraints.gridwidth = 1;
      constraints.gridheight = 1;
```

```
constraints.gridx = 0;
constraints.gridy = 0;

// add sliders with various decorations

JSlider slider = new JSlider();
addSlider(slider, "Plain");

slider = new JSlider();
slider.setPaintTicks(true);
slider.setMajorTickSpacing(20);
slider.setMinorTickSpacing(5);
addSlider(slider, "Ticks");

slider = new JSlider();
slider.setPaintTicks(true);
slider.setSnapToTicks(true);
slider.setMajorTickSpacing(20);
slider.setMinorTickSpacing(5);
addSlider(slider, "Snap to ticks");

slider = new JSlider();
slider.setPaintTicks(true);
slider.setMajorTickSpacing(20);
slider.setMinorTickSpacing(5);
slider.putClientProperty("JSlider.isFilled", Boolean.TRUE);
addSlider(slider, "Filled");

slider = new JSlider();
slider.setPaintTicks(true);
slider.setMajorTickSpacing(20);
slider.setMinorTickSpacing(5);
slider.putClientProperty("JSlider.isFilled", Boolean.TRUE);
slider.setInverted(true);
addSlider(slider, "Inverted");

slider = new JSlider();
slider.setPaintTicks(true);
slider.setPaintLabels(true);
slider.setMajorTickSpacing(20);
slider.setMinorTickSpacing(5);
addSlider(slider, "Labels");

slider = new JSlider();
slider.setPaintLabels(true);
slider.setPaintTicks(true);
slider.setMajorTickSpacing(20);
slider.setMinorTickSpacing(5);

Hashtable labelTable = new Hashtable();
labelTable.put(new Integer(0), new JLabel("A"));
labelTable.put(new Integer(20), new JLabel("B"));
```

```
      labelTable.put(new Integer(40), new JLabel("C"));
      labelTable.put(new Integer(60), new JLabel("D"));
      labelTable.put(new Integer(80), new JLabel("E"));
      labelTable.put(new Integer(100), new JLabel("F"));

      slider.setLabelTable(labelTable);
      addSlider(slider, "Custom labels");

      slider = new JSlider();
      slider.setPaintTicks(true);
      slider.setPaintLabels(true);
      slider.setSnapToTicks(true);
      slider.setMajorTickSpacing(20);
      slider.setMinorTickSpacing(20);

      labelTable = new Hashtable();

      // add card images

      labelTable.put(new Integer(0),
         new JLabel(new ImageIcon("9h.gif")));
      labelTable.put(new Integer(20),
         new JLabel(new ImageIcon("10h.gif")));
      labelTable.put(new Integer(40),
         new JLabel(new ImageIcon("jh.gif")));
      labelTable.put(new Integer(60),
         new JLabel(new ImageIcon("qh.gif")));
      labelTable.put(new Integer(80),
         new JLabel(new ImageIcon("kh.gif")));
      labelTable.put(new Integer(100),
         new JLabel(new ImageIcon("ah.gif")));

      slider.setLabelTable(labelTable);
      addSlider(slider, "Icon labels");
   }

   public void addSlider(JSlider s, String description)
   {  // create text field that is shown next to slider
      final TextField textField = new TextField(4);

      // update text field when the slider value changes
      s.addChangeListener(new ChangeListener()
         {  public void stateChanged(ChangeEvent event)
            {  JSlider source = (JSlider)event.getSource();
               textField.setText("" + source.getValue());
            }
         });

      // add three components into the next row

      constraints.gridx = 0;
      constraints.anchor = GridBagConstraints.WEST;
```

```
        constraints.fill = GridBagConstraints.NONE;
        constraints.weightx = 0;
        getContentPane().add(new JLabel(description), constraints);

        constraints.gridx++;
        constraints.anchor = GridBagConstraints.CENTER;
        constraints.fill = GridBagConstraints.HORIZONTAL;
        constraints.weightx = 100;
        getContentPane().add(s, constraints);

        constraints.gridx++;
        constraints.anchor = GridBagConstraints.WEST;
        constraints.fill = GridBagConstraints.NONE;
        constraints.weightx = 0;
        getContentPane().add(textField, constraints);

        // advance row
        constraints.gridy++;
    }

    private GridBagConstraints constraints;
}
```

javax.swing.JSlider

- `JSlider()`
- `JSlider(int direction)`
- `JSlider(int min, int max)`
- `JSlider(int min, int max, int initialValue)`
- `JSlider(int direction, int min, int max, int initialValue)`

  construct a horizontal slider with the given direction, minimum, maximum, and initial values.

Parameters:	`direction`	one of `SwingConstants.HORIZONTAL` or `SwingConstants.VERTICAL`. The default is horizontal.
	`min, max`	the minimum and maximum for the slider values. Defaults are 0 and 100.
	`initialValue`	the initial value for the slider. The default is 50.

- `void setPaintTicks(boolean b)`

  If `b` is true, then ticks are displayed.

- `void setMajorTickSpacing(int units)`
- `void setMinorTickSpacing(int units)`

  set major or minor ticks at multiples of the given slider units.

- `void setPaintLabels(boolean b)`

  If `b` is true, then tick labels are displayed.

- `slider.setLabelTable(Dictionary table)`

  sets the components to use for the tick labels. Each key/value pair in the table has the form `new Integer(`*value*`)/`*component*.

- `void setSnapToTicks(boolean b)`

  If `b` is true, then the slider snaps to the closest tick after each adjustment.

Progress Bars

A *progress bar* is a simple component—just a rectangle that is partially filled with color to indicate the progress of an operation. By default, progress is indicated by a string "*n* %". You can see a progress bar in the bottom right of Figure 6–37.

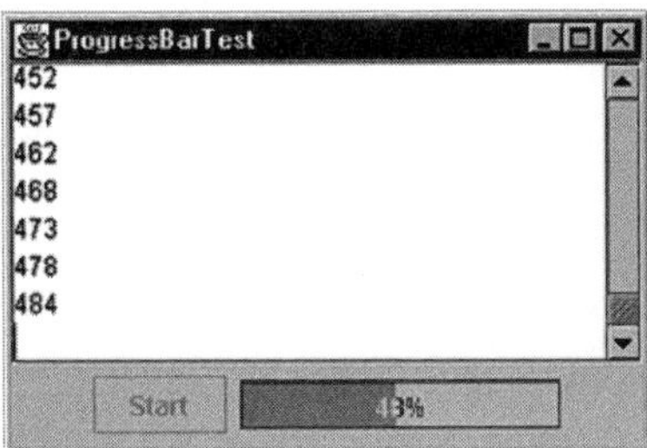

Figure 6–37: A progress bar

You construct a progress bar much as you construct a slider, by supplying the minimum and maximum value and an optional orientation:

```
progressBar = new JProgressBar(0, 1000);
progressBar = new JProgressBar(SwingConstants.VERTICAL, 0, 1000);
```

You can also set the minimum and maximum with the `setMinimum` and `setMaximum` methods.

Unlike a slider, the progress bar cannot be adjusted by the user. Your program needs to call `setValue` to update it.

If you call

```
progressBar.setStringPainted(true);
```

the progress bar computes the completion percentage and displays a string "*n* %". If you want to show a different string, you can supply it with the `setString` method:

```
if (progressBar.getValue() > 900)
   progressBar.setString("Almost Done");
```

The program in Example 6–14 shows a progress bar that monitors a simulated time-consuming activity.

The `SimulatedActivity` class implements a thread that increments a value `current` ten times per second. When it reaches a target value, the thread finishes. If you want to terminate the thread before it has reached its target, you should interrupt it.

```
class SimulatedActivity extends Thread
{  . . .
   public void run()
   {  while (current < target && !interrupted())
      {  try
         {  sleep(100);
         }
         catch(InterruptedException e)
         {  return;
         }
         current++;
      }
   }

   int current;
   int target;
}
```

When you click on the Start button, a new `SimulatedActivity` thread is started. To update the progress bar, it would appear to be an easy matter for the simulated activity thread to make calls to the `setValue` method. But that is not thread-safe. Recall from Chapter 1 that you should call Swing methods only from the event dispatch thread.

Instead, you can launch a timer that periodically polls the thread for a progress status and updates the progress bar. That is a realistic approach because in general a worker thread is not aware of the existence of the progress bar.

CAUTION: If a worker thread is aware of a progress bar that monitors its progress, remember that it cannot set the progress bar value directly. To set the value in the event dispatch thread, the worker thread can use the `SwingUtilities.invokeLater` method.

Recall from Chapter 1 that a Swing timer calls the `actionPerformed` method of its listeners and that these calls occur in the event dispatch thread. That means it is safe to update Swing components in the timer callback. Here is the timer callback from the example program. The current value of the simulated activity is displayed both in the text area and the progress bar. If the end of the simulation has been reached, the timer is stopped and the Start button is reenabled.

```
public void actionPerformed(ActionEvent event)
{  int current = activity.getCurrent();
   // show progress

   textArea.append(current + "\n");
```

```
      progressBar.setValue(current);

      // check if task is completed
      if (current == activity.getTarget())
      {  activityMonitor.stop();
         startButton.setEnabled(true);
      }
   }
```

Example 6–14 shows the full program code.

Example 6–14: ProgressBarTest.java

```
import java.awt.*;
import java.awt.event.*;
import java.util.*;
import javax.swing.*;
import javax.swing.event.*;

public class ProgressBarTest
{  public static void main(String[] args)
   {  JFrame frame = new ProgressBarFrame();
      frame.show();
   }
}

class ProgressBarFrame extends JFrame
{  public ProgressBarFrame()
   {  setTitle("ProgressBarTest");
      setSize(300, 200);
      addWindowListener(new WindowAdapter()
         {  public void windowClosing(WindowEvent e)
            {  System.exit(0);
            }
         } );

      Container contentPane = getContentPane();

      // this text area holds the activity output
      textArea = new JTextArea();

      // set up panel with button and progress bar

      JPanel panel = new JPanel();
      startButton = new JButton("Start");
      progressBar = new JProgressBar();
      progressBar.setStringPainted(true);
      panel.add(startButton);
      panel.add(progressBar);
      contentPane.add(new JScrollPane(textArea), "Center");
      contentPane.add(panel, "South");
```

```
      // set up the button action

      startButton.addActionListener(
         new ActionListener()
            {  public void actionPerformed(ActionEvent event)
               {  progressBar.setMaximum(1000);
                  activity = new SimulatedActivity(1000);
                  activity.start();
                  activityMonitor.start();
                  startButton.setEnabled(false);
               }
            });

      // set up the timer action

      activityMonitor = new Timer(500,
         new ActionListener()
            {  public void actionPerformed(ActionEvent event)
               {  int current = activity.getCurrent();

                  // show progress
                  textArea.append(current + "\n");
                  progressBar.setValue(current);

                  // check if task is completed
                  if (current == activity.getTarget())
                  {  activityMonitor.stop();
                     startButton.setEnabled(true);
                  }
               }
            });
   }

   private Timer activityMonitor;
   private JButton startButton;
   private JProgressBar progressBar;
   private JTextArea textArea;
   private SimulatedActivity activity;
}

class SimulatedActivity extends Thread
{  public SimulatedActivity(int t)
   {  current = 0;
      target = t;
   }

   public int getTarget()
   {  return target;
   }

   public int getCurrent()
```

```
   {  return current;
   }

   public void run()
   {  while (current < target && !interrupted())
      {  try
         {  sleep(100);
         }
         catch(InterruptedException e)
         {  return;
         }
         current++;
      }
   }

   private int current;
   private int target;
}
```

Progress Monitors

A progress bar is a very simple component that can be placed inside a window. In contrast, a `ProgressMonitor` is a complete dialog box that contains a progress bar (see Figure 6–38). The dialog contains OK and Cancel buttons. If you click either, the monitor dialog is closed. In addition, your program can query whether the user has canceled the dialog and terminate the monitored action. (Note that the class name does not start with a "`J`".)

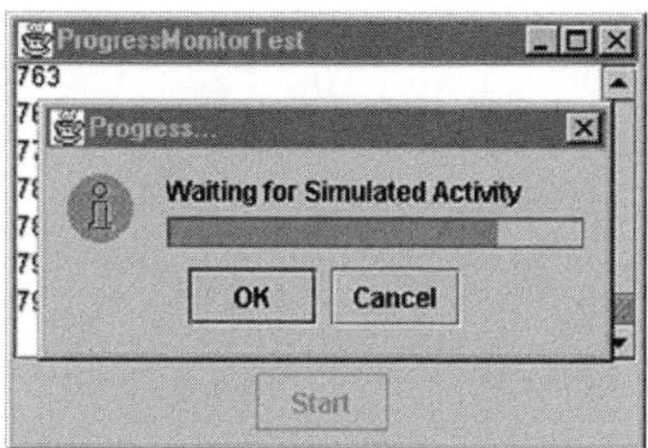

Figure 6–38: A progress monitor dialog

You construct a progress monitor by supplying the following:

- The parent component over which the dialog should pop up
- An object (which should be a string, icon, or component) that is displayed on the dialog
- An optional note to display below the object
- The minimum and maximum values

However, the progress monitor cannot measure progress or cancel an activity by itself. You still need to periodically set the progress value by calling the `setProgress` method. (This is the equivalent of the `setValue` method of the `JProgressBar` class.) As you update the progress value, you should also call the `isCanceled` method to see if the program user has clicked on the Cancel button.

When the monitored activity has concluded, you should call the `close` method to dismiss the dialog. You can reuse the same dialog by calling `start` again.

The example program looks very similar to that of the preceding section. We still need to launch a timer to watch over the progress of the simulated activity and update the progress monitor. Here is the timer callback.

```
public void actionPerformed(ActionEvent event)
{  int current = activity.getCurrent();

   // show progress
   textArea.append(current + "\n");
   progressDialog.setProgress(current);

   // check if task is completed or canceled
   if (current == activity.getTarget()
      || progressDialog.isCanceled())
   {  activityMonitor.stop();
      progressDialog.close();
      activity.interrupt();
      startButton.setEnabled(true);
   }
}
```

Note that there are two conditions for termination. The activity might have completed, or the user might have canceled it. In each of these cases, we close down

- the timer that monitored the activity;
- the progress dialog;
- the activity itself (by interrupting the thread).

If you run the program in Example 6–15, you can observe an interesting feature of the progress monitor dialog. The dialog doesn't come up immediately. Instead, it waits a for a short interval to see if the activity has already been completed or is likely to complete in less time than it would take for the dialog to appear. You control the timing as follows. Use the `setMillisToDecidePopup` method to set the number of milliseconds to wait between the construction of the dialog object and the decision whether to show the pop-up at all. The default value is 500 milliseconds. The `setMillisToPopup` is the time that you estimate that the dialog needs to pop up. The Swing designers set this value to a default of 2 seconds. Clearly they were mindful of the fact that Swing dialogs don't always come up as snappily as we all would like. You should probably not touch this value.

Example 6–15 shows the progress monitor in action, again measuring the progress of a simulated activity. As you can see, the progress monitor is convenient to use and only requires that you periodically query the thread that you want to monitor.

Example 6–15: ProgressMonitorTest.java

```
import java.awt.*;
import java.awt.event.*;
import java.util.*;
import javax.swing.*;
import javax.swing.event.*;

public class ProgressMonitorTest
{  public static void main(String[] args)
   {  JFrame frame = new ProgressMonitorFrame();
      frame.show();
   }
}

class ProgressMonitorFrame extends JFrame
{  public ProgressMonitorFrame()
   {  setTitle("ProgressMonitorTest");
      setSize(300, 200);
      addWindowListener(new WindowAdapter()
         {  public void windowClosing(WindowEvent e)
            {  System.exit(0);
            }
         } );

      Container contentPane = getContentPane();

      // this text area holds the activity output
      textArea = new JTextArea();

      // set up a button panel
      JPanel panel = new JPanel();
      startButton = new JButton("Start");
      panel.add(startButton);

      contentPane.add(new JScrollPane(textArea), "Center");
      contentPane.add(panel, "South");

      // set up the button action

      startButton.addActionListener(
         new ActionListener()
            {  public void actionPerformed(ActionEvent event)
               {  // start activity
                  activity = new SimulatedActivity(1000);
                  activity.start();

                  // launch progress dialog
```

```
                  progressDialog = new ProgressMonitor(
                     ProgressMonitorFrame.this,
                     "Waiting for Simulated Activity",
                     null, 0, activity.getTarget());

                  // start timer
                  activityMonitor.start();

                  startButton.setEnabled(false);
               }
            });

      // set up the timer action

      activityMonitor = new Timer(500,
         new ActionListener()
            {  public void actionPerformed(ActionEvent event)
               {  int current = activity.getCurrent();

                  // show progress
                  textArea.append(current + "\n");
                  progressDialog.setProgress(current);

                  // check if task is completed or canceled
                  if (current == activity.getTarget()
                     || progressDialog.isCanceled())
                  {  activityMonitor.stop();
                     progressDialog.close();
                     activity.interrupt();
                     startButton.setEnabled(true);
                  }
               }
            });
   }

   private Timer activityMonitor;
   private JButton startButton;
   private ProgressMonitor progressDialog;
   private JTextArea textArea;
   private SimulatedActivity activity;
}

class SimulatedActivity extends Thread
{  public SimulatedActivity(int t)
   {  current = 0;
      target = t;
   }

   public int getTarget()
   {  return target;
   }

   public int getCurrent()
```

```
    {  return current;
    }

    public void run()
    {  while (current < target && !interrupted())
       {  try
          {  sleep(100);
          }
          catch(InterruptedException e)
          {  return;
          }
          current++;
       }
    }

    private int current;
    private int target;
}
```

Monitoring the Progress of Input Streams

The Swing package contains a useful stream filter, `ProgressMonitorInputStream`, that you can use to automatically pop up a dialog that monitors how much of the stream has been read.

This filter is extremely easy to use. You sandwich in a `ProgressMonitorInputStream` between your usual sequence of filtered streams. (See Chapter 12 of Volume 1 for more information on streams.)

For example, suppose you read text from a file. You start out with a `FileInputStream`:

```
FileInputStream fileIn = new FileInputStream(f);
```

Normally, you would convert `fileIn` to an `InputStreamReader`.

```
InputStreamReader inReader = new InputStreamReader(fileIn);
```

However, to monitor the stream, first turn the file input stream into a stream with a progress monitor:

```
ProgressMonitorInputStream progressIn
   = new ProgressMonitorInputStream(parent, caption, fileIn);
```

You need to supply the parent component, a caption, and, of course, the stream to monitor. The `read` method of the progress monitor stream simply passes along the bytes and updates the progress dialog.

You now go on building your filter sequence:

```
InputStreamReader inReader = new InputStreamReader(progressIn);
```

That's all there is to it. When the file is read, the progress monitor automatically pops up. This is a very nice application of stream filtering.

CAUTION: The progress monitor stream uses the `available` method of the `InputStream` class to determine the total number of bytes in the stream. However, the `available` method only reports the number of bytes in the stream that are available *without blocking*. Progress monitors work well for files and HTTP URLs because their length is known in advance, but they don't work with all streams.

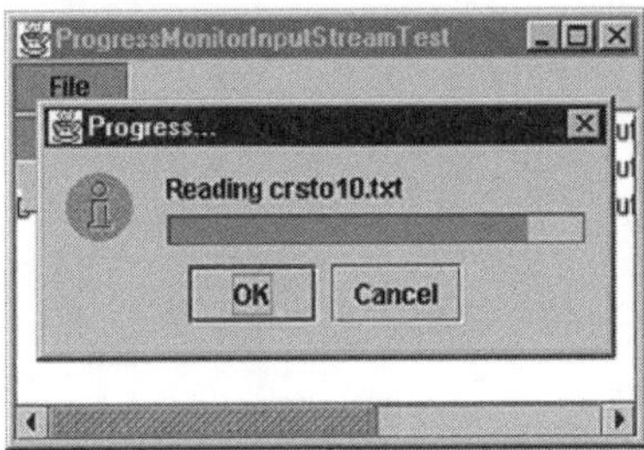

Figure 6–39: A progress monitor for an input stream

The program in Example 6–16 counts the lines in a file. If you read in a large file (such as "The Count of Monte Cristo" on the CD), then the progress dialog pops up.

Example 6–16: ProgressMonitorInputStreamTest.java

```
import java.awt.*;
import java.awt.event.*;
import java.io.*;
import java.util.*;
import javax.swing.*;
import javax.swing.event.*;

public class ProgressMonitorInputStreamTest
{  public static void main(String[] args)
   {  JFrame frame = new TextFrame();
      frame.show();
   }
}

class TextFrame extends JFrame
   implements ActionListener
{  public TextFrame()
   {  setTitle("ProgressMonitorInputStreamTest");
      setSize(300, 200);
      addWindowListener(new WindowAdapter()
         {  public void windowClosing(WindowEvent e)
            {  System.exit(0);
            }
         } );

      Container contentPane = getContentPane();
```

```
      // this text area contains line counts and error messages
      textArea = new JTextArea();
      contentPane.add(new JScrollPane(textArea), "Center");

      // set up menu

      JMenuBar menuBar = new JMenuBar();
      setJMenuBar(menuBar);
      JMenu fileMenu = new JMenu("File");
      menuBar.add(fileMenu);
      openItem = new JMenuItem("Open");
      openItem.addActionListener(this);
      fileMenu.add(openItem);
      exitItem = new JMenuItem("Exit");
      exitItem.addActionListener(this);
      fileMenu.add(exitItem);
   }

   public void actionPerformed(ActionEvent evt)
   {  Object source = evt.getSource();
      if (source == openItem)
      {  // have user select file

         JFileChooser chooser = new JFileChooser();
         chooser.setCurrentDirectory(new File("."));
         chooser.setFileFilter(
            new javax.swing.filechooser.FileFilter()
            {  public boolean accept(File f)
               {  String fname = f.getName().toLowerCase();
                  return fname.endsWith(".txt")
                     || f.isDirectory();
               }
               public String getDescription()
               { return "Text Files"; }
            });
         int r = chooser.showOpenDialog(this);
         if (r == JFileChooser.APPROVE_OPTION)
            readFile(chooser.getSelectedFile());
      }
      else if (source == exitItem)
         System.exit(0);
   }

   public void readFile(final File f)
   {  /* important: the monitored activity must be in a new
         thread. We define a thread class on the fly; the thread
         action is in the run method
      */

      Thread readThread = new Thread()
      {  public void run()
         {  try
```

```
            {  // set up stream and reader filter sequence

               FileInputStream fileIn = new FileInputStream(f);
               ProgressMonitorInputStream progressIn
                  = new ProgressMonitorInputStream(TextFrame.this,
                     "Reading " + f.getName(), fileIn);
               InputStreamReader inReader
                  = new InputStreamReader(progressIn);
               BufferedReader in = new BufferedReader(inReader);

               // read file and count lines

               int count = 0;
               String line;
               while ((line = in.readLine()) != null)
                  count++;
               textArea.append(f + ": " + count + " lines\n");
               fileIn.close();
            }
            catch(IOException e)
            {  textArea.append("Error " + e + "\n");
            }
         }
      };

      readThread.start();
   }

   private JTextArea textArea;
   private JMenuItem openItem;
   private JMenuItem exitItem;
}
```

`javax.swing.JProgressBar`

- `JProgressBar()`
- `JProgressBar(int direction)`
- `JProgressBar(int min, int max)`
- `JProgressBar(int direction, int min, int max)`

  construct a horizontal slider with the given direction, minimum, maximum, and initial values.

Parameters:	`direction`	one of `SwingConstants.HORIZONTAL` or `SwingConstants.VERTICAL`. The default is horizontal.
	`min, max`	the minimum and maximum for the progress bar values. Defaults are 0 and 100.

- `int getMinimum()`
- `int getMaximum()`
- `void setMinimum(int value)`
- `void setMaximum(int value)`

  get and set the minimum and maximum values.
- `int getValue()`
- `void setValue(int value)`

  get and set the current value.
- `String getString()`
- `void setString(String s)`

  get and set the string to be displayed in the progress bar. If the string is `null`, then a default string "*n* %" is displayed.
- `boolean isStringPainted()`
- `void setStringPainted(boolean b)`

  get and set the "string painted" property. If this property is `true`, then a string is painted on top of the progress bar. The default is `false`; no string is painted.

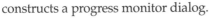

`javax.swing.ProgressMonitor` API

- `ProgressMonitor(Component parent, Object message, String note, int min, int max)`

  constructs a progress monitor dialog.

Parameters	`parent`	the parent component over which this dialog pops up
	`message`	the message object to display in the dialog
	`note`	the optional string to display under the message. If this value is `null`, then no space is set aside for the note, and a later call to `setNote` has no effect.
	`min, max`	the minumum and maximum values of the progress bar

- `void setNote(String note)`

  changes the note text.
- `void setProgress(int value)`

  sets the progress bar value to the given value.
- `void close()`

  closes this dialog.
- `boolean isCanceled()`

  returns `true` if the user canceled this dialog.

`javax.swing.ProgressMonitorInputStream`

- `ProgressMonitorInputStream(Component parent, Object message, InputStream in)`

  constructs an input stream filter with an associated progress monitor dialog.

Parameters	`parent`	the parent component over which this dialog pops up
	`message`	the message object to display in the dialog
	`in`	the input stream that is being monitored.

Tool Bars and Tool Tips

A tool bar is a button bar that gives quick access to the most commonly used commands in a program (see Figure 6–40).

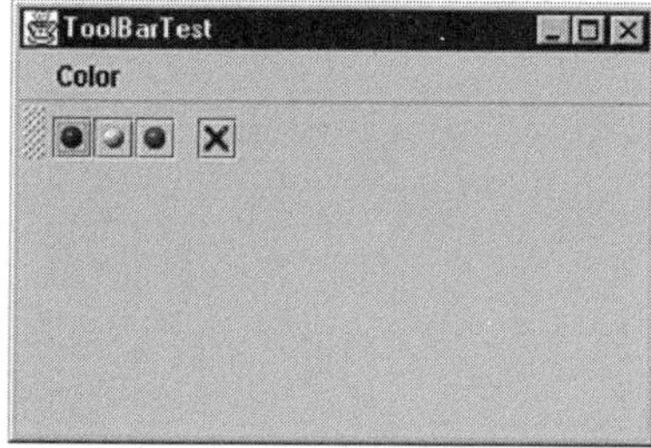

Figure 6–40: A tool bar

What makes tool bars special is that you can move them elsewhere. You can drag the tool bar to one of the four borders of the frame (see Figure 6–41). When you release the mouse button, the tool bar is dropped into the new location (see Figure 6–42).

NOTE: Tool bar dragging works if the tool bar is inside a container with a border layout, or any other layout manager that supports the `"North"`, `"East"`, `"South"`, and `"West"` constraints.

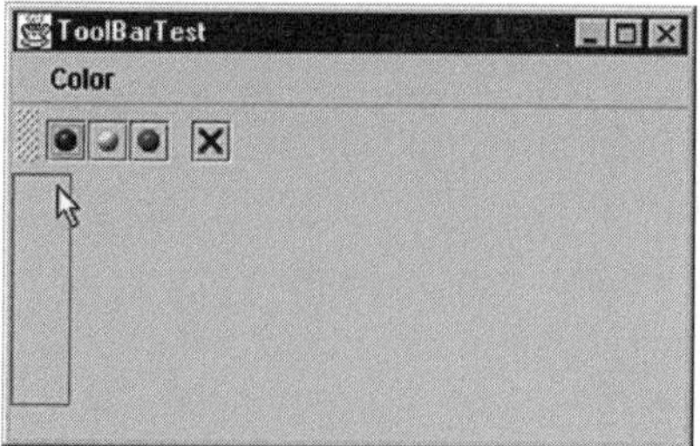

Figure 6–41: Dragging the tool bar

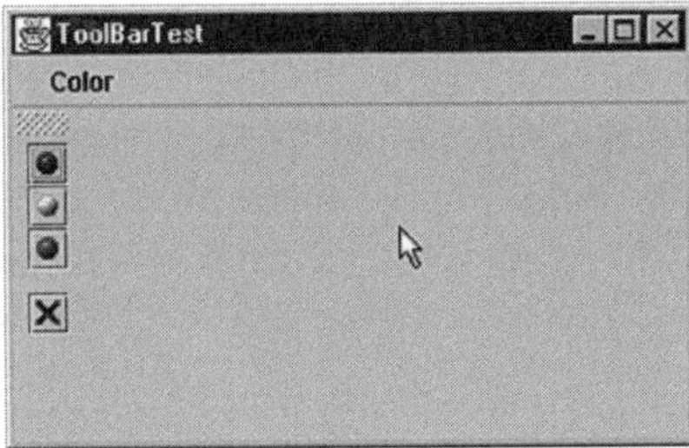

Figure 6–42: Dragging the tool bar to another border

The tool bar can even be completely detached from the frame. A detached tool bar is contained in its own frame (see Figure 6–43). When you close the frame containing a detached tool bar, the tool bar jumps back into the original frame.

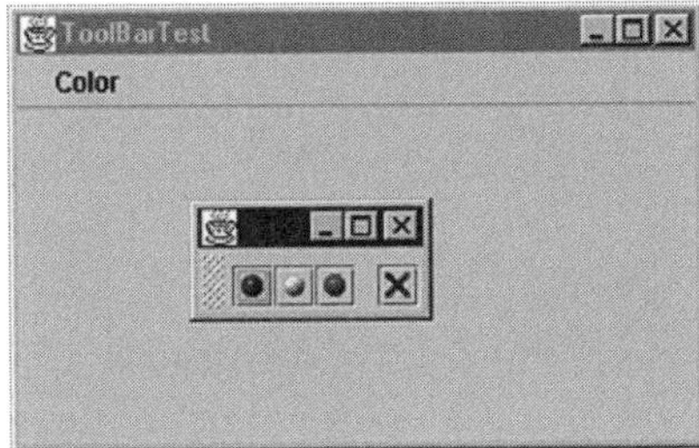

Figure 6–43: Detaching the tool bar

Tool bars are straightforward to program. You add components into the tool bar:

```
JToolBar bar = new JToolBar();
bar.add(blueButton);
```

You can separate groups of buttons with a separator:

```
bar.addSeparator();
```

For example, the tool bar in Figure 6–40 on page 426 has a separator between the third and fourth button.

Then, you add the tool bar to the container.

```
contentPane.add(bar, "North");
```

While most tool bars are made up of buttons, there is no restriction on the components that you can add to a tool bar. For example, combo boxes in tool bars are quite common.

CAUTION: In JDK 1.2, the tool bar buttons are much too wide when you use the Windows Look and Feel. The remedy is to call

```
button.setMargin(new Insets(0, 0, 0, 0));
```

for each button that you add to the tool bar.

If you followed Chapter 8 of Volume 1, then you will recall that we recommend the use of the `Action` interface to separate actions and the user interface that leads to them. The `Action` interface extends the `ActionListener` interface, and it supports a small lookup table to hold names, icons, and help information. The `AbstractAction` class implements all methods of the `Action` interface, except for the `actionPerformed` method, which you must supply in a subclass. Here is a typical action:

```
Action exitAction
   = new AbstractAction("Exit", new ImageIcon("exit.gif"))
      {  public void actionPerformed(ActionEvent event)
         {  System.exit(0);
         }
      };
```

You can add `Action` objects to menus:

```
menu.add(exitAction);
```

This operation automatically creates a menu item with the given name and icon, and the `actionPerformed` method is automatically called when the item is selected. Chapter 8 of Volume 1 shows how you can attach the same action object to a keystroke.

The `JToolBar` class also has a method to add an action. Unfortunately, the resulting tool bar looks rather unattractive because the action names are displayed under the icons (see Figure 6–44).

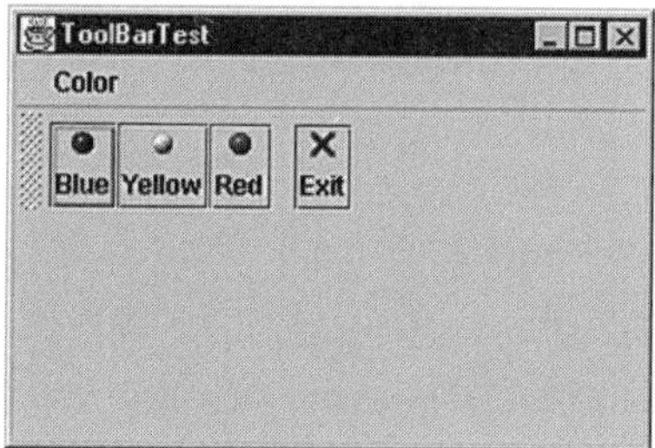

Figure 6–44: A tool bar with actions

Hopefully, a future version of Swing will add an option for tool bars to suppress these action names. In the meantime, we suggest that you use a helper class to make a tool bar button out of an action.

```
class ToolBarButton extends JButton
{  public ToolBarButton(Action a)
   {  super((Icon)a.getValue(Action.SMALL_ICON));
      addActionListener(a);
   }
}
```

Then, you can populate the tool bar with these buttons:

```
bar.add(new ToolBarButton(exitAction));
```

Tool Tips

A disadvantage of tool bars is that users are often mystified by the meanings of the tiny icons in tool bars. To solve this problem, *tool tips* were invented. A tool tip is activated when the cursor rests for a moment over a button. The tool tip text is displayed inside a colored rectangle. When the user moves the mouse away, the tool tip is removed.

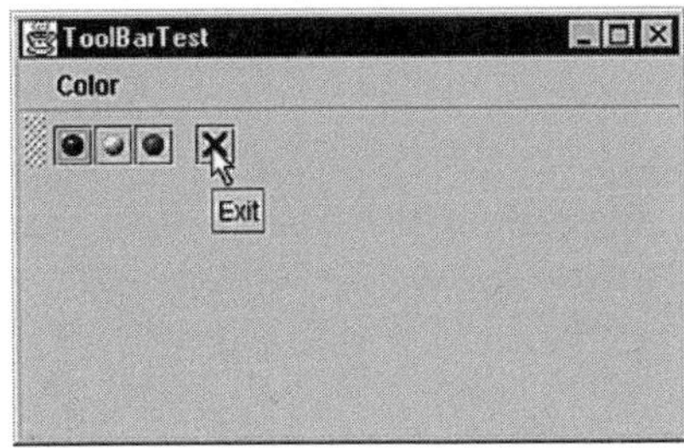

Figure 6–45: A tool tip

In Swing, you can add tool tips to any `JComponent` simply by calling the `setToolTipText` method:

```
exitButton.setToolTipText("Exit");
```

The `ToolBarButton` class in Example 6–17 tries to find an appropriate tool bar tip in the action table. If the action has a value associated with the key `Action.SHORT_DESCRIPTION`, then it is used. If not, the action name is displayed in the tool tip.

Example 6–17 is a program that shows how the same `Action` objects can be added to a menu and a tool bar. Note that the action names show up as the menu item names in the menu and as the tool tips in the tool bar.

Example 6–17: ToolBarTest.java

```
import java.awt.*;
import java.awt.event.*;
import java.beans.*;
import javax.swing.*;

public class ToolBarTest
{  public static void main(String[] args)
   {  JFrame frame = new ToolBarFrame();
      frame.show();
   }
```

```
}

/* the color action sets the background of its target to a
   given color
*/

class ColorAction extends AbstractAction
{  public ColorAction(String name, Icon icon,
      Color c, Component t)
   {  putValue(Action.NAME, name);
      putValue(Action.SMALL_ICON, icon);
      putValue(Action.SHORT_DESCRIPTION, name + " background");
      putValue("Color", c);
      target = t;
   }

   public void actionPerformed(ActionEvent evt)
   {  Color c = (Color)getValue("Color");
      target.setBackground(c);
      target.repaint();
   }

   private Component target;
}

/* the tool bar button is a button with an icon and no text
   suitable for addition into a tool bar. The tool tip is set
   to the short description of the action, or to the name
   if the short description is not available
*/

class ToolBarButton extends JButton
{  public ToolBarButton(Action a)
   {  super((Icon)a.getValue(Action.SMALL_ICON));

      String toolTip
         = (String)a.getValue(Action.SHORT_DESCRIPTION);
      if (toolTip == null)
         toolTip = (String)a.getValue(Action.NAME);
      if (toolTip != null)
         setToolTipText(toolTip);
      addActionListener(a);
   }
}

class ToolBarFrame extends JFrame
{  public ToolBarFrame()
   {  setTitle("ToolBarTest");
      setSize(300, 200);
      addWindowListener(new WindowAdapter()
         {  public void windowClosing(WindowEvent e)
```

```
         {  System.exit(0);
         }
      } );

   // add a panel for color change

   Container contentPane = getContentPane();
   JPanel panel = new JPanel();
   contentPane.add(panel, "Center");

   // set up actions

   Action blueAction = new ColorAction("Blue",
      new ImageIcon("blue-ball.gif"),
      Color.blue, panel);
   Action yellowAction = new ColorAction("Yellow",
      new ImageIcon("yellow-ball.gif"),
      Color.yellow, panel);
   Action redAction = new ColorAction("Red",
      new ImageIcon("red-ball.gif"),
      Color.red, panel);

   Action exitAction
      = new AbstractAction("Exit", new ImageIcon("exit.gif"))
         {  public void actionPerformed(ActionEvent event)
            {  System.exit(0);
            }
         };

   // populate tool bar

   JToolBar bar = new JToolBar();
   bar.add(new ToolBarButton(blueAction));
   bar.add(new ToolBarButton(yellowAction));
   bar.add(new ToolBarButton(redAction));
   bar.addSeparator();
   bar.add(new ToolBarButton(exitAction));
   contentPane.add(bar, "North");

   // populate menu

   JMenu menu = new JMenu("Color");
   menu.add(yellowAction);
   menu.add(blueAction);
   menu.add(redAction);
   menu.add(exitAction);
   JMenuBar menuBar = new JMenuBar();
   menuBar.add(menu);
   setJMenuBar(menuBar);
  }
}
```

javax.swing.JToolBar

- `void add(Action a)`

  constructs a new button inside the tool bar with name, icon, and action callback from the given action and adds the button to the end of the tool bar. Note that the name is displayed below the icon.
- `void addSeparator()`

  adds a separator to the end of the tool bar.

javax.swing.JComponent

- `void setToolTipText(String text)`

  sets the text that should be displayed as a tool tip when the mouse hovers over the component.

Component Organizers

We conclude the discussion of advanced Swing features with a presentation of components that help organize other components. These include the *split pane,* a mechanism for splitting an area into multiple parts whose boundaries can be adjusted, the *tabbed pane,* which uses tab dividers to allow a user to flip through multiple panels, and the *desktop pane,* which can be used to implement applications that display multiple *internal frames.*

Split Panes

Split panes are used to split a component into two parts, with an adjustable boundary in between. Figure 6–46 shows a frame with two split panes. The outer pane is split horizontally, with a text area on the bottom and another split pane on the top. That pane is split vertically, with a list on the left and a label containing an image on the right.

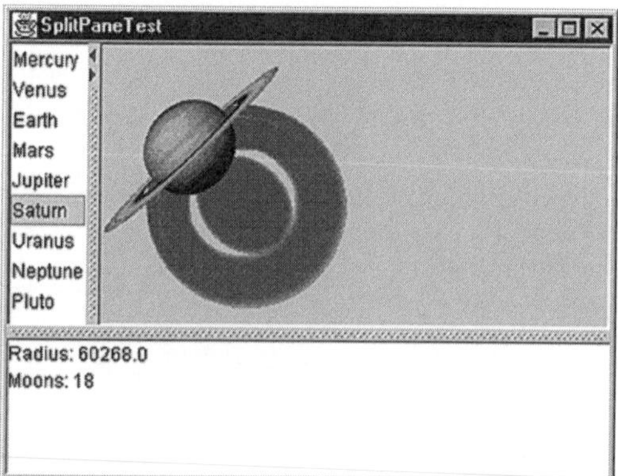

Figure 6–46: A frame with two nested split panes

You construct a split pane by specifying the orientation, one of `JSplitPane.HORIZONTAL_SPLIT` or `JSplitPane.VERTICAL_SPLIT`, followed by the two components. For example,

```
JSplitPane innerPane
    = new JSplitPane(JSplitPane.HORIZONTAL_SPLIT,
        planetList, planetImage);
```

That's all you have to do. If you like, you can add "one touch expand" icons to the splitter bar. You see those icons in the top pane in Figure 6–46. In the Metal look and feel, they are small triangles. If you click on one of them, the splitter moves all the way in the direction of the tip of the triangle, expanding one of the panes completely.

To add this capability, call

```
innerPane.setOneTouchExpandable(true);
```

The "continuous layout" feature continuously repaints the contents of both components as the user adjusts the splitter. That looks classier, but it can be slow. You turn on that feature with the call

```
innerPane.setContinuousLayout(true);
```

In the example program, we left the bottom splitter at the default (no continuous layout). When you drag it, you only move a black outline. When you are done, the components are repainted.

The program in Example 6–18 is very straightforward. It populates a list box with planets. When the user makes a selection, the planet image is displayed to the right and a description is placed in the text area on the bottom. When you run the program, adjust the splitters and try out the "one touch expansion" and "continuous layout" features.

Example 6–18: SplitPaneTest.java

```
import java.awt.*;
import java.awt.event.*;
import java.util.*;
import javax.swing.*;
import javax.swing.event.*;

public class SplitPaneTest
{  public static void main(String[] args)
   {  JFrame frame = new SplitPaneFrame();
      frame.show();
   }
}

class SplitPaneFrame extends JFrame
   implements ListSelectionListener
{  public SplitPaneFrame()
```

```
   {  setTitle("SplitPaneTest");
      setSize(400, 300);
      addWindowListener(new WindowAdapter()
         {  public void windowClosing(WindowEvent e)
            {  System.exit(0);
            }
         } );

      // set up components for planet names, images, descriptions

      planetList = new JList(planets);
      planetList.addListSelectionListener(this);

      planetImage = new JLabel();

      description = new JTextArea();

      // set up split panes

      JSplitPane innerPane
         = new JSplitPane(JSplitPane.HORIZONTAL_SPLIT,
            planetList, planetImage);

      innerPane.setContinuousLayout(true);
      innerPane.setOneTouchExpandable(true);

      JSplitPane outerPane
         = new JSplitPane(JSplitPane.VERTICAL_SPLIT,
            innerPane, description);

      getContentPane().add(outerPane, "Center");
   }

   public void valueChanged(ListSelectionEvent event)
   {  JList source = (JList)event.getSource();
      Planet value = (Planet)source.getSelectedValue();

      // update image and description

      planetImage.setIcon(value.getImage());
      description.setText(value.getDescription());
   }

   private JList planetList;
   private JLabel planetImage;
   private JTextArea description;
   private Planet[] planets =
      {  new Planet("Mercury", 2440, 0),
         new Planet("Venus", 6052, 0),
         new Planet("Earth", 6378, 1),
         new Planet("Mars", 3397, 2),
         new Planet("Jupiter", 71492, 16),
```

```
         new Planet("Saturn", 60268, 18),
         new Planet("Uranus", 25559, 17),
         new Planet("Neptune", 24766, 8),
         new Planet("Pluto", 1137, 1),
      };
}

class Planet
{  public Planet(String n, double r, int m)
   {  name = n;
      radius = r;
      moons = m;
      image = new ImageIcon(name + ".gif");
   }

   public String toString()
   {  return name;
   }

   public String getDescription()
   {  return "Radius: " + radius + "\nMoons: " + moons + "\n";
   }

   public ImageIcon getImage()
   {  return image;
   }

   private String name;
   private double radius;
   private int moons;
   private ImageIcon image;
}
```

javax.swing.JSplitPane

- `JSplitPane()`
- `JSplitPane(int direction)`
- `JSplitPane(int direction, boolean continuousLayout)`
- `JSplitPane(int direction, Component first, Component second)`
- `JSplitPane(int direction, boolean continuousLayout, Component first, Component second)`

  construct a new split pane.

Parameters:	`direction`	one of `HORIZONTAL_SPLIT` or `VERTICAL_SPLIT`
	`continousLayout`	`true` if the components are continuously updated when the splitter is moved
	`first, second`	the components to add

- `boolean isOneTouchExpandable()`
- `void setOneTouchExpandable(boolean b)`

  get and set the "one touch expandable" property. When this property is set, the splitter has two icons to completely expand one or the other component.

- `boolean isContinuousLayout()`
- `void setContinuousLayout(boolean b)`

  get and set the "continuous layout" property. When this property is set, then the components are continuously updated when the splitter is moved.

- `void setLeftComponent(Component c)`
- `void setTopComponent(Component c)`

  These operations have the same effect, to set `c` as the first component in the split pane.

- `void setRightComponent(Component c)`
- `void setBottomComponent(Component c)`

  These operations have the same effect, to set `c` as the second component in the split pane.

Tabbed Panes

Tabbed panes are a familiar user interface device to break up a complex dialog into subsets of related options. You can also use tabs to let a user flip through a set of documents or images (see Figure 6–47). That is what we will do in our sample program.

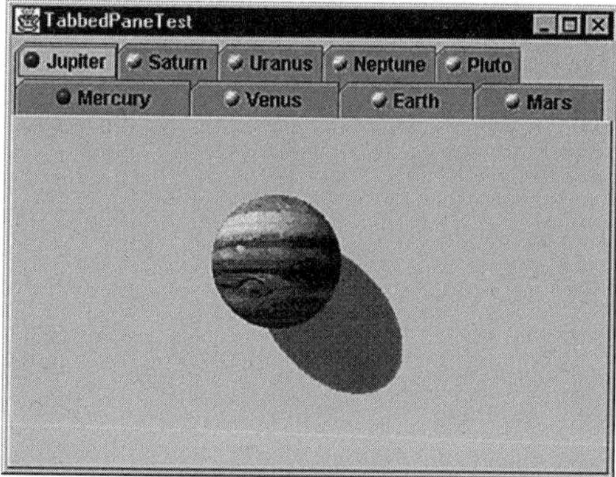

Figure 6–47: A tabbed pane

To create a tabbed pane, you first construct a `JTabbedPane` object, then you add tabs to it.

```
JTabbedPane tabbedPane = new JTabbedPane();
tabbedPane.addTab(title, icon, component);
```

The last parameter of the addTab method has type Component. If you want to add multiple components into the same tab, you first pack them up in a container, such as a JPanel.

The icon is optional; there is an addTab method that does not require an icon:

```
tabbedPane.addTab(title, component);
```

You can also add a tab in the middle of the tab collection with the insertTab method:

```
tabbedPane.insertTab(title, icon, component, index);
```

To remove a tab from the tab collection, use

```
tabPane.removeTabAt(index);
```

When you add a new tab to the tab collection, it is not automatically displayed. You must select it with the setSelectedIndex method. For example, here is how you show a tab that you just added to the end:

```
tabbedPane.setSelectedIndex(tabbedPane.getTabCount() - 1);
```

The example program shows a useful technique with tabbed panes. Sometimes, you want to update a component just before it is displayed. In our example program, we will load the planet image only when the user actually clicks on a tab.

To be notified whenever the user clicks on a new tab, you install a ChangeListener with the tabbed pane. Note that you must install the listener with the tabbed pane itself, not with any of the components.

```
tabbedPane.addChangeListener(listener);
```

When the user selects a tab, the stateChanged method of the change listener is called. You retrieve the tabbed pane as the source of the event. Call the getSelectedIndex method to find out which pane is about to be selected.

```
public void stateChanged(ChangeEvent event)
{  JTabbedPane pane = (JTabbedPane)event.getSource();
   int n = pane.getSelectedIndex();
   . . .
}
```

In Example 6–19, we first set all tab components to null. When a new tab is selected, we test if its component is still null. If so, we replace it with the image. (This happens instantaneously when you click on the tab. You will not see an empty pane.) Just for fun, we also change the icon from a yellow ball to a red ball to indicate which panes have been visited.

Example 6–19: TabbedPaneTest.java

```
import java.awt.*;
import java.awt.event.*;
import java.util.*;
import javax.swing.*;
```

```
import javax.swing.event.*;

public class TabbedPaneTest
{  public static void main(String[] args)
   {  JFrame frame = new TabbedPaneFrame();
      frame.show();
   }
}

class TabbedPaneFrame extends JFrame
   implements ChangeListener
{  public TabbedPaneFrame()
   {  setTitle("TabbedPaneTest");
      setSize(400, 300);
      addWindowListener(new WindowAdapter()
         {  public void windowClosing(WindowEvent e)
            {  System.exit(0);
            }
         } );

      tabbedPane = new JTabbedPane();
      tabbedPane.addChangeListener(this);

      /* we set the components to null and delay their
         loading until the tab is shown for the first time
      */

      ImageIcon icon = new ImageIcon("yellow-ball.gif");

      tabbedPane.addTab("Mercury", icon, null);
      tabbedPane.addTab("Venus", icon, null);
      tabbedPane.addTab("Earth", icon, null);
      tabbedPane.addTab("Mars", icon, null);
      tabbedPane.addTab("Jupiter", icon, null);
      tabbedPane.addTab("Saturn", icon, null);
      tabbedPane.addTab("Uranus", icon, null);
      tabbedPane.addTab("Neptune", icon, null);
      tabbedPane.addTab("Pluto", icon, null);

      getContentPane().add(tabbedPane, "Center");
   }

   public void stateChanged(ChangeEvent event)
   {  JTabbedPane pane = (JTabbedPane)event.getSource();

      // check if this tab still has a null component

      if (pane.getSelectedComponent() == null)
      {  // set the component to the image icon

         int n = pane.getSelectedIndex();
```

```
            String title = pane.getTitleAt(n);
            ImageIcon planetIcon = new ImageIcon(title + ".gif");
            pane.setComponentAt(n, new JLabel(planetIcon));

            // indicate that this tab has been visited--just for fun

            pane.setIconAt(n, new ImageIcon("red-ball.gif"));
         }
      }

   private JTabbedPane tabbedPane;
}
```

javax.swing.JTabbedPane

- `JTabbedPane()`
- `JTabbedPane(int placement)`

  construct a tabbed pane.

  Parameters: `placement` one of `SwingConstants.TOP`, `SwingConstants.LEFT`, `SwingConstants.RIGHT`, or `SwingConstants.BOTTOM`

- `void addTab(String title, Component component)`
- `void addTab(String title, Icon icon, Component c)`
- `void addTab(String title, Icon icon, Component c, String tooltip)`

  add a tab to the end of the tabbed pane.

- `void addTab(String title, Icon icon, Component c, String tooltip, int index)`

  inserts a tab to the tabbed pane at the given index.

- `void removeTabAt(int index)`

  removes the tab at the given index.

- `void setSelectedIndex(int index)`

  selects the tab at the given index.

- `int getSelectedIndex()`

  returns the index of the selected tab.

- `Component getSelectedComponent()`

  returns the component.

- `String getTitleAt(int index)`
- `void setTitleAt(int index, String title)`
- `Icon getIconAt(int index)`
- `void setIconAt(int index, Icon icon)`
- `Component getComponentAt(int index)`
- `void setComponentAt(int index, Component c)`

  get or set the title, icon, or component at the given index.

- `int indexOfTab(Icon icon)`
- `int indexOfTab(String title)`
- `int indexOfComponent(Component c)`

  return the index of the tab with the given title, icon, or component.
- `int getTabCount()`

  returns the total number of tabs in this tabbed pane.
- `void addChangeListener(ChangeListener listener)`

  adds a change listener that is notified when the user selects a different tab.

Desktop Panes and Internal Frames

Many applications present information in multiple windows that are all contained inside a large frame. If you minimize the application frame, all of its windows are hidden at the same time. In the Windows environment, this user interface is sometimes called the *multiple document interface* or MDI. Figure 6–48 shows a typical application that utilizes this interface.

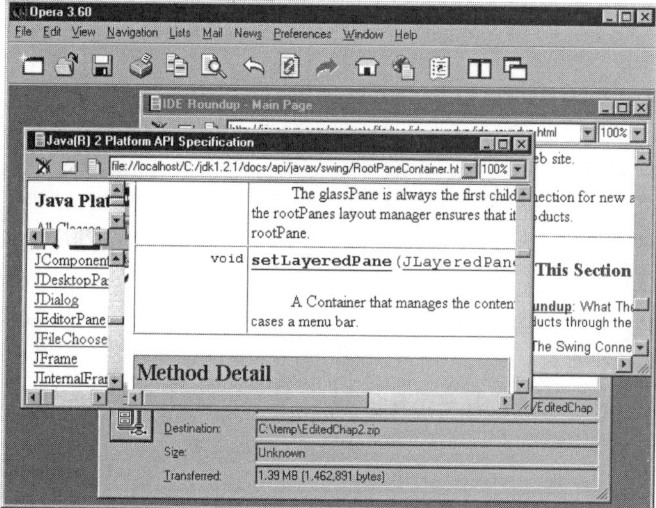

Figure 6–48: A multiple document interface application

For some time, this user interface style was very popular, but it has become less prevalent in recent years. In particular, most browsers display a separate top-level frame for each web page. (A conspicuous exception is the Opera browser, shown in Figure 6–48). Which is better? There are advantages and disadvantages to both approaches. MDI reduces window clutter. But having separate top-level windows means that you can use the buttons and hotkeys of the host windowing system to flip through your windows.

In the world of Java, where you can't rely on a rich host windowing system, it makes a lot of sense to have your application manage its frames.

Figure 6–49 shows a Java application with three internal frames. Two of them have decorations on the border to maximize and iconify them. The third is in its iconified state.

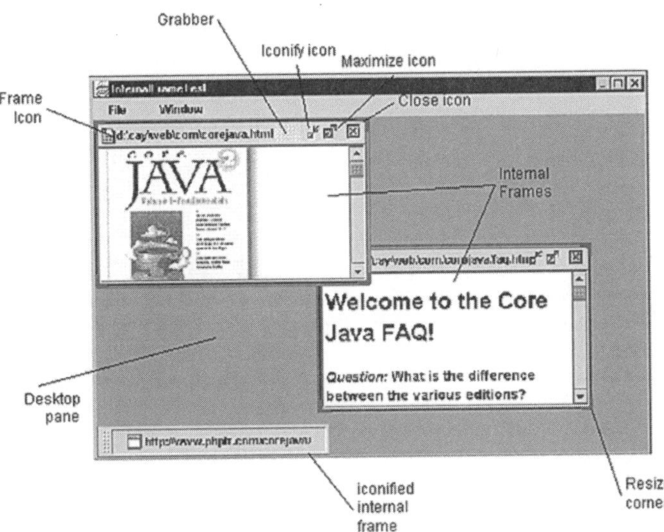

Figure 6–49: A Java application with three internal frames

In the Metal look and feel, the internal frames have distinctive "grabber" areas that you use to move the frames around. You can resize the windows by dragging the resize corners.

To achieve this capability, follow these steps:

1. Use a regular `JFrame` window for the application.
2. Set the content pane of the `JFrame` to a `JDesktopPane`.

```
desktop = new JDesktopPane();
setContentPane(desktop);
```

3. Construct `JInternalFrame` windows. You can specify whether you want the icons for resizing or closing the frame. Normally, you want all icons.

```
JInternalFrame iframe = new JInternalFrame(title,
   true, // resizable
   true, // closable
   true, // maximizable
   true); // iconifiable
```

4. Add components to the content pane of the frame.

```
iframe.getContentPane().add(c);
```

5. Set a frame icon. The icon is shown in the top-left corner of the frame.

```
iframe.setFrameIcon(icon);
```

NOTE: In the current version of the Metal look and feel, the frame icon is not displayed in iconized frames.

6. Set the size of the internal frame. As with regular frames, internal frames initially have a size of 0 by 0 pixels. Since you don't want to have all internal frames display on top of each other, you should use a variable position for the next frame. Use the `reshape` method to set both the position and size of the frame:

```
iframe.reshape(nextFrameX, nextFrameY, width, height);
```

7. As with `JFrames`, you need to make the frame visible.

```
iframe.setVisible(true);
```

NOTE: In earlier versions of Swing, internal frames were automatically visible and this call was not necessary.

8. Add the frame to the `JDesktopPane`:

```
desktop.add(iframe);
```

9. You probably want to make the new frame the *selected frame*. Of the internal frames on the desktop, only the selected frame receives keyboard focus. In the Metal look and feel, the selected frame has a blue title bar, whereas the other frames have a gray title bar. You use the `setSelected` method to select a frame. However, the "selected" property can be *vetoed*—the currently selected frame can refuse to give up focus. In that case, the `setSelected` method throws a `PropertyVetoException` that you need to handle.

```
try
{  iframe.setSelected(true);
}
catch(PropertyVetoException e)
{ // attempt was vetoed
}
```

10. You probably want to move the position for the next internal frame down so that it won't overlay over the existing frame. A good distance between frames is the height of the title bar, which you can obtain as

```
int frameDistance =
   iframe.getHeight() - iframe.getContentPane().getHeight()
```

11. Use that distance to determine the next internal frame position.

```
nextFrameX += frameDistance;
nextFrameY += frameDistance;
if (nextFrameX + width > desktop.getWidth())
   nextFrameX = 0;
```

```
if (nextFrameY + height > desktop.getHeight())
   nextFrameY = 0;
```

Cascading and tiling

In Windows, there are standard commands for *cascading* and *tiling* windows (see Figures 6–50 and 6–51). The Java `JDesktopPane` and `JInternalFrame` classes have no built-in support for these operations. In Example 6–20, we show you how you can implement these operations yourself.

To cascade all windows, you reshape windows to the same size and stagger their positions. The `getAllFrames` method of the `JDesktopPane` class returns an array of all internal frames.

```
JInternalFrame[] frames = desktop.getAllFrames();
```

However, you need to pay attention to the frame state. An internal frame can be in one of three states:

- Icon
- Resizable
- Maximum

You use the `isIcon` method to find out which internal frames are currently icons and should be skipped. However, if a frame is in the maximum state, you have to first set it to be resizable by calling `setMaximum(false)`. This is another property that can be vetoed. Therefore, you have to catch the `PropertyVetoException`.

The following loop cascades all internal frames on the desktop:

```
for (int i = 0; i < frames.length; i++)
{  if (!frames[i].isIcon())
   {  try
      {  /* try to make maximized frames resizable
            this might be vetoed
         */
         frames[i].setMaximum(false);
          frames[i].reshape(x, y, width, height);

         x += frameDistance;
         y += frameDistance;
         // wrap around at the desktop edge
         if (x + width > desktop.getWidth()) x = 0;
         if (y + height > desktop.getHeight()) y = 0;
      }
      catch(PropertyVetoException e)
      {}
   }
}
```

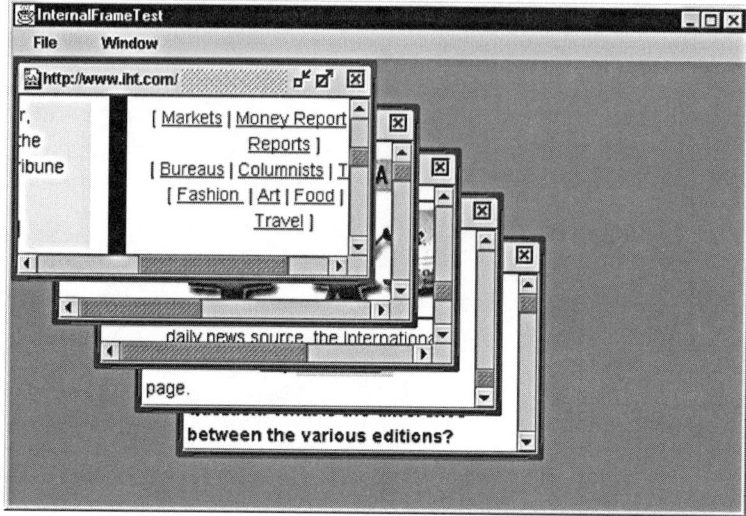

Figure 6–50: Cascaded internal frames

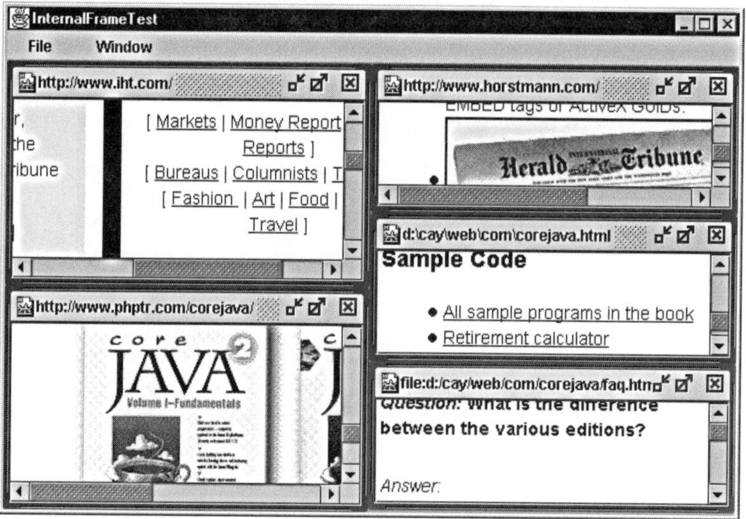

Figure 6–51: Tiled internal frames

Tiling frames is trickier, particularly if the number of frames is not a perfect square. First, count the number of frames that are not icons. Then, compute the number of columns as

```
int cols = (int)Math.sqrt(frameCount);
```

Then the number of rows is

```
int rows = frameCount / cols;
```

except that the last

```
extra = frameCount % cols
```

columns have `rows + 1` rows.

Here is the loop for tiling all frames on the desktop.

```
int width = desktop.getWidth() / cols;
int height = desktop.getHeight() / rows;
int r = 0;
int c = 0;
for (int i = 0; i < frames.length; i++)
{  if (!frames[i].isIcon())
   {  try
      {  frames[i].setMaximum(false);
         frames[i].reshape(c * width,
            r * height, width, height);
         r++;
         if (r == rows)
         {  r = 0;
            c++;
            if (c == cols - extra)
            {  // start adding an extra row
               rows++;
               height = desktop.getHeight() / rows;
            }
         }
      }
      catch(PropertyVetoException e)
      {}
   }
}
```

The example program shows another common frame operation: to move the selection from the current frame to the next frame that isn't an icon. The `JDesktopPane` class has no method to return the selected frame. Instead, you must traverse all frames and call `isSelected` until you find the currently selected frame. Then, look for the next frame in the sequence that isn't an icon, and try to select it by calling

```
frames[next].setSelected(true);
```

As before, that method can throw a `PropertyVetoException`, in which case you keep looking. If you come back to the original frame, then no other frame was selectable, and you give up. Here is the complete loop:

```
for (int i = 0; i < frames.length; i++)
{  if (frames[i].isSelected())
   {  /* find next frame that isn't an icon and can be
         selected
      */
      try
      {  int next = i + 1;
         while (next != i && frames[next].isIcon())
            next++;
```

```
            if (next == i) return;
               // all other frames are icons
            frames[next].setSelected(true);
            frames[next].toFront();
            return;
         }
         catch(PropertyVetoException e)
         {}
      }
   }
```

Vetoing property settings

Now that you have seen all these veto exceptions, you may wonder how your frames can issue a veto. The `JInternalFrame` class uses a general *JavaBeans* mechanism for monitoring the setting of properties. We discuss this mechanism in full in Chapter 8. For now, we just want to show you how your frames can veto requests for property changes.

Frames don't usually want to use a veto to protest iconization or loss of focus. But it is very common for frames to check if it is okay to *close* them. You close a frame with the `setClosed` method of the `JInternalFrame` class. Because the method is vetoable, it calls all registered *vetoable change listeners* before proceeding to make the change. That gives each of the listeners the opportunity to throw a `PropertyVetoException` and thereby terminate the call to `setClosed` before it changed any settings.

In our example program, we put up a dialog to ask the user whether it is okay to close the window (see Figure 6–52). If the user doesn't agree, the window stays open.

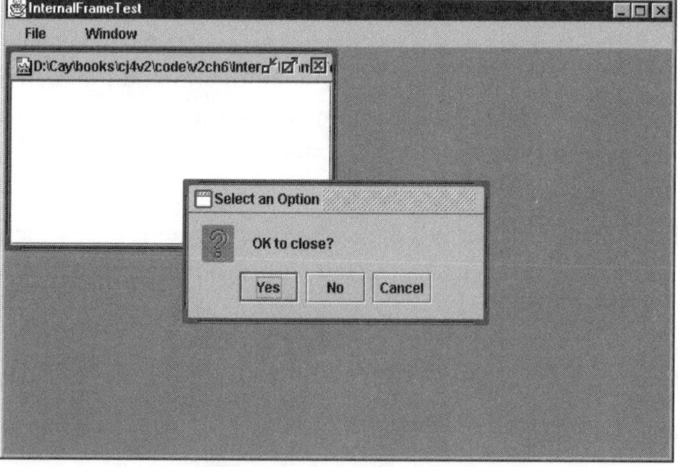

Figure 6–52: The user can veto the close property

Here is how you achieve such a notification.

1. Add a listener object to each frame. The object must belong to some class that implements the `VetoableChangeListener` interface. It is best to do that right after constructing the frame. In our example, we use the frame class that constructs the internal frames. Another option would be to use an anonymous inner class.

   ```
   iframe.addVetoableChangeListener(listener);
   ```

2. Implement the `vetoableChange` method, the only method required by the `VetoableChangeListener` interface. The method receives a `Property-ChangeEvent` object. Use the `getName` method to find the name of the property that is about to be changed (such as `"closed"` if the method call to veto is `setClosed(true)`. As you will see in Chapter 8, the property name is obtained by removing the `"set"` prefix from the method name and changing the next letter to lowercase.

   Use the `getNewValue` method to get the proposed new value.

   ```
   String name = event.getPropertyName();
   Object value = event.getNewValue();
   if (name.equals("closed") && value.equals(Boolean.TRUE))
   {   ask user for confirmation
   }
   ```

3. Simply throw a `PropertyVetoException` to block the property change. Return normally if you don't want to veto the change.

   ```
   class DesktopFrame extends JFrame
      implements VetoableChangeListener
   {  . . .
      public void vetoableChange(PropertyChangeEvent event)
         throws PropertyVetoException
      {  . . .
         if (not ok)
            throw new PropertyVetoException("reason", event);
         // return normally if ok
      }
   }
   ```

Dialogs in internal frames

If you use internal frames, you should not use the `JDialog` class for dialogs. Those dialogs have two disadvantages:

- They are heavyweight since they create a new frame in the windowing system.
- The windowing system does not know how to position them relative to the internal frame that spawned them.

Instead, for simple dialogs, use the `showInternal`*`Xxx`*`Dialog` methods of the `JOptionPane` class. They work exactly like the `show`*`Xxx`*`Dialog` methods, except they position a lightweight window over an internal frame.

As for more complex dialogs, construct them with a `JInternalFrame`. Unfortunately, then you have no built-in support for modal dialogs.

In our sample program, we use an internal dialog to ask the user whether it is okay to close a frame.

```
int result
   = JOptionPane.showInternalConfirmDialog(iframe,
      "OK to close?");
```

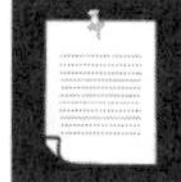

NOTE: If you simply want to be *notified* when a frame is closed, then you should not use the veto mechanism. Instead, install an `InternalFrameListener`. An internal frame listener works just like a `WindowListener`. When the internal frame is closing, the `internalFrameClosing` method is called instead of the familiar `windowClosing` method. The other six internal frame notifications (opened/closed, iconified/deiconified, activated/deactivated) also correspond to the window listener methods.

Outline dragging

One criticism that developers have leveled against internal frames is that performance has not been great. By far the slowest operation is to drag a frame with complex content across the desktop. The desktop manager keeps asking the frame to repaint itself as it is being dragged, which is quite slow.

Actually, if you use Windows or X Windows with a poorly written video driver, you'll experience the same problem. Window dragging appears fast on most systems because the video hardware supports the dragging operation by mapping the image inside the frame to different screen location during the dragging process.

To improve performance without greatly degrading the user experience, you can set "outline dragging" on. When the user drags the frame, only the outline of the frame is continuously updated (see Figure 6–53). The inside is repainted only when the user drops the frame to its final resting place.

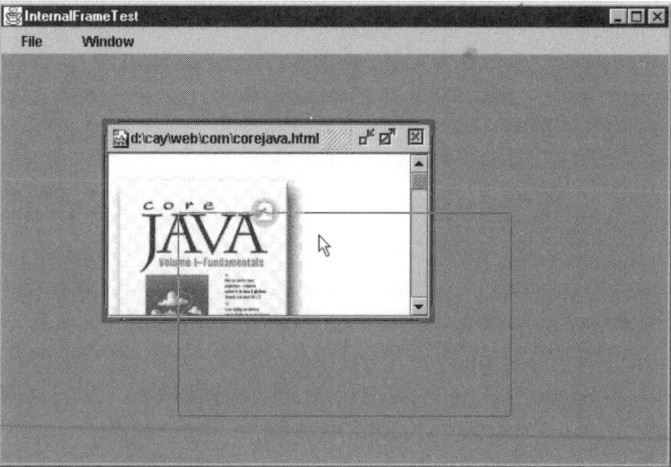

Figure 6–53: Outline dragging

To turn on outline dragging, use the magic incantation

```
desktop.putClientProperty("JDesktopPane.dragMode", "outline");
```

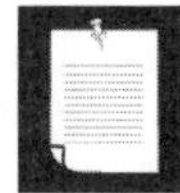

NOTE: This property is the equivalent of "continuous layout" in the `JSplitPane` class. It is curious that this behavior is exposed as a method in the `JSplitPane` class but hidden away in a property for the desktop pane.

In the sample program, you can use the Window -> Drag Outline check box menu selection to toggle outline dragging on or off.

NOTE: The internal frames on the desktop are managed by a `DesktopManager` class. You don't need to know about this class for normal programming. It is possible to implement different desktop behavior by installing a new desktop manager, but we won't cover that.

Example 6–20 populates a desktop with internal frames that show HTML pages. The File -> Open menu option pops up a file dialog for reading a local HTML file into a new internal frame. If you click on any link, the linked document is displayed in another internal frame. Try out the Window -> Cascade and Window -> Tile commands. This example concludes our discussion of advanced Swing features.

Example 6–20: InternalFrameTest.java

```
import java.awt.*;
import java.awt.event.*;
import java.beans.*;
import java.io.*;
import java.net.*;
import java.util.*;
import javax.swing.*;
import javax.swing.event.*;

public class InternalFrameTest
{  public static void main(String[] args)
   {  JFrame frame = new DesktopFrame();
      frame.show();
   }
}

class DesktopFrame extends JFrame
   implements ActionListener, VetoableChangeListener
{  public DesktopFrame()
   {  setTitle("InternalFrameTest");
      setSize(600, 400);
      addWindowListener(new WindowAdapter()
         {  public void windowClosing(WindowEvent e)
```

```
            {  System.exit(0);
            }
         } );

      desktop = new JDesktopPane();
      setContentPane(desktop);

      // set up menus

      JMenuBar menuBar = new JMenuBar();
      setJMenuBar(menuBar);
      JMenu fileMenu = new JMenu("File");
      menuBar.add(fileMenu);
      openItem = new JMenuItem("Open");
      openItem.addActionListener(this);
      fileMenu.add(openItem);
      exitItem = new JMenuItem("Exit");
      exitItem.addActionListener(this);
      fileMenu.add(exitItem);
      JMenu windowMenu = new JMenu("Window");
      menuBar.add(windowMenu);
      nextItem = new JMenuItem("Next");
      nextItem.addActionListener(this);
      windowMenu.add(nextItem);
      cascadeItem = new JMenuItem("Cascade");
      cascadeItem.addActionListener(this);
      windowMenu.add(cascadeItem);
      tileItem = new JMenuItem("Tile");
      tileItem.addActionListener(this);
      windowMenu.add(tileItem);
      dragOutlineItem = new JCheckBoxMenuItem("Drag Outline");
      dragOutlineItem.addActionListener(this);
      windowMenu.add(dragOutlineItem);
   }

   public void createInternalFrame(Component c, String t)
   {  JInternalFrame iframe = new JInternalFrame(t,
         true, // resizable
         true, // closable
         true, // maximizable
         true); // iconifiable

      iframe.getContentPane().add(c);
      desktop.add(iframe);

      iframe.setFrameIcon(new ImageIcon("document.gif"));

      // add listener to confirm frame closing
      iframe.addVetoableChangeListener(this);

      // position frame
      int width = desktop.getWidth() / 2;
```

```
      int height = desktop.getHeight() / 2;
      iframe.reshape(nextFrameX, nextFrameY, width, height);

      iframe.show();

      // select the frame--might be vetoed
      try
      {  iframe.setSelected(true);
      }
      catch(PropertyVetoException e)
      {}

      /* if this is the first time, compute distance between
         cascaded frames
      */

      if (frameDistance == 0)
         frameDistance = iframe.getHeight()
            - iframe.getContentPane().getHeight();

      // compute placement for next frame

      nextFrameX += frameDistance;
      nextFrameY += frameDistance;
      if (nextFrameX + width > desktop.getWidth())
         nextFrameX = 0;
      if (nextFrameY + height > desktop.getHeight())
         nextFrameY = 0;
   }

   public void cascadeWindows()
   {  JInternalFrame[] frames = desktop.getAllFrames();
      int x = 0;
      int y = 0;
      int width = desktop.getWidth() / 2;
      int height = desktop.getHeight() / 2;

      for (int i = 0; i < frames.length; i++)
      {  if (!frames[i].isIcon())
         {  try
            {  /* try to make maximized frames resizable
                  this might be vetoed
               */
               frames[i].setMaximum(false);
               frames[i].reshape(x, y, width, height);

               x += frameDistance;
               y += frameDistance;
               // wrap around at the desktop edge
               if (x + width > desktop.getWidth()) x = 0;
               if (y + height > desktop.getHeight()) y = 0;
            }
```

```
            catch(PropertyVetoException e)
            {}
         }
      }
   }

   public void tileWindows()
   {  JInternalFrame[] frames = desktop.getAllFrames();

      // count frames that aren't iconized
      int frameCount = 0;
      for (int i = 0; i < frames.length; i++)
      {  if (!frames[i].isIcon())
            frameCount++;
      }

      int rows = (int)Math.sqrt(frameCount);
      int cols = frameCount / rows;
      int extra = frameCount % rows;
         // number of columns with an extra row

      int width = desktop.getWidth() / cols;
      int height = desktop.getHeight() / rows;
      int r = 0;
      int c = 0;
      for (int i = 0; i < frames.length; i++)
      {  if (!frames[i].isIcon())
         {  try
            {  frames[i].setMaximum(false);
               frames[i].reshape(c * width,
                  r * height, width, height);
               r++;
               if (r == rows)
               {  r = 0;
                  c++;
                  if (c == cols - extra)
                  {  // start adding an extra row
                     rows++;
                     height = desktop.getHeight() / rows;
                  }
               }
            }
            catch(PropertyVetoException e)
            {}
         }
      }
   }

   public void selectNextWindow()
   {  JInternalFrame[] frames = desktop.getAllFrames();
      for (int i = 0; i < frames.length; i++)
      {  if (frames[i].isSelected())
```

```
        {  /* find next frame that isn't an icon and can be
              selected
           */
           try
           {  int next = i + 1;
              while (next != i && frames[next].isIcon())
                 next++;
              if (next == i) return;
                 // all other frames are icons or veto selection
              frames[next].setSelected(true);
              frames[next].toFront();
              return;
           }
           catch(PropertyVetoException e)
           {}
        }
     }
  }

  public void vetoableChange(PropertyChangeEvent event)
     throws PropertyVetoException
  {  JInternalFrame iframe = (JInternalFrame)event.getSource();
     String name = event.getPropertyName();
     Object value = event.getNewValue();

     // we only want to check attempts to close a frame

     if (name.equals("closed") && value.equals(Boolean.TRUE))
     {  // ask user if it is ok to close
        int result
           = JOptionPane.showInternalConfirmDialog(iframe,
              "OK to close?");

        // if the user doesn't agree, veto the close
        if (result == JOptionPane.CANCEL_OPTION)
           throw new PropertyVetoException("User canceled close",
              event);
     }
  }

  public Component createEditorPane(URL u)
  {  // create an editor pane that follows hyperlink clicks

     JEditorPane editorPane = new JEditorPane();
     editorPane.setEditable(false);
     editorPane.addHyperlinkListener(new HyperlinkListener()
        {  public void hyperlinkUpdate(HyperlinkEvent event)
           {  createInternalFrame(createEditorPane(event.getURL()),
                 event.getURL().toString());
           }
        });
     try
```

```
      {  editorPane.setPage(u);
      }
      catch(IOException e)
      {  editorPane.setText("Error: " + e);
      }
      return new JScrollPane(editorPane);
   }

   public void actionPerformed(ActionEvent evt)
   {  Object source = evt.getSource();
      if (source == openItem)
      {  // let user select file

         JFileChooser chooser = new JFileChooser();
         chooser.setCurrentDirectory(new File("."));
         chooser.setFileFilter(
            new javax.swing.filechooser.FileFilter()
            {  public boolean accept(File f)
               {  String fname = f.getName().toLowerCase();
                  return fname.endsWith(".html")
                     || fname.endsWith(".htm")
                     || f.isDirectory();
               }
               public String getDescription()
               { return "HTML Files"; }
            });
         int r = chooser.showOpenDialog(this);

         if (r == JFileChooser.APPROVE_OPTION)
         {  // open the file that the user selected

            String filename = chooser.getSelectedFile().getPath();
            try
            {  URL fileUrl = new URL("file:" + filename);
               createInternalFrame(createEditorPane(fileUrl),
                  filename);
            }
            catch(MalformedURLException e)
            {
            }
         }
      }
      else if (source == exitItem)
         System.exit(0);
      else if (source == nextItem)
         selectNextWindow();
      else if (source == cascadeItem)
         cascadeWindows();
      else if (source == tileItem)
         tileWindows();
      else if (source == dragOutlineItem)
      {  desktop.putClientProperty("JDesktopPane.dragMode",
```

```
            dragOutlineItem.isSelected() ? "outline" : null);
      }
   }

   private JDesktopPane desktop;

   private JMenuItem openItem;
   private JMenuItem exitItem;
   private JMenuItem nextItem;
   private JMenuItem cascadeItem;
   private JMenuItem tileItem;
   private JMenuItem dragOutlineItem;

   private int nextFrameX;
   private int nextFrameY;
   private int frameDistance;
}
```

`javax.swing.JDesktopPane`

- `JInternalFrame[] getAllFrames()`

  gets all internal frames in this desktop pane.

`javax.swing.JInternalFrame`

- `JInternalFrame()`
- `JInternalFrame(String title)`
- `JInternalFrame(String title, boolean resizable)`
- `JInternalFrame(String title, boolean resizable, boolean closable)`
- `JInternalFrame(String title, boolean resizable, boolean closable, boolean maximizable)`
- `JInternalFrame(String title, boolean resizable, boolean closable, boolean maximizable, boolean iconifiable)`

  construct a new internal frame.

Parameters	`title`	the string to display in the title bar
	`resizable`	`true` if the frame can be resized
	`closable`	`true` if the frame can be closed
	`maximizable`	`true` if the frame can be maximized
	`iconifiable`	`true` if the frame can be iconified

- `boolean isResizable()`
- `boolean isClosable()`
- `boolean isMaximizable()`
- `boolean isIconifiable()`

  get and set the `resizable`, `closable`, `maximizable`, and `iconifiable` properties. When the property is `true`, an icon appears in the frame title to resize, close, maximize, or iconify the internal frame.

- `boolean isIcon()`
- `void setIcon(boolean b)`
- `boolean isMaximum()`
- `void setMaximum(boolean b)`
- `boolean isClosed()`
- `void setClosed(boolean b)`

  get or set the `icon`, `maximum`, or `closed` property. When this property is `true`, the internal frame is iconified, maximized, or closed.
- `boolean isSelected()`
- `void setSelected(boolean b)`

  get or set the `selected` property. When this property is `true`, the current internal frame becomes the selected frame on the desktop.
- `void moveToFront()`
- `void moveToBack()`

  move this internal frame to the front or the back of the desktop.
- `void reshape(int x, int y, int width, int height)`

  moves and resizes this internal frame.

Parameters:	`x, y`	the top-left corner of the frame
	`width, height`	the width and height of the frame

- `Container getContentPane()`
- `void setContentPane(Container c)`

  get and set the content pane of this internal frame.
- `JDesktopPane getDesktopPane()`

  gets the desktop pane of this internal frame.
- `Icon getFrameIcon()`
- `void setFrameIcon(Icon anIcon)`

  get and set the frame icon that is displayed in the title bar.
- `boolean isVisible()`
- `void setVisible(boolean b)`

  get and set the "visible" property.
- `void show()`

  makes this internal frame visible and brings it to the front.

`javax.swing.JComponent`

- `void addVetoableChangeListener(VetoableChangeListener listener)`

  adds a vetoable change listener that is notified when an attempt is made to change a constrained property.

`java.beans.VetoableChangeListener`

- `void vetoableChange(PropertyChangeEvent event)`

  is called when the `set` method of a constrained property notifies the vetoable change listeners.

`java.beans.PropertyChangeEvent`

- `String getPropertyName()`

  returns the name of the property that is about to be changed.
- `Object getNewValue()`

  returns the proposed new value for the property.

`java.beans.PropertyVetoException`

- `PropertyVetoException(String reason, PropertyChangeEvent event)`

  constructs a property veto exception.

Parameters:	`reason`	the reason for the veto
	`event`	the vetoed event

Chapter 7

Advanced AWT

- The Rendering Pipeline
- Shapes
- Areas
- Strokes
- Paint
- Coordinate transformations
- Clipping
- Transparency and Composition
- Rendering Hints
- Image Manipulation
- Printing
- The Clipboard
- Drag and Drop

In Volume 1, you have seen how to use the methods of the `Graphics` class to create simple drawings. Those methods are sufficient for simple applets and applications, but they fall short for complex shapes or when you require complete control over the appearance of the graphics. The Java 2D API is a more recent class library that you can use to produce high-quality drawings. In this chapter, we give you an overview of that API.

We then turn to the topic of printing and show you how you can implement printing capabilities into your programs.

Finally, we cover two techniques for transferring data between programs: the system clipboard and the drag-and-drop mechanism. You can use these techniques to transfer data between two Java applications or between a Java application and a native program.

The Rendering Pipeline

The original JDK 1.0 had a very simple mechanism for drawing shapes. You select color and paint mode, and call methods of the `Graphics` class such as `drawRect` or `fillOval`. The Java 2D API supports many more options.

- You can easily produce a wide variety of *shapes.*
- You have control over the *stroke,* the pen that traces shape boundaries.
- You can *fill* shapes with solid colors, varying hues, and repeating patterns.
- You can use *transformations* to move, scale, rotate, or stretch shapes.
- You can *clip* shapes to restrict them to arbitrary areas.
- You can select *composition rules* to describe how to combine the pixels of a new shape with existing pixels.
- You can give *rendering hints* to make trade-offs between speed and drawing quality.

To draw a shape, you go through the following steps:

1. Obtain an object of the `Graphics2D` class. This class is a subclass of the `Graphics` class. If you use a version of the JDK that is Java 2D enabled, methods such as `paint` and `paintComponent` automatically receive an object of the `Graphics2D` class. Simply use a cast, as follows:

   ```
   public void paintComponent(Graphics g)
   {  Graphics2D g2 = (Graphics2D)g;
      . . .
   }
   ```

2. Use the `setRenderingHints` method to set rendering hints: trade-offs between speed and drawing quality.

   ```
   RenderingHints hints = . . .;
   g2.setRenderingHints(hints);
   ```

3. Use the `setStroke` method to set the *stroke.* The stroke is used to draw the outline of the shape. You can select the thickness and choose among solid and dotted lines.

   ```
   Stroke stroke = . . .;
   g2.setStroke(stroke);
   ```

4. Use the `setPaint` method to set the *paint.* The paint is used to fill areas such as the stroke path or the interior of a shape. You can create solid color paint, paint with changing hues, or tiled fill patterns.

   ```
   Paint paint = . . .;
   g2.setPaint(paint);
   ```

5. Use the `setClip` method to set the clipping region.

```
Shape clip = . . .;
g2.clip(clip);
```

6. Use the `setTransform` method to set a *transformation* from user space to device space. You use transformations if it is easier for you to define your shapes in a custom coordinate system than by using pixel coordinates.

```
AffineTransform transform = . . .;
g2.transform(transform);
```

7. Use the `setComposite` method to set a *composition rule* that describes how to combine the new pixels with the existing pixels.

```
Composite composite = . . .;
g2.setComposite(composite);
```

8. Create a shape. The Java 2D API supplies many shape objects and methods to combine shapes.

```
Shape shape = . . .;
```

9. Draw or fill the shape. If you draw the shape, its outline is stroked. If you fill the shape, the interior is painted.

```
g2.draw(shape);
g2.fill(shape);
```

Of course, in many practical circumstances, you don't need all these steps. There are reasonable defaults for the settings of the 2D graphics context. You only need to change the settings if you want to change the defaults.

In the following sections, you will see how to describe shapes, strokes, paints, transformations, and composition rules.

The various `set` methods simply set the state of the 2D graphics context. They don't cause any drawing. Similarly, when you construct `Shape` objects, no drawing takes place. A shape is only rendered when you call `draw` or `fill`. At that time, the new shape is computed in a *rendering pipeline* (see Figure 7–1).

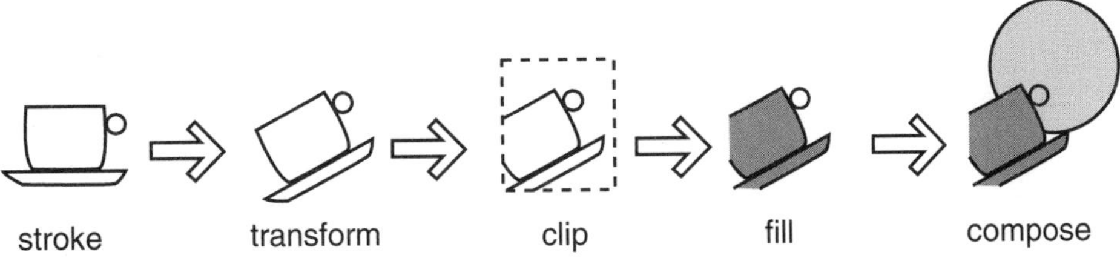

Figure 7–1: The rendering pipeline

In the rendering pipeline, the following steps take place to render a shape.

1. The path of the shape is stroked.

2. The shape is transformed.
3. The shape is clipped. If there is no intersection between the shape and the clipping area, then the process stops.
4. The remainder of the shape after clipping is filled.
5. The pixels of the filled shape are composed with the existing pixels. (In Figure 7–1, the circle is part of the existing pixels, and the cup shape is superimposed over it.)

In the next section, you will see how to define shapes. Then, we will turn to the 2D graphics context settings.

`java.awt.Graphics2D`

- `void draw(Shape s)`

  draws the outline of the given shape with the current stroke.

- `void fill(Shape s)`

  fills the interior of the given shape with the current paint.

Shapes

Here are some of the methods in the `Graphics` class to draw shapes:

```
drawLine
drawRectangle
drawRoundRect
draw3DRect
drawPolygon
drawPolyline
drawOval
drawArc
```

There are also corresponding `fill` methods. These methods have been in the `Graphics` class ever since JDK 1.0. The Java 2D API uses a completely different, object-oriented approach. Instead of methods, there are classes

```
Line2D
Rectangle2D
RoundRectangle2D
Ellipse2D
Arc2D
QuadCurve2D
CubicCurve2D
GeneralPath
```

These classes all implement the `Shape` interface.

To draw a shape, you first create an object of a class that implements the `Shape` interface and then call the `draw` method of the `Graphics2D` class.

The Line2D, Rectangle2D, RoundRectangle2D, Ellipse2D, and Arc2D classes correspond to the drawLine, drawRectangle, drawRoundRect, drawOval, and drawArc methods. (The concept of a "3D rectangle" has died the death that it so richly deserved—there is no analog to the draw3DRect method.) The Java 2D API supplies two additional classes: quadratic and cubic curves. We discuss these shapes later in this section. There is no Polygon2D class. Instead, the GeneralPath class describes paths that are made up from lines, quadratic and cubic curves. You can use a GeneralPath to describe a polygon; we'll show you how later in this section.

The Shape Class Hierarchy

There is a complexity when using the Java 2D shape classes. Unlike the JDK 1.0 draw methods, which used integer pixel coordinates, the Java 2D shapes use floating-point coordinates. That is a huge convenience because it allows you to specify your shapes in coordinates that are meaningful to you (such as millimeters or inches) and then translate to pixels. The Java 2D library uses single precision float quantities for many of its internal floating-point calculations. Single precision is sufficient—after all, the ultimate purpose of the geometric computations is to set pixels on the screen or printer. As long as any roundoff errors stay within one pixel, the visual outcome is not affected. Furthermore, float computations are faster on some platforms, and float values require half the storage than double values.

However, manipulating float values is sometimes inconvenient for the programmer because the Java programming language is adamant about requiring casts when converting double values into float values. For example, consider the following statement:

```
float f = 1.2; // Error
```

This statement does not compile. The constant 1.2 has type double, and the compiler is nervous about loss of precision. The remedy is to add an F suffix to the floating-point constant:

```
float f = 1.2F; // Ok
```

Now consider this statement:

```
Rectangle r = . . .
float f = r.getWidth(); // Error
```

This statement does not compile either, for the same reason. The getWidth method returns a double. This time, the remedy is to provide a cast:

```
float f = (float)r.getWidth(); // Ok
```

Because the suffixes and casts are a bit of a pain, the designers of the 2D library decided to supply *two versions* of each shape class: one with float coordinates for frugal programmers and one with double coordinates for the lazy ones. (In this book, we'll fall into the second camp and use double coordinates whenever we can.)

The library designers chose a curious, and initially confusing, method for packaging these choices. Consider the `Rectangle2D` class. This class has two subclasses, which are also static inner classes:

```
Rectangle2D.Float
Rectangle2D.Double
```

Figure 7–2 shows the inheritance diagram.

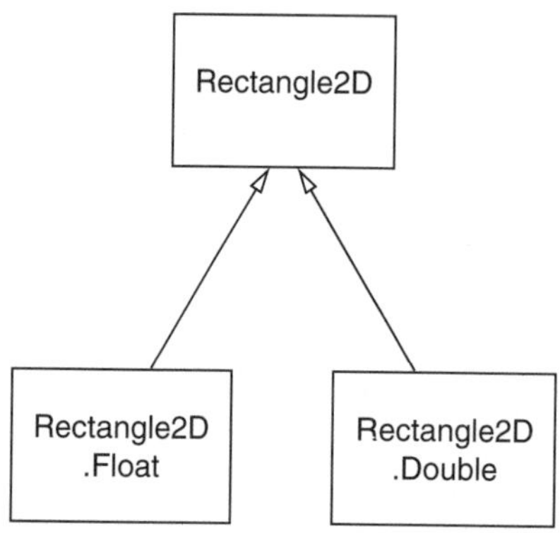

Figure 7–2: 2D rectangle classes

It is best to try to ignore the fact that the two concrete classes are static inner classes—that is just a gimmick to avoid names such as `FloatRectangle2D` and `DoubleRectangle2D`. (For more information on static inner classes, see Chapter 6 of Volume 1.)

When you construct a `Rectangle2D.Float` object, you supply the coordinates as `float` numbers. For a `Rectangle2D.Double` object, you supply them as `double` numbers.

```
Rectangle2D.Float floatRect = new Rectangle2D.Float(10.0F,
   25.0F, 22.5F, 20.0F);
Rectangle2D.Double doubleRect = new Rectangle2D.Double(10.0,
   25.0, 22.5, 20.0);
```

Actually, since both `Rectangle2D.Float` and `Rectangle2D.Double` extend the common `Rectangle2D` class, and the methods in the subclasses simply override methods in the `Rectangle2D` superclass, there is no benefit in remembering the exact shape type. You can simply use `Rectangle2D` variables to hold the rectangle references.

```
Rectangle2D floatRect = new Rectangle2D.Float(10.0F,
   25.0F, 22.5F, 20.0F);
Rectangle2D doubleRect = new Rectangle2D.Double(10.0,
   25.0, 22.5, 20.0);
```

That is, you only need to use the pesky inner classes when you construct the shape objects.

The construction parameters denote the top-left corner, width, and height of the rectangle.

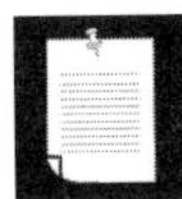

NOTE: Actually, the `Rectangle2D.Float` class has one additional method that is not inherited from `Rectangle2D`, namely, `setRect(float x, float y, float h, float w)`. You lose that method if you store the `Rectangle2D.Float` reference in a `Rectangle2D` variable. But it is not a big loss—the `Rectangle2D` class has a `setRect` method with `double` parameters.

The `Rectangle2D` methods use `double` parameters and return values. For example, the `getWidth` method returns a `double` value, even if the width is stored as a `float` in a `Rectangle2D.Float` object.

TIP: Simply use the `Double` shape classes to avoid dealing with `float` values altogether. However, if you are constructing thousands of shape objects, then you can consider using the `Float` classes to conserve memory.

What we just discussed for the `Rectangle2D` classes holds for the other shape classes as well. Furthermore, there is a `Point2D` class with subclasses `Point2D.Float` and `Point2D.Double`. Here is how to make a point object.

```
Point2D p = new Point2D.Double(10, 20);
```

TIP: The `Point2D` class is very useful—it is more object oriented to work with `Point2D` objects than with separate `x` and `y` values. Many constructors and methods accept `Point2D` parameters. We suggest that you use `Point2D` objects when you can—they usually makes geometric computations easier to understand.

The classes

```
Rectangle2D
RoundRectangle2D
Ellipse2D
Arc2D
```

all inherit from a common superclass `RectangularShape`. Admittedly, ellipses and arcs are not rectangular, but they have a *bounding rectangle* (see Figure 7–3).

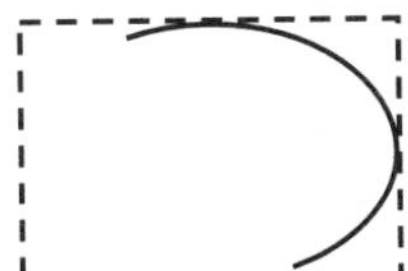

Figure 7–3: The bounding rectangle of an ellipse and an arc

The `RectangularShape` class defines over 20 methods that are common to these shapes, among them such useful methods as `getWidth`, `getHeight`, `getCenterX`, and `getCenterY` (but sadly, at the time of this writing, not a `getCenter` method that returns the center as a `Point2D` object).

Finally, there are a couple of legacy classes from JDK 1.0 that have been fit into the shape class hierarchy: The `Rectangle` and `Point` classes, which store a rectangle and a point with integer coordinates, extend the `Rectangle2D` and `Point2D` classes. The `Polygon` class now implements the `Shape` interface. You should nevertheless stay away from these classes in new code.

We will discuss the remaining shape classes,

```
QuadCurve2D
CubicCurve2D
GeneralPath
Area
```

in the next sections.

Figure 7–4 shows the relationships between the shape classes. However, the `Double` and `Float` subclasses are omitted. Legacy classes are marked with a gray fill.

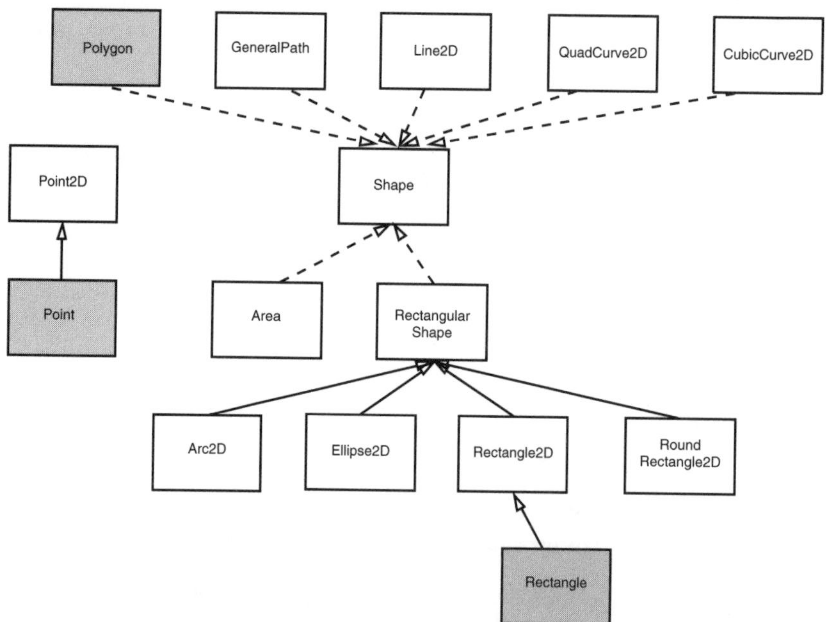

Figure 7–4: Relationships between the shape classes

```
java.awt.geom.RectangularShape
```

- `double getCenterX()`
- `double getCenterY()`
- `double getMinX()`
- `double getMinY()`
- `double getMaxX()`
- `double getMaxY()`

  return the center, minimum, or maximum x- or y-value of the enclosing rectangle.
- `double getWidth()`
- `double getHeight()`

  return the width or height of the enclosing rectangle.
- `double getX()`
- `double getY()`

  return the x- or y-coordinate of the top-left corner of the enclosing rectangle.

```
java.awt.geom.Rectangle2D.Double
```

- `Rectangle2D.Double(double x, double y, double w, double h)`

  constructs a rectangle with the given top-left corner, width, and height.

```
java.awt.geom.Rectangle2D.Float
```

- `Rectangle2D.Float(float x, float y, float w, float h)`

  constructs a rectangle with the given top-left corner, width, and height.

Using the Shape Classes

`Rectangle2D`, `RoundRectangle2D`, and `Ellipse2D` objects are simple to construct. You need to specify

- The x- and y-coordinates of the top-left corner
- The width and height

For example,

```
Rectangle2D r = new Rectangle2D.Double(150, 200, 100, 50);
```

constructs a rectangle with top-left corner (150, 200), width 100, and height 50.

For the `RoundRectangle2D` shape, you also need to specify the x- and y-dimension of the area that should be rounded (see Figure 7–5). For example, the call

```
RoundRectangle2D r = new RoundRectangle2D.Double(150, 200,
   100, 50, 20, 20);
```

produces a rounded rectangle with circles of radius 20 at each of the corners.

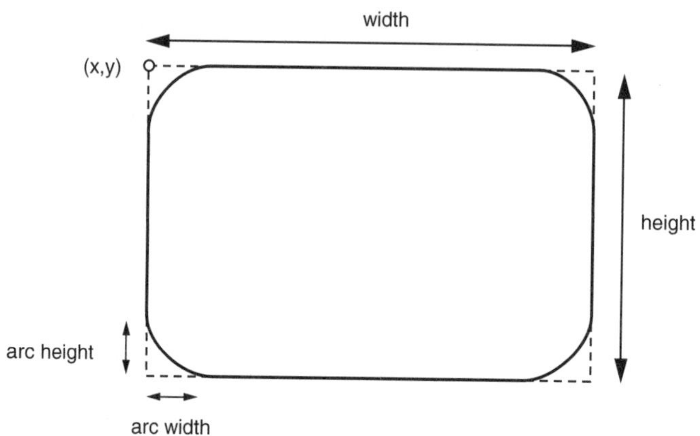

Figure 7–5: Constructing a `RoundRectangle2D`

However, sometimes you don't have the top-left corner readily available. It is quite common to have two diagonal corner points of a rectangle, but perhaps they aren't the top-left and bottom-right corners. You can't simply construct a rectangle as

```
Rectangle2D r = new Rectangle2D.Double(px, py,
   qx - px, qy - py); // Error
```

If `p` isn't the top-left corner, one or both of the coordinate differences will be negative and the rectangle will come out empty. In that case, first create a blank rectangle and use the `setFrameFromDiagonal` method.

```
Rectangle2D r = new Rectangle2D.Double();
r.setFrameFromDiagonal(px, py, qx, qy);
```

Or, even better, if you know the corner points as `Point2D` objects `p` and `q`,

```
r.setFrameFromDiagonal(p, q);
```

When constructing an ellipse, you usually know the center, width, and height, and not the corner points of the bounding rectangle (which don't even lie on the ellipse). There is a `setFrameFromCenter` method that uses the center point, but it still requires one of the four corner points. Thus, you will usually end up constructing an ellipse as follows:

```
Ellipse2D e = new Ellipse2D.Double(centerX - width / 2,
   centerY - height / 2, width, height);
```

To construct an arc, you specify the bounding box, followed by the start angle and the angle swept out by the arc (see Figure 7–6) and the closure type, one of `Arc2D.OPEN`, `Arc2D.PIE`, or `Arc2D.CHORD`.

```
Arc2D a = new Arc2D(x, y, width, height,
   startAngle, arcAngle, closureType);
```

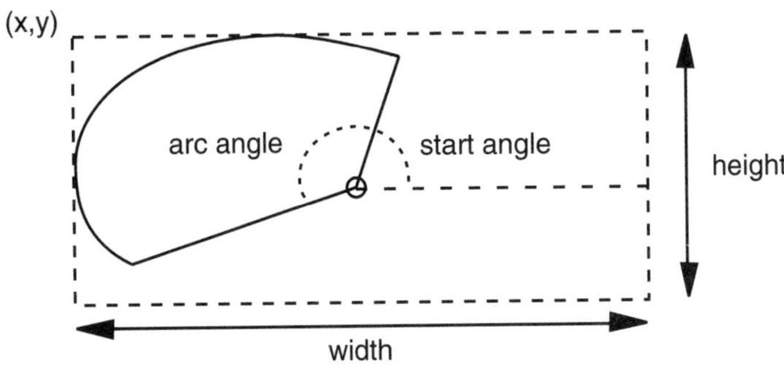

Figure 7–6: Constructing an elliptical arc

Figure 7–7 illustrates the arc types.

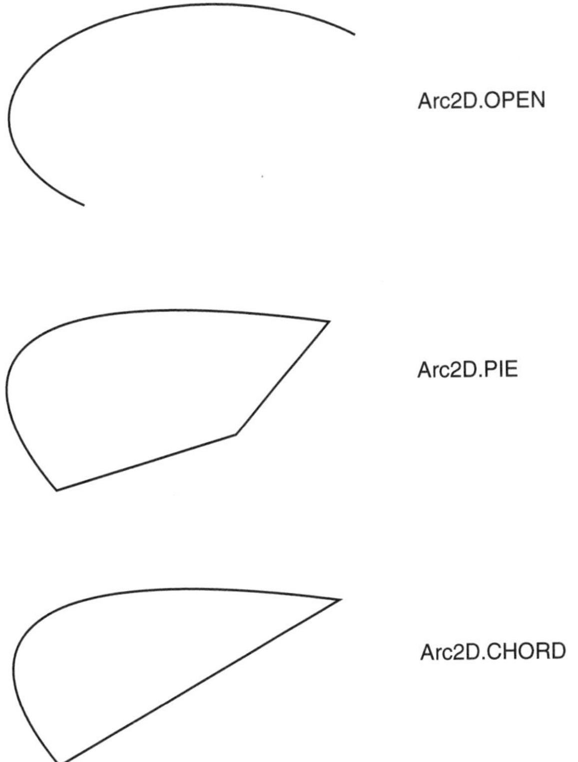

Figure 7–7: Arc types

However, the angles are not simply given in degrees, but they are distorted such that a 45 degree angle denotes the diagonal position, *even if width and height are not the same.* If you draw circular arcs (for example in a pie chart), then you don't need to worry about this. However, for elliptical arcs, be prepared for an adventure in trigonometry—see the sidebar for details.

Specifying Angles for Elliptical Arcs

The algorithm for drawing elliptical arcs uses distorted angles, which the caller must precompute. This sidebar tells you how. If you belong to the large majority of programmers who never draw elliptical arcs, just skip the sidebar. However, since the official documentation completely glosses over this topic, we thought it is worth recording it to save those who need this information a few hours of trigonometric agony.

You convert actual angles to distorted angles with the following formula.

```
distortedAngle = Math.atan2(Math.sin(angle) * width,
   Math.cos(angle) * height);
```

Sometimes (such as in the example program at the end of this section), you know an end point of the arc, or another point on the line joining the center of the ellipse and that end point. In that case, first compute

```
dx = p.getX() - center.getX();
dy = p.getY() - center.getY();
```

Then, the distorted angle is

```
distortedAngle = Math.atan2(-dy * width, dx * height);
```

(The minus sign in front of `dy` is necessary because in the pixel coordinate system, the y-axis points downwards, which leads to angle measurements that are clockwise, but you need to supply an angle that is measured counterclockwise.)

Convert the result from radian to degrees:

```
distortedAngle = Math.toDegrees(distortedAngle);
```

The result is a value between -180 and 180.

Compute both the distorted start and end angles in this way. Then, compute the difference between the two distorted angles.

If either the start angle or the difference is negative, add 360. Then, supply the start angle and the angle difference to the arc constructor.

```
Arc2D a = new Arc2D(x, y, width, height,
   distortedStartAngle, distortedAngleDifference,
   closureType);
```

Not only is the documentation vague on the exact nature of the distortion, it is also quite misleading in calling the distorted angle difference value the "arc angle." Except for the case of a circular arc, that value is neither the actual arc angle nor its distortion.

If you run the example program at the end of this section, then you can visually check that this calculation yields the correct values for the arc constructor (see Figure 7–10).

The Java 2D package supplies *quadratic* and *cubic* curves. In this chapter, we do not want to get into the mathematics of these curves. We suggest you get a feel for how the

curves look by running the program in Example 7–1. As you can see in Figures 7–8 and 7–9, quadratic and cubic curves are specified by two *end points* and one or two *control points*. Moving the control points changes the shape of the curves.

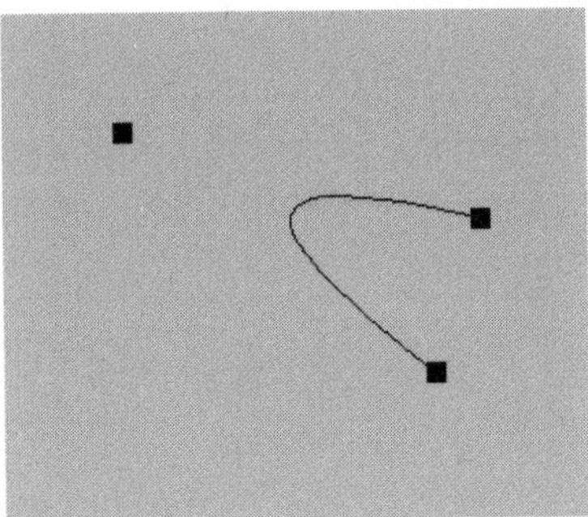

Figure 7–8: A quadratic curve

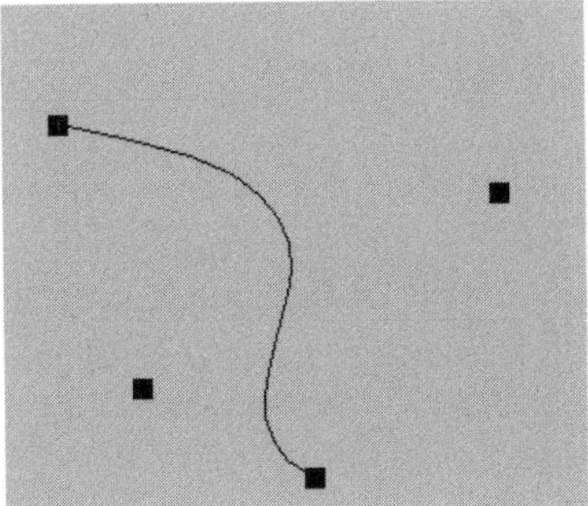

Figure 7–9: A cubic curve

To construct quadratic and cubic curves, you give the coordinates of the end points and the control points. For example,

```
QuadCurve2D q = new QuadCurve2D.Double(startX, startY,
   controlX, controlY, endX, endY);
CubicCurve2D c = new CubicCurve2D.Double(startX, startY,
   control1X, control1Y, control2X, control2Y, endX, endY);
```

Quadratic curves are not very flexible, and they are not commonly used in practice. Cubic curves (such as the Bezier curves drawn by the `CubicCurve3D` class) are, however, very common. By combining many cubic curves, so that the slopes at the connection points match, you can create complex smooth-looking curved shapes. For more information, we refer you to the book *Computer Graphics: Principles and Practice, Second Edition in C* by James D. Foley, Andries van Dam, Steven K. Feiner, et al. [Addison Wesley 1995].

You can build arbitrary sequences of line segments, quadratic curves, and cubic curves and store them in a GeneralPath object. You specify the first coordinate of the path with the moveTo method. For example,

```
GeneralPath path = new GeneralPath();
path.moveTo(10, 20);
```

Then, you extend the path by calling one of the methods lineTo, quadTo, or curveTo. These methods extend the path by a line, a quadratic curve, or a cubic curve. To call lineTo, supply the end point. For the two curve methods, supply the control points, then the end point. For example,

```
path.lineTo(20, 30);
path.curveTo(control1X, control1Y, control2X, control2Y, endX, endY);
```

You can close the path by calling the closePath method. It draws a line back to the last moveTo.

To make a polygon, simply call moveTo to go to the first corner point, followed by repeated calls to lineTo to visit the other corner points. Finally, call closePath to close the polygon. The program in Example 7–1 shows this in more detail.

A general path does not have to be connected. You can call moveTo at any time to start a new path segment.

Finally, you can use the append method to add arbitrary Shape objects to a general path. The outline of the shape is added to the end to the path. The second parameter of the append method is true if the new shape should be connected to the last point on the path, false if it should not be connected. For example, the call

```
Rectangle2D r = . . .;
path.append(r, false);
```

appends the outline of a rectangle to the path without connecting it to the existing path. But

```
path.append(r, false);
```

adds a straight line from the end point of the path to the starting point of the rectangle, and then adds the rectangle outline to the path.

The program in Example 7–1 lets you create sample paths. Figures 7–8 and 7–9 show sample runs of the program. You pick a shape maker from the combo box. The program contains shape makers for

- Straight lines
- Rectangles, round rectangles, and ellipses
- Arcs (showing lines for the bounding rectangle and the start and end angles, in addition to the arc itself)
- Polygons (using a GeneralPath)
- Quadratic and cubic curves

Use the mouse to adjust the control points. As you move them, the shape continuously repaints itself.

The program is a bit complex because it handles a multiplicity of shapes and it supports dragging of the control points.

An abstract superclass `ShapeMaker` encapsulates the commonality of the shape maker classes. Each shape has a fixed number of control points that the user can move around. The `getPointCount` method returns that value. The abstract method

```
Shape makeShape(Point2D[] points)
```

computes the actual shape, given the current positions of the control points. The `toString` method returns the class name so that the `ShapeMaker` objects can simply be dumped into a `JComboBox`.

To enable dragging of the control points, the `ShapePanel` class implements both the `MouseListener` and `MouseMotionListener` interfaces. If the mouse is pressed on top of a rectangle, subsequent mouse drags move the rectangle.

The majority of the shape maker classes are simple—their `makeShape` methods just construct and return the requested shape. However, the `ArcMaker` class needs to compute the distorted start and end angles. Furthermore, to demonstrate that the computation is indeed correct, the returned shape is a `GeneralPath` containing the arc itself, the bounding rectangle, and the lines from the center of the arc to the angle control points (see Figure 7–10).

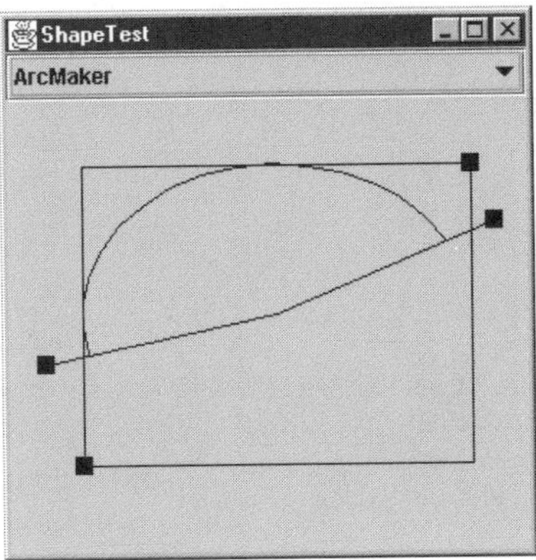

Figure 7–10: The ShapeTest program

Example 7–1: ShapeTest.java

```
import java.awt.*;
import java.awt.event.*;
import java.awt.geom.*;
import java.util.*;
```

```
import javax.swing.*;

public class ShapeTest
{  public static void main(String[] args)
   {  JFrame frame = new ShapeTestFrame();
      frame.show();
   }
}

class ShapeTestFrame extends JFrame
   implements ActionListener
{  public ShapeTestFrame()
   {  setTitle("ShapeTest");
      setSize(300, 300);
      addWindowListener(new WindowAdapter()
         {  public void windowClosing(WindowEvent e)
            {  System.exit(0);
            }
         } );

      Container contentPane = getContentPane();

      panel = new ShapePanel();
      contentPane.add(panel, "Center");
      comboBox = new JComboBox();
      comboBox.addItem(new LineMaker());
      comboBox.addItem(new RectangleMaker());
      comboBox.addItem(new RoundRectangleMaker());
      comboBox.addItem(new EllipseMaker());
      comboBox.addItem(new ArcMaker());
      comboBox.addItem(new PolygonMaker());
      comboBox.addItem(new QuadCurveMaker());
      comboBox.addItem(new CubicCurveMaker());
      comboBox.addActionListener(this);
      contentPane.add(comboBox, "North");
   }

   public void actionPerformed(ActionEvent event)
   {  ShapeMaker shapeMaker =
         (ShapeMaker)comboBox.getSelectedItem();
      panel.setShapeMaker(shapeMaker);
   }

   private JComboBox comboBox;
   private ShapePanel panel;
}

class ShapePanel extends JPanel
   implements MouseListener, MouseMotionListener
{  public ShapePanel()
   {  addMouseListener(this);
```

```
      addMouseMotionListener(this);
      current = -1;
   }

   public void setShapeMaker(ShapeMaker aShapeMaker)
   {  shapeMaker = aShapeMaker;
      int n = shapeMaker.getPointCount();
      points = new Point2D[n];
      for (int i = 0; i < n; i++)
      {  double x = generator.nextDouble() * getWidth();
         double y = generator.nextDouble() * getHeight();
         points[i] = new Point2D.Double(x, y);
      }
      repaint();
   }

   public void paintComponent(Graphics g)
   {  super.paintComponent(g);
      if (points == null) return;
      Graphics2D g2 = (Graphics2D)g;
      for (int i = 0; i < points.length; i++)
      {  double x = points[i].getX() - SIZE / 2;
         double y = points[i].getY() - SIZE / 2;
         g2.fill(new Rectangle2D.Double(x, y, SIZE, SIZE));
      }

      g2.draw(shapeMaker.makeShape(points));
   }

   public void mousePressed(MouseEvent event)
   {  Point p = event.getPoint();
      for (int i = 0; i < points.length; i++)
      {  double x = points[i].getX() - SIZE / 2;
         double y = points[i].getY() - SIZE / 2;
         Rectangle2D r = new Rectangle2D.Double(x, y, SIZE, SIZE);
         if (r.contains(p))
         {  current = i;
            return;
         }
      }
   }

   public void mouseReleased(MouseEvent event)
   {  current = -1;
   }

   public void mouseEntered(MouseEvent event)
   {
   }

   public void mouseExited(MouseEvent event)
```

```
      {
      }

      public void mouseClicked(MouseEvent event)
      {
      }

      public void mouseMoved(MouseEvent event)
      {
      }

      public void mouseDragged(MouseEvent event)
      {  if (current == -1) return;
         points[current] = event.getPoint();
         repaint();
      }


      private Point2D[] points;
      private static Random generator = new Random();
      private static int SIZE = 10;
      private int current;
      private ShapeMaker shapeMaker;
   }

   abstract class ShapeMaker
   {  public ShapeMaker(int aPointCount)
      {  pointCount = aPointCount;
      }

      public int getPointCount()
      {  return pointCount;
      }

      public abstract Shape makeShape(Point2D[] p);

      public String toString()
      {  return getClass().getName();
      }

      private int pointCount;
   }

   class LineMaker extends ShapeMaker
   {  public LineMaker() { super(2); }

      public Shape makeShape(Point2D[] p)
      {  return new Line2D.Double(p[0], p[1]);
      }
```

```
}

class RectangleMaker extends ShapeMaker
{  public RectangleMaker() { super(2); }

   public Shape makeShape(Point2D[] p)
   {  Rectangle2D s = new Rectangle2D.Double();
      s.setFrameFromDiagonal(p[0], p[1]);
      return s;
   }
}

class RoundRectangleMaker extends ShapeMaker
{  public RoundRectangleMaker() { super(2); }

   public Shape makeShape(Point2D[] p)
   {  RoundRectangle2D s
         = new RoundRectangle2D.Double(0, 0, 0, 0, 20, 20);
      s.setFrameFromDiagonal(p[0], p[1]);
      return s;
   }
}

class EllipseMaker extends ShapeMaker
{  public EllipseMaker() { super(2); }

   public Shape makeShape(Point2D[] p)
   {  Ellipse2D s = new Ellipse2D.Double();
      s.setFrameFromDiagonal(p[0], p[1]);
      return s;
   }
}

class ArcMaker extends ShapeMaker
{  public ArcMaker() { super(4); }

   public Shape makeShape(Point2D[] p)
   {  double centerX = (p[0].getX() + p[1].getX()) / 2;
      double centerY = (p[0].getY() + p[1].getY()) / 2;
      double width = Math.abs(p[1].getX() - p[0].getX());
      double height = Math.abs(p[1].getY() - p[0].getY());

      double distortedStartAngle
         = Math.toDegrees(Math.atan2(-(p[2].getY() - centerY)
           * width, (p[2].getX() - centerX) * height));
      double distortedEndAngle
         = Math.toDegrees(Math.atan2(-(p[3].getY() - centerY)
           * width, (p[3].getX() - centerX) * height));
      double distortedAngleDifference
         = distortedEndAngle - distortedStartAngle;
      if (distortedStartAngle < 0)
         distortedStartAngle += 360;
```

```
      if (distortedAngleDifference < 0)
         distortedAngleDifference += 360;

      Arc2D s = new Arc2D.Double(0, 0, 0, 0,
         distortedStartAngle, distortedAngleDifference,
         Arc2D.OPEN);
      s.setFrameFromDiagonal(p[0], p[1]);

      GeneralPath g = new GeneralPath();
      g.append(s, false);
      Rectangle2D r = new Rectangle2D.Double();
      r.setFrameFromDiagonal(p[0], p[1]);
      g.append(r, false);
      Point2D center = new Point2D.Double(centerX, centerY);
      g.append(new Line2D.Double(center, p[2]), false);
      g.append(new Line2D.Double(center, p[3]), false);
      return g;
   }
}

class PolygonMaker extends ShapeMaker
{  public PolygonMaker() { super(6); }

   public Shape makeShape(Point2D[] p)
   {  GeneralPath s = new GeneralPath();
      s.moveTo((float)p[0].getX(), (float)p[0].getY());
      for (int i = 1; i < p.length; i++)
         s.lineTo((float)p[i].getX(), (float)p[i].getY());
      s.closePath();
      return s;
   }
}

class QuadCurveMaker extends ShapeMaker
{  public QuadCurveMaker() { super(3); }

   public Shape makeShape(Point2D[] p)
   {  return new QuadCurve2D.Double(p[0].getX(), p[0].getY(),
         p[1].getX(), p[1].getY(), p[2].getX(), p[2].getY());
   }
}

class CubicCurveMaker extends ShapeMaker
{  public CubicCurveMaker() { super(4); }

   public Shape makeShape(Point2D[] p)
   {  return new CubicCurve2D.Double(p[0].getX(), p[0].getY(),
         p[1].getX(), p[1].getY(), p[2].getX(), p[2].getY(),
         p[3].getX(), p[3].getY());
   }
}
```

`java.awt.geom.RectangularShape`

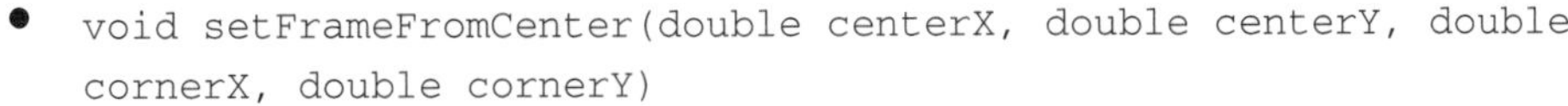

- `void setFrameFromCenter(double centerX, double centerY, double cornerX, double cornerY)`
- `void setFrameFromCenter(Point2D center, Point2D corner)`

  set the bounding rectangle of this rectangular shape to a new rectangle with the given center and corner points. The corner point need not be the top-left corner.

- `void setFrameFromDiagonal(double corner1X, double corner1Y, double corner2X, double corner2Y)`
- `void setFrameFromDiagonal(Point2D corner1, Point2D corner2)`

  set the bounding rectangle of this rectangular shape to a new rectangle with the given diametrically opposite corner points.

`java.awt.geom.RoundRectangle2D.Double`

- `RoundRectangle2D.Double(double x, double y, double w, double h, double arcWidth, double arcHeight)`

  constructs a round rectangle with the given bounding rectangle and arc dimensions.

Parameters:	`x, y`	top-left corner of bounding rectangle
	`w, h`	width and height of bounding rectangle
	`arcWidth`	the horizontal distance from the center to the end of the elliptical boundary arc
	`arcHeight`	the vertical distance from the center to the end of the elliptical boundary arc

`java.awt.geom.Ellipse2D.Double`

- `Ellipse2D.Double(double x, double y, double w, double h)`

  constructs a round rectangle with the given bounding rectangle.

Parameters:	`x, y`	top-left corner of bounding rectangle
	`w, h`	width and height of bounding rectangle

`java.awt.geom.Arc2D.Double`

- `Arc2D.Double(double x, double y, double w, double h, double startAngle, double arcAngle, int type)`

  constructs an arc with the given bounding rectangle, start, and arc angle and arc type.

Parameters:	`x,y`	top-left corner of bounding rectangle
	`w,h`	width and height of bounding rectangle
	`startAngle`	the angular measurement between the x-axis and the line joining the center of the bounding rectangle with the starting point of the arc, in radians, and distorted so that an "angle" of $\pi/4$ corresponds to the angle between the x-axis and line joining the center and top-right corner of the bounding rectangle
	`arcAngle`	the difference between the distorted end and start angles—see the sidebar on page 470. For a circular arc, this value equals the angle swept out by the arc.
	`type`	one of `Arc2D.OPEN`, `Arc2D.PIE`, and `Arc2D.CHORD`

`java.awt.geom.QuadCurve2D.Double`

- `QuadCurve2D.Double(double x1, double y1, double ctrlx, double ctrly, double x2, double y2)`

  constructs a quadratic curve from a start point, a control point, and an end point.

Parameters:	`x1,y1`	the start point
	`ctrlx,ctrly`	the control point
	`x2,y2`	the end points

`java.awt.geom.CubicCurve2D.Double`

- `CubicCurve2D.Double(double x1, double y1, double ctrlx1, double ctrly1, double ctrlx2, double ctrly2, double x2, double y2)`

  constructs a cubic curve from a start point, two control points, and an end point.

Parameters:	`x1,y1`	the start point
	`ctrlx1,ctrly1`	the first control point
	`ctrlx2,ctrly2`	the second control point
	`x2,y2`	the end points

`java.awt.geom.GeneralPath`

- `GeneralPath()`

  constructs an empty general path.

- `void moveTo(float x, float y)`

  makes `(x, y)` the *current point,* i.e., the starting point of the next segment.

- `void lineTo(float x, float y)`
- `void quadTo(float ctrlx, float ctrly, float x, float y)`
- `void curveTo(float ctrl1x, float ctrl1y, float ctrl2x, float ctrl2y, float x, float y)`

  draw a line, quadratic curve, or cubic curve from the current point to the end point `(x,y)`, and make that end point the current point.

- `void append(Shape s, boolean connect)`

  adds the outline of the given shape to the general path. If `connect` is `true`, the current point of the general point is connected to the starting point of the added shape by a straight line.

- `void closePath()`

  closes the path by drawing a straight line from the current point to the first point in the path.

Areas

In the preceding section, you saw how you can specify complex shapes by constructing general paths that are composed of lines and curves. By using a sufficient number of lines and curves, you can draw essentially any shape. For example, the shapes of characters in the fonts that you see on the screen and on your printouts are all made up of lines and cubic curves.

However, occasionally, it is easier to describe a shape by composing it from *areas,* such as rectangles, polygons, or ellipses. The Java 2D API supports four *constructive area geometry* operations that combine two areas to a new area:

- `add`—The combined area contains all points that are in the first or the second area.
- `subtract`—The combined area contains all points that are in the first but not the second area.
- `intersect`—The combined area contains all points that are in the first and the second area.
- `exclusiveOr`—The combined area contains all points that are in either the first or the second area, but not in both.

Figure 7–11 shows these operations.

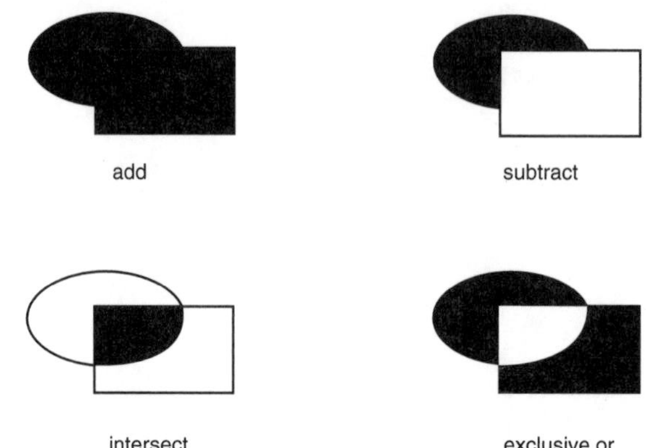

Figure 7–11: Constructive Area Geometry Operations

To construct a complex area, you start out with a default area object.

```
Area a = new Area();
```

Then, you combine the area with any shape:

```
a.add(new Rectangle2D.Double(. . .));
a.subtract(path);
. . .
```

The `Area` class implements the `Shape` interface. You can stroke the boundary of the area with the `draw` method or paint the interior with the `fill` method of the `Graphics2D` class.

The program in Example 7–2 shows the constructive area geometry operations. Select one of the four operations, and see the result of combining an ellipse and a rectangle with the operation that you selected (see Figure 7–12).

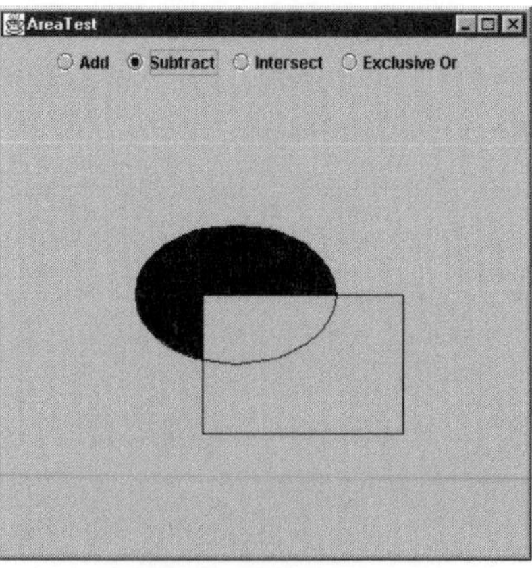

Figure 7–12: The AreaTest Program

Example 7-2: AreaTest.java

```
import java.awt.*;
import java.awt.event.*;
import java.awt.geom.*;
import java.util.*;
import javax.swing.*;

public class AreaTest
{  public static void main(String[] args)
   {  JFrame frame = new AreaTestFrame();
      frame.show();
   }
}

class AreaTestFrame extends JFrame
   implements ActionListener
{  public AreaTestFrame()
   {  setTitle("AreaTest");
      setSize(400, 400);
      addWindowListener(new WindowAdapter()
         {  public void windowClosing(WindowEvent e)
            {  System.exit(0);
            }
         } );

      Container contentPane = getContentPane();
      canvas = new AreaPanel();
      contentPane.add(canvas, "Center");

      JPanel buttonPanel = new JPanel();
      ButtonGroup group = new ButtonGroup();

      addButton = new JRadioButton("Add", true);
      buttonPanel.add(addButton);
      group.add(addButton);
      addButton.addActionListener(this);

      subtractButton = new JRadioButton("Subtract", false);
      buttonPanel.add(subtractButton);
      group.add(subtractButton);
      subtractButton.addActionListener(this);

      intersectButton = new JRadioButton("Intersect", false);
      buttonPanel.add(intersectButton);
      group.add(intersectButton);
      intersectButton.addActionListener(this);

      exclusiveOrButton = new JRadioButton("Exclusive Or", false);
      buttonPanel.add(exclusiveOrButton);
      group.add(exclusiveOrButton);
```

```
         exclusiveOrButton.addActionListener(this);

         contentPane.add(buttonPanel, "North");
      }

      public void actionPerformed(ActionEvent event)
      {  Object source = event.getSource();
         if (source == addButton)
            canvas.addAreas();
         else if (source == subtractButton)
            canvas.subtractAreas();
         else if (source == intersectButton)
            canvas.intersectAreas();
         else if (source == exclusiveOrButton)
            canvas.exclusiveOrAreas();
      }


      private AreaPanel canvas;
      private JRadioButton addButton;
      private JRadioButton subtractButton;
      private JRadioButton intersectButton;
      private JRadioButton exclusiveOrButton;
   }

   class AreaPanel extends JPanel
   {  public AreaPanel()
      {  area1
            = new Area(new Ellipse2D.Double(100, 100, 150, 100));
         area2
            = new Area(new Rectangle2D.Double(150, 150, 150, 100));
         addAreas();
      }

      public void paintComponent(Graphics g)
      {  super.paintComponent(g);
         Graphics2D g2 = (Graphics2D)g;
         g2.draw(area1);
         g2.draw(area2);
         g2.fill(area);
      }

      public void addAreas()
      {  area = new Area();
         area.add(area1);
         area.add(area2);
         repaint();
      }

      public void subtractAreas()
```

```
   {  area = new Area();
      area.add(area1);
      area.subtract(area2);
      repaint();
   }

   public void intersectAreas()
   {  area = new Area();
      area.add(area1);
      area.intersect(area2);
      repaint();
   }

   public void exclusiveOrAreas()
   {  area = new Area();
      area.add(area1);
      area.exclusiveOr(area2);
      repaint();
   }

   private Area area;
   private Area area1;
   private Area area2;
}
```

`java.awt.geom.Area`

- `void add(Area other)`
- `void subtract(Area other)`
- `void intersect(Area other)`
- `void exclusiveOr(Area other)`

  carry out the constructive area geometry operation with this area and the other area and set this area to the result.

Strokes

The `draw` operation of the `Graphics2D` class draws the boundary of a shape by using the currently selected *stroke*. By default, the stroke is a solid line that is one pixel wide. You can select a different stroke by calling the `setStroke` method. You supply an object of a class that implements the `Stroke` interface. The Java 2D API defines only one such class, called `BasicStroke`. In this section, we will look at the capabilities of the `BasicStroke` class.

You can construct strokes of arbitrary thickness. For example, here is how you draw lines that are 10 pixels wide.

```
g2.setStroke(new BasicStroke(10.0F));
g2.draw(new Line2D.Double(. . .));
```

When a stroke is more than a pixel thick, then the *end* of the stroke can have different styles. Figure 7–13 shows these so-called *end cap styles*. There are three choices:

- A *butt cap* simply ends the stroke at its end point.
- A *round cap* adds a half-circle to the end of the stroke.
- A *square cap* adds a half-square to the end of the stroke.

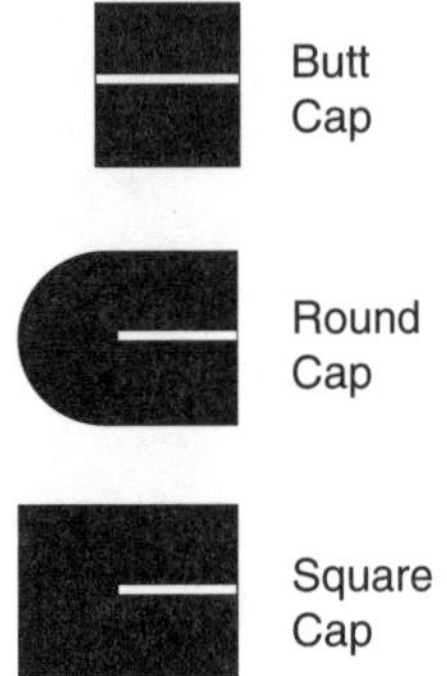

Figure 7–13: End Cap Styles

When two thick strokes meet, there are three choices for the *join style* (see Figure 7–14).

- A *bevel join* joins the strokes with a straight line that is perpendicular to the bisector of the angle between the two strokes.
- A *round join* extends each stroke to have a round cap.
- A *miter join* extends both strokes by adding a "spike."

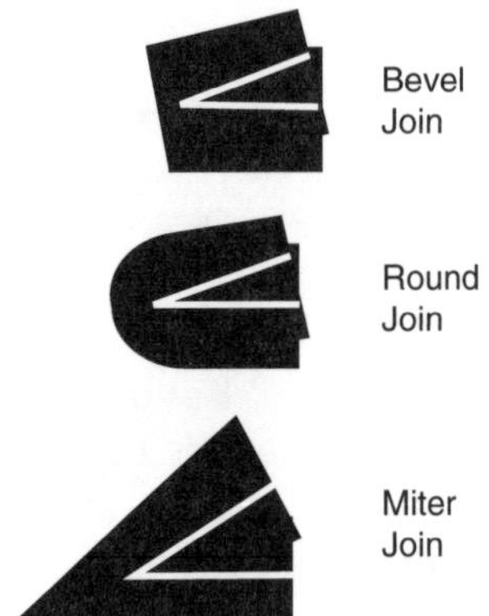

Figure 7–14: Join Styles

The miter join is not suitable for lines that meet at small angles. If two lines join with an angle that is less than the *miter limit,* then a bevel join is used instead. That usage prevents extremely long spikes. By default, the miter limit is ten degrees.

You specify these choices in the `BasicStroke` constructor, for example:

```
g2.setStroke(new BasicStroke(10.0F, BasicStroke.CAP_ROUND,
   BasicStroke.JOIN_ROUND));
```

```
g2.setStroke(new BasicStroke(10.0F, BasicStroke.CAP_BUTT,
   BasicStroke.JOIN_MITER, 15.0F /* miter limit */));
```

Finally, you can specify dashed lines by setting a *dash pattern.* In the program in Example 7–3, you can select a dash pattern that spells out SOS in morse code. The dash pattern is a `float[]` array of numbers that contains the lengths of the "on" and "off" strokes (see Figure 7–15).

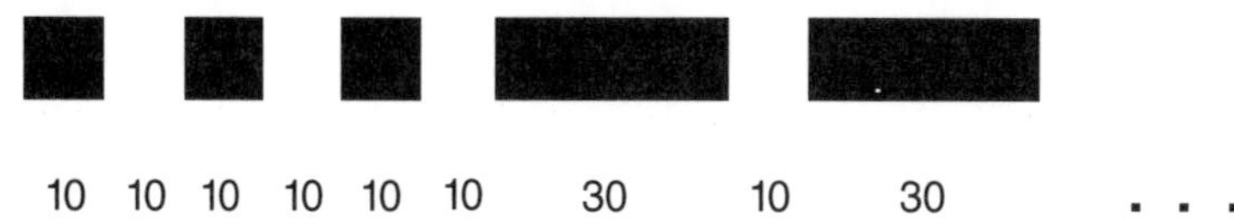

10 10 10 10 10 10 30 10 30 . . .

Figure 7–15: A dash pattern

You specify the dash pattern and a *dash phase* when constructing the `BasicStroke`. The dash phase indicates where in the dash pattern each line should start. Normally, you set this value to 0.

```
float[] dashPattern
   = { 10, 10, 10, 10, 10, 10, 30, 10, 30, ... };
g2.setStroke(new BasicStroke(10.0F, BasicStroke.CAP_BUTT,
   BasicStroke.JOIN_MITER, 10.0F /* miter limit */,
   dashPattern, 0 /* dash phase */));
```

NOTE: End cap styles are applied to the ends of *each dash* in a dash pattern.

The program in Example 7–3 lets you specify end cap styles, join styles, and dashed lines (see Figure 7–16). You can move the ends of the line segments to test out the miter limit: select the miter join, then move the line segment to form a very acute angle. You will see the miter join turn into a bevel join.

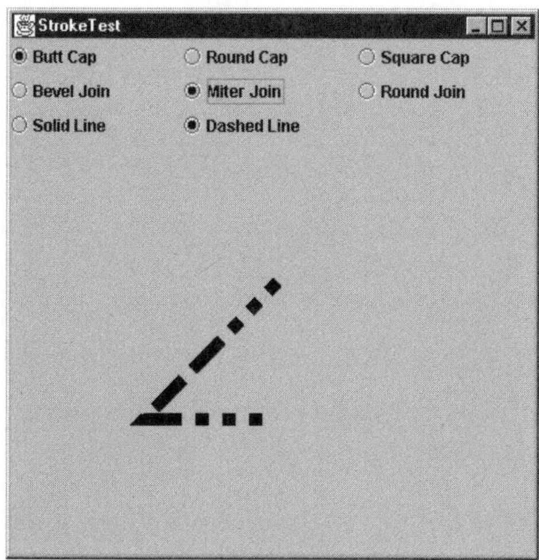

Figure 7–16: The StrokeTest program

The program is similar to the program in Example 7–1. The mouse listener remembers if you click on the end point of a line segment, and the mouse motion listener monitors the dragging of the end point. A set of radio buttons signal the user choices for the end cap style, join style, and solid or dashed line. The `paintComponent` method of the `StrokePanel` class constructs a `GeneralPath` consisting of the two line segments that join the three points that the user can move with the mouse. It then constructs a `BasicStroke`, according to the selections that the user made, and finally draws the path.

Example 7–3: StrokeTest.java

```
import java.awt.*;
import java.awt.event.*;
import java.awt.geom.*;
import java.util.*;
import javax.swing.*;

public class StrokeTest
{  public static void main(String[] args)
   {  JFrame frame = new StrokeTestFrame();
      frame.show();
   }
}

class StrokeTestFrame extends JFrame
   implements ActionListener
{  public StrokeTestFrame()
   {  setTitle("StrokeTest");
      setSize(400, 400);
      addWindowListener(new WindowAdapter()
         {  public void windowClosing(WindowEvent e)
            {  System.exit(0);
            }
         } );

      Container contentPane = getContentPane();
      canvas = new StrokePanel();
      contentPane.add(canvas, "Center");

      JPanel buttonPanel = new JPanel();
      buttonPanel.setLayout(new GridLayout(3, 3));
      ButtonGroup group1 = new ButtonGroup();

      buttCapButton = new JRadioButton("Butt Cap", true);
      buttonPanel.add(buttCapButton);
      group1.add(buttCapButton);
      buttCapButton.addActionListener(this);

      roundCapButton = new JRadioButton("Round Cap", false);
      buttonPanel.add(roundCapButton);
      group1.add(roundCapButton);
```

```
      roundCapButton.addActionListener(this);

      squareCapButton = new JRadioButton("Square Cap", false);
      buttonPanel.add(squareCapButton);
      group1.add(squareCapButton);
      squareCapButton.addActionListener(this);

      ButtonGroup group2 = new ButtonGroup();

      bevelJoinButton = new JRadioButton("Bevel Join", true);
      buttonPanel.add(bevelJoinButton);
      group2.add(bevelJoinButton);
      bevelJoinButton.addActionListener(this);

      miterJoinButton = new JRadioButton("Miter Join", false);
      buttonPanel.add(miterJoinButton);
      group2.add(miterJoinButton);
      miterJoinButton.addActionListener(this);

      roundJoinButton = new JRadioButton("Round Join", false);
      buttonPanel.add(roundJoinButton);
      group2.add(roundJoinButton);
      roundJoinButton.addActionListener(this);

      ButtonGroup group3 = new ButtonGroup();

      solidLineButton = new JRadioButton("Solid Line", true);
      buttonPanel.add(solidLineButton);
      group3.add(solidLineButton);
      solidLineButton.addActionListener(this);

      dashedLineButton = new JRadioButton("Dashed Line", false);
      buttonPanel.add(dashedLineButton);
      group3.add(dashedLineButton);
      dashedLineButton.addActionListener(this);

      contentPane.add(buttonPanel, "North");
   }

   public void actionPerformed(ActionEvent event)
   {  Object source = event.getSource();
      if (source == buttCapButton)
         canvas.setCap(BasicStroke.CAP_BUTT);
      else if (source == roundCapButton)
         canvas.setCap(BasicStroke.CAP_ROUND);
      else if (source == squareCapButton)
         canvas.setCap(BasicStroke.CAP_SQUARE);
      else if (source == bevelJoinButton)
         canvas.setJoin(BasicStroke.JOIN_BEVEL);
      else if (source == miterJoinButton)
         canvas.setJoin(BasicStroke.JOIN_MITER);
      else if (source == roundJoinButton)
```

```
            canvas.setJoin(BasicStroke.JOIN_ROUND);
         else if (source == solidLineButton)
            canvas.setDash(false);
         else if (source == dashedLineButton)
            canvas.setDash(true);
      }

      private StrokePanel canvas;
      private JRadioButton buttCapButton;
      private JRadioButton roundCapButton;
      private JRadioButton squareCapButton;
      private JRadioButton bevelJoinButton;
      private JRadioButton miterJoinButton;
      private JRadioButton roundJoinButton;
      private JRadioButton solidLineButton;
      private JRadioButton dashedLineButton;
}

class StrokePanel extends JPanel
   implements MouseListener, MouseMotionListener
{  public StrokePanel()
   {  addMouseListener(this);
      addMouseMotionListener(this);
      points = new Point2D[3];
      points[0] = new Point2D.Double(200, 100);
      points[1] = new Point2D.Double(100, 200);
      points[2] = new Point2D.Double(200, 200);
      current = -1;
      width = 10.0F;
   }

   public void paintComponent(Graphics g)
   {  super.paintComponent(g);
      Graphics2D g2 = (Graphics2D)g;
      GeneralPath path = new GeneralPath();
      path.moveTo((float)points[0].getX(),
         (float)points[0].getY());
      for (int i = 1; i < points.length; i++)
         path.lineTo((float)points[i].getX(),
            (float)points[i].getY());
      BasicStroke stroke;
      if (dash)
      {  float miterLimit = 10.0F;
         float[] dashPattern = { 10F, 10F, 10F, 10F, 10F, 10F,
            30F, 10F, 30F, 10F, 30F, 10F,
            10F, 10F, 10F, 10F, 10F, 30F };
         float dashPhase = 0;
         stroke = new BasicStroke(width, cap, join,
            miterLimit, dashPattern, dashPhase);
      }
      else
         stroke = new BasicStroke(width, cap, join);
```

```
      g2.setStroke(stroke);
      g2.draw(path);
   }

   public void setJoin(int j) { join = j; repaint(); }

   public void setCap(int c) { cap = c; repaint(); }

   public void setDash(boolean d) { dash = d; repaint(); }

   public void mousePressed(MouseEvent event)
   {  Point p = event.getPoint();
      for (int i = 0; i < points.length; i++)
      {  double x = points[i].getX() - SIZE / 2;
         double y = points[i].getY() - SIZE / 2;
         Rectangle2D r = new Rectangle2D.Double(x, y, SIZE, SIZE);
         if (r.contains(p))
         {  current = i;
            return;
         }
      }
   }

   public void mouseReleased(MouseEvent event)
   {  current = -1;
   }

   public void mouseEntered(MouseEvent event)
   {
   }

   public void mouseExited(MouseEvent event)
   {
   }

   public void mouseClicked(MouseEvent event)
   {
   }

   public void mouseMoved(MouseEvent event)
   {
   }

   public void mouseDragged(MouseEvent event)
   {  if (current == -1) return;
      points[current] = event.getPoint();
      repaint();
   }

   private Point2D[] points;
   private static int SIZE = 10;
   private int current;
   private float width;
```

```
    private int cap;
    private int join;
    private boolean dash;
}
```

java.awt.Graphics2D

- `void setStroke(Stroke s)`

  sets the stroke of this graphics context to the given object that implements the `Stroke` interface.

java.awt.geom.BasicStroke

- `BasicStroke(float width)`
- `BasicStroke(float width, int cap, int join)`
- `BasicStroke(float width, int cap, int join, float miterlimit)`
- `BasicStroke(float width, int cap, int join, float miterlimit, float[] dash, float dashPhase)`

  construct a stroke object with the given attributes.

Parameters:	`width`	the width of the pen
	`cap`	the end cap style, one of `CAP_BUTT`, `CAP_ROUND`, and `CAP_SQUARE`
	`join`	the join style, one of `JOIN_BEVEL`, `JOIN_MITER`, and `JOIN_ROUND`
	`miterlimit`	the angle, in degrees, below which a miter join is rendered as a bevel join
	`dash`	an array of the lengths of the alternating filled and blank portions of a dashed stroke
	`dashPhase`	the "phase" of the dash pattern. A segment of this length, preceding the starting point of the stroke, is assumed to have the dash pattern already applied.

Paint

When you fill a shape, its inside is covered with *paint*. You use the `setPaint` method to set the paint style to an object whose class implements the `Paint` interface. In the Java 2D API, there are three such classes:

- The `Color` class implements the `Paint` interface. To fill shapes with a solid color, simply call `setPaint` with a `Color` object, such as

  ```
  g2.setPaint(Color.red);
  ```

- The `GradientPaint` class varies colors by interpolating between two given color values (see Figure 7–17).
- The `TexturePaint` class fills an area with repetitions of an image (see Figure 7–18).

Figure 7–17: Gradient paint

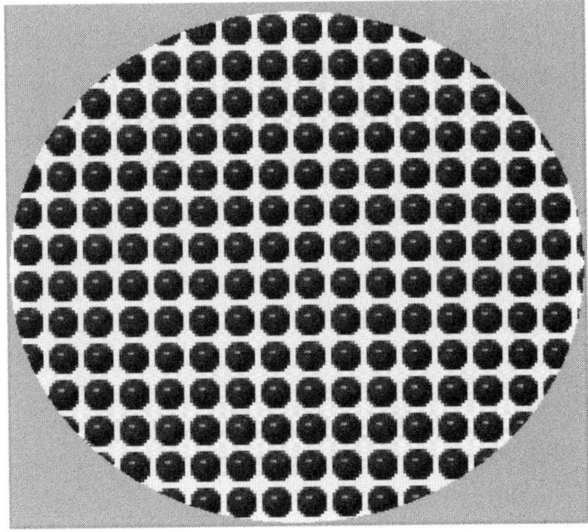

Figure 7–18: Texture paint

You construct a `GradientPaint` object by giving two points and the colors that you want at these two points.

```
g2.setPaint(new GradientPaint(p1, Color.red, p2, Color.blue));
```

Colors are interpolated along the line joining the two points. Colors are constant along lines that are perpendicular to that joining line. Points beyond an end point of the line are given the color at the end point.

Alternatively, if you call the `GradientPaint` constructor with `true` for the `cyclic` parameter,

```
g2.setPaint(new GradientPaint(p1, Color.red, p2, Color.blue, true));
```

then the color variation *cycles* and keeps varying beyond the end points.

To construct a `TexturePaint` object, you need to specify a `BufferedImage` and an *anchor* rectangle. The anchor rectangle is extended indefinitely in x- and y-directions to tile the entire coordinate plane. The image is scaled to fit into the anchor and then replicated into each tile.

We will introduce the `BufferedImage` class later in this chapter when we discuss images in detail. You create a `BufferedImage` object by giving the image size and the *image type*. The most common image type is `TYPE_INT_ARGB`, in which each pixel is specified by an integer that describes the *alpha* or transparency, red, green, and blue values. For example,

```
BufferedImage bufferedImage = new BufferedImage(width, height,
   TYPE_INT_ARGB);
```

Then, you obtain a graphics context to draw into the buffered image.

```
Graphics2D g2 = bufferedImage.createGraphics();
```

Any drawing operations on `g2` now fill the buffered image with pixels. When you are done, then you can create your `TexturePaint` object:

```
g2.setPaint(new TexturePaint(bufferedImage, anchorRectangle));
```

The program in Example 7–4 lets the user choose between a solid color paint, a gradient paint, and a texture paint. Then, an ellipse is filled with the specified paint. The texture paint reads in an image from a GIF file. Recall from Chapter 7 of Volume 1 that you need a media tracker to read in an image file.

```
Image image = Toolkit.getDefaultToolkit().getImage
        ("blue-ball.gif");
MediaTracker tracker = new MediaTracker(this);
tracker.addImage(image, 0);
try { tracker.waitForID(0); }
catch (InterruptedException e) {}
```

Once the image is acquired, we draw it inside a `BufferedImage`:

```
bufferedImage = new BufferedImage(image.getWidth(null),
   image.getHeight(null), BufferedImage.TYPE_INT_ARGB);
Graphics2D g2 = bufferedImage.createGraphics();
g2.drawImage(image, 0, 0, null);
```

To show the significance of the anchor rectangle, we specify the anchor to have twice the size of the image:

```
Rectangle2D anchor = new Rectangle2D.Double(0, 0,
   2 * bufferedImage.getWidth(),
   2 * bufferedImage.getHeight());
paint = new TexturePaint(bufferedImage, anchor);
```

As you can see when you select "Texture Paint", the image is scaled to fit the anchor, and it is then replicated to fill the shape. Tiles that meet the boundary of the shape are clipped.

Example 7-4: PaintTest.java

```
import java.awt.*;
import java.awt.event.*;
import java.awt.geom.*;
import java.awt.image.*;
import java.util.*;
import javax.swing.*;

public class PaintTest
{  public static void main(String[] args)
   {  JFrame frame = new PaintTestFrame();
      frame.show();
   }
}

class PaintTestFrame extends JFrame
   implements ActionListener
{  public PaintTestFrame()
   {  setTitle("PaintTest");
      setSize(400, 400);
      addWindowListener(new WindowAdapter()
         {  public void windowClosing(WindowEvent e)
            {  System.exit(0);
            }
         } );

      Container contentPane = getContentPane();
      canvas = new PaintPanel();
      contentPane.add(canvas, "Center");

      JPanel buttonPanel = new JPanel();
      ButtonGroup group = new ButtonGroup();

      colorButton = new JRadioButton("Color", true);
      buttonPanel.add(colorButton);
      group.add(colorButton);
      colorButton.addActionListener(this);

      gradientPaintButton
         = new JRadioButton("Gradient Paint", false);
      buttonPanel.add(gradientPaintButton);
      group.add(gradientPaintButton);
      gradientPaintButton.addActionListener(this);

      texturePaintButton
         = new JRadioButton("Texture Paint", false);
      buttonPanel.add(texturePaintButton);
      group.add(texturePaintButton);
```

```
      texturePaintButton.addActionListener(this);

      contentPane.add(buttonPanel, "North");
   }

   public void actionPerformed(ActionEvent event)
   {  Object source = event.getSource();
      if (source == colorButton)
         canvas.setColor();
      else if (source == gradientPaintButton)
         canvas.setGradientPaint();
      else if (source == texturePaintButton)
         canvas.setTexturePaint();
   }

   private PaintPanel canvas;
   private JRadioButton colorButton;
   private JRadioButton gradientPaintButton;
   private JRadioButton texturePaintButton;
}

class PaintPanel extends JPanel
{  public PaintPanel()
   {  Image image = Toolkit.getDefaultToolkit().getImage
         ("blue-ball.gif");
      MediaTracker tracker = new MediaTracker(this);
      tracker.addImage(image, 0);
      try { tracker.waitForID(0); }
      catch (InterruptedException e) {}
      bufferedImage = new BufferedImage(image.getWidth(null),
         image.getHeight(null), BufferedImage.TYPE_INT_ARGB);
      Graphics2D g2 = bufferedImage.createGraphics();
      g2.drawImage(image, 0, 0, null);

      setColor();
   }

   public void paintComponent(Graphics g)
   {  super.paintComponent(g);
      Graphics2D g2 = (Graphics2D)g;
      g2.setPaint(paint);
      Ellipse2D circle
         = new Ellipse2D.Double(0, 0, getWidth(), getHeight());
      g2.fill(circle);
   }

   public void setColor()
   {  paint = Color.red; // Color implements Paint
      repaint();
   }

   public void setGradientPaint()
   {  paint = new GradientPaint(0, 0, Color.red,
```

```
        (float)getWidth(), (float)getHeight(), Color.blue);
      repaint();
   }

   public void setTexturePaint()
   {  Rectangle2D anchor = new Rectangle2D.Double(0, 0,
         2 * bufferedImage.getWidth(),
         2 * bufferedImage.getHeight());
      paint = new TexturePaint(bufferedImage, anchor);
      repaint();
   }

   private Paint paint;
   private BufferedImage bufferedImage;
}
```

`java.awt.Graphics2D`

- `void setPaint(Paint s)`
  sets the paint of this graphics context to the given object that implements the `Paint` interface.

`java.awt.geom.GradientPaint`

- `GradientPaint(float x1, float y1, Color color1, float x2, float y2, Color color2)`
- `GradientPaint(float x1, float y1, Color color1, float x2, float y2, Color color2, boolean cyclic)`
- `GradientPaint(Point2D p1, Color color1, Point2D p2, Color color2)`
- `GradientPaint(Point2D p1, Color color1, Point2D p2, Color color2, boolean cyclic)`
  construct a gradient paint object that fills shapes with color such that the start point is colored with as `color1`, the end point is colored with `color2`, and the colors in between are linearly interpolated. Colors are constant along lines that are perpendicular to the line joining the start and the end point. By default, the gradient paint is not cyclic, that is, points beyond the start and end points are colored with the same color as the start and end point. If the gradient paint is *cyclic*, then colors continue to be interpolated, first returning back to the starting point color and then repeating indefinitely in both directions.

Parameters:	`x1`, `y1`, or `p1`	the start point
	`color1`	the color to use for the start point
	`x2`, `y2`, or `p2`	the end point
	`color2`	the color to use for the end point
	`cyclic`	`true` if the color change pattern repeats, `false` if the colors beyond the start and end point are constant

```
java.awt.geom.TexturePaint
```

- `TexturePaint(BufferedImage texture, Rectangle2D anchor)`
  creates a texture paint object.

  Parameters:

`texture`	the texture to use for filling shapes
`anchor`	the anchor rectangle that defines the tiling of the space to be painted. The rectangle is repeated indefinitely in x- and y-directions, and the texture image is scaled to fill each tile.

Coordinate Transformations

Suppose you need to draw an object such as an automobile. You know, from the manufacturer's specifications, the height, wheelbase, and total length. You could, of course, figure out all pixel positions, assuming some number of pixels per meter. However, there is an easier way. You can ask the graphics context to carry out the conversion for you.

```
g2.scale(pixelsPerMeter, pixelsPerMeter);
g2.draw(new Line2D.Double(coordinates in meters));
   // converts to pixels and draws scaled line
```

The `scale` method of the `Graphics2D` class sets the *coordinate transformation* of the graphics context to a scaling transformation. That transformation changes *user coordinates* (the units that the user specifies) to *device coordinates* (pixels). Figure 7–19 shows how the transformation works.

Coordinate transformations are very useful in practice. They allow you to work with convenient coordinate values. The graphics context takes care of the dirty work of transforming them to pixels.

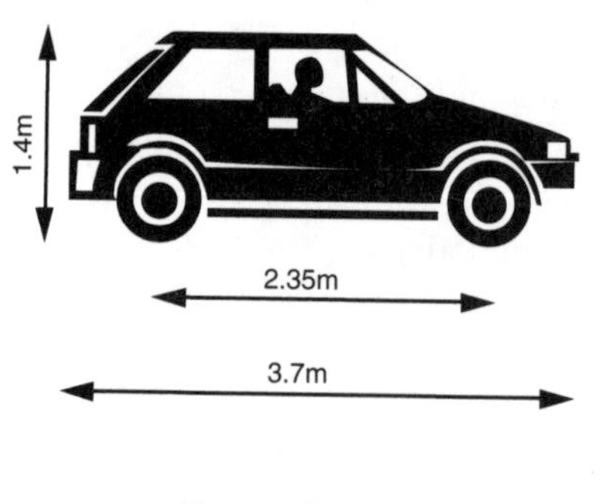

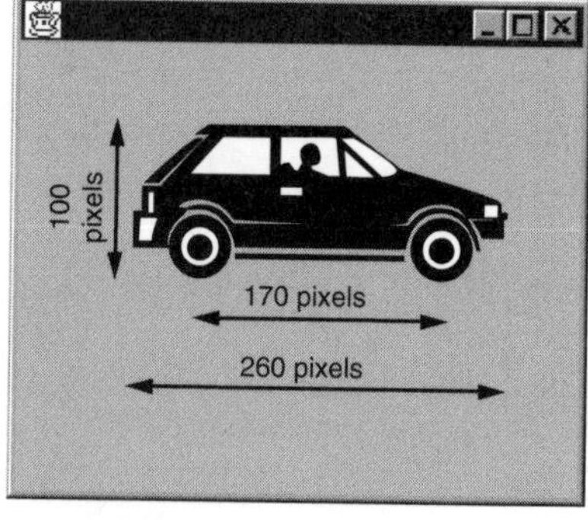

Figure 7–19: User and device coordinates

There are four fundamental transformations:

- Scaling: blowing up, or shrinking, all distances from a fixed point
- Rotation: rotating all points around a fixed center
- Translation: moving all points by a fixed amount
- Shear: leaving one line fixed and "sliding" the lines parallel to it by an amount that is proportional to the distance from the fixed line

Figure 7–20 shows how these four fundamental transformations act on a unit square.

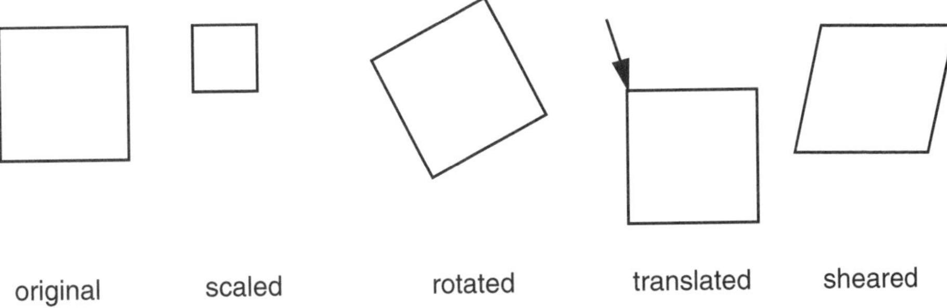

Figure 7–20: The fundamental transformations

The `scale`, `rotate`, `translate`, and `shear` methods of the `Graphics2D` class set the coordinate transformation of the graphics context to one of these fundamental transformations.

You can *compose* the transformations. For example, you may want to rotate shapes *and* double their size. Then, you need to supply both a rotation and a scaling transformation.

```
g2.rotate(angle);
g2.scale(2, 2);
g2.draw(. . .);
```

In this case, it does not matter in which order you supply the transformations. However, with most transformations, order does matter. For example, if you want to rotate and shear, then it makes a difference which of the transformations you supply first. You need to figure out what your intention is. The graphics context will apply the transformations in the order in which you supplied them.

You can supply as many transformations as you like. For example, consider the following sequence of transformations:

```
g2.translate(-x, -y);
g2.rotate(a);
g2.translate(x, y);
```

The first transformation moves the point (`x`, `y`) to the origin. The second transformation rotates with an angle `a` around the origin. The third transformation moves the origin back to (x, y). The overall effect is a rotation with center point (x, y)—see Figure 7–21. Because rotating about a point other than the origin is such a common operation, there is a shortcut:

```
g2.rotate(a, x, y);
```

If you know some matrix theory, you are probably aware that all rotations, translations, scalings, shears, and their compositions can be expressed by matrix transformations of the form

$$\begin{bmatrix} x_{\text{new}} \\ y_{\text{new}} \\ 1 \end{bmatrix} = \begin{bmatrix} a & c & e \\ b & d & f \\ 0 & 0 & 1 \end{bmatrix} \cdot \begin{bmatrix} x \\ y \\ 1 \end{bmatrix}$$

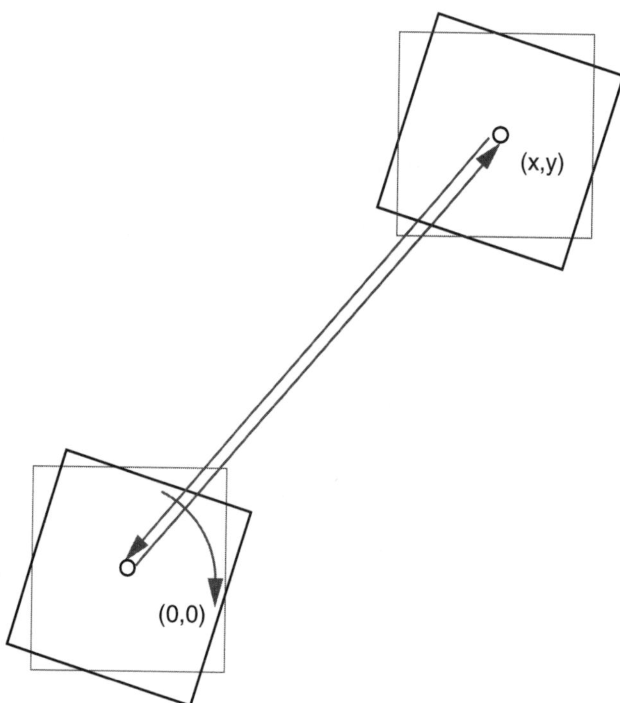

Figure 7–21: Composing transformations

Such a transformation is called an *affine transformation*. In the Java 2D API, the AffineTransform class describes such a transformation. If you know the components of a particular transformation matrix, you can construct it directly as

```
AffineTransform t = new AffineTransform(a, b, c, d, e, f);
```

There are also factory methods `getRotateInstance`, `getScaleInstance`, `getTranslateInstance`, and `getShearInstance` that construct the matrices that represent these transformation types. For example, the call

```
t = AffineTransform.getScaleInstance(2.0F, 0.5F);
```

returns a transformation that corresponds to the matrix

$$\begin{bmatrix} 2 & 0 & 0 \\ 0 & 0.5 & 0 \\ 0 & 0 & 1 \end{bmatrix}$$

Finally, there are instance methods `setToRotation`, `setToScale`, `setToTranslation`, and `setToShear` that set a transformation object to a new type. Here is an example.

```
t.setToRotation(angle); // sets t to a rotation
```

You can set the coordinate transformation of the graphics context to an `AffineTransform` object.

```
g2.setTransform(t); // replaces current transformation
```

However, in practice, you don't want to call the `setTransform` operation since it replaces any existing clipping shape that the graphics context may have. For example, a graphics context for printing in landscape mode already contains a 90 degree rotation transformation. If you call `setTransform`, you obliterate that rotation. Instead, call the `transform` method.

```
g2.transform(t); // composes current transformation with t
```

It composes the existing transformation with the new `AffineTransform` object.

If you just want to apply a transformation temporarily, then you should first get the old transformation, then compose with your new transformation, and finally restore the old transformation when you are done.

```
AffineTransform oldTransform = g2.getTransform();
   // save old transform
g2.transform(t); // apply temporary transform
   // now draw on g2
g2.setTransform(oldTransform); // restore old transform
```

The program in Example 7–5 lets the user choose among the four fundamental transformations. The `paintComponent` method draws a square, then applies the selected transformation and redraws the square. However, for a good visual appearance, we want to have the square and its transform appear on the *center* of the display panel. For that reason, the `paintComponent` method first sets the coordinate transformation to a translation.

```
g2.translate(getWidth() / 2, getHeight() / 2);
```

This translation moves the origin to the center of the component.

Then, the `paintComponent` method draws a square that is centered around the origin.

```
square = new Rectangle2D.Double(-50, -50, 100, 100);
. . .
g2.setPaint(Color.gray);
g2.draw(square);
```

However, because the graphics context applies the translation to the shape, the square is actually drawn with its center lying at the center of the component.

Next, the transformation that the user selected is composed with the current transformation, and the square is drawn once again.

```
g2.transform(t);
g2.setPaint(Color.black);
g2.draw(square);
```

The original square is drawn in gray, and the transformed one in black (see Figure 7–22).

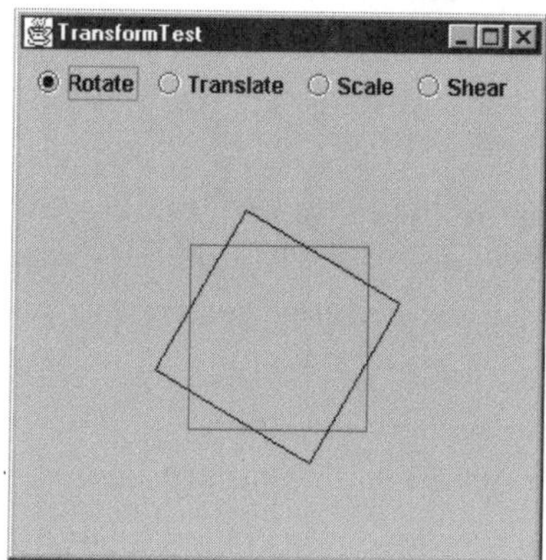

Figure 7–22: The TransformTest program

Example 7–5: TransformTest.java

```
import java.awt.*;
import java.awt.event.*;
import java.awt.geom.*;
import java.util.*;
import javax.swing.*;

public class TransformTest
{  public static void main(String[] args)
   {  JFrame frame = new TransformTestFrame();
      frame.show();
   }
```

```
}

class TransformTestFrame extends JFrame
   implements ActionListener
{  public TransformTestFrame()
   {  setTitle("TransformTest");
      setSize(300, 300);
      addWindowListener(new WindowAdapter()
         {  public void windowClosing(WindowEvent e)
            {  System.exit(0);
            }
         } );

      Container contentPane = getContentPane();
      canvas = new TransformPanel();
      contentPane.add(canvas, "Center");

      JPanel buttonPanel = new JPanel();
      ButtonGroup group = new ButtonGroup();

      rotateButton = new JRadioButton("Rotate", true);
      buttonPanel.add(rotateButton);
      group.add(rotateButton);
      rotateButton.addActionListener(this);

      translateButton = new JRadioButton("Translate", false);
      buttonPanel.add(translateButton);
      group.add(translateButton);
      translateButton.addActionListener(this);

      scaleButton = new JRadioButton("Scale", false);
      buttonPanel.add(scaleButton);
      group.add(scaleButton);
      scaleButton.addActionListener(this);

      shearButton = new JRadioButton("Shear", false);
      buttonPanel.add(shearButton);
      group.add(shearButton);
      shearButton.addActionListener(this);

      contentPane.add(buttonPanel, "North");
   }

   public void actionPerformed(ActionEvent event)
   {  Object source = event.getSource();
      if (source == rotateButton) canvas.setRotate();
      else if (source == translateButton) canvas.setTranslate();
      else if (source == scaleButton) canvas.setScale();
      else if (source == shearButton) canvas.setShear();
   }

   private TransformPanel canvas;
```

```
   private JRadioButton rotateButton;
   private JRadioButton translateButton;
   private JRadioButton scaleButton;
   private JRadioButton shearButton;
}

class TransformPanel extends JPanel
{  public TransformPanel()
   {  square = new Rectangle2D.Double(-50, -50, 100, 100);
      t = new AffineTransform();
      setRotate();
   }

   public void paintComponent(Graphics g)
   {  super.paintComponent(g);
      Graphics2D g2 = (Graphics2D)g;
      g2.translate(getWidth() / 2, getHeight() / 2);
      g2.setPaint(Color.gray);
      g2.draw(square);
      g2.transform(t);
         /* we don't use setTransform because we want
            to compose with the current translation
         */
      g2.setPaint(Color.black);
      g2.draw(square);
   }

   public void setRotate()
   {  t.setToRotation(Math.toRadians(30));
      repaint();
   }

   public void setTranslate()
   {  t.setToTranslation(20, 15);
      repaint();
   }

   public void setScale()
   {  t.setToScale(2.0, 1.5);
      repaint();
   }

   public void setShear()
   {  t.setToShear(-0.2, 0);
      repaint();
   }

   private Rectangle2D square;
   private AffineTransform t;
}
```

`java.awt.geom.AffineTransform`

- `AffineTransform(double a, double b, double c, double d, double e, double f)`
- `AffineTransform(float a, float b, float c, float d, float e, float f)`

  construct the affine transform with matrix

$$\begin{bmatrix} a & c & e \\ b & d & f \\ 0 & 0 & 1 \end{bmatrix}$$

- `AffineTransform(double[] m)`
- `AffineTransform(float[] m)`

  construct the affine transform with matrix

$$\begin{bmatrix} \texttt{m[0]} & \texttt{m[2]} & \texttt{m[4]} \\ \texttt{m[1]} & \texttt{m[3]} & \texttt{m[5]} \\ 0 & 0 & 1 \end{bmatrix}$$

- `static AffineTransform getRotateInstance(double a)`

  creates a counterclockwise rotation around the origin by the angle `a` (in radians). The transformation matrix is

$$\begin{bmatrix} \cos(\texttt{a}) & -\sin(\texttt{a}) & 0 \\ \sin(\texttt{a}) & \cos(\texttt{a}) & 0 \\ 0 & 0 & 1 \end{bmatrix}$$

- `static AffineTransform getRotateInstance(double a, double x, double y)`

  creates a counterclockwise rotation around the point `(x,y)` by the angle `a` (in radians).

- `static AffineTransform getScaleInstance(double sx, double sy)`

  creates a scaling transformation that scales the x-axis by `sx` and the y-axis by `sy`. The transformation matrix is

$$\begin{bmatrix} \texttt{sx} & 0 & 0 \\ 0 & \texttt{sy} & 0 \\ 0 & 0 & 1 \end{bmatrix}$$

- `static AffineTransform getShearInstance(double shx, double shy)`

  creates a shear transformation that shears the x-axis by `shx` and the y-axis by `shy`. The transformation matrix is

$$\begin{bmatrix} 1 & \mathtt{shx} & 0 \\ \mathtt{shy} & 1 & 0 \\ 0 & 0 & 1 \end{bmatrix}$$

- `static AffineTransform getTranslateInstance(double tx, double ty)`

  creates a translation that moves the x-axis by `tx` and the y-axis by `ty`. The transformation matrix is

$$\begin{bmatrix} 1 & 0 & \mathtt{tx} \\ 0 & 1 & \mathtt{ty} \\ 0 & 0 & 1 \end{bmatrix}$$

- `void setToRotation(double a)`
- `void setToRotation(double a, double x, double y)`
- `void setToScale(double sx, double sy)`
- `void setToShear(double sx, double sy)`
- `void setToTranslation(double tx, double ty)`

  set this affine transformation to a basic transformation with the given parameters. See the `get`*`Xxx`*`Instance` method for an explanation of the basic transformations and their parameters.

`java.awt.Graphics2D`

- `void setTransform(AffineTransform t)`

  replaces the existing coordinate transformation of this graphics context with `t`.

- `void transform(AffineTransform t)`

  composes the existing coordinate transformation of this graphics context with `t`.

- `void rotate(double a)`
- `void rotate(double a, double x, double y)`
- `void scale(double sx, double sy)`
- `void shear(double sx, double sy)`
- `void translate(double tx, double ty)`

  compose the existing coordinate transformation of this graphics context with a basic transformation with the given parameters. See the `AffineTransform.get`*`Xxx`*`Instance` method for an explanation of the basic transformations and their parameters.

Clipping

By setting a *clipping shape* in the graphics context, you constrain all drawing operations to the interior of that clipping shape.

```
g2.setClip(clipShape); // but see below
g2.draw(shape);
   // draws only the part that falls inside the clipping shape
```

However, in practice, you don't want to call the `setClip` operation since it replaces any existing clipping shape that the graphics context may have. For example, as you will see later in this chapter, a graphics context for printing comes with a clip rectangle that ensures that you don't draw on the margins. Instead, call the `clip` method.

```
g2.clip(clipShape); // better
```

The `clip` method intersects the existing clipping shape with the new one that you supply.

If you just want to apply a clipping area temporarily, then you should first get the old clip, then add your new clip, and finally restore the old clip when you are done:

```
Shape oldClip = g2.getClip(); // save old clip
g2.clip(clipShape); // apply temporary clip
// now draw on g2
g2.setClip(oldClip); // restore old clip
```

In Example 7–6, we show off the clipping capability with a rather dramatic drawing of a line pattern that is clipped by a complex shape, namely, the outline of a set of characters (see Figure 7–23).

Figure 7–23: The ClipTest program

To obtain character outlines, you need a *font render context*. Use the `getFontRenderContext` method of the `Graphics2D` class.

```
FontRenderContext context = g2.getFontRenderContext();
```

Next, create a `TextLayout` object from

- A string
- A font
- The font render context

```
TextLayout layout = new TextLayout("Hello", font, context);
```

This text layout object describes the layout of a sequence of characters, as rendered by a particular font render context. The layout depends on the font render context—the same characters will appear differently on a screen or a printer.

The methods

```
getAdvance()
getAscent()
getDescent()
getLeading()
```

of the `TextLayout` class describe the horizontal and vertical extent of the characters (see Figure 7–24). These methods replace the methods of the `FontMetrics` class that you saw in Chapter 7 of Volume 1. The `FontMetrics` class can only return integer measurements, which is not sufficient if these measurements have fractional values, which is not uncommon at small point sizes.

Figure 7–24: Text layout measurements

More importantly for our current application, the `getOutline` method returns a `Shape` object that describes the shape of the outline of the characters in the text layout. The outline shape starts at the origin (0, 0), which is not suitable for most drawing operations. Therefore, you need to supply an affine transform to the `getOutline` operation that specifies where you would like the outline to appear. We simply supply a translation that moves the base point to the point (0, 100).

```
AffineTransform transform
   = AffineTransform.getTranslateInstance(0, 100);
Shape outline = layout.getOutline(transform);
```

Then, we append the outline to the clipping shape.

```
GeneralPath clipShape = new GeneralPath();
clipShape.append(outline, false);
```

Finally, we set the clipping shape and draw a set of lines. The lines appear only inside the character boundaries.

```
g2.setClip(clipShape);
Point2D p = new Point2D.Double(0, 0);
for (int i = 0; i < NLINES; i++)
{  double x = . . .;
   double y = . . .;
   Point2D q = new Point2D.Double(x, y);
   g2.draw(new Line2D.Double(p, q)); // lines are clipped
}
```

Here is the complete program.

Example 7–6: ClipTest.java

```
import java.awt.*;
import java.awt.event.*;
import java.awt.font.*;
import java.awt.geom.*;
import java.util.*;
import javax.swing.*;

public class ClipTest
{  public static void main(String[] args)
   {  JFrame frame = new ClipTestFrame();
      frame.show();
   }
}

class ClipTestFrame extends JFrame
   implements ActionListener
{  public ClipTestFrame()
   {  setTitle("ClipTest");
      setSize(300, 300);
      addWindowListener(new WindowAdapter()
         {  public void windowClosing(WindowEvent e)
            {  System.exit(0);
            }
         } );

      Container contentPane = getContentPane();
      canvas = new ClipPanel();
      contentPane.add(canvas, "Center");

      JPanel buttonPanel = new JPanel();
      ButtonGroup group = new ButtonGroup();

      noClipButton = new JRadioButton("No Clip", true);
      buttonPanel.add(noClipButton);
      group.add(noClipButton);
```

```
         noClipButton.addActionListener(this);

         clipButton = new JRadioButton("Clip", false);
         buttonPanel.add(clipButton);
         group.add(clipButton);
         clipButton.addActionListener(this);

         contentPane.add(buttonPanel, "North");
      }

   public void actionPerformed(ActionEvent event)
   {  Object source = event.getSource();
      if (source == clipButton) canvas.setClip(true);
      else if (source == noClipButton) canvas.setClip(false);
   }

   private JRadioButton clipButton;
   private JRadioButton noClipButton;

   private ClipPanel canvas;
}

class ClipPanel extends JPanel
{  public void paintComponent(Graphics g)
   {  super.paintComponent(g);
      Graphics2D g2 = (Graphics2D)g;

      if (clip)
      {  FontRenderContext context = g2.getFontRenderContext();
         Font f = new Font("Serif", Font.PLAIN, 100);
         GeneralPath clipShape = new GeneralPath();

         TextLayout layout = new TextLayout("Hello", f, context);
         AffineTransform transform
            = AffineTransform.getTranslateInstance(0, 100);
         Shape outline = layout.getOutline(transform);
         clipShape.append(outline, false);

         layout = new TextLayout("World", f, context);
         transform
            = AffineTransform.getTranslateInstance(0, 200);
         outline = layout.getOutline(transform);
         clipShape.append(outline, false);

         g2.draw(clipShape);
         g2.clip(clipShape);
      }

      final int NLINES =50;
      Point2D p = new Point2D.Double(0, 0);
      for (int i = 0; i < NLINES; i++)
      {  double x = (2 * getWidth() * i) / NLINES;
```

```
         double y = (2 * getHeight() * (NLINES - 1 - i))
            / NLINES;
         Point2D q = new Point2D.Double(x, y);
         g2.draw(new Line2D.Double(p, q));
      }
   }

   public void setClip(boolean c)
   {  clip = c;
      repaint();
   }

   private boolean clip;
}
```

`java.awt.Graphics`

- `Shape getClip()`
  returns the current clipping shape.

`java.awt.Graphics2D`

- `void clip(Shape s)`
  intersects the current clipping shape with the shape `s`.
- `void setClip(Shape s)`
  sets the current clipping shape to the shape `s`.
- `FontRenderContext getFontRenderContext()`
  returns a font render context that is necessary for constructing `TextLayout` objects.

`java.awt.font.TextLayout`

- `TextLayout(String s, Font f, FontRenderContext context)`
  constructs a text layout object from a given string and font, using the font render context to obtain font properties for a particular device.
- `float getAdvance()`
  returns the width of this text layout.
- `float getAscent()`
- `float getDescent()`
  return the height of this text layout above and below the baseline.
- `float getLeading()`
  returns the distance between successive lines in the font used by this text layout.

Transparency and Composition

In the standard RGB color model, every color is described by its red, green, and blue components. However, it is also convenient to be able to describe areas of an image that are *transparent* or partially transparent. When you superimpose an image onto an existing drawing, the transparent pixels do not obscure the pixels under them at all, whereas partially transparent pixels are mixed with the pixels under them. Figure 7–25 shows the effect of overlaying a partially transparent rectangle on an image. You can still see the details of the image shine through from under the rectangle.

In the Java 2D API, transparency is described by an *alpha channel*. Each pixel has, in addition to its red, green, and blue color components, an alpha value between 0 (fully transparent) and 1 (fully opaque). For example, the rectangle in Figure 7–25 was filled with a pale yellow color with 50% transparency:

```
new Color(0.7F, 0.7F, 0.0F, 0.5F);
```

Figure 7–25: Overlaying a partially transparent rectangle on an image

Now let us look at what happens if you superimpose two shapes. You need to blend or *compose* the colors and alpha values of the source and destination pixels. Porter and Duff, two researchers in the field of computer graphics, have formulated twelve possible *composition rules* for this blending process. The Java 2D API implements eight of these rules. Before we go any further, we'd like to point out that only two of these rules have practical significance. If you find the rules arcane or confusing, just use the `SRC_OVER` rule. It is the default rule for a `Graphics2D` object, and it gives the most intuitive results.

Here is the theory behind the rules. Suppose you have a *source pixel* with alpha value a_S. In the image, there is already a *destination pixel* with alpha value a_D. You want to compose the two. The diagram in Figure 7–26 shows how to design a composition rule.

Porter and Duff consider the alpha value as the probability that the pixel color should be used. From the perspective of the source, there is a probability a_S that it wants to use the source color and a probability of $1 - a_S$ that it doesn't care. The same holds for the destination. When composing the colors, let us assume that the probabilities are independent. Then there are four cases, as shown in Figure 7–26. If the source wants to use the source color and the destination doesn't care, then it seems reasonable to let the source have its way. That's why the upper-right corner of the diagram is labeled "S." The probability for that event is $a_S \cdot (1 - a_D)$. Similarly, the lower-left corner is labeled "D." What should one do if both destination and source would like to select

their color? That's where the Porter-Duff rules come in. If we decide that the source is more important, then we label the lower-right corner with an "S" as well. That rule is called SRC_OVER. In that rule, you combine the source colors with a weight of a_S and the destination colors with a weight of $(1 - a_S) \cdot a_D$.

The visual effect is a blending of the source and destination, with preference given to the source. In particular, if a_S is 1, then the destination color is not taken into account at all. If a_S is zero, then the source pixel is completely transparent and the destination color is unchanged.

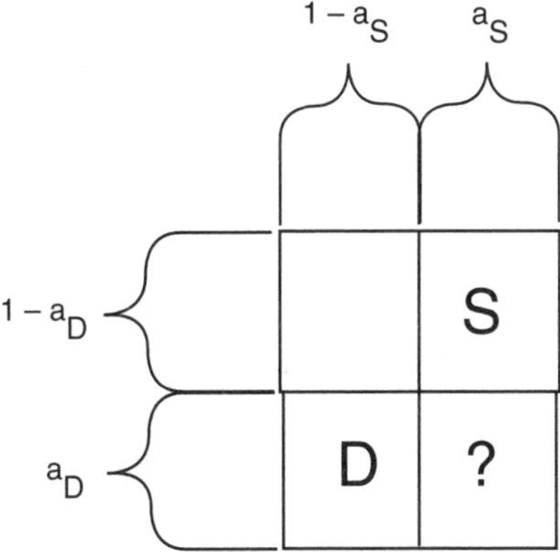

Figure 7–26: Designing a Composition Rule

There are other rules, depending on what letters you put in the boxes of the probability diagram. Table 7–1 and Figure 7–27 show all rules that are supported by the Java 2D API. The images in the figure show the results of the rules when a rectangular source region with an alpha of 0.75 is combined with an elliptical destination region with an alpha of 1.0.

Table 7–1 : The Porter-Duff Composition Rules

CLEAR	Source clears destination
SRC	Source overwrites destination and empty pixels
SRC_OVER	Source blends with destination and overwrites empty pixels
DST_OVER	Source overwrites empty pixels
SRC_IN	Source overwrites destination
SRC_OUT	Source clears destination and overwrites empty pixels
DST_IN	Source alpha modifies destination
DST_OUT	Source alpha complement modifies destination

As you can see, most of the other rules aren't very useful. Consider, as an extreme case, the DST_IN rule. It doesn't take the source color into account at all, but it uses

the alpha of the source to affect the destination. The `SRC` rule is potentially useful—it forces the source color to be used, turning off blending with the destination.

For more information on the Porter-Duff rules, see for example, *Foley, van Dam, Feiner, et al.,* Section 17.6.1.

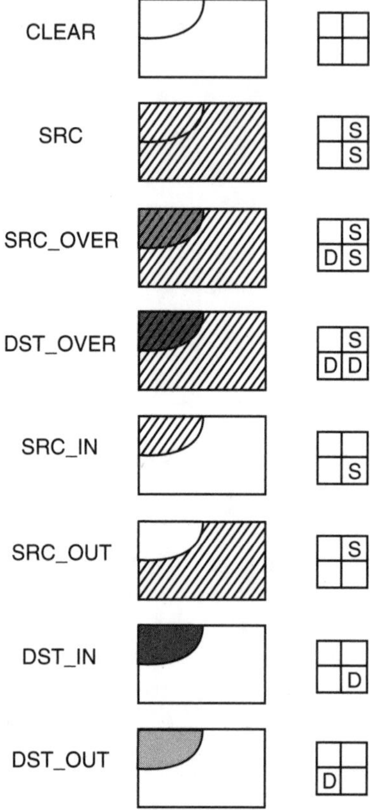

Figure 7–27: Porter-Duff Composition Rules

You use the `setComposite` method of the `Graphics2D` class to install an object of a class that implements the `Composite` interface. The Java 2D API supplies one such class, `AlphaComposite`, that implements the eight Porter-Duff rules in Figure 7–27.

The factory method `getInstance` of the `AlphaComposite` class yields an `AlphaComposite` object. You need to supply the rule and the alpha value to be used for source pixels. For example, consider the following code.

```
int rule = AlphaComposite.SRC_OVER;
float alpha = 0.5;
g2.setComposite(AlphaComposite.getInstance(rule, alpha));
g2.setPaint(Color.blue);
g2.fill(rectangle);
```

Then, the rectangle is painted with blue color and an alpha value of 0.5. Because the composition rule is SRC_OVER, it is transparently overlaid on over the existing image.

The program in Example 7–7 lets you explore these composition rules. Pick a rule from the combo box and use the slider to set the alpha value of the AlphaComposite object.

Furthermore, the program displays a verbal description of each rule. Note that the descriptions are computed from the composition rule diagrams. For example, a "DS" in the second row stands for "blends with destination."

The program has one important twist. There is no guarantee that the graphics context that corresponds to the screen has an alpha channel. (In fact, it generally does not.) When pixels are deposited to a destination without an alpha channel, then the pixel colors are multiplied with the alpha value and the alpha value is discarded. Since several of the Porter-Duff rules use the alpha values of the destination, a destination alpha channel is important. For that reason, we use a buffered image with the ARGB color model to compose the shapes. After the images have been composed, we draw the resulting image to the screen.

```
BufferedImage image = new BufferedImage(getWidth(),
   getHeight(), BufferedImage.TYPE_INT_ARGB);
Graphics2D gImage = image.createGraphics();
// now draw to gImage
g2.drawImage(image, null, 0, 0);
```

Here is the complete code for the program. Figure 7–28 shows the screen display. As you run the program, move the alpha slider from left to right to see the effect on the composed shapes. In particular, note that the only difference between the DST_IN and DST_OUT rules is how the destination (!) color changes when you change the source alpha.

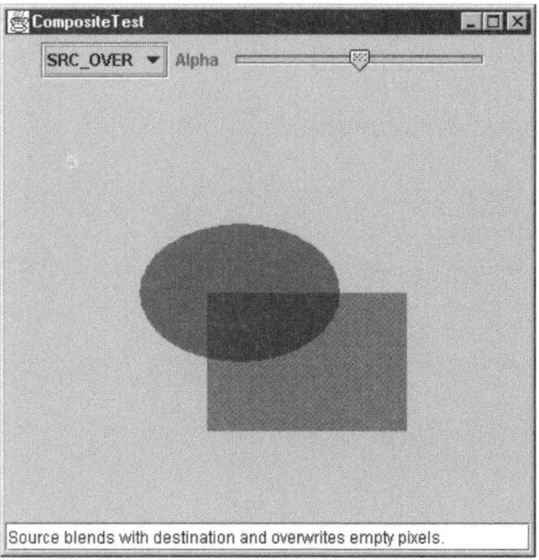

Figure 7–28: The CompositeTest program

Example 7-7: CompositeTest.java

```
import java.awt.*;
import java.awt.event.*;
import java.awt.image.*;
import java.awt.geom.*;
import java.util.*;
import javax.swing.*;
import javax.swing.event.*;

public class CompositeTest
{  public static void main(String[] args)
   {  JFrame frame = new CompositeTestFrame();
      frame.show();
   }
}

class CompositeTestFrame extends JFrame
   implements ActionListener, ChangeListener
{  public CompositeTestFrame()
   {  setTitle("CompositeTest");
      setSize(400, 400);
      addWindowListener(new WindowAdapter()
         {  public void windowClosing(WindowEvent e)
            {  System.exit(0);
            }
         } );

      Container contentPane = getContentPane();
      canvas = new CompositePanel();
      contentPane.add(canvas, "Center");

      ruleCombo = new JComboBox();
      ruleCombo.addItem("CLEAR");
      ruleCombo.addItem("SRC");
      ruleCombo.addItem("SRC_OVER");
      ruleCombo.addItem("DST_OVER");
      ruleCombo.addItem("SRC_IN");
      ruleCombo.addItem("SRC_OUT");
      ruleCombo.addItem("DST_IN");
      ruleCombo.addItem("DST_OUT");
      ruleCombo.addActionListener(this);

      alphaSlider = new JSlider();
      alphaSlider.addChangeListener(this);
      JPanel panel = new JPanel();
      panel.add(ruleCombo);
      panel.add(new JLabel("Alpha"));
      panel.add(alphaSlider);
      contentPane.add(panel, "North");

      explanation = new JTextField();
```

```
      contentPane.add(explanation, "South");

      canvas.setAlpha(alphaSlider.getValue());
      canvas.setRule(ruleCombo.getSelectedItem());
      explanation.setText(canvas.getExplanation());
   }

   public void stateChanged(ChangeEvent event)
   {  canvas.setAlpha(alphaSlider.getValue());
   }

   public void actionPerformed(ActionEvent event)
   {  canvas.setRule(ruleCombo.getSelectedItem());
      explanation.setText(canvas.getExplanation());
   }

   private CompositePanel canvas;
   private JComboBox ruleCombo;
   private JSlider alphaSlider;
   private JTextField explanation;
}

class CompositePanel extends JPanel
{  public CompositePanel()
   {  shape1 = new Ellipse2D.Double(100, 100, 150, 100);
      shape2 = new Rectangle2D.Double(150, 150, 150, 100);
   }

   public void paintComponent(Graphics g)
   {  super.paintComponent(g);
      Graphics2D g2 = (Graphics2D)g;

      BufferedImage image = new BufferedImage(getWidth(),
         getHeight(), BufferedImage.TYPE_INT_ARGB);
      Graphics2D gImage = image.createGraphics();
      gImage.setPaint(Color.red);
      gImage.fill(shape1);
      AlphaComposite composite
         = AlphaComposite.getInstance(rule, alpha);
      gImage.setComposite(composite);
      gImage.setPaint(Color.blue);
      gImage.fill(shape2);
      g2.drawImage(image, null, 0, 0);
   }

   public void setRule(Object r)
   {  if (r.equals("CLEAR"))
      {  rule = AlphaComposite.CLEAR;
         porterDuff1 = "  ";
         porterDuff2 = "  ";
      }
      else if (r.equals("SRC"))
```

```
   {  rule = AlphaComposite.SRC;
      porterDuff1 = " S";
      porterDuff2 = " S";
   }
   else if (r.equals("SRC_OVER"))
   {  rule = AlphaComposite.SRC_OVER;
      porterDuff1 = " S";
      porterDuff2 = "DS";
   }
   else if (r.equals("DST_OVER"))
   {  rule = AlphaComposite.DST_OVER;
      porterDuff1 = " S";
      porterDuff2 = "DD";
   }
   else if (r.equals("SRC_IN"))
   {  rule = AlphaComposite.SRC_IN;
      porterDuff1 = "  ";
      porterDuff2 = " S";
   }
   else if (r.equals("SRC_OUT"))
   {  rule = AlphaComposite.SRC_OUT;
      porterDuff1 = " S";
      porterDuff2 = "  ";
   }
   else if (r.equals("DST_IN"))
   {  rule = AlphaComposite.DST_IN;
      porterDuff1 = "  ";
      porterDuff2 = " D";
   }
   else if (r.equals("DST_OUT"))
   {  rule = AlphaComposite.DST_OUT;
      porterDuff1 = "  ";
      porterDuff2 = "D ";
   }
   repaint();
}

public void setAlpha(int a)
{  alpha = (float)a / 100.0F;
   repaint();
}

public String getExplanation()
{  String r = "Source ";
   if (porterDuff2.equals("  "))
      r += "clears";
   if (porterDuff2.equals(" S"))
      r += "overwrites";
   if (porterDuff2.equals("DS"))
      r += "blends with";
```

```
      if (porterDuff2.equals(" D"))
         r += "alpha modifies";
      if (porterDuff2.equals("D "))
         r += "alpha complement modifies";
      if (!porterDuff2.equals("DD"))
      {  r += " destination";
         if (!porterDuff1.equals("  ")) r += " and ";
      }
      if (porterDuff1.equals(" S"))
         r += "overwrites";
      if (!porterDuff1.equals("  "))
         r += " empty pixels";
      return r + ".";
   }

   private Shape shape1;
   private Shape shape2;
   private float alpha;
   private int rule;
   private String porterDuff1; // row 1 of the rule diagram
   private String porterDuff2; // row 2 of the rule diagram
}
```

`java.awt.Graphics2D`

- `void setComposite(Composite s)`

  sets the composite of this graphics context to the given object that implements the `Composite` interface.

`java.awt.AlphaComposite`

- `static AlphaComposite getInstance(int rule)`
- `static AlphaComposite getInstance(int rule, float alpha)`

  construct an alpha composite object.

Parameters:	`rule`	One of `CLEAR`, `SRC`, `SRC_OVER`, `DST_OVER`, `SRC_IN`, `SRC_OUT`, `DST_IN`, `DST_OUT`
	`alpha`	the alpha value for the source pixels

Rendering Hints

In the preceding sections you have seen that the rendering process is quite complex. While the Java 2D API is surprisingly fast in most cases, there are cases when you would like to have control over trade-offs between speed and quality. You achieve this by setting *rendering hints*. The `setRenderingHint` method of the `Graphics2D` class lets you set a single hint. The hint keys and values are declared in the `RenderingHints` class. Table 7–2 summarizes the choices.

Table 7–2: Rendering Hints

Key	Values	Explanation
KEY_ANTIALIASING	VALUE_ANTIALIAS_ON VALUE_ANTIALIAS_OFF VALUE_ANTIALIAS_ DEFAULT	Turn antialiasing for shapes on or off.
KEY_RENDERING	VALUE_RENDER_QUALITY VALUE_RENDER_SPEED VALUE_RENDER_DEFAULT	When available, select rendering algorithms for greater quality or speed.
KEY_DITHERING	VALUE_DITHER_ENABLE VALUE_DITHER_DISABLE VALUE_DITHER_DEFAULT	Turn dithering for colors on or off. Dithering approximates color values by drawing groups of pixels of similar colors.
KEY_TEXT_ ANTIALIASING	VALUE_TEXT_ANTIALIAS_ON VALUE_TEXT_ANTIALIAS_OFF VALUE_TEXT_ANTIALIAS_ DEFAULT	Turn antialiasing for fonts on or off.
KEY_FRACTIONAL- METRICS	VALUE_FRACTIONALMETRICS_ON VALUE_FRACTIONALMETRICS_OFF VALUE_FRACTIONALMETRICS_ DEFAULT	Turn the computation of fractional character dimensions on or off. Fractional character dimensions lead to better placement of characters.
KEY_ALPHA_ INTERPOLATION	VALUE_ALPHA_INTERPOLATION_ QUALITY VALUE_ALPHA_INTERPOLATION_ SPEED VALUE_ALPHA_INTERPOLATION_ DEFAULT	Turn precise computation of alpha composites on or off.
KEY_COLOR_ RENDERING	VALUE_COLOR_RENDER_ QUALITY VALUE_COLOR_RENDER_ SPEED VALUE_COLOR_RENDER_ DEFAULT	Select quality or speed for color rendering.
KEY_INTERPOLA- TION	VALUE_INTERPOLATION_ NEAREST_NEIGHBOR VALUE_INTERPOLATION_ BILINEAR VALUE_INTERPOLATION_ BICUBIC	Select a rule for interpolating pixels when scaling images.

The most useful of these settings involves *antialiasing.* This is a technique to remove the "jaggies" from slanted lines and curves. As you can see in Figure 7–29, a slanted line must be drawn as a "staircase" of pixels. Especially on low-resolution screens, this can look ugly. But if, rather than drawing each pixel completely on or off, you color in the pixels that are partially covered, with the color value

proportional to the area of the pixel that the line covers, then the result looks much smoother. This technique is called antialiasing. Of course, antialiasing takes a bit longer because it takes time to compute all those color values.

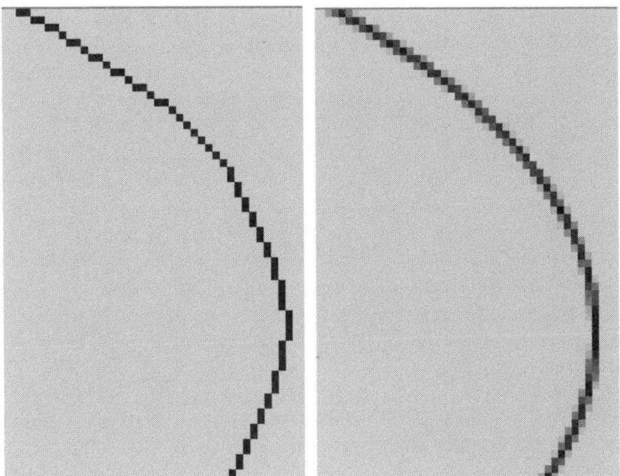

Figure 7–29: Antialiasing

For example, here is how you can request the use of antialiasing.

```
g2.setRenderingHint(RenderingHints.KEY_ANTIALIASING,
   VALUE_ANTIALIAS_ON);
```

It also makes sense to use antialiasing for fonts.

```
g2.setRenderingHint(RenderingHints.KEY_TEXT_ANTIALIASING,
   VALUE_TEXT_ANTIALIAS_ON);
```

The other rendering hints are not as commonly used.

You can also put a bunch of key/value hint pairs into a map and set them all at once by calling the `setRenderingHints` method. Any collection class implementing the map interface will do, but you may as well use the `RenderingHints` class itself. It implements the `Map` interface and supplies a default map implementation if you pass `null` to the constructor. For example,

```
RenderingHints hints = new RenderingHints(null);
hints.put(RenderingHints.KEY_ANTIALIASING,
   VALUE_ANTIALIAS_ON);
hints.put(RenderingHints.KEY_TEXT_ANTIALIASING,
   VALUE_TEXT_ANTIALIAS_ON);
g2.setRenderingHints(hints);
```

That is the technique that we use in Example 7–8. The program draws an image that we thought might benefit from some of the hints. You can turn various rendering hints on or off. Not all platforms support all the hints, so you should not expect every one of the settings to have an effect. On Windows 98, antialiasing smooths out the ellipse, and text antialiasing improves the look of the italic font. If text antialiasing is turned on, then selecting fractional text metrics moves the characters of the string closer together. The other hints had no effect for Windows 98, but they might with other platforms or with more complex images.

Figure 7–30 shows a screen capture of the program.

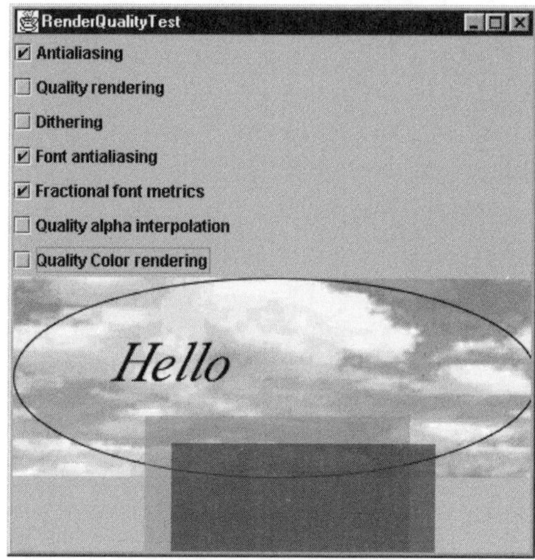

Figure 7–30: The RenderingHints program

Example 7–8: RenderQualityTest.java

```
import java.awt.*;
import java.awt.event.*;
import java.awt.geom.*;
import java.util.*;
import javax.swing.*;

public class RenderQualityTest
{  public static void main(String[] args)
   {  JFrame frame = new RenderQualityTestFrame();
      frame.show();
   }
}

class RenderQualityTestFrame extends JFrame
   implements ActionListener
{  public RenderQualityTestFrame()
   {  setTitle("RenderQualityTest");
      setSize(400, 400);
      addWindowListener(new WindowAdapter()
         {  public void windowClosing(WindowEvent e)
            {  System.exit(0);
```

```
         }
      } );

      checkBoxContainer = Box.createVerticalBox();

      antiAliasingBox
         = makeCheckBox("Antialiasing");
      qualityRenderingBox
         = makeCheckBox("Quality rendering");
      ditheringBox
         = makeCheckBox("Dithering");
      textAntiAliasingBox
         = makeCheckBox("Font antialiasing");
      fractionalMetricsBox
         = makeCheckBox("Fractional font metrics");
      qualityAlphaInterpolationBox
         = makeCheckBox("Quality alpha interpolation");
      qualityColorRenderingBox
         = makeCheckBox("Quality Color rendering");

      Container contentPane = getContentPane();
      canvas = new RenderQualityPanel();
      contentPane.add(canvas, "Center");
      contentPane.add(checkBoxContainer, "North");
   }

   JCheckBox makeCheckBox(String title)
   {  JCheckBox box = new JCheckBox(title);
      box.addActionListener(this);
      checkBoxContainer.add(box);
      return box;
   }

   public void actionPerformed(ActionEvent event)
   {  // get values from all check boxes
      RenderingHints hints = new RenderingHints(null);
      hints.put(RenderingHints.KEY_ANTIALIASING,
         antiAliasingBox.isSelected()
            ? RenderingHints.VALUE_ANTIALIAS_ON
            : RenderingHints.VALUE_ANTIALIAS_OFF);
      hints.put(RenderingHints.KEY_RENDERING,
         qualityRenderingBox.isSelected()
            ? RenderingHints.VALUE_RENDER_QUALITY
            : RenderingHints.VALUE_RENDER_SPEED);
      hints.put(RenderingHints.KEY_DITHERING,
         ditheringBox.isSelected()
            ? RenderingHints.VALUE_DITHER_ENABLE
            : RenderingHints.VALUE_DITHER_DISABLE);
      hints.put(RenderingHints.KEY_TEXT_ANTIALIASING,
         textAntiAliasingBox.isSelected()
            ? RenderingHints.VALUE_TEXT_ANTIALIAS_ON
```

```
               : RenderingHints.VALUE_TEXT_ANTIALIAS_OFF);
         hints.put(RenderingHints.KEY_FRACTIONALMETRICS,
            fractionalMetricsBox.isSelected()
               ? RenderingHints.VALUE_FRACTIONALMETRICS_ON
               : RenderingHints.VALUE_FRACTIONALMETRICS_OFF);
         hints.put(RenderingHints.KEY_ALPHA_INTERPOLATION,
            qualityAlphaInterpolationBox.isSelected()
               ? RenderingHints.VALUE_ALPHA_INTERPOLATION_QUALITY
               : RenderingHints.VALUE_ALPHA_INTERPOLATION_SPEED);
         hints.put(RenderingHints.KEY_COLOR_RENDERING,
            qualityColorRenderingBox.isSelected()
               ? RenderingHints.VALUE_COLOR_RENDER_QUALITY
               : RenderingHints.VALUE_COLOR_RENDER_SPEED);
         canvas.setRenderingHints(hints);
      }

      private RenderQualityPanel canvas;
      private JCheckBox antiAliasingBox;
      private JCheckBox qualityRenderingBox;
      private JCheckBox ditheringBox;
      private JCheckBox textAntiAliasingBox;
      private JCheckBox fractionalMetricsBox;
      private JCheckBox qualityAlphaInterpolationBox;
      private JCheckBox qualityColorRenderingBox;
      private Box checkBoxContainer;
   }

   class RenderQualityPanel extends JPanel
   {  public RenderQualityPanel()
      {  Random generator = new Random();
         color1 = new Color(0.7F, 0.7F, 0.0F, 0.5F);
         color2 = new Color(0.0F, 0.3F, 0.3F, 0.5F);
         image = Toolkit.getDefaultToolkit().getImage
            ("clouds.jpg");
         MediaTracker tracker = new MediaTracker(this);
         tracker.addImage(image, 0);
         try { tracker.waitForID(0); }
         catch (InterruptedException e) {}
      }

      public void paintComponent(Graphics g)
      {  super.paintComponent(g);
         Graphics2D g2 = (Graphics2D)g;
         g2.setRenderingHints(hints);

         g2.drawImage(image, 0, 0, null);
         g2.draw(new Ellipse2D.Double(0, 0,
            image.getWidth(null), image.getHeight(null)));
         g2.setFont(new Font("Serif", Font.ITALIC, 40));
         g2.drawString("Hello", 75, 75);
         g2.setPaint(color1);
         g2.translate(0,-80);
         g2.fill(new Rectangle2D.Double(100, 100, 200, 100));
```

```
      g2.setPaint(color2);
      g2.fill(new Rectangle2D.Double(120, 120, 200, 100));
   }

   public void setRenderingHints(RenderingHints h)
   {  hints = h;
      repaint();
   }

   private RenderingHints hints = new RenderingHints(null);
   private Color color1;
   private Color color2;
   private Image image;
}
```

`java.awt.Graphics2D`

- `void setRenderingHint(RenderingHints.Key key, Object value)`
  sets a rendering hint for this graphics context.
- `void setRenderingHints(Map m)`
  sets all rendering hints whose key/value pairs are stored in the map.

`java.awt.RenderingHints`

- `RenderingHints(Map m)`
  constructs a rendering hints map for storing rendering hints. If `m` is `null`, a default map implementation is provided.

Image Manipulation

Suppose you have an image and you would like to improve its appearance. You then need to access the individual pixels of the image and replace them with other pixels. Or perhaps you want to compute the pixels of an image from scratch, for example, to show the result of physical measurements or a mathematical computation. The `BufferedImage` class gives you control over the pixels in an image, and classes that implement the `BufferedImageOp` interface let you transform images.

This is a major change from the image support in JDK 1.0. At that time, the image classes were optimized to support *incremental rendering*. The original purpose of the classes was to render GIF and JPEG images that are downloaded from the web, a scan line at a time, as soon as partial image data is available. In fact, scan lines can be *interlaced*, with all even scan lines coming first, followed by the odd scan lines. That mechanism lets a browser display an approximation of the image quickly while fetching the remainder of the image data. The `ImageProducer`, `ImageFilter`, and `ImageConsumer` interfaces in JDK 1.0 expose all the complexities of incremental rendering. Writing an image manipulation that fit well into that framework was quite complex.

Fortunately, the need for using these classes has completely gone away. The Java 2 platform replaces the "push model" of JDK 1.0 with a "direct" model that lets you access pixels directly and conveniently. We only cover the direct model in this chapter. The only disadvantage of the direct model is that it requires all image pixels to be in memory. (In practice, the "push model" had the same restriction. It would have required fiendish cunning to write image manipulation algorithms that processed pixels as they became available. Most users of the old model simply buffered the entire image before processing it.) Future versions of the Java platform may support a "pull" model where a processing pipeline can reduce memory consumption and increase speed by only fetching and processing pixels when they are actually needed.

Accessing Image Data

Most of the images that you manipulate are simply read in from an image file—they were either produced by a device such as a digital camera or scanner, or constructed by a drawing program. In this section, we will show you a different technique for constructing an image, namely, to build up an image a pixel at a time.

To create an image, construct a `BufferedImage` object in the usual way.

```
image = new BufferedImage(width, height,
   BufferedImage.TYPE_INT_ARGB);
```

Now, call the `getRaster` method to obtain an object of type `WritableRaster`. You use this object to access and modify the pixels of the image.

```
WritableRaster raster = image.getRaster();
```

The `setPixel` method lets you set an individual pixel. The complexity here is that you can't simply set the pixel to a `Color` value but that you must know how the buffered image specifies color values. That depends on the *type* of the image. If your image has a type of `TYPE_INT_ARGB`, then each pixel is described by four values, for red, green, blue, and alpha, each of which is between 0 and 255. You need to supply them in an array of four integers.

```
int[] black = { 0, 0, 0, 255 };
raster.setPixel(i, j, black);
```

In the lingo of the Java 2D API, these values are called the *sample values* of the pixel.

CAUTION: There are also `setPixel` methods that take array parameters of types `float[]` and `double[]`. However, the values that you need to place into these arrays are *not* normalized color values between 0.0 and 1.0.

```
float[] red = { 1.0F, 0.0F, 0.0F, 1.0F };
raster.setPixel(i, j, red); // ERROR
```

You need to supply values between 0 and 255, no matter what the type of the array is.

You can supply batches of pixels with the `setPixels` method. Specify the starting pixel position and the width and height of the rectangle that you want to set. Then, supply an array that contains the sample values for all pixels. For example,

if your buffered image has a type of `TYPE_INT_ARGB`, then you supply the red, green, blue, and alpha value of the first pixel, then the red, green, blue, and alpha value for the second pixel, and so on.

```
int[] pixels = new int[4 * width * height];
pixels[0] = . . . // red value for first pixel
pixels[1] = . . . // green value for first pixel
pixels[2] = . . . // blue value for first pixel
pixels[3] = . . . // alpha value for first pixel
. . .
raster.setPixels(x, y, width, height, pixels);
```

Conversely, to read a pixel, you use the `getPixel` method. Supply an array of four integers to hold the sample values.

```
int[] sample = new int[4];
raster.getPixel(x, y, sample);
Color c = new Color(sample[0], sample[1], sample[2], sample[3]);
```

You can read multiple pixels with the `getPixels` method.

```
raster.getPixels(x, y, width, height, samples);
```

If you use an image type other than `TYPE_INT_ARGB` and you know how that type represents pixel values, then you can still use the `getPixel`/`setPixel` methods. However, you have to know the encoding of the sample values in the particular image type.

If you need to manipulate an image with an arbitrary, unknown image type, then you have to work a bit harder. Every image type has a *color model* that can translate between sample value arrays and the standard RGB color model.

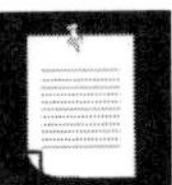

NOTE: The RGB color model isn't as standard as you might think. The exact look of a color value depends on the characteristics of the imaging device. Digital cameras, scanners, monitors, and LCD displays all have their own idiosyncrasies. As a result, the same RGB value can look quite different on different devices. The International Color Consortium (`www.color.org`) recommends that all color data be accompanied by an *ICC profile* that specifies how the colors map to a standard form such as the 1931 CIE XYZ color specification. That specification was designed in 1931 by the Commission Internationale de l'Eclairage or CIE (`www.cie.co.at/cie`), the international organization in charge of providing technical guidance in all matters of illumination and color. The specification is a standard method for representing all colors that the human eye can perceive as a triple of coordinates called X, Y, Z. (See, for example, *Foley, van Dam, Feiner, et al.*, Chapter 13, for more information on the 1931 CIE XYZ specification.) However, ICC profiles are complex. A simpler proposed standard, called sRGB (`http://www.w3.org/Graphics/Color/sRGB.html`), specifies an exact mapping between RGB values and 1931 CIE XYZ values that was designed to work well with typical color monitors. The Java 2D API uses that mapping when converting between RGB and other color spaces.

The `getColorModel` method returns the color model.

```
ColorModel model = image.getColorModel();
```

To find the color value of a pixel, you call the `getDataElements` method of the `Raster` class. That call returns an `Object` that contains a color model specific description of the color value.

```
Object data = raster.getDataElements(x, y, null);
```

NOTE: The object that is returned by the `getDataElements` method is actually an array of sample values. You don't need to know that to process it, but it explains why the method is called `getDataElements`.

The color model can translate the object to standard ARGB values. The `getRGB` method returns an `int` values that has the alpha, red, green, and blue values packed in four blocks of 8 bits each. You can construct a `Color` value out of that integer with the `Color(int argb, boolean hasAlpha)` constructor.

```
int argb = model.getRGB(data);
Color color = new Color(argb, true);
```

When you want to set a pixel to a particular color, you have to reverse these steps. The `getRGB` method of the `Color` class yields an `int` value with the alpha, red, green, and blue values. Supply that value to the `getDataElements` method of the `ColorModel` class. The return value is an `Object` that contains the color-model-specific description of the color value. Pass the object to the `setDataElements` method of the `WritableRaster` class.

```
int argb = color.getRGB();
Object data = model.getDataElements(argb, null);
raster.setDataElements(x, y, data);
```

To illustrate how to use these methods to build an image from individual pixels, we bow to tradition and draw a Mandelbrot set, as shown in Figure 7–31.

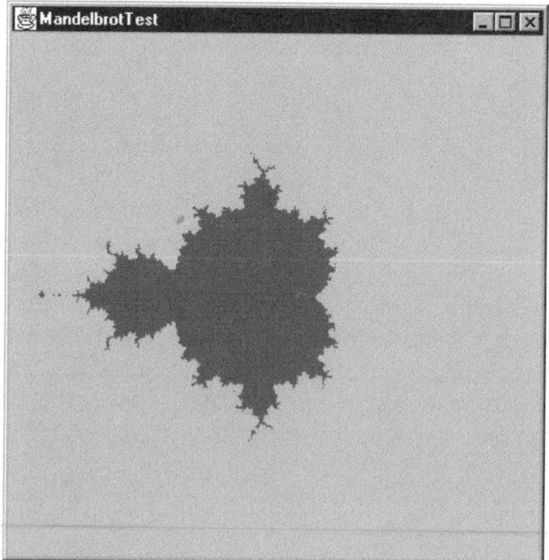

Figure 7–31: A Mandelbrot set

The idea of the Mandelbrot set is that you associate with each point in the plane a sequence of numbers. If that sequence stays bounded, you color the point. If it "escapes to infinity," you leave it transparent. The formulas for the number sequences come ultimately from the mathematics of complex numbers. We just take them for granted. For more on the mathematics of fractals, there are hundreds of books out there; one that is quite thick and comprehensive is *Chaos and Fractals: New Frontiers of Science* by Heinz-Otto Peitgen, Hartmut Jurgens, and Dietmar Saupe [Springer Verlag 1992].

Here is how you can construct the simplest Mandelbrot set. For each point (a,b), you look at sequences that start with (x, y) = (0, 0) and iterate:

$$x_{\text{new}} = x^2 - y^2 + a$$
$$y_{\text{new}} = 2 \cdot x \cdot y + b$$

Check whether the sequence stays bounded or "escapes to infinity," that is, whether x and y keep getting larger. It turns out that if x or y ever get larger than 2, then the sequence escapes to infinity. Only the pixels that correspond to points (a,b) leading to a bounded sequence are colored.

Example 7–9 shows the code. In this program, we demonstrate how to use the `ColorModel` class for translating `Color` values into pixel data. That process is independent of the image type. Just for fun, change the color type of the buffered image to `TYPE_BYTE_GRAY`. You don't need to change any other code—the color model of the image automatically takes care of the conversion from colors to sample values.

Example 7–9: MandelbrotTest.java

```
import java.awt.*;
import java.awt.event.*;
import java.awt.image.*;
import javax.swing.*;

public class MandelbrotTest
{  public static void main(String[] args)
   {  JFrame frame = new MandelbrotFrame();
      frame.show();
   }
}

class MandelbrotFrame extends JFrame
{  public MandelbrotFrame()
   {  setTitle("MandelbrotTest");
      setSize(400, 400);
      addWindowListener(new WindowAdapter()
         {  public void windowClosing(WindowEvent e)
```

```
               {  System.exit(0);
               }
            } );

         Container contentPane = getContentPane();
         contentPane.add(new MandelbrotPanel(), "Center");
      }
   }

   class MandelbrotPanel extends JPanel
   {  public void paintComponent(Graphics g)
      {  super.paintComponent(g);
         BufferedImage image = new BufferedImage(getWidth(),
            getHeight(), BufferedImage.TYPE_INT_ARGB);
         generate(image);
         g.drawImage(image, 0, 0, null);
      }

      public void generate(BufferedImage image)
      {  int width = image.getWidth();
         int height = image.getHeight();
         WritableRaster raster = image.getRaster();
         ColorModel model = image.getColorModel();

         Color fractalColor = Color.red;
         int argb = fractalColor.getRGB();
         Object colorData = model.getDataElements(argb, null);

         for (int i = 0; i < width; i++)
            for (int j = 0; j < height; j++)
            {  double a = XMIN + i * (XMAX - XMIN) / width;
               double b = YMIN + j * (YMAX - YMIN) / height;
               if (!escapesToInfinity(a, b))
                  raster.setDataElements(i, j, colorData);
            }
      }

      private boolean escapesToInfinity(double a, double b)
      {  double x = 0.0;
         double y = 0.0;
         int iterations = 0;
         do
         {  double xnew = x * x - y * y + a;
            double ynew = 2 * x * y + b;
            x = xnew;
            y = ynew;
            iterations++;
            if (iterations == MAX_ITERATIONS) return false;
         }
         while (x <= 2 && y <= 2);
         return true;
```

```
    }

    private static final double XMIN = -2;
    private static final double XMAX = 2;
    private static final double YMIN = -2;
    private static final double YMAX = 2;
    private static final int MAX_ITERATIONS = 16;
}
```

`java.awt.image.BufferedImage`

- `BufferedImage(int width, int height, int imageType)`

  constructs a buffered image object.

  Parameters:

`width, height`	the image dimensions
`imageType`	a type such as `TYPE_INT_RGB`, `TYPE_INT_ARGB`, `TYPE_BYTE_GRAY`, `TYPE_BYTE_INDEXED`, `TYPE_USHORT_555_RGB`, and so on

- `ColorModel getColorModel()`

  returns the color model of this buffered image.

- `WritableRaster getRaster()`

  gets the raster for accessing and modifying pixels of this buffered image.

`java.awt.image.Raster`

- `Object getDataElements(int x, int y, Object data)`

  returns the sample data for a raster point, in an array whose element type and length depends on the color model. If `data` is not `null`, it is assumed to be an array that is appropriate for holding sample data and it is filled. If `data` is `null`, a new array is allocated.

  Parameters:

`x, y`	the pixel location
`data`	`null` or an array that is suitable for being filled with the sample data for a pixel. Its element type and length depend on the color model.

- `int[] getPixel(int x, int y, int w, int h, int[] sampleValues)`
- `float[] getPixel(int x, int y, int w, int h, float[] sampleValues)`
- `double[] getPixel(int x, int y, int w, int h, double[] sampleValues)`
- `int[] getPixels(int x, int y, int w, int h, int[] sampleValues)`
- `float[] getPixels(int x, int y, int w, int h, float[] sampleValues)`

- `double[] getPixels(int x, int y, int w, int h, double[] sampleValues)`

  return the sample values for a raster point, or a rectangle of raster points, in an array whose length depends on the color model. If `sampleValues` is not `null`, it is assumed to be sufficiently long for holding the sample values and it is filled. If `sampleValues` is `null`, a new array is allocated. These methods are only useful if you know the meaning of the sample values for a color model.

Parameters:	`x,y`	the raster point location, or the top-left corner of the rectangle
	`w,h`	the width and height of the rectangle of raster points
	`sampleValues`	`null` or an array that is sufficiently long to be filled with the sample values

`java.awt.image.WritableRaster`

- `void setDataElements(int x, int y, Object data)`

  sets the sample data for a raster point.

Parameters:	`x, y`	the pixel location
	`data`	an array filled with the sample data for a pixel. Its element type and length depend on the color model.

- `void setPixel(int x, int y, int w, int h, int[] sampleValues)`
- `void setPixel(int x, int y, int w, int h, float[] sampleValues)`
- `void setPixel(int x, int y, int w, int h, double[] sampleValues)`
- `void setPixels(int x, int y, int w, int h, int[] sampleValues)`
- `void setPixels(int x, int y, int w, int h, float[] sampleValues)`
- `void setPixels(int x, int y, int w, int h, double[] sampleValues)`

  set the sample values for a raster point or a rectangle of raster points. These methods are only useful if you know the encoding of the sample values for a color model.

Parameters:	`x,y`	the raster point location, or the top-left corner of the rectangle
	`w,h`	the width and height of the rectangle of raster points
	`sampleValues`	an array filled with the sample data. Its element type and length depend on the color model.

java.awt.image.ColorModel

- `int getRGB(Object data)`

  returns the ARGB value that corresponds to the sample data passed in `data`.

Parameters:	`data`	an array filled with the sample data for a pixel. Its element type and length depend on the color model.

- `Object getDataElements(int argb, Object data);`

  returns the sample data for a color value. If `data` is not `null`, it is assumed to be an array that is appropriate for holding sample data and it is filled. If `data` is `null`, a new array is allocated.

Parameters:	`argb`	the color value
	`data`	`null` or an array that is suitable for being filled with the sample data for a color value. Its element type and length depend on the color model.

java.awt.Color

- `Color(int argb, boolean hasAlpha)`

  creates a color with the specified combined ARGB value if `hasAlpha` is `true` or the specified RGB value if `hasAlpha` is `false`.

- `int getRGB()`

  returns the ARGB color value corresponding to this color.

Filtering Images

In the preceding section, you saw how to build up an image from scratch. However, often you want to access image data for a different reason: you already have an image and you want to improve it in some way.

Of course, you can use the `getPixel`/`getDataElements` methods that you saw in the preceding section to read the image data, manipulate them, and then write them back. But fortunately Java 2 technology already supplies a number of *filters* that carry out common image processing operations for you.

The image manipulations all implement the `BufferedImageOp` interface. After you construct the operation, you simply call the `filter` method to transform an image into another.

```
BufferedImageOp op = . . .;
BufferedImage filteredImage
```

```
    = new BufferedImage(image.getWidth(), image.getHeight(),
        image.getType());
op.filter(image, filteredImage);
```

Some operations can transform an image in place (`op.filter(image, image)`), but most can't.

There are five classes that implement the `BufferedImageOp` interface:

```
AffineTransformOp
RescaleOp
LookupOp
ColorConvertOp
ConvolveOp
```

The `AffineTransformOp` carries out an affine transformation on the pixels. For example, here is how you can rotate an image about its center.

```
AffineTransform transform
    = AffineTransform.getRotateInstance(Math.toRadians(angle),
        image.getWidth() / 2, image.getHeight() / 2);
AffineTransformOp op
    = new AffineTransformOp(transform, interpolation);
op.filter(image, filteredImage);
```

The `AffineTransformOp` constructor requires an affine transform and an *interpolation* strategy. Interpolation is necessary to determine pixels in the target image if the source pixels are transformed somewhere between target pixels. For example, if you rotate source pixels, then they will generally not fall exactly onto target pixels. There are two interpolation strategies: `AffineTransformOp.TYPE_BILINEAR` and `AffineTransformOp.TYPE_NEAREST_NEIGHBOR`. Bilinear interpolation takes a bit longer but looks better.

The program in Example 7–10 lets you rotate an image by 5 degrees (see Figure 7–32).

Figure 7–32: A rotated image

The `RescaleOp` carries out a rescaling operation

$$x_{new} = a \cdot x + b$$

for all sample values x in the image. Sample values that are too large or small after the rescaling are set to the largest or smallest legal value. If the image is in ARGB

format, the scaling is carried out separately for the red, green, and blue values, but not for the alpha values. The effect of rescaling with $a > 1$ is to brighten the image. You construct the RescaleOp by specifying the scaling parameters and optional rendering hints. In Example 7–10, we use

```
float a = 1.5f;
float b = -20.0f;
RescaleOp op = new RescaleOp(a, b, null);
```

The LookupOp operation lets you specify an arbitrary mapping of sample values. You supply a table that specifies how each value should be mapped. In the example program, we compute the *negative* of all colors, changing the color c to $255 - c$.

The LookupOp constructor requires an object of type LookupTable and a map of optional hints. The LookupTable class is abstract. There are two concrete subclasses: ByteLookupTable and ShortLookupTable. Since RGB color values are bytes, we use the ByteLookupTable. You construct such a table from an array of bytes and an integer offset into that array. Here is how we construct the LookupOp for the example program.

```
byte negative[] = new byte[256];
for (int i = 0; i < 256; i++)
   negative[i] = (byte)(255 - i);
ByteLookupTable table = new ByteLookupTable(0, negative);
LookupOp op = new LookupOp(table, null);
```

The lookup is applied to each color value separately, but not to the alpha value.

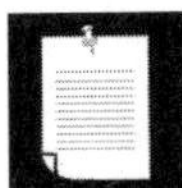

NOTE: You cannot apply a LookupOp to an image with an indexed color model. (In those images, each sample value is an offset into a color palette).

The ColorConvertOp is useful for color space conversions. We do not discuss it here.

The most powerful of the transformations is the ConvolveOp, which carries out a mathematical *convolution*. We do not want to get too deeply into the mathematical details of convolution, but the basic idea is simple. Consider, for example, the *blur filter* (see Figure 7–33).

Figure 7–33: Blurring an image

The blurring is achieved by replacing each pixel with the *average* value from the pixel and its eight neighbors. Intuitively, it makes sense why this operation would blur out the picture. Mathematically, the averaging can be expressed as a convolution operation with the following *kernel:*

$$\begin{bmatrix} \frac{1}{9} & \frac{1}{9} & \frac{1}{9} \\ \frac{1}{9} & \frac{1}{9} & \frac{1}{9} \\ \frac{1}{9} & \frac{1}{9} & \frac{1}{9} \end{bmatrix}$$

The kernel of a convolution is a matrix that tells what weights should be applied to the neighboring values. The kernel above leads to a blurred image. A different kernel

$$\begin{bmatrix} 0 & -1 & 0 \\ -1 & 4 & -1 \\ 0 & -1 & 0 \end{bmatrix}$$

carries out *edge detection,* locating areas of color changes (see Figure 7–34). Edge detection is an important technique for analyzing photographic images.

Figure 7–34: Edge detection

To construct a convolution operation, you first set up an array of the values for the kernel and construct a `Kernel` object. Then, construct a `ConvolveOp` object from the kernel and use it for filtering.

```
float[] elements =
   {  0.0f, -1.0f, 0.0f,
     -1.0f,  4.f, -1.0f,
      0.0f, -1.0f, 0.0f
   };
Kernel kernel = new Kernel(3, 3, elements);
ConvolveOp op = new ConvolveOp(kernel);
op.filter(image, filteredImage);
```

The program in Example 7–10 allows a user to load in a GIF or JPEG image and to carry out the image manipulations that we discussed. Thanks to the power of the image operations that the Java 2D API provides, the program is very simple.

NOTE: At the time of this writing, the Java platform has no official support for saving images in GIF or JPEG format. However, there is a package, `com.sun.image.codec.jpeg`, that is part of the JDK from Sun Microsystems and that supports saving images in JPEG format. You can find more information about this package at `http://java.sun.com/products/jdk/1.2/docs/guide/2d/api-jpeg/overview-summary.html`. You can find a GIF encoder at `www.acme.com/java`.

Example 7–10: ImageProcessingTest.java

```
import javax.swing.*;
import java.awt.*;
import java.awt.event.*;
import java.awt.geom.*;
import java.awt.image.*;
import java.io.*;

public class ImageProcessingTest
{  public static void main(String[] args)
   {  JFrame frame = new ImageProcessingFrame();
      frame.show();
   }
}

class ImageProcessingFrame extends JFrame
   implements ActionListener
{  public ImageProcessingFrame()
   {  setTitle("ImageProcessingTest");
      setSize(300, 400);
      addWindowListener(new WindowAdapter()
         {  public void windowClosing(WindowEvent e)
            {  System.exit(0);
            }
         } );

      Container contentPane = getContentPane();
      panel = new ImageProcessingPanel();
      contentPane.add(panel, "Center");

      JMenu fileMenu = new JMenu("File");
      openItem = new JMenuItem("Open");
      openItem.addActionListener(this);
      fileMenu.add(openItem);

      exitItem = new JMenuItem("Exit");
      exitItem.addActionListener(this);
      fileMenu.add(exitItem);

      JMenu editMenu = new JMenu("Edit");
      blurItem = new JMenuItem("Blur");
      blurItem.addActionListener(this);
      editMenu.add(blurItem);
```

```
      sharpenItem = new JMenuItem("Sharpen");
      sharpenItem.addActionListener(this);
      editMenu.add(sharpenItem);

      brightenItem = new JMenuItem("Brighten");
      brightenItem.addActionListener(this);
      editMenu.add(brightenItem);

      edgeDetectItem = new JMenuItem("Edge detect");
      edgeDetectItem.addActionListener(this);
      editMenu.add(edgeDetectItem);

      negativeItem = new JMenuItem("Negative");
      negativeItem.addActionListener(this);
      editMenu.add(negativeItem);

      rotateItem = new JMenuItem("Rotate");
      rotateItem.addActionListener(this);
      editMenu.add(rotateItem);

      JMenuBar menuBar = new JMenuBar();
      menuBar.add(fileMenu);
      menuBar.add(editMenu);
      setJMenuBar(menuBar);
   }

   public void actionPerformed(ActionEvent evt)
   {  Object source = evt.getSource();
      if (source == openItem)
      {  JFileChooser chooser = new JFileChooser();
         chooser.setCurrentDirectory(new File("."));

         chooser.setFileFilter(new
            javax.swing.filechooser.FileFilter()
            {  public boolean accept(File f)
               {  String name = f.getName().toLowerCase();
                  return name.endsWith(".gif")
                     || name.endsWith(".jpg")
                     || name.endsWith(".jpeg")
                     || f.isDirectory();
               }
               public String getDescription()
               {  return "Image files";
               }
            });

         int r = chooser.showOpenDialog(this);
         if(r == JFileChooser.APPROVE_OPTION)
         {  String name
               = chooser.getSelectedFile().getAbsolutePath();
            panel.loadImage(name);
```

```
         }
      }
      else if (source == exitItem) System.exit(0);
      else if (source == blurItem) panel.blur();
      else if (source == sharpenItem) panel.sharpen();
      else if (source == brightenItem) panel.brighten();
      else if (source == edgeDetectItem) panel.edgeDetect();
      else if (source == negativeItem) panel.negative();
      else if (source == rotateItem) panel.rotate();
   }

   private ImageProcessingPanel panel;
   private JMenuItem openItem;
   private JMenuItem exitItem;
   private JMenuItem blurItem;
   private JMenuItem sharpenItem;
   private JMenuItem brightenItem;
   private JMenuItem edgeDetectItem;
   private JMenuItem negativeItem;
   private JMenuItem rotateItem;
}

class ImageProcessingPanel extends JPanel
{  public void paintComponent(Graphics g)
   {  super.paintComponent(g);
      if (image != null)
         g.drawImage(image, 0, 0, null);
   }

   public void loadImage(String name)
   {  Image loadedImage
         = Toolkit.getDefaultToolkit().getImage(name);
      MediaTracker tracker = new MediaTracker(this);
      tracker.addImage(loadedImage, 0);
      try { tracker.waitForID(0); }
      catch (InterruptedException e) {}
      image = new BufferedImage(loadedImage.getWidth(null),
         loadedImage.getHeight(null), BufferedImage.TYPE_INT_RGB);
      Graphics2D g2 = image.createGraphics();
      g2.drawImage(loadedImage, 0, 0, null);

      repaint();
   }

   private void filter(BufferedImageOp op)
   {  BufferedImage filteredImage
         = new BufferedImage(image.getWidth(), image.getHeight(),
            image.getType());
      op.filter(image, filteredImage);
      image = filteredImage;
      repaint();
```

```
}

private void convolve(float[] elements)
{  Kernel kernel = new Kernel(3, 3, elements);
   ConvolveOp op = new ConvolveOp(kernel);
   filter(op);
}

public void blur()
{  float weight = 1.0f/9.0f;
   float[] elements = new float[9];
   for (int i = 0; i < 9; i++)
      elements[i] = weight;
   convolve(elements);
}

public void sharpen()
{  float[] elements =
      {  0.0f, -1.0f, 0.0f,
         -1.0f,  5.f, -1.0f,
         0.0f, -1.0f, 0.0f
      };
   convolve(elements);
}

void edgeDetect()
{  float[] elements =
      {  0.0f, -1.0f, 0.0f,
         -1.0f,  4.f, -1.0f,
         0.0f, -1.0f, 0.0f
      };
   convolve(elements);
}

public void brighten()
{  float a = 1.5f;
   float b = -20.0f;
   RescaleOp op = new RescaleOp(a, b, null);
   filter(op);
}

void negative()
{  byte negative[] = new byte[256];
   for (int i = 0; i < 256; i++)
      negative[i] = (byte)(255 - i);
   ByteLookupTable table = new ByteLookupTable(0, negative);
   LookupOp op = new LookupOp(table, null);
   filter(op);
}

void rotate()
{  AffineTransform transform
```

```
            = AffineTransform.getRotateInstance(Math.toRadians(5),
               image.getWidth() / 2, image.getHeight() / 2);
         AffineTransformOp op = new AffineTransformOp(transform,
            AffineTransformOp.TYPE_BILINEAR);
         filter(op);
      }

   private BufferedImage image;
}
```

java.awt.image.BufferedImageOp

- `BufferedImage filter(BufferedImage source, BufferedImage dest)`

  applies the image operation to the source image and stores the result in the destination image. If `dest` is `null`, a new destination image is created. The destination image is returned.

java.awt.image.AffineTransformOp

- `AffineTransformOp(AffineTransform t, int interpolationType)`

  constructs an affine transform operator.

Parameters:	`t`	an affine transform
	`interpolationType`	one of `TYPE_BILINEAR` or `TYPE_NEAREST_NEIGHBOR`

java.awt.image.RescaleOp

- `RescaleOp(float a, float b, RenderingHints hints)`

  constructs a rescale operator.

Parameters	`a, b`	coefficients of the transformation $x_{new} = a \cdot x + b$ that is applied to the sample values
	`hints`	rendering hints for color matching; can be `null`

java.awt.image.LookupOp

- `LookupOp(LookupTable table, RenderingHints hints)`

  constructs a lookup operator.

Parameters	`table`	the table for mapping the sample values
	`hints`	rendering hints for color matching; can be `null`

`java.awt.image.ByteLookupTable`

- `ByteLookupTable(int offset, byte[] data)`
  constructs a byte lookup table.

Parameters:	`offset`	position of first data value to be used
	`data`	the table data

`java.awt.image.ConvolveOp`

- `ConvolveOp(Kernel kernel)`
- `ConvolveOp(Kernel kernel, int edgeCondition, RenderingHints hints)`
  construct a convolution operator.

Parameters:	`kernel`	the kernel matrix for the convolution
	`edgeCondition`	specifies how edge values should be treated: one of `EDGE_NO_OP` and `EDGE_ZERO_FILL`. Edge values need to be treated specially because they don't have sufficient neighboring values to compute the convolution. The default is `EDGE_ZERO_FILL`.
	`hints`	rendering hints for color matching; can be `null`

`java.awt.image.Kernel`

- `Kernel(int width, int height, float[] data)`
  constructs a kernel.

Parameters:	`width, height`	dimensions of the kernel matrix
	`data`	entries of the kernel matrix

Printing

The original Java Development Kit had no support for printing at all. It was not possible to print from applets, and you had to get a third-party library if you wanted to print in an application. JDK 1.1 introduced very lightweight printing support, just enough to produce simple printouts, as long as you were not too particular about the print quality. The 1.1 printing model was designed to allow browser vendors to print the surface of an applet as it appears on a web page (which, however, the browser vendors have not embraced). Apart from that, it is best if the 1.1 printing model sinks into the obscurity it so richly deserves.

The Java 2 platform finally has the beginnings of a robust printing model that is fully integrated with 2D graphics. In this section, we show you how you can

easily print a drawing on a single sheet of paper, how you can manage a multi-page printout, and how you can benefit from the elegance of the Java 2D imaging model and easily generate a print preview dialog.

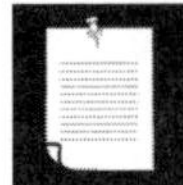

NOTE: The Java 2 platform also has support for printing user interface components. We do not cover this topic because it is mostly of interest to implementors of browsers, screen grabbers, and so on. For more information on printing components, see for example Marty Hall's tutorial at `www.apl.jhu.edu/~hall/java/Swing-Tutorial/Swing-Tutorial-Printing.html`.

Printing Single Sheets

To generate a printout, you need to take care of at least two items.

- You need to supply an object that implements the `Printable` interface.
- You need to start a print job.

The `Printable` interface has a single method:

```
int print(Graphics g, PageFormat format, int page)
```

That method is called whenever the print engine needs to have a page formatted for printing. Your code draws the text and image that need to be printed onto the graphics context. The page format tells you the paper size and the print margins. The page number tells you which page you need to render.

To start a print job, you use the `PrinterJob` class. First, you call the static `getPrinterJob` method to get a print job object. Call the `defaultPage` method to obtain a default page format and then use the `setPrintable` method to set the `Printable` object that renders the page contents.

```
PrinterJob printJob = PrinterJob.getPrinterJob();
pageFormat = printJob.defaultPage();
printJob.setPrintable(printable, pageFormat);
```

CAUTION: There is a class `PrintJob` that handles JDK 1.1 style printing. That class is now obsolete. Do not confuse it with the `PrinterJob` class.

Before starting the print job, you should call the `printDialog` method to display a print dialog (see Figure 7–35). That dialog gives the user a chance to select the page range that should be printed. More importantly, the print dialog lets the user change printer settings. The print dialog is a native dialog since many printer manufacturers supply a custom dialog, written for display by the host operating system, to select advanced printing features (such as color, collating, two-sided printing, and so on).

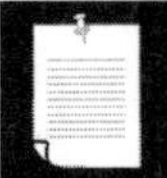

NOTE: It would make more sense if the Java platform provided its own dialog for page selection and used a native dialog only for printer settings. This may happen at some point in the future.

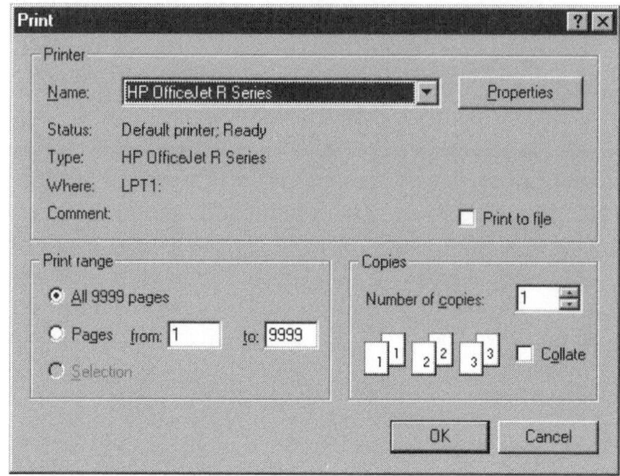

Figure 7–35: A print dialog

When you make a print job out of a `Printable` object, then the print job does not know how many pages you want to print. It simply keeps calling the `print` method. As long as the `print` method returns the value `Printable.PAGE_EXISTS`, the print job keeps producing pages. When the `print` method returns `Printable.NO_SUCH_PAGE`, the print job stops.

CAUTION: The page numbers that the print job passes to the `print` method start with page 0.

Therefore, the print job doesn't have an accurate page count until after the printout is complete. For that reason, the print dialog displays a page range of 1–9999. You will see in the next section how to avoid this blemish by supplying a `Book` object to the print job.

The `printDialog` method returns `true` if the user clicked "OK", and `false` if the user canceled the dialog. If the user accepted, call the `print` method of the `PrintJob` class to start the printing process. The `print` method may throw a `PrinterException`. Here is the outline of the printing code.

```
if (printJob.printDialog())
{  try
   {  printJob.print();
   }
   catch (PrinterException exception)
   {  . . .
   }
}
```

During the printing process, the print job repeatedly calls the `print` method of the `Printable` object. The print job is allowed to make multiple calls *for the same page*. You should therefore not count pages inside the `print` method but always rely on the page number parameter. There is a good reason why the print

job may call the `print` method repeatedly for the same page. Some printers, in particular dot-matrix and inkjet printers, use *banding*. They print one band at a time, advance the paper, and then print the next band. The print job may use banding even for laser printers that print a full page at a time—it gives the print job a way of managing the size of the spool file.

If the print job needs the `Printable` object to print a band, then it sets the clip area of the graphics context to the requested band and calls the `print` method. Its drawing operations will be clipped against the band rectangle, and only those drawing elements that show up in the band will be rendered. Your `print` method does not need to be aware of that process, with one caveat: it should *not* interfere with the clip area.

CAUTION: The `Graphics` object that your `print` method gets is also clipped against the page margins. If you replace the clip area, you can draw outside the margins. Especially in a printer graphics context, you need to respect the clipping area. Call `clip`, not `setClip`, to further restrict the clipping area. If you must remove a clip area, then make sure to call `getClip` at the beginning of your `print` method, and restore that clip area.

The `PageFormat` parameter of the `print` method contains information about the printed page. The methods

```
getWidth
getHeight
```

return the paper size, measured in *points*. One point is 1/72 of an inch. (An inch equals 25.4 millimeters.) For example, A4 paper is approximately 595 by 842 points, and US letter size paper is 612 by 792 points.

Points are a common measurement in the printing trade in the United States. Much to the chagrin of the rest of the world, the printing package uses point units for two purposes. Paper sizes and paper margins are measured in points. And the default unit for all print graphics contexts is one point. You can verify that in the example program at the end of this section. The program prints two lines of text that are 72 units apart from another. Run the example program and measure the distance between the baselines. They are exactly 1 inch or 25.4 millimeters apart.

The `getWidth` and `getHeight` methods of the `PageFormat` class give you the complete paper size. Not all of the paper area is printable. Users typically select margins, and even if they don't, printers need to somehow grip the sheets of paper on which they print and therefore have a small unprintable area around the edges. The methods

```
getImageableWidth
getImageableHeight
```

tell you the dimensions of the area that you can actually fill. However, the margins need not be symmetrical, so you also need to know the top-left corner of the imageable area (see Figure 7–36), which is obtained by the methods

```
getImageableX
getImageableY
```

TIP: The graphics context that you receive in the `print` method is clipped to exclude the margins. But in the versions of the JDK that we tested, the origin of the coordinate system is nevertheless the top-left corner of the paper. It makes sense to translate the coordinate system to start at the top-left corner of the imageable area. Simply start your `print` method with

```
g.translate(pageFormat.getImageableX(),
   pageFormat.getImageableY());
```

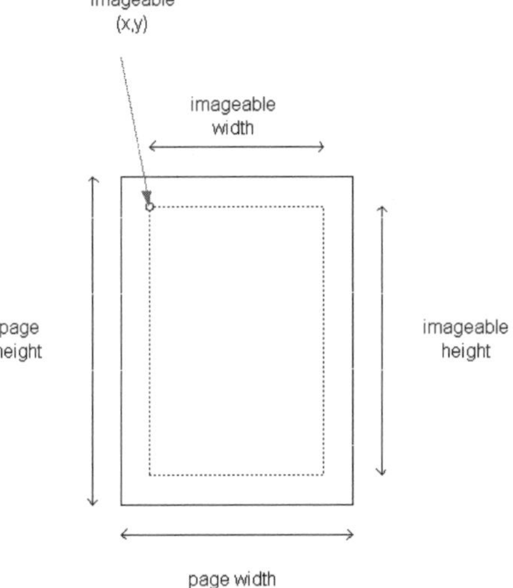

Figure 7–36: Page format measurements

If you want to have your users choose the settings for the page margins or have them switch between portrait and landscape orientation, then you can call the `pageDialog` method of the `PrintJob` class. Figure 7–37 shows a page format dialog for the Windows operating system.

You pass a default `PageFormat` object to the `pageDialog` method. The method clones that object, modifies it according to the user selections in the dialog, and returns the cloned object.

```
PageFormat defaultFormat = printJob.defaultPage();
PageFormat selectedFormat = printJob.pageDialog(defaultFormat);
```

NOTE: In the versions of the JDK that we tested on Windows, the page format dialog was not properly initialized with the values of the page format that was passed to the `pageDialog` method. That may be rectified in the future. It is also possible that a future version of the JDK will supply its own dialog for page setup instead of relying on a native dialog.

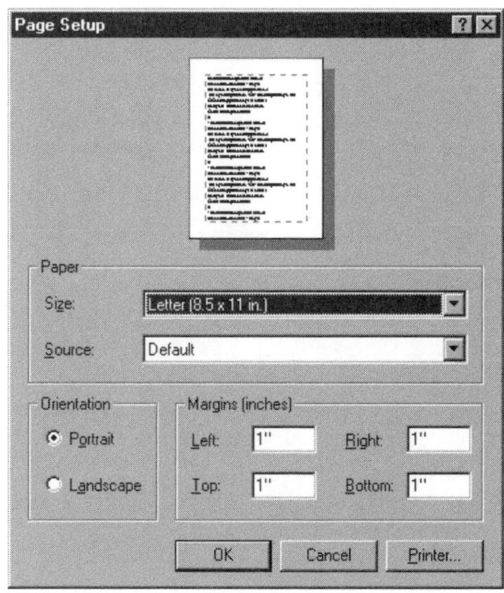

Figure 7–37: A page setup dialog

Example 7–11 shows you how to render the same set of shapes on the screen and on the printed page. A subclass of `JPanel` implements the `Printable` interface. Both the `paintComponent` and the `print` methods call the same method to carry out the actual drawing.

```
class PrintPanel extends JPanel implements Printable
{  public void paintComponent(Graphics g)
   {  super.paintComponent(g);
      Graphics2D g2 = (Graphics2D)g;
      drawPage(g2);
   }

   public int print(Graphics g, PageFormat pf, int page)
      throws PrinterException
   {  if (page >= 1) return Printable.NO_SUCH_PAGE;
      Graphics2D g2 = (Graphics2D)g;
      g2.translate(pf.getImageableX(), pf.getImageableY());
      drawPage(g2);
      return Printable.PAGE_EXISTS;
```

```
    }

    public void drawPage(Graphics2D g2)
    {  // shared drawing code goes here
          . . .
    }
    . . .
}
```

CAUTION: JDK 1.2 does not set the paint to black when setting up a printer graphics context. If your pages come out all white, add a line `gc.setPaint(Color.black)` at the top of the `print` method. This problem has been fixed in JDK 1.3.

This example displays and prints the same image as Example 7–6, namely the outline of the message "Hello, World" that is used as a clipping area for a pattern of lines (see Figure 7–23 on page 507).

Click on the Print button to start printing or on the Page setup button to bring up the page setup dialog. Example 7–11 shows the code.

CAUTION: This program prints a rectangle around the imageable area. We found that on some printers the imageable area was not properly centered, even though we specified equal margins. We suspect that the printing mechanism failed to take into account the unprintable area around the paper margins.

Example 7–11: PrintTest.java

```
import java.awt.*;
import java.awt.event.*;
import java.awt.font.*;
import java.awt.geom.*;
import java.awt.print.*;
import java.util.*;
import javax.swing.*;

public class PrintTest
{  public static void main(String[] args)
   {  JFrame frame = new PrintTestFrame();
      frame.show();
   }
}

class PrintTestFrame extends JFrame
   implements ActionListener
{  public PrintTestFrame()
   {  setTitle("PrintTest");
      setSize(300, 300);
      addWindowListener(new WindowAdapter()
         {  public void windowClosing(WindowEvent e)
            {  System.exit(0);
```

```
            }
         } );

      Container contentPane = getContentPane();
      canvas = new PrintPanel();
      contentPane.add(canvas, "Center");

      JPanel buttonPanel = new JPanel();
      printButton = new JButton("Print");
      buttonPanel.add(printButton);
      printButton.addActionListener(this);

      pageSetupButton = new JButton("Page setup");
      buttonPanel.add(pageSetupButton);
      pageSetupButton.addActionListener(this);

      contentPane.add(buttonPanel, "North");
   }

   public void actionPerformed(ActionEvent event)
   {  Object source = event.getSource();
      if (source == printButton)
      {  PrinterJob printJob = PrinterJob.getPrinterJob();
         if (pageFormat == null)
            pageFormat = printJob.defaultPage();
         printJob.setPrintable(canvas, pageFormat);
         if (printJob.printDialog())
         {  try
            {  printJob.print();
            }
            catch (PrinterException exception)
            {  JOptionPane.showMessageDialog(this, exception);
            }
         }
      }
      else if (source == pageSetupButton)
      {  PrinterJob printJob = PrinterJob.getPrinterJob();
         if (pageFormat == null)
            pageFormat = printJob.defaultPage();
         pageFormat = printJob.pageDialog(pageFormat);
      }
   }

   private JButton printButton;
   private JButton pageSetupButton;

   private PrintPanel canvas;
   private PageFormat pageFormat;
}

class PrintPanel extends JPanel
```

```
   implements Printable
{  public void paintComponent(Graphics g)
   {  super.paintComponent(g);
      Graphics2D g2 = (Graphics2D)g;
      drawPage(g2);
   }

   public int print(Graphics g, PageFormat pf, int page)
      throws PrinterException
   {  if (page >= 1) return Printable.NO_SUCH_PAGE;
      Graphics2D g2 = (Graphics2D)g;
      g2.setPaint(Color.black);
      g2.translate(pf.getImageableX(), pf.getImageableY());
      g2.draw(new Rectangle2D.Double(0, 0,
         pf.getImageableWidth(), pf.getImageableHeight()));

      drawPage(g2);
      return Printable.PAGE_EXISTS;
   }

   public void drawPage(Graphics2D g2)
   {  FontRenderContext context = g2.getFontRenderContext();
      Font f = new Font("Serif", Font.PLAIN, 72);
      GeneralPath clipShape = new GeneralPath();

      TextLayout layout = new TextLayout("Hello", f, context);
      AffineTransform transform
         = AffineTransform.getTranslateInstance(0, 72);
      Shape outline = layout.getOutline(transform);
      clipShape.append(outline, false);

      layout = new TextLayout("World", f, context);
      transform
         = AffineTransform.getTranslateInstance(0, 144);
      outline = layout.getOutline(transform);
      clipShape.append(outline, false);

      g2.draw(clipShape);
      g2.clip(clipShape);

      final int NLINES =50;
      Point2D p = new Point2D.Double(0, 0);
      for (int i = 0; i < NLINES; i++)
      {  double x = (2 * getWidth() * i) / NLINES;
         double y = (2 * getHeight() * (NLINES - 1 - i))
            / NLINES;
         Point2D q = new Point2D.Double(x, y);
         g2.draw(new Line2D.Double(p, q));
      }
   }
}
```

`java.awt.print.Printable`

- `int print(Graphics g, PageFormat format, int pageNumber)`
  renders a page and returns `PAGE_EXISTS`, or returns `NO_SUCH_PAGE`.

Parameters:	`g`	the graphics context onto which the page is rendered
	`format`	the format of the page to draw on
	`pageNumber`	the number of the requested page

`java.awt.print.PrinterJob`

- `static PrinterJob getPrinterJob()`
  returns a printer job object.
- `PageFormat defaultPage()`
  returns the default page format for this printer.
- `PageFormat pageDialog(PageFormat defaults)`
  displays the page setup dialog and returns a clone of `defaults`, with the changes that the user requested in the dialog.
- `boolean printDialog()`
  brings up the print dialog to give the user an opportunity to select the pages to be printed and to change the print settings of the host environment. Returns `true` if the user accepts the dialog.
- `void setPrintable(Printable p)`
- `void setPrintable(Printable p, PageFormat format)`
  set the `Printable` of this print job and an optional page format.
- `void print()`
  prints the current `Printable` by repeatedly calling its `print` method and sending the rendered pages to the printer, until no more pages are available.

`java.awt.print.PageFormat`

- `double getWidth()`
- `double getHeight()`
  return the width and height of the page.
- `double getImageableWidth()`
- `double getImageableHeight()`
  return the width and height of the imageable area of the page.
- `double getImageableX()`
- `double getImageableY()`
  return the position of the top-left corner of the imageable area.

- `int getOrientation()`

  returns one of `PORTRAIT`, `LANDSCAPE`, `REVERSE_LANDSCAPE`. Page orientation is transparent to programmers since the page format and graphics context settings automatically reflect the page orientation.

Printing Multiple Pages

In practice, you don't usually want to pass a raw `Printable` object to a print job. Instead, you should obtain an object of a class that implements the `Pageable` interface. The Java platform supplies one such class, called `Book`. A book is made up of sections, each of which is a `Printable`. You make a book by adding `Printable` objects and their page counts.

```
Book book = new Book();
Printable coverPage = . . .;
Printable bodyPages = . . .;
book.append(coverPage, pageFormat); // append 1 page
book.append(bodyPages, pageFormat, pageCount);
```

Then, you use the `setPageable` method to pass the `Book` object to the print job.

```
printJob.setPageable(book);
```

Now the print job knows exactly how many pages to print. Then, the print dialog displays an accurate page range, and the user can select the entire range or subranges.

CAUTION: When the print job calls the `print` methods of the `Printable` sections, it passes the current page number of the *book*, and not of each *section*, as the current page number. That is a huge pain—each section must know the page counts of the preceding sections in order to make sense of the page number parameter. As with some of the other oddities of the printing interface, it is conceivable that this behavior will change as the Java platform designers gain more understanding of printing issues.

From a programmer's perspective, the biggest challenge about using the `Book` class is that you need to know how many pages each section will have when you print it. Your `Printable` class needs a *layout algorithm* that computes the layout of the material on the printed pages. Before printing starts, invoke that algorithm to compute the page breaks and the page count. You can retain the layout information so you have it handy during the printing process.

You must guard against the possibility that the user has changed the page format. If that happens, you must recompute the layout, even if the information that you want to print has not changed.

Example 7–12 shows how to produce a multipage printout. This program prints a message in very large characters on a number of pages (see Figure 7–38). You can then trim the margins and tape the pages together to form a banner.

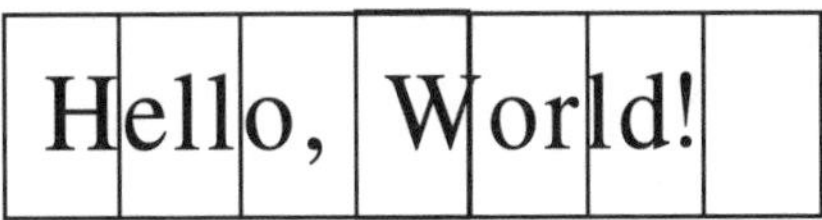

Figure 7–38: A banner

The `layoutPages` method of the `Banner` class computes the layout. We first lay out the message string in a 72 point font. Then, we compute the height of the resulting string and compare it against the imageable height of the page. We derive a scale factor from these two measurements. When printing the string, we will magnify it by that scale factor.

CAUTION: To lay out your information precisely, you usually need access to the printer graphics context. Unfortunately, there is no way to obtain that graphics context until printing actually starts. In our example program, we make do with the screen graphics context and hope that the font metrics of the screen and printer match.

The `getPageCount` method of the `Banner` class first calls the layout method. Then it scales up the width of the string and divides it by the imageable width of each page. The quotient, rounded up to the next integer, is the page count.

It sounds like it might be difficult to print the banner since characters can be broken across multiple pages. However, thanks to the power of the Java 2D API, this turns out not to be a problem at all. When a particular page is requested, we simply use the `translate` method of the `Graphics2D` class to shift the top-left corner of the string to the left. Then, we set a clip rectangle that equals the current page (see Figure 7–39). Finally, we scale the graphics context with the scale factor that the layout method computed.

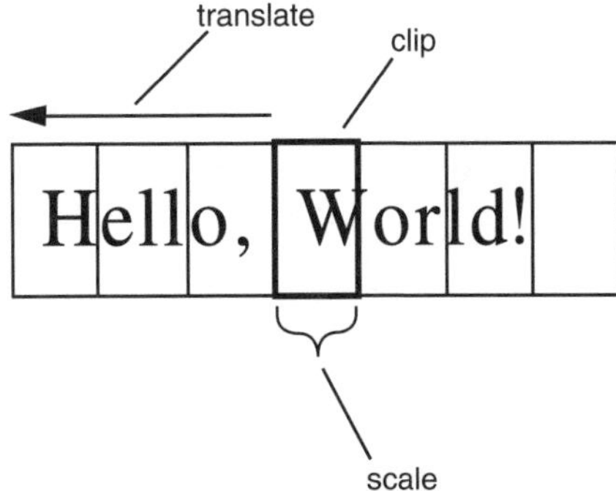

Figure 7–39: Printing a page of a banner

This example shows the power of transformations. The drawing code is kept simple, and the transformation does all the work of placing the drawing at the appropriate place. Finally, the clip cuts away the part of the image that falls outside the page. In the next section, you will see another compelling use of transformations, to display a print preview.

Print Preview

Most professional programs have a print preview mechanism that lets you look at your pages on the screen so that you won't waste paper on a printout that you don't like. The printing classes of the Java platform do not supply a standard "print preview" dialog. But it is easy to design your own (see Figure 7–40). In this section, we show you how. The `PrintPreviewDialog` class in Example 7–12 is completely generic—you can reuse it to preview any kind of printout.

To construct a `PrintPreviewDialog`, you supply either a `Printable` or a `Book`, together with a `PageFormat` object. The surface of the dialog contains a `PrintPreviewCanvas`. As you use the "Next" and "Previous" buttons to flip through the pages, the `paintComponent` method calls the `print` method of the `Printable` object for the requested page.

Normally, the `print` method draws the page context on a printer graphics context. However, we pass the screen graphics context, suitably scaled so that the entire printed page fits inside a small screen rectangle.

```
float xoff = . . .; // left of page
float yoff = . . .; // top of page
float scale = . . .; // to fit printed page onto screen
g2.translate(xoff, yoff);
g2.scale(scale, scale);
Printable printable = book.getPrintable(currentPage);
printable.print(g2, pageFormat, currentPage);
```

The `print` method never knows that it doesn't actually produce printed pages. It simply draws onto the graphics context, thereby producing a microscopic print preview on the screen. This is a very compelling demonstration of the power of the Java 2D imaging model.

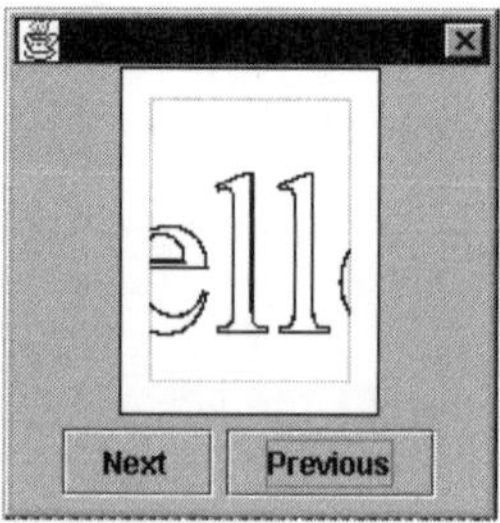

Figure 7–40: A print preview dialog

Example 7–12 contains the code for the banner printing program and the print preview dialog. Type "Hello, World!" into the text field and look at the print preview; then print out the banner.

Example 7–12: BookTest.java

```
import java.awt.*;
import java.awt.event.*;
import java.awt.font.*;
import java.awt.geom.*;
import java.awt.print.*;
import java.util.*;
import javax.swing.*;

public class BookTest
{  public static void main(String[] args)
   {  JFrame frame = new BookTestFrame();
      frame.show();
   }
}

class BookTestFrame extends JFrame
   implements ActionListener
{  public BookTestFrame()
   {  setTitle("BookTest");
      setSize(300, 100);
      addWindowListener(new WindowAdapter()
         {  public void windowClosing(WindowEvent e)
            {  System.exit(0);
            }
         } );

      Container contentPane = getContentPane();
      text = new JTextField();
      contentPane.add(text, "South");

      JPanel buttonPanel = new JPanel();

      printButton = new JButton("Print");
      buttonPanel.add(printButton);
      printButton.addActionListener(this);

      pageSetupButton = new JButton("Page setup");
      buttonPanel.add(pageSetupButton);
      pageSetupButton.addActionListener(this);

      printPreviewButton = new JButton("Print preview");
      buttonPanel.add(printPreviewButton);
      printPreviewButton.addActionListener(this);
```

```
      contentPane.add(buttonPanel, "North");
   }

   public Book makeBook()
   {  if (pageFormat == null)
      {  PrinterJob printJob = PrinterJob.getPrinterJob();
         pageFormat = printJob.defaultPage();
      }
      Book book = new Book();
      String message = text.getText();
      Banner banner = new Banner(message);
      int pageCount
         = banner.getPageCount((Graphics2D)getGraphics(),
            pageFormat);
      book.append(new CoverPage(message + " (" + pageCount
         + " pages)"), pageFormat);
      book.append(banner, pageFormat, pageCount);
      return book;
   }

   public void actionPerformed(ActionEvent event)
   {  Object source = event.getSource();
      if (source == printButton)
      {  PrinterJob printJob = PrinterJob.getPrinterJob();
         printJob.setPageable(makeBook());
         if (printJob.printDialog())
         {  try
            {  printJob.print();
            }
            catch (Exception exception)
            {  JOptionPane.showMessageDialog(this, exception);
            }
         }
      }
      else if (source == pageSetupButton)
      {  PrinterJob printJob = PrinterJob.getPrinterJob();
         if (pageFormat == null)
            pageFormat = printJob.defaultPage();
         pageFormat = printJob.pageDialog(pageFormat);
      }
      else if (source == printPreviewButton)
      {  PrintPreviewDialog dialog
            = new PrintPreviewDialog(makeBook());
         dialog.show();
      }
   }

   private JButton printButton;
   private JButton pageSetupButton;
```

```
   private JButton printPreviewButton;

   private JTextField text;
   private PageFormat pageFormat;
}

class Banner implements Printable
{  public Banner(String m)
   {  message = m;
   }

   public int getPageCount(Graphics2D g2, PageFormat pf)
   {  if (message.equals("")) return 0;
      layoutPages(g2, pf);
      float width = scale * layout.getAdvance();
      int pages = (int)Math.ceil(width / pf.getImageableWidth());
      return pages;
   }

   public int print(Graphics g, PageFormat pf, int page)
      throws PrinterException
   {  Graphics2D g2 = (Graphics2D)g;
      g2.setPaint(Color.black);
      if (page > getPageCount(g2, pf))
         return Printable.NO_SUCH_PAGE;
      g2.translate(pf.getImageableX(), pf.getImageableY());

      drawPage(g2, pf, page);
      return Printable.PAGE_EXISTS;
   }

   public void layoutPages(Graphics2D g2, PageFormat pf)
   {  if (message.equals("")) return;
      FontRenderContext context = g2.getFontRenderContext();
      Font f = new Font("Serif", Font.PLAIN, 72);
      layout = new TextLayout(message, f, context);
      float ascent = layout.getAscent();
      float descent = layout.getDescent();
      float height = ascent + descent;
      scale = (float)pf.getImageableHeight() / height;
   }

   public void drawPage(Graphics2D g2, PageFormat pf, int page)
   {  if (message.equals("")) return;
      page--; // account for cover page
      layoutPages(g2, pf);

      drawCropMarks(g2, pf);
      g2.clip(new Rectangle2D.Double(0, 0,
         pf.getImageableWidth(), pf.getImageableHeight()));
```

```
      g2.translate(-page * pf.getImageableWidth(), 0);
      g2.scale(scale, scale);
      AffineTransform transform
         = AffineTransform.getTranslateInstance(0,
            layout.getAscent());
      Shape outline = layout.getOutline(transform);
      g2.draw(outline);
   }

   public void drawCropMarks(Graphics2D g2, PageFormat pf)
   {  final double C = 36; // crop mark length = 1/2 inch
      double w = pf.getImageableWidth();
      double h = pf.getImageableHeight();
      g2.draw(new Line2D.Double(0, 0, 0, C));
      g2.draw(new Line2D.Double(0, 0, C, 0));
      g2.draw(new Line2D.Double(w, 0, w, C));
      g2.draw(new Line2D.Double(w, 0, w - C, 0));
      g2.draw(new Line2D.Double(0, h, 0, h - C));
      g2.draw(new Line2D.Double(0, h, C, h));
      g2.draw(new Line2D.Double(w, h, w, h - C));
      g2.draw(new Line2D.Double(w, h, w - C, h));
   }

   private String message;
   private float scale;
   private float width;
   private TextLayout layout;
}

class CoverPage implements Printable
{  public CoverPage(String t)
   {  title = t;
   }

   public int print(Graphics g, PageFormat pf, int page)
      throws PrinterException
   {  if (page >= 1) return Printable.NO_SUCH_PAGE;
      Graphics2D g2 = (Graphics2D)g;
      g2.setPaint(Color.black);
      g2.translate(pf.getImageableX(), pf.getImageableY());
      FontRenderContext context = g2.getFontRenderContext();
      Font f = g2.getFont();
      TextLayout layout = new TextLayout(title, f, context);
      float ascent = layout.getAscent();
      g2.drawString(title, 0, ascent);
      return Printable.PAGE_EXISTS;
   }

   private String title;
```

```
}

class PrintPreviewDialog extends JDialog
   implements ActionListener
{  public PrintPreviewDialog(Printable p, PageFormat pf,
      int pages)
   {  Book book = new Book();
      book.append(p, pf, pages);
      layoutUI(book);
   }

   public PrintPreviewDialog(Book b)
   {  layoutUI(b);
   }

   public void layoutUI(Book book)
   {  setSize(200, 200);

      Container contentPane = getContentPane();
      canvas = new PrintPreviewCanvas(book);
      contentPane.add(canvas, "Center");

      JPanel buttonPanel = new JPanel();

      nextButton = new JButton("Next");
      buttonPanel.add(nextButton);
      nextButton.addActionListener(this);

      previousButton = new JButton("Previous");
      buttonPanel.add(previousButton);
      previousButton.addActionListener(this);

      closeButton = new JButton("Close");
      buttonPanel.add(closeButton);
      closeButton.addActionListener(this);

      contentPane.add(buttonPanel, "South");
   }

   public void actionPerformed(ActionEvent event)
   {  Object source = event.getSource();
      if (source == nextButton)
      {  canvas.flipPage(1);
      }
      else if (source == previousButton)
      {  canvas.flipPage(-1);
      }
      else if (source == closeButton)
      {  setVisible(false);
      }
   }
```

```
    private JButton nextButton;
    private JButton previousButton;
    private JButton closeButton;
    private PrintPreviewCanvas canvas;
}

class PrintPreviewCanvas extends JPanel
{   public PrintPreviewCanvas(Book b)
    {   book = b;
        currentPage = 0;
    }

    public void paintComponent(Graphics g)
    {   super.paintComponent(g);
        Graphics2D g2 = (Graphics2D)g;
        PageFormat pageFormat = book.getPageFormat(currentPage);

        double xoff; // x offset of page start in window
        double yoff; // y offset of page start in window
        double scale; // scale factor to fit page in window
        double px = pageFormat.getWidth();
        double py = pageFormat.getHeight();
        double sx = getWidth() - 1;
        double sy = getHeight() - 1;
        if (px / py < sx / sy) // center horizontally
        {   scale = sy / py;
            xoff = 0.5 * (sx - scale * px);
            yoff = 0;
        }
        else // center vertically
        {   scale = sx / px;
            xoff = 0;
            yoff = 0.5 * (sy - scale * py);
        }
        g2.translate((float)xoff, (float)yoff);
        g2.scale((float)scale, (float)scale);

        // draw page outline (ignoring margins)
        Rectangle2D page = new Rectangle2D.Double(0, 0, px, py);
        g2.setPaint(Color.white);
        g2.fill(page);
        g2.setPaint(Color.black);
        g2.draw(page);

        Printable printable = book.getPrintable(currentPage);
        try
        {   printable.print(g2, pageFormat, currentPage);
        }
        catch (PrinterException exception)
```

```
      {  g2.draw(new Line2D.Double(0, 0, px, py));
         g2.draw(new Line2D.Double(0, px, 0, py));
      }
   }

   public void flipPage(int by)
   {  int newPage = currentPage + by;
      if (0 <= newPage && newPage < book.getNumberOfPages())
      {  currentPage = newPage;
         repaint();
      }
   }

   private Book book;
   private int currentPage;
}
```

java.awt.print.PrinterJob

API

- `void setPageable(Pageable p)`

  sets a `Pageable` (such as a `Book`) to be printed.

java.awt.print.Book

- `void append(Printable p, PageFormat format)`
- `void append(Printable p, PageFormat format, int pageCount)`

  append a section to this book. If the page count is not specified, the first page is added.

- `Printable getPrintable(int page)`

  gets the printable for the specified page.

The Clipboard

One of the most powerful and convenient user interface mechanisms of graphical user interface environments (such as Windows and X Window System) *is cut and paste.* You select some data in one program and cut or copy it to the clipboard. Then, you select another program and paste the clipboard contents into that application. Using the clipboard, you can transfer text, images, or other data from one document to another, or, of course, from one place in a document to another place in the same document. Cut and paste is so natural that most computer users never think about it.

However, in JDK 1.0, there was no support for cut and paste. You could not cut and paste between Java applications. For example, if you have a browser written in the Java programming language, then you could not copy text and images from a web page and transfer them into a word processor based on Java technology.

JDK 1.1 implemented a rudimentary clipboard mechanism. That mechanism (which has not been materially improved in the Java 2 platform) is the topic of this section.

Even though the clipboard is conceptually simple, implementing clipboard services is actually harder than you might think. Suppose you copy text from a word processor into the clipboard. If you paste that text into another word processor, then you expect that the fonts and formatting will stay intact. That is, the text in the clipboard needs to retain the formatting information. But if you paste the text into a plain text field, then you expect that just the characters are pasted in, without additional formatting codes.

The system clipboard of a graphical user interface environment can hold the clipboard data in multiple formats, and the program that provides the data must negotiate the data format with the program that consumes the data.

Furthermore, individual programs usually have their own local clipboards. When you cut and paste text inside a word processor, then the word processor saves the data in its own format in a *local clipboard*. There is no universal standard for exchanging formatted text. When text is pasted onto the system clipboard, some formatting information is usually lost. While this loss is tolerable for text interchange from one word processor to another, it is not acceptable for moving data within one word processor. Program users have the legitimate expectation that no information is lost when they move information from one place in a document to another place in the same document. To achieve perfect information transfer within a program, a local clipboard is required whenever that information is richer than the data that can be stored in the clipboard.

The system clipboard implementations of Microsoft Windows, OS/2 and the Macintosh are similar, but, of course, there are slight differences. And the X Window System clipboard mechanism is much more limited—cutting and pasting of anything but plain text is only sporadically supported. These differences are a major challenge for programs written in the Java programming language. Such a program is supposed to run unmodified on many platforms. As so often, Java technology must cater to the lowest common denominator, and again, as so often, that lowest common denominator is the X Window System. Since the X Window System has no standard method for storing graphics on the clipboard, programs in the Java programming language are currently limited to storing only text on the system clipboard. You will learn in this chapter how such a program can place text onto the system clipboard and how to retrieve text that was placed there by another program.

However, when copying data from one Java program to another, you can overcome the plain text limitation. Consider what happens if you attach a graphical

image to an e-mail message. The attachment is automatically encoded into a text format, using the MIME (Multipurpose Internet Mail Extensions) standard.

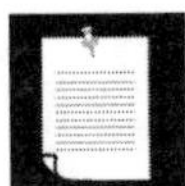

NOTE: For an HTML version of the RFC (Request for Comment) that defines the MIME format, see, for example, `http://www.oac.uci.edu/indiv/ehood/MIME`.

MIME-compliant mailers know how to encode attachments into plain text and how to decode the MIME format and present the attachments to the user. Of course, if you use an ancient mail reader (such as the original Unix `mail` program), then the attachments will simply show up as strange-looking text.

It is possible to use the same approach to transfer data from one program in the Java programming language to another by placing encoded data onto the clipboard. Of course, it makes no sense to paste that text into a program that does not know about this encoding. But if the target program can understand the header that describes the encoding format, then it can decode the information. Currently, Java technology has no support for this transfer method. Although MIME data types describe data formats, the data transfer mechanism does not currently make full use of the MIME standard to encode data. We found it reasonable to extend that mechanism and to encode clipboard data in MIME format as well. We give you a sample program that shows how you can easily exchange arbitrary serializable objects between Java applications through the system clipboard by using this approach. Perhaps, in the future, a similar mechanism will be officially used for data transfer between programs in the Java programming language.

Finally, the Java data transfer API supports a local clipboard that you can use to store arbitrary Java objects. Naturally, this is not nearly as difficult as transferring data between programs. Why can't you simply store the clipboard data in a global variable? The Java mechanism also supports data format negotiation. (In the data transfer API, the data formats are called *flavors*.)

Table 7–3 summarizes the data transfer capabilities of the new clipboard mechanism.

Table 7–3: Capabilities of the Java data transfer mechanism

Transfer	Format
Between a program in Java programming language and a native program	Text
Between two cooperating programs in the Java programming language	Text-encoded data
Within one program in the Java programming language	Any object

Classes and Interfaces for Data Transfer

Data transfer in the Java technology is implemented in a package called `java.awt.datatransfer`. Table 7–4 contains brief descriptions of the parts of this package.

Table 7–4: Classes in the java.awt.datatransfer package

`Transferable` interface	Objects that can be transferred must implement this interface.
`Clipboard` class	A class that encapsulates a clipboard. Transferable objects are the only items that can be put on or taken off a clipboard. The system clipboard is a concrete example of a `Clipboard`.
`ClipboardOwner` interface	A class that wants to be able to copy data to a clipboard must implement this interface.
`DataFlavor` class	A way of identifying the type (or "flavor") of the data that was placed on a clipboard.
`StringSelection` class	The only concrete class that Java1.1 supplies that implements `Transferable` and, as a convenience, `ClipboardOwner`. Used to transfer text strings.
`UnsupportedFlavor-Exception`	Thrown by a `Transferable` when it can't give you data in that flavor.

Transferring Text

The best way to get comfortable with the data transfer classes is to start with the simplest (and, in fact, currently the only) supported situation: transferring text to and from the system clipboard. The idea of the following program is simple. First we get a reference to the system clipboard.

```
Clipboard clipboard =
   Toolkit.getDefaultToolkit().getSystemClipboard();
```

For strings to be transferred to the clipboard, they need to be wrapped into `StringSelection` objects. The constructor takes the text you want to transfer.

```
StringSelection selection = new StringSelection(text);
```

The actual transfer is done by a call to `setContents`, which takes a `StringSelection` object and a `ClipBoardOwner` as parameters. If you are not interested in designating a clipboard owner, you can set the second parameter to `null`.

```
clipboard.setContents(selection, null);
```

For simple text, you don't need a clipboard owner. Clipboard ownership enables "delayed formatting" of complex data. If a program transfers simple data (such as a string), then it simply sets the clipboard contents and moves on to do the next

thing. However, if a program wants to place complex data that can be formatted in multiple flavors onto the clipboard, then it may not actually want to prepare all the flavors, since there is a good chance that most of them are never needed. However, then it needs to be able to hang on to the clipboard data so that it can create the flavors later when they are requested. The clipboard owner is notified (by calling its `lostOwnership` method) when the contents of the clipboard change. That tells it that the information is no longer needed.

In our sample programs, we don't need to worry about clipboard ownership.

Here is the complete set of instructions to place a string onto the system clipboard.

```
String text = . . .
StringSelection selection = new StringSelection(text);
clipboard.setContents(selection, null);
```

Let us look at the reverse operation, reading a string from the clipboard. Call the `getContents` method of the clipboard to get a Transferable object.

```
Transferable contents = clipBoard.getContents(this);
```

The parameter of the `getContents` call is an `Object` reference of the requesting object. It is not clear why the clipboard collects this information.

The return value of `getContents` may be `null`. That indicates that the clipboard is either empty or that it has no data that the Java platform knows how to retrieve.

The `Transferable` object can tell you in which flavors the clipboard information is available. We will discuss the details of flavor discovery later. For now, we only want the standard flavor called `DataFlavor.stringFlavor`. Use the `isDataFlavorSupported` method to find out whether that the flavor that you want is actually available.

Finally, you pass the desired flavor to the `getTransferData` method. The method call must be enclosed in a `try` block because the method threatens to throw an `UnsupportedFlavorException` if the requested flavor is not available, or an `IOException` if it cannot read the data.

```
DataFlavor flavor = DataFlavor.stringFlavor;
if (selection.isDataFlavorSupported(flavor))
{  try
   {  String text = (String)(selection.getTransferData(flavor);
      do something with text;
   }
   catch(Exception e)
   {  . . .
   }
}
```

Example 7–13 is a program that demonstrates cutting and pasting between a Java application and the system clipboard. Figure 7–41 shows a screen shot. If you select an area of text in the text area and click on Copy, then the selected text is copied to the system clipboard. As Figure 7–42 shows, the copied text does indeed get stored on the system clipboard. When you subsequently click on the Paste button, the contents of the clipboard (which may come from a native program) are pasted at the cursor position.

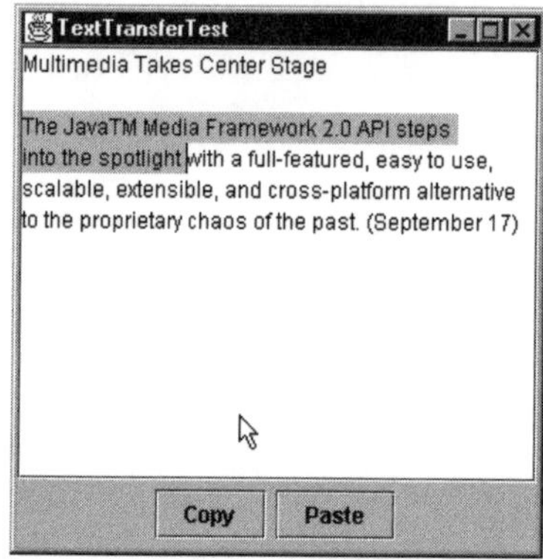

Figure 7–41: The TextTransferTest program

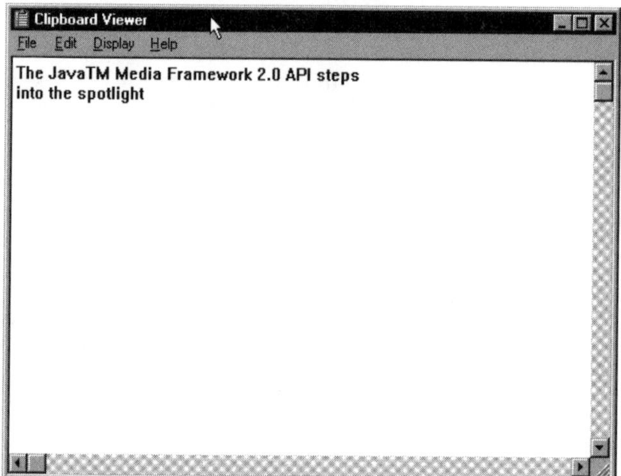

Figure 7–42: The Windows clipboard viewer after a copy

Example 7–13: TextTransferTest.java

```
import java.io.*;
import java.awt.*;
import java.awt.datatransfer.*;
import java.awt.event.*;
import javax.swing.*;

public class TextTransferTest
```

```
{  public static void main(String[] args)
   {  JFrame frame = new TextTransferFrame();
      frame.show();
   }
}

class TextTransferFrame extends JFrame
   implements ActionListener
{  public TextTransferFrame()
   {  setTitle("TextTransferTest");
      setSize(300, 300);
      addWindowListener(new WindowAdapter()
         {  public void windowClosing(WindowEvent e)
            {  System.exit(0);
            }
         } );

      Container contentPane = getContentPane();

      textArea = new JTextArea();
      contentPane.add(new JScrollPane(textArea), "Center");
      JPanel panel = new JPanel();
      copyButton = new JButton("Copy");
      panel.add(copyButton);
      copyButton.addActionListener(this);
      pasteButton = new JButton("Paste");
      panel.add(pasteButton);
      pasteButton.addActionListener(this);
      contentPane.add(panel, "South");
      sysClipboard
         = Toolkit.getDefaultToolkit().getSystemClipboard();
   }

   public void actionPerformed(ActionEvent event)
   {  Object source = event.getSource();
      if (source == copyButton) copy();
      else if (source == pasteButton) paste();
   }

   private void copy()
   {  String text = textArea.getSelectedText();
      if (text.equals("")) text = textArea.getText();
      StringSelection selection = new StringSelection(text);
      sysClipboard.setContents(selection, null);
   }

   private void paste()
   {  String text;
      Transferable contents = sysClipboard.getContents(this);
      if (contents == null) return;
      try
      {  text = (String)(contents.getTransferData
```

```
            (DataFlavor.stringFlavor));
         textArea.replaceSelection(text);
      }
      catch(Exception e)
      {  textArea.append("Error: " + e);
      }
   }

   private JTextArea textArea;
   private JButton copyButton;
   private JButton pasteButton;
   private Clipboard sysClipboard;
}
```

`java.awt.Toolkit`

- `Clipboard getSystemClipboard()`
  gets the system clipboard.

`java.awt.datatransfer.Clipboard`

- `Transferable getContents(Object requester)`
  gets the clipboard contents.

Parameters:	`requester`	the object requesting the clipboard contents

- `void setContents(Transferable contents, ClipboardOwner owner)`
  puts contents on the clipboard.

Parameters:	`contents`	the `Transferable` encapsulating the contents
	`owner`	the object to be notified (via its `lostOwnership` method) when new information is placed on the clipboard

`java.awt.datatransfer.ClipboardOwner`

- `void lostOwnership(Clipboard clipboard, Transferable contents)`
  notifies this object that it is no longer the owner of the contents of the clipboard.

Parameters:	`clipboard`	the clipboard onto which the contents were placed
	`contents`	the item that this owner had placed onto the clipboard

java.awt.datatransfer.Transferable

- `boolean isDataFlavorSupported(DataFlavor flavor)`

  returns `true` if the specified flavor is one of the supported data flavors; `false` otherwise.

- `Object getTransferData(DataFlavor flavor)`

  returns the data, formatted in the requested flavor. Throws an `UnsupportedFlavorException` if the flavor requested is not supported.

Building a Transferable

Objects that you want to transfer via the clipboard must implement the `Transferable` interface. The `StringSelection` class is currently the only public class in the Java standard library that implements the `Transferable` interface. We will first build an `ImageSelection` class that can be used to transfer images through the local clipboard. Finally, we will build up the machinery to construct a `Transferable` for serializable Java objects.

The Transferable Interface and Data Flavors

You can find out all data flavors that a transferable object supports:

```
DataFlavor[] flavors = transferable.getTransferDataFlavors()
```

A `DataFlavor` is defined by two characteristics:

- A MIME type name (such as `"image/gif"`)
- A representation class for accessing the data (such as `InputStream`)

In addition, every data flavor has a human-readable name (such as `"GIF Image"`).

The representation class can be specified with a `class` parameter in the MIME type, for example,

```
image/gif; class=java.awt.Image
```

NOTE: This is just an example to show the syntax. There is currently no support for transferring GIF image data.

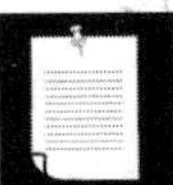

If no `class` parameter is given, then the representation class is `InputStream`.

Sun Microsystems defined a MIME type

```
application/x-java-serialized-object
```

for transferring serialized Java objects.

NOTE: The `x-` prefix indicates that this is an experimental name, not one that is sanctioned by IANA, the organization that assigns standard MIME type names.

For example, the standard `stringFlavor` data flavor is described by the MIME type

```
application/x-java-serialized-object; class=java.lang.String
```

`java.awt.datatransfer.DataFlavor`

- `DataFlavor(String mimeType, String humanPresentableName)`
  creates a data flavor that describes stream data in a format described by a MIME type.

Parameters:	`mimeType`	a MIME type string
	`humanPresentableName`	a more readable version of the name

- `DataFlavor(Class class, String humanPresentableName)`
  creates a data flavor that describes a Java platform class. Its MIME type is `application/x-java-serialized-object; class = class name.`

Parameters:	`class`	the class that is retrieved from the `Transferable`
	`humanPresentableName`	a readable version of the name

- `String getMimeType()`
  returns the MIME type string for this data flavor.
- `boolean isMimeTypeEqual(String mimeType)`
  tests whether this data flavor has the given MIME type.
- `String getHumanPresentableName()`
  returns the human-presentable name for the data format of this data flavor.
- `Class getRepresentationClass()`
  returns a `Class` object that represents the class of the object that a `Transferable` will return when called with this data flavor. This is either the `class` parameter of the MIME type or `InputStream`.

`java.awt.datatransfer.Transferable`

- `DataFlavor[] getTransferDataFlavors()`
  returns an array of the supported flavors.

Building an Image Transferable

Let us put the information of the preceding section to work and design a transferable image class. Right now, we only want to transfer images inside a single program; that is, we will just use a local clipboard.

Here's what you need to do:

1. Define a class `ImageSelection` that implements the `Transferable` interface.
```
class ImageSelection implements Transferable { . . . }
```
2. Define the single supported flavor as a class flavor for the class `java.awt.image`, with a human-presentable name of `"AWT Image"`. Construct a static object `imageFlavor` to represent that flavor.
```
public static final DataFlavor imageFlavor
   = new DataFlavor(java.awt.Image.class, "AWT Image");
```
3. Make the `getTransferDataFlavors` method return an array with the single entry, `imageFlavor` of type `DataFlavor`.
```
private static DataFlavor[] flavors = { imageFlavor };
public DataFlavor[] getTransferDataFlavors()
{  return flavors;
}
```
4. Have the `isDataFlavorSupported` check whether the requested flavor is equal to the `imageFlavor` object.
```
public boolean isDataFlavorSupported(DataFlavor flavor)
{  return flavor.equals(imageFlavor);
}
```
5. Have the `ImageSelection` constructor accept and store an object of type `Image`.
```
public ImageSelection(Image image)
{  theImage = image;
}
private Image theImage;
```
6. Return a reference to the stored `Image` object as the value of `getTransferData`.
```
public synchronized Object getTransferData
   (DataFlavor flavor)
   throws UnsupportedFlavorException
{  if(flavor.equals(imageFlavor))
   {  return theImage;
   }
   else
   {  throw new UnsupportedFlavorException(flavor);
   }
}
```

See Example 7–14 for the complete source code.

Of course, all this is a bit underwhelming. The `ImageSelection` class is simply a wrapper for `Image` objects.

This class, to be more interesting, would need to be able to deliver its contents in more than one flavor, for example, as an `Image` object and a GIF file. Then, you would see some real work in the `getTransferData` method. It would look like this:

```
public synchronized Object getTransferData
   (DataFlavor flavor)
```

```
    throws UnsupportedFlavorException
{   if(flavor.equals(imageFlavor))
    {  return theImage;
    }
    else if(flavor.equals(gifFlavor))
    {  byte[] gifBytes = . . .;
          // translate image to GIF format
       return new ByteArrayInputStream(gifBytes);
    }
    else
    {  throw new UnsupportedFlavorException(flavor);
    }
}
```

We will not do that work here, since it is a bit tedious to compute the GIF format of an image.

Using the `ImageSelection` *Class*

The program of Example 7–14 creates two windows. You can load an image file into each window, or you can copy and paste between the windows, with the Edit | Copy and Edit | Paste menu options (see Figure 7–43). Coding the copy and paste operations using the `ImageSelection` class is not much different than using the `StringSelection` class.

```
private void copyIt()
{  ImageSelection selection = new ImageSelection(theImage);
   localClipboard.setContents(selection, null);
}

private void pasteIt()
{  Transferable selection
      = localClipboard.getContents(this);
   try
   {  theImage = (Image)selection.getTransferData
         (ImageSelection.imageFlavor);
      repaint();
   }
   catch(Exception e) {}
}
```

In this case, `selection` is an `ImageSelection` instance. We obviously also need to cast the return value of `getTransferData` to an `Image` this time rather than to a string, and use a call to `repaint()` rather than adding the result to the text area. Note that we are using a local clipboard rather than the system clipboard. It is constructed as

```
static Clipboard localClipboard = new Clipboard("local");
```

We cannot use the system clipboard because, at this time, Java technology can transfer only text into the system clipboard.

Example 7–14 shows the full code for the example.

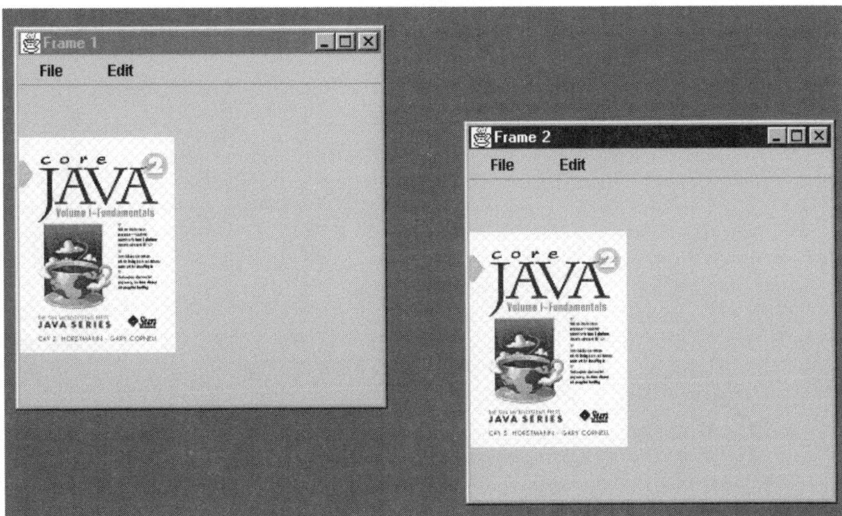

Figure 7–43: The `ImageTransferTest` program

Example 7–14: ImageTransferTest.java

```
import java.io.*;
import java.awt.*;
import java.awt.datatransfer.*;
import java.awt.event.*;
import javax.swing.*;

public class ImageTransferTest
{  public static void main(String[] args)
   {  JFrame frame1 = new ImageTransferFrame();
      JFrame frame2 = new ImageTransferFrame();
      frame1.setTitle("Frame 1");
      frame2.setTitle("Frame 2");
      frame1.show();
      frame2.show();
   }
}

class ImageTransferFrame extends JFrame
   implements ActionListener
{  public ImageTransferFrame()
   {  setSize(300, 300);
      addWindowListener(new WindowAdapter()
         {  public void windowClosing(WindowEvent e)
            {  System.exit(0);
```

```
         }
      } );

      Container contentPane = getContentPane();
      label = new JLabel();
      contentPane.add(label, "Center");

      JMenu fileMenu = new JMenu("File");
      openItem = new JMenuItem("Open");
      openItem.addActionListener(this);
      fileMenu.add(openItem);

      exitItem = new JMenuItem("Exit");
      exitItem.addActionListener(this);
      fileMenu.add(exitItem);

      JMenu editMenu = new JMenu("Edit");
      copyItem = new JMenuItem("Copy");
      copyItem.addActionListener(this);
      editMenu.add(copyItem);

      pasteItem = new JMenuItem("Paste");
      pasteItem.addActionListener(this);
      editMenu.add(pasteItem);

      JMenuBar menuBar = new JMenuBar();
      menuBar.add(fileMenu);
      menuBar.add(editMenu);
      setJMenuBar(menuBar);
   }

   public void actionPerformed(ActionEvent evt)
   {  Object source = evt.getSource();
      if (source == openItem)
      {  JFileChooser chooser = new JFileChooser();
         chooser.setCurrentDirectory(new File("."));

         chooser.setFileFilter(new
            javax.swing.filechooser.FileFilter()
            {  public boolean accept(File f)
               {  String name = f.getName().toLowerCase();
                  return name.endsWith(".gif")
                     || name.endsWith(".jpg")
                     || name.endsWith(".jpeg")
                     || f.isDirectory();
               }
               public String getDescription()
               {  return "Image files";
               }
```

```
            });

         int r = chooser.showOpenDialog(this);
         if(r == JFileChooser.APPROVE_OPTION)
         {  String name
               = chooser.getSelectedFile().getAbsolutePath();
            setImage(Toolkit.getDefaultToolkit().getImage(name));
         }
      }
      else if (source == exitItem) System.exit(0);
      else if (source == copyItem) copy();
      else if (source == pasteItem) paste();
   }

   private void copy()
   {  ImageSelection selection = new ImageSelection(theImage);
      localClipboard.setContents(selection, null);
   }

   private void paste()
   {  Transferable contents
         = localClipboard.getContents(this);
      if (contents == null) return;
      try
      {  Image image = (Image)contents.getTransferData
            (ImageSelection.imageFlavor);
         setImage(image);
      }
      catch(Exception e) {}
   }

   public void setImage(Image image)
   {  theImage = image;
      label.setIcon(new ImageIcon(image));
   }

   private static Clipboard localClipboard
      = new Clipboard("local");
   private Image theImage;
   private JLabel label;
   private JMenuItem openItem;
   private JMenuItem exitItem;
   private JMenuItem copyItem;
   private JMenuItem pasteItem;
}

class ImageSelection implements Transferable
{  public ImageSelection(Image image)
   {  theImage = image;
```

```
   }

   public DataFlavor[] getTransferDataFlavors()
   {  return flavors;
   }

   public boolean isDataFlavorSupported(DataFlavor flavor)
   {  return flavor.equals(imageFlavor);
   }

   public synchronized Object getTransferData
      (DataFlavor flavor)
      throws UnsupportedFlavorException
   {  if(flavor.equals(imageFlavor))
      {  return theImage;
      }
      else
      {  throw new UnsupportedFlavorException(flavor);
      }
   }

   public static final DataFlavor imageFlavor
      = new DataFlavor(java.awt.Image.class, "AWT Image");

   private static DataFlavor[] flavors = { imageFlavor };
   private Image theImage;
}
```

Transferring Java Objects via the System Clipboard

Now, suppose you want to paste the images by using the *system* clipboard rather than a private clipboard. This capability would have the nice consequence that the image would persist and so you could paste images between different programs in the Java programming language even if the original program was finished.

Unfortunately, the system clipboard can currently only be used to transfer `StringSelection` data from one program to another.

In this section, we show you how to overcome this limitation by encoding objects into text strings and placing those text strings onto the system clipboard. This method works for any *serializable* Java object. We choose the following simple text encoding:

```
Content-type: application/x-java-serialized-object;
   class=java.util.Serializable
Content-length: length

serialized object data in BASE64 encoding
```

For example,

```
Content-type: application/x-java-serialized-object;
   class=java.util.Serializable
Content-length: 80311
```


```
rO0ABXNyAAZCaXRtYXA8A5/mgeUpsAIAA0kABmhlaWdodEkABXdpZHRoWwAGcGl4ZWxzdAACW014
cAAAAIwAAABqdXIAAltJTbpgJnbqsqUCAAB4cAAAOfj////////////////////////////////
...
```


The BASE64 encoding is a commonly used method to encode binary data as printable characters. The exact encoding scheme is not important. You can find a description in the MIME RFC, and the code in Example 7–15 contains classes to carry out the encoding and decoding.

Because the system clipboard class can get only text from the clipboard, we designed a special `MimeClipboard` class. This class delegates storage and retrieval requests to another clipboard, typically the system clipboard, and it handles the data encoding and decoding.

```
class MimeClipboard extends Clipboard
{  public MimeClipboard(Clipboard cb)
   {  . . .
      clip = cb;
   }

   public synchronized void setContents(Transferable contents,
      ClipboardOwner owner)
   {  encode data and put on clip
   }

   public synchronized Transferable getContents
      (Object requestor)
   {  get data from clip and decode
   }

   private Clipboard clip;
}
```

We also use a transfer wrapper `SerializableSelection` for serializable objects—it is exactly analogous to the `ImageSelection` class of the preceding section. When a `Transferable` object is placed onto a `MimeClipboard`, the following happens:

1. If the `Transferable` object is a `StringSelection`, then it is simply put on the clipboard.

2. Otherwise, if the `Transferable` is of the type `SerializableSelection`, then the object is serialized into a sequence of bytes. The serialized bytes are encoded in BASE64, the MIME header is added, and the resulting string is placed on the clipboard.

```
public synchronized void setContents(Transferable
   contents, ClipboardOwner owner)
{  if (contents instanceof SerializableSelection)
   {  try
      {  DataFlavor flavor
            = SerializableSelection.serializableFlavor;
         Serializable obj = (Serializable)
            contents.getTransferData(flavor);
         String enc = encode(obj);
         String header = "Content-type: "
            + flavor.getMimeType()
            + "\nContent-length: "
            + enc.length() + "\n\n";
         StringSelection selection
            = new StringSelection(header + enc);
         clip.setContents(selection, owner);
      }
      catch(UnsupportedFlavorException e) {}
      catch(IOException e) {}
   }
   else clip.setContents(contents, owner);
}
```

When a `Transferable` object is read from the clipboard, these steps are reversed.

1. The `StringSelection` is obtained from the system clipboard.
2. If the string doesn't start with `Content-type`, then the string selection object is returned.
3. Otherwise, the BASE64 data is converted to binary and read as object stream data. The resulting object is wrapped into a `SerializableSelection` transfer object, which is returned.

```
public synchronized Transferable getContents
   (Object requestor)
{  Transferable contents = clip.getContents(requestor);

   if (contents instanceof StringSelection)
   {  String data = (String)contents.getTransferData
            (DataFlavor.stringFlavor);

      if (!data.startsWith("Content-type: "))
         return contents;
      int start = . . .; // skip three newlines
```

```
            Serializable obj = decode(data.substring(start));
            SerializableSelection selection
               = new SerializableSelection(obj);
            return selection;
         }
         else return contents;
      }
```

Admittedly, this mechanism can't transfer an ordinary string that starts with `Content-type`. It would not be difficult to enhance the mechanism to overcome this problem. However, we leave this enhancement as an exercise for the reader.

You use this clipboard just like any other clipboard:

```
Clipboard mimeClipboard
   = new MimeClipboard
   (Toolkit.getDefaultToolkit().getSystemClipboard());
. . .
private void copyIt()
{  SerializableSelection selection
      = new SerializableSelection(theBitmap);
   mimeClipboard.setContents(selection, null);
}
```

To encode an object, we serialize it to a stream. The `Base64OutputStream` class encodes all bytes written to it into BASE64. We layer an `ObjectOutputStream` on top of it. Here is the code from the encode method.

```
ByteArrayOutputStream bOut
   = new ByteArrayOutputStream();
Base64OutputStream b64Out
   = new Base64OutputStream(bOut);
ObjectOutputStream out
   = new ObjectOutputStream(b64Out);
out.writeObject(obj);
out.close();
String s = bOut.toString("8859_1");
```

To decode, we follow the same approach. A `Base64InputStream` has its read method defined to turn BASE64 characters into bytes, and an `ObjectInputStream` reads the serialized object data from that stream. Here is the code from the `decode` method.

```
byte[] bytes = s.getBytes("8859_1");
ByteArrayInputStream bIn
   = new ByteArrayInputStream(bytes);
Base64InputStream b64In
   = new Base64InputStream(bIn);
ObjectInputStream in
   = new ObjectInputStream(b64In);
Object obj = in.readObject();
```

When this technique is put to work for transferring images, there is a minor technical setback: the `Image` class does not implement `Serializable`. To overcome this problem, we designed a serializable class `Bitmap` that holds the pixels of an image.

```
class Bitmap implements Serializable
{  public Bitmap(BufferedImage image)
   {  type = image.getType();
      width = image.getWidth();
      height = image.getHeight();
      WritableRaster raster = image.getRaster();
      data = raster.getDataElements(0, 0, width, height, null);
   }

   public BufferedImage getImage()
   {  BufferedImage image
         = new BufferedImage(width, height, type);
      WritableRaster raster = image.getRaster();
      raster.setDataElements(0, 0, width, height, data);
      return image;
   }

   private int type;
   private int width;
   private int height;
   private Object data;
}
```

Remember from Chapter 12 of Volume 1 that we need not actually write any methods for serialization and deserialization. The serialization mechanism will automatically serialize the `width` and `height` fields and the array of pixels.

Now we have all the pieces together to write a program that can copy an image to the system clipboard. The program in Example 7–15 does just that. Run the program, load an image, and copy it into the clipboard. Then, close the program and run it again. Select Edit | Paste and watch how the image transfers into the new instance of the program. Or, run several copies of the program, as in Figure 7–44, and copy and paste between them.

If you use the clipboard viewer or if you simply select Paste in your word processor, you can see the MIME encoding of the clipboard data (see Figure 7–45). However, what you cannot do is have the bitmap in the clipboard pasted as an image into your word processor. The system clipboard does not know that the data is actually an image, and it does not understand the encoding. For the same reason, you cannot select an image in your web browser, copy it into the clipboard, and paste it into our example program. As mentioned previously, it is currently not possible to transfer anything other than text between a program in the Java programming language and a native application.

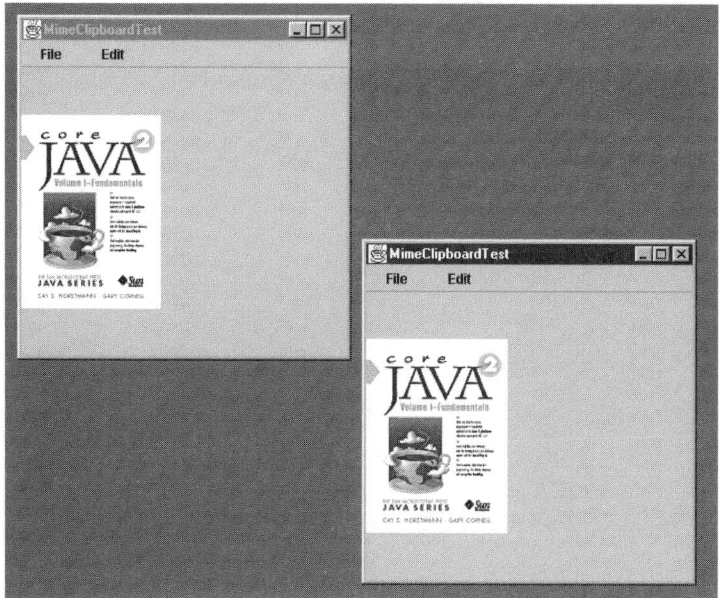

Figure 7–44: Data is copied between two instances of the `MimeClipboardTest` program

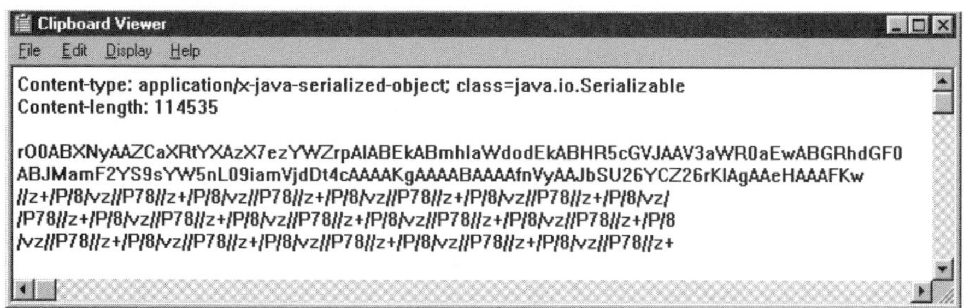

Figure 7–45: The clipboard contents after an image is copied

Example 7–15: MimeClipboardTest.java

```
import java.io.*;
import java.awt.*;
import java.awt.image.*;
import java.awt.event.*;
import java.awt.datatransfer.*;
import javax.swing.*;

public class MimeClipboardTest
{  public static void main(String [] args)
```

```
    {  JFrame frame = new MimeClipboardFrame();
       frame.show();
    }
}

class MimeClipboardFrame extends JFrame
   implements ActionListener
{  public MimeClipboardFrame()
   {  setSize(300, 300);
      setTitle("MimeClipboardTest");
      addWindowListener(new WindowAdapter()
         {  public void windowClosing(WindowEvent e)
            {  System.exit(0);
            }
         } );

      Container contentPane = getContentPane();
      label = new JLabel();
      contentPane.add(label, "Center");

      JMenu fileMenu = new JMenu("File");
      openItem = new JMenuItem("Open");
      openItem.addActionListener(this);
      fileMenu.add(openItem);

      exitItem = new JMenuItem("Exit");
      exitItem.addActionListener(this);
      fileMenu.add(exitItem);

      JMenu editMenu = new JMenu("Edit");
      copyItem = new JMenuItem("Copy");
      copyItem.addActionListener(this);
      editMenu.add(copyItem);

      pasteItem = new JMenuItem("Paste");
      pasteItem.addActionListener(this);
      editMenu.add(pasteItem);

      JMenuBar menuBar = new JMenuBar();
      menuBar.add(fileMenu);
      menuBar.add(editMenu);
      setJMenuBar(menuBar);
   }

   public void actionPerformed(ActionEvent evt)
   {  Object source = evt.getSource();
      if (source == openItem)
      {  JFileChooser chooser = new JFileChooser();
         chooser.setCurrentDirectory(new File("."));

         chooser.setFileFilter(new
```

```
         javax.swing.filechooser.FileFilter()
         {  public boolean accept(File f)
            {  String name = f.getName().toLowerCase();
               return name.endsWith(".gif")
                  || name.endsWith(".jpg")
                  || name.endsWith(".jpeg")
                  || f.isDirectory();
            }
            public String getDescription()
            {  return "Image files";
            }
         });

      int r = chooser.showOpenDialog(this);
      if(r == JFileChooser.APPROVE_OPTION)
      {  String name
            = chooser.getSelectedFile().getAbsolutePath();
         setImage(Toolkit.getDefaultToolkit().getImage(name));
      }
   }
   else if (source == exitItem) System.exit(0);
   else if (source == copyItem) copy();
   else if (source == pasteItem) paste();
}

private void copy()
{  MediaTracker tracker = new MediaTracker(this);
   tracker.addImage(theImage, 0);
   try { tracker.waitForID(0); }
   catch (InterruptedException e) {}
   BufferedImage image
      = new BufferedImage(theImage.getWidth(null),
         theImage.getHeight(null),
         BufferedImage.TYPE_INT_RGB);
   Graphics2D g2 = image.createGraphics();
   g2.drawImage(theImage, 0, 0, null);

   Bitmap bitmap = new Bitmap(image);
   SerializableSelection selection
      = new SerializableSelection(bitmap);
   mimeClipboard.setContents(selection, null);
}

private void paste()
{  Transferable selection
      = mimeClipboard.getContents(this);
   try
   {  Bitmap bitmap = (Bitmap)selection.getTransferData
         (SerializableSelection.serializableFlavor);
      setImage(bitmap.getImage());
   }
   catch(Exception e) {}
```

```
   }

   public void setImage(Image image)
   {  theImage = image;
      label.setIcon(new ImageIcon(image));
   }

   private static Clipboard mimeClipboard
      = new MimeClipboard
         (Toolkit.getDefaultToolkit().getSystemClipboard());
   private Image theImage;
   private JLabel label;
   private JMenuItem openItem;
   private JMenuItem exitItem;
   private JMenuItem copyItem;
   private JMenuItem pasteItem;
}

class Bitmap implements Serializable
{  public Bitmap(BufferedImage image)
   {  type = image.getType();
      width = image.getWidth();
      height = image.getHeight();
      WritableRaster raster = image.getRaster();
      data = raster.getDataElements(0, 0, width, height, null);
   }

   public BufferedImage getImage()
   {  BufferedImage image
         = new BufferedImage(width, height, type);
      WritableRaster raster = image.getRaster();
      raster.setDataElements(0, 0, width, height, data);
      return image;
   }

   private int type;
   private int width;
   private int height;
   private Object data;
}

class SerializableSelection implements Transferable
{  public SerializableSelection(Serializable object)
   {  theObject = object;
   }

   public boolean isDataFlavorSupported(DataFlavor flavor)
   {  return flavor.equals(serializableFlavor);
   }

   public synchronized Object getTransferData
```

```
      (DataFlavor flavor)
      throws UnsupportedFlavorException
   {  if(flavor.equals(serializableFlavor))
      {  return theObject;
      }
      else
      {  throw new UnsupportedFlavorException(flavor);
      }
   }

   public DataFlavor[] getTransferDataFlavors()
   {  return flavors;
   }

   public static final DataFlavor serializableFlavor
      = new DataFlavor(java.io.Serializable.class,
      "Serializable Object");

   private static DataFlavor[] flavors
      = { serializableFlavor };

   private Serializable theObject;
}

class MimeClipboard extends Clipboard
{  public MimeClipboard(Clipboard cb)
   {  super("MIME/" + cb.getName());
      clip = cb;
   }

   public synchronized void setContents(Transferable contents,
      ClipboardOwner owner)
   {  if (contents instanceof SerializableSelection)
      {  try
         {  DataFlavor flavor
               = SerializableSelection.serializableFlavor;
            Serializable obj = (Serializable)
               contents.getTransferData(flavor);
            String enc = encode(obj);
            String header = "Content-type: "
               + flavor.getMimeType()
               + "\nContent-length: "
               + enc.length() + "\n\n";
            StringSelection selection
               = new StringSelection(header + enc);
            clip.setContents(selection, owner);
         }
         catch(UnsupportedFlavorException e)
         {}
         catch(IOException e)
         {}
      }
```

```
      else clip.setContents(contents, owner);
   }

   public synchronized Transferable getContents
      (Object requestor)
   {  Transferable contents = clip.getContents(requestor);

      if (contents instanceof StringSelection)
      {  String data = null;
         try
         {  data = (String)contents.getTransferData
               (DataFlavor.stringFlavor);
         }
         catch(UnsupportedFlavorException e)
         { return contents; }
         catch(IOException e)
         { return contents; }

         if (!data.startsWith("Content-type: "))
            return contents;
         int start = -1;
         // skip three newlines
         for (int i = 0; i < 3; i++)
         {  start = data.indexOf('\n', start + 1);
            if (start < 0) return contents;
          }
         Serializable obj = decode(data.substring(start));
         SerializableSelection selection
            = new SerializableSelection(obj);
         return selection;
      }
      else return contents;
   }

   public static String encode(Serializable obj)
   {  ByteArrayOutputStream bOut
         = new ByteArrayOutputStream();
      try
      {  Base64OutputStream b64Out
            = new Base64OutputStream(bOut);
         ObjectOutputStream out
            = new ObjectOutputStream(b64Out);
         out.writeObject(obj);
         out.close();
         return bOut.toString("8859_1");
      }
      catch (IOException exception)
      {  return null;
      }
   }

   public static Serializable decode(String s)
```

```
   {  try
      {  byte[] bytes = s.getBytes("8859_1");
         ByteArrayInputStream bIn
            = new ByteArrayInputStream(bytes);
         Base64InputStream b64In
            = new Base64InputStream(bIn);
         ObjectInputStream in
            = new ObjectInputStream(b64In);
         Object obj = in.readObject();
         in.close();
         return (Serializable)obj;
      }
      catch(Exception e)
      {  return null;
      }
   }

   private Clipboard clip;
}

/* BASE64 encoding encodes 3 bytes into 4 characters.
   |11111122|22223333|33444444|
   Each set of 6 bits is encoded according to the
   toBase64 map. If the number of input bytes is not
   a multiple of 3, then the last group of 4 characters
   is padded with one or two = signs. Each output line
   is at most 76 characters.
*/

class Base64OutputStream extends FilterOutputStream
{  public Base64OutputStream(OutputStream out)
   {  super(out);
   }

   public void write(int c) throws IOException
   {  inbuf[i] = c;
      i++;
      if (i == 3)
      {  super.write(toBase64[(inbuf[0] & 0xFC) >> 2]);
         super.write(toBase64[((inbuf[0] & 0x03) << 4) |
            ((inbuf[1] & 0xF0) >> 4)]);
         super.write(toBase64[((inbuf[1] & 0x0F) << 2) |
            ((inbuf[2] & 0xC0) >> 6)]);
         super.write(toBase64[inbuf[2] & 0x3F]);
         col += 4;
         i = 0;
         if (col >= 76)
         {  super.write('\n');
            col = 0;
         }
      }
```

```
   }

   public void flush() throws IOException
   {  if (i == 1)
      {  super.write(toBase64[(inbuf[0] & 0xFC) >> 2]);
         super.write(toBase64[(inbuf[0] & 0x03) << 4]);
         super.write('=');
         super.write('=');
      }
      else if (i == 2)
      {  super.write(toBase64[(inbuf[0] & 0xFC) >> 2]);
         super.write(toBase64[((inbuf[0] & 0x03) << 4) |
            ((inbuf[1] & 0xF0) >> 4)]);
         super.write(toBase64[(inbuf[1] & 0x0F) << 2]);
         super.write('=');
      }
      i = 0;
   }

   private static char[] toBase64 =
   {  'A', 'B', 'C', 'D', 'E', 'F', 'G', 'H',
      'I', 'J', 'K', 'L', 'M', 'N', 'O', 'P',
      'Q', 'R', 'S', 'T', 'U', 'V', 'W', 'X',
      'Y', 'Z', 'a', 'b', 'c', 'd', 'e', 'f',
      'g', 'h', 'i', 'j', 'k', 'l', 'm', 'n',
      'o', 'p', 'q', 'r', 's', 't', 'u', 'v',
      'w', 'x', 'y', 'z', '0', '1', '2', '3',
      '4', '5', '6', '7', '8', '9', '+', '/'
   };

   private int col = 0;
   private int i = 0;
   private int[] inbuf = new int[3];
}


class Base64InputStream extends FilterInputStream
{  public Base64InputStream(InputStream in)
   {  super(in);
   }

   public int read(byte[] b, int off, int len) throws IOException
   {  if (len > b.length - off) len = b.length - off;
      for (int i = 0; i < len; i++)
      {  int ch = read();
         if (ch == -1) return i;
         b[i + off] = (byte)ch;
      }
```

```
      return len;
   }

   public int read(byte[] b) throws IOException
   {  return read(b, 0, b.length);
   }

   public int read() throws IOException
   {  int r;
      if (i == 0)
      {  // skip whitespace
         do
         {  ch[0] = super.read();
            if (ch[0] == -1) return -1;
         }
         while (Character.isWhitespace((char)ch[0]));
         ch[1] = super.read();
         if (ch[1] == -1) return -1;
         i++;
         r = (fromBase64[ch[0]] << 2)
            | (fromBase64[ch[1]] >> 4);
      }
      else if (i == 1)
      {  ch[2] = super.read();
         if (ch[2] == '=' || ch[2] == -1) return -1;
         i++;
         r = ((fromBase64[ch[1]] & 0x0F) << 4)
            | (fromBase64[ch[2]] >> 2);
      }
      else
      {  ch[3] = super.read();
         if (ch[3] == '=' || ch[3] == -1) return -1;
         i = 0;
         r = ((fromBase64[ch[2]] & 0x03) << 6)
            | fromBase64[ch[3]];
      }
      return r;
   }

   private static int[] fromBase64 =
   {  -1, -1, -1, -1, -1, -1, -1, -1,
      -1, -1, -1, -1, -1, -1, -1, -1,
      -1, -1, -1, -1, -1, -1, -1, -1,
      -1, -1, -1, -1, -1, -1, -1, -1,
      -1, -1, -1, -1, -1, -1, -1, -1,
      -1, -1, -1, 62, -1, -1, -1, 63,
      52, 53, 54, 55, 56, 57, 58, 59,
      60, 61, -1, -1, -1, -1, -1, -1,
      -1,  0,  1,  2,  3,  4,  5,  6,
```

```
         7,   8,   9, 10, 11, 12, 13, 14,
        15, 16, 17, 18, 19, 20, 21, 22,
        23, 24, 25, -1, -1, -1, -1, -1,
        -1, 26, 27, 28, 29, 30, 31, 32,
        33, 34, 35, 36, 37, 38, 39, 40,
        41, 42, 43, 44, 45, 46, 47, 48,
        49, 50, 51, -1, -1, -1, -1, -1
    };

    int i = 0;
    int[] ch = new int[4];
}
```

Drag and Drop

When you use cut and paste to transmit information between two programs, then the clipboard acts as an intermediary. The *drag and drop* metaphor cuts out the middleman and lets two programs communicate directly. The Java 2 platform offers basic support for drag and drop. You can carry out drag and drop operations between Java applications and native applications. This section shows you how to write a Java application that is a drop target and an application that is a drag source.

Before going deeper into the Java platform support for drag and drop, let us have a quick look at the drag and drop user interface. We'll use the Windows Explorer and WordPad programs as examples—on another platform, you can experiment with locally available programs with drag and drop capabilities.

You initiate a *drag operation* with a *gesture* inside a *drag source*—usually, by first selecting one or more elements and then dragging the selection away from its initial location (see figure Figure 7–46).

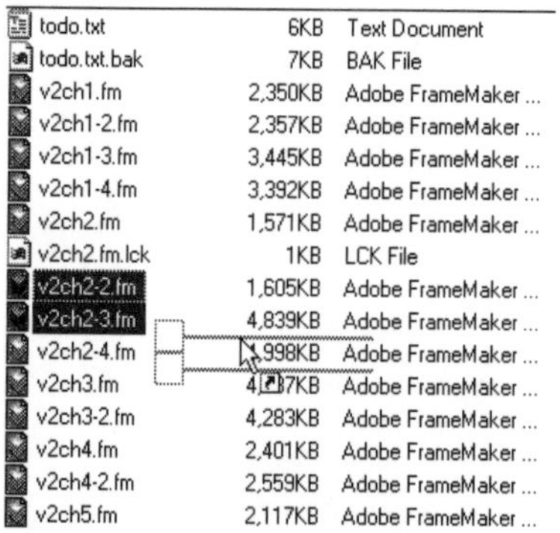

todo.txt	6KB	Text Document
todo.txt.bak	7KB	BAK File
v2ch1.fm	2,350KB	Adobe FrameMaker ...
v2ch1-2.fm	2,357KB	Adobe FrameMaker ...
v2ch1-3.fm	3,445KB	Adobe FrameMaker ...
v2ch1-4.fm	3,392KB	Adobe FrameMaker ...
v2ch2.fm	1,571KB	Adobe FrameMaker ...
v2ch2.fm.lck	1KB	LCK File
v2ch2-2.fm	1,605KB	Adobe FrameMaker ...
v2ch2-3.fm	4,839KB	Adobe FrameMaker ...
v2ch2-4.fm	998KB	Adobe FrameMaker ...
v2ch3.fm	4,[illegible]7KB	Adobe FrameMaker ...
v2ch3-2.fm	4,283KB	Adobe FrameMaker ...
v2ch4.fm	2,401KB	Adobe FrameMaker ...
v2ch4-2.fm	2,559KB	Adobe FrameMaker ...
v2ch5.fm	2,117KB	Adobe FrameMaker ...

Figure 7–46: Initiating a drag operation

When you release the mouse button over a drop target that accepts the drop operation, then the drop target queries the drag source for information about the

dropped elements, and it initiates some operation. For example, if you drop a file icon from Windows Explorer to WordPad, then WordPad opens the file. However, if you drag a file icon on top of a directory icon in Windows Explorer, then it moves the file into that directory.

If you hold down the SHIFT or CTRL key while dragging, then the type of the drop action changes from a *move action* to a *copy action,* and a copy of the file is placed into the directory. If you hold down *both* SHIFT and CTRL keys, then a *link* to the file is placed into the directory. (Other platforms may use other keyboard combinations for these operations.)

Thus, there are three types of drop actions with different gestures.

- Move
- Copy
- Link

The intention of the link action is to establish a reference to the dropped element. Such links typically require support from the host operating system (such as symbolic links for files or object linking for document components) and don't usually make a lot of sense in cross-platform programs. In this section, we'll focus on using drag and drop for copying and moving.

Not all programs are sensitive to the drop action types. For example, if you drop a file onto WordPad, it ignores the action type and always opens the file.

There is usually some visual feedback for the drag operation. Minimally, the cursor shape will change. As the cursor moves over possible *drop targets,* the cursor shape indicates whether the drop is possible or not. If a drop is possible, the cursor shape also indicates the type of the drop action. Figure 7–47 shows several cursor shapes over drop targets.

Figure 7–47: Cursor shapes over drop targets

You can also drag other elements besides file icons. For example, you can select text in WordPad and drag it. Try dropping text fragments into willing drop targets and see how they react.

NOTE: This experiment shows a disadvantage of drag and drop as a user interface mechanism. It can be difficult for users to anticipate what you can drag, where you can drop it, and what happens when you do. Because the default "move" action can remove the original, many users are understandably cautious about experimenting with drag and drop.

Drop Targets

In this section, we will construct a simple Java application that is a drop target. The example program does nothing useful; it simply demonstrates how you can detect that a user would like to initiate a drop, how to accept the drop, and how to analyze the data that is being dropped.

You can designate any AWT component to be a drop target. To do so, you need to construct a `DropTarget` object and pass the component and a drop target listener to the constructor. The constructor registers the object with the drag and drop system.

```
DropTarget target = new DropTarget(component, listener);
```

You can activate or deactivate the target with the `setActive` method. By default, the target is active.

```
target.setActive(b);
```

You can call the `setDefaultActions` method to set the drop operations that you want to accept by default. The operations are

```
DndConstants.ACTION_COPY
DndConstants.ACTION_MOVE
DndConstants.ACTION_COPY_OR_MOVE
DndConstants.ACTION_LINK
```

By default, all operations are allowed.

Now you need to implement a drop target listener. The `DropTargetListener` interface has five methods:

```
void dragEnter(DropTargetDragEvent event)
void dragExit(DropTargetEvent event)
void dragOver(DropTargetDragEvent event)
void dropActionChanged(DropTargetDragEvent event)
void drop(DropTargetDropEvent event)
```

The `dragEnter` and `dragExit` methods are called when the cursor enters or exits the drop target component. In the `dragEnter` method, you have the chance to set the cursor shape to indicate whether the drop target is willing to accept the drop.

You don't usually worry about the `dragExit` method. However, if you built up some elaborate mechanism for visual feedback, then you can dispose of it in this method.

The `dragOver` method is called continuously as the user moves the mouse over the drop target component. You can use it to give detailed visual feedback about the effect of a drop. For example, if the drop target is a tree component, you can highlight the node under the cursor or even open up a subtree if the cursor hovers over a node.

The `dropActionChanged` method is called if the user changes the action gesture. For example, if the user presses or lifts the SHIFT or CTRL keys while moving the

mouse over the drop target component, then this method is called. That gives you a chance to modify the visual feedback and match it to the changed action.

The most important method is the `drop` method. It is called when the user has committed to a drop by finishing the drop gesture, usually by releasing the mouse button. Note that this method is called whether or not you previously indicated that you would accept the drop.

Look carefully at the parameters of the `DropTargetListener` methods. Three of them are a `DropTarget`**`Drag`**`Event`. However, the `drop` method receives a `DropTarget`**`Drop`**`Event` and the `dragExit` method receives a `DropTargetEvent`. The `DropTargetEvent` class is the superclass of the other two event classes. It has only one method, `getDropTargetContext`, which returns a class with no interesting public methods. Since the purpose of a `dragExit` method is to do cleanup, you probably won't even look at the parameter.

The `DropTargetDragEvent` and `DropTargetDropEvent` classes each have the following methods:

```
int getDropAction()
Point getLocation()
DataFlavor[] getCurrentDataFlavors()
boolean isDataFlavorSupported(DataFlavor flavor)
```

You need these methods to test whether to encourage a drag or allow a drop, and how to give visual feedback.

Unfortunately, since the methods are not available in the common superclass, you'll have to implement the test logic twice, once for the drag and then again for the drop.

If you don't want to encourage a drag, you should call the `rejectDrag` method of the `DropTargetDragEvent` class in the `dragEnter` or `dropActionChanged` method. As a result, the cursor changes to a warning icon. If the user drops an item despite the warning, then you should call the `rejectDrop` method of the `DropTargetDropEvent` class.

The `getDropAction` method returns the drop action that the user intends to carry out. In many drag and drop operations, you don't want the action taken literally. For example, if you move a file icon into WordPad, then you don't want the drag source to delete the file. But you also don't want the drop target to insist that the user hold down a key when dragging. In this situation, the drop target should accept either copy or move actions. In the `drop` method, call the `acceptDrop` method of the `DropTargetDropEvent` with the *actual* action. If you call

```
event.acceptDrop(DnDConstants.ACTION_MOVE);
   // drag source deletes dragged items!
```

then the drag source will *delete* the dragged items.

TIP: Are you certain that your users understand the distinction between move and copy operations and the role of the SHIFT and CTRL modifiers? Do they realize that the default drag gesture (without a modifier) deletes the dragged items from the source? If not, you should accept a drop as

```
event.acceptDrop(DnDConstants.ACTION_COPY);
```

On the other hand, if you really want to make a distinction between move and copy, simply call

```
event.acceptDrop(event.getDropEvent()).
```

Here is an overview of a typical drop target listener:

```
class ADropTargetListener implements DropTargetListener
{  // convenience methods
   public boolean isDragAcceptable(DropTargetDragEvent event)
   {  look at drop action and available data flavors
   }

   public boolean isDropAcceptable(DropTargetDropEvent event)
   {  carry out the same test as in isDragAcceptable
   }

   // listener methods
   public void dragEnter(DropTargetDragEvent event)
   {  if (!isDragAcceptable(event))
      {  event.rejectDrag();
         return;
      }
   }

   public void dragExit(DropTargetEvent event)
   {
   }

   public void dragOver(DropTargetDragEvent event)
   {  // you can provide visual feedback here
   }

   public void dropActionChanged(DropTargetDragEvent event)
   {  if (!isDragAcceptable(event))
      {  event.rejectDrag();
         return;
      }
   }

   public void drop(DropTargetDropEvent event)
   {  if (!isDropAcceptable(event))
      {  event.rejectDrop();
         return;
      }
```

```
        event.acceptDrop(actual action);
        process data from drag source
        event.dropComplete(true);
     }
     . . .
  }
```

Once you accept a drop, you need to analyze the data from the drag source. The `getTransferable` method of the `DropTargetDropEvent` class returns a reference to a `Transferable` object. This is the same interface that is used for copy and paste.

You now go through the same process as you do when pasting data from a clipboard. However, the Java platform implementation supports more data flavors for the drag and drop mechanism than it does for the system clipboard.

If the data flavor `DataFlavor.javaFileListFlavor` is available, then the `Transferable` object yields a file list, an object of type `java.util.List` whose items are `File` objects. A file list describes a set of file icons that was dropped onto the target. Here is the code for retrieving the files:

```
DataFlavor[] flavors = transferable.getTransferDataFlavors();
DataFlavor flavor = flavors[i];
if (flavor.equals(DataFlavor.javaFileListFlavor))
{  java.util.List fileList
      = (java.util.List)transferable.getTransferData(flavor);
   Iterator iterator = fileList.iterator();
   while (iterator.hasNext())
   {  File f = (File)iterator.next();
      do something with f;
   }
}
```

The other flavor that can be dropped is text. However, unlike the clipboard, the drag and drop mechanism doesn't go through the effort of converting the text to Unicode and giving you a `stringFlavor`. Instead, you get a flavor with MIME type `text/plain`. You retrieve the text through an `InputStream`. Of course, an input stream is a sequence of bytes, whereas text is a sequence of characters. The `text/plain` MIME type contains a `charset` parameter that indicates the character encoding. In theory, you ought to be able to pass the input stream and the character encoding to the `InputStreamReader` constructor and then read the input a character at a time.

```
if (flavor.isMimeTypeEqual("text/plain"))
{  String charset = flavor.getParameter("charset");
   InputStream inStream
      = (InputStream)transferable.getTransferData(flavor);
   InputStreamReader in
     = new InputStreamReader(inStream, charset); // Doesn't work
```

```
        int ch;
        while ((ch = in.read()) != -1)
        {  do something with ch
        }
    }
```

However, the MIME encoding names are different from the ones expected by the `InputStreamReader`.

We have encountered two character encodings, with MIME types

```
text/plain; charset=ascii
text/plain; charset=unicode
```

The `InputStreamReader` does not know these character sets. You need to convert `ascii` to `8859_1` and `unicode` to `Unicode`.

CAUTION: Under Windows, you are going to run into a couple of problems with this approach. The input stream is terminated by a null character, and you should not read past it. The Unicode data doesn't start with a Unicode byte order marker that the `InputStreamReader` expects, resulting in a `sun.io.MalformedInputException`. The code in Example 7–16 shows a workaround, where we don't use an `InputStreamReader` but construct the Unicode characters from pairs of bytes. We assume that the absence of a byte order marker indicates Windows and thus little-endian byte ordering. Hopefully, a future version of the drag and drop implementation will shield users from this hassle and simply return a `stringFlavor`.

Depending on the drag source, you may also find data in the formats

```
text/html
text/enriched
```

You read the data in the same way.

Our sample program does not attempt to do anything useful. It simply lets you drop items onto a text area. When you start dragging over the text area, the drop action is displayed. Once you initiate a drop, the dropped data is displayed. If the data is in text format, the program reads both `ascii` and `unicode` encodings.

In our sample program, we will not give any visual feedback of the dragging process beyond the change to a warning cursor that automatically happens when calling the `rejectDrag` method.

The purpose of this program is simply to give you a drop target for experimentation. Try dropping a selection of file names from Windows Explorer or a text fragment from WordPad (see Figure 7–48). Also see how a link attempt is rejected. If you depress both the SHIFT and CTRL keys, then a warning icon appears when you drag an item over the text area.

Example 7–16 shows the complete program.

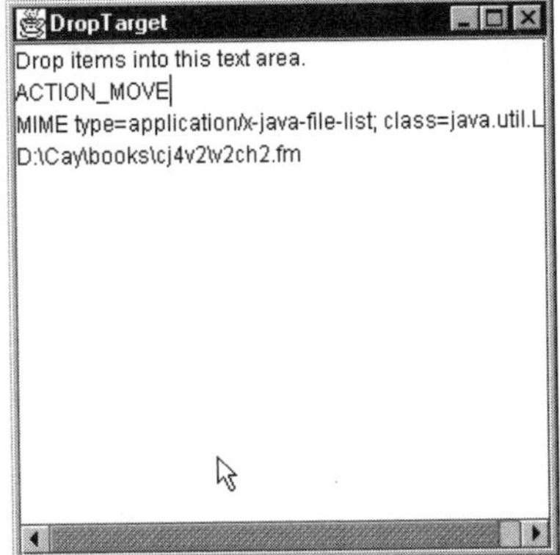

Figure 7–48: The DropTargetTest program

Example 7–16: DropTargetTest.java

```
import java.awt.*;
import java.awt.datatransfer.*;
import java.awt.event.*;
import java.awt.dnd.*;
import java.io.*;
import java.util.*;
import javax.swing.*;

public class DropTargetTest
{  public static void main(String[] args)
   {  JFrame frame = new DropTargetFrame();
      frame.show();
   }
}

class DropTargetFrame extends JFrame
{  public DropTargetFrame()
   {  setTitle("DropTarget");
      setSize(300, 300);
      addWindowListener(new WindowAdapter()
         {  public void windowClosing(WindowEvent e)
            {  System.exit(0);
            }
         } );

      Container contentPane = getContentPane();
      JTextArea textArea
         = new JTextArea("Drop items into this text area.\n");

      new DropTarget(textArea,
         new TextDropTargetListener(textArea));
      contentPane.add(new JScrollPane(textArea), "Center");
   }
```

```
}

class TextDropTargetListener implements DropTargetListener
{  public TextDropTargetListener(JTextArea ta)
   {  textArea = ta;
   }

   public void dragEnter(DropTargetDragEvent event)
   {  int a = event.getDropAction();
      if ((a & DnDConstants.ACTION_COPY) != 0)
         textArea.append("ACTION_COPY\n");
      if ((a & DnDConstants.ACTION_MOVE) != 0)
         textArea.append("ACTION_MOVE\n");
      if ((a & DnDConstants.ACTION_LINK) != 0)
         textArea.append("ACTION_LINK\n");

      if (!isDragAcceptable(event))
      {  event.rejectDrag();
         return;
      }
   }

   public void dragExit(DropTargetEvent event)
   {
   }

   public void dragOver(DropTargetDragEvent event)
   {  // you can provide visual feedback here
   }

   public void dropActionChanged(DropTargetDragEvent event)
   {  if (!isDragAcceptable(event))
      {  event.rejectDrag();
         return;
      }
   }

   public void drop(DropTargetDropEvent event)
   {  if (!isDropAcceptable(event))
      {  event.rejectDrop();
         return;
      }

      event.acceptDrop(DnDConstants.ACTION_COPY);

      Transferable transferable = event.getTransferable();

      DataFlavor[] flavors
         = transferable.getTransferDataFlavors();
      for (int i = 0; i < flavors.length; i++)
      {  DataFlavor d = flavors[i];
```

```
textArea.append("MIME type=" + d.getMimeType() + "\n");

try
{  if (d.equals(DataFlavor.javaFileListFlavor))
   {  java.util.List fileList = (java.util.List)
         transferable.getTransferData(d);
      Iterator iterator = fileList.iterator();
      while (iterator.hasNext())
      {  File f = (File)iterator.next();
         textArea.append(f + "\n");
      }
   }
   else if (d.equals(DataFlavor.stringFlavor))
   {  String s = (String)
         transferable.getTransferData(d);
      textArea.append(s + "\n");
   }
   else if (d.isMimeTypeEqual("text/plain"))
   {  String charset = d.getParameter("charset");
      InputStream in = (InputStream)
         transferable.getTransferData(d);

      boolean more = true;
      int ch;
      if (charset.equals("ascii"))
      {  do
         {  ch = in.read();
            if (ch != 0 && ch != -1)
               textArea.append("" + (char)ch);
            else more = false;
         } while (more);
      }
      else if (charset.equals("unicode"))
      {  boolean littleEndian = true;
            // if no byte ordering mark, we assume
            // Windows is the culprit
         do
         {  ch = in.read();
            int ch2 = in.read();
            if (ch != -1 && littleEndian)
               ch = (ch & 0xFF) | ((ch2 & 0xFF) << 8);
            if (ch == 0xFFFE)
               littleEndian = false;
            else if (ch != 0 && ch != -1)
               textArea.append("" + (char)ch);
            else more = false;
         } while (more);
      }

      textArea.append("\n");
   }
}
```

```
         catch(Exception e)
         {  textArea.append("Error: " + e + "\n");
         }
      }
      event.dropComplete(true);
   }

   public boolean isDragAcceptable(DropTargetDragEvent event)
   {  // usually, you check the available data flavors here
      // in this program, we accept all flavors
      return (event.getDropAction()
         & DnDConstants.ACTION_COPY_OR_MOVE) != 0;
   }

   public boolean isDropAcceptable(DropTargetDropEvent event)
   {  // usually, you check the available data flavors here
      // in this program, we accept all flavors
      return (event.getDropAction()
         & DnDConstants.ACTION_COPY_OR_MOVE) != 0;
   }

   private JTextArea textArea;
}
```

`java.awt.dnd.DropTarget`

- `DropTarget(Component c, DropTargetListener listener)`

  constructs a drop target that coordinates the drag and drop action onto a component.

Parameters:	`c`	the drop target
	`listener`	the listener to be notified in the drop process

- `void setActive(boolean b)`

  activates or deactivates this drop target.

- `void setDefaultActions(int actions)`

  sets the actions that are permissible by default for this drop target. `actions` is a bit mask composed of constants defined in the `DnDConstants` class such as `ACTION_COPY`, `ACTION_MOVE`, `ACTION_COPY_OR_MOVE`, or `ACTION_LINK`.

`java.awt.dnd.DropTargetListener`

- `void dragEnter(DropTargetDragEvent event)`

  is called when the cursor enters the drop target.

- `void dragExit(DropTargetEvent event)`

  is called when the cursor exits the drop target.

- `void dragOver(DropTargetDragEvent event)`

  is called when the cursor moves over the drop target.

- `void dropActionChanged(DropTargetDragEvent event)`
  is called when the user changes the drop action while the cursor is over the drop target.
- `void drop(DropTargetDropEvent event)`
  is called when the user drops items into the drop target.

`java.awt.dnd.DropTargetDragEvent`

- `int getDropAction()`
  gets the currently selected drop action. Possible values are defined in the `DnDConstants` class.
- `void acceptDrag(int action)`
  This method should be called if the drop target wants to accept a drop action that is different from the currently selected action.
- `void rejectDrag()`
  notifies the drag and drop mechanism that this component rejects the current drop attempt.
- `Point getLocation()`
  returns the current location of the mouse over the drop target.
- `DataFlavor[] getCurrentDataFlavors()`
  returns the data flavors that the drag source can deliver.
- `boolean isDataFlavorSupported(DataFlavor flavor)`
  tests whether drag source supports the given flavor.

`java.awt.dnd.DropTargetDropEvent`

- `int getDropAction()`
  gets the currently selected drop action. Possible values are defined in the `DnDConstants` class.
- `void acceptDrop(int action)`
  This method should be called if the drop target has carried out a drop action that is different from the currently selected action.
- `void rejectDrop()`
  notifies the drag and drop mechanism that this component rejects the drop.
- `void dropComplete(boolean success)`
  notifies the drag source that the drop is complete and whether it was successful.
- `Point getLocation()`
  returns the current location of the mouse over the drop target.

- `DataFlavor[] getCurrentDataFlavors()`
  returns the data flavors that the drag source can deliver.
- `boolean isDataFlavorSupported(DataFlavor flavor)`
  tests whether drag source supports the given flavor.

Drag Sources

Now that you saw how to implement a program that contains a drop target, we want to show you how to implement a drag source.

The program in Example 7–17 fills a `JList` with all files in the current directory (see Figure 7–49.) The list component is a drag source. You can drag file items from the list component to any drop target that is willing to accept a list of files.

To turn a component into a drag source, you need to obtain a `DragSource` object—you can simply call the static `DragSource.getDefaultDragSource` method. Then, call the `createDefaultDragGestureRecognizer` method and supply it with

- The component that you want to turn into a drag source
- The drop actions that you want to allow
- An object that implements the `DragGestureListener` interface

For example,

```
DragSource dragSource = DragSource.getDefaultDragSource();
dragSource.createDefaultDragGestureRecognizer(component,
   DnDConstants.ACTION_COPY_OR_MOVE, dragGestureListener);
```

The `DragGestureListener` interface has a single method, `dragGestureRecognized`. The gesture recognizer calls that method as soon as it has noticed that the user wants to initiate a drag operation. In that method, you need to build the `Transferable` that the drop target will ultimately read in its `drop` method. Once you have assembled the `Transferable`, you call the `startDrag` method of the `DragGestureEvent` class. You supply an optional cursor, or `null` if you want to use the default drag cursor, followed by the `Transferable` and an object that implements the `DragSourceListener` interface. For example,

```
event.startDrag(null, transferable, dragSourceListener);
```

The drag source listener is notified repeatedly as the drag operation progresses. We will look at it shortly, but first we want to show you how to build a `Transferable` that can hold a list of files.

You need to define a class that implements the `Transferable` interface and supports the standard flavor `DataFlavor.javaFileListFlavor`. The `getTransferData` method needs to return an object of a class implementing the `java.util.List` interface that is filled with `File` elements. Here is a simple version of such a class. We simply store an array of files in an `ArrayList` and return that list when the flavor matches `DataFlavor.javaFileListFlavor`.

```
class FileListTransferable implements Transferable
{  public FileListTransferable(Object[] files)
   {  // turn the array into an ArrayList
      fileList = new ArrayList(Arrays.asList(files));
   }

   public synchronized Object getTransferData
      (DataFlavor flavor)
      throws UnsupportedFlavorException
   {  if(flavor.equals(DataFlavor.javaFileListFlavor))
      {  return fileList;
      }
      else
      {  throw new UnsupportedFlavorException(flavor);
      }
   }

   public DataFlavor[] getTransferDataFlavors()
   {  return new DataFlavor[] { DataFlavor.javaFileListFlavor };
   }

   public boolean isDataFlavorSupported(DataFlavor flavor)
   {  return flavor.equals(DataFlavor.javaFileListFlavor);
   }

   private ArrayList fileList;
}
```

The class in Example 7–17 is a little more complex because it also supports the `stringFlavor`.

Now let us return to the `DragSourceListener` interface. The interface has five methods.

```
void dragEnter(DragSourceDragEvent event)
void dragOver(DragSourceDragEvent event)
void dragExit(DragSourceEvent event)
void dropActionChanged(DragSourceDragEvent event)
void dragDropEnd(DragSourceDropEvent event)
```

You can use the first four methods to give the user visual feedback of the drag operation. However, generally, such feedback should be the role of the drop target. We will use these methods in our sample program. However, the last method, `dragDropEnd`, is very important. This method is called when the `drop` method has finished. For a move operation, you need to check whether the drop has succeeded. In that case, you need to update the drag source. (For a copy operation, you probably don't have to do anything.)

Here is the `dragDropEnd` method for our example program. When a move has succeeded, we remove the moved items from the list model.

```
public void dragDropEnd(DragSourceDropEvent event)
{  if (event.getDropSuccess())
```

```
        {  int action = event.getDropAction();
           if (action == DnDConstants.ACTION_MOVE)
           {  for (int i = 0; i < draggedValues.length; i++)
                 model.removeElement(draggedValues[i]);
           }
        }
     }
```

In this method, we rely on the `drop` method to tell us what drop was actually carried out. Recall that the `drop` method can change a move action to a copy action if the source allowed both actions. The `event.getDropAction` of the `DragSourceDropEvent` class returns the action that the drop target reported when calling the `acceptDrop` method of the `DropTargetDropEvent`.

Try out the program in Example 7–17 and drag file items to various drop targets, such as the program in Example 7–16 or a native program such as Windows Explorer or WordPad.

NOTE: When you try the dragging, you have to be careful that the drag gesture doesn't interfere with the normal mouse effects of the list control. Select one or more items. Press the mouse button on a selected item and move the mouse *sideways*, until it leaves the list component. Now the drag gesture is recognized. *After* the mouse has left the list component, depress the SHIFT or CTRL key to modify the drop action.

CAUTION: The default drop action is a *move*. If you drag a file item from the list component and drop it into Windows Explorer, then Explorer moves the file into the target folder.

As you have seen, support for the system clipboard and the drag and drop mechanism are still very much a work in progress. The basics work, but, hopefully, future versions of the Java platform will offer more robust and comprehensive support.

In this section, we have covered the basic mechanics of the drag and drop mechanism. For more information, particularly about programming visual feedback, we recommend the book *Core Swing: Advanced Programming* by Kim Topley [Prentice Hall 2000].

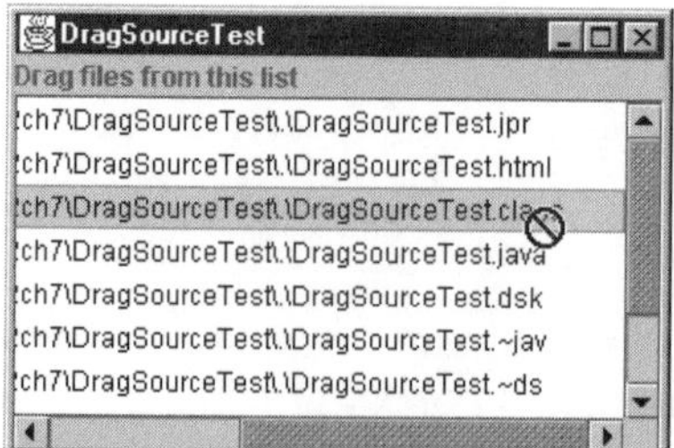

Figure 7–49: The DragSourceTest program

Example 7-17: DragSourceTest.java

```
import java.awt.*;
import java.awt.datatransfer.*;
import java.awt.dnd.*;
import java.awt.event.*;
import java.io.*;
import java.util.*;
import javax.swing.*;

public class DragSourceTest
{  public static void main(String[] args)
   {  JFrame frame = new DragSourceFrame();
      frame.show();
   }
}

class DragSourceFrame extends JFrame
   implements DragSourceListener, DragGestureListener
{  public DragSourceFrame()
   {  setTitle("DragSourceTest");
      setSize(300, 200);
      addWindowListener(new WindowAdapter()
         {  public void windowClosing(WindowEvent e)
            {  System.exit(0);
            }
         } );

      Container contentPane = getContentPane();
      File f = new File(".").getAbsoluteFile();
      File[] files = f.listFiles();
      model = new DefaultListModel();
      for (int i = 0; i < files.length; i++)
         model.addElement(files[i]);
      fileList = new JList(model);
      contentPane.add(new JScrollPane(fileList), "Center");
      contentPane.add(new JLabel("Drag files from this list"),
         "North");

      DragSource dragSource = DragSource.getDefaultDragSource();
      dragSource.createDefaultDragGestureRecognizer(fileList,
         DnDConstants.ACTION_COPY_OR_MOVE, this);
   }

   // DragGestureListener method

   public void dragGestureRecognized(DragGestureEvent event)
   {  draggedValues = fileList.getSelectedValues();
      Transferable transferable
         = new FileListTransferable(draggedValues);
      event.startDrag(null, transferable, this);
```

```
   }

   // DragSourceListener methods

   public void dragEnter(DragSourceDragEvent event)
   {
   }

   public void dragOver(DragSourceDragEvent event)
   {
   }

   public void dragExit(DragSourceEvent event)
   {
   }

   public void dropActionChanged(DragSourceDragEvent event)
   {
   }

   public void dragDropEnd(DragSourceDropEvent event)
   {  if (event.getDropSuccess())
      {  int action = event.getDropAction();
         if (action == DnDConstants.ACTION_MOVE)
         {  for (int i = 0; i < draggedValues.length; i++)
               model.removeElement(draggedValues[i]);
         }
      }
   }

   private JList fileList;
   private DefaultListModel model;
   private Object[] draggedValues;
}

class FileListTransferable implements Transferable
{  public FileListTransferable(Object[] files)
   {  fileList = new ArrayList(Arrays.asList(files));
   }

   public DataFlavor[] getTransferDataFlavors()
   {  return flavors;
   }

   public boolean isDataFlavorSupported(DataFlavor flavor)
   {  return Arrays.asList(flavors).contains(flavor);
   }

   public synchronized Object getTransferData
      (DataFlavor flavor)
      throws UnsupportedFlavorException
   {  if(flavor.equals(DataFlavor.javaFileListFlavor))
```

```
      {  return fileList;
      }
      else if(flavor.equals(DataFlavor.stringFlavor))
      {  return fileList.toString();
      }
      else
      {  throw new UnsupportedFlavorException(flavor);
      }
   }

   private static DataFlavor[] flavors =
      {  DataFlavor.javaFileListFlavor,
         DataFlavor.stringFlavor
      };

   private java.util.List fileList;
}
```

`java.awt.dnd.DragSource`

- `static DragSource getDefaultDragSource()`
  gets a `DragSource` object to coordinate drag actions on components.
- `DragGestureRecognizer createDefaultDragGestureRecognizer(Component component, int actions, DragGestureListener listener)`
  creates a drag gesture recognizer.

Parameters:	`component`	the drag source
	`actions`	the permissible drop actions
	`listener`	the listener to be notified when a drag gesture has been recognized

`java.awt.dnd.DragGestureListener`

- `void dragGestureRecognized(DragGestureEvent event)`
  is called when the drag gesture recognizer has recognized a gesture.

`java.awt.dnd.DragGestureEvent`

- `void startDrag(Cursor dragCursor, Transferable transferable, DragSourceListener listener)`
  starts the drag action.

Parameters:	`dragCursor`	an optional cursor to use for the drag. May be `null`, in which case a default cursor is used
	`transferable`	the data to be transferred to the drop target
	`listener`	the listener to be notified of the drag process

`java.awt.dnd.DragSourceListener`

- `void dragEnter(DragSourceDragEvent event)`
  is called when the drag cursor enters the drag source.
- `void dragExit(DragSourceEvent event)`
  is called when the drag cursor exits the drag source.
- `void dragOver(DragSourceDragEvent event)`
  is called when the drag cursor moves over the drag source.
- `void dropActionChanged(DragSourceDragEvent event)`
  is called when the user changed the drop action.
- `void dragDropEnd(DragSourceDropEvent event)`
  is called after the drag and drop operation was completed or canceled.

`java.awt.dnd.DragSourceDropEvent`

- `boolean getDropSuccess()`
  returns `true` if the drop target reported a successful drop.
- `int getDropAction()`
  returns the action that the drop target actually carried out.

Chapter 8

JavaBeans™

- ▼ Why Beans?
- ▼ The Bean Writing Process
- ▼ The BDK and the BeanBox
- ▼ Building an Image Viewer Application via Beans
- ▼ Naming Patterns for Bean Properties and Events
- ▼ Bean Property Types
- ▼ Adding Custom Bean Events
- ▼ Property Editors
- ▼ Going Beyond Naming Patterns—Building a BeanInfo Class
- ▼ Customizers
- ▼ The Bean Context

The official definition of a bean, as given in the JavaBeans specification, is: "A bean is a reusable software component based on Sun's JavaBeans specification that can be manipulated visually in a builder tool."

Once you implement a bean, others can use it in a builder environment such as JBuilder, VisualAge, or Visual Café, to produce applications or applets more efficiently.

We will not tell you how to use those environments—you should refer to the documentation that the vendors provide. This chapter explains what you need to know about beans in order to *implement* them so that other programmers can use your beans easily.

Why Beans?

Programmers coming from a Windows background (specifically, Visual Basic or Delphi) will immediately know why beans are so important. Programmers coming from an environment where the tradition is to "roll your own" for everything may not understand at once. In our experience, programmers who do not come from a Visual Basic background often find it hard to believe that Visual Basic is one of the most successful examples of reusable object technology. One reason for the popularity of Visual Basic becomes clear if you consider how you build a Visual Basic application. For those who have never worked with Visual Basic, here, in a nutshell, is how you do it:

1. You build the interface by dropping components (called *controls* in Visual Basic) onto a form window.
2. Through *property sheets,* you set properties of the components such as height, color, or other behavior.
3. The property sheets also list the events to which components can react. For some of those events, you write short snippets of event handling code.

For example, in Chapter 2 of Volume 1, we wrote a program that displays an image in a frame. It took a little over a page of code. Here's what you would do in Visual Basic to create a program with pretty much the same functionality.

1. Add two controls to a window: an *Image* control for displaying graphics and a *Common Dialog* control for selecting a file.
2. Set the *Filter* properties of the CommonDialog control so that only files that the Image control can handle will show up. This is done in what VB calls the Properties window, as shown in Figure 8–1.

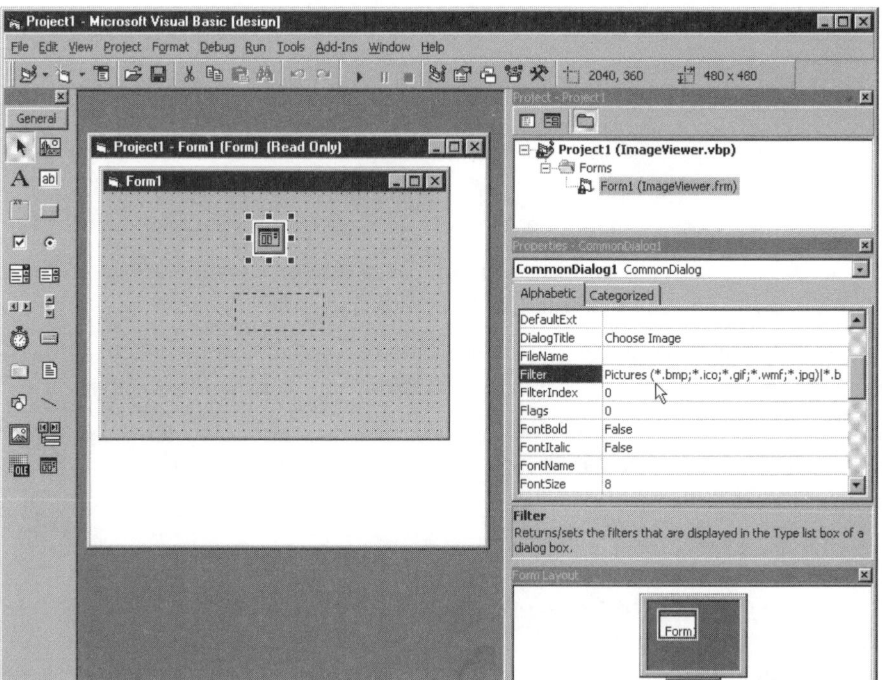

Figure 8–1: The Properties window in VB for an image application

Now, we need to write the five lines of VB code that will be activated when the project first starts running. This corresponds to an event called the `Form_Load`, so

the code goes in the `Form_Load` event procedure. The following code pops up the file dialog box—but only files with the right extension are shown because of how we set the filter property. After the user selects an image file, the code then tells the Image control to display it. All the code you need for this sequence looks like this:

```
Private Sub Form_Load()
  On Error Resume Next
  CommonDialog1.ShowOpen
  Image1.Picture = LoadPicture(CommonDialog1.FileName)
End Sub
```

That's it. The layout activity, combined with these five lines of code give essentially the same functionality as a page of Java programming language code. Clearly, it is a lot easier to learn how to drop down components and set properties than it is to write a page of code.

The point is that right now the Java programming language is still a tool used mostly by top-notch, object-oriented programmers. And, realistically, even such programmers are unlikely to be as productive as a good Visual Basic programmer for designing the user interface of a small- to medium-sized application. The JavaBeans technology enables vendors to create environments that make it dramatically easier to develop user interfaces for Java applications.

Note that we do not want to imply that Visual Basic is a good solution for every problem. It is clearly optimized for a particular kind of problems—UI-intensive Windows programs. In contrast, Java technology will always have a much wider range of uses. And the good news is that with the advent of JavaBeans technology, some of the benefits of Visual Basic-style application building are on the horizon for programmers. In particular:

1. Beans with the same functionality as the most common Visual Basic controls are readily available.
2. Java technology builder tools have come much closer to the ease of use of the Visual Basic environment.

NOTE: Once you have built a bean, users of *any* environment enabled for JavaBeans technology can readily use it. They can even, through the magic of the "Beans to ActiveX Bridge," use them in Visual Basic and Delphi (`http://java.sun.com/beans/bridge`).

The Bean-Writing Process

Most of the rest of this chapter shows you the techniques that you will use to write beans. Before we go into details, we give an overview of the process. First, we want to stress that writing a bean is not technically difficult—there are only a few new classes and interfaces for you to master.

In particular, the simplest kind of bean is really nothing more than a Java platform class that follows some fairly strict naming conventions for its event listeners and its methods. Example 8–1 shows the code for an ImageViewer Bean that could give a builder environment based on Java technology the same functionality as the Visual Basic image control that we mentioned in the previous section.

Example 8–1: ImageViewerBean.java

```
import java.awt.*;
import java.io.*;
import javax.swing.*;

public class ImageViewerBean extends JPanel
   implements Serializable
{  public void setFileName(String f)
   {  fileName = f;
      image = Toolkit.getDefaultToolkit().getImage(fileName);
      MediaTracker tracker = new MediaTracker(this);
      tracker.addImage(image, 0);
      try { tracker.waitForID(0); }
      catch (InterruptedException e) {}
      repaint();
   }

   public String getFileName()
   {  return fileName;
   }

   public void paint(Graphics g)
   {  if (image == null)
      {  g.drawRect(0, 0, getWidth() - 1, getHeight() - 1);
      }
      else
         g.drawImage(image, 0, 0, this);
   }

   public Dimension getPreferredSize()
   {  if (image == null)
         return new Dimension(MINSIZE, MINSIZE);
      return new Dimension(image.getWidth(null),
         image.getHeight(null));
   }

   private static final int MINSIZE = 50;
   private Image image = null;
   private String fileName = "";
}
```

When you look at this code, notice that it really doesn't look any different from any other well-designed Java platform class. For example, all accessor methods begin with `get`, all mutator methods begin with `set`. As you will soon see, builder tools use this standard naming convention to discover *properties*. For example, `fileName` is a property of this bean because it has `get` and `set` methods. In this particular example, the `fileName` property is stored in an instance variable that is

also called `fileName`. However, a property doesn't have to be stored in an instance variable—the `get` method can compute it in some other way.

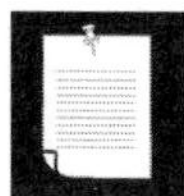

NOTE: For full support in a bean environment, beans should have a default constructor (or no constructor at all, in which case a default constructor is automatically provided), and they should be serializable. This allows the environment to instantiate new beans and to save beans between sessions. However, these are just practical recommendations, not requirements.

One point that you need to keep in mind when you read through the examples in this chapter is that real-world beans are much more elaborate and tedious to code than our brief examples, for two reasons.

1. Beans need to be usable by less-than-expert programmers. Such people will access most of the functionality of your bean with a visual design tool that uses essentially no programming. You need to expose *lots of properties* to make it easy to customize the bean behavior.
2. The same bean needs to be usable in a wide *variety of contexts*. A bean that is too simplistic to be usable in the real world won't get much respect. Of course, that is why people can charge hundreds of dollars for a professional component, such as a full-featured chart control. For example, at the time of this writing, a popular chart control has
   - 60 properties
   - 47 events
   - 14 methods
   - 178 pages of documentation

Obviously, a chart control is about as full featured a control as one can imagine, but even a bean as simple as a text field for entering numbers turns out to be not quite so simple to code as one might first imagine.

Consider, for example, what should happen as the user types digits into the text field. Should the new numbers be *immediately* reported to the listeners? On the one hand, this approach is attractive because it gives instant feedback to the user of your bean. But many applications restrict the range for valid entries, and partial entries that can go into an eventual valid entry might not themselves be valid.

For example, suppose a listener wanted to receive only even numbers from the input field. If a user tried to enter `256`, the listener could *veto* the invalid input `25`, and the user would never get past the veto. So, in this case, incremental update is a bad idea because the incremental value could be vetoed even though the eventual entry would not have been. In cases like this, your bean should report the value to listeners only when the user has finished entering the number, that is, when the user presses ENTER or if the text field loses focus.

If you are writing a program for a single application, then you will simply choose one behavior or the other. But if you are building a bean, you aren't programming for yourself but for a wide audience of users with different needs. Therefore, it would be best to add a property called something like `incrementalUpdate` and implement both behaviors, depending on the value of that property. Add a few more options like this, and even a simple `IntTextBean` will end up with a dozen properties.

Fortunately, you need to master only a small number of concepts to write beans with a rich set of behaviors. The example beans in this chapter, while not trivial, are kept simple enough to illustrate the necessary concepts.

TIP: You will find full-featured beans available for sale from many programming product stores, bundled with Java development environments, or for free at sites such as `www.gamelan.com` and the IBM alphaWorks site `http://alphaworks.ibm.com`. Also, all Swing components are beans.

The BDK and the BeanBox

Before we get into the mechanics of writing beans, we want you to see how you might use or test them. The `ImageViewerBean` is a perfectly usable bean, but outside a builder environment it can't show off any of its special features. In particular, the only way to use it in an ordinary program in the Java programming language would be to write a class that instantiates it and calls the `setFileName` method. So, the question is how can we show off the power of this simple bean? This question, in turn, leads to the question of what bean builder tool to use. A number of good environments are available, but they act quite differently from each other. Rather than favor the product of one particular vendor, we use the least common denominator environment, the so-called BeanBox, that is part of the Bean Developer Kit (or BDK). The BeanBox is not very full featured, but it is available on many platforms and it lets you test simple beans. Moreover, if you get your bean working in the BeanBox, then it should work in other development environments without any changes.

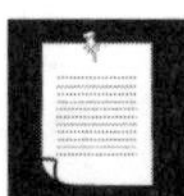

NOTE: At this time, the BDK installation is separate from the JDK installation. You may need to obtain it from the Java web site (`http://java.sun.com/beans`). Be sure that you have installed it before going any further.

CAUTION: Under Windows, do not install the BDK into the `Program Files` directory. If you do, then the space in the directory name will give you grief later. Just install the BDK into a directory such as `bdk` or `bdk1.1`.

Using the BeanBox

We will assume that you installed the BDK into the `bdk` directory. The BeanBox is automatically installed into a subdirectory called `beanbox`. This directory has a batch file (`run.bat`) to start up the BeanBox under Windows and a shell script (`run.sh`) for Unix systems. When you start up the BeanBox, you'll see a message box that looks like Figure 8–2. The message indicates that the BeanBox loads JAR files—as you will soon see, beans are packaged into JAR files. (See chapter 10 of Volume 1 for more information on JAR files.)

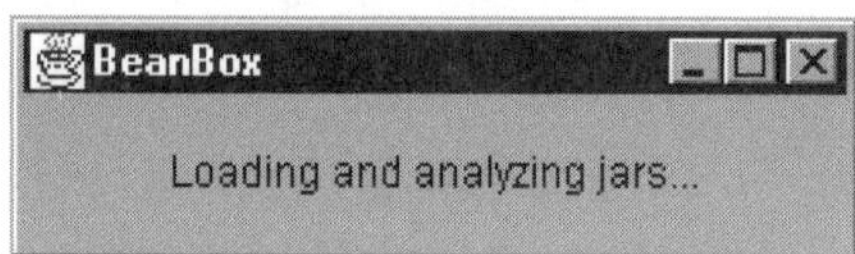

Figure 8–2: The "Analyzing Jars" message box

The actual BeanBox consists of four independently resizable and movable windows, as shown in Figure 8–3. The Toolbox lists all the beans that the BeanBox knows about. (See below for how to add new beans to the BeanBox.) As you can see in Figure 8–3, some beans have associated icons that show up in the left side of the Toolbox as well. The window marked BeanBox is where you will drop the beans and where you will connect them so that events in one trigger actions in another. The window marked Properties-BeanBox is the *property sheet* where you control the properties of your beans. This is a vital part of component-based development tools since setting properties at design time is how you set the initial state of a component.

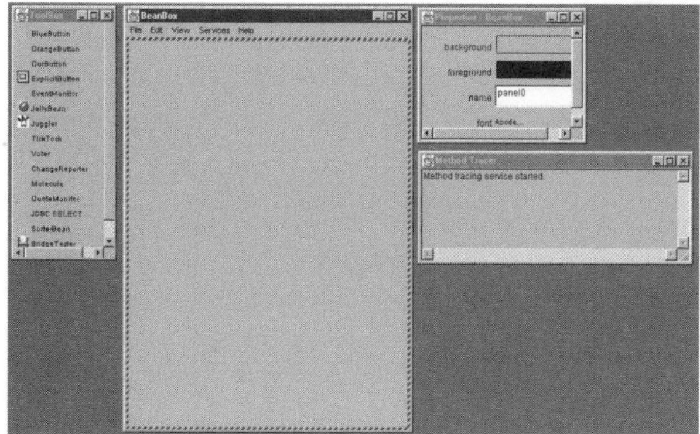

Figure 8–3: The parts of the BeanBox

For example, you can reset the `name` property of the panel used for the BeanBox by simply typing in a new name into the property sheet. Changing the `name` property is simple—you just edit a string in a text field.

But properties don't have to be strings; they can be values of any Java platform type. To make it possible for users to set values for properties of any type, builder tools access specialized *property editors*. (Property editors either come with the builder or are supplied by the bean developer. You'll see how to write your own property editors later in this chapter.)

To see a simple property editor at work, try to reset the background color of the BeanBox window as follows:

1. Click in the box marked "background" in the property sheet. This brings up a property editor for editing objects of type `Color`, as shown in Figure 8–4.
2. Choose a new color either by entering new digits (in the range 0–255) in the first box or by making a selection via the choice box in the editor.

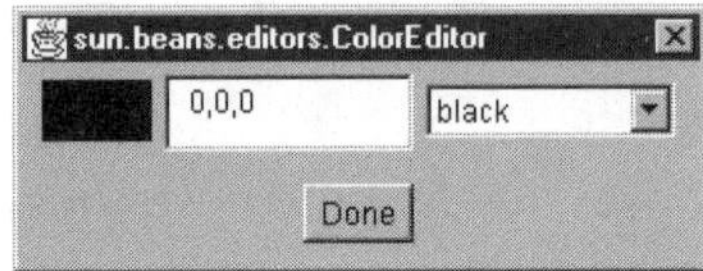

Figure 8–4: Using a property editor to set properties

Notice that you'll immediately see the change to the background color.

Using a Bean in the BeanBox

Using a bean that the BeanBox knows about is not hard:

1. Select the bean in the Toolbox. (The cursor will become a crosshair).
2. Click on the spot in the BeanBox window where you want the bean to go.

The user interface is not very clever. It neither gives you a clue as to which bean you selected nor lets you cancel the operation once you start it.

Once you have a bean in the BeanBox window, click in it to select it. A hatched border indicates that the bean is selected (see Figure 8–5—the bottom button is selected).

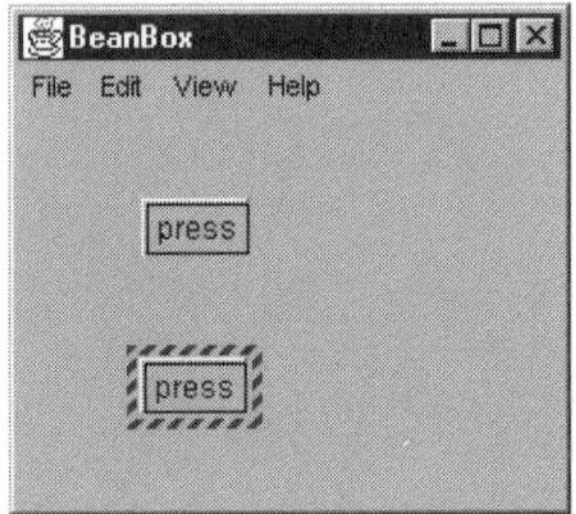

Figure 8–5: A selected bean versus an unselected bean

You can move selected beans around the BeanBox window by:

1. Moving the mouse cursor to the boundary. (You may have to try various spots—you'll know you are at the right place when the cursor changes to a four-headed arrow, as shown in Figure 8–6.)
2. Dragging the bean to the new location.

Figure 8–6: A bean ready for moving

Similarly, you can resize most beans by moving the cursor to one of the corners (it will change to a two-sided arrow) and dragging the boundary of the bean to be the size that you want.

TIP: To remove a bean that you inadvertently placed on the BeanBox window:

1. Select the bean.
2. Choose the menu option Edit -> Cut.

Building a Simple Application in the BeanBox

We explain later in this chapter how builder tools such as the BeanBox can know what properties a bean supports or what events it triggers. For now though, we simply want to show you that it all works. For this, we will follow tradition and hook up Start and Stop buttons to the juggling, tooth-shaped character shown in the Juggler bean. Here are the steps to follow (see Figure 8–7 for what the results might look like).

1. Add two "ExplicitButton" beans to the BeanBox window.
2. Set the Label property of one to Start and the other to Stop.
3. Add the Juggler bean to the BeanBox. Notice that it immediately starts juggling.

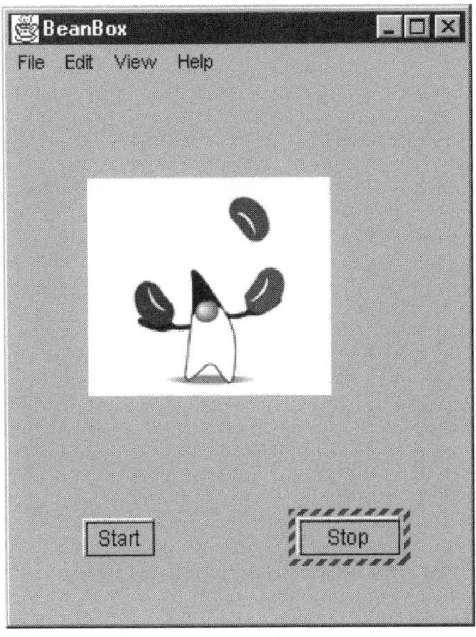

Figure 8–7: The BeanBox window for our Stop/Start Juggler application

Since the Juggler is already annoyingly juggling, let's hook up the "Stop" button first.

1. Select the "Stop" button.

2. Choose Edit -> Events -> button push (see Figure 8–8). Choose the `actionPerformed` event from this submenu.

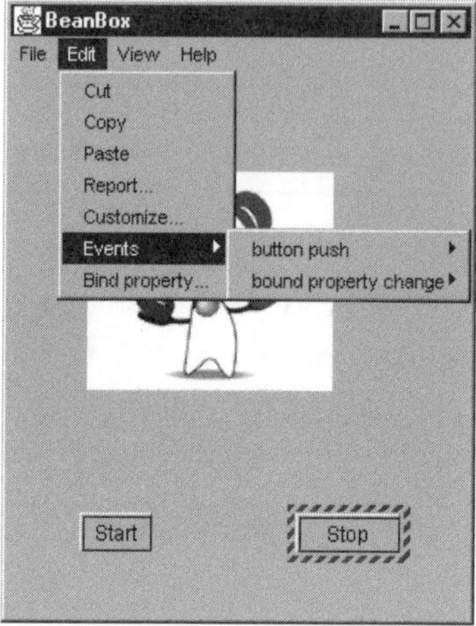

Figure 8–8: The possible events for the Stop Button window for our Stop/Start Juggler application

Now, when you move the mouse cursor on the BeanBox window, you'll see a red line growing from the Stop button (see Figure 8–9).

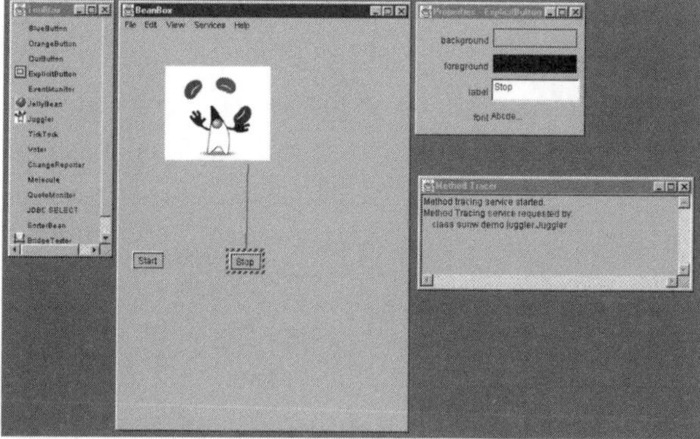

Figure 8–9: The marker for an event hookup

Now, choose the Juggler bean. You'll see a window like that shown in Figure 8–10 where you can select the method you want to hook up to the `actionPerformed` event.

We wanted to stop the juggling, so just choose `stopJuggling` in the dialog box shown in Figure 8–10. After you click on OK, the BeanBox will generate the

needed adapter code. (Look inside the `tmp\sunw\beanbox` directory below the location where the BeanBox is stored.)

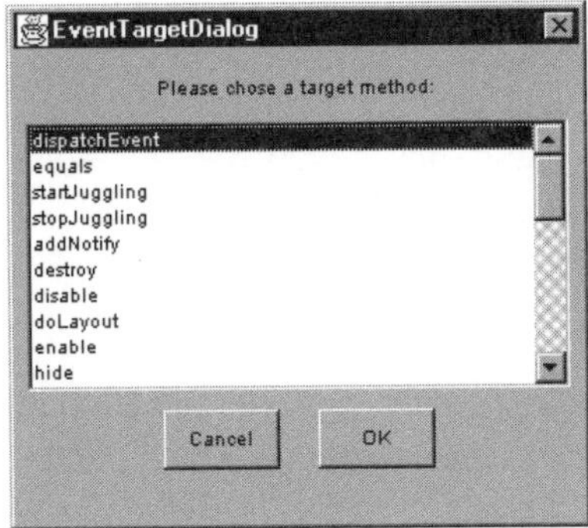

Figure 8–10: The target method dialog

Here is what the code looks like:

```
// Automatically generated event hookup file.

package tmp.sunw.beanbox;
import sunw.demo.juggler.Juggler;
import java.awt.event.ActionListener;
import java.awt.event.ActionEvent;

public class ____Hookup_146ca316c4 implements
java.awt.event.ActionListener, java.io.Serializable {

    public void setTarget(sunw.demo.juggler.Juggler t) {
        target = t;
    }

    public void actionPerformed(java.awt.event.ActionEvent
            arg0) {
        target.stopJuggling(arg0);
    }

    private sunw.demo.juggler.Juggler target;
}
```

Notice that the adapter class is given a strange-looking computer-generated name.

The key is that the `actionPerformed` method calls the `stopJuggling` method of the `Juggler` class. Thus, clicking the "Stop" button really does stop the juggler.

Saving and Restoring the State of the BeanBox

As you might expect, the BeanBox uses object serialization to save the state of your BeanBox.

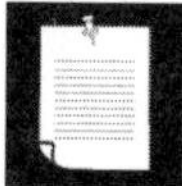

NOTE: It is essential that a builder tool be able to save the state of a bean (such as the current property settings), so design your beans so that their current state is serializable (see Chapter 12 of Volume 1).

To save the state of an application that you are testing in the BeanBox, choose File -> Save and fill in the File dialog box as desired. To restore the state of the BeanBox, make sure the BeanBox is clear of any beans (choose File -> Clear), then choose File -> Open to reload the previous application.

Building an Applet from the BeanBox

To deploy your BeanBox experiment, you can create an *applet* that others can run in a browser or the applet viewer. Here is how you can build an applet.

1. Choose File -> Make Applet.
2. In the Dialog Box (Figure 8–11) that pops up, you can give the JAR file a new name or simply accept the default choice.

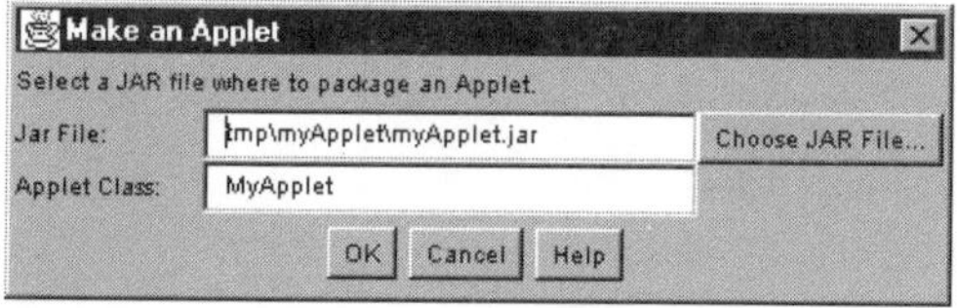

Figure 8–11: The applet creation dialog

That's it. The BeanBox will generate the needed HTML code (`myApplet.html` is the default name). You can load the HTML file in your favorite Java technology enabled browser or the applet viewer (see Figure 8–12).

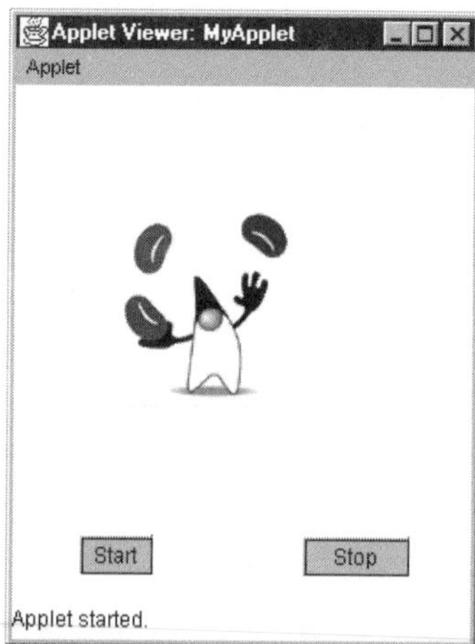

Figure 8–12: The connected beans as an applet in the applet viewer

Adding Beans to the Toolbox

To make any bean usable in a builder tool, package all class files that are used by the bean code into a JAR file. Unlike the JAR files for an applet that you saw previously, a JAR file for a bean needs a manifest file that specifies which class files in the archive are beans and should be included in the Toolbox. For example, here is the manifest file `ImageViewerBean.mf` for the ImageViewerBean.

```
Name: ImageViewerBean.class
Java-Bean: True
```

If your bean contains multiple class files, you only mention in the manifest those class files that are beans and that you want to have displayed in the toolbox.

To make the JAR file, follow these steps:

1. Edit the manifest file.
2. Gather all needed class files in a directory.
3. Run the `jar` tool as follows:

   ```
   jar cfm JarFile ManifestFile *.class
   ```

   For example,

   ```
   jar cfm ImageViewerBean.jar ImageViewerBean.mf *.class
   ```

You can also add other items, such as GIF files, to the JAR file.

TIP: If you prefer to build a make file to create the needed JAR file, look at the demo directory below the `bdk` directory for some sample make (`.mk`) files.

Finally, to make the BeanBox's Toolbox aware of your JAR file that contains the bean, copy the JAR file to the `jars` subdirectory of the BDK or choose File -> Load Jar in the BeanBox window.

Building an Image Viewer Application via Beans

We have shown you enough BeanBox techniques so that you can use the two beans on the CD that give you the equivalent of the Visual Basic ImageViewer program. To see these beans at work, add the `ImageViewerBean` and the `FileNameBean` JAR files to the BeanBox by choosing File -> Load Jar or by copying the JAR file to the `jars` subdirectory of the `bdk` directory.

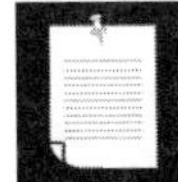

NOTE: You have already seen the code for the `ImageViewerBean`. The code for the `FileNameBean` is a lot more sophisticated. We'll analyze it in depth later in this chapter. For now, all you have to know is that clicking on the ellipsis will open a standard File Open dialog box where you can enter the name of the file.

If you add the `ImageViewerBean`, then, as you can see from Figure 8–13, you can choose a file name for a GIF or JPEG file. Once you do so, the `ImageViewerBean` automatically displays the bean.

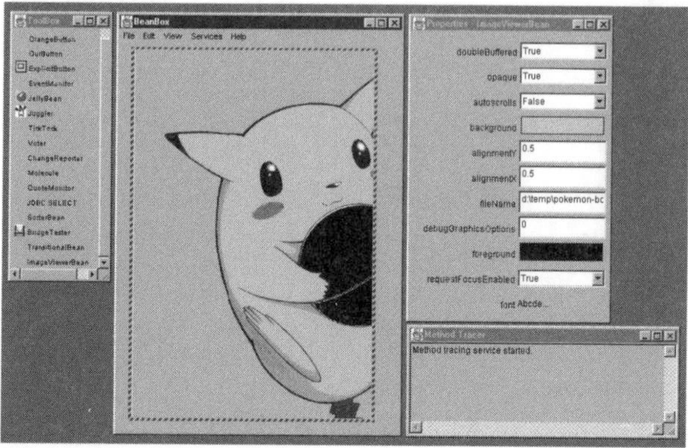

Figure 8–13: The `ImageViewerBean` at work

NOTE: If you look at the property sheet on the right in Figure 8–13, you will find a large number of mysterious properties such as `autoscrolls` and `requestFocusEnabled`. These are inherited from the `JPanel` superclass. You will see later in this chapter how you can suppress them from the property sheet.

CAUTION: If you look into the shell window from which you started the BeanBox, you will see mysterious messages such as

```
Warning: Can't find public property editor for property "next-
FocusableComponent". Skipping.
```

The automatic property discovery in the BeanBox was tricked into believing that there was a property called `nextFocusableComponent`, and then it didn't know how to display a component value in the property sheet. You will see later in this chapter how to tell the BeanBox which are the true properties of the bean.

To imitate the functionality of the Visual Basic program, we don't want to hook up events, as we did for the juggler. Instead, we link together the respective `fileName` properties of the beans. The idea is that a change in the `fileName` property of the `FileNameBean` is immediately reflected in the current value of the `fileName` property of `ImageViewerBean`. (Of course, this actually happens through a `PropertyChange` event; we discuss these kinds of events a little later in this chapter.) This file name change, in turn, results in the `ImageViewerBean` immediately displaying the right image—exactly as the VB program did.

NOTE: We describe the way it is supposed to work in the BeanBox. Be sure to use the most updated version of the BeanBox. Some versions do not update the image, some versions do not update the property sheet, and, unfortunately, some do neither.

To hook up the properties in the respective beans:

1. Select the `FileNameBean`.
2. Choose Edit -> Bind Property.
3. In the resulting dialog box that pops up (Figure 8–14), choose the `fileName` property.
4. Click on OK.

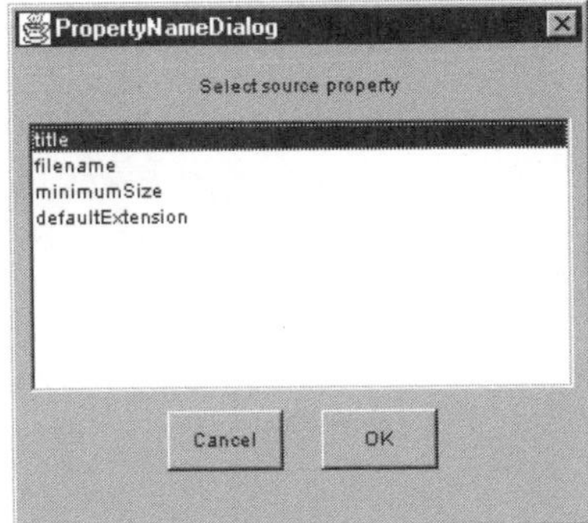

Figure 8–14: The Bind PropertyNameDialog box for `FileNameBean`

Now, the magic red line should appear, and you stretch it to reach the `ImageViewerBean`.

Click when the magic line reaches to the `ImageViewerBean`. The BeanBox will then pop up another dialog box (see Figure 8–15). Click on `fileName` and select "Ok. "

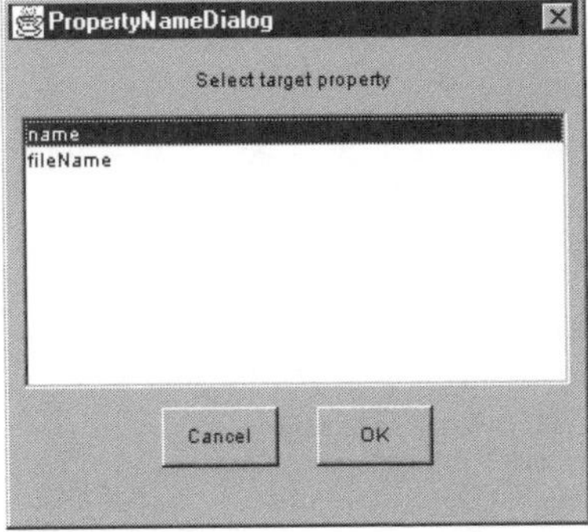

Figure 8–15: The PropertyNameDialog box for the `ImageViewerBean`

At this point, the two `fileName` properties are hooked up, so you can use the `FileNameBean` to update the image by clicking on the ellipsis and choosing the name of a GIF file (see Figure 8–16).

Figure 8–16: The result of hooking up the `fileName` properties

Naming Patterns for Bean Properties and Events

First, we want to stress there is *no* cosmic beans class that you extend to build your beans. Visual beans directly or indirectly extend the `Component` class, but nonvisual beans don't have to extend any particular superclass. Remember, a bean is simply *any* class that can be manipulated in a visual design tool. The design tool does not look at the superclass to determine the bean nature of a class, but it analyzes the names of its methods. To enable this analysis, the method names for beans must follow certain patterns.

NOTE: There is a `java.beans.Beans` class, but all methods in it are static. Extending it would, therefore, be rather pointless, even though you will see it done occasionally, supposedly for greater "clarity." Clearly, since a bean can't extend both `Beans` and `Component`, this approach can't work for visual beans. In fact, the `Beans` class contains methods that are designed to be called by builder tools, for example, to check whether the tool is operating at design time or run time.

Other languages for visual design environments, such as Visual Basic and Delphi, have special keywords such as "Property" and "Event" to express these concepts directly. The designers of the Java specification decided not to add keywords to the language in order to support visual programming. Therefore, they needed an alternative so that a builder tool could analyze a bean to learn its properties or events. Actually, there are two alternate mechanisms. If the bean writer uses standard naming patterns for properties and events, then the builder tool can use the reflection mechanism to understand what properties and events the bean is supposed to expose. Alternatively, the bean writer can supply a *bean information* class that tells the builder tool about the properties and events of the bean. We'll start out using the naming patterns because they are easy to use. You'll see later in this chapter how to supply a bean information class.

NOTE: Although the documentation calls these standard naming patterns "design patterns," these are really only naming conventions and have nothing to do with the design patterns that are used in object-oriented programming.

The naming pattern for properties is simple: Any pair of methods

```
public X getPropertyName()
public void setPropertyName(X x)
```

corresponds to a read/write property of type `X`.

For example, in our `ImageViewerBean`, there is only one `read/write` property (for the file name to be viewed), with the following methods:

```
public String getFileName()
public void setFileName(String f)
```

If you have a `get` method but not an associated `set` method, you define a read-only property.

Be careful with the capitalization pattern you use for your method names. The designers of the JavaBeans specification decided that the name of the property in our example would be `fileName`, with a lowercase `f`, even though the `get` and `set` methods contain an uppercase `F` (`getFileName`, `setFileName`). The bean analyzer performs a process called *decapitalization* to derive the property name. (That is, the first character after `get` or `set` is converted to lower case.) The rationale is that this process results in method and property names that are more natural to programmers.

NOTE: The `get` and `set` methods you create can do more than simply get and set a private data field. Like any Java method, they can carry out arbitrary actions. For example, the `setFileName` method of the `ImageViewerBean` class not only sets the value of the `fileName` data field, but it also opens the file and loads the image.

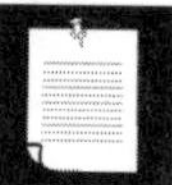

NOTE: In Visual Basic, properties also come from `get` and `set` methods. (Delphi uses `read` and `write`.) But, in both these languages there is a `Property` keyword so that the compiler doesn't have to second-guess the programmer's intentions by analyzing method names. And using a keyword in those languages has another advantage: Using a property name on the left-hand side of an assignment automatically calls the `set` method. Using a property name in an expression automatically calls the `get` method. For example, in VB you can write

```
imageBean.fileName = "corejava.gif"
```

instead of

```
imageBean.setFileName("corejava.gif");
```

There is one exception to the `get/set` naming pattern. Properties that have Boolean values should use an `is/set` naming pattern, as in the following examples:

```
public boolean isPropertyName()
public void setPropertyName(boolean b)
```

For example, an animation might have a property `running`, with two methods

```
public boolean isRunning()
public void setRunning(boolean b)
```

The `setRunning` method would start and stop the animation. The `isRunning` method would report its current status. (The juggler bean does not have such a property, however.)

For events, the naming pattern is even simpler. A bean builder environment will infer that your bean generates events when you supply methods to add and remove event listeners. Suppose your bean generates events of type *EventName*`Event`. (All events must end in `Event`.) Then, the listener interface must be called *EventName*`Listener`, and the methods to add and remove a listener must be called.

```
public void addEventNameListener(EventNameListener e)
public void removeEventNameListener(EventNameListener e)
```

If you look at the code for the `ImageViewerBean`, you'll see that it has no events to expose. Later, we will see a timer bean that generates `TimerEvent` objects and has the following methods to manage event listeners:

```
public void addTimerListener(TimerListener e)
public void removeTimerListener(TimerListener e)
```

NOTE: What do you do if your class has a pair of `get` and `set` methods that don't correspond to a property or event that you want users to manipulate in a property sheet? In your own classes, you can of course avoid that situation by renaming your methods. But if you extend another class, then you inherit the method names from the superclass. This happens, for example, when your bean extends `JPanel`—a large number of uninter-

esting properties show up in the property sheet. This shows that naming patterns are really a lousy way for designating properties. You will see later in this chapter how you can override the automatic property discovery process by supplying *bean information* that specifies exactly which methods correspond to properties.

Bean Property Types

A sophisticated bean will have lots of different kinds of properties that it should expose in a builder tool for a user to set at design time or get at run time. It can also trigger both standard and custom events. Properties can be as simple as the `fileName` property that you saw in the `ImageViewerBean` and the `FileNameBean` or as sophisticated as a color value or even an array of data points—we encounter both of these cases later in this chapter. Furthermore, properties can fire events, as you will see in this section.

Getting the properties of your beans right is probably the most complex part of building a bean because the model is quite rich. The JavaBeans specification allows four types of properties, which we illustrate by various examples.

Simple Properties

A simple property is one that takes a single value such as a string or a number. The `fileName` property of the ImageViewer is an example of a simple property. Simple properties are easy to program: just use the `set/get` naming convention we indicated earlier. For example, if you look at the code in Example 8–1, you can see that all it took to implement a simple string property is:

```
public void setFileName(String f)
{  fileName = f;
   image = Toolkit.getDefaultToolkit().getImage(fileName);
   . . . // use media tracker to wait for image loading
   repaint();
}

public String getFileName()
{  return fileName;
}
```

Notice that, as far as the JavaBeans specification is concerned, we also have a read-only property of this bean because we have a method with this signature inside the class

```
public Dimension getPreferredSize()
```

without a corresponding `setPreferredSize` method. You would not normally be able to see read-only properties at design time in a property sheet.

TIP: In the version of the BeanBox we are working with, you have to initialize private data members explicitly to non-`null` values, or the BeanBox simply won't display them, leaving you to wonder whether you misspelled something. For example,

```
public String getProp() { return prop; }
public void setProp(String p) { prop = p; )
. . .
private String prop;
   // initialized with null--BeanBox won't display prop
```

Instead, when the BeanBox loads the bean, it will display an error message in the console window. Be sure to check those error messages if a property doesn't show up in the property sheet.

Indexed Properties

An indexed property is one that gets or sets an array. A chart bean (see below) would use an indexed property for the data points. With an indexed property, you supply two pairs of `get` and `set` methods: one for the array and one for individual entries. They must follow the pattern:

```
X[] getPropertyName()
void setPropertyName(X[] x)
X getPropertyName(int i)
void setPropertyName(int i, X x)
```

Here's an example of the indexed property we use in the chart bean that you will see later in this chapter.

```
public double[] getValues() { return values; }
public void setValues(double[] v) { values = v; }
public double getValues(int i) { return values[i]; }
public void setValues(int i, double v) { values[i] = v; }
. . .
private double[] values;
```

The `get`/`set` functions that set individual array entries can assume that `i` is within the legal range. Builder tools will not call them with an index that is less than 0 or larger than the length of the array. In particular, the

```
setPropertyName(int i, X[] x)
```

method cannot be used to *grow* the array. To grow the array, you must manually build a new array and then pass it to this method:

```
setPropertyName(X[] x)
```

As a practical matter, however, the `get` and `set` methods can still be called programmatically, not just by the builder environment. Therefore, it is best to add some error checking, after all. For example, here is the code that we really use in the `ChartBean` class.

```
public double getValues(int i)
{  if (0 <= i && i < values.length) return values[i];
```

```
    return 0;
}

public void setValues(int i, double value)
{  if (0 <= i && i < values.length) values[i] = value;
}
```

NOTE: As we write this, the BeanBox's property sheet does not support indexed properties. That is, they don't show up on the property sheet, and you can't set them in the builder. You will see later in this chapter how to overcome this limitation by supplying a property editor for arrays.

Bound Properties

Bound properties tell interested listeners that their value has changed. For example, the `fileName` property in the `FileNameBean` is a bound property. When the file name changes, then the `ImageViewerBean` is automatically notified and it loads the new file.

To implement a bound property, you must implement two mechanisms.

1. Whenever the value of the property changes, the bean must send a `PropertyChange` event to all registered listeners. This change can occur when the `set` method is called or when the program user carries out an action, such as editing text or selecting a file.
2. To enable interested listeners to register themselves, the bean has to implement the following two methods:

```
void addPropertyChangeListener(PropertyChangeListener
   listener)
void removePropertyChangeListener(PropertyChangeListener
   listener)
```

The `java.beans` package has a convenience class, called `PropertyChangeSupport`, that manages the listeners for you. To use this convenience class, your bean must have a data field of this class that looks like this:

```
private PropertyChangeSupport changeSupport
   = new PropertyChangeSupport(this);
```

You delegate the task of adding and removing property change listeners to that object.

```
public void addPropertyChangeListener(PropertyChangeListener
   listener)
{  changeSupport.addPropertyChangeListener(listener);
}

public void removePropertyChangeListener(PropertyChangeListener
   listener)
{  changeSupport.removePropertyChangeListener(listener);
}
```

Whenever the value of the property changes, use the `firePropertyChange` method of the `PropertyChangeSupport` object to deliver an event to all the registered listeners. That method has three parameters: the name of the property, the old value, and the new value. For example,

```
changeSupport.firePropertyChange("fileName",
   oldValue, newValue);
```

The values must be objects. If the property type is not an object, then you must use an object wrapper. For example,

```
changeSupport.firePropertyChange("running",
   new Boolean(false), new Boolean(true));
```

TIP: If your bean extends any Swing class that ultimately extends the `JComponent` class, then you do *not* need to implement the `addPropertyChangeListener` and `removePropertyChangeListener` methods. These methods are already implemented in the `JComponent` superclass.

To notify the listeners of a property change, simply call the `firePropertyChange` method of the `JComponent` superclass:

```
firePropertyChange("propertyName", oldValue, newValue);
```

For your convenience, that method is overloaded for the types `boolean`, `byte`, `char`, `double`, `float`, `int`, `long`, and `short`. If `oldValue` and `newValue` belong to these types, you do not need to use object wrappers.

Other beans that want to be notified when the property value changes must implement the `PropertyChangeListener` interface. That interface contains only one method:

```
void propertyChange(PropertyChangeEvent event)
```

The code in the `propertyChange` method is triggered whenever the property value changes, provided, of course, that you have added the recipient to the property change listeners of the bean that generates the event. The `PropertyChangeEvent` object encapsulates the old and new value of the property, obtainable with

```
Object oldValue = event.getOldValue();
Object newValue = event.getNewValue();
```

If the property type is not a class type, then the returned objects are the usual wrapper types. For example, if a `boolean` property is changed, then a `Boolean` is returned and you need to retrieve the Boolean value with the `booleanValue` method.

Thus, a listening object must follow this model:

```
class Listener implements PropertyChangeListener
{  public Listener()
   {  bean.addPropertyChangeListener(this);
   }

   void propertyChange(PropertyChangeEvent event)
```

```
      {  Object newValue = event.getNewValue();
         . . .
      }
      . . .
   }
```

You may be wondering how the ImageViewerBean got notified when the file name in the FileNameBean changed. After all, there is no listener method in the ImageViewerBean source code. In this case, the BeanBox registered itself as a property change listener to the FileNameBean, and *it* called the setFileName method of the ImageViewerBean in its propertyChange listener method.

Example 8–2 is the full code for the FileNameBean. Since the FileNameBean extends the JPanel class, we did not have to explicitly use a PropertyChange-Support object. Instead, we rely on the ability of the JPanel class to manage property change listeners.

Example 8–2: FileNameBean.java

```
import java.awt.*;
import java.awt.event.*;
import java.beans.*;
import java.io.*;
import javax.swing.*;

public class FileNameBean extends JPanel
   implements Serializable
{  public FileNameBean()
   {  dialogButton = new JButton("...");
      nameField = new JTextField("");

      chooser = new JFileChooser();
      chooser.setCurrentDirectory(new File("."));

      chooser.setFileFilter(
         new javax.swing.filechooser.FileFilter()
         {  public boolean accept(File f)
            {  String name = f.getName().toLowerCase();
               return name.endsWith("." + defaultExtension)
                  || f.isDirectory();
            }
            public String getDescription()
            {  return defaultExtension + " files";
            }
         });

      setLayout(new GridBagLayout());
      GridBagConstraints gbc = new GridBagConstraints();
      gbc.weightx = 100;
      gbc.weighty = 100;
      gbc.anchor = GridBagConstraints.WEST;
      gbc.fill = GridBagConstraints.BOTH;
```

```
      add(nameField, gbc, 0, 0, 1, 1);
      dialogButton.addActionListener(
         new ActionListener()
         {  public void actionPerformed(ActionEvent evt)
            {  showFileDialog();
            }
         });
      nameField.setEditable(false);
      gbc.weightx = 0;
      gbc.anchor = GridBagConstraints.EAST;
      gbc.fill = GridBagConstraints.NONE;
      add(dialogButton, gbc, 1, 0, 1, 1);
   }

   public void add(Component c, GridBagConstraints gbc,
      int x, int y, int w, int h)
   {  gbc.gridx = x;
      gbc.gridy = y;
      gbc.gridwidth = w;
      gbc.gridheight = h;
      add(c, gbc);
   }

   public void showFileDialog()
   {  int r = chooser.showOpenDialog(null);
      if(r == JFileChooser.APPROVE_OPTION)
      {  String name
            = chooser.getSelectedFile().getAbsolutePath();
         setFileName(name);
      }
   }

   public void setFileName(String newValue)
   {  String oldValue = nameField.getText();
      firePropertyChange("fileName", oldValue, newValue);
      nameField.setText(newValue);
   }

   public String getFileName()
   {  return nameField.getText();
   }

   public Dimension getMinimumSize()
   {  return new Dimension(XMINSIZE, YMINSIZE);
   }

   public String getDefaultExtension()
   {  return defaultExtension;
   }

   public void setDefaultExtension(String s)
   {  defaultExtension = s;
```

```
   }

   private static final int XMINSIZE = 200;
   private static final int YMINSIZE = 20;
   private JButton dialogButton;
   private JTextField nameField;
   private JFileChooser chooser;
   private String defaultExtension = "gif";
}
```

`java.beans.PropertyChangeListener`

- `void propertyChange(PropertyChangeEvent event)`

  is called when a property change event is fired.

  Parameters: `event` the property change event

`java.beans.PropertyChangeSupport`

- `PropertyChangeSupport(Object sourceBean)`

  constructs the (convenience) `PropertyChangeSupport` object.

  Parameters: `sourceBean` the bean that is the source of the property change (usually `this`)

- `void addPropertyChangeListener(PropertyChangeListener listener)`

  registers an interested listener for the bound property.

  Parameters: `listener` the object that wants to be notified of a change in the bound property

- `void removePropertyChangeListener(PropertyChangeListener listener)`

  removes a previously registered interested listener for the bound property.

  Parameters: `listener` the object to be removed from the list of listeners

- `void firePropertyChange(String propertyName, Object oldValue, Object newValue)`

  sends a `PropertyChangeEvent` to registered listeners.

  Parameters:

`propertyName`	the name of the property
`oldValue`	the old value
`newValue`	the new value

- `PropertyChangeEvent(Object source, String propertyName, Object`

`java.beans.PropertyChangeEvent`

`oldValue, Object newValue)`
constructs a new `PropertyChangeEvent` object.

Parameters:	`Object`	the bean source for the property
	`propertyName`	the name of the property
	`oldValue`	the old value
	`newValue`	the new value

- `Object getNewValue()`
  returns the new value of the property.
- `Object getOldValue();`
  returns the previous value of the property.
- `String getPropertyName()`
  returns the name of the property.

`javax.swing.JComponent`

- `void addPropertyChangeListener(String propertyName, Property-ChangeListener listener)`
  registers an interested listener for the bound property.

Parameters:	`propertyName`	the name of the property to listen to
	`listener`	the object that wants to be notified of a change in the bound property

- `void addPropertyChangeListener(PropertyChangeListener listener)`
  registers an interested listener for all bound properties of this component.

Parameters:	`listener`	the object that wants to be notified of a change in the bound property

- `void removePropertyChangeListener(PropertyChangeListener listener)`
  removes a previously registered interested listener for the bound property.

Parameters:	`propertyName`	the name of the property to listen to
	`listener`	the object to be removed from the list of listeners

- `void removePropertyChangeListener(PropertyChangeListener listener)`
  removes a previously registered interested listener for the bound properties of this component.

Parameters:	`listener`	the object to be removed from the list of listeners

- `void firePropertyChange(String propertyName, Xxx oldValue, Xxx newValue)`

  sends a `PropertyChangeEvent` to registered listeners.

Parameters:	`propertyName`	the name of the property
	`oldValue`	the old value
	`newValue`	the new value

Constrained Properties

A constrained property is the most interesting of the properties, and also the most complex to implement. Such a property is constrained by the fact that *any* listener can "veto" proposed changes, forcing it to revert to the old setting.

For example, consider a text field to enter a number, implemented as a bean `IntTextBean`. A consumer of that number may have restrictions on the value; for example, perhaps the number must be between 0 and 255. Such a restriction would be easy to implement: add a `minValue` and `maxValue` to the `IntTextBean`. However, the restriction may be more complex than that. Perhaps the number should be even. Or, it may depend on another number that also changes. In that case, no simple property of the `IntTextBean` is able to distinguish good user inputs from bad ones. Instead, the bean should notify its consumers of the new value and give the consumers the chance to *veto* the change. A property that can be vetoed is called a *constrained* property.

We will put this concept to use with a *range bean* (see Figure 8–17). This bean contains two `IntTextBean` fields to specify the lower and the upper bound of a range. (You might use such a bean in a print dialog where the user can specify the range of pages to be printed.) If the user enters a `to` value that is less than the current `from` value (or a `from` value that is greater than the current `to` value), then the `RangeBean` vetoes the change.

Figure 8–17: The range bean

In this example, the `IntTextBean` is the producer of the vetoable event, and the `RangeBean` is the consumer that may issue a veto.

To build a constrained property, your bean must have the following two methods to let it register `VetoableChangeListener` objects:

```
public void addVetoableChangeListener(VetoableChangeListener
   listener);
public void removeVetoableChangeListener(VetoableChangeListener
   listener);
```

Just as there is a convenience class to manage property change listeners, there is a convenience class, called `VetoableChangeSupport`, that manages vetoable change listeners. Your bean should contain an object of this class.

```
private VetoableChangeSupport vetoSupport
   = new VetoableChangeSupport(this);
```

Adding and removing listeners should be delegated to this object. For example:

```
public void addVetoableChangeListener(VetoableChangeListener
   listener)
{  vetoSupport.addVetoableChangeListener(listener);
}
public void removeVetoableChangeListener(VetoableChangeListener
   listener)
{  vetoSupport.removeVetoableChangeListener(listener);
}
```

TIP: The `JComponent` class has some support for constrained properties, but it is not as extensive as that for bound properties. The `JComponent` class keeps a single listener list for vetoable change listeners, not a separate list for each property. And the `fireVetoableChange` method is not overloaded for basic types. If your bean extends `JComponent` and has a single constrained property (as is often the case), then the listener support of the `JComponent` superclass is entirely adequate, and you do not need a separate `VetoableChangeSupport` object.

An object that is able to veto changes needs to implement the `VetoableChangeListener` interface. That interface contains one method:

```
void vetoableChange(PropertyChangeEvent event)
   throws PropertyVetoException
```

This method receives a `PropertyChangeEvent` object, from which it can retrieve the current value and the proposed new value with the `getOldValue` and `getNewValue` methods.

Notice that the `vetoableChange` method throws an exception. A listener indicates its disapproval with the proposed change by throwing a `PropertyVetoException`. This exception forces the bean that produced the event to abandon the new value.

To see how to implement the `VetoableChangeListener` interface, look at the code for the `RangeBean` class. It implements the needed method with the following code.

```
public void vetoableChange(PropertyChangeEvent event)
   throws PropertyVetoException
{  int v = ((Integer)event.getNewValue()).intValue();
   if (event.getSource() == from && v > to.getValue())
      throw new PropertyVetoException("from > to", event);
   if (event.getSource() == to && v < from.getValue())
      throw new PropertyVetoException("to < from", event);
}
```

It is highly recommended that constrained properties are also bound properties. That is, your bean should have methods to add `PropertyChangeListener` objects in addition to `VetoableChangeListener` objects. You saw how to implement those methods in the preceding section.

To update a constrained property value, a bean uses the following two-phase approach:

1. Notify all vetoable change listeners of the *intent* to change the property value. (Use the `fireVetoableChange` method of the `VetoableChange-Support` class.)
2. If none of the vetoable change listeners has thrown a `PropertyVetoEx-ception`, then update the value of the property.
3. Notify all property change listeners to *confirm* that a change has occurred.

Here is a typical example from the `IntTextBean` code.

```
public void setValue(int v) throws PropertyVetoException
{  Integer oldValue = new Integer(getValue());
   Integer newValue = new Integer(v);
   vetoSupport.fireVetoableChange("value", oldValue, newValue);
   // survived, therefore no veto
   value = v;
   setText("" + v);
   changeSupport.firePropertyChange("value", oldValue,
      newValue);
}
```

It is important that you don't change the property value until all the registered vetoable change listeners have agreed with the proposed change. Conversely, a vetoable change listener should never assume that a change that it agrees with is actually happening. The only reliable way to get notified when a change is actually happening is through a property change listener.

Example 8–3 shows the code for the integer text bean that allows its values to be vetoed—it is based on the `IntTextField` class from Volume 1. Example 8–4 shows the code for the `RangeBean`. A range bean contains two `IntTextBean` objects and vetoes the change if it would result in an invalid range.

Activate the range bean and then type a value into the `from` field that is larger than the value in the `to` field. Then, press ENTER. You will see that the contents of the `from` field instantly revert to the old value. Also, if you look inside the console from which you started the BeanBox, you will see a message:

```
WARNING: Vetoed; reason is: from > to
```

Here is what happens in detail:

1. You type a value into the edit field for the `from` property.
2. The BeanBox calls the `setFrom` method of the `RangeBean` class.
3. The `setFrom` method calls the `setValue` method of the `IntTextBean` class.

4. The `setValue` method notifies its vetoable listeners, in our case, the `RangeBean`.
5. The `vetoableChange` method of the `RangeBean` class throws a `PropertyVetoException`.
6. The `setValue` method of the `IntTextBean` class does not catch the exception, and the value is not updated.
7. The BeanBox captures the exception and displays the warning message.
8. The BeanBox calls `getValue` to restore the original value in the text field.

Here is another experiment to try. Rather than typing into the property sheet, type directly into the `from` text field. Try typing in a lower bound that is greater than the upper bound, and then leave the text field by pressing TAB or clicking the mouse elsewhere. The `IntTextBean` will pop up a dialog that displays the veto message to the user (see Figure 8–18).

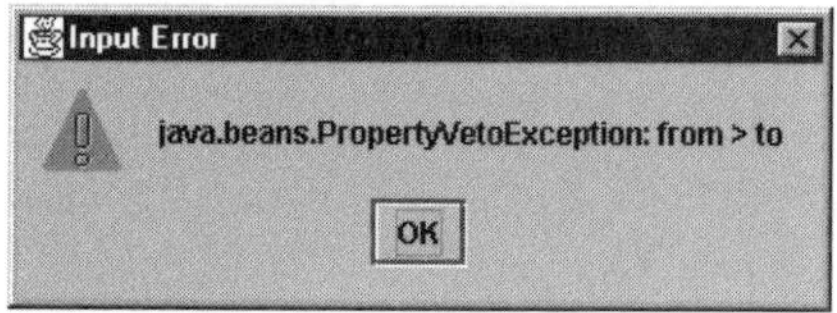

Figure 8–18: A Veto Message

This error is trapped in a different way. The text field sets a *focus listener* that tracks focus events. When the text field gains focus, the original value is saved. When it gives up the focus, then the `editComplete` method is called.

```
public IntTextBean(int defval, int size)
{  super("" + defval, size);
   addFocusListener(new FocusListener()
      {  public void focusGained(FocusEvent event)
         {  if (!event.isTemporary())
            {  lastValue = getValue();
            }
         }
         public void focusLost(FocusEvent event)
         {  if (!event.isTemporary())
            {  editComplete();
            }
         }
      });
}
```

The `editComplete` method is similar to the `setValue` method; however, if a property change was vetoed, it restores the original value and resets the focus to the text field.

```
public void editComplete()
{  Integer oldValue = new Integer(lastValue);
   Integer newValue = new Integer(getValue());
```

```
        try
        {  fireVetoableChange("value", oldValue, newValue);
           // survived, therefore no veto
           firePropertyChange("value", oldValue, newValue);
        }
        catch(PropertyVetoException e)
        {  // someone didn't like it
           JOptionPane.showMessageDialog(this, "" + e,
              "Input Error", JOptionPane.WARNING_MESSAGE);
           setText("" + lastValue);
           requestFocus();
        }
     }
```

CAUTION: The `requestFocus` method does not work for Swing components in JDK 1.2—see bug #4128659 in the "bug parade" at `http://developer.java.sun.com` for details.

Whenever you build a constrained property into your bean, keep in mind that the bean may have multiple listeners, any of which can veto the change. Therefore, a constrained property that isn't bound doesn't make much sense. Listeners need to be notified when a proposed property change has actually been accepted by all listeners. For this reason, we strongly suggest that all your constrained properties be bound.

Example 8–3: IntTextBean.java

```
import java.awt.*;
import java.awt.event.*;
import java.beans.*;
import java.io.*;
import javax.swing.*;
import javax.swing.text.*;

public class IntTextBean extends JTextField
   implements Serializable
{  public IntTextBean()
   {  this(0, 10);
   }

   public IntTextBean(int defval, int size)
   {  super("" + defval, size);
      addFocusListener(new FocusListener()
         {  public void focusGained(FocusEvent event)
            {  if (!event.isTemporary())
               {  lastValue = getValue();
               }
            }
```

```
            public void focusLost(FocusEvent event)
            {  if (!event.isTemporary())
               {  editComplete();
               }
            }
         });
   }

   public void editComplete()
   {  Integer oldValue = new Integer(lastValue);
      Integer newValue = new Integer(getValue());
      try
      {  fireVetoableChange("value", oldValue, newValue);
         // survived, therefore no veto
         firePropertyChange("value", oldValue, newValue);
      }
      catch(PropertyVetoException e)
      {  // someone didn't like it
         JOptionPane.showMessageDialog(this, "" + e,
            "Input Error", JOptionPane.WARNING_MESSAGE);
         setText("" + lastValue);
         requestFocus();
            // doesn't work in all JDK versions--see bug #4128659
      }
   }

   public int getValue()
   {  try
      {  return Integer.parseInt(getText());
      }
      catch (NumberFormatException exception)
      {  return 0;
      }
   }

   public void setValue(int v) throws PropertyVetoException
   {  Integer oldValue = new Integer(getValue());
      Integer newValue = new Integer(v);
      fireVetoableChange("value", oldValue, newValue);
      // survived, therefore no veto
      setText("" + v);
      firePropertyChange("value", oldValue, newValue);
   }

   protected Document createDefaultModel()
   {  return new IntTextDocument();
   }

   public Dimension getMinimumSize()
   {  return new Dimension(XMINSIZE, YMINSIZE);
```

```
   }

   private int lastValue;
   private static final int XMINSIZE = 50;
   private static final int YMINSIZE = 20;
}

class IntTextDocument extends PlainDocument
{  public void insertString(int offs, String str,
      AttributeSet a)
      throws BadLocationException
   {  if (str == null) return;
      String oldString = getText(0, getLength());
      String newString = oldString.substring(0, offs)
         + str + oldString.substring(offs);
      try
      {  Integer.parseInt(newString + "0");
         super.insertString(offs, str, a);
      }
      catch(NumberFormatException e)
      {
      }
   }
}
```

Example 8–4: RangeBean.java

```
import java.awt.*;
import java.beans.*;
import java.io.*;
import javax.swing.*;

public class RangeBean extends JPanel
   implements VetoableChangeListener, Serializable
{  public RangeBean()
   {  add(new JLabel("From"));
      add(from);
      add(new JLabel("To"));
      add(to);

      from.addVetoableChangeListener(this);
      to.addVetoableChangeListener(this);
   }

   public void vetoableChange(PropertyChangeEvent event)
      throws PropertyVetoException
   {  int v = ((Integer)event.getNewValue()).intValue();
      if (event.getSource() == from && v > to.getValue())
         throw new PropertyVetoException("from > to", event);
      if (event.getSource() == to && v < from.getValue())
         throw new PropertyVetoException("to < from", event);
```

```
    }

    public int getFrom() { return from.getValue(); }
    public int getTo() { return to.getValue(); }

    public void setFrom(int v) throws PropertyVetoException
    {  from.setValue(v);
    }

    public void setTo(int v) throws PropertyVetoException
    {  to.setValue(v);
    }

    private IntTextBean from = new IntTextBean();
    private IntTextBean to = new IntTextBean();
}
```

java.beans.VetoableChangeListener

- `void vetoableChange(PropertyChangeEvent event)`

  is called when a property is about to be changed. It should throw a `PropertyVetoException` if the change is not acceptable.

Parameters:	`event`	the event object describing the property change

`java.beans.VetoableChangeSupport`

- `VetoableChangeSupport(Object sourceBean)`

  constructs the (convenience) `VetoableChangeSupport` object.

Parameters:	`sourceBean`	the bean that is the source of the vetoable change (usually `this`)

- `void addVetoableChangeListener(VetoableChangeListener listener)`

  registers an interested listener for the constrained property.

Parameters:	`listener`	the bean that wants to have a chance to veto the constrained property

- `void removeVetoableChangeListener(VetoableChangeListener listener)`

  removes a previously registered interested listener for the constrained property.

Parameters:	`listener`	the bean to be removed from the list of listeners

- `void fireVetoableChange(String propertyName, Object oldValue, Object newValue)`

  sends a (convenience) `PropertyChangeEvent` to registered listeners prior to updating the property value.

Parameters:	`propertyName`	the name of the property
	`oldValue`	the current value
	`newValue`	the proposed new value

`javax.swing.JComponent`

- `void addVetoableChangeListener(PropertyChangeListener listener)`

  registers an interested listener for all constrained properties of this component.

Parameters:	`listener`	the object that wants to be notified of a change in the bound property

- `void removeVetoableChangeListener(PropertyChangeListener listener)`

  removes a previously registered interested listener for the constrained properties of this component.

Parameters:	`listener`	the object to be removed from the list of listeners

- `void fireVetoableChange(String propertyName, Object oldValue, Object newValue)`

  sends a `PropertyChangeEvent` to registered listeners.

Parameters:	`propertyName`	the name of the property
	`oldValue`	the old value
	`newValue`	the new value

`java.beans.PropertyVetoException`

API

- `PropertyVetoException(String reason, PropertyChangeEvent event)`

  creates a new `PropertyVetoException`.

Parameters:	`reason`	a string that describes the reason for the veto
	`event`	the `PropertyChangeEvent` for the constrained property you want to veto

- `PropertyChangeEvent getPropertyChangeEvent()`

  returns the `PropertyChangeEvent` used to construct the exception.

Adding Custom Bean Events

When you add a bound or constrained property to a bean, you also enable the bean to fire events whenever the value of that property changes. However, there are other events that a bean can send out, for example,

- When the program user has clicked on a control within the bean

- When new information is available
- Or, simply when some amount of time has elapsed

Unlike the `PropertyChangeEvent` events, these events belong to custom classes and need to be captured by custom listeners.

Here is how to write a bean that generates custom events. (Please consult Chapter 8 of Volume 1 for more details on event-handling in the Java platform.) Be sure to follow the first two steps precisely or the introspection mechanism will not recognize that you are trying to define a custom event.

1. Write a class *Custom*`Event` that extends `EventObject`. (The event name must end in `Event` in order for a builder to use the naming patterns to find it.)
2. Write an interface *Custom*`Listener` with a single notification method. That notification method can have any name, but it must have a single parameter of type *Custom*`Event` and return type `void`.
3. Supply the following two methods in the bean:

```
public void addCustomListener(CustomListener e)
public void removeCustomListener(CustomListener e)
```

CAUTION: If your event class doesn't extend `EventObject`, chances are that your code will compile just fine because none of the methods of the `EventObject` class are actually needed, and none of the various other methods ever try to cast the event objects to the `EventObject` class. However, your bean will mysteriously fail—the introspection mechanism will not recognize the events.

To implement the methods needed for adding, removing, and delivering custom events, you can no longer rely on convenience classes that automatically manage the event listeners. Instead, you need to collect and manage all the event listeners, for example, in a `Vector`. Moreover, when delivering the event, you also need to call the notification method for all the collected listeners. This call can lead to a synchronization problem—it is possible that one thread tries to add or remove a listener at the same time that another thread is handling an event delivery to it. For that reason, synchronize access to the collection of listeners. The following code shows how you can provide the needed synchronization.

```
public synchronized void addCustomListener
   (CustomListener l)
{  listeners.addElement(l);
}

public synchronized void removeCustomListener
   (CustomListener l)
{  listeners.removeElement(l);
}

public void fireCustomEvent(CustomEvent event)
{  Vector currentListeners = null;
   synchronized(this)
```

```
      {  currentListeners = (Vector)listeners.clone();
      }
      for (int i = 0; i < currentListeners.size(); i++)
      {  CustomListener listener
            = (CustomListener)currentListeners.elementAt(i);
         listener.notifyMethod(event);
      }
   }
   . . .
   private Vector listeners = new Vector();
```

The code for the synchronization is a bit tricky. Why don't we just make fire-*Custom*Event into a synchronized method as well? Then, we could be sure that no listeners were added or removed as the events were fired. However, that opens us up to the potential for deadlocks because, in some cases, the notify-Method might call add*Custom*Listener or remove*Custom*Listener. Since it is not called in a separate thread, that call would give rise to a deadlock. Therefore, we first clone the vector. Only the block of code that performs the cloning is synchronized. Of course, now only the listeners that have been registered at the outset of the delivery process are notified. And if one listener is removed before the delivery process is completed, that listener is still called. This in turn means that there is no absolute guarantee that event deliveries will cease immediately when a listener removes itself from an event source. Conversely, if a listener is added during the delivery process of an event, the newly added listener is not a part of the cloned vector and thus is not notified of the same event.

TIP: If you don't want to implement the listener list by hand, you can use a javax.swing.EventListenerList. See Chapter 6 for details.

Now, let's apply this technique to implementing a TimerBean. This bean should send TimerEvent objects to its listeners. (This is a modification of the Timer class from Chapter 2.) Timer events are generated at regular intervals, measured in milliseconds, provided that the running property is set to true. The interval length is determined by the interval property. Examples 8–5 through 8–7 show the code for the following:

- The TimerEvent class, the custom event that is generated by this bean
- The TimerListener class with a notification method that we called timeElapsed
- The TimerBean with methods addTimerListener and removeTimer-Listener

Here is how you can test the bean. Drop a timer bean into the BeanBox. (This is an *invisible bean* with no paint method—it is just displayed as a string "TimerBean" by the BeanBox.) Then, drop an EventMonitor bean into the BeanBox. Select the TimerBean and choose Edit -> Events from the BeanBox menu. Note that there is a submenu `timer` with a child menu `timeElapsed`. These menus show that the introspection method has correctly identified the custom event. Select the `timeElapsed` method. Then, a red line appears. Connect it to the `EventMonitor`. A dialog asks you which method should be called when the event notification occurs. Choose the only method available, `initiateEventSourceMonitoring`. Now, select the `TimerBean` once again. In the property sheet, set the `running` property to `true` and watch the text area in the `EventMonitor` bean. Once every second, a notification message is displayed (see Figure 8–19).

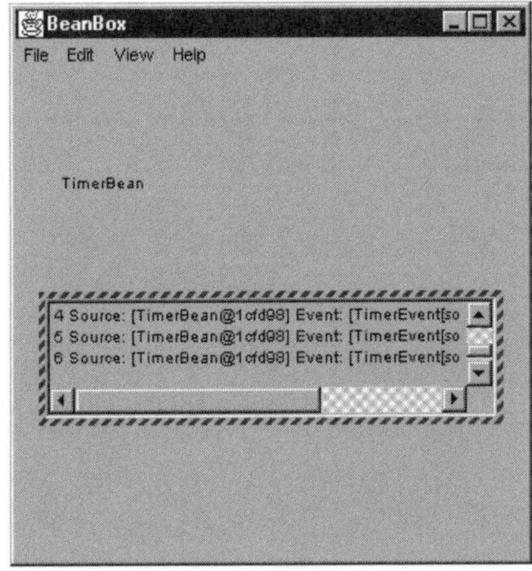

Figure 8–19: The BeanBox monitors a custom event

Here's the complete code for the `TimerBean`.

Example 8–5: TimerBean.java

```
import java.awt.*;
import java.util.*;
import java.io.*;

public class TimerBean implements Runnable, Serializable
{  public int getInterval() { return interval; }
   public void setInterval(int i) { interval = i; }

   public boolean isRunning() { return runner != null; }
   public void setRunning(boolean b)
   {  if (b && runner == null)
      {  runner = new Thread(this);
         runner.start();
      }
      else if (!b && runner != null)
      {  runner.interrupt();
         runner = null;
      }
```

```
   }

   public synchronized void addTimerListener
      (TimerListener l)
   {  timerListeners.addElement(l);
   }

   public synchronized void removeTimerListener
      (TimerListener l)
   {  timerListeners.removeElement(l);
   }

   public void fireTimerEvent(TimerEvent evt)
   {  Vector currentListeners = null;
      synchronized(this)
      {  currentListeners = (Vector)timerListeners.clone();
      }
      for (int i = 0; i < currentListeners.size(); i++)
      {  TimerListener listener
            = (TimerListener)currentListeners.elementAt(i);
         listener.timeElapsed(evt);
      }
   }

   public void run()
   {  if (interval <= 0) return;
      try
      {  while (!interrupted())
         {  Thread.sleep(interval);
            fireTimerEvent(new TimerEvent(this));
         }
      }
      catch(InterruptedException e)
      {
      }
   }

   private int interval = 1000;
   private Vector timerListeners = new Vector();
   private Thread runner;
}
```

Example 8–6: TimerListener.java

```
import java.util.*;

public interface TimerListener extends EventListener
{  public void timeElapsed(TimerEvent evt);
}
```

Example 8–7: TimerEvent.java

```
import java.util.*;

public class TimerEvent extends EventObject
{  public TimerEvent(Object source)
   {  super(source);
      now = new Date();
   }

   public Date getDate() { return now; }

   private Date now;
}
```

Property Editors

If you add an integer or string property to a bean, then that property is automatically displayed in the bean's property sheet. But what happens if you add a property whose values cannot easily be edited in a text field, for example, a date or a `Color`? Then, you need to provide a separate component that the user can use to specify the property value. Such components are called *property editors.* For example, a property editor for a date object might be a calendar that lets the user scroll through the months and pick a date. A property editor for a `Color` object would let the user select the red, green, and blue components of the color.

Actually, the BeanBox already has a property editor for colors—you saw it in Figure 8–4. Also, of course, there are property editors for basic types such as `String` (a text field) and `boolean` (a choice list with values `true` and `false`). These property editors are registered with the *property editor manager.* You can add property editors to the manager with the static `registerEditor` method of the `PropertyEditorManager` class. You supply the class to which the editor applies and the class of the editor.

```
PropertyEditorManager.registerEditor(Date.class,
   CalendarSelector.class);
```

You can use the `findEditor` method in the `PropertyEditorManager` class to check whether a property editor exists for a given type in your builder tool. That method does the following:

1. It looks first to see which property editors are already registered with it. (These will be the editors supplied by the builder tool and the editors that you supplied by calling `registerEditor`.)
2. Then, it looks for a class whose name consists of the name of the type plus the word `Editor`.
3. If neither lookup succeeds, then `findEditor` returns `null`.

For example, if a `CalendarSelector` class is registered for `Date` objects, then it would be used to edit a `Date` property.

The BeanBox also uses the `findEditor` method to locate an editor for each type it displays in a property sheet. But before looking for a generic editor, it checks whether you requested a specific editor in the *bean information* of your bean. The bean info is a collection of miscellaneous information about your bean. For example, if you have a property whose type is `int` or `String` but whose legal values are restricted in some way, you may not want to use the general-purpose property editor that is supplied by the BeanBox. Instead, you can supply a specific editor for a particular property by naming it in the bean info.

The process for supplying a specific property editor is slightly involved. First, you create a bean info class to accompany your bean. The name of the class must be the name of the bean, followed by the word `BeanInfo`. That class must implement the `BeanInfo` interface, an interface with eight methods. It is simplest to extend the `SimpleBeanInfo` class instead. This convenience class has do-nothing implementations for the eight methods. For example,

```
// bean info class for ChartBean
class ChartBeanBeanInfo
   extends SimpleBeanInfo
{ . . .
}
```

To request a specific editor for a particular bean, you override the `getPropertyDescriptors` method. That method returns an array of `PropertyDescriptor` objects. You create one object for each property that should be displayed on a property editor, *even those for which you just want the default editor.*

You construct a `PropertyDescriptor` by supplying the name of the property and the class of the bean that contains it.

```
PropertyDescriptor descriptor
   = new PropertyDescriptor("titlePosition", ChartBean.class);
```

To request a specific editor for the property, you call the `setPropertyEditorClass` method of the `PropertyDescriptor` class.

```
descriptor.setPropertyEditorClass(TitlePositionEditor.class);
```

Next, you build an array of descriptors for properties of your bean. For example, the chart bean that we discuss in this section has four properties:

- A `String` property, `title`
- An `int` property, `titlePosition`
- A `double[]` property, `values`
- A `boolean` property, `inverse`

Figure 8–20 shows the chart bean. You can see the title on the top. Its position can be set to left, center, or right. The `values` property specifies the graph values. If the `inverse` property is true, then the background is colored and the bars of the chart are white. Example 8–8 lists the code for the chart bean; the bean is simply a modification of the chart applet in Volume 1, Chapter 10.

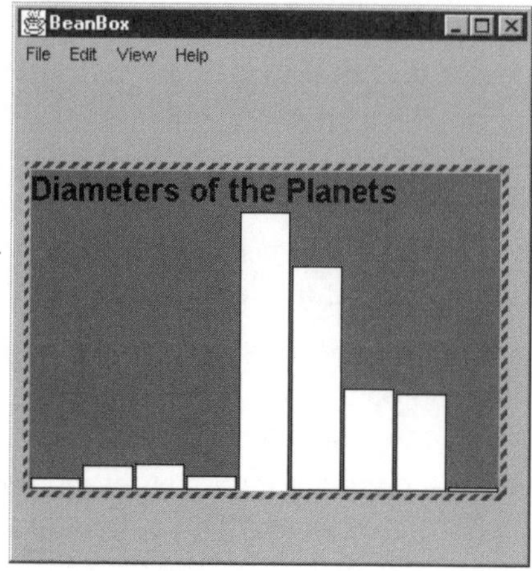

Figure 8–20: The chart bean

The code in Example 8–9 shows the `ChartBeanBeanInfo` class that specifies the property editors for these properties. It achieves the following:

1. In the `static` block, the `DoubleArrayEditor` is registered as an editor for any `double[]` array.
2. The `getPropertyDescriptors` method returns a descriptor for each property. The `title` and `values` properties are used with the default editors, that is, the string editor that comes with the BeanBox and the `DoubleArrayEditor` that was registered in the `static` block.
3. The `titlePosition` and `inverse` properties use special editors of type `TitlePositionEditor` and `InverseEditor`, respectively.

Figure 8–21 shows the resulting property sheet. You'll see in the following sections how to implement these kinds of editors.

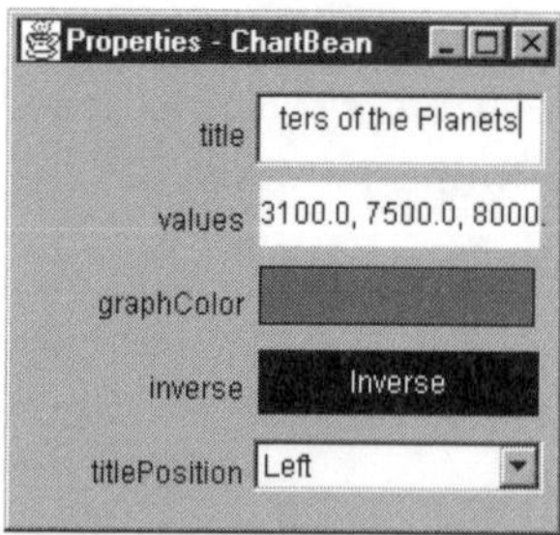

Figure 8–21: The property sheet for the chart bean

Example 8–8: ChartBean.java

```
import java.awt.*;
import java.util.*;
```

```
import java.beans.*;
import java.io.*;
import javax.swing.*;

public class ChartBean extends JPanel
   implements Serializable
{  public void paint(Graphics g)
   {  if (values == null || values.length == 0) return;
      int i;
      double minValue = 0;
      double maxValue = 0;
      for (i = 0; i < values.length; i++)
      {  if (minValue > getValues(i)) minValue = getValues(i);
         if (maxValue < getValues(i)) maxValue = getValues(i);
      }
      if (maxValue == minValue) return;

      Dimension d = getSize();
      int clientWidth = d.width;
      int clientHeight = d.height;
      int barWidth = clientWidth / values.length;

      g.setColor(inverse ? color : Color.white);
      g.fillRect(0, 0, clientWidth, clientHeight);
      g.setColor(Color.black);

      Font titleFont = new Font("SansSerif", Font.BOLD, 20);
      FontMetrics titleFontMetrics
         = g.getFontMetrics(titleFont);

      int titleWidth = titleFontMetrics.stringWidth(title);
      int y = titleFontMetrics.getAscent();
      int x;
      if (titlePosition == LEFT)
         x = 0;
      else if (titlePosition == CENTER)
         x = (clientWidth - titleWidth) / 2;
      else
         x = clientWidth - titleWidth;

      g.setFont(titleFont);
      g.drawString(title, x, y);

      int top = titleFontMetrics.getHeight();
      double scale = (clientHeight - top)
         / (maxValue - minValue);
      y = clientHeight;

      for (i = 0; i < values.length; i++)
      {  int x1 = i * barWidth + 1;
         int y1 = top;
         int height = (int)(getValues(i) * scale);
```

```
         if (getValues(i) >= 0)
            y1 += (int)((maxValue - getValues(i)) * scale);
         else
         {  y1 += (int)(maxValue * scale);
            height = -height;
         }

         g.setColor(inverse ? Color.white : color);
         g.fillRect(x1, y1, barWidth - 2, height);
         g.setColor(Color.black);
         g.drawRect(x1, y1, barWidth - 2, height);
      }
   }
   public void setTitle(String t) { title = t; }
   public String getTitle() { return title; }


   public double[] getValues() { return values; }

   public void setValues(double[] v) { values = v; }

   public double getValues(int i)
   {  if (0 <= i && i < values.length) return values[i];
      return 0;
   }

   public void setValues(int i, double value)
   {  if (0 <= i && i < values.length) values[i] = value;
   }

   public boolean isInverse()
   {  return inverse;
   }

   public void setTitlePosition(int p) { titlePosition = p; }

   public int getTitlePosition()
   {  return titlePosition;
   }

   public void setInverse(boolean b) { inverse = b; }

   public Dimension getMinimumSize()
   {  return new Dimension(MINSIZE, MINSIZE);
   }

   public void setGraphColor(Color c) { color = c; }
   public Color getGraphColor() { return color; }

   private static final int LEFT = 0;
   private static final int CENTER = 1;
```

```
   private static final int RIGHT = 2;

   private static final int MINSIZE = 50;
   private double[] values = { 1, 2, 3 };
   private String title = "Title";
   private int titlePosition = CENTER;
   private boolean inverse;
   private Color color = Color.red;
}
```

Example 8–9: ChartBeanBeanInfo.java

```
import java.beans.*;

public class ChartBeanBeanInfo extends SimpleBeanInfo
{  public PropertyDescriptor[] getPropertyDescriptors()
   {  try
      {  PropertyDescriptor titlePositionDescriptor
            = new PropertyDescriptor("titlePosition",
               ChartBean.class);
         titlePositionDescriptor.setPropertyEditorClass
            (TitlePositionEditor.class);
         PropertyDescriptor inverseDescriptor
            = new PropertyDescriptor("inverse",
               ChartBean.class);
         inverseDescriptor.setPropertyEditorClass
            (InverseEditor.class);

         return new PropertyDescriptor[]
         {  new PropertyDescriptor("title",
               ChartBean.class),
            titlePositionDescriptor,
            new PropertyDescriptor("values",
               ChartBean.class),
            new PropertyDescriptor("graphColor",
               ChartBean.class),
            inverseDescriptor
         };
      }
      catch(IntrospectionException e)
      {  System.out.println("Error: " + e);
         return null;
      }
   }

   static
   {  PropertyEditorManager.registerEditor(double[].class,
         DoubleArrayEditor.class);
   }
}
```

`java.beans.PropertyEditorManager`

- `static PropertyEditor findEditor(Class targetType)`

  returns a property editor for the given type, or `null` if none is registered.

  Parameters: `targetType` the `Class` object for the type to be edited, such as `Class.Color`

- `static void registerEditor(Class targetType, Class editorClass)`

  registers an editor class to edit values of the given type.

  Parameters: `targetType` the `Class` object for the type to be edited

  `editorClass` the `Class` object for the editor class (`null` will unregister the current editor)

`java.beans.PropertyDescriptor`

- `PropertyDescriptor(String name, Class beanClass)`

  constructs a `PropertyDescriptor` object.

  Parameters: `name` the name of the property

  `beanClass` the class of the bean to which the property belongs

- `void setPropertyEditorClass(Class editorClass)`

  sets the class of the property editor to be used with this property.

`java.beans.BeanInfo`

- `PropertyDescriptor[] getPropertyDescriptors()`

  returns a descriptor for each property that should be displayed in the property sheet for the bean.

Writing a Property Editor

Before we begin showing you how to write a property editor, we want to point out that while each property editor works with a value of one specific type, it can nonetheless be quite elaborate. For example, a color property editor (which edits an object of type `Color`) could use sliders or a palette (or both) to allow the user to edit the color in a more congenial way.

Next, any property editor you write must implement the `PropertyEditor` interface, an interface with 12 methods. As with the `BeanInfo` interface, you will not want to do this directly. Instead, it is far more convenient to extend the convenience `PropertyEditorSupport` class that is supplied with the standard library. This support class comes with methods to add and remove property change listeners, and with default

versions of all other methods of the PropertyEditor interface. For example, our editor for editing the title position of a chart in our chart bean starts out like this:

```
// property editor class for title position
class TitlePositionEditor
   extends PropertyEditorSupport
{ . . .
}
```

Note that if a property editor class has a constructor, it must also supply a default constructor, that is, one without arguments.

Finally, before we get into the mechanics of actually writing a property editor, we want to point out that the editor is under the control of the builder, not the bean. The builder adheres to the following procedure to display the current value of the property:

1. It instantiates property editors for each property of the bean.
2. It asks the *bean* to tell it the current value of the property.
3. It then asks the *property editor* to display the value.

The property editor can either use text-based or graphically based methods to actually display the value. We discuss these methods next.

Simple Property Editors

Simple property editors work with text strings. You override the setAsText and getAsText methods. For example, our chart bean has a property that lets you set where the title should be displayed: Left, Center, or Right. These choices are implemented as integer constants.

```
private static final int LEFT = 0;
private static final int CENTER = 1;
private static final int RIGHT = 2;
```

But of course, we don't want them to appear as numbers 0, 1, 2 in the text field—unless we are competing for the User Interface Hall of Horrors. Instead, we define a property editor whose getAsText method returns the value as a string. The method calls the getValue method of the PropertyEditor to find the value of the property. Since this is a generic method, the value is returned as an Object. If the property type is a basic type, we need to return a wrapper object. In our case, the property type is int, and the call to getValue returns an Integer.

```
class TitlePositionEditor
   extends PropertyEditorSupport
{  public String getAsText()
   {  int i = ((Integer)getValue()).intValue();
      if (0 <= i && i < options.length) return options[i];
      return "";
   }
   . . .
   private String[] options = { "Left", "Center", "Right" };
}
```

Now, the text field displays one of these fields. When the user edits the text field, this triggers a call to the `setAsText` method to update the property value by invoking the `setValue` method. It, too, is a generic method whose parameter is of type `Object`. To set the value of a numeric type, we need to pass a wrapper object.

```
public void setAsText(String s)
{  for (int i = 0; i < options.length; i++)
   {  if (options[i].equals(s))
      {  setValue(new Integer(i));
         return;
      }
   }
}
```

Actually, this property editor is not a good choice for the `titlePosition` property, unless, of course, we are also competing for the User Interface Hall of Shame. The user may not know what the legal choices are. It would be better to display all valid settings (see Figure 8–22). The `PropertyEditorSupport` class gives a simple method to display the selections in a property editor. We simply write a `getTags` method that returns an array of strings.

```
public String[] getTags() { return options; }
```

The default `getTags` method returns `null`. By returning a non-`null` value, we indicate a choice field instead of a text field.

We still need to supply the `getAsText` and `setAsText` methods. The `getTags` method simply specifies the values to be displayed in the `Choice` field. The `getAsText`/`setAsText` methods translate between the strings and the data type of the property (which may be a string, an integer, or a completely different type).

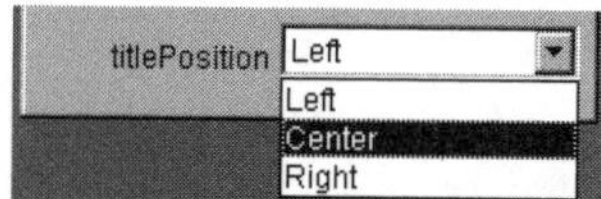

Figure 8–22: The TitlePositionEditor at work

Example 8–10 lists the complete code for the property editor (see Example 8–8 for the code for the actual bean).

Example 8–10: TitlePositionEditor.java

```
import java.beans.*;

public class TitlePositionEditor
   extends PropertyEditorSupport
{  public String getAsText()
   {  int value = ((Integer)getValue()).intValue();
```

```
      return options[value];
   }

   public void setAsText(String s)
   {  for (int i = 0; i < options.length; i++)
      {  if (options[i].equals(s))
         {  setValue(new Integer(i));
            return;
         }
      }
   }

   public String[] getTags() { return options; }

   private String[] options = { "Left", "Center", "Right" };
}
```

java.beans.PropertyEditorSupport

- `Object getValue()`

  returns the current value of the property. Basic types are wrapped into object wrappers.

- `void setValue(Object newValue)`

  sets the property to a new value. Basic types must be wrapped into object wrappers.

Parameters:	`newValue`	the new value of the object; should be a newly created object that the property can own

- `String getAsText()`

  Override this method to return a string representation of the current value of the property. The default returns `null` to indicate that the property cannot be represented as a string.

- `void setAsText(String text)`

  Override this method to set the property to a new value that is obtained by parsing the text. May throw an `IllegalArgumentException` if the text does not represent a legal value or if this property cannot be represented as a string.

- `String[] getTags()`

  Override this method to return an array of all possible string representations of the property values so they can be displayed in a Choice box. The default returns `null` to indicate that there is not a finite set of string values.

GUI-Based Property Editors

More sophisticated property types can't be edited as text. Instead, they are represented in two ways. The property sheet contains a small area (which otherwise would hold a text box or choice field) onto which the property editor will draw a graphical representation of the current value. When the user clicks on that area, a custom editor dialog box pops up (see Figure 8–23). The dialog box contains a component to edit the property values, supplied by the property editor, and a button labeled Done, supplied by the BeanBox.

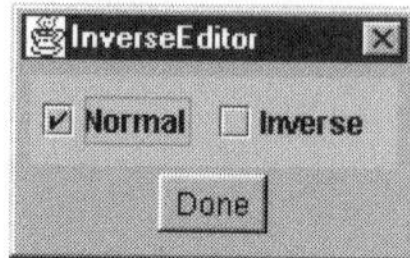

Figure 8–23: A custom editor dialog

To build a GUI-based property editor:

1. Tell the builder tool that you will paint the value and not use a string.
2. "Paint" the value the user enters onto the GUI.
3. Tell the builder tool that you will be using a GUI-based property editor.
4. Build the GUI.
5. Write the code to validate what the user tries to enter as the value.

For the first step, you override the `getAsText` method in the `PropertyEditor` interface to return `null` and the `isPaintable` method to return `true`.

```
public String getAsText()
{  return null;
}
public boolean isPaintable()
{  return true;
}
```

Then, you implement the `paintValue` procedure. It receives a `Graphics` handle and the coordinates of the rectangle inside which you can paint. Note that this rectangle is typically small, so you can't have a very elaborate representation. To graphically represent the `inverse` property, we draw the string `"Inverse"` in white letters with a black background or the string `"Normal"` in black letters with a white background (see Figure 8–21).

```
public void paintValue(Graphics g, Rectangle box)
{  boolean isInverse = ((Boolean)getValue()).booleanValue();
   String s = isInverse ? "Inverse" : "Normal";
   g.setColor(isInverse ? Color.black : Color.white);
   g.fillRect(box.x, box.y, box.width, box.height);
   g.setColor(isInverse ? Color.white : Color.black);
   FontMetrics fm = g.getFontMetrics();
   int w = fm.stringWidth(s);
   int x = box.x;
   if (w < box.width) x += (box.width - w) / 2;
   int y = box.y + (box.height - fm.getHeight()) / 2
```

```
        + fm.getAscent();
    g.drawString(s, x, y);
}
```

Of course, this graphical representation is not editable. The user must click on it to pop up a custom editor.

You indicate that you will have a custom editor by overriding the `supportsCustomEditor` in the `PropertyEditor` interface to return `true`.

```
public boolean supportsCustomEditor()
{  return true;
}
```

Now, you write the code that builds up the component that will hold the custom editor. You will need to build a separate custom editor class for every property. For example, associated to our `InverseEditor` class is an `InverseEditorPanel` class (see Example 8–9) that describes a GUI with two radio buttons to toggle between normal and inverse mode. That code is straightforward. However, the GUI actions must update the property values. We did this as follows:

1. Have the custom editor constructor receive a reference to the property editor object and store it in a variable `editor`.
2. To read the property value, we have the custom editor call `editor.getValue()`.
3. To set the object value, we have the custom editor call `editor.setValue(newValue)` followed by `editor.firePropertyChange()`.

Next, the `getCustomEditor` method of the `PropertyEditor` interface constructs and returns an object of the custom editor class.

```
public Component getCustomEditor()
{  return new InverseEditorPanel(this);
}
```

Example 8–11 shows the complete code for the `InverseEditor` that displays the current setting in the property sheet. Example 8–12 lists the code implementing the pop-up editor panel.

The other custom editor that we built for the chart bean class lets you edit a `double[]` array. Recall that the BeanBox cannot edit array properties at all. We developed this custom editor to fill this obvious gap. That custom editor is a little involved. Figure 8–24 shows the custom editor in action. All array values are shown in the list box, prefixed by their array index. Clicking on an array value places it into the text field above it, and you can edit it. You can also resize the array. The code for the `DoubleArrayPanel` class that implements the GUI is listed in Example 8–14.

The code for the property editor class (shown in Example 8–13) is almost identical to that of the `InverseEditor`, except that we simply paint a string consisting of the first few array values, followed by . . ., in the `paintValue` method. And, of course, we return a different custom editor in the `getCustomEditor` method. These examples complete the code for the chart bean.

NOTE: Unfortunately, we have to *paint* the array values. It would be more convenient to return a string with the `getAsText` method. However, then the BeanBox assumes that you can edit that text, and it won't pop up a custom editor if you click on it, even if the `getCustomEditor` method is defined.

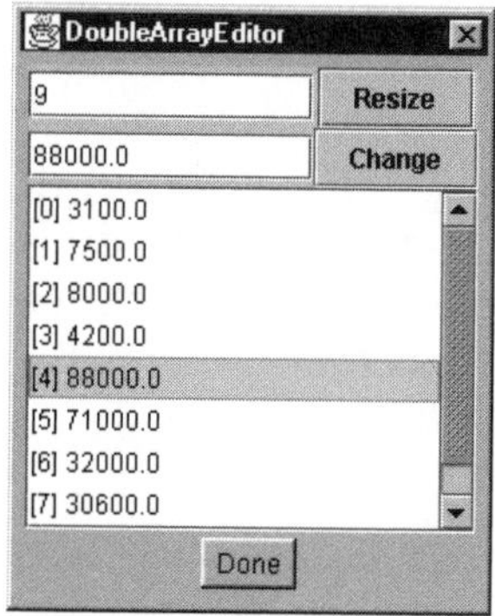

Figure 8–24: The custom editor dialog for editing an array

Example 8–11: InverseEditor.java

```
import java.awt.*;
import java.beans.*;

public class InverseEditor extends PropertyEditorSupport
{  public Component getCustomEditor()
   {  return new InverseEditorPanel(this);
   }

   public boolean supportsCustomEditor()
   {  return true;
   }

   public boolean isPaintable()
   {  return true;
   }

   public void paintValue(Graphics g, Rectangle box)
   {  boolean isInverse = ((Boolean)getValue()).booleanValue();
      String s = isInverse ? "Inverse" : "Normal";
      g.setColor(isInverse ? Color.black : Color.white);
      g.fillRect(box.x, box.y, box.width, box.height);
      g.setColor(isInverse ? Color.white : Color.black);
      FontMetrics fm = g.getFontMetrics();
```

```
      int w = fm.stringWidth(s);
      int x = box.x;
      if (w < box.width) x += (box.width - w) / 2;
      int y = box.y + (box.height - fm.getHeight()) / 2
         + fm.getAscent();
      g.drawString(s, x, y);
   }

   public String getAsText()
   {  return null;
   }
}
```

Example 8–12: InverseEditorPanel.java

```
import java.awt.*;
import java.awt.event.*;
import java.text.*;
import java.lang.reflect.*;
import java.beans.*;
import javax.swing.*;

public class InverseEditorPanel extends JPanel
{  public InverseEditorPanel(PropertyEditorSupport ed)
   {  editor = ed;
      ButtonGroup g = new ButtonGroup();
      boolean isInverse
         = ((Boolean)editor.getValue()).booleanValue();
      normal = new JCheckBox("Normal", !isInverse);
      inverse = new JCheckBox("Inverse", isInverse);

      g.add(normal);
      g.add(inverse);
      add(normal);
      add(inverse);

      ActionListener buttonListener =
         new ActionListener()
         {  public void actionPerformed(ActionEvent event)
            {  editor.setValue(new Boolean(inverse.isSelected()));
               editor.firePropertyChange();
            }
         };

      normal.addActionListener(buttonListener);
      inverse.addActionListener(buttonListener);
   }

   private JCheckBox normal;
   private JCheckBox inverse;
   PropertyEditorSupport editor;
}
```

Example 8–13: DoubleArrayEditor.java

```
import java.awt.*;
import java.beans.*;

public class DoubleArrayEditor extends PropertyEditorSupport
{  public Component getCustomEditor()
   {  return new DoubleArrayEditorPanel(this);
   }

   public boolean supportsCustomEditor()
   {  return true;
   }

   public boolean isPaintable()
   {  return true;
   }

   public void paintValue(Graphics g, Rectangle box)
   {  double[] values = (double[]) getValue();
      String s = "";
      for (int i = 0; i < 3; i++)
      {  if (values.length > i) s = s + values[i];
         if (values.length > i + 1) s = s + ", ";
      }
      if (values.length > 3) s += "...";

      g.setColor(Color.white);
      g.fillRect(box.x, box.y, box.width, box.height);
      g.setColor(Color.black);
      FontMetrics fm = g.getFontMetrics();
      int w = fm.stringWidth(s);
      int x = box.x;
      if (w < box.width) x += (box.width - w) / 2;
      int y = box.y + (box.height - fm.getHeight()) / 2
         + fm.getAscent();
      g.drawString(s, x, y);
   }

   public String getAsText()
   {  return null;
   }
}
```

Example 8–14: DoubleArrayEditorPanel.java

```
import java.awt.*;
import java.awt.event.*;
import java.text.*;
import java.lang.reflect.*;
import java.beans.*;
```

```
import javax.swing.*;
import javax.swing.event.*;

public class DoubleArrayEditorPanel extends JPanel
{  public DoubleArrayEditorPanel(PropertyEditorSupport ed)
   {  editor = ed;
      setArray((double[])ed.getValue());

      setLayout(new GridBagLayout());
      GridBagConstraints gbc = new GridBagConstraints();

      gbc.weightx = 100;
      gbc.weighty = 0;
      gbc.fill = GridBagConstraints.HORIZONTAL;

      add(sizeField, gbc, 0, 0, 1, 1);
      add(valueField, gbc, 0, 1, 1, 1);

      gbc.fill = GridBagConstraints.NONE;

      add(sizeButton, gbc, 1, 0, 1, 1);
      add(valueButton, gbc, 1, 1, 1, 1);

      sizeButton.addActionListener(
         new ActionListener()
         {  public void actionPerformed(ActionEvent event)
            {  changeSize();
            }
         });

      valueButton.addActionListener(
         new ActionListener()
         {  public void actionPerformed(ActionEvent event)
            {  changeValue();
            }
         });

      gbc.weighty = 100;
      gbc.fill = GridBagConstraints.BOTH;

      add(new JScrollPane(elementList), gbc, 0, 2, 2, 1);

      elementList.setSelectionMode(ListSelection-
Model.SINGLE_SELECTION);

      elementList.addListSelectionListener(
         new ListSelectionListener()
         {  public void valueChanged(ListSelectionEvent event)
            {  int i = elementList.getSelectedIndex();
               if (i < 0) return;
               valueField.setText("" + array[i]);
            }
```

```
      });

   elementList.setModel(model);
   elementList.setSelectedIndex(0);
}

public void add(Component c, GridBagConstraints gbc,
   int x, int y, int w, int h)
{  gbc.gridx = x;
   gbc.gridy = y;
   gbc.gridwidth = w;
   gbc.gridheight = h;
   add(c, gbc);
}

public void changeSize()
{  fmt.setParseIntegerOnly(true);
   int s = 0;
   try
   {  s = fmt.parse(sizeField.getText()).intValue();
      if (s < 0)
         throw new ParseException("Out of bounds", 0);
   }
   catch(ParseException e)
   {  JOptionPane.showMessageDialog(this, "" + e,
         "Input Error", JOptionPane.WARNING_MESSAGE);
      sizeField.requestFocus();
      return;
   }
   if (s == array.length) return;
   setArray((double[])arrayGrow(array, s));
   editor.setValue(array);
   editor.firePropertyChange();
}

public void changeValue()
{  double v = 0;
   fmt.setParseIntegerOnly(false);
   try
   {  v = fmt.parse(valueField.getText()).doubleValue();
   }
   catch(ParseException e)
   {  JOptionPane.showMessageDialog(this, "" + e,
         "Input Error", JOptionPane.WARNING_MESSAGE);
      valueField.requestFocus();
      return;
   }
   int currentIndex = elementList.getSelectedIndex();
   setArray(currentIndex, v);
   editor.firePropertyChange();
}

static Object arrayGrow(Object a, int newLength)
```

```
{  Class cl = a.getClass();
   if (!cl.isArray()) return null;
   Class componentType = a.getClass().getComponentType();
   int length = Array.getLength(a);

   Object newArray = Array.newInstance(componentType,
      newLength);
   System.arraycopy(a, 0, newArray, 0,
      Math.min(length, newLength));
   return newArray;
}

public double[] getArray()
{  return (double[])array.clone();
}

public void setArray(double[] v)
{  if (v == null) array = new double[0];
   else array = v;
   model.setArray(array);
   sizeField.setText("" + array.length);
   if (array.length > 0)
   {  valueField.setText("" + array[0]);
      elementList.setSelectedIndex(0);
   }
   else
      valueField.setText("");
}

public double getArray(int i)
{  if (0 <= i && i < array.length) return array[i];
   return 0;
}

public void setArray(int i, double value)
{  if (0 <= i && i < array.length)
   {  model.setValue(i, value);
      elementList.setSelectedIndex(i);
      valueField.setText("" + value);
   }
}

private PropertyEditorSupport editor;
private double[] array;
private NumberFormat fmt = NumberFormat.getNumberInstance();
private JTextField sizeField = new JTextField(4);
private JTextField valueField = new JTextField(12);
private JButton sizeButton = new JButton("Resize");
private JButton valueButton = new JButton("Change");
private JList elementList = new JList();
private DoubleArrayListModel model = new DoubleArrayListModel();
```

```
}

class DoubleArrayListModel extends AbstractListModel
{  public int getSize()
   {  return array.length;
   }

   public Object getElementAt(int i)
   {  return "[" + i + "] " + array[i];
   }

   public void setArray(double[] a)
   {  int oldLength = array == null ? 0 : array.length;
      array = a;
      int newLength = array == null ? 0 : array.length;
      if (oldLength > 0) fireIntervalRemoved(this, 0, oldLength);
      if (newLength > 0) fireIntervalAdded(this, 0, newLength);
   }

   public void setValue(int i, double value)
   {  array[i] = value;
      fireContentsChanged(this, i, i);
   }

   double[] array;
}
```

Summing Up

For every property editor you write, you have to choose one of three ways to display and edit the property value:

- As a text string (define `getAsText` and `setAsText`)
- As a choice field (define `getAsText`, `setAsText`, and `getTags`)
- Graphically, by painting it (define `isPaintable`, `paintValue`, `supportsCustomEditor`, and `getCustomEditor`)

You saw examples of all three cases in the chart bean.

Finally, some property editors might want to support a method called `getJavaInitializationString`. With this method, you can give the builder tool the Java programming language code that sets a property to allow automatic code generation. We did not show you an example for this method.

`java.beans.PropertyEditorSupport`

- `boolean isPaintable()`

  Override this method to return `true` if the class uses the `paintValue` method to display the property.

- `void paintValue(Graphics g, Rectangle box)`

  Override this method to represent the value by drawing into a graphics context in the specified place on the component used for the property sheet.

Parameters:	`g`	the graphics object to draw onto
	`box`	a rectangle object that represents where on the Property Sheet component to draw the value.

- `boolean supportsCustomEditor()`
  Override this method to return `true` if the property editor has a custom editor.
- `Component getCustomEditor()`
  Override this method to return the component that contains a customized GUI for editing the property value.
- `String getJavaInitializationString()`
  Override this method to return a Java programming language code string that can be used to generate code that initializes the property value. Examples are `"0"`,`"new Color(64, 64, 64)"`.

Going Beyond Naming Patterns—Building a `BeanInfo` Class

You have already seen that if you use the standard naming conventions for the members of your bean, then a builder tool can use reflection to determine the properties, events, and methods of your bean. This process makes it simple to get started with bean programming but is rather limiting in the end. As your beans become in any way complex, there *will* be features of your bean that naming patterns and reflection will simply not reveal. (Not to mention that using English naming patterns as the basis for all GUI builders in all languages for all times seems to be rather against the spirit of providing support for your international customers.) Moreover, as we already mentioned, there may well be `get/set` pairs that you do *not* want to expose as bean properties.

Luckily, the JavaBeans specification allows a far more flexible and powerful mechanism for storing information about your bean for use by a builder. As with many features of beans, the mechanism is simple in theory but can be tedious to carry out in practice. The idea is that you again use an object that implements the `BeanInfo` interface. (Recall that we used one feature of the `BeanInfo` class when we supplied property editors for the chart bean class.)

When you implement this interface to describe your bean, a builder tool will look to the methods from the `BeanInfo` interface to tell it (potentially quite detailed) information about the properties, events, and methods your bean supports. The `BeanInfo` is supposed to free you from the tyranny of naming patterns. Somewhat ironically, the JavaBeans specification does require that you use a naming pattern to associate a `BeanInfo` object to the bean. You specify the name of the bean info class by adding `BeanInfo` to the name of the bean. For example, the bean info class associated to the class `ChartBean` *must* be named `ChartBeanBeanInfo`. The bean info class must be part of the same package as the bean itself.

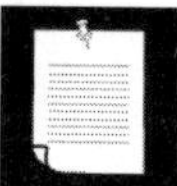

NOTE: Any descriptions you supply in the bean info associated to your bean override any information that the builder might obtain by reflecting on the member names. Moreover, if you supply information about a feature set (such as the properties that your bean supports), you must then provide information about all the properties in the associated bean info.

As you already saw, you won't normally write from scratch a class that implements the `BeanInfo` interface. Instead, you will probably turn again to the `SimpleBeanInfo` convenience class that has empty implementations (returning `null`) for all the methods in the `BeanInfo` interface. This practice is certainly convenient—just override the methods you really want to change. Moreover, this convenience class includes a useful method called `loadImage` that you can use to load an image (such as an icon—see below) for your bean. We use the `SimpleBeanInfo` class for all our examples of `BeanInfo` classes. For example, our `ChartBeanBeanInfo` class starts out:

```
public class ChartBeanBeanInfo extends SimpleBeanInfo
```

NOTE: That the methods in the `SimpleBeanInfo` class return `null` is actually quite important. This is exactly how the builder tool knows how to use naming patterns to find out the members of that feature set. A non-`null` return value turns off the reflective search.

For a taste of what you can do with the bean info mechanism, let's start with an easy-to-use, but most useful, method in the `BeanInfo` interface: the `getIcon` method that lets you give your bean a custom icon. This is useful since builder tools will usually want to have an icon for the bean for some sort of palette. In the BeanBox, the icon shows up to the left of the bean name in its Toolbox—see Figure 8–3. Actually, you can specify separate icon bitmaps. The `BeanInfo` interface has four constants that cover the standard sizes.

```
ICON_COLOR_16x16
ICON_COLOR_32x32
ICON_MONO_16x16
ICON_MONO_32x32
```

Here is an example of how you might use the `loadImage` convenience method in the `SimpleBeanInfo` class to add an icon to a class:

```
public Image getIcon(int iconType)
{  String name = "";
   if (iconType == BeanInfo.ICON_COLOR_16x16)
      name = "COLOR_16x16";
   else if (iconType == BeanInfo.ICON_COLOR_32x32)
      name = "COLOR_32x32";
   else if (iconType == BeanInfo.ICON_MONO_16x16)
      name = "MONO_16x16";
   else if (iconType == BeanInfo.ICON_MONO_32x32)
```

```
        name = "MONO_32x32";
    else return null;
    return loadImage("ChartBean_" + name + ".gif");
}
```

where we have cleverly named the image files to be

```
ChartBean_COLOR_16x16.gif
ChartBean_COLOR_32x32.gif
```

and so on.

`FeatureDescriptor` *Objects*

The key to using any of the more advanced features of the `BeanInfo` class is the `FeatureDescriptor` class and its various subclasses. As its name suggests, a `FeatureDescriptor` object provides information about a feature. Examples of features are properties, events, methods, and so on. More precisely, the `FeatureDescriptor` class is the superclass for all descriptors, and it factors out the common operations that you need to deal with when trying to describe any feature. For example, the name of the feature is obtained through the `getName` method. Since this method is in the superclass, it works for all feature descriptors, no matter what they describe. Here are the subclasses of the `FeatureDescriptor` class.

- `BeanDescriptor`
- `EventSetDescriptor`
- `MethodDescriptor`
- `ParameterDescriptor`
- `PropertyDescriptor` (with a further subclass—`IndexedPropertyDescriptor`)

These classes all work basically the same. You create a descriptor object for each member you are trying to describe, and you collect all descriptors of a feature set in an array and return it as the return value of one of the `BeanInfo` methods.

For example, to turn off reflection for event sets, you'll return an array of `EventSetDescriptor` objects in your bean info class.

```
class MyBeanBeanInfo extends SimpleBeanInfo
{  public EventSetDescriptor[] getEventSetDescriptors()
   {  . . .
   }
   . . .
}
```

Next, you'll construct all the various `EventSetDescriptor` objects that will go into this array. Generally, all the constructors for the various kinds of `FeatureDescriptor` objects work in the same way. In particular, for events, the most common constructor takes:

- The class of the bean that has the event
- The base name of the event

- The class of the EventListener interface that corresponds to the event
- The methods in the specified EventListener interface that are triggered by the event

Other constructors let you specify the methods of the bean that should be used to add and remove EventListener objects.

A good example of all this can be found in the BeanInfo class associated with the ExplicitButtonBean that ships with the BDK. Let's analyze the code that creates the needed event descriptors for this bean. The ExplicitButtonBean fires two events: when the button is pushed and when the state of the button has changed. Here's how you build these two EventSetDescriptor objects associated to these two events:

```
EventSetDescriptor push = new EventSetDescriptor(beanClass,
   "actionPerformed",
   java.awt.event.ActionListener.class,
   "actionPerformed");

EventSetDescriptor changed = new EventSetDescriptor(beanClass,
   "propertyChange",
   java.beans.PropertyChangeListener.class,
   "propertyChange");
```

The next step is to set the various display names for the events for the EventSetDescriptor. In the code for the ExplicitButton in the BeanInfo class, this is done by

```
push.setDisplayName("button push");
changed.setDisplayName("bound property change");
```

Actually, it is a little messier to code the creation of the needed EventSetDescriptor objects than the above fragments indicate because all constructors for feature descriptor objects can throw an IntrospectionException. So, you actually have to build the array of descriptors in a try/catch block, as the following code indicates.

```
public EventSetDescriptor[] getEventSetDescriptors()
{  try
   {   EventSetDescriptor push = new
          EventSetDescriptor(beanClass,
            "actionPerformed",
            java.awt.event.ActionListener.class,
            "actionPerformed");

       EventSetDescriptor changed = new
          EventSetDescriptor(beanClass,
            "propertyChange",
            java.beans.PropertyChangeListener.class,
            "propertyChange");

       push.setDisplayName("button push");
```

```
            changed.setDisplayName("bound property change");

            return new EventSetDescriptor[] { push, changed };
        } catch (IntrospectionException e)
        {   throw new Error(e.toString());
        }
    }
```

This particular event set descriptor is needed because the event descriptors differ from the standard naming pattern. Specifically, there are two differences:

- The listener classes are not the name of the bean + `Listener`.
- The display names are not the same as the event names.

To summarize: When any feature of your bean differs from the standard naming pattern, you must do the following:

- Create feature descriptors for *all* features in that set (events, properties, methods).
- Return an array of the descriptors in the appropriate `BeanInfo` method.

java.beans.BeanInfo

- `EventSetDescriptor[] getEventSetDescriptors()`
- `MethodDescriptor[] getMethodDescriptors()`
- `PropertyDescriptor[] getPropertyDescriptors()`

  return an array of the specified descriptor objects. A return of `null` signals the builder to use the naming conventions and reflection to find the member. The `getPropertyDescriptors` method returns a mixture of plain and indexed property descriptors. Use `instanceof` to check if a specific `PropertyDescriptor` is an `IndexedPropertyDescriptor`.

- `Image getIcon(int iconType)`

  returns an image object that can be used to represent the bean in toolboxes, tool bars, and the like. There are four constants, as described earlier, for the standard types of icons.

Parameters:	`iconType`	the type of icon to use (16 x 16 color, 32 x 32 color, etc.)

- `int getDefaultEventIndex()`
- `int getDefaultPropertyIndex()`

  A bean can have a default event or property. Both of these methods return the array index that specifies which element of the descriptor array to use as that default member, or –1 if no default exists. A bean builder environment can visually enhance the default feature, for example, by placing it first in a list of features or by displaying its name in boldface.

- `BeanInfo[] getAdditionalBeanInfo()`

  returns an array of `BeanInfo` objects or `null`. Use this method when you want some information about your bean to come from `BeanInfo` classes for other beans. For example, you might use this method if your bean aggregated lots of other beans. The current `BeanInfo` class rules in case of conflict.

`java.beans.SimpleBeanInfo`

- `Image loadImage(String resourceName)`

  returns an image object file associated to the resource. Currently only GIFs are supported.

  Parameters: `resourceName` a path name (taken relative to the directory containing the current class)

`java.beans.FeatureDescriptor`

- `String getName()`

  returns the name used in the bean's code for the member.

- `void setName(String name)`

  sets the programmatic name for the feature.

  Parameters: `name` the name of the feature

- `String getDisplayName()`

  returns a localized display name for the feature. The default value is the value returned by `getName`. However, currently there is no explicit support for supplying feature names in multiple locales.

- `void setDisplayName(String displayName)`

  sets the localized display name for the feature.

  Parameters: `displayName` the name to use

- `String getShortDescription()`

  returns a localized string that a builder tool can use to provide a short description for this feature. The default value is the return value of `getDisplayName`.

- `void setShortDescription(String text)`

  sets the descriptive string (short—usually less than 40 characters) that describes the feature.

  Parameters: `text` the localized short description to associate with this feature

- `void setValue(String attributeName, Object value)`

  associates a named attribute to this feature.

Parameters:	`attributeName`	the name of the attribute whose value you are setting

- `Object getValue(String attributeName)`

  gets the value of the feature with the given name.

Parameters:	`attributeName`	the name for the attribute to be retrieved

- `Enumeration attributeNames()`

  returns an enumeration object that contains names of any attributes registered with `setValue`.

- `void setExpert(boolean b)`

  lets you supply an expert flag that a builder can use to determine whether to hide the feature from a naïve user. (Not every builder is likely to support this feature.)

Parameters:	`b`	`true` if you intend that this feature be used only by experts

- `boolean isExpert()`

  returns `true` if this feature is marked for use by experts.

- `void setHidden(boolean b)`

  marks a feature for use only by the builder tool.

Parameters:	`b`	`true` if you want to hide this feature

- `boolean isHidden()`

  returns `true` if the user of the builder shouldn't see this feature but the builder tool needs to be aware of it.

`java.beans.EventSetDescriptor`

API

- `EventSetDescriptor(Class sourceClass, String eventSetName, Class listener, String listenerMethod)`

  constructs an `EventSetDescriptor`. This constructor assumes that you follow the standard pattern for the names of the event class and the names of the methods to add and remove event listeners. Throws an `IntrospectionException` if an error occurred during introspection.

Parameters:	`sourceClass`	the class firing the event
	`eventSetName`	the name of the event
	`listener`	the listener interface to which these events get delivered
	`listenerMethod`	the method triggered when the event gets delivered to a listener

- `EventSetDescriptor(Class sourceClass, String eventSetName, Class listener, String[] listenerMethods, String addListenerMethod, String removeListenerMethod)`

  is the most general constructor for an `EventSetDescriptor`. Throws an `IntrospectionException` if an error occurred during introspection.

Parameters:		
	`sourceClass`	the class firing the event
	`eventSetName`	the name of the event
	`listener`	the listener interface to which these events get delivered
	`listenerMethods`	the methods of the listener interface triggered when the event gets delivered to a listener
	`addListenerMethod`	the method to add a listener to the bean
	`removeListenerMethod`	the method to remove a listener from the bean

- `Method getAddListenerMethod()`

  returns the method used to register the listener.

- `Method getRemoveListenerMethod()`

  returns the method used to remove a registered listener for the event.

- `Method[] getListenerMethods()`
- `MethodDescriptor[] getListenerMethodDescriptors()`

  return an array of `Method` or `MethodDescriptor` objects for the methods triggered in the listener interface.

- `Class getListenerType()`

  returns a `Class` object for the target listener interface associated with the event.

- `void setUnicast(boolean b)`

  is set to `true` if this event can be propagated to only one listener.

- `boolean isUnicast()`

  is set to `true` if the event set is unicast (default is `false`).

`java.beans.PropertyDescriptor`

- `PropertyDescriptor(String propertyName, Class beanClass)`
- `PropertyDescriptor(String propertyName, Class beanClass, String getMethod, String setMethod)`

  construct a `PropertyDescriptor` object. The methods throw an `IntrospectionException` if an error occurred during introspection. The first

constructor assumes that you follow the standard convention for the names of the `get` and `set` methods.

Parameters:	`propertyName`	the name of the property
	`beanClass`	the `Class` object for the bean being described
	`getMethod`	the name of the `get` method
	`setMethod`	the name of the `set` method

- `Class getPropertyType()`
  returns a `Class` object for the property type.
- `Method getReadMethod()`
  returns the `get` method.
- `Method getWriteMethod()`
  returns the `set` method.
- `void setBound(boolean b)`
  is set to `true` if this property fires a `PropertyChangeEvent` when its value is changed.
- `boolean isBound()`
  returns `true` if this is a bound property.
- `void setConstrained(boolean b)`
  is set to `true` if this property fires a `VetoableChangeEvent` before its value is changed.
- `boolean isConstrained()`
  returns `true` if this is a constrained property.

`java.beans.IndexedPropertyDescriptor` API

- `IndexedPropertyDescriptor(String propertyName, Class beanClass)`
- `IndexedPropertyDescriptor(String propertyName, Class beanClass, String getMethod, String setMethod, String indexedGetMethod, String indexedSetMethod)`
  construct an `IndexedPropertyDescriptor` for the index property. The methods throw an `IntrospectionException` if an error occurred during introspection. The first constructor assumes that you follow the standard convention for the names of the `get` and `set` methods.

Parameters:	`propertyName`	the name of the property
	`beanClass`	the `Class` object for the bean being described
	`getMethod`	the name of the `get` method

`setMethod`	the name of the `set` method
`indexedGetMethod`	the name of the indexed `get` method
`indexedSetMethod`	the name of the indexed `set` method

- `Class getIndexedPropertyType()`
  returns the Java platform class that describes the type of the indexed values of the property, that is, the return type of the indexed `get` method.
- `Method getIndexedReadMethod()`
  returns the indexed `get` method.
- `Method getIndexedWriteMethod()`
  returns the indexed `set` method.

`java.beans.MethodDescriptor`

- `MethodDescriptor(Method method)`
- `MethodDescriptor(Method method, ParameterDescriptor[] parameterDescriptors)`
  construct a method descriptor for the given method with the associated parameters; throw an `IntrospectionException` if an error occurred during introspection.

Parameters:	`method`	method object
	`parameterDescriptors`	an array of parameter descriptors that describe the parameters for the method

- `Method getMethod()`
  returns the method object for that method.
- `ParameterDescriptor[] getParameterDescriptors()`
  returns an array of parameter descriptor objects for the methods parameters.

`java.beans.ParameterDescriptor`

- `ParameterDescriptor()`
  creates a new parameter descriptor object. Parameter descriptors carry no information beyond that stored in the `FeatureDescriptor` superclass.

Customizers

A property editor, no matter how sophisticated, is responsible for allowing the user to set one property at a time. Especially if certain properties of a bean relate to each other, it may be more user friendly to give users a way to edit multiple

properties at the same time. To enable this feature, you supply a *customizer* instead of (or in addition to) multiple property editors.

In the example program for this section, we develop a customizer for the chart bean. The customizer lets you set several properties of the chart bean at once, and it lets you specify a file from which to read the data points for the chart. Figure 8–25 shows you one pane of the customizer for the ChartBean.

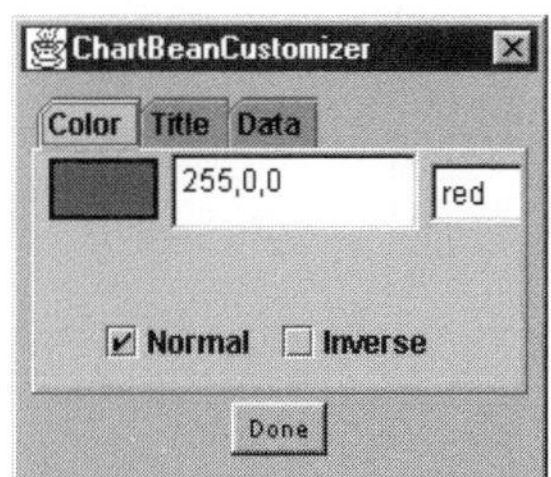

Figure 8–25: The customizer for the ChartBean

To add a customizer to your bean, you *must* supply a `BeanInfo` class and override the `getBeanDescriptor` method, as shown in the following example.

```
public BeanDescriptor getBeanDescriptor()
{  return new BeanDescriptor(ChartBean.class,
      ChartBeanCustomizer.class);
}
```

The general procedure for your customizers follows the same model.

1. Override the `getBeanDescriptor` method by returning a new `BeanDescriptor` object for your bean.
2. Specify the customizer class as the second parameter of the constructor for the `BeanDescriptor` object.

Note that you need not follow any naming pattern for the customizer class. The builder can locate it by

1. Finding the associated `BeanInfo` class
2. Invoking its `getBeanDescriptor` method
3. Calling the `getCustomizerClass` method

(Nevertheless, it is customary to name the customizer as *`BeanName`*`Customizer`.)

Example 8–15 has the code for the `ChartBeanBeanInfo` class that references the `ChartBeanCustomizer`. You will see in the next section how that customizer is implemented.

Example 8–15: ChartBeanBeanInfo.java

```
import java.awt.*;
import java.beans.*;
```

```
public class ChartBeanBeanInfo extends SimpleBeanInfo
{  public BeanDescriptor getBeanDescriptor()
   {  return new BeanDescriptor(ChartBean.class,
         ChartBeanCustomizer.class);
   }

   public Image getIcon(int iconType)
   {  String name = "";
      if (iconType == BeanInfo.ICON_COLOR_16x16)
         name = "COLOR_16x16";
      else if (iconType == BeanInfo.ICON_COLOR_32x32)
         name = "COLOR_32x32";
      else if (iconType == BeanInfo.ICON_MONO_16x16)
         name = "MONO_16x16";
      else if (iconType == BeanInfo.ICON_MONO_32x32)
         name = "MONO_32x32";
      else return null;
      return loadImage("ChartBean_" + name + ".gif");
   }
}
```

java.beans.BeanInfo

- `BeanDescriptor getBeanDescriptor()`
  returns a `BeanDescriptor` object that describes features of the bean.

java.beans.BeanDescriptor

- `BeanDescriptor(Class beanClass, Class customizerClass)`
  constructs a `BeanDescriptor` object for a bean that has a customizer.

Parameters:	`beanClass`	the `Class` object for the bean
	`customizerClass`	the `Class` object for the bean's customizer

- `Class getBeanClass()`
  returns the `Class` object that defines the bean.
- `Class getCustomizerClass()`
  returns the `Class` object that defines the bean's customizer.

Writing a Customizer Class

Any customizer class you write must implement the `Customizer` interface. There are only three methods in this interface:

- The `setObject` method, which takes a parameter that specifies the bean being customized
- The `addPropertyChangeListener` and `removePropertyChangeListener` methods, which manage the collection of listeners that are notified when a property is changed in the customizer

It is a good idea to update the visual appearance of the target bean by broadcasting a `PropertyChangeEvent` whenever the user changes any of the property values, not just when the user is at the end of the customization process.

Unlike property editors, customizers are not automatically displayed. In the BeanBox, you must select Edit -> Customize to pop up the customizer of a bean. At that point, the BeanBox will call the `setObject` method of the customizer that takes the bean being customized as a parameter. Notice that your customizer is thus created before it is actually linked to an instance of your bean. Therefore, you cannot assume any information about the state of a bean in the customizer, and you must provide a default constructor, that is, one without arguments.

There are three parts to writing a customizer class:

1. Building the visual interface;
2. Initializing the customizer in the `setObject` method;
3. Updating the bean by firing property change events when the user changes properties in the interface.

By definition, a customizer class is visual. It must, therefore, extend `Component` or a subclass of `Component`, such as `JPanel`. Since customizers typically present the user with many options, it is often handy to use the tabbed pane interface. We use this approach and have the customizer extend the `JTabbedPane` interface.

CAUTION: We had quite a bit of grief with placing a `JTabbedPane` inside the customizer dialog of the BeanBox. The BeanBox uses the old AWT components. Somehow the events became entangled between the AWT and Swing components and clicking on the tabs did not flip the panes. By trial and error, we found that trapping the tab clicks and calling `validate` fixed this problem. Presumably, in the long run, this issue will go away when all bean environments use Swing.

The customizer gathers the information in three panes:

- Graph color and inverse mode
- Title and title position
- Data points

Of course, developing this kind of user interface can be tedious to code—our example devotes over 100 lines just to set it up in the constructor. However, this task requires only the usual Swing programming skills, and we won't dwell on the details here.

There is one trick that is worth keeping in mind. You often need to edit property values in a customizer. Rather than implementing a new interface for setting the property value of a particular class, you can simply locate an existing property editor and add it to your user interface! For example, in our `ChartBean` customizer, we need to set the graph color. Since we know that the BeanBox has a perfectly good property editor for colors, we locate it as follows:

```
PropertyEditor colorEditor
   = PropertEditorManager.findEditor(Color.Class);
```

We then call `getCustomEditor` to get the component that contains the user interface for setting the colors.

```
Component colorEditorComponent = colorEditor.getCustomEditor();
// now add this component to the UI
```

Once we have all components laid out, we initialize their values in the `setObject` method. The `setObject` method is called when the customizer is displayed. Its parameter is the bean that is being customized. To proceed, we store that bean reference—we'll need it later to notify the bean of property changes. Then, we initialize each user interface component. Here is a part of the `setObject` method of the chart bean customizer that does this initialization.

```
public void setObject(Object obj)
{  bean = (ChartBean)obj;
   titleField.setText(bean.getTitle());
   colorEditor.setValue(bean.getGraphColor());
   . . .
}
```

Finally, we hook up event handlers to track the user's activities. Whenever the user changes the value of a component, the component fires an event that our customizer must handle. The event handler must update the value of the property in the bean and must also fire a `PropertyChangeEvent` so that other listeners (such as the property sheet) can be updated. Let us follow that process with a couple of user interface elements in the chart bean customizer.

When the user types a new title, we want to update the title property. We attach a `DocumentListener` to the text field into which the user types the title.

```
titleField.getDocument().addDocumentListener(
   new DocumentListener()
   {  public void changedUpdate(DocumentEvent event)
      {  setTitle(titleField.getText());
      }
      public void insertUpdate(DocumentEvent event)
      {  setTitle(titleField.getText());
      }
      public void removeUpdate(DocumentEvent event)
      {  setTitle(titleField.getText());
      }
   });
```

The three listener methods call the `setTitle` method of the customizer. That method calls the bean to update the property value and then fires a property change event. (This update is necessary only for properties that are not bound.) Here is the code for the `setTitle` method.

```
public void setTitle(String newValue)
{  if (bean == null) return;
   String oldValue = bean.getTitle();
   bean.setTitle(newValue);
   firePropertyChange("title", oldValue, newValue);
}
```

When the color value changes in the color property editor, we want to update the graph color of the bean. We track the color changes by attaching a listener to the property editor. Perhaps confusingly, that editor also sends out property change events.

```
colorEditor.addPropertyChangeListener(
   new PropertyChangeListener()
   {  public void propertyChange(PropertyChangeEvent
         event)
      {  setGraphColor((Color)colorEditor.getValue());
      }
   });
```

Whenever the color value of the color property editor changes, we call the `setGraphColor` method of the customizer. That method updates the `graphColor` property of the bean and fires a different property change event that is associated with the `graphColor` property.

```
public void setGraphColor(Color newValue)
{  if (bean == null) return;
   Color oldValue = bean.getGraphColor();
   bean.setGraphColor(newValue);
   firePropertyChange("graphColor", oldValue, newValue);
}
```

Example 8–16 provides the full code of the chart bean customizer.

This particular customizer just set properties of the bean. In general, customizers can call any methods of the bean, whether or not they are property setters. That is, customizers are more general than property editors. (Some beans may have features that are not exposed as properties and that can be edited only through the customizer.)

Example 8–16: ChartBeanCustomizer.java

```
import java.awt.*;
import java.awt.event.*;
import java.beans.*;
import java.io.*;
import java.text.*;
import java.util.*;
import javax.swing.*;
import javax.swing.event.*;

public class ChartBeanCustomizer extends JTabbedPane
   implements Customizer
{  public ChartBeanCustomizer()
   {  data = new JTextArea();
```

```
JPanel dataPane = new JPanel();
dataPane.setLayout(new BorderLayout());
dataPane.add(new JScrollPane(data), "Center");
JButton dataButton = new JButton("Set data");
dataButton.addActionListener(
   new ActionListener()
   {  public void actionPerformed(ActionEvent event)
      {  setData(data.getText());
      }
   });
JPanel p = new JPanel();
p.add(dataButton);
dataPane.add(p, "South");

JPanel colorPane = new JPanel();
colorPane.setLayout(new BorderLayout());

normal = new JCheckBox("Normal", true);
inverse = new JCheckBox("Inverse", false);
p = new JPanel();
p.add(normal);
p.add(inverse);
ButtonGroup g = new ButtonGroup();
g.add(normal);
g.add(inverse);
normal.addActionListener(
   new ActionListener()
   {  public void actionPerformed(ActionEvent event)
      {  setInverse(false);
      }
   });

inverse.addActionListener(
   new ActionListener()
   {  public void actionPerformed(ActionEvent event)
      {  setInverse(true);
      }
   });

colorEditor
   = PropertyEditorManager.findEditor(Color.class);
colorEditor.addPropertyChangeListener(
   new PropertyChangeListener()
   {  public void propertyChange(PropertyChangeEvent
         event)
      {  setGraphColor((Color)colorEditor.getValue());
      }
   });

colorPane.add(colorEditor.getCustomEditor(), "North");
```

```
colorPane.add(p, "South");

JPanel titlePane = new JPanel();
titlePane.setLayout(new BorderLayout());

g = new ButtonGroup();
position = new JCheckBox[3];
position[0] = new JCheckBox("Left", false);
position[1] = new JCheckBox("Center", true);
position[2] = new JCheckBox("Right", false);

p = new JPanel();
for (int i = 0; i < position.length; i++)
{  final int value = i;
   p.add(position[i]);
   g.add(position[i]);
   position[i].addActionListener(
      new ActionListener()
      {  public void actionPerformed(ActionEvent event)
         {  setTitlePosition(value);
         }
      });
}

titleField = new JTextField();
titleField.getDocument().addDocumentListener(
   new DocumentListener()
   {  public void changedUpdate(DocumentEvent evt)
      {  setTitle(titleField.getText());
      }
      public void insertUpdate(DocumentEvent evt)
      {  setTitle(titleField.getText());
      }
      public void removeUpdate(DocumentEvent evt)
      {  setTitle(titleField.getText());
      }
   });

titlePane.add(titleField, "North");
titlePane.add(p, "South");
addTab("Color", colorPane);
addTab("Title", titlePane);
addTab("Data", dataPane);

addChangeListener(
   // workaround for a JTabbedPane bug in JDK 1.2
   new ChangeListener()
   {  public void stateChanged(ChangeEvent event)
      {  validate();
      }
   });
```

```
   }

   public void setData(String s)
   {  StringTokenizer tokenizer = new StringTokenizer(s);

      int i = 0;
      double[] values = new double[tokenizer.countTokens()];
      while (tokenizer.hasMoreTokens())
      {  String token = tokenizer.nextToken();
         try
         {  values[i] = Double.parseDouble(token);
            i++;
         }
         catch (NumberFormatException exception)
         {
         }
      }
      setValues(values);
   }

   public void setTitle(String newValue)
   {  if (bean == null) return;
      String oldValue = bean.getTitle();
      bean.setTitle(newValue);
      firePropertyChange("title", oldValue, newValue);
   }

   public void setTitlePosition(int i)
   {  if (bean == null) return;
      Integer oldValue = new Integer(bean.getTitlePosition());
      Integer newValue = new Integer(i);
      bean.setTitlePosition(i);
      firePropertyChange("titlePosition", oldValue, newValue);
   }

   public void setInverse(boolean b)
   {  if (bean == null) return;
      Boolean oldValue = new Boolean(bean.isInverse());
      Boolean newValue = new Boolean(b);
      bean.setInverse(b);
      firePropertyChange("inverse", oldValue, newValue);
   }

   public void setValues(double[] newValue)
   {  if (bean == null) return;
      double[] oldValue = bean.getValues();
      bean.setValues(newValue);
      firePropertyChange("values", oldValue, newValue);
   }

   public void setGraphColor(Color newValue)
   {  if (bean == null) return;
```

```
        Color oldValue = bean.getGraphColor();
        bean.setGraphColor(newValue);
        firePropertyChange("graphColor", oldValue, newValue);
    }

    public void setObject(Object obj)
    {   bean = (ChartBean)obj;

        data.setText("");
        double[] values = bean.getValues();
        for (int i = 0; i < values.length; i++)
            data.append(values[i] + "\n");

        normal.setSelected(!bean.isInverse());
        inverse.setSelected(bean.isInverse());

        titleField.setText(bean.getTitle());

        for (int i = 0; i < position.length; i++)
            position[i].setSelected(i == bean.getTitlePosition());

        colorEditor.setValue(bean.getGraphColor());
    }

    public Dimension getPreferredSize()
    {   return new Dimension(200, 120);
    }

    private ChartBean bean;
    private PropertyEditor colorEditor;

    private JTextArea data;
    private JCheckBox normal;
    private JCheckBox inverse;
    private JCheckBox[] position;
    private JTextField titleField;
}
```

java.beans.Customizer

API

- `void setObject(Object bean)`

  specifies the bean to customize.

The Bean Context

In this section, we show you how you can write beans that take advantage of their environment. This is useful to implement beans that interact with other beans or with services that the BeanBox provides. In particular, you will see how to implement a bean that can change the value of an arbitrary integer property of another bean and how a bean can use the *message trace service* that the BeanBox provides.

Advanced Uses of Introspection

From the point of view of the JavaBeans specification, introspection is simply the process by which a builder tool finds out which properties, methods, and events a bean supports. Introspection is carried out in two ways:

- By searching for classes and methods that follow certain naming patterns
- By querying the `BeanInfo` of a class

Normally, introspection is an activity that is reserved for bean environments. The bean environment uses introspection to learn about beans, but the beans themselves don't need to carry out introspection. However, there are some cases when one bean needs to use introspection to analyze other beans. A good example is when you want to tightly couple two beans on a form in a builder tool. Consider, for example, a spin bean, a small control element with two buttons, to increase or decrease a value (see Figure 8–26).

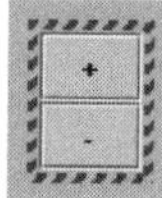

Figure 8–26: The spin bean

A spin bean by itself is not useful. It needs to be coupled with another bean. For example, a spin bean can be coupled to an integer text bean. Each time the user clicks on one of the buttons of the spin bean, the integer value is incremented or decremented. We will call the coupled bean the *buddy* of the spin bean. The buddy does not have to be an `IntTextBean`. It can be any other bean with an integer property.

You use the customizer of the spin bean to attach the buddy (see Figure 8–27).

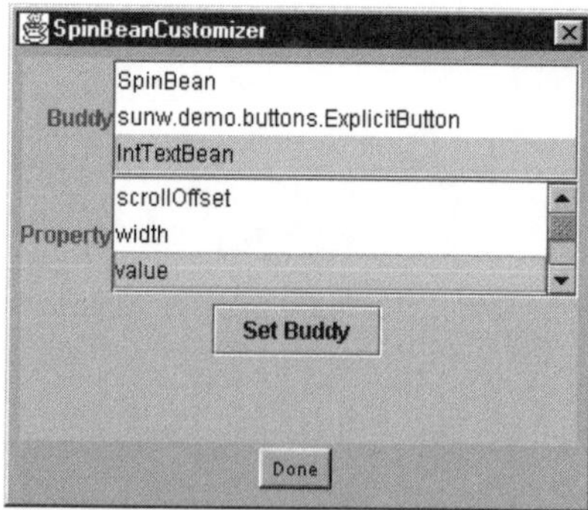

Figure 8–27: The customizer of the `SpinBean`

Here is how you can try it out.

1. Add the `SpinBean` and an `IntTextBean` on the form.

2. Pop up the customizer of the spin bean by selecting it and selecting Edit -> Customize from the menu.
3. Select the `IntTextBean` in the Buddy list.
4. Watch how all the `int` properties in the Property list are automatically filled in (see Figure 8–27).
5. Select `value` and click on Set Buddy.
6. Click on "Done".
7. Then, click on "+" and "–" and watch the integer text field value increase and decrease (see Figure 8–28).

Figure 8–28: The `SpinBean` coupled with an `IntTextBean` buddy

It looks easy, but there were two challenges to implementing this customization.

- How do you find all properties of a bean whose values are of type `int`?
- How do you program the getting and setting of a property if you know it only at run time?

We use introspection (that is, the reflection API) to solve both of these problems. To analyze the properties of a bean, first get the bean info by calling the static `getBeanInfo` method of the `Introspector` class.

```
BeanInfo info
   = Introspector.getBeanInfo(buddy.getClass());
```

Once we have the bean info, we can obtain an array of property descriptors:

```
PropertyDescriptor[] props = info.getPropertyDescriptors();
```

In the spin bean customizer, the next step is to loop through this array, picking out all properties of type `int` and adding their names to a list component.

```
for (int i = 0; i < props.length; i++)
{  Class propertyType = props[i].getPropertyType();
   if (int.class.equals(propertyType))
   {  String name = props[i].getName();
      propModel.addElement(name);
   }
}
```

This code shows how you can find out about the properties of a bean.

Next, we need to be able to get and set the property that the user selected. We obtain the `get` and `set` methods by calls to `getReadMethod` and `getWriteMethod`:

```
Method getMethod = prop.getReadMethod();
Method setMethod = prop.getWriteMethod();
```

(Why is it called `getReadMethod`? Probably because `getGetMethod` sounds too silly.)

Now, we invoke the methods to get a value, increment it, and set it. This process again uses the reflection API—see, for example, Chapter 5 of Volume 1. Note that we must use an `Integer` wrapper around the `int` value.

```
int value = ((Integer)getMethod.invoke(buddy,
   null)).intValue();
value += increment;
setMethod.invoke(buddy,
   new Object[] { new Integer(value) });
```

Could we have avoided reflection if we had demanded that the buddy have methods `getValue` and `setValue`? No. You can only call

```
int value = buddy.getValue();
```

when the compiler knows that `buddy` is an object of a type that has a `getValue` method. But `buddy` can be of any type—there is no type hierarchy for beans. Whenever one bean is coupled with another arbitrary bean, then you need to use introspection.

Finding Sibling Beans

In the preceding section, you saw how the spin bean buttons were able to change the value of the buddy component. However, there is another unrelated issue—how can the spin bean customizer present all possible buddies to the user?

It is a bit more difficult to enumerate all beans on a form than you might think. In the BeanBox, for example, you can't simply call

```
Component[] siblings = getParent().getComponents()
```

to get all the siblings of a bean. The reason you can't do this is that the BeanBox surrounds every bean by a panel within a panel. (We suspect that is done to detect mouse clicks that select the bean and to draw the outline around a selected bean.) So, in the BeanBox, we'd have to write

```
Component[] siblings
   = getParent().getParent().getParent().getComponents()
```

However, there is no guarantee that this solution would work in another builder environment—since those environments might be smart enough not to need all these extra panels.

In the Java 2 platform, we can solve this problem. The JavaBeans architecture now supports the concept of a *bean context.* Bean contexts express the *logical* containment between beans and bean containers, which, as you just saw, can be quite different from the physical containment.

A bean context can hold beans, services, and other bean contexts, just like an AWT container can hold components and other containers (see Figure 8–29).

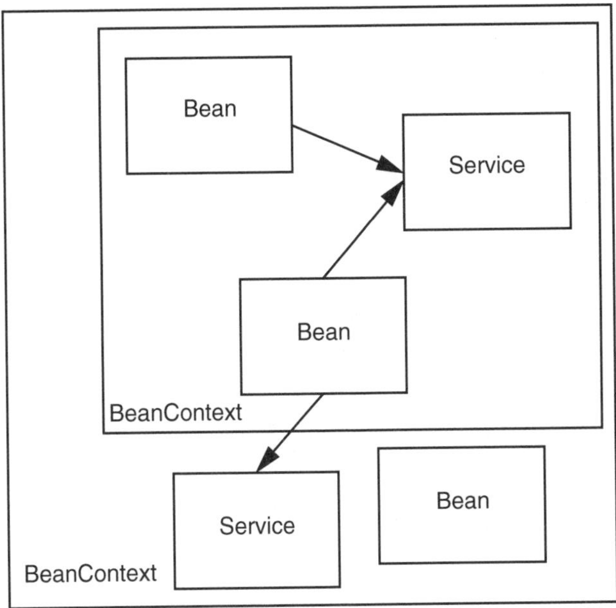

Figure 8–29: Bean Contexts

Currently, nested bean contexts aren't common. At best, you can expect that your beans live in a single bean context, the builder environment. For example, the BeanBox in BDK 1.1 is a bean context. The BeanBox provides a *message tracing service* that beans can use to display logging messages. Other bean contexts may provide different services. In the next section, we show you how your beans can use the message tracing service.

NOTE: Future versions of the BDK will supply an InfoBus service. See `http://java.sun.com/beans/infobus/index.html` for more information on the InfoBus technology.

CAUTION: Not all currently available builder environments place their beans into a bean context. Even if your environment uses a bean context, it may not supply the message tracing service. Therefore, the example program may not work in your favorite environment.

To communicate with its surrounding bean context, a bean can implement the `BeanContextChild` interface. That interface has six methods:

```
void setBeanContext(BeanContext bc)
BeanContext getBeanContext()
void addPropertyChangeListener(String name,
   PropertyChangeListener listener)
void removePropertyChangeListener(String name,
   PropertyChangeListener listener)
void addVetoableChangeListener(String name,
   VetoableChangeListener listener)
void removeVetoableChangeListener(String name,
   VetoableChangeListener listener)
```

A bean context calls the `setBeanContext` method when it begins managing your bean. You can hold on to the `BeanContext` parameter value and use it whenever you need to access the ambient bean context.

Since it is tedious to implement the change listeners, a convenience class `BeanContextChildSupport` implements these methods for you. However, there is a technical issue if you want to use this convenience class. Since your bean can't simultaneously extend a component class and the `BeanContextChildSupport` class, you use a proxy mechanism. Follow these steps:

1. Implement the `BeanContextProxy` interface.
2. Construct an instance variable of type `BeanContextChildSupport`.

   ```
   private BeanContextChildSupport childSupport
      = new BeanContextChildSupport();
   ```

3. Return that instance variable in the `getBeanContextProxy` method of the `BeanContextProxy` interface.

   ```
   public BeanContextChild getBeanContextProxy()
   {  return childSupport;
   }
   ```

   The bean context calls this method to retrieve the proxy object. Then, it invokes the `BeanContextChild` methods on the returned object rather than the bean itself.

4. Call the `getBeanContext` method of the `childSupport` object whenever you want to know the current bean context.

   ```
   BeanContext context = childSupport.getBeanContext();
   ```

Figure 8–30 shows the relationships between these classes.

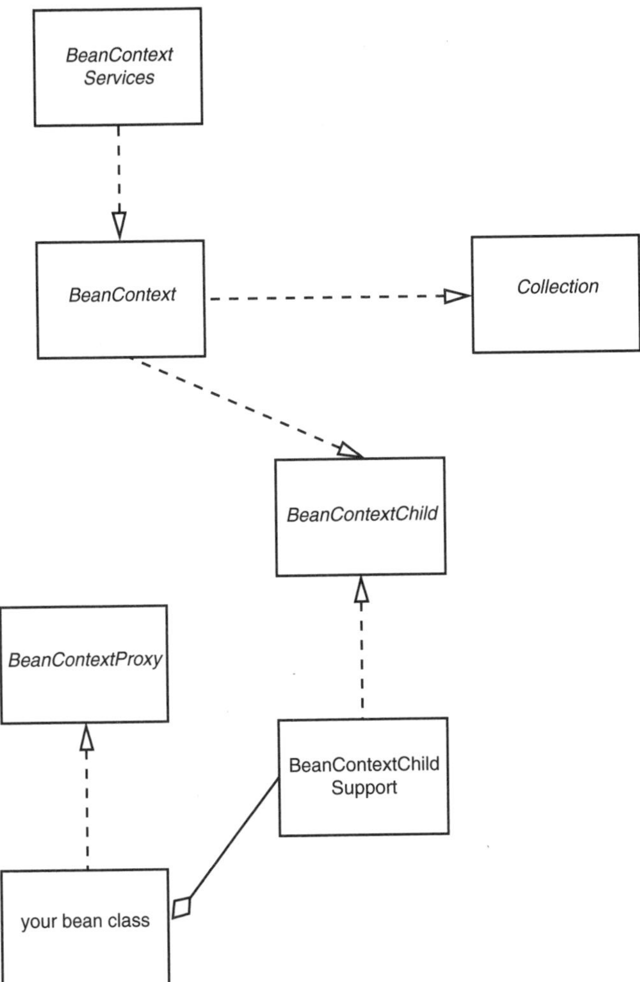

Figure 8–30: Relationships between the bean context classes

Once you have the bean context, you can enumerate all beans that it contains. The `BeanContext` class implements the `Collection` interface. Therefore, you can simply enumerate the beans as follows:

```
Iterator iter = beanContext.iterator();
while (iter.hasNext())
{  Object buddy = iter.next();
   do something with buddy
}
```

From a user interface perspective, our approach—to list the types of the potential buddies—is still not satisfactory. If there is more than one sibling of the same class in the form, then the user cannot tell them apart. It would be nice if we could physically move the spin bean next to its buddy or draw a box around the selected buddy, but the `BeanContext` does not expose position information. (It is useless to ask the buddy about its location. It only knows its location with respect to its enclosing panel.) Perhaps a future version of the JavaBeans specification will allow such manipulations.

Using Bean Context Services

In this section, we want to show you how your beans can access services that a bean context provides. You have to know the class that provides the service that you want. For example, the message tracer service that the BeanBox provides is implemented by the class `sunw.demo.methodtracer.MethodTracer`. First, you need to make sure that the bean context implements the `BeanContextServices` interface—not all bean contexts do.

```
if (beanContext implements BeanContextServices)
{  BeanContextServices services
      = (BeanContextServices)beanContext;
   . . .
}
```

Then, you ask the bean context if it supports the desired service.

```
tracerClass = Class.forName
   ("sunw.demo.methodtracer.MethodTracer");
if (services.hasService(tracerClass))
{  . . .
}
```

If you run this bean in an environment other than the BeanBox, the `hasService` call may simply return `false`.

Finally, you need to get the object that carries out the service. You call the `getService` method with five parameters:

- The object that implements the `ChildBeanContext` interface; usually the proxy `BeanContextChildSupport` object
- The requesting object
- The class of the service that you want to obtain
- An auxiliary object to select the right service, if the service requires it, or `null` otherwise
- A `BeanContextServiceRevokedListener` object that is called when the service ceases to be available.

Here is a typical call.

```
BeanContextServiceRevokedListener revokedListener =
   new BeanContextServiceRevokedListener()
   {  public void serviceRevoked
         (BeanContextServiceRevokedEvent event)
      {  tracer = null;
      }
```

```
    };
  tracer = services.getService(childSupport, this, tracerClass,
     null, revokedListener);
```

Note that you typically do not have the service class available when you compile your program. For example, the class file for the `MethodTracer` class is not part of the standard runtime library, and the compiler will not find it even if you try to import the `sunw.demo.methodtracer` package.

For that reason, we use reflection to call service methods. The following statements call the `logText` method of the `MethodTracer` class to display a message in the method tracer window.

```
if (tracer != null)
{  String text = "spin: value=" + value
      + " increment=" + increment;
   Method logText = tracerClass.getMethod("logText",
      new Class[] { String.class });
   logText.invoke(tracer, new Object[] { text });
}
```

Of course, we don't call the method if the bean context doesn't support the service. If it does, we use the `invoke` method to call it through the reflection mechanism.

When you try out this example, watch the Message Tracer window. It contains a message for each click on one of the spin buttons (see Figure 8–31).

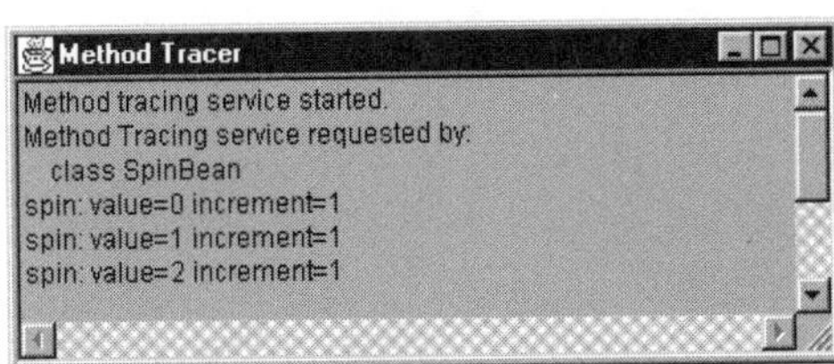

Figure 8–31: The Message Tracer window

Examples 8–17 through 8–19 contain the full code for the SpinBean, including the needed bean info class to hook in the customizer.

Example 8–17: SpinBean.java

```
import java.awt.*;
import java.awt.event.*;
import java.beans.*;
import java.beans.beancontext.*;
import java.lang.reflect.*;
import java.io.*;
import java.util.*;
import javax.swing.*;

public class SpinBean extends JPanel
```

```
   implements Serializable, BeanContextProxy
{  public SpinBean()
   {  setLayout(new GridLayout(2, 1));
      JButton plusButton = new JButton("+");
      JButton minusButton = new JButton("-");
      add(plusButton);
      add(minusButton);
      plusButton.addActionListener(
         new ActionListener()
         {  public void actionPerformed(ActionEvent evt)
            {  spin(1);
            }
         });
      minusButton.addActionListener(
         new ActionListener()
         {  public void actionPerformed(ActionEvent evt)
            {  spin(-1);
            }
         });

      childSupport =
         new BeanContextChildSupport()
         {  public void setBeanContext(BeanContext context)
               throws PropertyVetoException
            {  super.setBeanContext(context);
               setTracer(context);
            }
         };
   }

   public BeanContextChild getBeanContextProxy()
   {  return childSupport;
   }

   public void setBuddy(Component b, PropertyDescriptor p)
   {  buddy = b;
      prop = p;
   }

   public void spin(int increment)
   {  if (buddy == null) return;
      if (prop == null) return;
      Method readMethod = prop.getReadMethod();
      Method writeMethod = prop.getWriteMethod();
      try
      {  int value = ((Integer)readMethod.invoke(buddy,
            null)).intValue();

         if (tracer != null)
         {  String text = "spin: value=" + value
               + " increment=" + increment;
            Method logText = tracerClass.getMethod("logText",
```

```
            new Class[] { String.class });
         logText.invoke(tracer, new Object[] { text });
      }

      value += increment;
      writeMethod.invoke(buddy,
         new Object[] { new Integer(value) });
   }
   catch(Exception e)
   {
   }
}

public void setTracer(BeanContext context)
{  try
   {  BeanContextServices services
         = (BeanContextServices)context;
      tracerClass = Class.forName
         ("sunw.demo.methodtracer.MethodTracer");
      if (services.hasService(tracerClass))
      {  BeanContextServiceRevokedListener revokedListener =
            new BeanContextServiceRevokedListener()
            {  public void serviceRevoked
                  (BeanContextServiceRevokedEvent event)
               {  tracer = null;
               }
            };
         tracer = services.getService(childSupport, this,
            tracerClass, null, revokedListener);
      }
   }
   catch (Exception exception)
   {  tracer = null;
   }
}

public Dimension getPreferredSize()
{  return new Dimension(MINSIZE, MINSIZE);
}

private static final int MINSIZE = 20;
private Component buddy;
private PropertyDescriptor prop;
private Object tracer;
private Class tracerClass;
private BeanContextChildSupport childSupport;
}
```

Example 8–18: SpinBeanCustomizer.java

```
import java.awt.*;
import java.awt.event.*;
```

```
import java.beans.*;
import java.beans.beancontext.*;
import java.io.*;
import java.text.*;
import java.util.*;
import javax.swing.*;
import javax.swing.event.*;

public class SpinBeanCustomizer extends JPanel
   implements Customizer
{  public SpinBeanCustomizer()
   {  setLayout(new GridBagLayout());
      GridBagConstraints gbc = new GridBagConstraints();
      gbc.weightx = 0;
      gbc.weighty = 100;
      gbc.fill = GridBagConstraints.NONE;
      gbc.anchor = GridBagConstraints.EAST;
      add(new JLabel("Buddy"), gbc, 0, 0, 1, 1);
      add(new JLabel("Property"), gbc, 0, 1, 1, 1);
      gbc.weightx = 100;
      gbc.anchor = GridBagConstraints.WEST;
      gbc.fill = GridBagConstraints.BOTH;
      buddyModel = new DefaultListModel();
      propModel = new DefaultListModel();
      buddyList = new JList(buddyModel);
      propList = new JList(propModel);
      add(new JScrollPane(buddyList), gbc, 1, 0, 1, 1);
      add(new JScrollPane(propList), gbc, 1, 1, 1, 1);
      JButton setButton = new JButton("Set Buddy");
      JPanel p = new JPanel();
      p.add(setButton);
      add(p, gbc, 0, 2, 2, 1);

      buddyList.addListSelectionListener(
         new ListSelectionListener()
         {  public void valueChanged(ListSelectionEvent event)
            {  findBuddyMethods();
            }
         });

      setButton.addActionListener(
         new ActionListener()
         {  public void actionPerformed(ActionEvent event)
            {  int buddyIndex = buddyList.getSelectedIndex();
               if (buddyIndex < 0) return;
               int propIndex = propList.getSelectedIndex();
               if (propIndex < 0) return;
              bean.setBuddy(buddies[buddyIndex], props[propIndex]);
            }
         });
```

```
   }

   public void add(Component c, GridBagConstraints gbc,
      int x, int y, int w, int h)
   {  gbc.gridx = x;
      gbc.gridy = y;
      gbc.gridwidth = w;
      gbc.gridheight = h;
      add(c, gbc);
   }

   public void findBuddyMethods()
   {  int buddyIndex = buddyList.getSelectedIndex();
      if (buddyIndex < 0) return;
      Component buddy = buddies[buddyIndex];
      propModel.removeAllElements();
      try
      {  BeanInfo info
            = Introspector.getBeanInfo(buddy.getClass());
         props = info.getPropertyDescriptors();
         int j = 0;
         for (int i = 0; i < props.length; i++)
         {  Class propertyType = props[i].getPropertyType();
            if (int.class.equals(propertyType))
            {  String name = props[i].getName();
               propModel.addElement(name);
               props[j++] = props[i];
            }
         }
      }
      catch(IntrospectionException e){}
   }

   public Dimension getPreferredSize()
   {  return new Dimension(300, 200);
   }

   public void setObject(Object obj)
   {  bean = (SpinBean)obj;
      BeanContext context
         = bean.getBeanContextProxy().getBeanContext();
      buddies = new Component[context.size()];
      buddyModel.removeAllElements();
      Iterator iter = context.iterator();
      int i = 0;
      while (iter.hasNext())
      {  Object buddy = iter.next();
         if (buddy instanceof Component)
         {  buddies[i] = (Component)buddy;
            String className = buddies[i].getClass().getName();
```

```
                buddyModel.addElement(className);
                i++;
            }
        }
    }

    public void addPropertyChangeListener
        (PropertyChangeListener l)
    {   support.addPropertyChangeListener(l);
    }

    public void removePropertyChangeListener
        (PropertyChangeListener l)
    {   support.removePropertyChangeListener(l);
    }

    private SpinBean bean;
    private PropertyChangeSupport support
        = new PropertyChangeSupport(this);
    private JList buddyList;
    private JList propList;
    private DefaultListModel buddyModel;
    private DefaultListModel propModel;
    private PropertyDescriptor[] props;
    private Component[] buddies;
}
```

Example 8–19: SpinBeanBeanInfo.java

```
import java.awt.*;
import java.beans.*;

public class SpinBeanBeanInfo extends SimpleBeanInfo
{   public BeanDescriptor getBeanDescriptor()
    {   return new BeanDescriptor(SpinBean.class,
            SpinBeanCustomizer.class);
    }
}
```

`java.beans.Introspector`

- `String decapitalize(String name)`

  converts a string to the Java platform naming convention. `SillyMethod` becomes `sillyMethod`, for example. (When there are two consecutive capitals, nothing happens.)

- `BeanInfo getBeanInfo(Class beanClass)`

  gets the `BeanInfo` class associated to the bean or creates one on-the-fly, using the naming convention discussed earlier in this chapter; throws an `IntrospectionException` if the introspection fails.

`java.beans.beancontext.BeanContextChild`

- `void setBeanContext(BeanContext bc)`

  is called when a bean context adds this bean as a child. Must fire a property change event with property name `"beanContext"` to all vetoable listeners, then to all property change listeners.

- `BeanContext getBeanContext()`

  returns the current bean context for this bean.

- `void addPropertyChangeListener(String name, PropertyChange-Listener listener)`

  adds a listener for the named property.

- `void removePropertyChangeListener(String name, PropertyChange-Listener listener)`

  removes a listener for the named property.

- `void addVetoableChangeListener(String name, VetoableChangeListener listener)`

  adds a vetoable listener for the named property.

- `void removeVetoableChangeListener(String name, VetoableChangeListener listener)`

  removes a vetoable listener for the named property.

`java.beans.beancontext.BeanContextChildSupport`

- `BeanContext getBeanContext()`

  returns the current bean context for this bean.

`javax.beans.beancontext.BeanContextProxy`

- `BeanContextChild getBeanContextProxy()`

  returns the proxy object that handles the `BeanContextChild` methods.

`javax.beans.beancontext.BeanContextServices`

- `boolean hasService(Class cl)`

  tests whether this bean context supports the service carried out by the given class.

- `Object getService(BeanContextChild child, Object requestor, Class cl, Object selector, BeanContextServiceRevokedListener listener)`

  gets the object that carries out a bean context service.

Parameters:	`child`	the bean context child object that is linked as the child of the bean context

`requestor`	the object requesting the service
`cl`	the service class
`selector`	an optional object to locate or instantiate the service
`listener`	the listener to be notified when the service is no longer available

javax.beans.beancontext.BeanContextServiceRevokedListener

- `void serviceRevoked(BeanContextServiceRevokedEvent event)`

  is called when a service is revoked. You need to make sure the service is no longer called after this notification.

javax.beans.beancontext.BeanContextServiceRevokedEvent

- `Class getServiceClass()`

  gets the class that carries out the revoked service.

- `boolean isServiceClass(Class cl)`

  tests whether the given class object describes the class that carries out the revoked service.

Chapter 9

Security

- Class Loaders
- Bytecode Verification
- Security Managers and Permissions
- The Java Security Package
- Authentication
- The Java Authentication Framework
- Code Signing
- Encryption

When Java technology first appeared on the scene, the excitement was not about a well-crafted programming language but about the possibility of safely executing applets that are delivered over the Internet (see Chapter 10 of Volume 1, for more information about applets). Obviously, delivering executable applets is practical only when the recipients are sure that the code can't wreak havoc on their machines. For this reason, security was and is a major concern of both the designers and the users of Java technology. This means that unlike the case with other languages and systems where security was implemented as an afterthought or a reaction to break-ins, security mechanisms are an integral part of Java technology.

Three mechanisms in Java technology help ensure safety:

- Language design features (bounds checking on arrays, legal type conversions only, no pointer arithmetic, and so on);
- An access control mechanism that controls what the code can do (such as file access, network access, and so on);

- Code signing, whereby code authors can use standard cryptographic algorithms to authenticate Java programming language code. Then, the users of the code can determine exactly who created the code and whether the code has been altered after it was signed.

The Java virtual machine checks for bad pointers, invalid array offsets, and so on. The other steps require controlling what goes to the Java virtual machine.

When class files are loaded into the virtual machine, they are checked for integrity. We show you in detail how that process works. More importantly, we show you how to control what goes to the virtual machine by building your own *class loader.*

For maximum security, both the default mechanism for loading a class and a custom class loader need to work with a *security manager* class that controls what actions code can perform. You'll see how to write your own security manager class.

Finally, you'll see the cryptographic algorithms supplied in the `java.security` package, which allow for code signing and user authentication.

As always, we focus on those topics that are of greatest interest to application programmers. For an in-depth view, we recommend the book *Inside Java 2 Platform Security* by Li Gong [Addison-Wesley 1999].

Class Loaders

A Java programming language compiler converts source into the machine language of a hypothetical machine, called the *virtual machine.* The virtual machine code is stored in a class file with a `.class` extension. Class files contain the code for all the methods of one class. These class files need to be interpreted by a program that can translate the instruction set of the virtual machine into the machine language of the target machine.

Note that the virtual machine interpreter loads only those class files that are needed for the execution of a program. For example, suppose program execution starts with `MyProgram.class`. Here are the steps that the virtual machine carries out.

1. The virtual machine has a mechanism for loading class files, for example, by reading the files from disk or by requesting them from the Web; it uses this mechanism to load the contents of the `MyProgram` class file.
2. If the `MyProgram` class has data fields or superclasses of another class type, these class files are loaded as well. (The process of loading all the classes that a given class depends on is called *resolving* the class.)
3. The virtual machine then executes the `main` method in `MyProgram` (which is static, so no instance of a class needs to be created).
4. If the `main` method or a method that `main` calls requires additional classes, these are loaded next.

In addition to loading the classes that a particular program requires, the virtual machine must load *system classes.* The virtual machine knows how to load the system classes (for example, from the JAR file `rt.jar`), using a *bootstrap class loader* that is a part of the virtual machine and usually implemented in C. You have no control over this class loading process. However, you can supply a custom *class loader* to load application classes. The most common example of a class loader is the applet class loader. The applet class loader knows how to load class files across a network and how to authenticate signed JAR files.

NOTE: A browser uses separate instances of the applet class loader class for each web page. The virtual machine keeps track of the class loader that was used for each class. Classes with the same name but with different class loader objects are considered different classes. This allows the virtual machine to separate classes from different web pages.

A custom class loader like the applet class loader replaces the built-in mechanism for locating and loading class files. It lets you carry out specialized security checks before you pass the bytecodes to the virtual machine. For example, you can write a class loader that can refuse to load a class that has not been marked as "paid for." The next section shows you how.

Writing Your Own Class Loader

A class loader is an implementation of the abstract class `ClassLoader`. The `loadClass` method in this class determines how to load the top-level class. Once a class is loaded through class loader, all other classes that it references are also loaded through that same class loader.

To write your own class loader, you simply override the method

```
loadClass(String className, boolean resolve)
```

Your implementation of this method must:

1. Check whether this class loader has already loaded this class. For this purpose, your class loader needs to keep a record of the classes that it has previously loaded.
2. If it is a new class, you need to check whether it is a system class. Otherwise, load the bytecodes for the class from the local file system or from some other source.
3. Call the `defineClass` method of the `ClassLoader` superclass to present the bytecodes to the virtual machine.

If the `resolve` flag is set, you must call the `resolveClass` method of the `ClassLoader` superclass. Your class loader will be called again to load any other classes that this class refers to. (Your `loadClass` method might be called with `resolve` set to `false` if the virtual machine merely attempts to find out if a class exists, but every class must be fully resolved before you can create an instance or call a method.)

Usually, a class loader uses a map (such as a hash table) to store the references to the already loaded classes. The following code example shows the framework of the `loadClass` method of a typical class loader.

```
public class TypicalClassLoader extends ClassLoader
{  protected synchronized Class loadClass(String name, boolean
      resolve)
      throws ClassNotFoundException
   {  // check if class already loaded
      Class cl = (Class)classes.get(name);

      if (cl == null) // new class
      {  try
         {  // check if system class
            return findSystemClass(name);
         }
         catch (ClassNotFoundException e) {}
         catch (NoClassDefFoundError e) {}

         // load class bytes--details depend on class loader

         byte[] classBytes = loadClassBytes(name);
         if (classBytes == null)
            throw new ClassNotFoundException(name);

         cl = defineClass(name, classBytes, 0,
            classBytes.length);
         if (cl == null) throw new ClassNotFoundException(name);

         classes.put(name, cl); // remember class
      }

      if (resolve) resolveClass(cl);

      return cl;
   }

   private byte[] loadClassBytes(String name)
   {  . . .
   }

   private Map classes = new HashMap();
}
```

In the program of Example 9–1, we implement a class loader that loads encrypted class files. The program asks the user for the name of the first class to load (that is, the class containing `main`) and the decryption key. It then uses a special class loader to load the specified class and calls the `main` method. The class loader decrypts the specified class and all nonsystem classes that are referenced by it. Finally, the program calls the `main` method of the loaded class (see Figure 9–1).

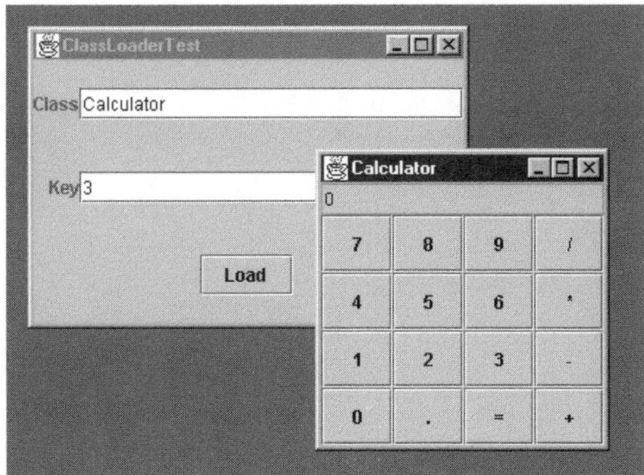

Figure 9–1: The `ClassLoaderTest` program

For simplicity, we ignore 2,000 years of progress in the field of cryptography and use the venerable Caesar cipher for encrypting the class files—so that we can safely export this book.

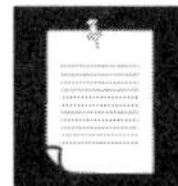

NOTE: David Kahn's wonderful book *The Code Breakers,* (Macmillan, NY, 1967, p. 84) refers to Suetonius as a historical source for the Caesar cipher. Caesar shifted the 24 letters of the Roman alphabet by 3 letters. At the time of this writing, the U.S. government restricts the export of strong encryption methods. Therefore, we use Caesar's method for our example since it is so weak that it is presumably legal for export.

Our version of the Caesar cipher has as a key a number between 1 and 255. To decrypt, simply add that key to every byte and reduce modulo 256. The `Caesar.java` program of Example 9–2 carries out the encryption.

In order not to confuse the regular class loader, we use a different extension, `.caesar`, for the encrypted class files.

To decrypt, the class loader simply subtracts the key from every byte. On the CD-ROM for this book, you will find four class files, encrypted with a key value of 3—the traditional choice. You cannot load these classes via the regular bytecode interpreter, but you can run the encrypted program by using the custom class loader defined in our `ClassLoaderTest` program.

Encrypting class files has a number of practical uses (provided, of course, that you use a cipher stronger than the Caesar cipher). Without the decryption key, the class files are useless. They can neither be executed by a standard bytecode interpreter nor readily disassembled.

This means that you can use a custom class loader to authenticate the user of the class or to ensure that a program has been paid for before it will be allowed to run.

Of course, encryption is only one application of a custom class loader. You can use other types of class loaders to solve other problems, for example, controlling whether your code is only run by authorized users.

Example 9–1: ClassLoaderTest.java

```
import java.util.*;
import java.io.*;
import java.lang.reflect.*;
import java.awt.*;
import java.awt.event.*;
import javax.swing.*;

public class ClassLoaderTest
{  public static void main(String[] args)
   {  Frame f = new ClassLoaderFrame();
      f.show();
   }
}

class ClassLoaderFrame extends JFrame
{  public ClassLoaderFrame()
   {  setTitle("ClassLoaderTest");
      setSize(300, 200);
      addWindowListener(new WindowAdapter()
         {  public void windowClosing(WindowEvent e)
            {  System.exit(0);
            }
         } );
      getContentPane().setLayout(new GridBagLayout());
      GridBagConstraints gbc = new GridBagConstraints();
      gbc.weightx = 0;
      gbc.weighty = 100;
      gbc.fill = GridBagConstraints.NONE;
      gbc.anchor = GridBagConstraints.EAST;
      add(new JLabel("Class"), gbc, 0, 0, 1, 1);
      add(new JLabel("Key"), gbc, 0, 1, 1, 1);
      gbc.weightx = 100;
      gbc.fill = GridBagConstraints.HORIZONTAL;
      gbc.anchor = GridBagConstraints.WEST;
      add(nameField, gbc, 1, 0, 1, 1);
      add(keyField, gbc, 1, 1, 1, 1);
      gbc.fill = GridBagConstraints.NONE;
      gbc.anchor = GridBagConstraints.CENTER;
      JButton loadButton = new JButton("Load");
      add(loadButton, gbc, 0, 2, 2, 1);
      loadButton.addActionListener(
         new ActionListener()
         {  public void actionPerformed(ActionEvent event)
            {  runClass(nameField.getText(), keyField.getText());
            }
```

```
         });
   }

   public void add(Component c, GridBagConstraints gbc,
      int x, int y, int w, int h)
   {  gbc.gridx = x;
      gbc.gridy = y;
      gbc.gridwidth = w;
      gbc.gridheight = h;
      getContentPane().add(c, gbc);
   }

   public void runClass(String name, String key)
   {  try
      {  ClassLoader loader
            = new CryptoClassLoader(Integer.parseInt(key));
         Class c = loader.loadClass(name);
         String[] args = new String[] {};

         Method m = c.getMethod("main",
            new Class[] { args.getClass() });
         m.invoke(null, new Object[] { args });
      }
      catch (Throwable e)
      {  JOptionPane.showMessageDialog(this, e);
      }
   }

   private JTextField keyField = new JTextField("3", 4);
   private JTextField nameField = new JTextField(30);
}

class CryptoClassLoader extends ClassLoader
{  public CryptoClassLoader(int k)
   {  key = k;
   }

   protected synchronized Class loadClass(String name,
      boolean resolve) throws ClassNotFoundException
   {  // check if class already loaded
      Class cl = (Class)classes.get(name);

      if (cl == null) // new class
      {  try
         {  // check if system class
            return findSystemClass(name);
         }
         catch (ClassNotFoundException e) {}
         catch (NoClassDefFoundError e) {}

         // load class bytes--details depend on class loader
```

```
            byte[] classBytes = loadClassBytes(name);
            if (classBytes == null)
               throw new ClassNotFoundException(name);

            cl = defineClass(name, classBytes,
               0, classBytes.length);
            if (cl == null)
               throw new ClassNotFoundException(name);

            classes.put(name, cl); // remember class
         }

         if (resolve) resolveClass(cl);

         return cl;
      }

   private byte[] loadClassBytes(String name)
   {  String cname = name.replace('.', '/') + ".caesar";
      FileInputStream in = null;
      try
      {  in = new FileInputStream(cname);
         ByteArrayOutputStream buffer
            = new ByteArrayOutputStream();
         int ch;
         while ((ch = in.read()) != -1)
         {  byte b = (byte)(ch - key);
            buffer.write(b);
         }
         in.close();
         return buffer.toByteArray();
      }
      catch (IOException e)
      {  if (in != null)
         {  try { in.close(); } catch (IOException e2) { }
         }
         return null;
      }
   }

   private Map classes = new HashMap();
   private int key;
}
```

Example 9–2: Caesar.java

```
import java.io.*;

public class Caesar
{  public static void main(String[] args)
   {  if (args.length != 3)
      {  System.out.println("USAGE: java Caesar in out key");
```

```
            return;
         }

         try
         {  FileInputStream in = new FileInputStream(args[0]);
            FileOutputStream out = new FileOutputStream(args[1]);
            int key = Integer.parseInt(args[2]);
            int ch;
            while ((ch = in.read()) != -1)
            {  byte c = (byte)(ch + key);
               out.write(c);
            }
            in.close();
            out.close();
         }
         catch(IOException e)
         {  System.out.println("Error: " + e);
         }
      }
   }
```

java.lang.ClassLoader

- `Class defineClass(String name, byte data[], int offset, int length)`
  adds a new class to the virtual machine.

  Parameters:

	`name`	the name of the class. Use `.` as package name separator, and don't use a `.class` suffix
	`data`	an array holding the bytecodes of the class
	`offset`	the start of the bytecodes in the array
	`length`	the length of the bytecodes in the array

- `void loadClass(String name, boolean resolve)`
  is implemented by a class extending `ClassLoader`. It obtains the bytecodes for the class and then calls `defineClass` and, if the `resolve` flag is `true`, `resolveClass`. The class loader should implement a cache to ensure that previously loaded classes are not loaded again.

  Parameters:

	`name`	the name of the class. Use `.` as package name separator, and don't use a `.class` suffix
	`resolve`	`true` if the `resolveClass` method needs to be called after the class is loaded

- `void resolveClass(Class c)`
  should be called by `loadClass` if the `resolve` flag is `true`. It keeps loading dependent classes until all the classes that the class refers to either directly or

indirectly are fully known to the virtual machine. Once the class is resolved, the virtual machine can create objects of the class and can call class methods.

Parameters: `c` the class to be resolved

- `Class findSystemClass(String name)`
  finds the system class with the specified name and loads it if necessary. A system class is a class loaded from the local file system in a platform-dependent way, using the value of the `CLASSPATH` environment variable. System classes have no class loader.

  Parameters: `name` the name of the class. Use `.` as package name separator, and don't use a `.class` suffix

Bytecode Verification

When a class loader presents the bytecodes of a newly loaded Java platform class to the virtual machine, these bytecodes are first inspected by a *verifier*. The verifier checks that the instructions cannot perform actions that are obviously damaging. All classes except for system classes are verified. However, you can deactivate verification with the undocumented `-noverify` option.

For example,

```
java -noverify Hello
```

Here are some of the checks that the verifier carries out:

- That variables are initialized before they are used;
- That method calls match the types of object references;
- That rules for accessing private data and methods are not violated;
- That local variable accesses fall within the runtime stack;
- That the runtime stack does not overflow.

If any of these checks fail, then the class is considered corrupted and will not be loaded.

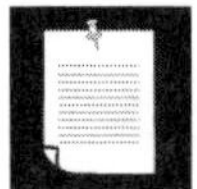

NOTE: If you are familiar with Gödel's theorem, you may wonder how the verifier can prove that a class file is free from type mismatches, uninitialized variables, and stack overflows. Gödel's theorem states that it is impossible to design algorithms whose inputs are program files and whose output is a Boolean value that states whether the input program has a particular property (such as being free from stack overflows). Is this a conflict between the public relations department at Sun Microsystems and the laws of logic? No—in fact, the verifier is *not* a decision algorithm in the sense of Gödel. If the verifier accepts a program, it is indeed safe. However, there may be many programs that the verifier rejects even though they would actually be safe.

This strict verification is an important security consideration. Accidental errors, such as uninitialized variables, can easily wreak havoc if they are not caught.

More importantly, in the wide open world of the Internet, you must be protected against malicious programmers who create evil effects on purpose. For example, by modifying values on the runtime stack or by writing to the private data fields of system objects, a program can break through the security system of a browser.

However, you may wonder why there is a special verifier to check all these features. After all, the compiler would never allow you to generate a class file in which an uninitialized variable is used or in which a private data field is accessed from another class. Indeed, a class file generated by a compiler for the Java programming language always passes verification. However, the bytecode format used in the class files is well documented, and it is an easy matter for someone with some experience in assembly programming and a hex editor to manually produce a class file that contains valid but unsafe instructions for the Java virtual machine. Once again, keep in mind that the verifier is always guarding against maliciously altered class files, not just checking the class files produced by a compiler.

Here's an example of how to construct such an altered class file. We start with the program `VerifierTest.java` of Example 9–3. This is a simple program that calls a method and displays the method result. The program can be run both as a console program and as an applet. The `fun` method itself just computes 1 + 2.

```
static int fun()
{  int m;
   int n;
   m = 1;
   n = 2;
   int r = m + n;
   return r;
}
```

As an experiment, try to compile the following modification of this program:

```
static int fun()
{  int m = 1;
   int n;
   m = 1;
   m = 2;
   int r = m + n;
   return r;
}
```

In this case, `n` is not initialized, and it could have any random value. Of course, the compiler detects that problem and refuses to compile the program. To create a bad class file, we have to work a little harder. First, run the `javap` program to find out how the compiler translates the `fun` method. The command

```
javap -c VerifierTest
```

shows the bytecodes in the class file in mnemonic form.

```
Method int fun()
   0 iconst_1
   1 istore_0
   2 iconst_2
   3 istore_1
   4 iload_0
   5 iload_1
   6 iadd
   7 istore_2
   8 iload_2
   9 ireturn
```

We will use a hex editor to change instruction 3 from `istore_1` to `istore_0`. That is, local variable 0 (which is `m`) is initialized twice, and local variable 1 (which is `n`) is not initialized at all. We need to know the hexadecimal values for these instructions. These values are readily available from *The Java Virtual Machine* by Tim Lindholm and Frank Yellin [Addison-Wesley, 1997].

```
   0 iconst_1 04
   1 istore_0 3B
   2 iconst_2 05
   3 istore_1 3C
   4 iload_0  1A
   5 iload_1  1B
   6 iadd     60
   7 istore_2 3D
   8 iload_2  1C
   9 ireturn  AC
```

We will use Hex Workshop (which is included in the companion CD-ROM for this book), our favorite hex editor, to carry out the modification. In Figure 9–2, you see the class file `VerifierTest.class` loaded into Hex Workshop, with the bytecodes of the `fun` method highlighted.

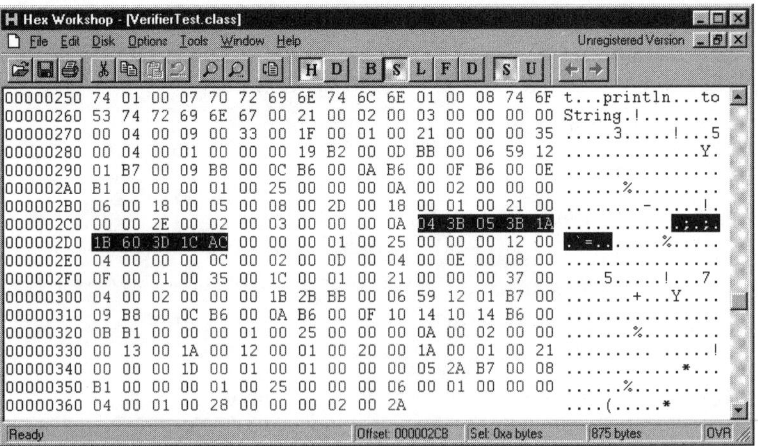

Figure 9–2: Modifying bytecodes with a hex editor

We simply change 3C to 3B and save the class file. (If you don't want to run the hex editor yourself, you can find the edited `VerifierTest.class` on the CD-ROM. Just make sure not to compile the `VerifierTest` source file again.)

Try running the `VerifierTest` program. You get an error message:

```
Exception in thread "main" java.lang.VerifyError: (class: Verifi-
erTest, method:fun signature: ()I) Accessing value from unini-
tialized register 1
```

That is good—the virtual machine detected our modification.

Now run the program with the `-noverify` option. The `fun` method returns a seemingly random value. This is actually 2 plus the value that happened to be stored in the variable `n`, which never was initialized. Here is a typical printout:

```
1 + 2 = 15102330
```

To see how browsers handle verification, we wrote this program to run either as an application or an applet. Load the applet into a browser, using a file URL such as

```
file:///C:/CoreJavaBook/v2ch9/VerifierTest/VerifierTest.html
```

Then, you see an error message displayed indicating that verification has failed (see Figure 9–3).

Example 9–3: VerifierTest.java

```
import java.awt.*;
import java.applet.*;

public class VerifierTest extends Applet
{  public static void main(String[] args)
   {  System.out.println("1 + 2 == " + fun());
   }

   static int fun()
   {  int m;
      int n;
      m = 1;
      n = 2;
      // used hex editor to change to "m = 2" in class file
      int r = m + n;
      return r;
   }

   public void paint(Graphics g)
   {  g.drawString("1 + 2 == " + fun(), 20, 20);
   }
}
```

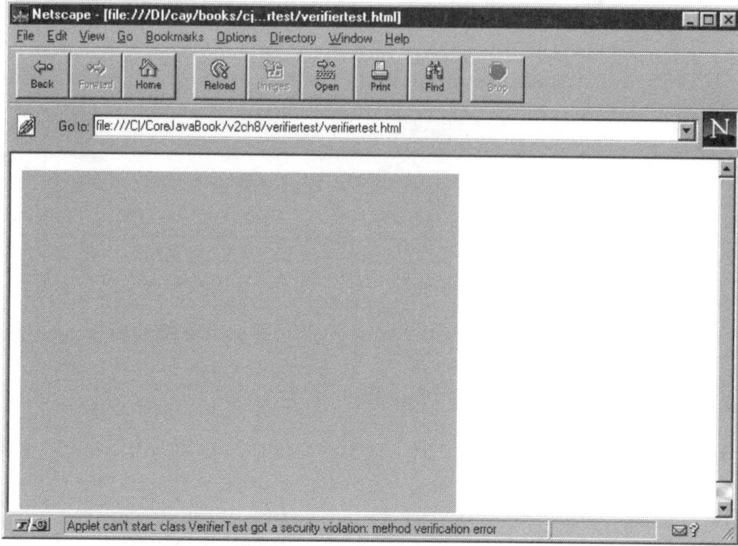

Figure 9–3: Loading a corrupted class file raises a method verification error

Security Managers and Permissions

Once a class has been loaded into the virtual machine by a class loader or by the default class loading mechanism and checked by the verifier, the third security mechanism of the Java platform springs into action: the *security manager.* A security manager is a class that controls whether a specific operation is permitted. Operations checked by a security manager include:

- Whether the current thread can create a new class loader;
- Whether the current thread can create a subprocess;
- Whether the current thread can halt the virtual machine;
- Whether the current thread can load a dynamic link library;
- Whether a class can access a member of another class;
- Whether the current thread can access a specified package;
- Whether the current thread can define classes in a specified package;
- Whether the current thread can access or modify system properties;
- Whether the current thread can read from or write to a specified file;
- Whether the current thread can delete a specified file;
- Whether the current thread can accept a socket connection from a specified host and port number;
- Whether the current thread can open a socket connection to the specified host and port number;

- Whether the current thread can wait for a connection request on a specified local port number;
- Whether the current thread can use IP multicas;t
- Whether the current thread can invoke a `stop`, `suspend`, `resume`, `destroy`, `setPriority/setMaxPriority`, `setName`, or `setDaemon` method of a given thread or thread group;
- Whether the current thread can set a socket or stream handler factory;
- Whether a class can start a print job;
- Whether a class can access the system clipboard;
- Whether a class can access the AWT event queue;
- Whether the current thread is trusted to bring up a top-level window.

The default behavior when running Java applications is that *no* security manager is installed, so all these operations are permitted. The appletviewer, on the other hand, immediately installs a security manager (called `AppletSecurity`) that is quite restrictive.

For example, applets are not allowed to exit the virtual machine. If they try calling the `exit` method, then a security exception is thrown. Here is what happens in detail. The `exit` method of the `Runtime` class calls the `checkExit` method of the security manager. Here is the entire code of the `exit` method.

```
public void exit(int status)
{  SecurityManager security = System.getSecurityManager();
   if (security != null)
       security.checkExit(status);
   exitInternal(status);
}
```

The security manager now checks if the exit request came from the browser or an individual applet. If the security manager agrees with the exit request, then the `checkExit` method simply returns, and normal processing continues. However, if the security manager doesn't want to grant the request, the `checkExit` method throws a `SecurityException`.

The `exit` method continues only if no exception occurred. It then calls the *private native* `exitInternal` method that actually terminates the virtual machine. There is no other way of terminating the virtual machine, and since the `exitInternal` method is private, it cannot be called from any other class. Thus, any code that attempts to exit the virtual machine must go through the `exit` method and thus through the `checkExit` security check without triggering a security exception.

Clearly, the integrity of the security policy depends on careful coding. The providers of system services in the standard library must be careful to always consult the security manager before attempting any sensitive operation.

When you run a Java application, the default is that no security manager is running. Your program can install a specific security manager by a call to the static `setSecurityManager` method in the `System` class. Once your program installs a security manager, any attempt to install a second security manager only succeeds if the first security manager agrees to be replaced. This is clearly essential; otherwise, a bad applet could install its own security manager. Thus, while it is possible to have multiple class loaders, a program in the Java programming language can be governed by only one security manager. It is up to the implementor of that security manager to decide whether to grant all classes the same access or whether to take the origins of the classes into account before deciding what to do.

The default security manager of the Java 2 platform allows both programmers and system administrators fine-grained control over individual security permissions. We describe these features in the following section. First, we give you an overview of the Java 2 platform security model. Then, we show you how you can control permissions with *policy files.* Finally, you will see how you can define your own permission types and how you can extend the default security manager class.

Java 2 Platform Security

JDK 1.0 had a very simple security model: local classes had full permissions, and remote classes were confined to the *sandbox:* the applet security manager denied all access to local resources. JDK 1.1 implemented a slight modification: remote code that was signed by a trusted entity was granted the same permissions as local classes. However, both versions of the JDK provided an all-or-nothing approach. Programs either had full access or they had to play in the sandbox.

The Java 2 platform has a much more flexible mechanism. A *security policy* maps *code sources to permission sets* (see Figure 9–4).

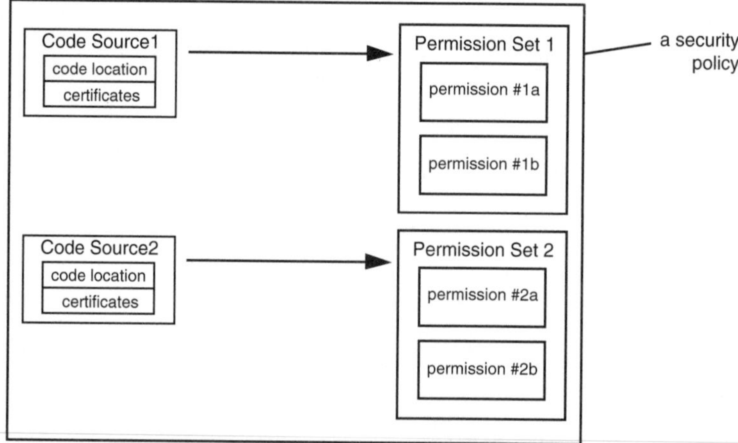

Figure 9–4: A security policy

A *code source* has two properties: the *code location* (for example, a code base URL or a JAR file) and *certificates*. You will see later in this chapter how code can be certified by trusted parties.

A *permission* is any property that is checked by a security manager. The JDK 1.2 implementation supports a number of permission classes, each of which encapsulates the details of a particular permission. For example, the following instance of the `FilePermission` class states that it is ok to read and write any file in the `/tmp` directory.

```
FilePermission p = new FilePermission("/tmp/*", "read,write");
```

More importantly, the default implementation of the `Policy` class in JDK 1.2 reads permissions from a *permission file*. Inside a permission file, the same read permission is expressed as

```
permission java.io.FilePermission "/tmp/*", "read,write";
```

We discuss permission files in the next section.

Figure 9–5 shows the hierarchy of permission classes in JDK 1.2.

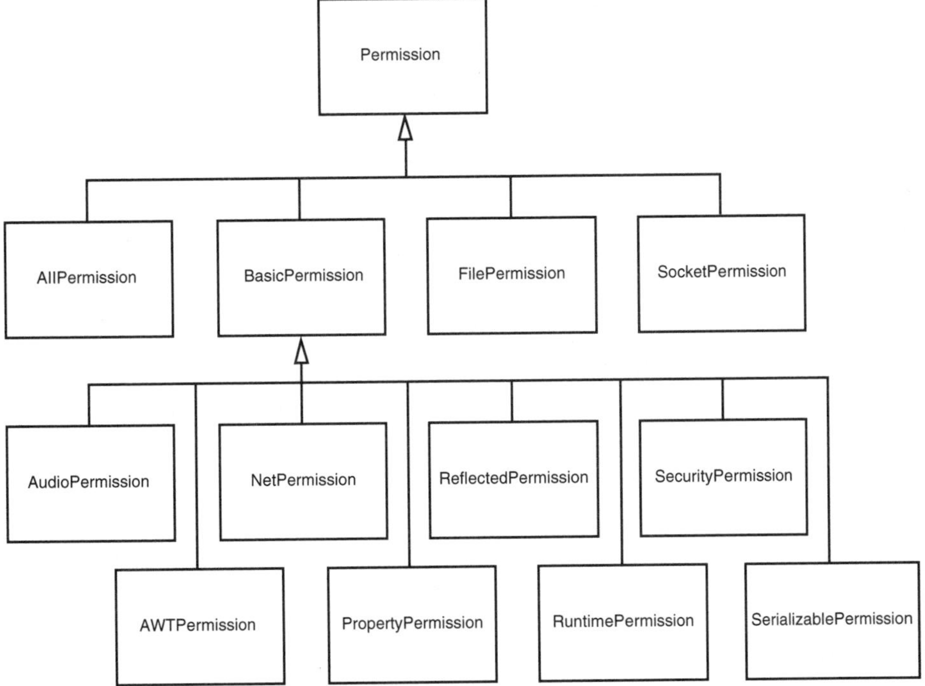

Figure 9–5: Permission hierarchy in JDK 1.2

In the preceding section, you saw that the `SecurityManager` class has security check methods such as `checkExit`. These methods exist only for the convenience of the programmer and for backward compatibility. All of them call one of the two following methods:

```
void checkPermission(Permission p)
void checkPermission(Permission p, Object context)
```

The second method is used if one thread carries out a security check for another thread. The `context` encapsulates the call stack at the time of the check. (See Gong's book for details on how to generate and use these context objects.)

For example, here is the source code for the `checkExit` method.

```
public void checkExit()
{  checkPermission(new RuntimePermission("exitVM"));
}
```

Each security manager is free to provide its own implementation of the `checkPermission` method. However, the JDK provides a "standard model" of how to carry out permission checks. For the remainder of this section, we describe this standard model. The standard model relies on two classes:

```
java.security.SecureClassLoader
java.lang.SecurityManager
```

These are the superclasses of the class loader and security manager that are used in all practical settings (such as applets and remote method invocation). In principle, you can install your own class loader and security manager. However, that is a complex undertaking that few programmers will want to attempt. It is much more common to extend the standard classes.

The standard model relies on a `Policy` object to map code sources to permissions. There can be only one `Policy` object in effect at any given time. The static `getPolicy` method of the `Policy` class gets the current policy.

```
Policy currentPolicy = Policy.getPolicy();
```

The principal method of the `Policy` class is the `getPermissions` method that returns the permission collection for a particular code source.

```
PermissionCollection permissions
   = currentPolicy.getPermissions(codeBase);
```

Each class has a *protection domain,* an object that encapsulates both the code source and the collection of permissions of the class. The `getProtectionDomain` method of the `Class` class returns that domain.

```
ProtectionDomain domain
   = anObject.getClass().getProtectionDomain();
```

The `getCodeSource` and `getPermissions` methods of the `ProtectionDomain` method return the code source and permission collection.

In the standard model, the permission collection is entirely dependent on the code source. The protection domain is set when the `SecureClassLoader` loads the

class. The SecureClassLoader queries the current policy for the permissions that match the code source. It then creates a ProtectionDomain object with the given code source and permissions. Finally, it passes that object to the defineClass method. Figure 9–6 shows the relationships between these security classes.

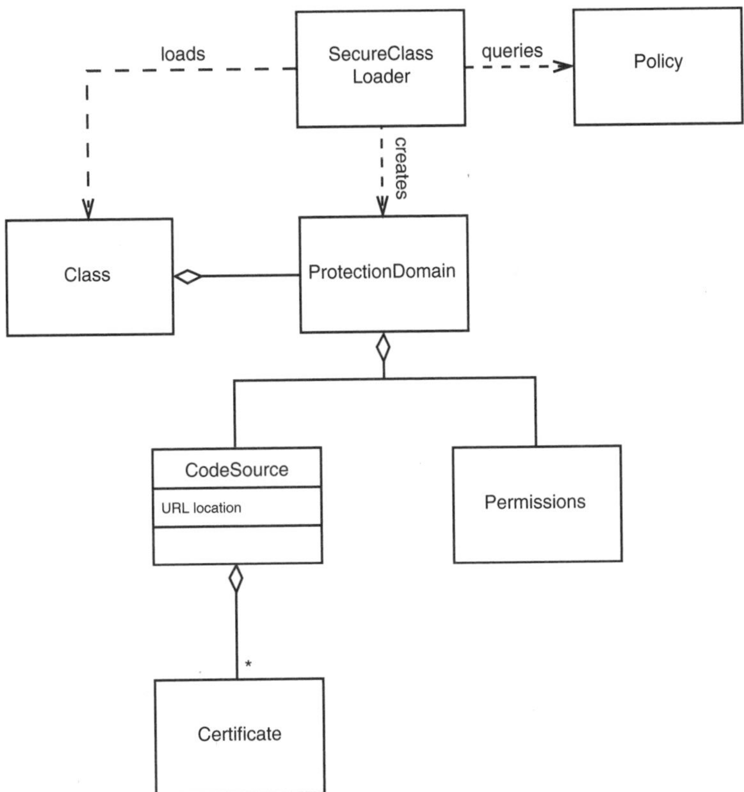

Figure 9–6: Relationship between security classes

When the SecurityManager needs to check a permission, it looks at the classes of all methods currently on the call stack. It then gets the protection domains of all classes and asks each protection domain if its permission collection allows the operation that is currently being checked. If all domains agree, then the check passes. Otherwise, a SecurityException is thrown.

Why do all methods on the call stack need to allow a particular operation? Let us work through an example. Suppose the init method of an applet wants to open a file. It might call

```
Reader in = new FileReader(name);
```

The FileReader constructor calls the FileInputStream constructor, which calls the checkRead method of the security manager, which finally calls `checkPermission` with a `FilePermission(name, "read")` object. Table 9–1 shows the call stack.

Table 9–1: Call stack during permission checking

Class	Method	Code Source	Permissions
`SecurityManager`	`SecurityManager`	`null`	`AllPermission`
`SecurityManager`	`checkRead`	`null`	`AllPermission`
`FileInputStream`	constructor	`null`	`AllPermission`
`FileReader`	constructor	`null`	`AllPermission`
applet	`init`	applet code source	applet permissions
. . .			

The `FileInputStream` and `SecurityManager` classes are *system classes* whose `CodeSource` is `null` and whose permissions consist of an instance of the `AllPermission` class, which allows all operations. Clearly, their permissions alone can't determine the outcome of the check. As you can see, the `checkPermission` method must take into account the restricted permissions of the applet class. By checking the entire call stack, the security mechanism ensures that one class can never ask another class to carry out a sensitive operation on its behalf.

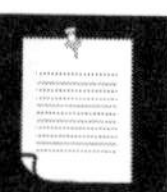

NOTE: This brief discussion of permission checking shows you the basic concepts. However, there are a number of technical details that we omit here. With security, the devil lies in the details, and we encourage you to read the book by Li Gong for more information. For a more critical view of the Java platform security model, see the book *Securing Java* by Gary McGraw and Ed Felten (John Wiley & Sons 1999). You can find an online version of that book at `http://www.securingjava.com`.

`java.lang.SecurityManager`

- `void checkPermission(Permission p)`
- `void checkPermission(Permission p, Object context)`

  check whether the current security policy permits the given permission. The second method receives an object that encapsulates the call stack. That method is used if one thread asks another thread to carry out a permission check on its behalf.

java.security.Policy

- `static Policy getPolicy()`
  gets the current policy object, or `null` if no security policy is in effect.
- `PermissionCollection getPermissions(CodeSource source)`
  gets the permissions associated with the given code source.

java.lang.Class

- `ProtectionDomain getProtectionDomain()`
  gets the protection domain for this class, or `null` if this class was loaded without a protection domain.

java.lang.ClassLoader

- `Class defineClass(String name, byte data[], int offset, int length, ProtectionDomain domain)`
  adds a new class to the virtual machine.

Parameters:		
	`name`	the name of the class. Use `.` as package name separator, and don't use a `.class` suffix
	`data`	an array holding the bytecodes of the class
	`offset`	the start of the bytecodes in the array
	`length`	the length of the bytecodes in the array
	`domain`	the protection domain for this class

java.security.ProtectionDomain

- `ProtectionDomain(CodeSource source, PermissionCollection collections)`
  constructs a protection domain with the given code source and permissions.
- `CodeSource getCodeSource()`
  gets the code source of this protection domain.
- `PermissionCollection getPermissions()`
  gets the permissions of this protection domain.

java.security.PermissionCollection

- `void add(Permission p)`
  adds a permission to this permission collection.
- `Enumeration elements()`
  returns an enumeration to iterate through all permissions in this collection.

`java.security.CodeSource`

- `Certificate[] getCertificates()`
  gets the certificates for class file signature associated with this code source.
- `URL getLocation()`
  gets the location of class files associated with this code source.

Security Policy Files

In the preceding section, you saw how the `SecureClassLoader` assigns permissions when loading classes, by asking a `Policy` object to look up the permissions for the code source of each class. In principle, you can install your own `Policy` class to carry out the mapping from code sources to permissions. However, in this section, you will learn about the standard policy class that the JDK 1.2 interpreter uses.

NOTE: The policy class is set in the file `java.security` in the `jre/lib` subdirectory of the JDK home directory. By default, this file contains the line

```
policy.provider=sun.security.provider.PolicyFile
```

You can supply your own policy class and install it by changing this file.

The standard policy reads *policy files* that contain instructions for mapping code sources to permissions. You have seen these policy files in Chapter 5, where they were required to grant network access to programs that use the `RMISecurity-Manager`. Here is a typical policy file:

```
grant codeBase "www.horstmann.com/classes"
{  permission java.io.FilePermission "/tmp/*", "read,write";
}
```

This file grants permission to read and write files in the `/tmp` directory to all code that was downloaded from `www.horstmann.com/classes`.

You can install policy files in standard locations. By default, there are two locations:

- the file `java.policy` in the Java platform home directory
- the file `.java.policy` (notice the period at the beginning of the file name) in the user home directory

NOTE: You can change the locations of these files in the `java.security` configuration file. The defaults are specified as

```
policy.url.1=file:${java.home}/lib/security/java.policy
policy.url.2=file:${user.home}/.java.policy
```

A system administrator can modify the `java.security` file and specify policy URLs that reside on another server and that cannot be edited by users. There can be any number of policy URLs (with consecutive numbers) in the policy file. The permissions of all files are combined.

During testing, we don't like to constantly modify these standard files. Therefore, we prefer to explicitly name the policy file that is required for each application. Simply place the permissions into a separate file, say, `MyApp.policy`, and start the interpreter as

```
java -Djava.security.policy=MyApp.policy MyApp
```

For applets, you use instead

```
appletviewer -J-Djava.security.policy=MyApplet.policy MyApplet.html
```

(You can use the `-J` option of the `appletviewer` to pass any command-line argument to the interpreter.)

In these examples, the `MyApp.policy` file is added to the other policies in effect. If you add a second equals sign, such as

```
java -Djava.security.policy==MyApp.policy MyApp
```

then your application uses *only* the specified policy file and the standard policy files are ignored.

CAUTION: An easy mistake during testing is to accidentally leave a `.java.policy` file that grants a lot of permissions, perhaps even `AllPermission`, in the current directory. If you find that your application doesn't seem to pay attention to the restrictions in your policy file, check for a left-behind `.java.policy` file in your current directory. If you use a Unix system, this is a particularly easy mistake to make because files whose names start with a period are not displayed by default.

As you saw previously, by default, Java applications do not install a security manager. Therefore, you won't see the effect of policy files until you install one. You can, of course, add a line

```
System.setSecurityManager(new SecurityManager());
```

into your `main` method. Or you can add the command-line option `-Djava.security.manager` when starting the interpreter.

```
java -Djava.security.manager
   -Djava.security.policy=MyApp.policy MyApp
```

In the remainder of this section, you will see in detail how to describe permissions in the policy file. We will describe the entire policy file format, except for code certificates, which we cover later in this chapter.

A policy file contains a sequence of `grant` entries. Each entry has the following form:

```
grant codesource
{  permission_1;
```

```
        permission_2;
        . . .
    }
```

The code source contains a code base (which can be omitted if the entry applies to code from all sources) and the names of trusted certificate signers (which can be omitted if signatures are not required for this entry).

The code base is specified as

```
codeBase "url"
```

If the URL ends in a `/`, then it refers to a directory. Otherwise, it is taken to be the name of a JAR file. For example

```
grant codeBase "www.horstmann.com/classes/" { . . . }
grant codeBase "www.horstmann.com/classes/MyApp.jar" { . . . }
```

The code base is an URL and should always contain forward slashes as file separators, even for file URLs in Windows. For example,

```
grant codeBase "file:C:/myapps/classes/"
```

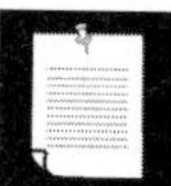

NOTE: Everyone knows that `http` URLs start with two slashes (`http://`). But there seems sufficient confusion about `file` URLs that the policy file reader accepts two forms of file URLs, namely, `file://`*`localFile`* and `file:`*`localFile`*. Furthermore, a slash before a Windows drive letter is optional. That is, all of the following are acceptable:

```
file:C:/dir/filename.ext
file:/C:/dir/filename.ext
file://C:/dir/filename.ext
file:///C:/dir/filename.ext
```

Actually, we tested that `file:////C:/dir/filename.ext` is acceptable as well, and we have no explanation for that. In the Solaris operating environment, you should use the form

```
file:/dir/filename.ext
```

The permissions have the following structure:

```
permission className targetName, actionList;
```

The class name is the fully qualified class name of the permission class (such as `java.io.FilePermission`). The *target name* is a permission-specific value, for example, a file or directory name for the file permission or a host and port for a socket permission. The *action list* is also permission-specific. It is a list of actions, such as `read` or `connect`, separated by commas. Some permission classes don't need target names and action lists. Table 9–2 lists the standard permissions and their actions.

Table 9–2 : Permissions and their associated targets and actions

Permission	Target	Action

`java.io.FilePermission`	file target (see text)	`read,`
		`write,`
		`execute,`
		`delete`

`java.net.SocketPermission`	socket target (see text)	`accept,`
		`connect,`
		`listen,`
		`resolve`

`java.util.PropertyPermission`	property target (see text)	`read,` `write`

`java.lang.RuntimePermission`	`createClassLoader`
	`getClassLoader`
	`setContextClassLoader`
	`createSecurityManager`
	`setSecurityManager`
	`exitVM`
	`setFactory`
	`setIO`
	`modifyThread`
	`modifyThreadGroup`
	`getProtectionDomain`
	`readFileDescriptor`
	`writeFileDescriptor`
	`loadLibrary.`*`libraryName`*
	`accessClassInPackage.`*`packageName`*
	`defineClassInPackage.`*`packageName`*
	`accessDeclaredMembers.`*`className`*
	`queuePrintJob`
	`stopThread`	

`java.awt.AWTPermission`	`showWindowWithoutWarningBanner`
	`accessClipboard`
	`accessEventQueue`
	`listenToAllAWTEvents`
	`readDisplayPixels`	

`java.net.NetPermission`	`setDefaultAuthenticator`
	`specifyStreamHandler`
	`requestPasswordAuthentication`	

`java.lang.reflect.Reflect-` `Permission`	`suppressAccessChecks`	
`java.io.SerializablePermission`	`enableSubclassImplementation` `enableSubstitution`	

`java.security.SecurityPermission`	`getPolicy`
	`setPolicy`
	`getProperty.`*`key`*
	`setProperty.`*`key`*
	`insertProvider.`*`providerName`*
	`removeProvider.`*`providerName`*
	`setSystemScope`
	`setIdentityPublicKey`
	`setIdentityInfo`
	`setIdentityCertificate`
	`removeIdentityCertificate`
	`printIdentity`
	`clearProviderProperties.`*`provider-`*
	`Name`
	`putProviderProperty.`*`providerName`*
	`removeProviderProperty.`*`provider-`*
	`Name`
	`getSignerPrivateKey`
	`setSignerKeyPair`	

`java.security.AllPermission`		

As you can see from Table 9–2, most permissions simply permit a particular operation. You can think of the operation as the target with an implied action `"permit"`. These permission classes all extend the `BasicPermission` class (see Figure 9–5 on page 717). However, the targets for the file, socket, and property permissions are more complex, and we need to investigate them in detail.

File permission targets can have the following form:

file	a file
directory/	a directory
directory/*	all files in the directory
*	all files in the current directory
directory/-	all files in the directory or one of its subdirectories
-	all files in the current directory or one of its subdirectories
<<ALL FILES>>	all files in the file system

For example, the following permission entry gives access to all files the directory `/myapp` and any of its subdirectories.

```
permission java.io.FilePermission "/myapp/-",
   "read,write,delete";
```

You must use the `\\` escape sequence to denote a backslash in a Windows file name.

```
permission java.io.FilePermission "c:\\myapp\\-",
   "read,write,delete";
```

Socket permission targets consist of a host and a port range. Host specifications have the following form:

hostname or *IPaddress*	a single host
`localhost` or the empty string	the local host
*.*domainSuffix*	any host whose domain ends with the given suffix
*	all hosts

Port ranges are optional and have the form

:*n*	a single port
:*n*-	all ports numbered *n* and above
:-*n*	all ports numbered *n* and below
:*n1*-*n2*	all ports in the given range

Here is an example:

```
permission java.net.SocketPermission
   "*.horstmann.com:8000-8999", "connect";
```

Finally, property permission targets can have one of two forms:

property	a specific property
propertyPrefix.*	all properties with the given prefix

Examples are "java.home" and "java.vm.*".

For example, the following permission entry allows a program to read all properties that start with java.vm.

```
permission java.util.PropertyPermission "java.vm.*", "read";
```

You can use system properties in policy files. The token ${*property*} is replaced by the property value. For example, ${user.home} is replaced by the home directory of the user. Here is an typical use of this system property in a permission entry.

```
permission java.io.FilePermission "${user.home}" "read,write";
```

To create platform-independent policy files, it is a good idea to use the file.separator property instead of explicit / or \\ separators. To make this simpler, the special notation ${/} is a shortcut for ${file.separator}. For example,

```
permission java.io.FilePermission "${user.home}${/}-"
   "read,write";
```

is a portable entry for granting permission to read and write in the user's home directory and any of its subdirectories.

The JDK comes with a rudimentary tool, called policytool, that you can use to edit policy files. When you start the tool, you can read in a policy file. The tool then displays all code sources that have permissions assigned to them (see Figure 9–7). When you click the "Edit Policy Entry" button, then all permissions for that code source are displayed (see Figure 9–8). If you select a permission and click the "Edit Permission" button, you get a dialog that lets you edit the properties of a permission entry (see Figure 9–9). As you can see, the dialog displays the valid choices for targets and actions, which can be a convenience.

Of course, this tool is not suitable for end users who would be completely mystified by most of the settings. We view it as a proof of concept for an administration tool that might be used by system administrators who don't want to worry about the exact file format of the policy files. Still, what's missing is a sensible set of categories (such as low, medium, or high security) that is meaningful to nonexperts. As a general observation, we believe that the Java 2 platform certainly contains all the pieces for a fine-grained security model, but that it could benefit from some polish in delivering these pieces to end users and system administrators.

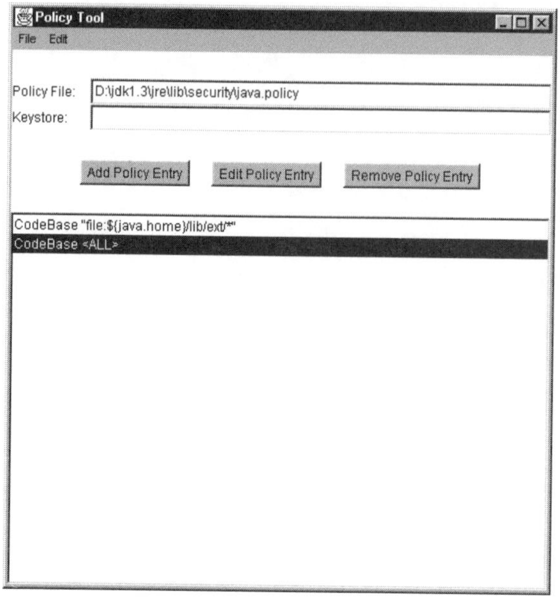

Figure 9–7: The policy tool displaying code sources

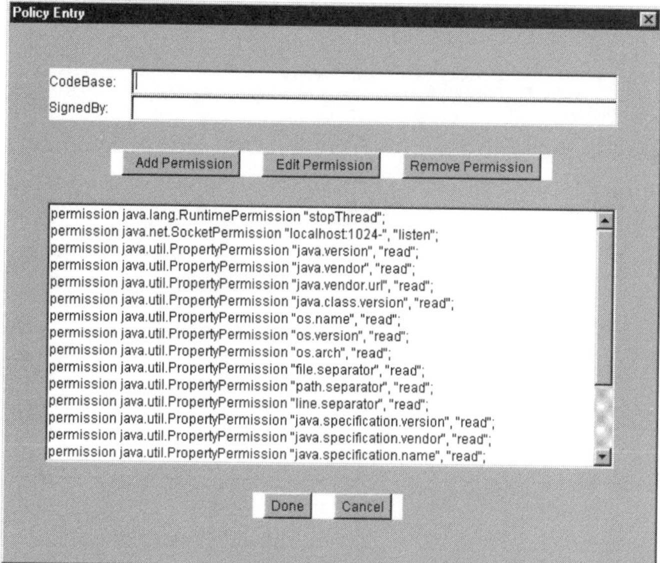

Figure 9–8: The policy tool displaying the permissions for a code source

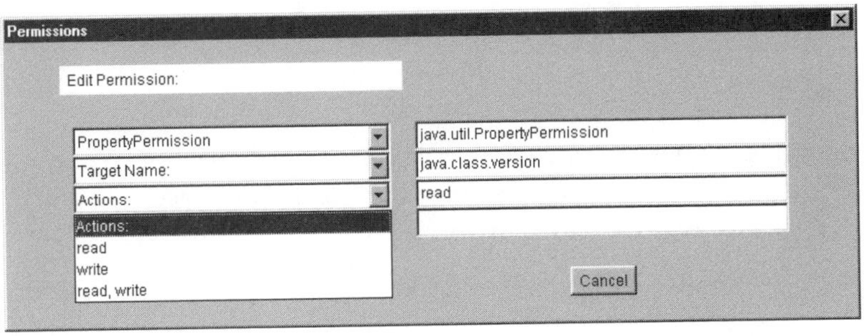

Figure 9–9: Editing a permission with the policy tool

Custom Permissions

In this section, you will see how you can supply your own permission class that users can refer to in their policy files.

To implement your permission class, you extend the `Permission` class and supply the following methods:

a constructor with two `String` parameters, for the target and the action list

```
String getActions()
boolean equals()
int hashCode()
boolean implies(Permission other)
```

The last method is the most important. Permissions have an *ordering,* in which more general permissions *imply* more specific ones. Consider the file permission

```
p1 = new FilePermission("/tmp/-", "read, write");
```

This permission allows reading and writing of any file in the `/tmp` directory and any of its subdirectories.

Here are some more-specific permissions that this permission implies:

```
p2 = new FilePermission("/tmp/-", "read");
p3 = new FilePermission("/tmp/aFile", "read, write");
p4 = new FilePermission("/tmp/aDirectory/-", "write");
```

In other words, a file permission `p1` implies another file permission `p2` if

1. the target file set of `p1` contains the target file set of `p2`;
2. the action set of `p1` contains the action set of `p2`.

Here is an example of the use of the the `implies` method. When the `FileInputStream` constructor wants to open a file for reading, it checks whether it has permission to do so. To carry out that check, a *specific* file permission object is passed to the the `checkPermission` method:

```
checkPermission(new FilePermission(fileName, "read"));
```

The security manager now asks all applicable permissions whether they imply this permission. If any one of them implies it, then the check passes.

In particular, the `AllPermission` implies all other permissions.

If you define your own permission classes, then you need to define a suitable notion of implication for your permission objects. Suppose, for example, that you define a `TVPermission` for a set-top box powered by Java technology. A permission

```
new TVPermission("Tommy:2-12:1900-2200", "watch,record")
```

might allow Tommy to watch and record television channels 2–12 between 19:00 and 22:00. You need to implement the `implies` method so that this permission implies a more specific one, such as

```
new TVPermission("Tommy:4:2000-2100", "watch")
```

Implementing a Permission Class

In the next sample program, we implement a new permission for monitoring the insertion of text into a text area. The program ensures that you cannot add "bad words" such as *sex, drugs,* and C++ into a text area. We use a custom permission class so that the list of bad words can be supplied in a policy file.

The following subclass of `JTextArea` asks the security manager whether it is ok to add new text.

```
class WordCheckTextArea extends JTextArea
{  public void append(String text)
   {  WordCheckPermission p
         = new WordCheckPermission(text, "insert");
      SecurityManager manager = System.getSecurityManager();
      if (manager != null) manager.checkPermission(p);
      super.append(text);
   }
}
```

If the security manager grants the `WordCheckPermission`, then the text is appended. Otherwise, the `checkPermission` method throws an exception.

Word check permissions have two possible actions: `insert` (the permission to insert a specific text) and `avoid` (the permission to add any text that avoids certain bad words). You should run this program with the following policy file:

```
grant
{  permission WordCheckPermission "sex,drugs,C++", "avoid";
};
```

This policy file grants the permission to insert any text that avoids the bad words *sex, drugs,* and C++.

When designing the `WordCheckPermission` class, we must pay particular attention to the `implies` method. Here are the rules that control whether permission `p1` implies permission `p2`.

1. If `p1` has action `avoid` and `p2` has action `insert`, then the target of `p2` must avoid all words in `p1`. For example, the permission

   ```
   WordCheckPermission "sex,drugs,C++", "avoid"
   ```

   implies the permission

   ```
   WordCheckPermission "Mary had a little lamb", "insert"
   ```

2. If `p1` and `p2` both have action `avoid`, then the word set of `p2` must contain all words in the word set of `p1`. For example, the permission

   ```
   WordCheckPermission "sex,drugs,C++", "avoid"
   ```

   implies the permission

   ```
   WordCheckPermission "sex,drugs", "avoid"
   ```

3. If `p1` and `p2` both have action `insert`, then the text of `p1` must contain the text of `p2`. For example, the permission

   ```
   WordCheckPermission "Mary had a little lamb", "insert"
   ```

   implies the permission

   ```
   WordCheckPermission "a little lamb", "insert"
   ```

You can find the implementation of this class in Example 9–5.

Note that you retrieve the permission target with the confusingly named `getName` method of the `Permission` class.

Since permissions are described by a pair of strings in policy files, permission classes need to be prepared to parse these strings. In particular, we use the following method to transform the comma-separated list of bad words of an `avoid` permission into a genuine `Set`.

```
public Set badWordSet()
{  StringTokenizer tokenizer
      = new StringTokenizer(getName(), ",");
   Set set = new HashSet();
   while (tokenizer.hasMoreTokens())
      set.add(tokenizer.nextToken());
   return set;
}
```

This code allows us to use the `equals` and `containsAll` methods to compare sets. As you saw in Chapter 2, the `equals` method of a set class finds two sets to be equal if they contain the same elements in any order. For example, the sets resulting from `"sex,drugs,C++"` and `"C++,drugs,sex"` are equal.

CAUTION: Make sure that your permission class is a public class. The policy file loader cannot load classes with package visibility outside the boot class path, and it silently ignores any classes that it cannot find.

The program in Example 9–5 shows how the `WordCheckPermission` class works. Type any text into the text field and press the "Insert" button. If the security check passes, the text is appended to the text area. If not, an error message appears (see Figure 9–10).

Make sure to start the program with the appropriate policy file.

```
java -Djava.security.policy=PermissionTest.policy
   PermissionTest
```

Otherwise, all attempts to insert text will fail.

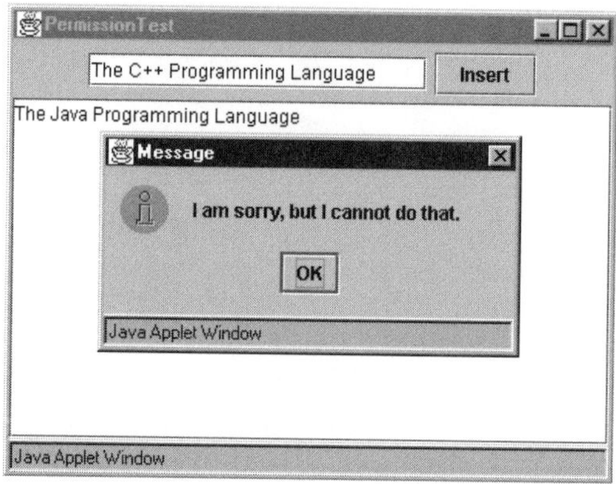

Figure 9–10: The `PermissionTest` program

CAUTION: If you carefully look at Figure 9–10, you will see that the frame window has a warning border with the misleading caption `"Java Applet Window."` The window caption is determined by the `showWindowWithoutWarningBanner` target of the `java.awt.AWTPermission`. If you like, you can edit the policy file to grant that permission.

Example 9–4: PermissionTest.java

```
import java.awt.*;
import java.awt.event.*;
import java.io.*;
import java.net.*;
import java.security.*;
import java.util.*;
import javax.swing.*;

public class PermissionTest
{  public static void main(String[] args)
   {  System.setSecurityManager(new SecurityManager());
      JFrame f = new PermissionTestFrame();
      f.show();
   }
```

```
}

class PermissionTestFrame extends JFrame
{  public PermissionTestFrame()
   {  setTitle("PermissionTest");
      setSize(400, 300);
      addWindowListener(
         new WindowAdapter()
         {  public void windowClosing(WindowEvent e)
            {  System.exit(0);
            }
         });

      textField = new JTextField(20);
      JPanel panel = new JPanel();
      panel.add(textField);
      JButton openButton = new JButton("Insert");
      panel.add(openButton);
      openButton.addActionListener(
         new ActionListener()
         {  public void actionPerformed(ActionEvent event)
            {  insertWords(textField.getText());
            }
         });

      Container contentPane = getContentPane();
      contentPane.add(panel, "North");

      textArea = new WordCheckTextArea();
      contentPane.add(new JScrollPane(textArea), "Center");
   }

   public void insertWords(String words)
   {  try
      {  textArea.append(words + "\n");
      }
      catch (SecurityException e)
      {  JOptionPane.showMessageDialog(this,
            "I am sorry, but I cannot do that.");
      }
   }

   private JTextField textField;
   private WordCheckTextArea textArea;
}

class WordCheckTextArea extends JTextArea
{  public void append(String text)
   {  WordCheckPermission p
         = new WordCheckPermission(text, "insert");
      SecurityManager manager = System.getSecurityManager();
      if (manager != null) manager.checkPermission(p);
      super.append(text);
```

```
   }
}
```

Example 9–5: WordCheckPermission.java

```
import java.security.*;
import java.util.*;

public class WordCheckPermission extends Permission
{  public WordCheckPermission(String target, String anAction)
   {  super(target);
      action = anAction;
   }

   public String getActions() { return action; }

   public boolean equals(Object other)
   {  if (other == null) return false;
      if (!getClass().equals(other.getClass())) return false;
      WordCheckPermission b = (WordCheckPermission)other;
      if (!action.equals(b.action)) return false;
      if (action.equals("insert"))
         return getName().equals(b.getName());
      else if (action.equals("avoid"))
         return badWordSet().equals(b.badWordSet());
      else return false;
   }

   public int hashCode()
   {  return getName().hashCode() + action.hashCode();
   }

   public boolean implies(Permission other)
   {  if (!(other instanceof WordCheckPermission)) return false;
      WordCheckPermission b = (WordCheckPermission)other;
      if (action.equals("insert"))
      {  return b.action.equals("insert") &&
            getName().indexOf(b.getName()) >= 0;
      }
      else if (action.equals("avoid"))
      {  if (b.action.equals("avoid"))
         {  return b.badWordSet().containsAll(badWordSet());
         }
         else if (b.action.equals("insert"))
         {  Iterator iter = badWordSet().iterator();
            while (iter.hasNext())
            {  String badWord = (String)iter.next();
               if (b.getName().indexOf(badWord) >= 0)
                  return false;
            }
            return true;
         }
         else return false;
```

```
      }
      else return false;
   }

   public Set badWordSet()
   {  StringTokenizer tokenizer
         = new StringTokenizer(getName(), ",");
      Set set = new HashSet();
      while (tokenizer.hasMoreTokens())
         set.add(tokenizer.nextToken());
      return set;
   }

   private String action;
}
```

java.security.Permission

- `Permission(String name)`
  constructs a permission with the given target name.
- `String getName()`
  returns the target name of this permission.
- `boolean implies(Permission other)`
  checks whether this permission implies the other permission. That is the case if the other permission describes a more specific condition that is a consequence of the condition described by this permission.

A Custom Security Manager

In this section, we show you how to build a simple yet complete security manager. We call it the `WordCheckSecurityManager`. It monitors all file access and ensures that you can't open a text file if it contains forbidden words such as *sex*, *drugs*, and C++.

We monitor file access by overriding the `checkPermission` method of the standard security manager class. If the permission isn't a file read permission, then we simply call `super.checkPermission`. To check that it is permissible to read from a file, we open the file and scan its contents. We grant access to the file only when it doesn't contain any of the forbidden words. (We only monitor files with extension `.txt` since we don't want to block access to system and property files.)

```
public class WordCheckSecurityManager extends SecurityManager
{  public void checkPermission(Permission p)
   {  if (p instanceof FilePermission
         && p.getActions().equals("read"))
      {  String fileName = p.getName();
         if (containsBadWords(fileName))
```

```
                throw new SecurityException("Bad words in "
                    + fileName);
            }
            else super.checkPermission(p);
        }
        . . .
    }
```

NOTE: Another way of being notified of file read requests is to override the `checkRead` method. The `SecurityManager` class implements this method to call the `checkPermission` method with a `FilePermission` object. There are close to 30 methods for other security checks that all call the `checkPermission` method—see the API note at the end of this section. These methods exist for historical reasons. The permission system has been introduced in the Java 2 platform. We recommend that you do not override these methods but instead carry out all permission checks in the `checkPermission` method.

There is just one catch in our file check scenario. Consider one possible flow of events.

- A method of some class opens a file.
- Then, the security manager springs into action and uses its `checkPermission` method.
- The `checkPermission` method calls the `containsBadWords` method.

But the `containsBadWords` method must itself read the file in order to check its contents, which calls the security manager again! This would result in an infinite regression unless the security manager has a way of finding out in which context it was called. The `getClassContext` method is the way to find out how the method was called. This method returns an array of class objects that gives all the classes whose calls are currently pending. For example, when the security manager is called for the first time, that array is

```
class WordCheckSecurityManager
class SecurityManager
class java.io.FileInputStream
class java.io.FileReader
class SecurityManagerFrame
. . .
class java.awt.EventDispatchThread
```

The class at index 0 gives the currently executing call. Unfortunately, you only get to see the classes, not the names of the pending methods. When the security manager itself attempts to open the file, it is called again and the `getClassContext` method returns the following array.

```
class WordCheckSecurityManager
class SecurityManager
```

```
class java.io.FileInputStream
class java.io.FileReader
class WordCheckSecurityManager
class WordCheckSecurityManager
class SecurityManager
class java.io.FileInputStream
class java.io.FileReader
class SecurityManagerFrame
. . .
class java.awt.EventDispatchThread
```

In this case, the security manager should permit the file access. How can we do this? We could test whether

```
getClassContext()[0] == getClassContext()[4]
```

but this approach is fragile. Here's an obvious case of where it can go wrong: Imagine that if the implementation changed, for example, so the `FileReader` constructor calls the security manager directly, then the test would be meaningless because the positions would not be the same in the array. It is far more robust to test whether *any* of the pending calls came from the same security manager.

Here is a method that carries out this test. Since this method is called from `checkPermission`, there are at least two copies of the security manager class on the call stack. We skip these first and then look for another instance of the same security manager.

```
boolean inSameManager()
{  Class[] cc = getClassContext();

   // skip past current set of calls to this manager
   int i = 0;
   while (i < cc.length && cc[0] == cc[i])
      i++;

   // check if there is another call to this manager
   while (i < cc.length)
   {  if (cc[0] == cc[i]) return true;
      i++;
   }
   return false;
}
```

We call this method in the `checkPermission` method. If we find that the security manager is invoked recursively, then we do not call the `containsBadWords` method again.

```
if (p instanceof FilePermission
   && p.getActions().equals("read"))
{  if (inSameManager())
      return;
   String fileName = p.getName();
   if (containsBadWords(fileName))
```

```
        throw new SecurityException("Bad words in "
           + fileName);
  }
```

Example 9–6 shows a program that puts this security manager to work. The security manager is installed in the `main` method. When running the program, you can specify a file. The program will load its contents into the text area. However, if the file fails the security check, the program catches the security exception and displays a message instead (see Figure 9–11). For example, you can display "Alice in Wonderland," but the program refuses to load "The Count of Monte Cristo."

NOTE: You may wonder why we don't use a `JFileChooser` to select a file name. The `JFileChooser` class tries to read the files that it displays, probably to find out which of them are files and which are directories.

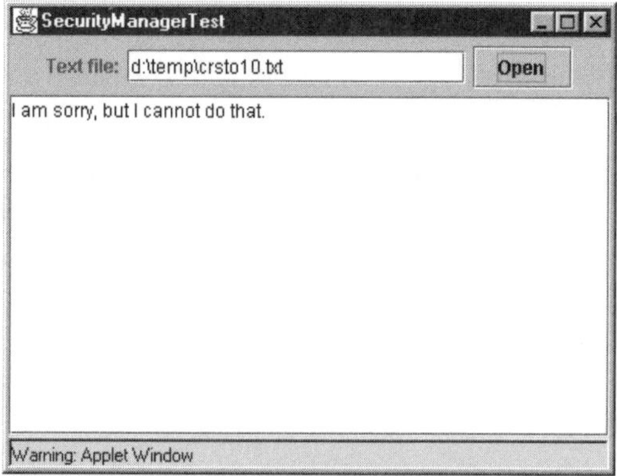

Figure 9–11: The `SecurityManagerTest` program

You need to be careful how you invoke this program. The `WordCheckSecurityManager` class itself needs to be given `AllPermission`. The reason for this is subtle. The `WordCheckSecurityManager` class calls the `SecurityManager` superclass for all permissions other than file read permissions. When the `SecurityManager` class evaluates a permission, it looks whether *all methods on the call stack* should be granted that particular permission. The `WordCheckSecurityManager` is one of those classes. But it is not a system class, so you must explicitly grant it all permissions without also granting all permissions to the other classes of the program.

To separate the `WordCheckSecurityManager` class files from the other class files, make a JAR file containing just that class file.

```
jar cvf WordCheck.jar WordCheckSecurityManager.class
```

The delete the `WordCheckSecurityManager.class` file.

Next, create a policy file, `WordCheck.policy`, with the following contents:

```
grant codeBase "file:WordCheck.jar"
{  permission java.security.AllPermission;
};
```

This policy grants all permissions to the classes in the `WordCheck.jar` file. Finally, start the application as follows:

```
java -Djava.security.policy=WordCheck.policy
   -classpath WordCheck.jar;. SecurityManagerTest.java
```

TIP: If you are thinking of changing the security manager in your own programs, you should first investigate whether you can instead use the standard security manager and a custom permission, as described in the preceding section. Writing a security manager is error prone and can cause subtle security flaws. It is much better to use the standard security manager and augment the permission system instead.

Example 9–6: SecurityManagerTest.java

```
import java.awt.*;
import java.awt.event.*;
import java.io.*;
import java.net.*;
import java.util.*;
import javax.swing.*;

public class SecurityManagerTest
{  public static void main(String[] args)
   {  System.setSecurityManager(new WordCheckSecurityManager());
      JFrame f = new SecurityManagerFrame();
      f.show();
   }
}

class SecurityManagerFrame extends JFrame
{  public SecurityManagerFrame()
   {  setTitle("SecurityManagerTest");
      setSize(400, 300);
      addWindowListener(
         new WindowAdapter()
         {  public void windowClosing(WindowEvent e)
            {  System.exit(0);
            }
         });

      fileNameField = new JTextField(20);
      JPanel panel = new JPanel();
      panel.add(new JLabel("Text file:"));
      panel.add(fileNameField);
```

```
      JButton openButton = new JButton("Open");
      panel.add(openButton);
      openButton.addActionListener(
         new ActionListener()
         {  public void actionPerformed(ActionEvent event)
            {  loadFile(fileNameField.getText());
            }
         });

      Container contentPane = getContentPane();
      contentPane.add(panel, "North");

      fileText = new JTextArea();
      contentPane.add(new JScrollPane(fileText), "Center");
   }

   public void loadFile(String filename)
   {  try
      {  fileText.setText("");
         BufferedReader in
            = new BufferedReader(new FileReader(filename));
         String s;
         while ((s = in.readLine()) != null)
         fileText.append(s + "\n");
         in.close();
      }
      catch (IOException e)
      {  fileText.append(e + "\n");
      }
      catch (SecurityException e)
      {  fileText.append("I am sorry, but I cannot do that.");
      }
   }

   private JTextField fileNameField;
   private JTextArea fileText;
}
```

Example 9–7: WordCheckSecurityManager.java

```
import java.io.*;
import java.security.*;

public class WordCheckSecurityManager extends SecurityManager
{  public void checkPermission(Permission p)
   {  if (p instanceof FilePermission
         && p.getActions().equals("read"))
      {  if (inSameManager())
            return;
         String fileName = p.getName();
         if (containsBadWords(fileName))
```

```
            throw new SecurityException("Bad words in "
               + fileName);
      }
      else super.checkPermission(p);
   }

   boolean inSameManager()
   {  Class[] cc = getClassContext();

      // skip past current set of calls to this manager
      int i = 0;
      while (i < cc.length && cc[0] == cc[i])
         i++;

      // check if there is another call to this manager
      while (i < cc.length)
      {  if (cc[0] == cc[i]) return true;
         i++;
      }
      return false;
   }

   boolean containsBadWords(String fileName)
   {  if (!fileName.toLowerCase().endsWith(".txt")) return false;
         // only check text files
      BufferedReader in = null;
      try
      {  in = new BufferedReader(new FileReader(fileName));
         String s;
         while ((s = in.readLine()) != null)
         {  for (int i = 0; i < badWords.length; i++)
            if (s.toLowerCase().indexOf(badWords[i]) != -1)
               return true;
         }
         in.close();
         return false;
      }
      catch(IOException e)
      {  return true;
      }
      finally
      {  if (in != null)
            try { in.close(); } catch (IOException e) {}
      }
   }

   private String[] badWords = { "sex", "drugs", "c++" };
}
```

`java.lang.System`

- `void setSecurityManager(SecurityManager s)`
  sets the security manager for remainder of this application. If `s` is `null`, no action is taken. This method throws a security exception if the current security manager does not permit the installation of a new security manager.
- `SecurityManager getSecurityManager()`
  gets the system security manager; returns `null` if none is installed.

`java.lang.SecurityManager`

- `Class[] getClassContext()`
  returns an array of the classes for the currently executing methods. The element at position 0 is the class of the currently running method, the element at position 1 is the class of the caller of the current method, and so on. Only the class names, not the method names, are available.
- `void checkCreateClassLoader()`
  checks whether the current thread can create a class loader.
- `void checkAccess(Thread g)`
  checks whether the current thread can invoke the `stop`, `suspend`, `resume`, `setPriority`, `setName`, and `setDaemon` methods on the thread `g`.
- `void checkAccess(ThreadGroup g)`
  checks whether the current thread can invoke the `stop`, `suspend`, `resume`, `destroy`, and `setMaxPriority` methods on the thread group `g`.
- `void checkExit(int status)`
  checks whether the current thread can exit the virtual machine with status code `status`.
- `void checkExec(String cmd)`
  checks whether the current thread can execute the system command `cmd`.
- `void checkLink(String lib)`
  checks whether the current thread can dynamically load the library `lib`.
- `void checkRead(FileDescriptor fd)`
- `void checkRead(String file)`
- `void checkWrite(FileDescriptor fd)`
- `void checkWrite(String file)`
- `void checkDelete(String file)`
  These methods check whether the current thread can read, write, or delete the given file.

- `void checkRead(String file, Object context)`
  checks whether another thread can read the given file. The other thread must have called `getSecurityContext`, and the return value of that call is passed as the value of the `context` parameter.
- `void checkConnect(String host, int port)`
  checks whether the current thread can connect to the given host at the given port.
- `void checkConnect(String host, int port, Object context)`
  checks whether another thread can connect to the given host at the given port. The other thread must have called `getSecurityContext`, and the return value of that call is passed as the `context` parameter.
- `void checkListen(int port)`
  checks whether the current thread can listen for a connection to the given local port.
- `void checkAccept(String host, int port)`
  checks whether the current thread can accept a socket connection from the given host and port.
- `void checkSetFactory()`
  checks whether the current thread can set the socket or stream handler factory.
- `void checkPropertiesAccess()`
- `void checkPropertyAccess(String key)`
  These methods check whether the current thread can access the system properties or the system property with the given key.
- `void checkSecurityAccess(String key)`
  checks whether the current thread can access the security property with the given key.
- `boolean checkTopLevelWindow(Object window)`
  returns `true` if the given window can be displayed without a security warning.
- `void checkPrintJobAccess()`
  checks whether the current thread can access print jobs.
- `void checkSystemClipboardAccess()`
  checks whether the current thread can access the system clipboard.
- `void checkAwtEventQueueAccess()`
  checks whether the current thread can access the AWT event queue.
- `void checkPackageAccess(String pkg)`
  checks whether the current thread can load classes from the given package. This method is called from the `loadClass` method of some class loaders.

- `void checkPackageDefinition(String pkg)`
  checks whether the current thread can define new classes that are in the given package. This method is often called from the `loadClass` method of a custom class loader.
- `void checkMemberAccess(Class cl, int member_id)`
  checks whether the current thread can access a member of a class. (See Chapter 11 for information on how to obtain member IDs.)

The `java.security` Package

As we said earlier, applets were what started the craze over the Java platform. In practice, people discovered that although they could write animated applets like the famous "nervous text" applet, applets could not do a whole lot of useful stuff in the JDK 1.0 security model. For example, because applets under JDK 1.0 were so closely supervised, they couldn't do much good on a corporate intranet, even though relatively little risk attaches to executing an applet from your company's secure intranet. It quickly became clear to Sun that for applets to become truly useful, it was important for users to be able to assign *different* levels of security, depending on where the applet originated. If an applet comes from a trusted supplier and it has not been tampered with, the user of that applet can then decide whether to give the applet more privileges.

This added control is now possible because of the applet-signing mechanism in Java 1.1. To give more trust to an applet, we need to know two things:

1. Where did the applet come from?
2. Was the code corrupted in transit?

In the past 50 years, mathematicians and computer scientists have developed sophisticated algorithms for ensuring the integrity of data and for electronic signatures. The `java.security` package contains implementations of many of these algorithms. Fortunately, you don't need to understand the underlying mathematics to use the algorithms in the `java.security` package. In the next sections, you will see how message digests can detect changes in data files and how digital signatures can prove the identity of the signer.

Message Digests

A message digest is a digital fingerprint of a block of data. For example, the so-called SHA1 (secure hash algorithm #1) condenses any data block, no matter how long, into a sequence of 160 bits (20 bytes). As with real fingerprints, one hopes that no two messages have the same SHA1 fingerprint. Of course, that cannot be true—there are only 2^{160} SHA1 fingerprints, so there must be some messages with the same fingerprint. But 2^{160} is so large that the probability of duplication occurring is negligible. How negligible? According to James Walsh in *True Odds—How Risks Affect Your Everyday Life* [Merritt Publishing 1996], the chance that you will

die from being struck by lightning is about one in 30,000. Now, think of 9 other people, for example, your 9 least favorite managers or professors. The chance that you and *all of them* will die from lightning strikes is higher than that of a forged message having the same SHA1 fingerprint as the original. (Of course, more than 10 people, none of whom you are likely to know, will die from lightning. But we are talking about the far slimmer chance that *your particular choice* of people will be wiped out.)

A message digest has two essential properties.

1. If one bit or several bits of the data are changed, then the message digest also changes.
2. A forger who is in possession of a given message cannot construct a fake message that has the same message digest as the original.

The second property is again a matter of probabilities, of course. Consider the following message by the billionaire father:

> *"Upon my death, my property shall be divided equally among my children; however, my son George shall receive nothing."*

That message has an SHA1 fingerprint of

```
2D 8B 35 F3 BF 49 CD B1 94 04 E0 66 21 2B 5E 57 70 49 E1 7E
```

The distrustful father has deposited the message with one attorney and the fingerprint with another. Now, suppose George can bribe the lawyer holding the message. He wants to change the message so that Bill gets nothing. Of course, that changes the fingerprint to a completely different bit pattern:

```
2A 33 0B 4B B3 FE CC 1C 9D 5C 01 A7 09 51 0B 49 AC 8F 98 92
```

Can George find some other wording that matches the fingerprint? If he had a been the proud owner of a billion computers from the time the Earth was formed, each computing a million messages a second, he would not yet have found a message he could substitute.

A number of algorithms have been designed to compute these message digests. The two best-known are SHA1, the secure hash algorithm developed by the National Institute of Standards and Technology, and MD5, an algorithm invented by Ronald Rivest of MIT. Both algorithms scramble the bits of a message in ingenious ways. For details about these algorithms, see, for example, *Network and Internetwork Security* by William Stallings [Prentice-Hall 1995]. Note that recently, subtle regularities have been discovered in MD5, and some cryptographers recommend avoiding it and using SHA1 for that reason. (Both algorithms are easy to compute.)

The Java programming language implements both SHA1 and MD5. The `MessageDigest` class is a *factory* for creating objects that encapsulate the fingerprinting algorithms. It has a static method, called `getInstance`, that returns an object of a class that extends the `MessageDigest` class. This means the `MessageDigest` class serves double duty:

- As a factory class;
- As the superclass for all message digest algorithms.

For example, here is how you obtain an object that can compute SHA fingerprints.

```
MessageDigest alg = MessageDigest.getInstance("SHA-1");
```

(To get an object that can compute MD5, use the string `"MD5"` as the argument to `getInstance`.)

After you have obtained a `MessageDigest` object, you feed it all the bytes in the message by repeatedly calling the `update` method. For example, the following code passes all bytes in a file to the `alg` object created above to do the fingerprinting:

```
FileInputStream in = new FileInputStream(f);
int ch;

while ((ch = in.read()) != -1)
   alg.update((byte)ch);
```

When you are done, call the `digest` method. This method pads the input—as required by the fingerprinting algorithm—does the computation, and returns the digest as an array of bytes.

```
byte[] hash = alg.digest();
```

The program in Example 9–8 computes a message digest, using either SHA or MD5. You can load the data to be digested from a file, or you can type a message in the text area. Figure 9–12 shows the application.

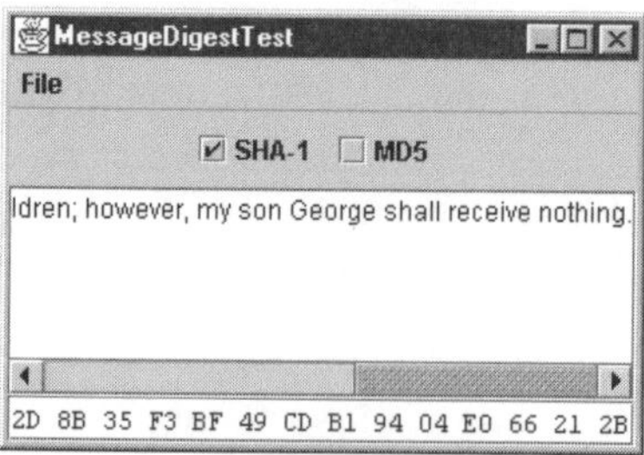

Figure 9–12: Computing a message digest

Example 9–8: MessageDigestTest.java

```
import java.io.*;
import java.security.*;
import java.awt.*;
import java.awt.event.*;
```

```
import javax.swing.*;

public class MessageDigestTest
{  public static void main(String[] args)
   {  JFrame f = new MessageDigestFrame();
      f.show();
   }
}

class MessageDigestFrame extends JFrame
{  public MessageDigestFrame()
   {  setTitle("MessageDigestTest");
      setSize(400, 200);
      addWindowListener(
         new WindowAdapter()
         {  public void windowClosing(WindowEvent e)
            {  System.exit(0);
            }
         });

      JPanel panel = new JPanel();
      ButtonGroup group = new ButtonGroup();
      ActionListener listener =
         new ActionListener()
         {  public void actionPerformed(ActionEvent event)
            {  JCheckBox b = (JCheckBox)event.getSource();
               setAlgorithm(b.getText());
            }
         };
      addCheckBox(panel, "SHA-1", group, true, listener);
      addCheckBox(panel, "MD5", group, false, listener);

      Container contentPane = getContentPane();

      contentPane.add(panel, "North");
      contentPane.add(new JScrollPane(message), "Center");
      contentPane.add(digest, "South");
      digest.setFont(new Font("Monospaced", Font.PLAIN, 12));

      setAlgorithm("SHA-1");

      JMenuBar menuBar = new JMenuBar();
      JMenu menu = new JMenu("File");
      JMenuItem fileDigestItem = new JMenuItem("File digest");
      fileDigestItem.addActionListener(
         new ActionListener()
         {  public void actionPerformed(ActionEvent event)
            {  loadFile();
            }
         });
      menu.add(fileDigestItem);
      JMenuItem textDigestItem
```

```
         = new JMenuItem("Text area digest");
      textDigestItem.addActionListener(
         new ActionListener()
         {  public void actionPerformed(ActionEvent event)
            {  String m = message.getText();
               computeDigest(m.getBytes());
            }
         });
      menu.add(textDigestItem);
      menuBar.add(menu);
      setJMenuBar(menuBar);
   }

   public void addCheckBox(Container c, String name,
      ButtonGroup g, boolean selected, ActionListener listener)
   {  JCheckBox b = new JCheckBox(name, selected);
      c.add(b);
      g.add(b);
      b.addActionListener(listener);
   }

   public void setAlgorithm(String alg)
   {  try
      {  currentAlgorithm = MessageDigest.getInstance(alg);
         digest.setText("");
      }
      catch(NoSuchAlgorithmException e)
      {  digest.setText("" + e);
      }
   }

   public void loadFile()
   {  JFileChooser chooser = new JFileChooser();
      chooser.setCurrentDirectory(new File("."));

      int r = chooser.showOpenDialog(this);
      if(r == JFileChooser.APPROVE_OPTION)
      {  String name
            = chooser.getSelectedFile().getAbsolutePath();
         computeDigest(loadBytes(name));
      }
   }

   public byte[] loadBytes(String name)
   {  FileInputStream in = null;

      try
      {  in = new FileInputStream(name);
         ByteArrayOutputStream buffer
            = new ByteArrayOutputStream();
         int ch;
         while ((ch = in.read()) != -1)
```

```
            buffer.write(ch);
         return buffer.toByteArray();
      }
      catch (IOException e)
      {  if (in != null)
         {  try { in.close(); } catch (IOException e2) {}
         }
         return null;
      }
   }

   public void computeDigest(byte[] b)
   {  currentAlgorithm.reset();
      currentAlgorithm.update(b);
      byte[] hash = currentAlgorithm.digest();
      String d = "";
      for (int i = 0; i < hash.length; i++)
      {  int v = hash[i] & 0xFF;
         if (v < 16) d += "0";
         d += Integer.toString(v, 16).toUpperCase() + " ";
      }
      digest.setText(d);
   }

   private JTextArea message = new JTextArea();
   private JTextField digest = new JTextField();
   private MessageDigest currentAlgorithm;
}
```

java.security.MessageDigest

- `static MessageDigest getInstance(String algorithm)`
  returns a `MessageDigest` object that implements the specified algorithm. Throws a `NoSuchAlgorithmException` if the algorithm is not provided.

Parameters:	`algorithm`	the name of the algorithm, such as `"SHA-1"` or `"MD5"`

- `void update(byte input)`
- `void update(byte[] input)`
- `void update(byte[] input, int offset, int len)`
  update the digest, using the specified bytes.
- `byte[] digest()`
  completes the hash computation, returns the computed digest, and resets the algorithm object.
- `void reset()`
  resets the digest.

Digital Signatures

In the last section, you saw how to compute a message digest, a fingerprint for the original message. If the message is altered, then the fingerprint of the altered message will not match the fingerprint of the original. If the message and its fingerprint are delivered separately, then the recipient can check whether the message has been tampered with. However, if both the message and the fingerprint were intercepted, it is an easy matter to modify the message and then recompute the fingerprint. After all, the message digest algorithms are publicly known, and they don't require any secret keys. In that case, the recipient of the forged message and the recomputed fingerprint would never know that the message has been altered. In this section, you will see how *digital signatures can authenticate* a message. When a message is authenticated, you *know*

- The message was not altered.
- The message came from the claimed sender.

To understand how digital signatures work, we need to explain a few concepts from the field called *public key cryptography.* Public key cryptography is based on the notion of a *public* key and *private* key. The idea is that you tell everyone in the world your public key. However, only you hold the private key, and it is important that you safeguard it and don't release it to anyone else. The keys are matched by mathematical relationships, but it is believed to be practically impossible to compute one from the other. That is, even though everyone knows your public key, they can't compute your private key in your lifetime, no matter how many computing resources they have available.

It may seem difficult to believe that nobody can compute the private key from the public keys, but nobody has ever found an algorithm to do this for the encryption algorithms that are in common use today. If the keys are sufficiently long, brute force—simply trying all possible keys—would require more computers than can be built from all the atoms in the solar system, crunching away for thousands of years. Of course, it is possible that someone could come up with algorithms for computing keys that are much more clever than brute force. For example, the RSA algorithm (the encryption algorithm invented by Rivest, Shamir, and Adleman) depends on the difficulty of factoring large numbers. For the last 20 years, many of the best mathematicians have tried to come up with good factoring algorithms, but so far with no success. For that reason, most cryptographers believe that keys with a "modulus" of 2,000 bits or more are currently completely safe from any attack.

There are two kinds of public/private key pairs: for *encryption* and for *authentication.* If anyone sends you a message that was encrypted with your public encryption key, then you can decrypt it with your private decryption key, but nobody else can. Conversely, if you sign a message with your private authentication key, then anyone else can verify the signature by checking with your public key. The

verification passes only for messages that you signed and it fails if anyone else used his key to sign the message. (Kahn remarks in the new edition of his book *The Code Breakers* that this was the first *new* idea in cryptography in hundreds of years.)

Many cryptographic algorithms, such as RSA and DSA (the Digital Signature Algorithm), use this idea. The exact structure of the keys and what it means for them to match depend on the algorithm. For example, here is a matching pair of public and private DSA keys.

Public key:

```
p: fca682ce8e12caba26efccf7110e526db078b05edecbcd1eb4a208f3ae16
17ae01f35b91a47e6df63413c5e12ed0899bcd132acd50d99151bdc43ee7375
92e17

q: 962eddcc369cba8ebb260ee6b6a126d9346e38c5

g: 678471b27a9cf44ee91a49c5147db1a9aaf244f05a434d6486931d2d1427
1b9e35030b71fd73da179069b32e2935630e1c2062354d0da20a6c416e50be79
4ca4

y: c0b6e67b4ac098eb1a32c5f8c4c1f0e7e6fb9d832532e27d0bdab9ca2d2a
8123ce5a8018b8161a760480fadd040b927281ddb22cb9bc4df596d7de4d1b97
7d50
```

Private key:

```
p: fca682ce8e12caba26efccf7110e526db078b05edecbcd1eb4a208f3ae16
17ae01f35b91a47e6df63413c5e12ed0899bcd132acd50d99151bdc43ee73759
2e17

q: 962eddcc369cba8ebb260ee6b6a126d9346e38c5

g: 678471b27a9cf44ee91a49c5147db1a9aaf244f05a434d6486931d2d1427
1b9e35030b71fd73da179069b32e2935630e1c2062354d0da20a6c416e50be79
4ca4

x: 146c09f881656cc6c51f27ea6c3a91b85ed1d70a
```

There is a mathematical relationship between these keys, but the exact nature of the relationship is not interesting for practical programming. (If you are interested, you can look it up in *Network and Internetwork Security* by William Stallings [Prentice-Hall 1995] or *The Handbook of Cryptography* mentioned earlier.)

The obvious question is how to generate the pair of keys. Usually, this is done by feeding the result of some random process in to a deterministic procedure that returns the key pair to you. Luckily, how to get a random key pair for public key cryptography is not a question anyone but cryptographers and mathematicians need to worry about.

Here is how it works in practice. Suppose Alice wants to send Bob a message, and Bob wants to know this message came from Alice and not an impostor. Alice writes the message and then *signs* the message digest with her private key. Bob gets a copy of her public key. Bob then applies the public key to *verify* the signature. If the verification passes, then Bob can be assured of two facts:

1. The original message has not been altered
2. The message was signed by Alice, the holder of the private key that matches the public key that Bob used for verification

See Figure 9–13.

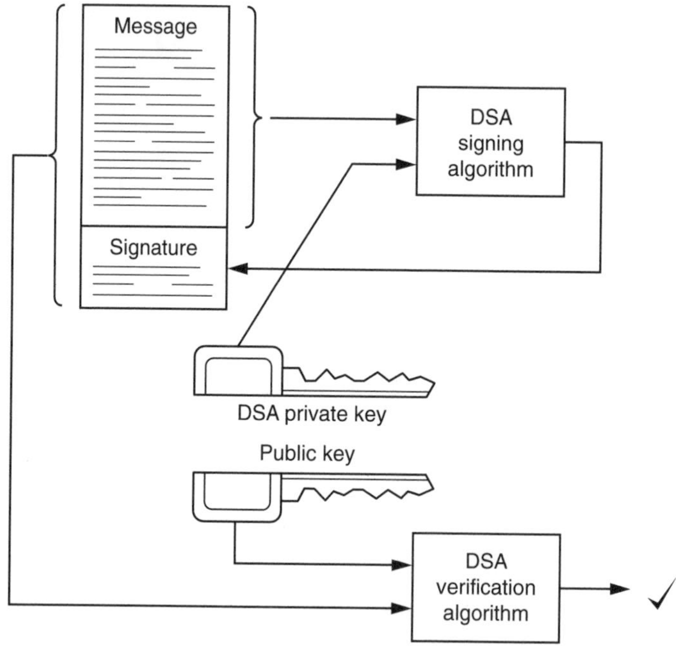

Figure 9–13: Public key signature exchange using DSA

You can see why security for private keys is all-important. If someone steals Alice's private key or if a government can require her to turn it over, then she is in trouble. The thief or a government agent can impersonate her by sending messages, money transfer instructions, and so on, that others will believe to have come from Alice.

The Java security package comes with DSA. If you want to use RSA, you'll need to buy the classes from RSA (`www.rsa.com`). Let us put the DSA algorithm to work. Actually, there are three algorithms:

1. To generate a key pair
2. To sign a message
3. To verify a signature

Of course, you generate a key pair only once and then use it for signing and verifying many messages. To generate a new random key pair, make sure you use *truly random* numbers. For example, the regular random number generator in the `Random` class, seeded by the current date and time, is not random enough. (The

jargon says the basic random number generator in `java.util` is not "cryptographically secure.") For example, supposing the computer clock is accurate to 1/10 of a second; then, there are at most 864,000 seeds per day. If an attacker knows the day a key was issued (as can often be deduced from the expiration date), then it is an easy matter to generate all possible seeds for that day.

The `SecureRandom` class generates random numbers that are far more secure than those produced by the `Random` class. You still need to provide a seed to start the number sequence at a random spot. The best method for doing this is to obtain random input from a hardware device such as a white-noise generator. Another reasonable source for random input is to ask the user to type away aimlessly on the keyboard. But each keystroke should contribute only one or two bits to the random seed. Once you gather such random bits in an array of bytes, you pass it to the `setSeed` method.

```
SecureRandom secrand = new SecureRandom();
byte[] b = new byte[20];
// fill with truly random bits
secrand.setSeed(b);
```

If you don't seed the random number generator, then it will compute its own 20-byte seed by launching threads, putting them to sleep, and measuring the exact time when they are awakened.

NOTE: This is an innovative algorithm that, at this point, is *not* known to be safe. And, in the past, algorithms that relied on timing other components of the computer, such as hard disk access time, were later shown not to be completely random.

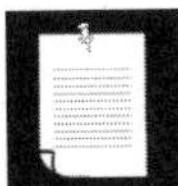

Once you seed the generator, you can then draw random bytes with the `nextBytes` method.

```
byte[] randomBytes = new byte[64];
secrand.nextBytes(randomBytes);
```

Actually, to compute a new DSA key, you don't compute the random numbers yourself. You just pass the random number generator object to the DSA key generation algorithm.

To make a new key pair, you need a `KeyPairGenerator` object. Just as with the `MessageDigest` class of the preceding section, the `KeyPairGenerator` class is both a factory class and the superclass for actual key pair generation algorithms. To get a DSA key pair generator, you call the `getInstance` method with the string `"DSA"`.

```
KeyPairGenerator keygen = KeyPairGenerator.getInstance("DSA");
```

The returned object is actually an object of the class `sun.security.provider.DSAKeyPairGenerator`, which is a subclass of `KeyPairGenerator`.

To generate keys, you must initialize the key generation algorithm object with the key strength and a secure random number generator. Note that the key strength is not the length of the generated keys but the size of one of the building blocks of the key. In the case of DSA, it is the number of bits in the modulus, one of the mathematical quantities that makes up the public and private keys. Suppose you want to generate a key with a modulus of 512 bits:

```
SecureRandom secrand = new SecureRandom();
secrand.setSeed(...);
keygen.initialize(512, secrand);
```

Now you are ready to generate key pairs.

```
KeyPair keys = keygen.generateKeyPair();
KeyPair morekeys = keygen.generateKeyPair();
```

Each key pair has a public and a private key.

```
PublicKey pubkey = keys.getPublic();
PrivateKey privkey = keys.getPrivate();
```

To sign a message, you need a signature algorithm object. You use the `Signature` factory class:

```
Signature signalg = Signature.getInstance("DSA");
```

Signature algorithm objects can be used both to sign and to verify a message. To prepare the object for message signing, use the `initSign` method and pass the private key to the signature algorithm.

```
signalg.initSign(privkey);
```

Now, you use the `update` method to add bytes to the algorithm objects, in the same way as with the message digest algorithm.

```
while ((ch = in.read()) != -1)
   signalg.update((byte)ch);
```

Finally, you can compute the signature with the `sign` method. The signature is returned as an array of bytes.

```
byte[] signature = signalg.sign();
```

The recipient of the message must obtain a DSA signature algorithm object and prepare it for signature verification by calling the `initVerify` method with the public key as parameter.

```
Signature verifyalg = Signature.getInstance("DSA");
verifyalg.initVerify(pubkey);
```

Then, the message must be sent to the algorithm object.

```
while ((ch = in.read()) != -1)
   verifyalg.update((byte)ch);
```

Finally, you can verify the signature.

```
boolean check = verifyalg.verify(signature);
```

If the `verify` method returns `true`, then the signature was a valid signature of the message that was signed with the matching private key. That is, both the sender and the contents of the message have been authenticated.

Example 9–9 demonstrates the key generation, signing, and verification processes.

Example 9–9: SignatureTest.java

```
import java.security.*;

public class SignatureTest
{  public static void main(String[] args)
   {  try
      {  KeyPairGenerator keygen
            = KeyPairGenerator.getInstance("DSA");
         SecureRandom secrand = new SecureRandom();
         keygen.initialize(512, secrand);

         KeyPair keys1 = keygen.generateKeyPair();
         PublicKey pubkey1 = keys1.getPublic();
         PrivateKey privkey1 = keys1.getPrivate();

         KeyPair keys2 = keygen.generateKeyPair();
         PublicKey pubkey2 = keys2.getPublic();
         PrivateKey privkey2 = keys2.getPrivate();

         Signature signalg = Signature.getInstance("DSA");
         signalg.initSign(privkey1);
         String message
            = "Pay authors a bonus of $20,000.";
         signalg.update(message.getBytes());
         byte[] signature = signalg.sign();
         Signature verifyalg = Signature.getInstance("DSA");
         verifyalg.initVerify(pubkey1);
         verifyalg.update(message.getBytes());
         if (!verifyalg.verify(signature))
            System.out.print("not ");
         System.out.println("signed with private key 1");

         verifyalg.initVerify(pubkey2);
         verifyalg.update(message.getBytes());
         if (!verifyalg.verify(signature))
            System.out.print("not ");
         System.out.println("signed with private key 2");
      }
      catch(Exception e)
      {  System.out.println("Error " + e);
      }
   }
}
```

java.security.KeyPairGenerator

- `static KeyPairGenerator getInstance(String algorithm)`
  returns a `KeyPairGenerator` object that implements the specified algorithm. Throws a `NoSuchAlgorithmException` if the algorithm is not provided.

  Parameters: `algorithm` the name of the algorithm, such as `"DSA"`

- `void initialize(int strength, SecureRandom random)`

  Parameters: `strength` an algorithm-specific measurements, typically, the number of bits of one of the algorithm parameters

  `random` the source of random bits for generating keys

- `KeyPair generateKeyPair()`
  generates a new key pair.

java.security.KeyPair

- `PrivateKey getPrivate()`
  returns the private key from the key pair.
- `PublicKey getPublic()`
  returns the public key from the key pair.

java.security.Signature

- `static Signature getInstance(String algorithm)`
  returns a `Signature` object that implements the specified algorithm. Throws a `NoSuchAlgorithmException` if the algorithm is not provided.

  Parameters: `algorithm` the name of the algorithm, such as `"DSA"`

- `void initSign(PrivateKey privateKey)`
  initializes this object for signing. Throws an `InvalidKeyException` if the key type does not match the algorithm type.

  Parameters: `privateKey` the private key of the identity whose signature is being computed

- `void update(byte input)`
- `void update(byte[] input)`
- `void update(byte[] input, int offset, int len)`
  update the message buffer, using the specified bytes.
- `byte[] sign()`
  completes the signature computation and returns the computed signature.

- `void initVerify(PublicKey publicKey)`
  initializes this object for verification. Throws an `InvalidKeyException` if the key type does not match the algorithm type.

  Parameters: `publicKey` the public key of the identity to be verified

- `boolean verify(byte[] signature)`
  checks whether the signature is valid.

Authentication

Suppose you get a message from your friend, signed by your friend with his private key, using the method we just showed you. You may already have his public key, or you can easily get it by asking him for a copy or by getting it from your friend's web page. Then, you can verify that the message was in fact authored by your friend and has not been tampered with. Now, suppose you get a message from a stranger who claims to represent a famous software company, urging you to run the program that is attached to the message. The stranger even sends you a copy of his public key so you can verify that he authored the message. You check that the signature is valid. This proves that the message was signed with the matching private key and that it has not been corrupted.

Be careful: *you still have no idea who wrote the message.* Anyone could have generated a pair of public and private keys, signed the message with the private key, and sent the signed message and the public key to you. The problem of determining the identity of the sender is called the *authentication problem.*

The usual way to solve the authentication problem is simple. Suppose the stranger and you have a common acquaintance whom you both trust. Suppose the stranger meets your acquaintance in person and hands over a disk with the public key. Your acquaintance later meets you, assures you that he met the stranger and that the stranger indeed works for the famous software company, and then gives you the disk (see Figure 9–14). That way, your acquaintance vouches for the authenticity of the stranger.

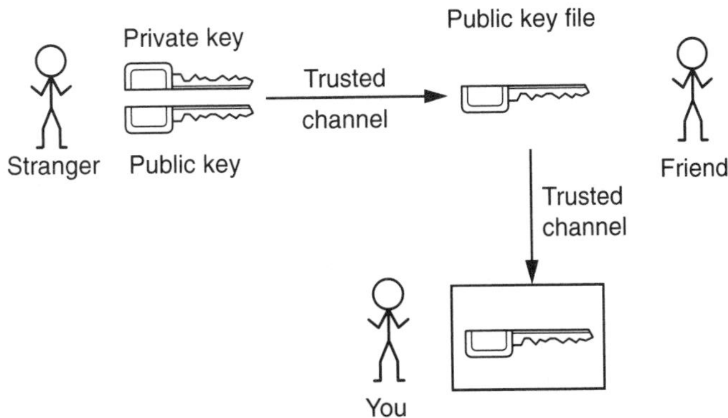

Figure 9–14 : Authentication through a trusted intermediary

In fact, your acquaintance does not actually need to meet you. Instead, he can apply his private signature to the stranger's public key file (see Figure 9–15).

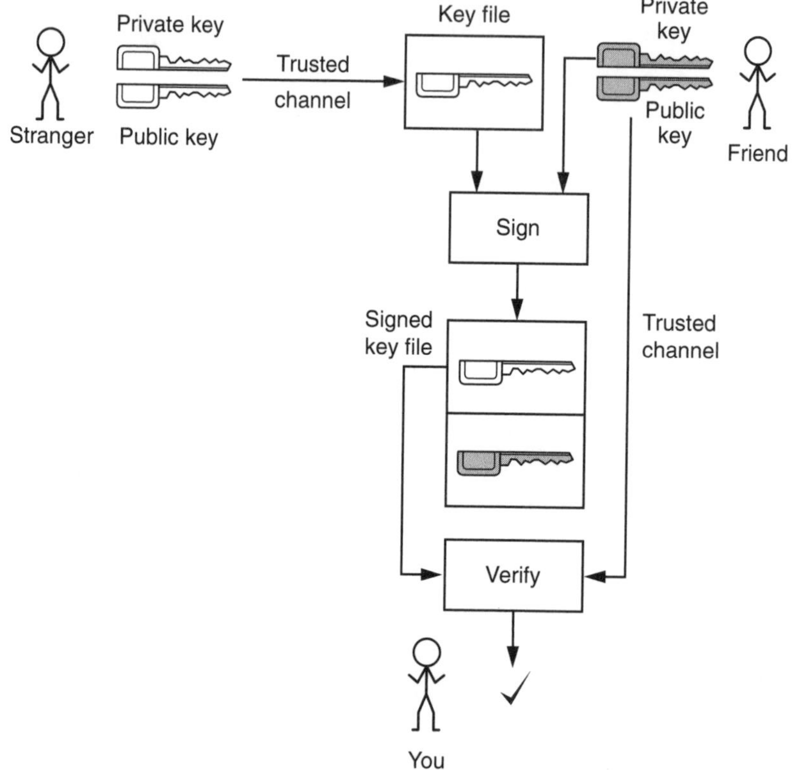

Figure 9–15: Authentication through a trusted intermediary's signature

When you get the public key file, you verify the signature of your acquaintance, and because you trust him, you are confident that he did check the stranger's credentials before applying his signature.

However, you may not have a common acquaintance. Some trust models assume that there is always a "chain of trust"—a chain of mutual acquaintances—so that you trust every member of that chain. In practice, of course, that isn't always true. You may trust your acquaintance, Alice, and you know that Alice trusts Bob, but you don't know Bob and aren't sure that you trust him. Other trust models assume that there is a benevolent big brother in whom we all trust. Some companies are working to become such big brothers, such as Verisign, Inc. (`www.verisign.com`), and, yes, the United States Postal Service.

You will often encounter digital signatures that are signed by one or more entities who will vouch for the authenticity, and you will need to evaluate to what degree you trust the authenticators. You might place a great deal of trust in Verisign, perhaps because you read their ponderous certification practice statements, or because you heard that they require multiple people with black attache cases to come together into a secure chamber whenever new master keys are to be minted.

However, you should have realistic expectations about what is actually being authenticated. Stratton Sclavos, the CEO of Verisign, does not personally meet every individual who has a public key that is authenticated by Verisign. More likely, that individual just filled out a form on a web page (see Figure 9–16).

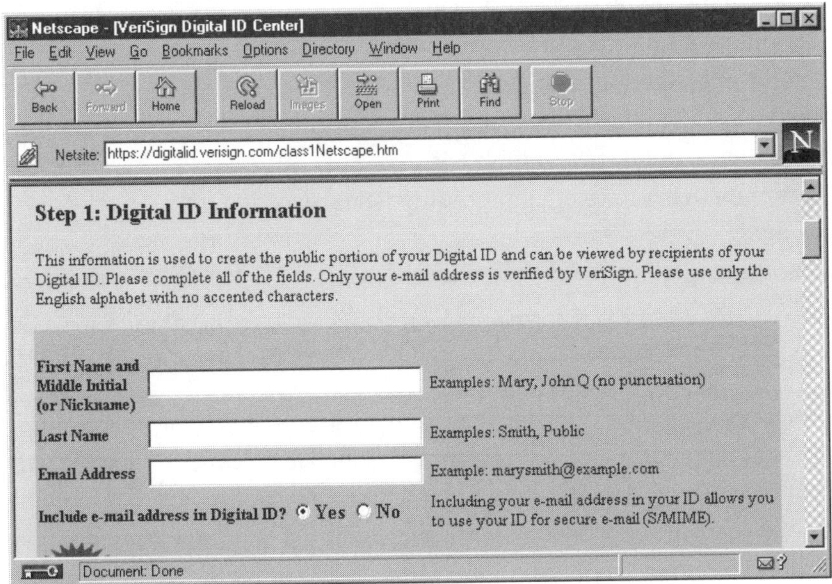

Figure 9–16: Request for a digital ID

Such a form asks the requestor to specify the name, organization, country, and e-mail address. Typically, the key (or instructions on how to fetch the key) is mailed to that e-mail address. Thus, you can be reasonably assured that the e-mail address is genuine, but the requestor could have filled in *any* name and organization. With a "class 1" ID from Verisign, that information is not verified. There are more stringent classes of IDs. For example, with a "class 3" ID, Verisign will require an individual requestor to appear before a notary public, and it will check the financial rating of a corporate requestor. Other authenticators will have different procedures. Thus, when you receive an authenticated message, it is important that you understand what, in fact, is being authenticated.

The X.509 Certificate Format

One of the most common formats for signed certificates is the X.509 format. X.509 certificates are widely used by Verisign, Microsoft, Netscape, and many other companies, for signing e-mail messages, authenticating program code, and certifying many other kinds of data. The X.509 standard is part of the X.500 series of recommendations for a directory service by the international telephone standards body, the CCITT. In its simplest form, an X.509 certificate contains the following data:

- Version of certificate format;
- Serial number of certificate;
- Signature algorithm identifier (algorithm ID + parameters of the algorithm used to sign the certificate);
- Name of the signer of the certificate;
- Period of validity (begin/end date);
- Name of the identity being certified;
- Public key of identity being certified (algorithm ID + parameters of the algorithm + public key value);
- Signature (hash code of all preceding fields, encoded with private key of signer).

Thus, the signer guarantees that a certain identity has a particular public key.

Extensions to the basic X.509 format make it possible for the certificates to contain additional information. For more information on the structure of X.509 certificates, see `http://www.ietf.cnri.reston.va.us/ids.by.wg/X.509.html`. Peter Gutmann's web site (`http://www.cs.auckland.ac.nz/~pgut001/pubs/x509guide.txt`) contains an entertaining and informative description of the many discrepancies in the X.509 format, as it is implemented by different vendors.

The precise structure of X.509 certificates is described in a formal notation, called "abstract syntax notation #1" or ASN.1. Figure 9–17 shows the ASN.1 definition of version 3 of the X.509 format. The exact syntax is not important for us, but, as you can see, ASN.1 gives a precise definition of the structure of a certificate file. The *basic encoding rules*, or BER, describe precisely how to save this structure in a binary file. That is, BER describes how to encode integers, character strings, bit strings, and constructs such as `SEQUENCE`, `CHOICE`, and `OPTIONAL`.

Actually, the BER rules are not unique; there are several ways of specifying some elements. The *distinguished encoding rules* (DER) remove these ambiguities. For a readable description of the BER encoding format, we recommend *A Layman's Guide to a Subset of ASN.1, BER, and DER* by Burton S. Kaliski, Jr., available from `http://www.rsa.com/rsalabs/pubs/PKCS/`. You can find the source code for a useful program for dumping BER encoded files at `http://www.cs.auckland.ac.nz/~pgut001/dumpasn1.c`.

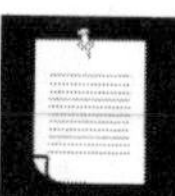

NOTE: You can find more information on ASN.1 in *ASN.1—Communication Between Heterogeneous Systems* by Olivier Dubuisson (Academic Press 2000) and *ASN.1 Complete* by John Larmouth (`www.nokalva.com/asn1/larmouth.html`).

```
Certificate  ::=  SEQUENCE  {
      tbsCertificate          TBSCertificate,
      signatureAlgorithm      AlgorithmIdentifier,
      signature               BIT STRING  }

   TBSCertificate  ::=  SEQUENCE  {
      version         [0]   EXPLICIT Version DEFAULT v1,
      serialNumber          CertificateSerialNumber,
      signature             AlgorithmIdentifier,
      issuer                Name,
      validity              Validity,
      subject               Name,
      subjectPublicKeyInfo  SubjectPublicKeyInfo,
      issuerUniqueID  [1]  IMPLICIT UniqueIdentifier OPTIONAL,
                            -- If present, version must be v2
                                or v3
      subjectUniqueID [2]  IMPLICIT UniqueIdentifier OPTIONAL,
                           -- If present, version must be v2
                                or v3
      extensions      [3]  EXPLICIT Extensions OPTIONAL
                          -- If present, version must be v3
      }

   Version  ::=  INTEGER  {  v1(0), v2(1), v3(2)  }

   CertificateSerialNumber  ::=  INTEGER

   Validity ::= SEQUENCE {
      notBefore      CertificateValidityDate,
      notAfter       CertificateValidityDate }

   CertificateValidityDate ::= CHOICE {
      utcTime        UTCTime,
      generalTime    GeneralizedTime }

   UniqueIdentifier  ::=  BIT STRING

   SubjectPublicKeyInfo  ::=  SEQUENCE  {
      algorithm            AlgorithmIdentifier,
      subjectPublicKey     BIT STRING  }

   Extensions  ::=  SEQUENCE OF Extension

   Extension  ::=  SEQUENCE  {
      extnID      OBJECT IDENTIFIER,
      critical    BOOLEAN DEFAULT FALSE,
      extnValue   OCTET STRING  }
```

Figure 9-17: ASN.1 definition of X.509v3

Generating Certificates

The JDK comes with the `keytool` program, which is a command-line tool to generate and manage a set of certificates. We expect that ultimately the functionality of this tool will be embedded in other, more user-friendly programs. But right now, we will use `keytool` to show how Alice can sign a document and send it to Bob, and how Bob can verify that the document really was signed by Alice and not an impostor. We do not discuss all of the `keytool` features—see the JDK documentation for complete information.

The `keytool` program manages *key stores,* databases of certificates, and private keys. Each entry in the key store has an *alias.* Here is how Alice creates a keystore `alice.store` and generates a key pair with alias `alice`.

```
keytool -genkey -keystore alice.store -alias alice
```

When creating or opening a keystore, you will be prompted for a keystore password. For this example, just use `password`. If you were to use the `keytool`-generated keystore for any serious purpose, you would need to choose a good password and safeguard this file —it contains private signature keys.

When generating a key, you will be prompted for the following information:

```
Enter keystore password:  password
What is your first and last name?
  [Unknown]:  Alice Lee
What is the name of your organizational unit?
  [Unknown]:  Engineering Department
What is the name of your organization?
  [Unknown]:  ACME Software
What is the name of your City or Locality?
  [Unknown]:  Cupertino
What is the name of your State or Province?
  [Unknown]:  CA
What is the two-letter country code for this unit?
  [Unknown]:  US
Is <CN=Alice Lee, OU=Engineering Department, O=ACME Software,
L=Cupertino, ST=CA, C=US> correct?
  [no]:  Y
```

The `keytool` uses X.500 distinguished names, with components Common Name (CN), Organizational Unit (OU), Organization (O), Location (L), State (ST), and Country (C) to identify key owners and certificate issuers.

Finally, you need to specify a key password, or press ENTER to use the key store password as the key password.

Suppose Alice wants to give her public key to Bob. She needs to export a certificate file:

```
keytool -export -keystore alice.store -alias alice -file alice.cert
```

Now Alice can send the certificate to Bob. When Bob receives the certificate, he can print it:

```
keytool -printcert -file alice.cert
```

The printout looks like this:

```
Owner: CN=Alice Lee, OU=Engineering Department, O=ACME Software,
L=Cupertino, ST=CA, C=US

Issuer: CN=Alice Lee, OU=Engineering Department, O=ACME Software,
L=Cupertino, ST=CA, C=US

Serial number: 38107867

Valid from: Fri Oct 22 07:44:55 PDT 1999 until: Thu Jan 20
06:44:55 PST 2000

Certificate fingerprints:

MD5: 5D:00:0F:95:01:30:B4:FE:18:CE:9A:35:0F:C9:90:DD

SHA1:F8:C2:7C:E2:0B:1F:69:E2:6C:31:9A:F6:35:FA:A3:4F:83:81:6A:6A
```

This certificate is *self-signed*. Therefore, Bob cannot use another trusted certificate to check that this certificate is valid. Instead, he can call up Alice and have her read the certificate fingerprint over the phone.

Some certificate issuers publish certificate fingerprints on their web sites. For example, the JRE includes a key store `cacerts` in the `jre/lib/security` directory. It contains certificates from Thawte and VeriSign. To list the contents of a keystore, use the `-list` option:

```
keytool -list -keystore jre/lib/security/cacerts
```

The password for this keystore is `changeit`. One of the certificates in this keystore is

```
thawtepremiumserverca, Fri Feb 12 12:15:26 PST 1999, trustedCertEntry,
Certificate fingerprint (MD5):
06:9F:69:79:16:66:90:02:1B:8C:8C:A2:C3:07:6F:3A
```

You can check that your certificate is valid by visiting the Thawte web site at `http://www.thawte.com/certs/trustmap.html`.

NOTE: Of course, this check requires that you trust that your copy of `keytool` (and the JRE code in `rt.jar` that the `keytool` program calls) has not been tampered with. If you are paranoid, you may want to copy the file to another machine (using a trusted file copy program) and check it on that machine with a freshly downloaded copy of the JDK.

Once Bob trusts the certificate, he can import it into his keystore.

```
keytool -import -keystore bob.store -alias alice -file alice.cert
```

CAUTION: Never import a certificate into a keystore that you don't fully trust. Once a certificate is added to the keystore, any program that uses the keystore assumes that the certificate can be used to verify signatures.

Now Alice can start sending signed documents to Bob. The `jarsigner` tool signs and verifies JAR files. Alice simply adds the document to be signed into a JAR file.

```
jar cvf document.jar document.txt
```

Then she uses the `jarsigner` tool to add the signature to the file. She needs to specify the keystore, the JAR file and the alias of the key to use.

```
jarsigner -keystore alice.store document.jar alice
```

When Bob receives the file, he uses the `-verify` option of the `jarsigner` program.

```
jarsigner -verify -keystore bob.store document.jar
```

Bob does not need to specify the key alias. The `jarsigner` program finds the X.500 name of the key owner in the digital signature and looks for matching certificates in the keystore.

If the JAR file is not corrupted and the signature matches, then the `jarsigner` program prints

```
jar verified.
```

Otherwise, the program displays an error message.

Signing Certificates

In the preceding section, you saw how to use a self-signed certificate to distribute a public key to another party. However, the recipient of the certificate needed to ensure that the certificate was valid by verifying the fingerprint with the issuer. More commonly, a certificate is signed by a trusted intermediary.

The JDK does not contain tools for certificate signing. In this section, you will see how to write a program that signs a certificate with a private key from a keystore. This program is useful in its own right, and it shows you how to write programs that access to the contents of certificates and keystores.

Before looking inside the program code, let's see how to put it to use. Suppose Alice wants to send her colleague Cindy a signed message. But Cindy doesn't want to call up everyone who sends her a signature file to verify the signature fingerprint. There needs to be an entity that Cindy trusts to verify signatures. In this example, we will suppose that Cindy trusts the Information Resources Department at ACME Software

to perform this service. To simulate this process, you'll need to create an added keystore `acmesoft.store`. Generate a key and export the self-signed certificate.

```
keytool -genkey -keystore acmesoft.store -alias acmeroot
keytool -export -alias acmeroot -keystore acmesoft.store
   -file acmeroot.cert
```

Then add it to Cindy's key store.

```
keytool -import -alias acmeroot -keystore cindy.store
   -file acmeroot.cert
```

Cindy still needs to verify the fingerprint of that *root certificate,* but from now on, she can simply accept all certificates that are signed by it.

For Alice to send messages to Cindy and to everyone else at ACME Software, she needs to bring her certificate to the Information Resources Department and have it signed. However, the `keytool` program in the JDK does not have this functionality. That is where the certificate signer program in Example 9–10 comes in. The program reads a certificate file and signs it with a private key in a key store. An authorized staff member at ACME Software would verify Alice's identity and generate a signed certificate as follows:

```
java CertificateSigner -keystore acmesoft.store -alias acmeroot
   -infile alice.cert -outfile alice_signedby_acmeroot.cert
```

The certificate signer program must have access to the ACME Software keystore, and the staff member must know the keystore password. Clearly this is a sensitive operation.

Now Alice gives the file `alice_signedby_acmeroot.cert` file to Cindy and to anyone else in ACME Software. Alternatively, ACME Software can simply store the file in a company directory. Remember, this file contains Alice's public key and an assertion by ACME Software that this key really belongs to Alice.

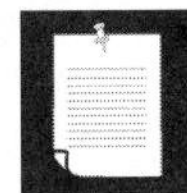

NOTE: The `keytool` program supports a different mechanism for key signing. The `-certreq` option produces a certificate request in a standard format that can be processed by certificate authorities such as Thawte and Verisign or local authorities running software such as the Netscape certificate server.

When Cindy imports the signed certificate into her key store, the key store verifies that the key was signed by a trusted root key that is already present in the key store and she is not asked to verify the certificate fingerprint.

CAUTION: This scenario is for illustrative purposes only. The `keytool` is really not suitable as a tool for end-users. The `keytool` silently accepts certificates that are signed by a party that it already trusts, and it asks the user to confirm those that it cannot verify. It never rejects a certificate. It is all too easy for a confused user to accept an invalid certificate.

Once Cindy has added the root certificate and the certificates of the people who regularly send her documents, she never has to worry about the keystore again.

Now let us look at the source code of Example 9–10. First, we load the keystore. The `getInstance` factory method of the `KeyStore` class creates a keystore instance of the appropriate type. The `keytool`-generated keystore has a type of `"JKS"`. The provider of this keystore type is `"SUN"`.

```
KeyStore store = KeyStore.getInstance("JKS", "SUN");
```

Now, we need to load the keystore data. The `load` method requires an input stream and a password. Note that the password is specified as a `char[]` array, not a string. The JVM can keep strings around for a long time before they are garbage collected. Hackers could potentially find these strings, for example, by examining the contents of swap files. But character arrays can be cleared immediately after they are used.

Here is the code for loading the keystore. Note that we fill the password with spaces immediately after use.

```
InputStream in = . . .;
char[] password = . . .;
store.load(in, password);
Arrays.fill(password, ' ');
in.close();
```

Next, we use the `getKey` method to retrieve the private key for signing. The `getKey` method requires the key alias and key password. Its return type is `Key`, and we cast it to `PrivateKey` since we know that the retrieved key is a private key.

```
char[] keyPassword = . . .;
PrivateKey issuerPrivateKey
   = (PrivateKey)store.getKey(alias; keyPassword);
Arrays.fill(keyPassword, ' ');
```

Now we are ready to read in the certificate that needs to be signed. The `CertificateFactory` class can read in certificates from an input stream. First, you need to get a factory of the appropriate type:

```
CertificateFactory factory
  = CertificateFactory.getInstance("X.509");
```

Then, call the `generateCertificate` method with an input stream:

```
in = new FileInputStream(inname);
X509Certificate inCert
   = (X509Certificate)factory.generateCertificate(in);
in.close();
```

The return type of the `generateCertificate` method is the abstract `Certificate` class that is the superclass of concrete classes such as `X509Certificate`. Since we know that the input file actually contains an `X509Certificate`, we use a cast.

CAUTION: There are two types called `Certificate`: a deprecated interface in the `java.security` package, and an abstract class in the `java.security.cert` package, which is the class that you want to use. If you import both the `java.security` and the `java.security.cert` package into your program, you need to resolve the ambiguity and explicitly reference the `java.security.cert.Certificate` class.

The purpose of this program is to sign the bytes in the certificate. You retrieve the bytes with the `getTBSCertificate` method:

```
byte[] inCertBytes = inCert.getTBSCertificate();
```

Next, we need the distinguished name of the issuer, which we will need to insert into the signed certificate. The name is stored in the issuer certificate in the keystore. You fetch certificates from the keystore with the `getCertificate` method. Since certificates are public information, you only supply the alias, not a password.

```
X509Certificate issuerCert
   = (X509Certificate)store.getCertificate(alias);
```

The `getCertificate` method has return type `Certificate`, but once again we know that the returned value is actually an `X509Certificate`. We obtain the issuer identity from the certificate by calling the `getSubjectDN` method. That method returns an object of some type that implements the `Principal` interface. Conceptually, a *principal* is a real-world entity such as a person, organization, or company.

```
Principal issuer = issuerCert.getSubjectDN();
```

We also retrieve the name of the signing algorithm.

```
String issuerSigAlg = issuerCert.getSigAlgName()
```

Now we must leave the realm of the standard security library. The standard library contains no methods for generating new certificates. Libraries for certificate generation are available from third-party vendors such as RSA Inc. However, we will use the classes in the `sun.security.x509` package. The usual caveats apply. This package might not be supplied by third-party vendors of Java technology, and Sun Microsystems might change the behavior at any time.

The following code segment carries out these steps:

- Generates a certificate information object from the bytes in the certificate that is to be signed;
- Sets the issuer name;
- Creates the certificate and signs it with the issuer's private key;
- Saves the signed certificate to a file

```
X509CertInfo info = new X509CertInfo(inCertBytes);
info.set(X509CertInfo.ISSUER,
```

```
      new CertificateIssuerName((X500Name)issuer));
   X509CertImpl outCert = new X509CertImpl(info);
   outCert.sign(issuerPrivateKey, issuerSigAlg);
   outCert.derEncode(out);
```

We will not discuss the use of these classes in detail since we do not recommend the use of Sun libraries for production code. A future version of the JDK may contain classes for certificate generation. In the meantime, you may want to rely on third-party libraries or simply use existing certificate generation software.

Example 9–10: CertificateSigner.java

```
import java.io.*;
import java.security.*;
import java.security.cert.*;
import java.util.*;

import sun.security.x509.X509CertInfo;
import sun.security.x509.X509CertImpl;
import sun.security.x509.X500Name;
import sun.security.x509.CertificateIssuerName;

public class CertificateSigner
{  public static void main(String[] args)
   {  String ksname = null; // the keystore name
      String alias = null; // the private key alias
      String inname = null; // the input file name
      String outname = null; // the output file name
      for (int i = 0; i < args.length; i += 2)
      {  if (args[i].equals("-keystore"))
            ksname = args[i + 1];
         else if (args[i].equals("-alias"))
            alias = args[i + 1];
         else if (args[i].equals("-infile"))
            inname = args[i + 1];
         else if (args[i].equals("-outfile"))
            outname = args[i + 1];
         else usage();
      }

      if (ksname == null || alias == null ||
         inname == null || outname == null) usage();

      try
      {  PushbackReader console = new PushbackReader(new
            InputStreamReader(System.in));

         KeyStore store = KeyStore.getInstance("JKS", "SUN");
         InputStream in = new FileInputStream(ksname);
         char[] password
            = readPassword(console, "Keystore password");
```

```
        store.load(in, password);
        Arrays.fill(password, ' ');
        in.close();

        char[] keyPassword
           = readPassword(console, "Key password for " + alias);
        PrivateKey issuerPrivateKey
           = (PrivateKey)store.getKey(alias, keyPassword);
        Arrays.fill(keyPassword, ' ');

        if (issuerPrivateKey == null)
           error("No such private key");

        in = new FileInputStream(inname);

        CertificateFactory factory
           = CertificateFactory.getInstance("X.509");


        X509Certificate inCert
           = (X509Certificate)factory.generateCertificate(in);
        in.close();
        byte[] inCertBytes = inCert.getTBSCertificate();

        X509Certificate issuerCert
           = (X509Certificate)store.getCertificate(alias);
        Principal issuer = issuerCert.getSubjectDN();
        String issuerSigAlg = issuerCert.getSigAlgName();

        FileOutputStream out = new FileOutputStream(outname);

        X509CertInfo info = new X509CertInfo(inCertBytes);
        info.set(X509CertInfo.ISSUER,
           new CertificateIssuerName((X500Name)issuer));

        X509CertImpl outCert = new X509CertImpl(info);
        outCert.sign(issuerPrivateKey, issuerSigAlg);
        outCert.derEncode(out);

        out.close();
     }
     catch (Exception exception)
     {  System.out.println(exception);
     }
  }

  public static char[] readPassword(PushbackReader in,
     String prompt) throws IOException
  {  System.out.print(prompt + ": ");
     System.out.flush();
     final int MAX_PASSWORD_LENGTH = 100;
     int length = 0;
```

```
      char[] buffer = new char[MAX_PASSWORD_LENGTH];

      while (true)
      {  int ch = in.read();
         if (ch == '\r' || ch == '\n' || ch == -1
            || length == MAX_PASSWORD_LENGTH)
         {  if (ch == '\r') // handle DOS "\r\n" line ends
            {  ch = in.read();
               if (ch != '\n' && ch != -1) in.unread(ch);
            }
            char[] password = new char[length];
            System.arraycopy(buffer, 0, password, 0, length);
            Arrays.fill(buffer, ' ');
            return password;
         }
         else
         {  buffer[length] = (char)ch;
            length++;
         }
      }
   }

   public static void error(String message)
   {  System.out.println(message);
      System.exit(1);
   }

   public static void usage()
   {  System.out.println("Usage: java CertificateSigner"
         + " -keystore keyStore -alias issuerKeyAlias"
         + " -infile inputFile -outfile outputFile");
      System.exit(1);
   }
}
```

`java.security.Principal`

- `String getName()`
  returns the name of this principal.

`java.security.KeyStore`

- `static getInstance(String type)`
- `static getInstance(String type, String provider)`
  These messages construct a keystore object of the given type. If no provider is specified, the default provider is used. To work with keystores generated by the `keytool`, specify `"JKS"` as the type and `"SUN"` as the provider.
- `void load(InputStream in, char[] password)`
  loads a keystore from a stream. The password is kept in a character array so that it does not become part of the JVM string pool.

- `Key getKey(String alias, char[] password)`
  returns a private key with the given alias that is stored in this keystore.
- `Certificate getCertificate(String alias)`
  returns a certificate for a public key with the given alias that is stored in this keystore.

`java.security.cert.CertificateFactory`

- `CertificateFactory getInstance(String type)`
  creates a certificate factory for the given type. The type is a certificate type such as `"X509"`.
- `Certificate generateCertificate(InputStream in)`
  loads a certificate from an input stream.

`java.security.cert.Certificate`

- `PublicKey getPublicKey()`
  returns the public key that is being guaranteed by this certificate.
- `byte[] getEncoded()`
  gets the encoded form of this certificate.
- `String getType()`
  returns the type of this certificate, such as `"X509"`.

`java.security.cert.X509Certificate`

- `Principal getSubjectDN()`
- `Principal getIssuerDN()`
  get the owner (or subject) and issuer distinguished names from the certificate.
- `Date getNotBefore()`
- `Date getNotAfter()`
  get the validity period start and end dates of the certificate.
- `BigInteger getSerialNumber()`
  gets the serial number value from the certificate.
- `String getSigAlgName()`
- `byte[] getSignature()`
  get the signature algorithm name and the owner signature from the certificate.
- `byte[] getTBSCertificate()`
  gets the DER-encoded certificate information that needs to be signed by the certificate issuer.

Code Signing

One of the most important uses of authentication technology is signing executable programs. If you download a program, you are naturally concerned about damage that a program can do. For example, the program could have been infected by a virus. If you know where the code comes from *and* that it has not been tampered with since it left its origin, then your comfort level will be a lot higher than without this knowledge. In fact, if the program was also written in the Java programming language, you can then use this information to make a rational decision about what privileges you will allow that program to have. You might just want it to run in a sandbox as a regular applet, or you might want to grant it a different set of rights and restrictions. For example, if you download a word processing program, you might want to grant it access to your printer and to files in a certain subdirectory. But you may not want to give it the right to make network connections, so that the program can't try to send your files to a third party without your knowledge.

You now know how to implement this sophisticated scheme.

- First, use authentication to verify where the code came from.
- Then, run the code with a security policy that enforces the permissions that you want to grant the program, depending on its origin.

Signing JAR Files

At this point, code signing is still somewhat platform dependent. If you use JDK 1.1 applets with Netscape or Internet Explorer, you need to use the Netscape or Microsoft tools to sign your applets. See `www.securingjava.com/appdx-c/` or `www.suitable.com/Doc_CodeSigning.shtml` for more information on this topic.

In this section, we show you how to sign applets for use with the Java Plug-in. There are two scenarios:

1. Signed intranet applets
2. Signed internet applets

In the first scenario, a system administrator installs certificates and policy files on local machines. Whenever the Java Plug-in loads a signed applet, it consults the keystore for signatures and the policy file for the applet permissions. Installing the certificates and policies is straightforward and can be done once per desktop. End users can then run signed corporate applets outside the sandbox. Whenever a new applet is created or an existing applet is updated, it must be signed and deployed on the web server. However, no desktops need to be touched as the applets evolve. We think this is a reasonable scenario that can be an attractive alternative over deploying corporate applications on every desktop.

In the second scenario, software vendors obtain certificates that are signed by certificate authorities such as Thawte and Verisign. When an end user visits a web site that contains a signed applet, a dialog pops up that identifies the software

vendor and gives the end user two choices: to run the applet with full privileges, or to confine it to the sandbox. We discuss this scenario in detail later.

For the remainder of this section, we describe how you can build policy files that grant specific permissions to applets from known sources. Building and deploying these policy files is not for casual end users. However, system administrators can carry out these tasks in preparation for distributing intranet applets.

Suppose ACME Software wants its users to run certain applets that require local file access. Since these applets cannot run inside the sandbox, ACME Software needs to install policy files on employee machines. As you saw earlier in this chapter, ACME could identify the applets by their code base. But that means that ACME would need to update the policy files each time the applet code is moved to a different web server. Instead, ACME decides to *sign* the JAR files that contain the applet code.

To make a signed JAR file, first add your class files to a JAR file.

```
jar cvf MyApplet.jar *.class
```

Then run the `jarsigner` tool and specify the JAR file and the alias of the private key:

```
jarsigner -keystore acmesoft.store MyApplet.jar acmeroot
```

In this example, the JAR file is signed with the self-signed root key. In practice, it would be more likely that ACME issues its programmers individual keys that are themselves signed by the root key.

Of course, the keystore containing the root key must be kept at a safe place. Let's make a second keystore `certs.store` for certificates and add the `acmeroot` certificate into it.

```
keytool -export -keystore acmesoft.store -alias acmeroot -file
   acmeroot.cert
keytool -import -keystore certs.store -alias acmeroot -file
   acmeroot.cert
```

Next, you need to create a policy file that gives the permission for all applets that are signed with signatures in that keystore.

You need to include the location of your keystore in the policy file. Add a line

```
keystore "keystoreURL", "keystoreType";
```

to the top of the policy file. The type is `JKS` if the keystore was generated by `keytool`.

```
keystore "file:certs.store", "JKS";
```

Then add `signedBy "alias"` to one or more `grant` clauses in the policy file. For example,

```
grant signedBy "acmeroot"
{  permission java.io.FilePermission "<<ALL FILES>>", "read";
   . . .
};
```

Any signed code that can be verified with the public key associated with the alias is now granted these permissions.

You can try this out with the applet in Example 9–11. The applet tries to read from a local file (see Figure 9–18). The default security policy lets the applet read files from its code base and any subdirectories. Use `appletviewer` to run the applet and verify that you can view files from the code base directory, but not from other directories.

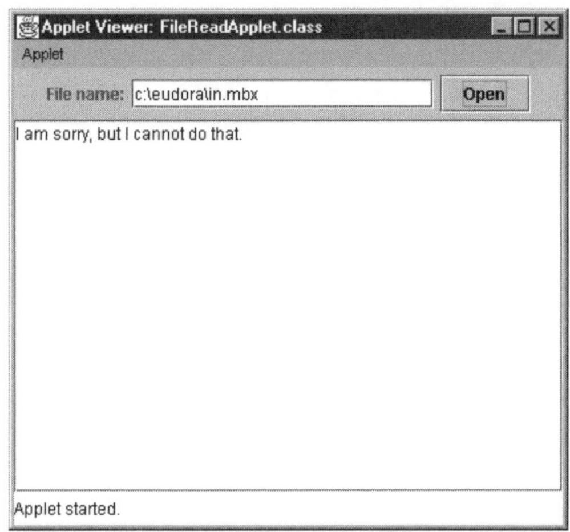

Figure 9–18: The `FileReadApplet` program

Now place the applet in a JAR file and sign it with the `acmeroot` key. Then create a policy file `applets.policy` with the contents:

```
keystore "file:certs.store", "JKS";
grant signedBy "acmeroot"
{  permission java.io.FilePermission "<<ALL FILES>>", "read";
};
```

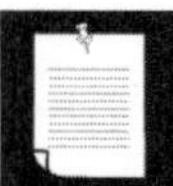

NOTE: You can also use the `policytool` to create the policy file.

For this test, make sure that the keystore, policy file, and JAR file are all in the same directory.

Finally, tell the appletviewer to use the policy file:

```
appletviewer -J-Djava.security.policy=applets.policy
   FileReadApplet.html
```

Now the applet can read all files.

This shows that the signing mechanism works. To actually deploy this mechanism, you need to find appropriate places for the security files. We take up that topic in the next section.

As a final test, you may want to test your applet inside the Java Plug-in. Then, you need to modify the file `java.security` in the `jre/lib/security` directory. Locate the section

```
# The default is to have a single system wide policy file,
# and a policy file in the user's home directory.
policy.url.1=file:${java.home}/lib/security/java.policy
policy.url.2=file:${user.home}/.java.policy
```

Add a line with a file URL for the policy file, such as

```
policy.url.3=file:///home/test/applet.policy
```

CAUTION: Be sure to modify the correct `java.security` file. The plug-in uses the virtual machine in the JRE, *not* the one belonging to the JDK. For example, under Windows, the JRE files are located inside the `\Program Files\JavaSoft` directory.

If you use the plug-in in Netscape 4 or Internet Explorer, you also need to change the HTML file to load the plug-in with an `EMBED` or `OBJECT` tag. Opera and Netscape 5 automatically load the plug-in when you use the `APPLET` tag. (See Chapter 10 of Volume 1 for more information on how to load the plug-in.)

CAUTION: If you test your applet with the Java Plug-in instead of the appletviewer, then you need to be aware that the plug-in only reads the policy file *once*, when it is loaded for the first time. If you made a mistake in your policy file or keystore, then you need to close down the browser, fix your mistake, and restart the browser. Simply reloading the web page containing the applet does *not* work.

Example 9–11: FileReadApplet.java

```
import java.awt.*;
import java.awt.event.*;
import java.io.*;
import java.util.*;
import javax.swing.*;

public class FileReadApplet extends JApplet
{  public FileReadApplet()
   {  fileNameField = new JTextField(20);
      JPanel panel = new JPanel();
      panel.add(new JLabel("File name:"));
      panel.add(fileNameField);
      JButton openButton = new JButton("Open");
      panel.add(openButton);
      openButton.addActionListener(
         new ActionListener()
         {  public void actionPerformed(ActionEvent event)
            {  loadFile(fileNameField.getText());
            }
```

```
         });

      Container contentPane = getContentPane();
      contentPane.add(panel, "North");

      fileText = new JTextArea();
      contentPane.add(new JScrollPane(fileText), "Center");
   }

   public void loadFile(String filename)
   {  try
      {  fileText.setText("");
         BufferedReader in
            = new BufferedReader(new FileReader(filename));
         String s;
         while ((s = in.readLine()) != null)
         fileText.append(s + "\n");
         in.close();
      }
      catch (IOException e)
      {  fileText.append(e + "\n");
      }
      catch (SecurityException e)
      {  fileText.append("I am sorry, but I cannot do that.");
      }
   }

   private JTextField fileNameField;
   private JTextArea fileText;
}
```

Deployment Tips

The first decision you need to make is where to deploy policy files. There are two default locations:

- `java.policy` in the `${java.home}/lib/security` directory
- `.java.policy` in the `${user.home}` directory

We don't think either is a good choice. Instead, we recommend that you edit the `java.security` file in the `${java.home}/jre/lib/security` directory and add a line to include a third policy file, such as:

```
policy.url.3=http://intranet.acmesoft.com/admin/applet.policy
```

Then, you can set up a policy file on an intranet server. That is an advantage since you only need to manage a file in a single location.

Similarly, inside the policy file, you can specify the keystore location with an URL:

```
keystore "http://intranet.acmesoft.com/admin/certs.store", "JKS";
```

Add the certificate for the public key for corporate intranet applications to that keystore.

NOTE: You could add certificates to the `cacerts` keystore in the JRE. But then you would need to keep updating the JRE on every desktop when you change the keystore. We recommend that you don't touch to the `cacerts` file.

Finally, sign the JAR files that contain the code for your intranet applications with the matching private key.

We suggest that you don't simply grant `AllPermission` to intranet applets but that you augment the "sandbox" rights by specific privileges, such as accessing all directories inside a particular subdirectory, printing, network access within the intranet, and so on.

The deployment sounds a bit complex, but it is actually quite manageable. You need to minimally customize the Java Plug-in configuration on each desktop. The rest can be managed remotely. There are two benefits. At no time do you place a burden on your users to make solitary security decisions. And you have fine-grained control over the privileges of the remote code that your users execute.

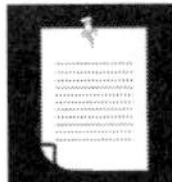

NOTE: Because Java platform security combines authentication and control over code permissions, it offers a far more comprehensive security model than does Microsoft's ActiveX technology. ActiveX code is authenticated, but once it gains permission to run, it cannot be controlled at all.

Software Developer Certificates

Up to now, we discussed scenarios where applets are delivered in an intranet and a system administrator configures a security policy that controls the privileges of the applets. However, that strategy only works with applets from known sources.

Suppose you surf the Internet and you encounter a web site that offers to run an applet from an unfamiliar vendor, provided you grant it the permission to do so (see Figure 9–19). Such an applet is signed with a *software developer* certificate that is issued by a certificate authority such as Thawte or Verisign. The pop-up dialog identifies the software developer and the certificate issuer. You now have two choices:

- To run the applet with full privileges, or
- To confine the applet to the sandbox.

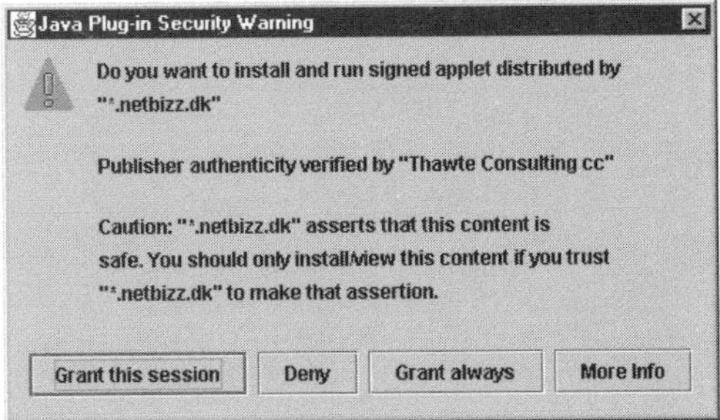

Figure 9–19: Launching a signed applet

What facts do you have at your disposal that might influence your decision? Here is what you know:

1. Thawte sold a certificate to the software developer.
2. The applet really was signed with that certificate, and it hasn't been modified in transit.
3. The certificate really was signed by Thawte—it was verified by the public key in the local `cacerts` file.

Does that tell you whether the code is safe to run? Do you trust the vendor if all you know is the vendor name (*.netbizz.dk) and the fact that Thawte sold them a software developer certificate? Presumably Thawte went to some degree of trouble to assure itself that *.netbizz.dk is not an outright cracker. However, no certificate issuer carries out a comprehensive audit of the honesty and competence of software vendors.

In the situation of an unknown vendor, an end user is ill-equipped to make an intelligent decision whether to let this applet run outside the sandbox, with all permissions of a local application. If the vendor is a well-known company, then the user can at least take the past track record of the company into account.

We don't like situations where a program demands "give me all rights, or I won't run at all." Naive users are too often cowed into granting access that can put them into danger. Would it help if the applet explained what rights it needs and seeks specific permission for those rights? Unfortunately, as you have seen, that can get pretty technical. It doesn't seem reasonable for an end user to have to ponder whether an applet should really have the right to inspect the AWT event queue. Perhaps, a future version of a plug-in can define permission sets that are meaningful to an end user. Until that time, we remain unenthusiastic about applets that are signed with software developer certificates.

If you want to deploy your applets to the world at large and you think that your users trust you enough that they will allow your applets to run with full permissions on their machine, then you may want to purchase a certificate from Thawte or Verisign and use it to sign your applets. See `http://java.sun.com/products/plugin/1.2/docs/nsobjsigning.html` for more information.

Encryption

In this chapter, we have discussed one important cryptographic technique that is implemented with the Java platform security API, namely, authentication through digital signatures. A second important aspect of security is *encryption*. When information is authenticated, the information itself is plainly visible. The digital signature merely verifies that the information has not been changed. In contrast, when information is encrypted, it is not visible. It can only be decrypted with a matching key.

Authentication is sufficient for code signing—there is no need for hiding the code. But encryption is necessary when applets or applications transfer confidential information, such as credit card numbers and other personal data.

However, the Java 2 Standard Edition does not currently have support for encryption. If you need encryption, you need to get the Java Cryptographic Extensions (JCE). JCE only supports a small number of encryption algorithms, such as the DES (Data Encryption Standard) algorithm. This is a symmetric-key, freely usable algorithm with a key length of 56 bits. If you want stronger algorithms, you will need to license them from a cryptographic service provider such as RSA Security Inc. Unfortunately, the Java Cryptographic Extensions are only available in the United States and Canada, and cryptography algorithms can carry steep licensing fees.

A major reason for the lack of encryption support in the standard Java library is the export restriction imposed by the United States government. It is a crime in the United States to export cryptographic products without an export license. Until recently, export licenses have been granted only for low-grade security, which can be broken relatively easily. The situation is only slowly improving, with increasing numbers of export licenses for high-grade keys for banking and commerce applications. At one time, there were even efforts by the White House to pass legislation that would make it illegal for any American to use encryption that did not have a back door for law-enforcement agencies. In our opinion, these efforts are ultimately futile and counterproductive. Encryption software, without trapdoors for law enforcement and with very high grades of security is widely available over the Internet, and the Internet knows no national borders.

Furthermore, the RSA algorithm (the most commonly used encryption algorithms using highly secure public/private key pairs) has been protected by patents. If you want to use the RSA algorithm, you need a license from RSA Security Inc., and you will probably need to pay them a substantial fee. For that reason, the Java Cryptography Extensions do not contain the RSA algorithm. That situation may change soon. The RSA patent expires in October 2000, at which point the algorithm passes into the public domain and can be implemented freely.

We hope that strong encryption soon becomes a part of the standard Java library, so that developers can write code instead of dealing with export and patent restrictions. In the meantime, if you reside in the United States or Canada, you can download the JCE from `http://java.sun.com/products/jce`. Alternatively, you can find sources for cleanroom® implementations at the web page `http://java.sun.com/products/jce/jce12_providers.html`.

Chapter 10

Internationalization

- LOCALES
- NUMBERS AND CURRENCIES
- DATE AND TIME
- TEXT
- RESOURCE BUNDLES
- GRAPHICAL USER INTERFACE LOCALIZATION

There's a big world out there; we hope that lots of its inhabitants will be interested in your application or applet. The Internet, after all, effortlessly spans the barriers between countries. On the other hand, when you write your applet in U.S. English, using the ASCII character set, *you* are putting up a barrier. For example, even within countries that can function using the ASCII character set, things as basic as dates and numbers are displayed differently. To a German speaker, 3/4/95 means something different than it does to an English speaker. Or, an applet like our calculator from Chapter 10 of Volume 1 could confuse people who do not use the "." to separate the integer and fractional parts of a number.

Now, it is true that many Internet users are able to read English, but they will certainly be more comfortable with applets or applications that are written in their own language and that present data in the format they are most familiar with. Imagine, for example, that you could write a retirement calculator applet that would change how it displays its results *depending on the location of the machine that is downloading it*. This kind of applet is immediately more valuable—and smart companies will recognize its value.

The Java programming language was the first language designed from the ground up to support internationalization. From the beginning, it had the one essential feature needed for effective internationalization: it used Unicode for all strings. Unicode support makes it easy to write programs in the Java programming language that manipulate strings in any one of multiple languages.

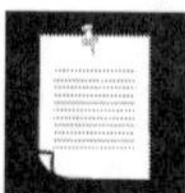

NOTE: The best source for Unicode character tables is *The Unicode Standard, Version 2.0, Addison-Wesley, 1996.* You can also see many of the code charts at `www.unicode.org`.

Many programmers believe that all they need to do to internationalize their application is to support Unicode and to translate the messages in the user interface. However, as you will see in this chapter, there is a lot more to internationalizing programs than just Unicode support. Operating systems and even browsers may not necessarily be Unicode-ready. For example, it is almost always necessary to have a translation layer between the character sets and fonts of the host machine and the Unicode-centric Java virtual machine. Also, dates, times, currencies—even numbers—are formatted differently in different parts of the world. You need an easy way to configure menu and button names, message strings, and keyboard shortcuts for different languages. You need to trigger the changes in a way that is based on information the ambient machine can report to your program.

In this chapter, you'll see how to write internationalized Java applications and applets. You will see how to localize date and time, numbers and text, and graphical user interfaces, and you'll look at the tools that the JDK offers for writing internationalized programs. (And, by the way, you will see how to write a retirement calculator applet that can change how it displays its results *depending on the location of the machine that is downloading it.*)

Locales

When you look at an application that is adapted to an international market, the most obvious difference you notice is the language. This observation is actually a bit too limiting for true internationalization: Countries can share a common language, but you still may need to do some work to make computer users of both countries happy.[1]

In all cases, menus, button labels, and program messages will need to be translated to the local language; they may also need to be rendered in a different script. There are many more subtle differences, for example, numbers are formatted quite differently in English and in German. The number

```
123,456.78
```

1. "We have really everything in common with America nowadays, except, of course, language." Oscar Wilde.

should be displayed as

```
123.456,78
```

to a German user. That is, the role of the decimal point and the decimal comma separator are reversed! There are similar variations in the display of dates. In the United States, dates are somewhat irrationally displayed as month/day/year. Germany uses the more sensible order of day/month/year, whereas in China, the usage is year/month/day. Thus, the date

```
3/22/61
```

should be presented as

```
22.03.1961
```

to a German user. Of course, if the month names are written out explicitly, then the difference in languages becomes apparent. The English

```
March 22, 1961
```

should be presented as

```
22. März 1961
```

in German or

1961年3月22日

in Chinese.

You saw in volume 1 that the `java.text` class has methods that can format numbers, currencies, and dates. These methods can, in fact, do much more when you give them a parameter that describes the location. To invoke these methods in a non-country-specific way, you only have to supply objects of the `Locale` class. A *locale* describes

- A language
- A location
- Optionally, a variant

For example, in the United States, you use a locale with

language=English, location=United States.

In Germany, you use a locale with

language=German, location=Germany.

Switzerland has four official languages (German, French, Italian, and Rhaeto-Romance). A German speaker in Switzerland would want to use a locale with

language=German, location=Switzerland

This locale would make formatting work similarly to how it would work for the German locale; however, currency values would be expressed in Swiss francs, not German marks.

Variants are, fortunately, rare and are needed only for exceptional or system-dependent situations. For example, the Norwegians are having a hard time agreeing on the spelling of their language (a derivative of Danish). They use two spelling rule sets: a traditional one called Bokmål and a new one called Nynorsk. The traditional spelling would be expressed as a variant

language=Norwegian, location=Norway, variant=Bokmål

It is also possible to encode platform-dependent information in the variant.

To express the language and location in a concise and standardized manner, the Java programming language uses codes that were defined by the International Standards Organization. The local language is expressed as a lowercase two-letter code, following ISO-639, and the country code is expressed as an uppercase two-letter code, following ISO-3166. Tables 10–1 and 10–2 show some of the most common codes.

NOTE: For a full list of ISO-639 codes, see, for example, `http://www.ics.uci.edu/pub/ietf/http/related/iso639.txt`. You can find a full list of the ISO-3166 codes at a number of sites, including `http://www.niso.org/3166.html`.

Table 10–1: Common ISO-639 language codes

Language	Code
Chinese	`zh`
Danish	`da`
Dutch	`nl`
English	`en`
French	`fr`
Finnish	`fi`
German	`de`
Greek	`el`
Italian	`it`
Japanese	`ja`
Korean	`ko`
Norwegian	`no`
Portuguese	`pt`
Spanish	`sp`
Swedish	`sv`
Turkish	`tr`

Table 10–2: Common ISO-3166 country codes

Country	Code
Austria	AT
Belgium	BE
Canada	CA
China	CN
Denmark	DK
Finland	FI
Germany	DE
Great Britain	GB
Greece	GR
Ireland	IE
Italy	IT
Japan	JP
Korea	KR
the Netherlands	NL
Norway	NO
Portugal	PT
Spain	ES
Sweden	SE
Switzerland	CH
Taiwan	TW
Turkey	TR
United States	US

These codes do seem a bit random, especially since some of them are derived from local languages (German = Deutsch = `de`, Chinese = zhongwen = `zh`), but they are, at least, standardized.

To describe a locale, you concatenate the language, country code, and variant (if any) and pass this string to the constructor of the `Locale` class. The variant is optional.

```
Locale germanGermany = new Locale("de", "DE");
Locale germanSwitzerland = new Locale("de", "CH");
Locale norwegianNorwayBokmål = new Locale("no", "NO", "B");
```

If you want to specify a locale that describes a language only and not a location, use an empty string as the second argument of the constructor.

```
Locale german = new Locale("de", "");
```

These kinds of locales can be used only for language-dependent lookups. Since the locales do not specify the location where German is spoken, you cannot use them to determine local currency and date formatting preferences.

For your convenience, the JDK predefines a number of locale objects:

```
Locale.CANADA
Locale.CANADA_FRENCH
Locale.CHINA
Locale.FRANCE
Locale.GERMANY
Locale.ITALY
Locale.JAPAN
Locale.KOREA
Locale.PRC
Locale.TAIWAN
Locale.UK
Locale.US
```

The JDK also predefines a number of language locales that specify just a language without a location.

```
Locale.CHINESE
Locale.ENGLISH
Locale.FRENCH
Locale.GERMAN
Locale.ITALIAN
Locale.JAPANESE
Locale.KOREAN
Locale.SIMPLIFIED_CHINESE
Locale.TRADITIONAL_CHINESE
```

Besides constructing a locale or using a predefined one, you have two other methods for obtaining a locale object.

The static `getDefault` method of the `Locale` class gets the default locale as stored by the local operating system. Similarly, in an applet, the `getLocale` method returns the locale of the user viewing the applet. Finally, all locale-dependent utility classes can return an array of the locales they support. For example,

```
Locale[] supportedLocales = DateFormat.getAvailableLocales();
```

returns all arrays that the `DateFormat` class can handle. For example, in Java 1.1, the `DateFormat` class knows how to format dates in Chinese but not in Vietnamese. Therefore, the `getAvailableLocales()` returns the Chinese locales but no Vietnamese ones.

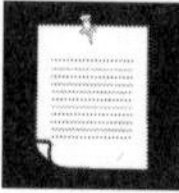

NOTE: We do not discuss how to create new language-specific elements. If you need to build a Brooklyn- or Texas-centric locale, please consult the JDK documentation.

Once you have a locale, what can you do with it? Not much, as it turns out. The only useful methods in the `Locale` class are the ones for identifying the language and country codes. The most important one is `getDisplayName`. It returns a string describing the locale. This string does not contain the cryptic two-letter codes, but it is in a form that can be presented to a user, such as

```
German (Switzerland)
```

Actually, there is a problem here. The display name is issued in the default locale. That may not be appropriate. If your user already selected German as the preferred language, you probably want to present the string in German. You can do just that by giving the German locale as a parameter: The code

```
Locale loc = new Locale("de", "CH");
System.out.println(loc.getDisplayName(Locale.GERMAN));
```

prints out

```
Deutsch (Schweiz)
```

But the real reason you need a `Locale` object is to feed it to locale-aware methods. For example, the `toLowerCase` and `toUpperCase` methods of the `String` class can take an argument of type `Locale` because the rules for forming uppercase letters differ by locale. In France, accents are generally dropped for uppercase letters. But in French-speaking Canada, they are retained. For example, the upper case of "étoile" (star) in France would be "ETOILE," but in Canada it would be "ÉTOILE."

```
String star = "étoile";
String fr = star.toUpperCase(Locale.FRANCE);
// should return "ETOILE"
String ca = star.toUpperCase(Locale.CANADA_FRENCH);
// returns "ÉTOILE"
```

Well, not quite: actually, this is the way it is *supposed* to work, but in the version of JDK 1.3 that we have, the `toUpperCase` method does not pay attention to the French locale. Still, we hope we have given you an idea of what you *will* be able to do with a `Locale` object. (Actually, you can give a `Locale` object to many other methods that carry out locale-specific tasks. You will see many examples in the following sections.)

`java.util.Locale`

- `static Locale getDefault()`
  returns the default locale.
- `static void setDefault(Locale l)`
  sets the default locale.
- `String getDisplayName()`
  returns a name describing the locale, expressed in the current locale.

- `String getDisplayName(Locale l)`
  returns a name describing the locale, expressed in the given locale.
- `String getLanguage()`
  returns the language code, a lowercase two-letter ISO-639 code.
- `String getDisplayLanguage()`
  returns the name of the language, expressed in the current locale.
- `String getDisplayLanguage(Locale l)`
  returns the name of the language, expressed in the given locale.
- `String getCountry()`
  returns the country code as an uppercase two-letter ISO-3166 code.
- `String getDisplayCountry()`
  returns the name of the country, expressed in the current locale.
- `String getDisplayCountry(Locale l)`
  returns the name of the country, expressed in the given locale.
- `String getVariant()`
  returns the variant string.
- `String getDisplayVariant()`
  returns the name of the variant, expressed in the current locale.
- `String getDisplayVariant(Locale l)`
  returns the name of the variant, expressed in the given locale.
- `String toString()`
  returns a description of the locale, with the language, country, and variant separated by underscores (e.g., `"de_CH"`).

Numbers and Currencies

We already mentioned how number and currency formatting is highly locale dependent. The Java programming language supplies a collection of formatter objects that can format and parse numeric values in the `java.text` class. You go through the following steps to format a number for a particular locale.

1. Get the locale object, as described in the preceding section.
2. Use a "factory method" to obtain a formatter object.
3. Use the formatter object for formatting and parsing.

The factory methods are static methods of the `NumberFormat` class that take a `Locale` argument. There are three factory methods: `getNumberInstance`, `getCurrencyInstance`, and `getPercentInstance`. These methods return objects that can format and parse numbers, currency amounts, and percentages, respectively. For example, here is how you can format a currency value in German.

```
Locale loc = new Locale("de", "DE");
NumberFormat currFmt = NumberFormat.getCurrencyInstance(loc);
double amt = 123456.78;
System.out.println(currFmt.format(amt));
```

This code prints

```
123.456,78 DM
```

Note that the currency symbol is `DM` and that it is placed at the end of the string. Also, note the reversal of decimal points and decimal commas.

Conversely, if you want to read in a number that was entered or stored with the conventions of a certain locale, then you use the `parse` method, which automatically uses the default locale. For example, the following code parses the value that the user typed into a text field. The `parse` method can deal with decimal points and commas, as well as digits in other languages.

```
TextField inputField;
. . .
NumberFormat fmt = NumberFormat.getNumberInstance();
// get number formatter for default locale
Number input = fmt.parse(inputField.getText().trim());
double x = input.doubleValue();
```

The return type of `parse` is the abstract type `Number`. The returned object is either a `Double` or a `Long` wrapper object, depending on whether the parsed number was a floating-point number. If you don't care about the distinction, you can simply use the `doubleValue` method of the `Number` class to retrieve the wrapped number.

If the number is not in the correct form, the method throws a `ParseException`. For example, leading white space in the string is *not* allowed. (Call `trim` to remove it.) However, any characters that follow the number in the string are simply ignored, so no exception is thrown.

Note that the classes returned by the `get`*`Xxx`*`Instance` factory methods are not actually of type `NumberFormat`. The `NumberFormat` type is an abstract class, and the actual formatters belong to one of its subclasses. The factory methods merely know how to locate the object that belongs to a particular locale.

It is quite obvious that it takes effort to produce a formatter object for a particular locale. Although the JDK supports only a limited number of localized formatters, more should follow over time, and you can, of course, write your own.

You can get a list of the currently supported locales with the static `getAvailableLocales` method. That method returns an array of the locales for which number formatter objects can be obtained.

The sample program for this section lets you experiment with number formatters (see Figure 10–1). The combo box at the top of the figure contains all locales with number formatters. You can choose between number, currency, and percentage formatters. Each time you make another choice, the number in the text field is reformatted. If you go through a few locales, then you get a good impression of how many ways there are to format a number or currency value. You can also type a different number and click on the Parse button to call the `parse` method, which tries to parse what you entered. If your input is successfully parsed, then it is passed to `format` and the result is displayed. If parsing fails, then a "Parse error" message is displayed in the text field.

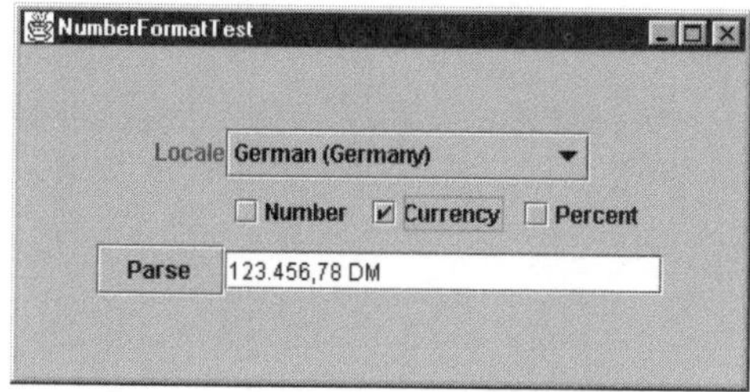

Figure 10–1: The `NumberFormatTest` program

The code, shown in Example 10–1, is fairly straightforward. In the constructor, we call `NumberFormat.getAvailableLocales`. For each locale, we call `getDisplayName`, and we fill a combo box with the strings that the `getDisplayName` method returns. Whenever the user selects another locale or clicks on one of the radio buttons, we create a new formatter object and update the text field. When the user clicks on the Parse button, we call the `parse` method to do the actual parsing, based on the locale selected.

Example 10–1: NumberFormatTest.java

```
import java.awt.*;
import java.awt.event.*;
import java.text.*;
import java.util.*;
import javax.swing.*;

public class NumberFormatTest
{  public static void main(String[] args)
   {  JFrame frame = new NumberFormatFrame();
      frame.show();
   }
}

class NumberFormatFrame extends JFrame
{  public NumberFormatFrame()
   {  setSize(400, 200);
      setTitle("NumberFormatTest");

      addWindowListener(new WindowAdapter()
```

```
         {  public void windowClosing(WindowEvent e)
            {  System.exit(0);
            }
         } );

      getContentPane().setLayout(new GridBagLayout());

      ActionListener listener =
         new ActionListener()
         {  public void actionPerformed(ActionEvent event)
            {  updateDisplay();
            }
         };

      JPanel p = new JPanel();
      addCheckBox(p, numberCheckBox, cbGroup, listener, true);
      addCheckBox(p, currencyCheckBox, cbGroup, listener, false);
      addCheckBox(p, percentCheckBox, cbGroup, listener, false);

      GridBagConstraints gbc = new GridBagConstraints();
      gbc.fill = GridBagConstraints.NONE;
      gbc.anchor = GridBagConstraints.EAST;
      add(new JLabel("Locale"), gbc, 0, 0, 1, 1);
      add(p, gbc, 1, 1, 1, 1);
      add(parseButton, gbc, 0, 2, 1, 1);
      gbc.anchor = GridBagConstraints.WEST;
      add(localeCombo, gbc, 1, 0, 1, 1);
      gbc.fill = GridBagConstraints.HORIZONTAL;
      add(numberText, gbc, 1, 2, 1, 1);

      locales = NumberFormat.getAvailableLocales();
      for (int i = 0; i < locales.length; i++)
         localeCombo.addItem(locales[i].getDisplayName());
      localeCombo.setSelectedItem(
         Locale.getDefault().getDisplayName());
      currentNumber = 123456.78;
      updateDisplay();

      localeCombo.addActionListener(listener);

      parseButton.addActionListener(
         new ActionListener()
         {  public void actionPerformed(ActionEvent event)
            {  String s = numberText.getText();
               try
               {  Number n = currentNumberFormat.parse(s);
                  if (n != null)
                  {  currentNumber = n.doubleValue();
                     updateDisplay();
                  }
                  else
                  {  numberText.setText("Parse error: " + s);
                  }
               }
               catch(ParseException e)
```

```
            {  numberText.setText("Parse error: " + s);
            }
         }
      });
   }

   public void add(Component c, GridBagConstraints gbc,
      int x, int y, int w, int h)
   {  gbc.gridx = x;
      gbc.gridy = y;
      gbc.gridwidth = w;
      gbc.gridheight = h;
      getContentPane().add(c, gbc);
   }

   public void addCheckBox(Container p, JCheckBox checkBox,
      ButtonGroup g, ActionListener listener, boolean v)
   {  checkBox.setSelected(v);
      checkBox.addActionListener(listener);
      g.add(checkBox);
      p.add(checkBox);
   }

   public void updateDisplay()
   {  Locale currentLocale = locales[
         localeCombo.getSelectedIndex()];
      currentNumberFormat = null;
      if (numberCheckBox.isSelected())
         currentNumberFormat
            = NumberFormat.getNumberInstance(currentLocale);
      else if (currencyCheckBox.isSelected())
         currentNumberFormat
            = NumberFormat.getCurrencyInstance(currentLocale);
      else if (percentCheckBox.isSelected())
         currentNumberFormat
            = NumberFormat.getPercentInstance(currentLocale);
      String n = currentNumberFormat.format(currentNumber);
      numberText.setText(n);
   }

   private Locale[] locales;

   private double currentNumber;

   private JComboBox localeCombo = new JComboBox();
   private JButton parseButton = new JButton("Parse");
   private JTextField numberText = new JTextField(30);
   private JCheckBox numberCheckBox = new JCheckBox("Number");
   private JCheckBox currencyCheckBox = new JCheckBox("Currency");
   private JCheckBox percentCheckBox = new JCheckBox("Percent");
   private ButtonGroup cbGroup = new ButtonGroup();
   private NumberFormat currentNumberFormat;
}
```

`java.text.NumberFormat`

- `static Locale[] getAvailableLocales()`
  returns an array of `Locale` objects for which `NumberFormat` formatters are available.
- `static NumberFormat getNumberInstance()`
- `static NumberFormat getNumberInstance(Locale l)`
- `static NumberFormat getCurrencyInstance()`
- `static NumberFormat getCurrencyInstance(Locale l)`
- `static NumberFormat getPercentInstance()`
- `static NumberFormat getPercentInstance(Locale l)`
  These methods return a formatter for numbers, currency amounts, or percentage values for the current locale or for the given locale.
- `String format(double x)`
- `String format(long x)`
  These methods return the string resulting from formatting the given floating-point number or integer.
- `Number parse(String s)`
  parses the given string and returns the number value, as a `Double` if the input string described a floating-point number, and as a `Long` otherwise. The beginning of the string must contain a number; no leading white space is allowed. The number can be followed by other characters, which are ignored. Throws a `ParseException` if parsing was not successful.
- `void setParseIntegerOnly(boolean b)`
- `boolean getParseIntegerOnly()`
  These methods set or get a flag to indicate whether this formatter should parse only integer values.
- `void setGroupingUsed(boolean b)`
- `boolean isGroupingUsed()`
  These methods set or get a flag to indicate whether this formatter emits and recognizes decimal separators (such as `100,000`).
- `void setMinimumIntegerDigits(int n)`
- `int getMinimumIntegerDigits()`
- `void setMaximumIntegerDigits(int n)`
- `int getMaximumIntegerDigits()`
- `void setMinimumFractionDigits(int n)`
- `int getMinimumFractionDigits()`
- `void setMaximumFractionDigits(int n)`
- `int getMaximumFractionDigits()`
  These methods set or get the maximum or minimum number of digits allowed in the integer or fractional part of a number.

Date and Time

When you are formatting date and time, there are four locale-dependent issues you need to worry about:

- The names of months and weekdays should be presented in the local language.
- There will be local preferences for the order of year, month, and day.
- The Gregorian calendar may not be the local preference for expressing dates.
- The time zone of the location must be taken into account.

The Java `DateFormat` class handles these issues. It is easy to use and quite similar to the `NumberFormat` class. First, you get a locale. You can use the default locale or call the static `getAvailableLocales` method to obtain an array of locales that support date formatting. Then, you call one of the three factory methods:

```
fmt = DateFormat.getDateInstance(dateStyle, loc);
fmt = DateFormat.getTimeInstance(timeStyle, loc);
fmt = DateFormat.getDateTimeInstance(dateStyle, timeStyle, loc);
```

To specify the desired style, these factory methods have a parameter that is one of the following constants:

`DateFormat.DEFAULT`

`DateFormat.FULL` (e.g., Thursday, September 18, 1997 8:42:46 o'clock A.M. PDT for the U.S. locale)

`DateFormat.LONG` (e.g., September 18, 1997 8:42:46 A.M. PDT for the U.S. locale)

`DateFormat.MEDIUM` (e.g., Sep 18, 1997 8:42:46 A.M. for the U.S. locale)

`DateFormat.SHORT` (e.g., 9/18/97 8:42 A.M. for the U.S. locale)

The factory method returns a formatting object that you can then use to format dates.

```
Date now = new Date();
String s = fmt.format(now);
```

Just as with the `NumberFormat` class, you can use the `parse` method to parse a date that the user typed. For example, the following code parses the value that the user typed into a text field.

```
TextField inputField;
. . .
DateFormat fmt = DateFormat.getDateInstance(DateFormat.MEDIUM);
   // get date formatter for default locale
Date input = fmt.parse(inputField.getText().trim());
```

If the number was not typed correctly, this code throws a `ParseException`. Note that leading white space in the string is *not* allowed here, either. You should again call `trim` to remove it. However, any characters that follow the number in the string will again be ignored. Unfortunately, the user must type the date exactly in the expected format. For example, if the format is set to `MEDIUM` in the U.S. locale, then dates are expected to look like

```
Sep 18, 1997
```

If the user types

```
Sep 18 1997
```

(without the comma), or the short format,

```
9/18/97
```

then a parse error results.

A `lenient` flag interprets dates leniently. For example, `February 30, 1999` will be automatically converted to `March 2, 1999`. This seems dangerous, but, unfortunately, it is the default. You should probably turn off this feature. The calendar object that is used to interpret the parsed date will throw an `IllegalArgumentException` when the user enters an invalid day/month/year combination.

Example 10–2 shows the `DateFormat` class in action. You can select a locale and see how the date and time are formatted in different places around the world. If you see question-mark characters in the output, then you don't have the fonts installed for displaying characters in the local language. For example, if you pick a Chinese locale, the date may be expressed as

```
1997?9?19?
```

Figure 10–2 shows the program running under Chinese Windows; as you can see, it correctly displays the output.

You can also experiment with parsing. Type in a date or time, click the Parse lenient checkbox if desired, and click on the Parse date or Parse time button.

The only mysterious feature about the code is probably the `EnumCombo` class. We used this class to solve the following technical problem. We wanted to fill a combo with values such as `Short`, `Medium`, and `Long` and then automatically convert the user's selection to integer values `DateFormat.SHORT`, `DateFormat.MEDIUM`, and `DateFormat.LONG`. To do this, we convert the user's choice to upper case, replace all spaces with underscores, and then use reflection to find the value of the static field with that name. (See Chapter 5 of Volume 1 for more details about reflection.)

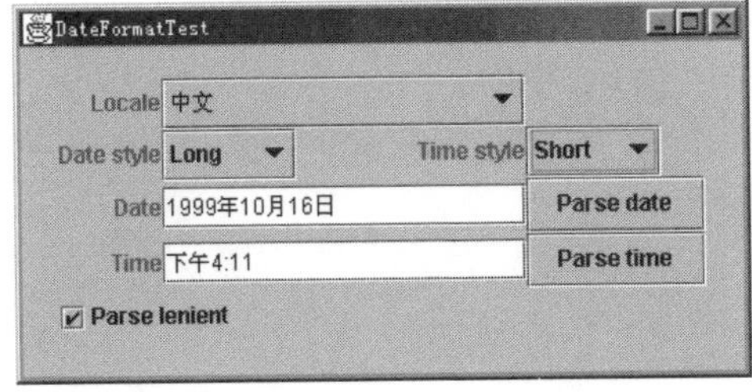

Figure 10–2: The `DateFormatTest` program running under Chinese Windows

Example 10–2: DateFormatTest.java

```
import java.awt.*;
import java.awt.event.*;
import java.text.*;
import java.util.*;
import javax.swing.*;

public class DateFormatTest
{  public static void main(String[] args)
   {  JFrame frame = new DateFormatFrame();
      frame.show();
   }
}

class DateFormatFrame extends JFrame
{  public DateFormatFrame()
   {  setSize(400, 200);
      setTitle("DateFormatTest");

      addWindowListener(new WindowAdapter()
         {  public void windowClosing(WindowEvent e)
            {  System.exit(0);
            }
         } );

      getContentPane().setLayout(new GridBagLayout());
      GridBagConstraints gbc = new GridBagConstraints();
      gbc.fill = GridBagConstraints.NONE;
      gbc.anchor = GridBagConstraints.EAST;
      add(new JLabel("Locale"), gbc, 0, 0, 1, 1);
      add(new JLabel("Date style"), gbc, 0, 1, 1, 1);
      add(new JLabel("Time style"), gbc, 2, 1, 1, 1);
      add(new JLabel("Date"), gbc, 0, 2, 1, 1);
      add(new JLabel("Time"), gbc, 0, 3, 1, 1);
      gbc.anchor = GridBagConstraints.WEST;
      add(localeCombo, gbc, 1, 0, 2, 1);
      add(dateStyleCombo, gbc, 1, 1, 1, 1);
      add(timeStyleCombo, gbc, 3, 1, 1, 1);
      add(dateParseButton, gbc, 3, 2, 1, 1);
      add(timeParseButton, gbc, 3, 3, 1, 1);
      add(lenientCheckbox, gbc, 0, 4, 2, 1);
      gbc.fill = GridBagConstraints.HORIZONTAL;
      add(dateText, gbc, 1, 2, 2, 1);
      add(timeText, gbc, 1, 3, 2, 1);

      locales = DateFormat.getAvailableLocales();
      for (int i = 0; i < locales.length; i++)
         localeCombo.addItem(locales[i].getDisplayName());
      localeCombo.setSelectedItem(
         Locale.getDefault().getDisplayName());
      currentDate = new Date();
      currentTime = new Date();
      updateDisplay();
```

```
      ActionListener listener =
         new ActionListener()
         {  public void actionPerformed(ActionEvent event)
            {  updateDisplay();
            }
         };

      localeCombo.addActionListener(listener);
      dateStyleCombo.addActionListener(listener);
      timeStyleCombo.addActionListener(listener);

      dateParseButton.addActionListener(
         new ActionListener()
         {  public void actionPerformed(ActionEvent event)
            {  String d = dateText.getText();
               try
               {  currentDateFormat.setLenient
                     (lenientCheckbox.isSelected());
                  Date date = currentDateFormat.parse(d);
                  currentDate = date;
                  updateDisplay();
               }
               catch(ParseException e)
               {  dateText.setText("Parse error: " + d);
               }
               catch(IllegalArgumentException e)
               {  dateText.setText("Argument error: " + d);
               }
            }
         });

      timeParseButton.addActionListener(
         new ActionListener()
         {  public void actionPerformed(ActionEvent event)
            {  String t = timeText.getText();
               try
               {  currentDateFormat.setLenient
                     (lenientCheckbox.isSelected());
                  Date date = currentTimeFormat.parse(t);
                  currentTime = date;
                  updateDisplay();
               }
               catch(ParseException e)
               {  timeText.setText("Parse error: " + t);
               }
               catch(IllegalArgumentException e)
               {  timeText.setText("Argument error: " + t);
               }
            }
         });
   }

   public void add(Component c, GridBagConstraints gbc,
```

```
      int x, int y, int w, int h)
   {  gbc.gridx = x;
      gbc.gridy = y;
      gbc.gridwidth = w;
      gbc.gridheight = h;
      getContentPane().add(c, gbc);
   }

   public void updateDisplay()
   {  Locale currentLocale = locales[
         localeCombo.getSelectedIndex()];
      int dateStyle = dateStyleCombo.getValue();
      currentDateFormat
         = DateFormat.getDateInstance(dateStyle,
         currentLocale);
      String d = currentDateFormat.format(currentDate);
      dateText.setText(d);
      int timeStyle = timeStyleCombo.getValue();
      currentTimeFormat
         = DateFormat.getTimeInstance(timeStyle,
         currentLocale);
      String t = currentTimeFormat.format(currentTime);
      timeText.setText(t);
   }

   private Locale[] locales;

   private Date currentDate;
   private Date currentTime;
   private DateFormat currentDateFormat;
   private DateFormat currentTimeFormat;

   private JComboBox localeCombo = new JComboBox();
   private EnumCombo dateStyleCombo
      = new EnumCombo(DateFormat.class,
        new String[] { "Default", "Full", "Long",
        "Medium", "Short" });
   private EnumCombo timeStyleCombo
      = new EnumCombo(DateFormat.class,
        new String[] { "Default", "Full", "Long",
        "Medium", "Short" });
   private JButton dateParseButton = new JButton("Parse date");
   private JButton timeParseButton = new JButton("Parse time");
   private JTextField dateText = new JTextField(30);
   private JTextField timeText = new JTextField(30);
   private JTextField parseText = new JTextField(30);
   private JCheckBox lenientCheckbox
      = new JCheckBox("Parse lenient", true);
}

class EnumCombo extends JComboBox
{  public EnumCombo(Class cl, String[] labels)
   {  for (int i = 0; i < labels.length; i++)
```

```
      {  String label = labels[i];
         String name = label.toUpperCase().replace(' ', '_');
         int value = 0;
         try
         {  java.lang.reflect.Field f = cl.getField(name);
            value = f.getInt(cl);
         }
         catch(Exception e)
         {  label = "(" + label + ")";
         }
         table.put(label, new Integer(value));
         addItem(label);
      }
      setSelectedItem(labels[0]);
   }

   public int getValue()
   {  return ((Integer)table.get(getSelectedItem())).intValue();
   }

   private Map table = new HashMap();
}
```

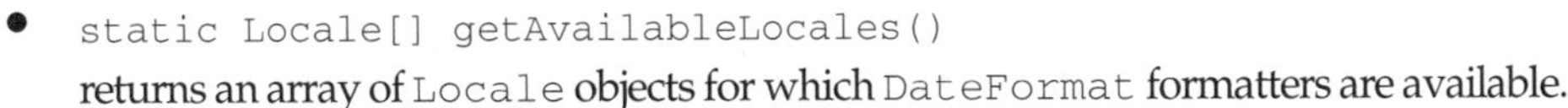

- `static Locale[] getAvailableLocales()`
  returns an array of `Locale` objects for which `DateFormat` formatters are available.
- `static DateFormat getDateInstance(int dateStyle)`
- `static DateFormat getDateInstance(int dateStyle, Locale l)`
- `static DateFormat getTimeInstance(int timeStyle)`
- `static DateFormat getDateTimeInstance(int timeStyle, Locale l)`
- `static DateFormat getDateTimeInstance(int dateStyle, int timeStyle)`
- `static DateFormat getDateTimeInstance(int dateStyle, int timeStyle, Locale l)`
  These methods return a formatter for date, time, or date and time for the default locale or the given locale.

Parameters:	`dateStyle`, `timeStyle`	one of `DEFAULT`, `FULL`, `LONG`, `MEDIUM`, `SHORT`

- `String format(Date d)`
  returns the string resulting from formatting the given date/time.
- `Date parse(String s)`
  parses the given string and returns the date/time described in it. The beginning of the string must contain a date or time; no leading white space is allowed. The date can be followed by other characters, which are ignored. Throws a `ParseException` if parsing was not successful.

- `void setLenient(boolean b)`
- `boolean isLenient()`

  These methods set or get a flag to indicate whether parsing should be lenient or strict. In lenient mode, dates such as `February 30, 1999` will be automatically converted to `March 2, 1999`. The default is lenient mode.

- `void setCalendar(Calendar cal)`
- `Calendar getCalendar()`

  These methods set or get the calendar object used for extracting year, month, day, hour, minute, and second from the `Date` object. Use this method if you do not want to use the default calendar for the locale (usually the Gregorian calendar).

- `void setTimeZone(TimeZone tz)`
- `TimeZone getTimeZone()`

  These methods set or get the time zone object used for formatting the time. Use this method if you do not want to use the default time zone for the locale. The default time zone is the time zone of the default locale, as obtained from the operating system. For the other locales, it is the preferred time zone in the geographical location.

- `void setNumberFormat(NumberFormat f)`
- `NumberFormat getNumberFormat()`

  These methods set or get the number format used for formatting the numbers used for representing year, month, day, hour, minute, and second.

Text

There are many localization issues to deal with when you display even the simplest text in an internationalized application. In this section, we work on the presentation and manipulation of text strings. For example, the sorting order for strings is clearly locale specific. Obviously, you also need to localize the text itself: directions, labels, and messages will all need to be translated. (Later in this chapter, you'll see how to build *resource bundles*. These let you collect a set of message strings that work for a particular language.)

Collation (Ordering)

Sorting strings in alphabetical order is easy when the strings are made up of only English ASCII characters. You just compare the strings with the `compareTo` method of the `String` class. The value of

```
a.compareTo(b)
```

is a negative number if `a` is lexicographically less than `b`, 0 if they are identical, and positive otherwise.

Unfortunately, unless all your words are in uppercase English ASCII characters, this method is useless. The problem is that the `compareTo` method in the Java programming language uses the values of the Unicode character to determine the

ordering. For example, lowercase characters have a higher Unicode value than do uppercase characters, and accented characters have even higher values. This leads to absurd results; for example, the following five strings are ordered according to the `compareTo` method:

```
America
Zulu
ant
zebra
Ångstrom
```

For dictionary ordering, you want to consider upper case and lower case to be equivalent. To an English speaker, the sample list of words would be ordered as

```
America
Ångstrom
ant
zebra
Zulu
```

However, that order would not be acceptable to a Danish user. In Danish, the letter Å is a different letter than the letter A, and it is collated *after* the letter Z! That is, a Danish user would want the words to be sorted as

```
America
ant
zebra
Zulu
Ångstrom
```

Fortunately, once you are aware of the problem, collation is quite easy. As always, you start by obtaining a `Locale` object. Then, you call the `getInstance` factory method to obtain a `Collator` object. Finally, you use the `compare` method of the collator, *not* the `compareTo` method of the `String` class, whenever you want to sort strings.

```
Locale loc = . . .;
Collator coll = Collator.getInstance(loc);
if (coll.compare(a, b) < 0) // a comes before b . . .;
```

Most importantly, the `Collator` class implements the `Comparator` interface. Therefore, you can pass a collator object to the `Collections.sort` method in order to sort a list of strings:

```
Collections.sort(strings, coll);
```

You can set a collator's *strength* to select how selective it should be. Character differences are classified as *primary, secondary,* and *tertiary.* For example, in English, the difference between "A" and "Z" is considered primary, the difference between "A" and "Å" is secondary, and between "A" and "a" is tertiary.

By setting the collator's strength to `Collator.PRIMARY`, you tell it to pay attention only to primary differences. By setting the strength to `Collator.SECONDARY`, the collator will take secondary differences into account. That is, two strings will be more likely to be considered different when the strength is set to "secondary." For example,

```
// assuming English locale
String a = "Angstrom";
String b = "Ångstrom";
coll.setStrength(Collator.PRIMARY);
if (coll.compare(a, b) == 0) System.out.print("same");
else System.out.print("different");
// will print "same"
coll.setStrength(Collator.SECONDARY);
if (coll.compare(a, b) == 0) System.out.print("same");
else System.out.print("different");
// will print "different"
```

Table 10–3 shows how a sample set of strings is sorted with the three collation strengths. Note that the strength indicates only whether two strings are considered identical.

Table 10–3: Collations with different strengths

Input	PRIMARY	SECONDARY	TERTIARY
`Ant,`	`Angstrom = Ångstrom,`	`Angstrom,`	`Angstrom,`
`ant,`	`Ant = ant,`	`Ångstrom,`	`Ångstrom,`
`Angstrom,`		`Ant = ant`	`Ant,`
`Ångstrom,`			`ant`

Finally, there is one technical setting, the *decomposition mode*. The default, "canonical decomposition," is appropriate for most use. If you choose "no decomposition," then accented characters are not decomposed into their base form + accent. This option is faster, but it gives correct results only when the input does not contain accented characters. (It never makes sense to sort accented characters by their Unicode values.) Finally, "full decomposition" analyzes Unicode variants, that is, Unicode characters that ought to be considered identical. For example, Japanese displays have two ways of showing English characters, called half-width and full-width. The half-width characters have normal character spacing, whereas the full-width characters are spaced in the same grid as the ideographs. (One could argue that this is a presentation issue and it should not have resulted in different Unicode characters, but we don't make the rules.) With full decomposition, half-width and full-width variants of the same letter are recognized as identical.

It is wasteful to have the collator decompose a string many times. If one string is compared many times against other strings, then you can save the decomposition in a *collation* key object. The `getCollationKey` method returns a `CollationKey` object that you can use for further, faster comparisons. Here is an example:

```
String a = . . .;
CollationKey aKey = coll.getCollationKey(a);
if (aKey.compareTo(coll.getCollationKey(b) == 0)
   // fast comparison
   . . .
```

The program in Example 10–3 lets you experiment with collation order. Type a word into the text field and click on Add to add it to the list of words. Each time you add another word or change the locale, strength, or decomposition mode, the list of words is sorted again. An = sign indicates words that are considered identical (see Figure 10–3).

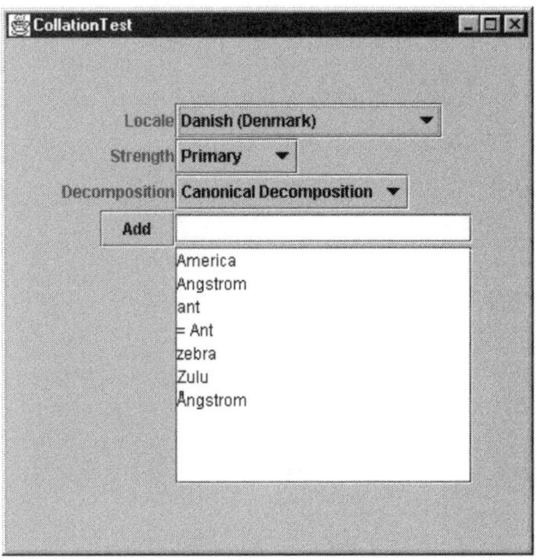

Figure 10–3: The `CollationTest` program

Example 10–3: CollationTest.java

```
import java.io.*;
import java.awt.*;
import java.awt.event.*;
import java.text.*;
import java.util.*;
import java.util.List;
import javax.swing.*;

public class CollationTest
{  public static void main(String[] args)
   {  JFrame frame = new CollationFrame();
      frame.show();
   }
}

class CollationFrame extends JFrame
{  public CollationFrame()
   {  setSize(400, 400);
      setTitle("CollationTest");

      addWindowListener(new WindowAdapter()
         {  public void windowClosing(WindowEvent e)
            {  System.exit(0);
            }
```

```
      } );

   getContentPane().setLayout(new GridBagLayout());
   GridBagConstraints gbc = new GridBagConstraints();
   gbc.fill = GridBagConstraints.NONE;
   gbc.anchor = GridBagConstraints.EAST;
   add(new JLabel("Locale"), gbc, 0, 0, 1, 1);
   add(new JLabel("Strength"), gbc, 0, 1, 1, 1);
   add(new JLabel("Decomposition"), gbc, 0, 2, 1, 1);
   add(addButton, gbc, 0, 3, 1, 1);
   gbc.anchor = GridBagConstraints.WEST;
   add(localeCombo, gbc, 1, 0, 1, 1);
   add(strengthCombo, gbc, 1, 1, 1, 1);
   add(decompositionCombo, gbc, 1, 2, 1, 1);
   gbc.fill = GridBagConstraints.HORIZONTAL;
   add(newWord, gbc, 1, 3, 1, 1);
   gbc.fill = GridBagConstraints.BOTH;
   add(new JScrollPane(sortedWords), gbc, 1, 4, 1, 1);

   locales = Collator.getAvailableLocales();
   for (int i = 0; i < locales.length; i++)
      localeCombo.addItem(locales[i].getDisplayName());
   localeCombo.setSelectedItem(
      Locale.getDefault().getDisplayName());

   strings.add("America");
   strings.add("ant");
   strings.add("Zulu");
   strings.add("zebra");
   strings.add("≈ngstrom");
   strings.add("Angstrom");
   strings.add("Ant");
   updateDisplay();

   addButton.addActionListener(
      new ActionListener()
      {  public void actionPerformed(ActionEvent event)
         {  strings.add(newWord.getText());
            updateDisplay();
         }
      });

   ActionListener listener =
      new ActionListener()
      {  public void actionPerformed(ActionEvent event)
         {  updateDisplay();
         }
      };

   localeCombo.addActionListener(listener);
   strengthCombo.addActionListener(listener);
   decompositionCombo.addActionListener(listener);
```

```
   }

   public void add(Component c, GridBagConstraints gbc,
      int x, int y, int w, int h)
   {  gbc.gridx = x;
      gbc.gridy = y;
      gbc.gridwidth = w;
      gbc.gridheight = h;
      getContentPane().add(c, gbc);
   }

   public void updateDisplay()
   {  Locale currentLocale = locales[
         localeCombo.getSelectedIndex()];

      currentCollator
         = Collator.getInstance(currentLocale);
      currentCollator.setStrength(strengthCombo.getValue());
      currentCollator.setDecomposition(
         decompositionCombo.getValue());

      Collections.sort(strings, currentCollator);

      sortedWords.setText("");
      for (int i = 0; i < strings.size(); i++)
      {  String s = (String)strings.get(i);
         if (i > 0
            && currentCollator.compare(s, strings.get(i - 1)) == 0)
         {  sortedWords.append("= ");
         }
         sortedWords.append(s + "\n");
      }
   }

   private Locale[] locales;
   private List strings = new ArrayList();
   private Collator currentCollator;

   private JComboBox localeCombo = new JComboBox();
   private EnumCombo strengthCombo
      = new EnumCombo(Collator.class,
        new String[] { "Primary", "Secondary", "Tertiary" });
   private EnumCombo decompositionCombo
      = new EnumCombo(Collator.class,
        new String[] { "Canonical Decomposition",
        "Full Decomposition", "No Decomposition" });
   private JTextField newWord = new JTextField(20);
   private JTextArea sortedWords = new JTextArea(10, 20);
   private JButton addButton = new JButton("Add");
}

class EnumCombo extends JComboBox
```

```
{  public EnumCombo(Class cl, String[] labels)
   {  for (int i = 0; i < labels.length; i++)
      {  String label = labels[i];
         String name = label.toUpperCase().replace(' ', '_');
         int value = 0;
         try
         {  java.lang.reflect.Field f = cl.getField(name);
            value = f.getInt(cl);
         }
         catch(Exception e)
         {  label = "(" + label + ")";
         }
         table.put(label, new Integer(value));
         addItem(label);
      }
      setSelectedItem(labels[0]);
   }

   public int getValue()
   {  return ((Integer)table.get(getSelectedItem())).intValue();
   }

   private Map table = new HashMap();
}
```

`java.text.Collator`

- `static Locale[] getAvailableLocales()`
  returns an array of `Locale` objects for which `Collator` objects are available.
- `static Collator getInstance()`
- `static Collator getInstance(Locale l)`
  These methods return a collator for the default locale or the given locale.
- `int compare(String a, String b)`
  returns a negative value if `a` comes before `b`, 0 if they are considered identical, a positive value otherwise.
- `boolean equals(String a, String b)`
  returns `true` if they are considered identical, `false` otherwise.
- `void setStrength(int strength) / int getStrength()`
  sets or gets the strength of the collator. Stronger collators tell more words apart. Strength values are `Collator.PRIMARY`, `Collator.SECONDARY`, and `Collator.TERTIARY`.
- `void setDecomposition(int decomp) / int getDecompositon()`
  sets or gets the decomposition mode of the collator. The more a collator decomposes a string, the more strict it will be in deciding whether two strings ought to be considered identical. Decomposition values are

`Collator.NO_DECOMPOSITION`, `Collator.CANONICAL_DECOMPOSITION`, and `Collator.FULL_DECOMPOSITION`.

- `CollationKey getCollationKey(String a)`
  returns a collation key that contains a decomposition of the characters in a form that can be quickly compared against another collation key.

`java.text.CollationKey`

- `int compareTo(CollationKey b)`
  returns a negative value if this key comes before `b`, 0 if they are considered identical, a positive value otherwise.

Text Boundaries

Consider a "sentence" in an arbitrary language: Where are its "words"? Answering this question sounds trivial, but once you deal with multiple languages, then just as with collation, it isn't as simple as you might think. Actually, the situation is even worse than you might think—consider the problem of determining where a *character starts and ends.* If you have a string such as `"Hello"`, then it is trivial to break it up into five individual characters: `H|e|l|l|o`. But accents throw a monkey wrench into this simple model. There are two ways of describing an accented character such as `ä`, namely, the character `ä` itself (Unicode `\u00E4`) or the character `a` followed by a combining diaeresis ¨ (Unicode `\u0308`). That is, the string with four Unicode characters `Ba¨r` is a sequence of three logical characters: `B|a¨|r`. This situation is still relatively easy; it gets much more complex for Asian languages such as the Korean Hangul script.

What about word breaks? Word breaks, of course, are at the beginning and the end of a word. In English, this is simple: sequences of characters are words. For example, the word breaks in

```
The quick, brown fox jump-ed over the lazy dog.
```

are

```
The| |quick|,| |brown| |fox| |jump-ed| |over| |the| |lazy| |dog.|
```

(The hyphen in `jump-ed` indicates a soft hyphen.)

Line boundaries are positions where a line can be broken on the screen or in printed text. In English text, this decision is relatively easy. Lines can be broken before a word or after a hyphen. For example, the line breaks in our sample sentence are

```
The |quick, |brown |fox |jump-|ed |over |the |lazy |dog.|
```

Note that line breaks are the points where a line *can* be broken, not the points where the lines are actually broken.

Determining character, word, and line boundaries is simple for European and Asian ideographic scripts, but it is quite complex for others, such as Devanagari, the script used to write classical Sanskrit and modern Hindi.

Finally, you will want to know about breaks between sentences. In English, for example, sentence breaks occur after periods, exclamation marks, and question marks.

Use the `BreakIterator` class to find out where you can break up text into components such as characters, words, lines, and sentences. You would use these classes when writing code for editing, displaying, and printing text.

Luckily, the break iterator class does not blindly break sentences at every period. It knows about the rules for periods inside quotation marks, and about "..." ellipses. For example, the string

```
The quick, brown fox jumped over the lazy "dog." And then
   ... what happened?
```

is broken into two sentences.

```
The quick, brown fox jumped over the lazy "dog." |And then
   ... what happened?|
```

Here is an example of how to program with break iterators. As always, you first get a break iterator with a static factory method. You can request one of four iterators to iterate through characters, words, lines, or sentences. Note that once you have a particular iterator object, such as one for sentences, it can iterate only through sentences. More generally, a break iterator can iterate only through the construct for which it was created. For example, the following code lets you analyze individual words:

```
Locale loc = . . .;
BreakIterator wordIter = BreakIterator.getWordInstance(loc);
```

Once you have an iterator, you give it a string to iterate through.

```
String msg = " The quick, brown fox";
wordIter.setText(msg);
```

Then, call the `first` method to get the offset of the first boundary.

```
int f = wordIter.first(); // returns 3
```

In our example, this call to `first` returns a 3—which is the offset of the first space inside the string. You keep calling the `next` method to get the offsets for the next tokens. You know there are no more tokens when a call to `next` returns the constant `BreakIterator.DONE`. For example, here is how you can iterate through the remaining word breaks.

```
int to;
while ((to = currentBreakIterator.next()) !=
   BreakIterator.DONE)
{  // do something with to
}
```

The program in Example 10–4 lets you type text into the text area on the top of the frame. Then, select the way you want to break the text (character, word, line, or sentence). You then see the text boundaries in the text area on the bottom (see Figure 10–4).

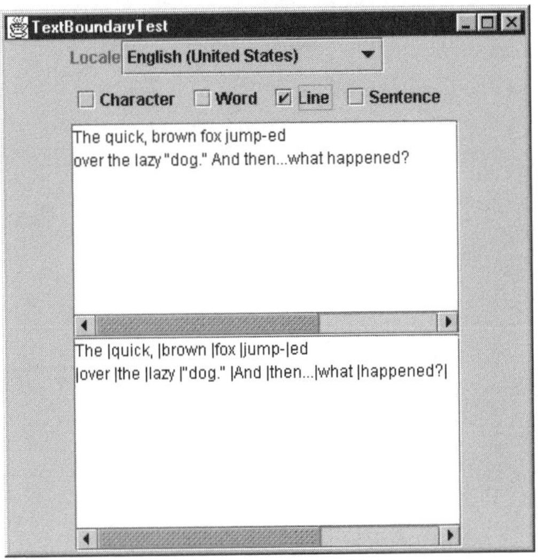

Figure 10–4: The `TextBoundaryTest` program

Example 10–4: TextBoundaryTest.java

```
import java.awt.*;
import java.awt.event.*;
import java.text.*;
import java.util.*;
import javax.swing.*;

public class TextBoundaryTest
{  public static void main(String[] args)
   {  JFrame frame = new TextBoundaryFrame();
      frame.show();
   }
}

class TextBoundaryFrame extends JFrame
{  public TextBoundaryFrame()
   {  setSize(400, 400);
      setTitle("TextBoundaryTest");

      addWindowListener(new WindowAdapter()
         {  public void windowClosing(WindowEvent e)
            {  System.exit(0);
            }
         } );

      ActionListener listener =
```

```
         new ActionListener()
         {  public void actionPerformed(ActionEvent event)
            {  updateDisplay();
            }
         };

      JPanel p = new JPanel();
      addCheckBox(p, characterCheckBox, cbGroup, listener, false);
      addCheckBox(p, wordCheckBox, cbGroup, listener, false);
      addCheckBox(p, lineCheckBox, cbGroup, listener, false);
      addCheckBox(p, sentenceCheckBox, cbGroup, listener, true);

      getContentPane().setLayout(new GridBagLayout());
      GridBagConstraints gbc = new GridBagConstraints();
      gbc.fill = GridBagConstraints.NONE;
      gbc.anchor = GridBagConstraints.EAST;
      add(new JLabel("Locale"), gbc, 0, 0, 1, 1);
      gbc.anchor = GridBagConstraints.WEST;
      add(localeCombo, gbc, 1, 0, 1, 1);
      add(p, gbc, 0, 1, 2, 1);
      gbc.fill = GridBagConstraints.BOTH;
      gbc.weighty = 100;
      add(new JScrollPane(inputText), gbc, 0, 2, 2, 1);
      add(new JScrollPane(outputText), gbc, 0, 3, 2, 1);


      locales = BreakIterator.getAvailableLocales();
      for (int i = 0; i < locales.length; i++)
         localeCombo.addItem(locales[i].getDisplayName());
      localeCombo.setSelectedItem(
         Locale.getDefault().getDisplayName());

      localeCombo.addActionListener(listener);

      inputText.setText("The quick, brown fox jump-ed\n"
        + "over the lazy \"dog.\" And then...what happened?");
      updateDisplay();
   }

   public void addCheckBox(Container p, JCheckBox checkBox,
      ButtonGroup g, ActionListener listener, boolean v)
   {  checkBox.setSelected(v);
      checkBox.addActionListener(listener);
      g.add(checkBox);
      p.add(checkBox);
   }

   public void add(Component c, GridBagConstraints gbc,
      int x, int y, int w, int h)
   {  gbc.gridx = x;
      gbc.gridy = y;
```

```
      gbc.gridwidth = w;
      gbc.gridheight = h;
      getContentPane().add(c, gbc);
   }

   public void updateDisplay()
   {  Locale currentLocale = locales[
         localeCombo.getSelectedIndex()];
      BreakIterator currentBreakIterator = null;
      if (characterCheckBox.isSelected())
         currentBreakIterator
            = BreakIterator.getCharacterInstance(currentLocale);
      else if (wordCheckBox.isSelected())
         currentBreakIterator
            = BreakIterator.getWordInstance(currentLocale);
      else if (lineCheckBox.isSelected())
         currentBreakIterator
            = BreakIterator.getLineInstance(currentLocale);
      else if (sentenceCheckBox.isSelected())
         currentBreakIterator
            = BreakIterator.getSentenceInstance(currentLocale);

      String text = inputText.getText();
      currentBreakIterator.setText(text);
      outputText.setText("");

      int from = currentBreakIterator.first();
      int to;
      while ((to = currentBreakIterator.next()) !=
         BreakIterator.DONE)
      {  outputText.append(text.substring(from, to) + "|");
         from = to;
      }
      outputText.append(text.substring(from));
   }

   private Locale[] locales;
   private BreakIterator currentBreakIterator;

   private JComboBox localeCombo = new JComboBox();
   private JTextArea inputText = new JTextArea(6, 40);
   private JTextArea outputText = new JTextArea(6, 40);
   private ButtonGroup cbGroup = new ButtonGroup();
   private JCheckBox characterCheckBox = new JCheckBox("Character");
   private JCheckBox wordCheckBox = new JCheckBox("Word");
   private JCheckBox lineCheckBox = new JCheckBox("Line");
   private JCheckBox sentenceCheckBox = new JCheckBox("Sentence");
}
```

`java.text.BreakIterator`

- `static Locale[] getAvailableLocales()`

  returns an array of `Locale` objects for which `BreakIterator` objects are available.

- `static BreakIterator getCharacterInstance()`
- `static BreakIterator getCharacterInstance(Locale l)`
- `static BreakIterator getWordInstance()`
- `static BreakIterator getWordInstance(Locale l)`
- `static BreakIterator getLineInstance()`
- `static BreakIterator getLineInstance(Locale l)`
- `static BreakIterator getSentenceInstance()`
- `static BreakIterator getSentenceInstance(Locale l)`

  These methods return a break iterator for characters, words, lines, and sentences for the default or the given locale.

- `void setText(String text)`
- `void setText(CharacterIterator text)`
- `CharacterIterator getText()`

  These methods set or get the text to be scanned.

- `int first()`

  moves the current boundary to the first boundary position in the scanned string and returns the index.

- `int next()`

  moves the current boundary to the next boundary position and returns the index. Returns `BreakIterator.DONE` if the end of the string has been reached.

- `int previous()`

  moves the current boundary to the previous boundary position and returns the index. Returns `BreakIterator.DONE` if the beginning of the string has been reached.

- `int last()`

  moves the current boundary to the last boundary position in the scanned string and returns the index.

- `int current()`

  returns the index of the current boundary.

- `int next(int n)`

  moves the current boundary to the `n`th boundary position from the current one and returns the index. If `n` is negative, then the position is set closer to the beginning to the string. Returns `BreakIterator.DONE` if the end or beginning of the string has been reached.

- `int following(int pos)`
  moves the current boundary to the first boundary position after offset `pos` in the scanned string and returns the index. The returned value is larger than `pos`, or it is equal to `BreakIterator.DONE`.

Message Formatting

In the early days of "mail-merge" programs, you had strings like:

```
"On {2}, a {0} destroyed {1} houses and caused {3} of
   damage."
```

where the numbers in braces were placeholders for actual names and values. This technique is actually very convenient for doing certain kinds of internationalization, and the Java programming language has a convenience `MessageFormat` class to allow formatting text that has a pattern. To use the class, follow these steps.

1. Write the pattern as a string. You can use up to 10 placeholders `{0}`...`{9}`. You can use each placeholder more than once.
2. Construct a `MessageFormat` object with the pattern string as the constructor parameter.
3. Build an array of objects to substitute for the placeholders. The number inside the braces refers to the index in the array of objects.
4. Call the `format` method with the array of objects as a parameter.

CAUTION: Steps 1 and 2 build a `MessageFormat` object that uses the *current locale* for fomatting numbers and dates. If you need to specify a different locale, you must *first* construct a `MessageFormat` object with a dummy pattern, then call the `setLocale` method, and finally call the `applyPattern` method with the actual pattern that you want to use.

```
MessageFormat format = new MessageFormat("");
format.setLocale(locale);
format.applyPattern(pattern);
```

Here is an example of these steps. We first supply the array of objects for the placeholders.

```
String pattern =
   "On {2}, a {0} destroyed {1} houses and caused {3} of
      damage.";
MessageFormat msgFmt = new MessageFormat(pattern);

Object[] msgArgs = {
   "hurricane",
   new Integer(99),
   new GregorianCalendar(1999, 0, 1).getTime(),
   new Double(10E7)
```

```
};
String msg = msgFmt.format(msgArgs);
System.out.println(msg);
```

The number of the placeholder refers to the index in the object array. For example, the first placeholder `{2}` is replaced with `msgArgs[2]`. Since we need to supply objects, we have to remember to wrap integers and floating-point numbers in their `Integer` and `Double` wrappers before passing them. Notice the cumbersome construction of the date that we used. The `format` method expects an object of type `Date`, but the `Date(int, int, int)` constructor is deprecated in favor of the `Calendar` class. Therefore, we have to create a `Calendar` object and then call the `getTime` (sic) method to convert it to a `Date` object.

This code prints:

```
On 1/1/99 12:00 AM, a hurricane destroyed 99 houses
   and caused 100,000,000 of damage.
```

That is a start, but it is not perfect. We don't want to display the time "12:00 AM," and we want the damage amount printed as a currency value. The way we do this is by supplying an (optional) format for some or all of the placeholders. There are two ways to supply formats:

- By adding them to the pattern string
- By calling the `setFormat` or `setFormats` method

Let's do the easy one first. We can set a format for each individual *occurrence* of a placeholder. In our example, we want the first occurrence of a placeholder (which is placeholder `{2}`) to be formatted as a date, without a time field. And we want the fourth placeholder to be formatted as a currency. Actually, the placeholders are numbered starting at 0, so we actually want to set the formats of placeholders 0 and 3. We will use the formatters that you saw earlier in this chapter, namely, `DateFormat.getDateInstance(loc)` and `NumberFormat.getCurrencyInstance(loc)`, where `loc` is the locale we want to use. Conveniently, all formatters have a common base class `Format`. The `setFormat` method of the `MessageText` class receives an integer, the 0-based count of the placeholder to which the format should be applied, and a `Format` reference.

To build the format we want, we simply set the formats of placeholders 0 and 3 and then call the `format` method.

```
msgFmt.setFormat(0,
   DateFormat.getDateInstance(DateFormat.LONG, loc));
msgFmt.setFormat(3, NumberFormat.getCurrencyInstance(loc));
String msg = msgFmt.format(msgArgs);
System.out.println(msg);
```

Now, the printout is

```
On January 1, 1999, a hurricane destroyed 99 houses
and caused $100,000,000.00 of damage.
```

Next, rather than setting the formats individually, we can pack them into an array. Use `null` if you don't need any special format.

```
Format argFormats[] =
{  DateFormat.getDateInstance(DateFormat.LONG, loc),
   null,
   null,
   NumberFormat.getCurrencyInstance(loc)
};

msgFmt.setFormats(argFormats);
```

Note that the `msgArgs` and the `argFormats` array entries *do not correspond to one another.* The `msgArgs` indexes correspond to the number inside the `{}` delimiters. The `argFormats` indexes correspond to the position of the `{}` delimiters inside the message string. This arrangement sounds cumbersome, but there is a reason for it. It is possible for the placeholders to be repeated in the string, and each occurrence may require a different format. Therefore, the formats must be indexed by position. For example, if the exact time of the disaster was known, we might use the date object twice, once to extract the day and once to extract the time.

```
String pattern =
   "On {2}, a {0} touched down at {2} and destroyed {1}
      houses.";
MessageFormat msgFmt = new MessageFormat(pattern);

Format argFormats[] =
{  DateFormat.getDateInstance(DateFormat.LONG, loc),
   null,
   DateFormat.getTimeInstance(DateFormat.SHORT, loc),
   null
};
msg.setFormats(argFormats);

Object[] msgArgs = {
   "hurricane",
   new Integer(99),
   new GregorianCalendar(1999, 0, 1, 11, 45, 0).getTime(),
};
String msg = msgFmt.format(msgArgs);
System.out.println(msg);
```

This example code prints:

```
On January 1, 1999, a hurricane touched down
at 11:45 AM and destroyed 99 houses.
```

Note that the placeholder `{2}` was printed twice, with two different formats!

Rather than setting placeholders dynamically, we can also set them in the message string. For example, here we specify the date and currency formats directly in the message pattern.

```
"On {2,date,long}, a {0} destroyed {1} houses
and caused {3,number,currency} of damage."
```

If you specify formats directly, you don't need to make a call to `setFormat` or `setFormats`. In general, you can make the placeholder index be followed by a type and a style. Separate the index, *type,* and *style* by commas. The type can be any of:

```
number
time
date
choice
```

If the type is `number`, then the style can be:

```
integer
currency
percent
```

or it can be a number format pattern such as `$,##0`. (See Chapter 3 of Volume 1 for a discussion of number format patterns.)

If the type is either `time` or `date`, then the style can be:

```
short
medium
long
full
```

or a date format pattern. (See the documentation of the `SimpleDateFormat` class for more information about the possible formats.)

Choice formats are more complex, and we take them up in the next section.

`java.text.MessageFormat`

- `MessageFormat(String pattern)`
  constructs a message format object with the specified pattern.
- `void applyPattern(String pattern)`
  sets the pattern of a message format object to the specified pattern.
- `void setLocale(Locale loc)`
- `Locale getLocale()`
  These methods set or get the locale to be used for the placeholders in the message. The locale is *only* used for subsequent patterns that you set by calling the `applyPattern` method.
- `void setFormats(Format[] formats)`
- `Format[] getFormats()`
  These methods set or get the formats to be used for the placeholders in the message.

- `void setFormat(int i, Format format)`
  sets the formats to be used for the `i`th placeholder in the message.
- `String format(String pattern, Object[] args)`
  formats the objects by using `args[i]` as input for placeholder `{i}`.

Choice Formats

Let's look closer at the pattern of the preceding section:

```
"On {2}, a {0} destroyed {1} houses and caused {3} of damage."
```

If we replace the disaster placeholder `{0}` with `"earthquake"`, then the sentence is not grammatically correct in English.

```
On January 1, 1999, a earthquake destroyed …
```

That means what we really want to do is integrate the article "a" into the placeholder:

```
"On {2}, {0} destroyed {1} houses and caused {3} of damage."
```

Then, the `{0}` would be replaced with `"a hurricane"` or `"an earthquake"`. That is especially appropriate if this message needs to be translated into a language where the gender of a word affects the article. For example, in German, the pattern would be

```
"{0} zerstörte am {2} {1} Häuser und richtete einen Schaden von
   {3} an."
```

The placeholder would then be replaced with the grammatically correct combination of article and noun, such as `"Ein Hurrikan"`, `"Eine Naturkatastrophe"`.

Now let us turn to the `{1}` parameter. If the disaster isn't all that catastrophic, then `{1}` might be replaced with the number 1, and the message would read:

```
On January 1, 1999, a mudslide destroyed 1 houses and …
```

We would ideally like the message to vary according to the placeholder value, so that it can read

```
no houses
one house
2 houses
. . .
```

depending on the placeholder value. The `ChoiceFormat` class was designed to let you do this. A `ChoiceFormat` object is constructed with two arrays:

- An array of *limits*
- An array of *format strings*

```
double[] limits = . . .;
String[] formatStrings = . . .;
ChoiceFormat choiceFmt = new ChoiceFormat(limits,
   formatStrings);
double input = . . .;
String s = choiceFmt.format(input);
```

The `limits` and `formatStrings` arrays must have the same length. The numbers in the `limits` array must be in ascending order. Then, the `format` method checks between which limits the input falls. If

```
limits[i] <= input && input < limits[i + 1]
```

then `formatStrings[i]` is used to format the input. If the input is at least as large as the last limit, then the last format string is used. And, if the input is less than `limits[0]`, then `formatStrings[0]` is used anyway.

For example, consider these limits and format strings:

```
double[] limits = {0, 1, 2};
String[] formatStrings = {"no houses", "one house", "many
   houses"};
```

Table 10–4 shows the return values of the call to

```
String selected = choiceFmt.format(input);
```

Table 10–4: String selected by `ChoiceFormat`

input	selected
`input < 0`	`"no houses"`
`0 <= input && input < 1`	`"no houses"`
`1 <= input && input < 2`	`"one house"`
`2 <= input`	`"many houses"`

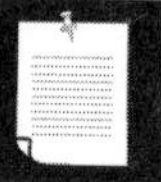

NOTE: This example shows that the designer of the `ChoiceFormat` class was a bit muddleheaded. If you have three strings, you need two limits to separate them. In general, you need *one fewer limit* than you have strings. Thus, the first limit is meaningless, and you can simply set the first and second limit to the same number. For example, the following code works fine:

```
double[] limits = {1, 1, 2};
String[] formatStrings = {"no houses", "one house", "many
   houses"};
ChoiceFormat choiceFmt = new ChoiceFormat(limits,
   formatStrings);
```

Of course, in our case, we don't want to return `"many houses"` if the number of houses is 2 or greater. We still want the value to be formatted. Here is the code to format the value.

```
double[] limits = {0, 1, 2};
String[] formatStrings = {"no houses", "one house", "{1}
   houses"};
ChoiceFormat choiceFmt = new ChoiceFormat(limits,
   formatStrings);
msgFmt.setFormat(2, choiceFmt);
```

That is, we create the choice format object and set it as the format to use for the third placeholder (because the count is 0-based).

Why do we use `{1}` in the format string? The usage is a little mysterious. When the message format applies the choice format on the placeholder, the choice format returns `"{1} houses"`. That string is then formatted again by the message format, and the answer is spliced into the result. As a rule, you should always feed back the same placeholder that was used to make the choice. Otherwise, you can create weird effects.

You can add formatting information to the returned string, for example,

```
String[] formatStrings
  = {"no houses", "one house", "{1, number, integer} houses"};
```

As you saw in the preceding section, it is also possible to express the choice format directly in a format string. When the format type is `choice`, then the next parameter is a list of pairs, each pair consisting of a limit and a format string, separated by a `#`. The pairs themselves are separated by `|`. Here is how to express the house format:

```
{1,choice,0#no houses|1#one house|2#{1} houses}
```

Thus, there are three sets of choices:

```
0#no houses
1#one house
2#{1} houses
```

The first one is used if the placeholder value is < 1, the second is used if the value is at least 1 but < 2, and the third is used if it is at least 2.

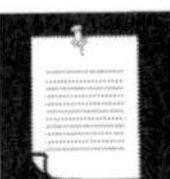

NOTE: As previously noted, the first limit is meaningless. But here you can't set the first and second limits to the same value; the format parser complains that

```
1#no houses|1#one house|2#{1} houses
```

is an invalid choice. In this case, you must set the first limit to any number that is strictly less than the second limit.

The syntax would have been a lot clearer if the designer of this class realized that the limits belong *between* the choices, such as

```
no houses|1|one house|2|{1} houses
// not the actual format
```

If we put the choice string inside the original message string, then we get the rather monstrous format instruction:

```
String pattern =
"On {2,date,long}, {0} destroyed {1,choice,0#no houses|1#one
   house|2#{1} houses}
and caused {3,number,currency} of damage.";
```

Or, in German,

```
String pattern =
"{0} zerstörte am {2,date,long} {1,choice,0#kein Haus|1#ein
   Haus|2#{1} Häuser}
und richtete einen Schaden von {3,number,currency} an.";
```

Note that the ordering of the words is different in German, but the array of objects you pass to the `format` method is the *same*. The order of the placeholders in the format string takes care of the changes in the word ordering.

`java.text.ChoiceFormat`

- `ChoiceFormat(String pattern)`
  constructs a choice format from a pattern string containing a `|` delimited set of pairs, each of which is of the form `limit#formatString`.
- `ChoiceFormat(double limits[], String formatStrings[])`
  constructs a choice format with the given limits and formats. The limits must be increasing. If `input` is the value to be formatted, then it is formatted with the `formatString[i]`, where `i` is the smallest index such that `limits[i] <= input`. However, all inputs that are less than `limits[1]` are formatted with `formatString[0]`.

Character Set Conversion

As you know, the Java programming language itself is fully Unicode based. However, operating systems typically have their own, homegrown, often incompatible, character encoding, such as ISO 8859-1 (an 8-bit code sometimes called the "ANSI" code) in the United States or BIG5 in Taiwan. So, the input that you receive from a user might be in a different encoding system, and the strings that you show to the user must eventually be encoded in a way that the local operating system understands.

Of course, *inside* your program, you should always use Unicode characters. You have to hope that the implementation of the Java virtual machine on that platform successfully converts input and output between Unicode and the local character set. For example, if you set a button label, you specify the string in Unicode, and it is up to the Java virtual machine to get the button to display your string correctly. Similarly, when you call `getText` to get user input from a text box, you get the string in Unicode, no matter how the user entered it.

However, *you* need to be careful with text files. Never read a text file one byte at a time! Always use the `InputStreamReader` or `FileReader` classes that were described in Chapter 1. These classes automatically convert from a particular character encoding to Unicode. By default, they use the local encoding scheme,

but as you saw in Chapter 1, you can specify the encoding in the constructor of the `InputStreamReader` class, for example,

```
InputStreamReader = new InputStreamReader(in, "8859_1");
```

Unfortunately, there is currently no connection between locales and character encodings. For example, if your user has selected the Chinese Traditional locale `zh_TW`, there is no method in the Java programming language that tells you that the BIG5 character encoding would be the most appropriate.

When writing text files, you need to decide:

- Is the output of the text file intended for humans to read or for use with other programs on their local machines?
- Is the output simply going to be fed into the same or another program?

If the output is intended for human consumption or a non-Unicode-enabled program, you'll need to convert it to the local character encoding by using a `PrintWriter`, as you saw in Chapter 1. Otherwise, just use the `writeUTF` method of the `DataOutputStream` to write the string in Unicode Text Format. Then, of course, the program reading the file must open it as a `DataInputStream` and read the string with the `readUTF` method.

TIP: In the case of input to a program in the Java programming language, an even better choice is to use serialization. Then, you never have to worry at all how strings are saved and loaded.

Of course, with both data streams and object streams, the output will not be in human-readable form.

International Issues and Source Files

It is worth keeping in mind that you, the programmer, will need to communicate with the Java compiler. And, *you do that with tools on your local system.* For example, you can use the Chinese version of Notepad to write your Java source code files. The resulting source code files are *not portable* because they use the local character encoding (GB or BIG5, depending on which Chinese operating system you use). Only the compiled class files are portable—they will automatically use the UTF encoding for identifiers and strings. That means that even when a program is compiling and running, three character encodings are involved:

- Source files: local encoding
- Class files: UTF
- Virtual machine: Unicode

To make your source files portable, restrict yourself to using the plain ASCII encoding. That is, you should change all non-ASCII characters to their equivalent Unicode encodings. For example, rather than using the string `"Häuser"`, use

"H\u0084user". The JDK contains a utility, `native2ascii`, that you can use to convert the native character encoding to plain ASCII. This utility simply replaces every non-ASCII character in the input with a `\u` followed by the four hex digits of the Unicode value. To use the `native2ascii` program, simply provide the input and output file names.

```
native2ascii Myfile.java Myfile.temp
```

You can convert the other way with the `-reverse` option:

```
native2ascii -reverse Myfile.java Myfile.temp
```

And you can specify another encoding with the `-encoding` option. The encoding name must be one of the ones listed in the encodings table in Chapter 12 of Volume 1.

```
native2ascii -encoding Cp437 Myfile.java Myfile.temp
```

Finally, we strongly recommend that you restrict yourself to plain ASCII class names. Since the name of the class also turns into the name of the *class file*, you are at the mercy of the local file system to handle any non-ASCII coded names—and it will almost certainly not do it right. For example, depressingly enough, Windows 95 uses yet another character encoding, the so-called *Code Page 437* or *original PC* encoding, for its file names. Windows 95 makes a valiant attempt to translate between ANSI and original names, but the JVM class loader does not. (NT is much better this way.) For example, if you make a class Bär, then the JDK class loader will complain that it "cannot find class BΣr." There is a reason for this behavior, but you don't want to know. Simply stick to ASCII for your class names until all computers around the world offer consistent support for Unicode.

Resource Bundles

When localizing an application, you'll probably have a dauntingly large number of message strings, button labels, and so on, that all need to be translated. To make this task feasible, you'll want to define the message strings in an external location, usually called a *resource*. The person carrying out the translation can then simply edit the resource files without having to touch the source code of the program.

NOTE: Java technology resources are not the same as Windows or Macintosh resources. A Windows executable program stores resources such as menus, dialog boxes, icons, and messages in a section separate from the program code. A resource editor can be used to inspect and update these resources without affecting the program code.

Java technology, unfortunately, does not have a mechanism for storing external resources in class files. Instead, all resource data must be put in a *class*, either as static variables or as return values of method calls. You create a different class for each locale, and then the `getBundle` method of the `ResourceBundle` class automatically locates the correct class for your locale.

NOTE: Chapter 10 of Volume 1 describes a concept of file resources, where data files, sounds, and images can be placed in a JAR file. The `getResource` method of the class `Class` finds the file, opens it and returns a URL to the resource. Why? When you write a program that needs access to files, it needs to *find* the files. By placing the files into the JAR file, you leave the job of finding the files to the class loader, which already knows how to locate the class files. While this mechanism does not directly support internationalization, it is useful for locating localized property files, and we take advantage of it in the next section.

Locating Resources

When localizing an application, you need to make a set of classes that describe the locale-specific items (such as messages, labels, and so on) for each locale that you want to support. Each of these classes must extend the class `ResourceBundle`. (You'll see a little later the details involved in designing these kinds of classes.) You also need to use a naming convention for these classes, where the name of the class corresponds to the locale. For example, resources specific for Germany go to the class `ProgramResources_de_DE`, while those that are shared by all German-speaking countries go into `ProgramResources_de`. Taiwan-specific resources go into `ProgramResources_zh_TW`, and any Chinese language strings go into `ProgramResources_zh`. In general, use

```
ProgramResources_language_country
```

for all country-specific resources, and use

```
ProgramResources_language
```

for all language-specific resources. Finally, as a fallback, you can put the U.S. English strings and messages into the class `ProgramResources`, without any suffix. Then, compile all these classes and store them with the other application classes for the project.

Once you have a class for the resource bundle, you load it with the command

```
ResourceBundle currentResources =
   ResourceBundle.getBundle("ProgramResources", currentLocale);
```

The `getBundle` method attempts to load the class that matches the current locale by language, country, and variant. If it is not successful, then the variant, country, and language are dropped in turn. That is, the `getBundle` method tries to load one of the following classes until it is successful.

```
ProgramResources_language_country_variant
ProgramResources_language_country
ProgramResources_language
ProgramResources
```

If all these attempts are unsuccessful, then the `getBundle` method tries all over again, only this time it uses the default locale instead of the current locale. If even these attempts fail, the method throws a `MissingResourceException`.

Once the getBundle method has located a class, say, ProgramResources_de_DE, it will still keep looking for ProgramResources_de and ProgramResources. If these classes exist, they become the *parents* of the ProgramResources_de_DE class in a *resource hierarchy*. Later, when looking up a resource, the getObject method will search the parents if the lookup was not successful in the current class. That is, if a particular resource was not found in ProgramResources_de_DE, then the ProgramResources_de and ProgramResources will be queried as well.

This is clearly a very useful service and one that would be tedious to program by hand. A resource mechanism of the Java programming language lets you locate the class that is the best match for localization information. It is very easy to add more and more localizations to an existing program: all you have to do is add additional resource classes.

Now that you know how a program can locate the correct resource, we show you how to place the language-dependent information into the resource class. Ultimately, it would be nice if you could get tools that even a nonprogrammer could use to define and modify resources. We hope and expect that developers of integrated Java programming environments will eventually provide such tools. But right now, creating resources still involves some programming. We take that up next.

Placing Resources into Bundles

In the Java programming language, you place resources inside classes that extend the ResourceBundle class. Each resource bundle implements a lookup table. When you design a program, you provide a key string for each setting you want to localize, and you use that key string to retrieve the setting. Use getString to retrieve a string resource.

```
String computeButtonLabel
   = resources.getString("computeButton");
```

However, a resource bundle can store objects of *any* kind. Not all localized settings are strings! You use the getObject method to retrieve arbitrary objects from the bundle.

```
Color backgroundColor
   = (Color)resources.getObject("backgroundColor");
double[] paperSize
   = (double[])resources.getObject("defaultPaperSize");
```

TIP: You do not need to place all resources for your application into a single bundle. You could have one bundle for button labels, one for error messages, and so on.

To implement your own resource bundle class, you need to implement two methods:

```
Enumeration getKeys()
Object handleGetObject(String key)
```

The `getObject` and `getString` methods call the `handleGetObject` method that you supply. For example, you can write the following classes to provide German and U.S. English resources.

```
public class ProgramResources extends ResourceBundle
   // place getKeys method in common superclass
{  public Enumeration getKeys()
   {  return Collections.enumeration(Arrays.asList(keys));
   }

   private String[] keys = { "computeButton", "backgroundColor",
      "defaultPaperSize"};
}

public class ProgramResources_de extends ProgramResources
{  public Object handleGetObject(String key)
   {  if (key.equals("computeButton"))
         return "Rechnen";
      else if (key.equals("backgroundColor")
         return Color.black;
      else if (key.equals("defaultPaperSize")
         return new double[] { 210, 297 };
   }
}

public class ProgramResources_en_US extends ProgramResources
{  public Object handleGetObject(String key)
   {  if (key.equals("computeButton"))
         return "Compute";
      else if (key.equals("backgroundColor")
         return Color.blue;
      else if (key.equals("defaultPaperSize")
         return new double[] { 216, 279 };
   }
}
```

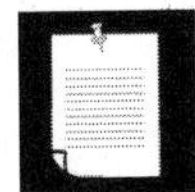

NOTE: Everyone on the planet, with the exception of the United States and Canada, uses ISO 216 paper sizes. For more information, see `http://www.cl.cam.ac.uk/~mgk25/iso-paper.html`. According to the U.S. Metric Association (`http://lamar.colostate.edu/~hillger`), there are only three countries in the world that have not yet officially adopted the metric system, namely, Liberia, Myanmar (Burma), and the United States of America. U.S. businesses that wish to extend their export market further need to go metric. See `http://ts.nist.gov/ts/htdocs/200/202/mpo_reso.htm` for a useful set of links to information about the metric (SI) system.

Of course, it is extremely tedious to write this kind of code for every resource bundle. The Java standard library provides two convenience classes, `ListResourceBundle` and `PropertyResourceBundle`, to make the job easier.

The ListResourceBundle lets you place all your resources into an object array, and then it does the lookup for you. You need to supply the following skeleton:

```
public class ProgramResources_language_country
   extends ListResourceBundle
{  public Object[][] getContents() { return contents;  }
   static final Object[][] contents =
   {  // localization information goes here
   }
}
```

For example,

```
public class ProgramResources_de
   extends ListResourceBundle
{  public Object[][] getContents() { return contents;  }
   static final Object[][] contents =
   {  { "computeButton", "Rechnen" },
      { "backgroundColor", Color.black },
      { "defaultPaperSize", new double[] { 210, 297 } }
   }
}

public class ProgramResources_en_US
   extends ListResourceBundle
{  public Object[][] getContents() { return contents;  }
   static final Object[][] contents =
   {  { "computeButton", "Compute" },
      { "backgroundColor", Color.blue },
      { "defaultPaperSize", new double[] { 216, 279 } }
   }
}
```

Note that you need not supply the getObject lookup method. The Java programming language provides it in the base class ListResourceBundle.

As an alternative, if all your settings are strings, you can use the more convenient PropertyResourceBundle. You place all your strings into a property file, as described in Chapter 2. This is simply a text file with one key/value pair per line. A typical file would look like this:

```
computeButton=Rechnen
backgroundColor=black
defaultPaperSize=210x297
```

Then, you open a stream to the property file and pass it to the PropertyResourceBundle constructor.

```
InputStream in = . . .; // open property file
PropertyResourceBundle currentResources
      = new PropertyResourceBundle(in);
```

Placing all resources into a text file is enormously attractive. It is much easier for the person performing the localization, especially if he or she is not familiar with the Java programming language, to understand a text file than a file with code.

The downside is that your program must parse strings (such as the paper size `"210x297"` in the example above.) The best solution is, therefore, to put the string resources into property files and use a `ListResourceBundle` for those resource objects that are not strings.

NOTE: Files for storing properties are always 7-bit ASCII files. If you need to place Unicode characters into a properties file, you need to encode them by using the `\uxxxx` encoding. For example, to specify `"colorName=Grün"`, use

```
colorName=Gr\u00FCn
```

You can use the `native2ascii` tool to generate these files.

We still have one remaining issue: How can the running program locate the file that contains the localized strings? Naturally, that file is best placed with the class files of the application, preferably inside a JAR file. Then, we can use the `getResourceAsStream` method of the `Class` class. The method will find the right file and open it.

```
in = Program.class.getResourceAsStream("ProgramProperties_de.
   properties");
PropertyResourceBundle currentResources
   = new PropertyResourceBundle(in);
```

It would be nice if the `PropertyResourceBundle` class could look for resource text files in the same way that the `ResourceBundle` class looks for class files. Unfortunately, it does not. Thus, you have to write a class file to accompany every text file. Fortunately, writing such a class file is completely mechanical. For example, here is the class file that loads `ProgramResources_de.properties`.

```
public class ProgramProperties_de
   extends PropertyResourceBundle
{  public ProgramProperties_de() throws IOException
   {  super(ProgramProperties_de.class.getResourceAsStream
         ("ProgramProperties_de.properties"));
   }
}
```

You need to produce two files: the class file and the property file, a text file containing key/value pairs. Place both the class file and property file in the same location in the directory or JAR file.

NOTE: In this section, you saw how to create resource bundles programmatically. Of course, a lot of the code is completely routine. The Java Internationalization and Localization Toolkit (`http://java.sun.com/products/jilkit`) is a tool that can help you manage the creation and maintenance of resource bundles.

java.util.ResourceBundle

- `static ResourceBundle getBundle(String baseName, Locale loc)`
- `static ResourceBundle getBundle(String baseName)`

  These methods load the resource bundle class with the given name, for the given locale or the default locale, and its parent classes. If the resource bundle classes are located in a package, then the base name must contain the full package name, such as `"intl.ProgramResources"`. The resource bundle classes must be `public` so that the `getBundle` method can access them.
- `Object getObject(String name)`

  looks up an object from the resource bundle or its parents.
- `String getString(String name)`

  looks up an object from the resource bundle or its parents and casts it as a string.
- `String[] getStringArray(String name)`

  looks up an object from the resource bundle or its parents and casts it as a string array.
- `Enumeration getKeys()`

  returns an enumeration object to enumerate the keys of this resource bundle. It enumerates the keys in the parent bundles as well.

java.util.PropertyResourceBundle

- `PropertyResourceBundle(InputStream in)`

  creates a resource bundle that contains the key/value pairs from the given input stream.

Graphical User Interface Localization

We have spent a lot of time showing you how to localize your applications. Now, we explain how localization requires you to change the kind of code you write. For example, you have to be much more careful how you code your event handlers for user interface events. Consider the following common style of programming:

```
public class MyApplet extends JApplet
   implements ActionListener
{  public void init()
   {  JButton cancelButton = new JButton("Cancel");
      cancelButton.addActionListener(this);
      . . .
   }
   public void actionPerformed(ActionEvent evt)
   {  String arg = evt.getActionCommand();
      if (arg.equals("Cancel"))
            doCancel();
      else . . .
   }
```

```
      . . .
   }
```

Many programmers write this kind of code, and it works fine as long as you never internationalize the interface. However, when the button name is translated to German, "Cancel" turns into "Abbrechen." Then, the name needs to be updated automatically in both the `init` method and the `actionPerformed` method. This is clearly error prone—it is a well-known corollary to Murphy's law in computer science that two entities that are supposed to stay in sync, won't. In this case, if you forget to update one of the occurrences of the string, then the button won't work. There are three ways you can eliminate this potential problem.

1. Use inner classes instead of separate `actionPerformed` procedures.
2. Identify components by their reference, not their label.
3. Use the `name` attribute to identify components.

Let us look at these three strategies one by one.

Rather than having one handler that handles many actions, you can easily define a separate handler for every component. For example,

```
public class MyApplet extends JApplet implements ActionListener
{  public void init()
   {  JButton cancelButton = new JButton("Cancel");
      cancelButton.addActionListener(
         new ActionListener()
            {  public void actionPerformed(ActionEvent e)
               {  doCancel();
               }
            });
      . . .
   }
   . . .
}
```

This code creates an inner class that listens just to the Cancel button. Since the button and its listener are now tightly joined, there is no more code to parse the button label. Hence, there is only one occurrence of the label string to localize.

We think this is the best solution to the problem of joining a user interface component and its associated handler code. You may not like inner classes, either because they are confusing to read or because each inner class results in an additional class file. The next choice, therefore, is to make the button into an instance variable and compare its reference against the source of the command.

```
public class MyApplet extends JApplet implements ActionListener
{  public void init()
   {  cancelButton = new JButton("Cancel");
      cancelButton.addActionListener(this);
      . . .
```

```
    }

    public void actionPerformed(ActionEvent evt)
    {  Object source = evt.getSource();
       if (source == cancelButton)
           doCancel();
       else . . .
    }
    . . .
    private JButton cancelButton;
}
```

This approach works fine too. Note that now every user interface element must be stored in an instance variable, and the `actionPerformed` method must have access to the variables.

Finally, you can give any class that inherits from `Component` (such as the `Button` class) a *name* property. This name may or may not be distinct from its label in a specific locale, but this is irrelevant; the name property stays constant *regardless* of locale changes. For example, if you give a cancel button the name `"cancel1"`, this is not a visual attribute of the button, it is simply a text string associated with the button. (Think of it as a property of the button—see Chapter 8 for more on properties.) When an action event is triggered, you first get the source and then you can find the name attribute of the source.

```
public class MyApplet extends JApplet implements ActionListener
{  public void init()
   {  JButton cancelButton = new JButton("Cancel");
      cancelButton.setName("cancel1");
      cancelButton.addActionListener(this);
      . . .
   }
   public void actionPerformed(ActionEvent evt)
   {  Component source = (Component)evt.getSource();
      if (source.getName().equals("cancel1"))
        doCancel();
      . . .
   }
   . . .
}
```

`java.awt.Component`

- `void setName(String s)`
- `String getName()`

  These methods set or get a component name, an arbitrary tag associated with the component.

Localizing an Applet

In this section, we apply the material from this chapter to localize a retirement calculator applet.

The applet calculates whether or not you are saving enough money for your retirement. You enter your age, how much money you save every month, and so on (see Figure 10–5).

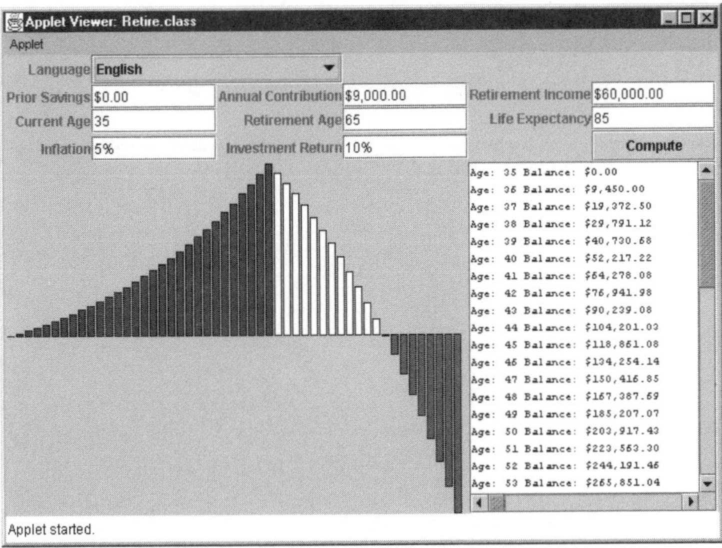

Figure 10–5: The retirement calculator in English

The text area and the graph show the balance of the retirement account for every year. If the numbers turn negative toward the later part of your life and the bars in the graph show up below the x-axis, you need to do something, for example, save more money, postpone your retirement, die earlier, or be younger.

The retirement calculator now works in three locales (English, German, and Chinese). Here are some of the highlights of the internationalization.

- The labels, buttons, and messages are translated into German and Chinese. You can find them in the classes `RetireResources_de`, `RetireResources_zh`. English is used as the fallback—see the `RetireResources` file. To generate the Chinese messages, we first typed the file, using Notepad running in Chinese Windows and then used the `native2ascii` utility to convert the characters to Unicode.
- Whenever the locale changes, we reset the labels and reformat the contents of the text fields.

- The text fields handle numbers, currency amounts, and percentages in the local format.
- The computation field uses a `MessageFormat`. The format string is stored in the resource bundle of each language.
- Just to show that it can be done, we use different colors for the bar graph, depending on the language chosen by the user.

Examples 10–5 through 10–8 show the code. Figures 10–6 and 10–7 show the outputs in German and Chinese. To see Chinese characters, you need to run the applet under Chinese Windows or manually install the Chinese fonts. Otherwise, all Chinese characters show up as "missing character" icons.

NOTE: This applet was harder to write than a typical localized application because the user can change the locale on-the-fly. The applet, therefore, had to be prepared to redraw itself whenever the user selects another locale. If you simply want to display your applet in the user's default locale, you will not need to work so hard. You can simply call `getLocale()` to find the locale of your user's system and then use it for the entire duration of the application.

In sum, while the localization mechanism of the Java programming language still has some rough edges, it does have one major virtue. Once you have organized your application for localization, it is extremely easy to add more localized versions. You simply provide more resource files, and they will be automatically loaded when a user wants them.

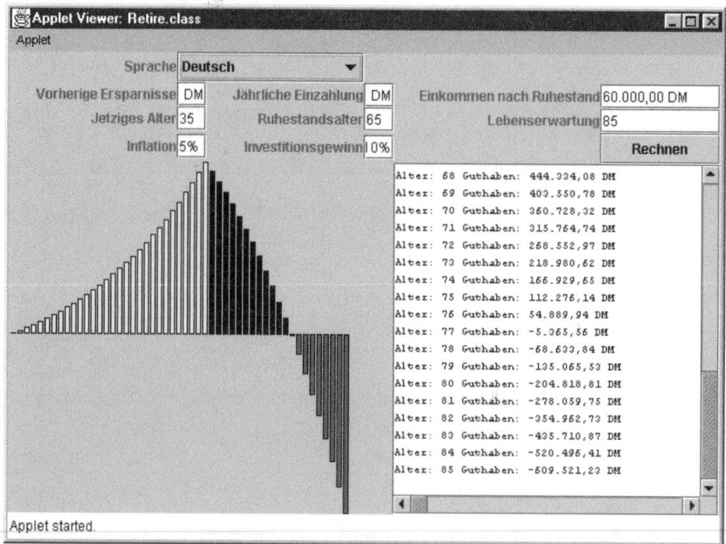

Figure 10–6: The retirement calculator in German

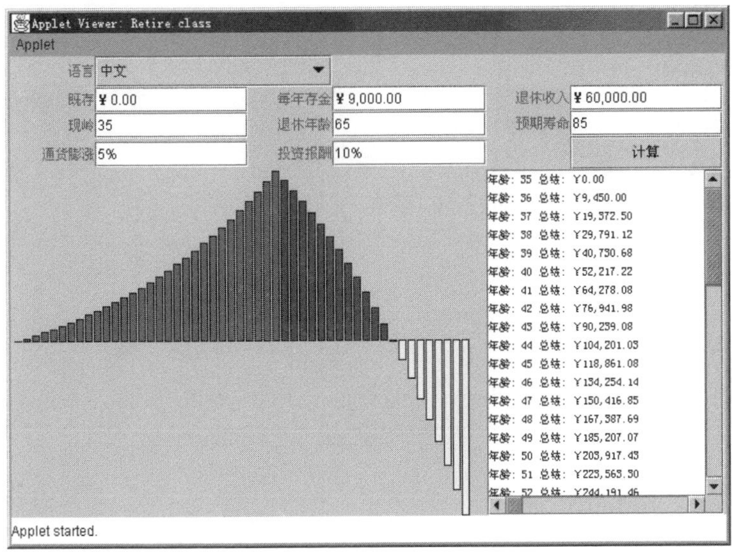

Figure 10–7: The retirement calculator in Chinese

Example 10–5: Retire.java

```
import java.awt.*;
import java.awt.event.*;
import java.applet.*;
import java.util.*;
import java.text.*;
import java.io.*;
import javax.swing.*;

public class Retire extends JApplet
{  public void init()
   {  GridBagLayout gbl = new GridBagLayout();
      getContentPane().setLayout(gbl);

      GridBagConstraints gbc = new GridBagConstraints();
      gbc.weightx = 100;
      gbc.weighty = 0;

      gbc.fill = GridBagConstraints.NONE;
      gbc.anchor = GridBagConstraints.EAST;
      add(languageLabel, gbc, 0, 0, 1, 1);
      add(savingsLabel, gbc, 0, 1, 1, 1);
      add(contribLabel, gbc, 2, 1, 1, 1);
      add(incomeLabel, gbc, 4, 1, 1, 1);
      add(currentAgeLabel, gbc, 0, 2, 1, 1);
      add(retireAgeLabel, gbc, 2, 2, 1, 1);
      add(deathAgeLabel, gbc, 4, 2, 1, 1);
      add(inflationPercentLabel, gbc, 0, 3, 1, 1);
```

```
add(investPercentLabel, gbc, 2, 3, 1, 1);

gbc.fill = GridBagConstraints.HORIZONTAL;
gbc.anchor = GridBagConstraints.WEST;
add(localeCombo, gbc, 1, 0, 2, 1);
add(savingsField, gbc, 1, 1, 1, 1);
add(contribField, gbc, 3, 1, 1, 1);
add(incomeField, gbc, 5, 1, 1, 1);
add(currentAgeField, gbc, 1, 2, 1, 1);
add(retireAgeField, gbc, 3, 2, 1, 1);
add(deathAgeField, gbc, 5, 2, 1, 1);
add(inflationPercentField, gbc, 1, 3, 1, 1);
add(investPercentField, gbc, 3, 3, 1, 1);

computeButton.setName("computeButton");
computeButton.addActionListener(
   new ActionListener()
   {  public void actionPerformed(ActionEvent event)
      {  getInfo();
         updateData();
         updateGraph();
      }
   });
add(computeButton, gbc, 5, 3, 1, 1);

gbc.weighty = 100;
gbc.fill = GridBagConstraints.BOTH;
add(retireCanvas, gbc, 0, 4, 4, 1);
add(new JScrollPane(retireText), gbc, 4, 4, 2, 1);
retireText.setEditable(false);
retireText.setFont(new Font("Monospaced", Font.PLAIN, 10));

info.setSavings(0);
info.setContrib(9000);
info.setIncome(60000);
info.setCurrentAge(35);
info.setRetireAge(65);
info.setDeathAge(85);
info.setInvestPercent(0.1);
info.setInflationPercent(0.05);

localeCombo.addActionListener(
   new ActionListener()
   {  public void actionPerformed(ActionEvent event)
      {  setCurrentLocale(localeCombo.getSelectedIndex());
      }
   });

locales = new Locale[]
```

```
      { Locale.US, Locale.CHINA, Locale.GERMANY };

   int localeIndex = 0; // US locale is default selection

   for (int i = 0; i < locales.length; i++)
      // if current locale one of the choices, we'll select it
      if (getLocale().equals(locales[i])) localeIndex = i;

   setCurrentLocale(localeIndex);
}

public void add(Component c, GridBagConstraints gbc,
   int x, int y, int w, int h)
{  gbc.gridx = x;
   gbc.gridy = y;
   gbc.gridwidth = w;
   gbc.gridheight = h;
   getContentPane().add(c, gbc);
}

public void setCurrentLocale(int localeIndex)
{  currentLocale
      = locales[localeIndex];

   localeCombo.removeAllItems();
   for (int i = 0; i < locales.length; i++)
   {  String language = locales[i].getDisplayLanguage(currentLocale);
      localeCombo.addItem(language);
   }
   localeCombo.setSelectedIndex(localeIndex);

   res = ResourceBundle.getBundle("RetireResources",
      currentLocale);
   currencyFmt
      = NumberFormat.getCurrencyInstance(currentLocale);
   numberFmt
      = NumberFormat.getNumberInstance(currentLocale);
   percentFmt
      = NumberFormat.getPercentInstance(currentLocale);

   updateDisplay();
   updateInfo();
   updateData();
   updateGraph();
}

public void updateDisplay()
{  languageLabel.setText(res.getString("language"));
   savingsLabel.setText(res.getString("savings"));
   contribLabel.setText(res.getString("contrib"));
   incomeLabel.setText(res.getString("income"));
   currentAgeLabel.setText(res.getString("currentAge"));
```

```
      retireAgeLabel.setText(res.getString("retireAge"));
      deathAgeLabel.setText(res.getString("deathAge"));
      inflationPercentLabel.setText
         (res.getString("inflationPercent"));
      investPercentLabel.setText
         (res.getString("investPercent"));
      computeButton.setText(res.getString("computeButton"));

      validate();
   }

   public void updateInfo()
   {  savingsField.setText(currencyFmt.format(info.getSavings()));
      contribField.setText(currencyFmt.format(info.getContrib()));
      incomeField.setText(currencyFmt.format(info.getIncome()));
      currentAgeField.setText(numberFmt.format(info.getCurrentAge()));
      retireAgeField.setText(numberFmt.format(info.getRetireAge()));
      deathAgeField.setText(numberFmt.format(info.getDeathAge()));
      investPercentField.setText(percentFmt.format
         (info.getInvestPercent()));
      inflationPercentField.setText(percentFmt.format
         (info.getInflationPercent()));
   }

   public void updateData()
   {  retireText.setText("");
      MessageFormat retireMsg = new MessageFormat("");
      retireMsg.setLocale(currentLocale);
      retireMsg.applyPattern(res.getString("retire"));

      for (int i = info.getCurrentAge(); i <= info.getDeathAge(); i++)
      {  Object[] args = { new Integer(i),
            new Double(info.getBalance(i)) };
         retireText.append(retireMsg.format(args) + "\n");
      }
   }

   public void updateGraph()
   {  retireCanvas.setColorPre((Color)res.getObject("colorPre"));
      retireCanvas.setColorGain((Color)res.getObject("colorGain"));
      retireCanvas.setColorLoss((Color)res.getObject("colorLoss"));
      retireCanvas.setInfo(info);
      repaint();
   }

   public void getInfo()
   {  try
      {  info.setSavings(currencyFmt.parse
            (savingsField.getText()).doubleValue());
         info.setContrib(currencyFmt.parse
            (contribField.getText()).doubleValue());
         info.setIncome(currencyFmt.parse
            (incomeField.getText()).doubleValue());
```

```
         info.setCurrentAge(numberFmt.parse
            (currentAgeField.getText()).intValue());
         info.setRetireAge(numberFmt.parse
            (retireAgeField.getText()).intValue());
         info.setDeathAge(numberFmt.parse
            (deathAgeField.getText()).intValue());
         info.setInvestPercent(percentFmt.parse
            (investPercentField.getText()).doubleValue());
         info.setInflationPercent(percentFmt.parse
            (inflationPercentField.getText()).doubleValue());
      }
      catch (ParseException exception)
      {
      }
   }

   private JTextField savingsField = new JTextField(10);
   private JTextField contribField = new JTextField(10);
   private JTextField incomeField = new JTextField(10);
   private JTextField currentAgeField = new JTextField(4);
   private JTextField retireAgeField = new JTextField(4);
   private JTextField deathAgeField = new JTextField(4);
   private JTextField inflationPercentField = new JTextField(6);
   private JTextField investPercentField = new JTextField(6);
   private JTextArea retireText = new JTextArea(10, 25);
   private RetireCanvas retireCanvas = new RetireCanvas();
   private JButton computeButton = new JButton();
   private JLabel languageLabel = new JLabel();
   private JLabel savingsLabel = new JLabel();
   private JLabel contribLabel = new JLabel();
   private JLabel incomeLabel = new JLabel();
   private JLabel currentAgeLabel = new JLabel();
   private JLabel retireAgeLabel = new JLabel();
   private JLabel deathAgeLabel = new JLabel();
   private JLabel inflationPercentLabel = new JLabel();
   private JLabel investPercentLabel = new JLabel();

   private RetireInfo info = new RetireInfo();

   private Locale[] locales;
   private Locale currentLocale;
   private JComboBox localeCombo = new JComboBox();
   private ResourceBundle res;
   private NumberFormat currencyFmt;
   private NumberFormat numberFmt;
   private NumberFormat percentFmt;
}

class RetireInfo
{  public double getBalance(int year)
   {  if (year < currentAge) return 0;
      else if (year == currentAge)
      {  age = year;
```

```
      balance = savings;
      return balance;
   }
   else if (year == age)
      return balance;
   if (year != age + 1)
      getBalance(year - 1);
   age = year;
   if (age < retireAge)
      balance += contrib;
   else
      balance -= income;
   balance = balance
      * (1 + (investPercent - inflationPercent));
   return balance;
}

public double getSavings()
{  return savings;
}

public double getContrib()
{  return contrib;
}

public double getIncome()
{  return income;
}

public int getCurrentAge()
{  return currentAge;
}

public int getRetireAge()
{  return retireAge;
}

public int getDeathAge()
{  return deathAge;
}

public double getInflationPercent()
{  return inflationPercent;
}

public double getInvestPercent()
{  return investPercent;
}

public void setSavings(double x)
{  savings = x;
```

```
   }

   public void setContrib(double x)
   {  contrib = x;
   }

   public void setIncome(double x)
   {  income = x;
   }

   public void setCurrentAge(int x)
   {  currentAge = x;
   }

   public void setRetireAge(int x)
   {  retireAge = x;
   }

   public void setDeathAge(int x)
   {  deathAge = x;
   }

   public void setInflationPercent(double x)
   {  inflationPercent = x;
   }

   public void setInvestPercent(double x)
   {  investPercent = x;
   }

   private double savings;
   private double contrib;
   private double income;
   private int currentAge;
   private int retireAge;
   private int deathAge;
   private double inflationPercent;
   private double investPercent;

   private int age;
   private double balance;
}

class RetireCanvas extends JPanel
{  public RetireCanvas()
   {  setSize(400, 200);
   }

   public void setInfo(RetireInfo newInfo)
   {  info = newInfo;
```

```
   }

   public void paint(Graphics g)
   {  if (info == null) return;

      double minValue = 0;
      double maxValue = 0;
      int i;
      for (i = info.getCurrentAge(); i <= info.getDeathAge(); i++)
      {  double v = info.getBalance(i);
         if (minValue > v) minValue = v;
         if (maxValue < v) maxValue = v;
      }
      if (maxValue == minValue) return;

      int barWidth = getWidth() / (info.getDeathAge()
         - info.getCurrentAge() + 1);
      double scale = getHeight() / (maxValue - minValue);

      for (i = info.getCurrentAge(); i <= info.getDeathAge(); i++)
      {  int x1 = (i - info.getCurrentAge()) * barWidth + 1;
         int y1;
         double v = info.getBalance(i);
         int height;
         int yOrigin = (int)(maxValue * scale);

         if (v >= 0)
         {  y1 = (int)((maxValue - v) * scale);
            height = yOrigin - y1;
         }
         else
         {  y1 = yOrigin;
            height = (int)(-v * scale);
         }

         if (i < info.getRetireAge())
            g.setColor(colorPre);
         else if (v >= 0)
            g.setColor(colorGain);
         else
            g.setColor(colorLoss);
         g.fillRect(x1, y1, barWidth - 2, height);
         g.setColor(Color.black);
         g.drawRect(x1, y1, barWidth - 2, height);
      }
   }

   public void setColorPre(Color color)
   {  colorPre = color;
   }

   public void setColorGain(Color color)
   {  colorGain = color;
```

```
   }

   public void setColorLoss(Color color)
   {  colorLoss = color;
   }

   private RetireInfo info = null;


   private Color colorPre;
   private Color colorGain;
   private Color colorLoss;
}
```

Example 10–6: RetireResources.java

```
import java.util.*;
import java.awt.*;

public class RetireResources
   extends java.util.ListResourceBundle
{  public Object[][] getContents() { return contents; }
   static final Object[][] contents =
   {  // BEGIN LOCALIZE
      { "language", "Language" },
      { "computeButton", "Compute" },
      { "savings", "Prior Savings" },
      { "contrib", "Annual Contribution" },
      { "income", "Retirement Income" },
      { "currentAge", "Current Age" },
      { "retireAge", "Retirement Age" },
      { "deathAge", "Life Expectancy" },
      { "inflationPercent", "Inflation" },
      { "investPercent", "Investment Return" },
      { "retire", "Age: {0,number} Balance: {1,number,currency}" },
      { "colorPre", Color.blue },
      { "colorGain", Color.white },
      { "colorLoss", Color.red }
      // END LOCALIZE
   };
}
```

Example 10–7: RetireResources_de.java

```
import java.util.*;
import java.awt.*;

public class RetireResources_de
   extends java.util.ListResourceBundle
{  public Object[][] getContents() { return contents; }
   static final Object[][] contents =
   {  // BEGIN LOCALIZE
      { "language", "Sprache" },
      { "computeButton", "Rechnen" },
```

```
         { "savings", "Vorherige Ersparnisse" },
         { "contrib", "J%hrliche Einzahlung" },
         { "income", "Einkommen nach Ruhestand" },
         { "currentAge", "Jetziges Alter" },
         { "retireAge", "Ruhestandsalter" },
         { "deathAge", "Lebenserwartung" },
         { "inflationPercent", "Inflation" },
         { "investPercent", "Investitionsgewinn" },
         { "retire", "Alter: {0,number} Guthaben: {1,number,currency}" },
         { "colorPre", Color.yellow },
         { "colorGain", Color.black },
         { "colorLoss", Color.red }

         // END LOCALIZE
      };
}
```

Example 10–8: RetireResources_zh.java

```
import java.util.*;
import java.awt.*;

public class RetireResources_zh
   extends java.util.ListResourceBundle
{  public Object[][] getContents() { return contents; }
   static final Object[][] contents =
   {  // BEGIN LOCALIZE
         { "language", "\u8bed\u8a00" },
         { "computeButton", "\u8ba1\u7b97" },
         { "savings", "\u65e2\u5b58" },
         { "contrib", "\u6bcf\u5e74\u5b58\u91d1" },
         { "income", "\u9000\u4f11\u6536\u5165" },
         { "currentAge", "\u73b0\u5cad" },
         { "retireAge", "\u9000\u4f11\u5e74\u9f84" },
         { "deathAge", "\u9884\u671f\u5bff\u547d" },
         { "inflationPercent", "\u901a\u8d27\u81a8\u6da8" },
         { "investPercent", "\u6295\u8d44\u62a5\u916c" },
         { "retire",
           "\u5e74\u9f84: {0,number} \u603b\u7ed3: {1,number,currency}" },
         { "colorPre", Color.red },
         { "colorGain", Color.blue },
         { "colorLoss", Color.yellow }

         // END LOCALIZE
   };
}
```

`java.awt.Applet`

- `Locale getLocale()`

  gets the current locale of the applet. The current locale is determined from the client computer that executes the applet.

Chapter 11

Native Methods

We hope that you are convinced that code written in the Java programming language has a number of advantages over code written in languages like C or C++—even for platform-specific applications. Here, of course, it is not portability that is the issue but rather features like these:

- You are more likely to produce bug-free code with the Java programming language than with C or C++.
- Multithreading is probably easier to code in the Java programming language than in most other languages.
- Networking code is a breeze.

Portability is simply a bonus that you may or may not want to take advantage of down the line.

While a "100% Pure Java" solution is nice in principle, realistically, for an application, there are situations where you will want to write (or use) code written in another language. (Such code is usually called *native* code.) There are three obvious reasons why this may be the right choice:

1. You have substantial amounts of tested and debugged code available in that language. Porting the code to the Java programming language would be time consuming, and the resulting code would need to be tested and debugged again.
2. Your application requires access to system features or devices, and using Java technology would be cumbersome, at best, or impossible, at worst.
3. Maximizing the speed of the code is essential. For example, the task may be time-critical, or it may be code that is used so often that optimizing it has a big payoff. This is actually the least plausible reason. With just-in-time compilation (JIT), intensive computations coded in the Java programming language are not that much slower than compiled C code.

If you are in one of these three situations, it *might* make sense to call the native code from programs written in the Java programming language. Of course, with the usual security manager in place, once you start using native code, you are restricted to applications rather than applets. In particular, the native code library you are calling must exist on the client machine, and it must work with the client machine architecture.

To make calling native methods possible, Java technology comes with hooks for working with system libraries, and the JDK has a few tools to relieve some (but not all) of the programming tedium.

NOTE: The language you use for your native code doesn't have to be C or C++; you could use code compiled with a FORTRAN compiler, if you have access to a binding between the Java and FORTRAN programming languages.

Still, keep in mind: If you use native methods, you lose portability. Even when you distribute your program as an application, you must supply a separate native method library for every platform you wish to support. This means you must also educate your users on how to install these libraries! Also, while users may trust that applets can neither damage data nor steal confidential information, they may not want to extend the same trust to code that uses native method libraries. For that reason, many potential users will be reluctant to use programs in the Java programming language that require native code. Aside from the security issue, native libraries are unlikely to be as safe as code written in the Java programming language, especially if they are written in a language like C or C++ that offers no protection against overwriting memory through invalid pointer usage. It is easy to write native methods that corrupt the Java virtual machine, compromise its security, or trash the operating system.

Thus, we suggest using native code only as a last resort. If you must gain access to a device, such as a serial port, in a program, then you may need to write native code. If you need to access an existing body of code, why not consider native methods as a stopgap measure and eventually port the code to the Java programming language? If you are concerned about efficiency, benchmark a Java platform implementation. In most cases, the speed using a just-in-time compiler will be sufficient. A talk at the 1996 JavaOne conference showed this clearly. The implementors of the cryptography library at Sun Microsystems reported that a pure Java platform implementation of their cryptographic functions was more than adequate. It was true that the code was not as fast as a C implementation would have been, but it turned out not to matter. The Java platform implementation was far faster than the network I/O. And this turns out to be the real bottleneck.

In summary, there is no point in sacrificing portability for a meaningless speed improvement; don't go native until you determine that you have no other choice.

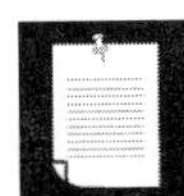

NOTE: In this chapter, we describe the so-called Java Native Interface (JNI) binding. An earlier language binding (sometimes called the raw native interface) was used with Java 1.0, and a variation of that earlier binding was used by the Microsoft Virtual Machine. Sun Microsystems has assured developers that the JNI binding described here is a permanent part of the Java platform, and that it needs to be supported by all Java virtual machines.

Finally, we use C as our language for native methods in this chapter because C is probably the language most often used for native methods. In particular, you'll see how to make the correspondence between Java data types, feature names, and function calls and those of C. (This correspondence is usually called the C *binding*.)

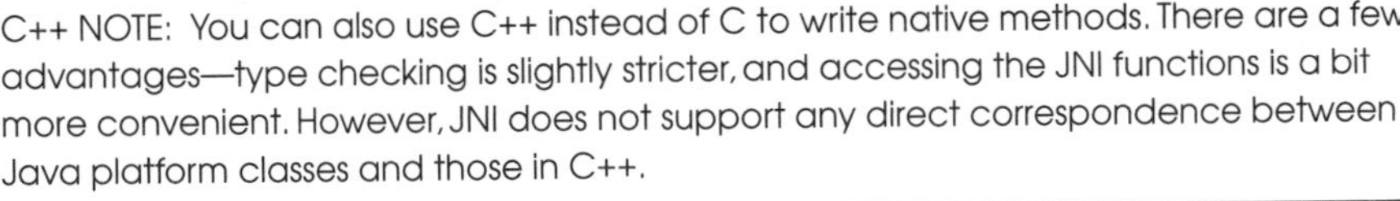

C++ NOTE: You can also use C++ instead of C to write native methods. There are a few advantages—type checking is slightly stricter, and accessing the JNI functions is a bit more convenient. However, JNI does not support any direct correspondence between Java platform classes and those in C++.

Calling a C Function from the Java Programming Language

Suppose you have a C function that does something you like and, for one reason or another, you don't want to bother reimplementing it in the Java programming language. For the sake of illustration, we'll assume it is the useful and venerable `printf` function. You want to be able to call `printf` from your programs. The Java programming language uses the keyword native for a native method, and you will obviously need to encapsulate the `printf` function in a class. So, you might write something like:

```
public class Printf
{  public native String printf(String s);
}
```

You actually can compile this class but when you go to use it in a program, then the virtual machine will tell you it doesn't know how to find `printf`—reporting an `UnsatisfiedLinkError`. So the trick is to give the run time enough information so that it can link in this class. As you will soon see, under the JDK this requires a three-step process:

1. Generate a C stub for a function that translates between the Java platform call and the actual C function. The stub does this translation by taking parameter information off the virtual machine stack and passing it to the compiled C function.
2. Create a special shared library and export the stub from it.
3. Use a special method, called `System.loadLibrary`. to tell the Java runtime environment to load the library from Step 2.

We now show you how to carry out these steps for various kinds of examples, starting from a trivial special-case use of `printf` and ending with a realistic example involving the registry function for Windows—platform-dependent functions that are obviously not available directly from the Java platform.

Working with the `printf` *Function*

Let's start with just about the simplest possible situation using `printf`: calling a native method that prints the message "Hello, Native World." Obviously we are not even tapping into the useful formatting features of `printf`! Still, this is a good way for you to test that your C compiler works as expected before you try implementing more ambitious native methods.

As we mentioned earlier, you first need to declare the native method in a class. The `native` keyword alerts the compiler that the method will be defined externally. Of course, native methods will contain no code in the Java programming language, and the method header is followed immediately by a terminating semicolon. This means, as you saw in the example above, native method declarations look similar to abstract method declarations.

```
class HelloNative
{  public native static void greeting();
   . . .
}
```

In this particular example, note that we also declare the native method as `static`. Native methods can be both static and nonstatic. This method takes no parameters; we do not yet want to deal with parameter passing, not even implicit parameters.

Next, write a corresponding C function. You must name that function *exactly* the way the Java runtime environment expects. Here are the rules:

1. Use the full Java method name, such as `HelloNative.greeting`. If the class is in a package, then prepend the package name, such as `com.horstmann.HelloNative.greeting`.

2. Replace every period with an underscore, and prepend the prefix `Java_`. For example, `Java_HelloNative_greeting` or `Java_com_horstmann_HelloNative_greeting`.
3. If the class name contains characters that are not ASCII letters or digits—that is, `'_'`, `'$'`, or Unicode characters with code > `'\u007F'`—replace them with `_0`*xxxx*, where *xxxx* is the sequence of four hexadecimal digits of the character's Unicode value.

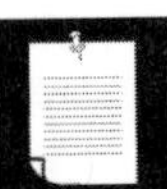

NOTE: If you *overload* native methods, that is, if you provide multiple native methods with the same name, then you must append a double underscore followed by the encoded argument types. We describe the encoding of the argument types later in this chapter. For example, if you have a native method, `greeting`, and another native method `greeting(int repeat)`, then the first one is called `Java_HelloNative_greeting__`, and the second, `Java_HelloNative_greeting__I`.

Actually, nobody does this by hand; instead, you should run the `javah` utility, which automatically generates the function names. To use `javah`, first, compile the source file (given in Example 11–3).

```
javac HelloNative.java
```

Next, call the `javah` utility to produce a C header file. The `javah` executable can be found in the `\jdk\bin` directory.

```
javah HelloNative
```

NOTE: If you are still using JDK1.1, be sure to use the `-jni` flag when running `javah`. Without that flag, the `javah` tool in JDK 1.1 generates the header file for the Java 1.0 binding. Starting with JDK 1.2, the JNI binding is the default.

Using `javah` creates a header file, `HelloNative.h`, as in Example 11–1.

Example 11–1: HelloNative.h

```
/* DO NOT EDIT THIS FILE - it is machine generated */
#include <jni.h>
/* Header for class HelloNative */

#ifndef _Included_HelloNative
#define _Included_HelloNative
#ifdef __cplusplus
extern "C" {
#endif
/*
 * Class:     HelloNative
 * Method:    greeting
 * Signature: ()V
```

```
 */
JNIEXPORT void JNICALL Java_HelloNative_greeting
  (JNIEnv *, jclass);

#ifdef __cplusplus
}
#endif
#endif
```

As you can see, this file contains the declaration of a function `Java_HelloNative_greeting`. (The strings `JNIEXPORT` and `JNICALL` are defined in the header file `jni.h`. They denote compiler-dependent specifiers for exported functions that come from a dynamically loaded library.)

Now, you simply have to copy the function prototype from the header file into the source file and give the implementation code for the function, as shown in Example 11–2.

Example 11–2: HelloNative.c

```
#include "HelloNative.h"
#include <stdio.h>

JNIEXPORT void JNICALL Java_HelloNative_greeting
  (JNIEnv* env, jclass cl)
{  printf("Hello, Native World!\n");
}
```

In this simple function, we ignore the `env` and `cl` arguments. You'll see their use later.

C++ NOTE: You can use C++ to implement native methods. However, you must then declare the functions that implement the native methods as extern "C". For example,

```
#include "HelloNative.h"
#include <stdio.h>

extern "C"
JNIEXPORT void JNICALL Java_HelloNative_greeting
   (JNIEnv* env, jclass cl)
{  printf("Hello, Native World!\n");
}
```

Next, compile the C code into a dynamically loaded library. For example, with the Microsoft C++ compiler under Windows, the command you use is

```
cl -Ic:\jdk\include -Ic:\jdk\include\win32 -LD HelloNative.c
   -FeHelloNative.dll
```

With the Sun compiler under the Solaris operating environment, the command to use is

```
cc -G -I/usr/local/jdk/include
   -I/usr/local/jdk/include/solaris
   HelloNative.c -o libHelloNative.so
```

(You may need to use different paths to specify the locations of the header files, depending on which directory contains the JDK.)

TIP: If you use the Microsoft C++ compiler to compile DLLs from a DOS shell, first run the batch file

```
c:\devstudio\vc\bin\vcvars32.bat
```

That batch file properly configures the command-line compiler by setting up the path and the environment variables needed by the compiler.

Finally, we need to add the call to the `System.loadLibrary` method that ensures that the virtual machine will load the library prior to the first use of the class. The easiest way to do this is to use a static initialization block in the class that contains the native method, as in Example 11–3:

Example 11–3: HelloNative.java

```
class HelloNative
{  public native static void greeting();
   static
   {  System.loadLibrary("HelloNative");
   }
}
```

Assuming you have followed all the steps given above, you are now ready to run the `HelloNativeTest` application shown in Example 11–4.

Example 11–4: HelloNativeTest.java

```
class HelloNativeTest
{  public static void main(String[] args)
   {  HelloNative.greeting();
   }
}
```

If you compile and run this program, the message "Hello, Native World!" is displayed in a terminal window.

Of course, this is not particularly impressive by itself. However, if you keep in mind that this message is generated by the C `printf` command and not by any Java programming language code, you will see that we have taken the first steps toward bridging the gap between the two languages!

NOTE: Some shared libraries for native code need to run initialization code. You can place any initialization code into a `JNI_OnLoad` method. Similarly, when the VM shuts down, it will call the `JNI_OnUnload` method if you provide it. The prototypes are

```
jint JNI_OnLoad(JavaVM* vm, void* reserved);
void JNI_OnUnload(JavaVM* vm, void* reserved);
```

The `JNI_OnLoad` method needs to return the minimum version of the VM that it requires, such as `JNI_VERSION_1_1`.

`java.lang.System`

- `void loadLibrary(String libname)`
  loads the library with the given name. The library is located in the library search path. The exact method for locating the library is operating-system dependent. Under Windows, this method searches first the current directory, then the directories listed in the `PATH` environment variable.
- `void load(String filename)`
  loads the library with the given file name. If the library is not found, then an `UnsatisfiedLinkError` is thrown.

Numeric Parameters and Return Values

When passing numbers between C and the Java programming language, you need to understand which types correspond to each other. For example, while C does have data types called `int` and `long`, their implementation is platform dependent. On some platforms, `int`s are 16-bit quantities, and on others they are 32-bit quantities. In the Java platform, of course, an `int` is *always* a 32-bit integer. For that reason, the Java Native Interface defines types `jint`, `jlong`, and so on. Table 11–1 shows the correspondence between Java types and C types.

Table 11–1: Java types and C types

Java Programming Language	C Programming Language	Bytes
boolean	jboolean	1
byte	jbyte	1
char	jchar	2
short	jshort	2
int	jint	4
long	jlong	8
float	jfloat	4
double	jdouble	8

In the header file `jni.h`, these types are declared with `typedef` statements as the equivalent types on the target platform. That header file also defines the constants `JNI_FALSE = 0` and `JNI_TRUE = 1`.

Using `printf` *for Formatting Numbers*

Recall that the Java library has no elegant way for formatted printing of floating-point numbers. Of course, you can use the `DecimalFormat` class (see Volume 1, Chapter 3) and build custom formats—we just don't think this is as easy as a simple call to `printf`. Since `printf` is quick, easy, and well known, let's suppose you decide to implement the same functionality via a call to the `printf` function in a native method.

We don't actually recommend this approach: the native code needs to be compiled for every target platform. We are using it because it shows off the techniques of passing parameters to a native method and obtaining a return value.

Example 11–5 shows a class called `Printf1` that uses a native method to print a floating-point number with a given field width and precision.

Example 11–5: Printf1.java

```
class Printf1
{  public static native int print(int width, int
      precision, double x);
   static
   {  System.loadLibrary("Printf1");
   }
}
```

Notice that when implementing the method in C, all `int` and `double` parameters are changed to `jint` and `jdouble`, as shown in Example 11–6.

Example 11–6: Printf1.c

```
#include "Printf1.h"
#include <stdio.h>

JNIEXPORT jint JNICALL Java_Printf1_print
  (JNIEnv* env, jclass cl, jint width, jint precision, jdouble x)
{  char fmt[30];
   jint ret;
   sprintf(fmt, "%%%d.%df", width, precision);
   ret = printf(fmt, x);
   return ret;
}
```

The function simply assembles a format string `"%w.pf"` in the variable `fmt`, then calls `printf`. It then returns the number of characters it printed.

Example 11–7 shows the test program that demonstrates the `Printf1` class.

Example 11–7: Printf1Test.java

```
class Printf1Test
{  public static void main(String[] args)
   {  int count = Printf1.print(8, 4, 3.14);
      count += Printf1.print(8, 4, (double)count);
      System.out.println();
      for (int i = 0; i < count; i++)
         System.out.print("-");
      System.out.println();
   }
}
```

String Parameters

Next, we want to consider how to transfer strings to and from native methods. As you know, strings in the Java programming language are sequences of 16-bit Unicode characters; C strings are null-terminated strings of 8-bit characters, so strings are quite different in the two languages. The Java Native Interface has two sets of functions, one that converts Java strings to UTF (Unicode Text Format) and one that converts them to arrays of Unicode characters, that is, to `jchar` arrays. The UTF format was discussed in Chapter 1—recall that ASCII characters are encoded "as is," but all other Unicode characters are encoded as 2-byte or 3-byte sequences.

If your C code already uses Unicode, you'll want to use the second set of conversion functions. On the other hand, if all your Java strings are restricted to ASCII characters, you can use the UTF conversion functions.

A native method with a `String` parameter actually receives a value of an opaque type called `jstring`. A native method with a return value of type `String` must return a value of type `jstring`. JNI functions are used to read and construct these `jstring` objects. For example, the `NewStringUTF` function makes a new `jstring` object out of a `char` array that contains UTF-encoded characters. Unfortunately, JNI functions have a somewhat odd calling convention. Here is a call to the `NewStringUTF` function.

```
JNIEXPORT jstring JNICALL Java_HelloNative_getGreeting
   (JNIEnv* env, jclass cl)
{  jstring jstr;
   char greeting[] = "Hello, Native World\n";
   jstr = (*env)->NewStringUTF(env, greeting);
   return jstr;
}
```

All calls to JNI functions use the `env` pointer that is the first argument of every native method. The `env` pointer is a pointer to a table of function pointers (see

Figure 11–1). Therefore, you must prefix every JNI call with `(*env)->` to actually dereference the function pointer. Furthermore, `env` is the first parameter of every JNI function. This setup is somewhat cumbersome, and it could have easily been made more transparent to C programmers. We suggest that you simply supply the `(*env)->` prefix without worrying about the table of function pointers.

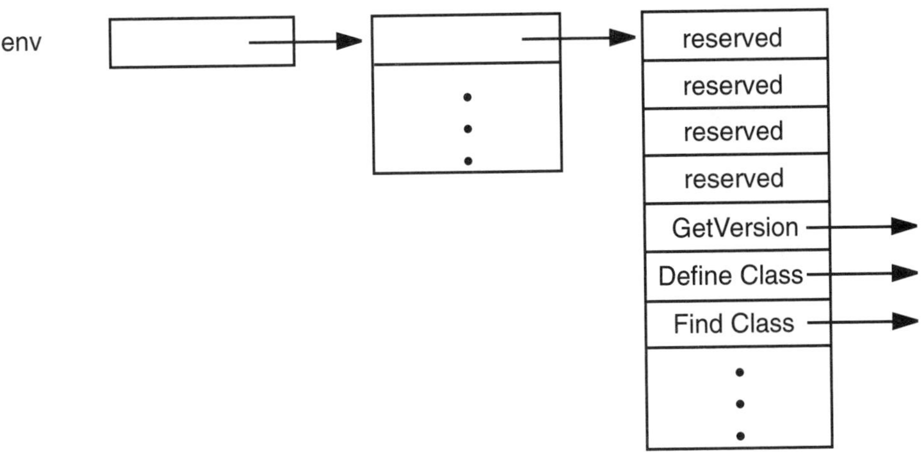

Figure 11–1: The env pointer

C++ NOTE: It is simpler to access JNI functions in C++. The C++ version of the `JNIEnv` class has inline member functions that take care of the function pointer lookup for you. For example, you can call the `NewStringUTF` function as

```
jstr = env->NewStringUTF(greeting);
```

Note that you omit the `JNIEnv` pointer from the parameter list of the call.

The `NewStringUTF` function lets you construct a new `jstring`. To read the contents of an existing `jstring` object, use the `GetStringUTFChars` function. This function returns a `const jbyte*` pointer to the UTF characters that describe the character string. Note that a specific virtual machine is free to use UTF for its internal string representation, so you may get a character pointer into the actual Java string. Since Java strings are meant to be immutable, it is *very* important that you treat the `const` seriously and do not try to write into this character array. On the other hand, if the virtual machine uses Unicode characters for its internal string representation, then this function call allocates a new memory block that will be filled with the UTF equivalents.

The virtual machine must know when you are finished using the UTF string, so that it can garbage-collect it. (The garbage collector runs in a separate thread, and it can interrupt the execution of native methods.) For that reason, you must call the `ReleaseStringUTFChars` function.

Alternatively, you can supply your own buffer to hold the string characters by calling the `GetStringRegion` or `GetStringUTFRegion` methods.

Finally, the `GetStringUTFLength` function returns the number of characters needed for the UTF encoding of the string.

Accessing Java strings from C code

- `jstring NewStringUTF(JNIEnv* env, const char bytes[])`
  returns a new Java string object from an UTF string, or `NULL` if the string cannot be constructed.

Parameters:	`env`	the JNI interface pointer
	`bytes`	the null-terminated UTF string

- `jsize GetStringUTFLength(JNIEnv* env, jstring string)`
  returns the number of characters required for the UTF encoding.

Parameters:	`env`	the JNI interface pointer
	`string`	a Java string object

- `const jbyte* GetStringUTFChars(JNIEnv* env, jstring string, jboolean* isCopy)`
  returns a pointer to the UTF encoding of a string, or `NULL` if the character array cannot be constructed. The pointer is valid until `ReleaseStringUTFChars` is called.

Parameters:	`env`	the JNI interface pointer
	`string`	a Java string object
	`isCopy`	points to a `jboolean` that is filled with `JNI_TRUE` if a copy is made; with `JNI_FALSE` otherwise

- `void ReleaseStringUTFChars(JNIEnv* env, jstring string, const jbyte bytes[])`
  informs the virtual machine that the native code no longer needs access to the Java string through `bytes`.

Parameters:	`env`	the JNI interface pointer
	`string`	a Java string object
	`bytes`	a pointer returned by `GetStringUTFChars`

- `void GetStringRegion(JNIEnv *env, jstring string, jsize start, jsize length, jchar *buffer)`
  copies a sequence of Unicode characters from a string to a user-supplied buffer.

Parameters:	`env`	the JNI interface pointer
	`string`	a Java string object

	`start`	the starting index
	`length`	the number of characters to copy
	`buffer`	the user-supplied buffer

- `void GetStringUTFRegion(JNIEnv *env, jstring string, jsize start, jsize length, jbyte *buffer)`
  copies a sequence of UTF8 characters from a string to a user-supplied buffer. The buffer must be long enough to hold the bytes. In the worst case, 3 × `length` bytes are copied.
- `jstring NewString(JNIEnv* env, const jchar chars[], jsize length)`
  returns a new Java string object from a Unicode string, or `NULL` if the string cannot be constructed.

Parameters:	`env`	the JNI interface pointer
	`chars`	the null-terminated UTF string
	`length`	the number of characters in the string

- `jsize GetStringLength(JNIEnv* env, jstring string)`
  returns the number of characters in the string.

Parameters:	`env`	the JNI interface pointer
	`string`	a Java string object

- `const jchar* GetStringChars(JNIEnv* env, jstring string, jboolean* isCopy)`
  returns a pointer to the Unicode encoding of a string, or `NULL` if the character array cannot be constructed. The pointer is valid until `ReleaseStringChars` is called.

Parameters:	`env`	the JNI interface pointer
	`string`	a Java string object
	`isCopy`	is either `NULL` or points to a `jboolean` that is filled with `JNI_TRUE` if a copy is made; with `JNI_FALSE` otherwise

- `void ReleaseStringChars(JNIEnv* env, jstring string, const jchar chars[])`
  informs the virtual machine that the native code no longer needs access to the Java string through chars.

Parameters:	`env`	the JNI interface pointer
	`string`	a Java string object
	`chars`	a pointer returned by `GetStringChars`

Calling `sprintf` *in a Native Method*

Let us put these functions we just described to work and write a class that calls the C function `sprintf`. We would like to call the function as shown in Example 11–8.

Example 11–8: Printf2Test.java

```
class Printf2Test
{  public static void main(String[] args)
   {  double price = 44.95;
      double tax = 7.75;
      double amountDue = price * (1 + tax / 100);

      String s = Printf2.sprint("Amount due = %8.2f",
         amountDue);
      System.out.println(s);
   }
}
```

Example 11–9 shows the class with the native `sprintf` method.

Example 11–9: Printf2.java

```
class Printf2
{  public static native String sprint(String format, double x);
   static
   {  System.loadLibrary("Printf2");
   }
}
```

Therefore, the C function that formats a floating-point number has the prototype

```
JNIEXPORT jstring JNICALL Java_Printf2_sprint
  (JNIEnv* env, jclass cl, jstring format, jdouble x)
```

Example 11–10 shows the code for the C implementation. Note the calls to `GetStringUTFChars` to read the format argument, `NewStringUTF` to generate the return value, and `ReleaseStringUTFChars` to inform the virtual machine that access to the string is no longer required.

Example 11–10: Printf2.c

```
#include "Printf2.h"
#include <string.h>
#include <stdlib.h>
#include <float.h>

char* find_format(const char format[])
/**
 * @param format a string containing a printf format specifier
 * (such as "%8.2f"). Substrings "%%" are skipped.
 * @return a pointer to the format specifier (skipping the '%')
 * or NULL if there wasn't a unique format specifier
```

```
 */
{  char* p;
   char* q;

   p = strchr(format, '%');
   while (p != NULL && *(p + 1) == '%') /* skip %% */
      p = strchr(p + 2, '%');
   if (p == NULL) return NULL;
   /* now check that % is unique */
   p++;
   q = strchr(p, '%');
   while (q != NULL && *(q + 1) == '%') /* skip %% */
      q = strchr(q + 2, '%');
   if (q != NULL) return NULL; /* % not unique */
   q = p + strspn(p, " -0+#"); /* skip past flags */
   q += strspn(q, "0123456789"); /* skip past field width */
   if (*q == '.') { q++; q += strspn(q, "0123456789"); }
      /* skip past precision */
   if (strchr("eEfFgG", *q) == NULL) return NULL;
      /* not a floating point format */
   return p;
}

JNIEXPORT jstring JNICALL Java_Printf2_sprint
  (JNIEnv* env, jclass cl, jstring format, jdouble x)
{  const char* cformat;
   char* fmt;
   jstring ret;

   cformat = (*env)->GetStringUTFChars(env, format, NULL);
   fmt = find_format(cformat);
   if (fmt == NULL)
      ret = format;
   else
   {  char* cret;
      int width = atoi(fmt);
      if (width == 0) width = DBL_DIG + 10;
      cret = (char*)malloc(strlen(cformat) + width);
      sprintf(cret, cformat, x);
      ret = (*env)->NewStringUTF(env, cret);
      free(cret);
   }
   (*env)->ReleaseStringUTFChars(env, format, cformat);
   return ret;
}
```

In this function, we chose to keep the error handling simple. If the format code to print a floating-point number is not of the form `%w.pc`, where `c` is one of the characters `e`, `E`, `f`, `g`, or `G`, then what we simply do is *not* format the number. You will see later how to make a native method throw an exception.

Accessing Object Fields

All the native methods that you saw so far were static methods with number and string parameters. We next consider native methods that operate on objects. As an exercise, we will implement a method of the `Employee` class that was introduced in Chapter 4 of Volume 1, using a native method. Again, this is not something you would normally want to do, but it does illustrate how to access object fields from a native method when you need to do so.

Consider the `raiseSalary` method. In the Java programming language, the code was simple.

```
public void raiseSalary(double byPercent)
{  salary *= 1 + byPercent / 100;
}
```

Let us rewrite this as a native method. Unlike the previous examples of native methods, this is not a static method. Running `javah` gives the following prototype.

```
JNIEXPORT void JNICALL Java_Employee_raiseSalary
   (JNIEnv *, jobject, jdouble);
```

Note the second argument. It is no longer of type `jclass` but of type `jobject`. In fact, it is the equivalent of the `this` reference. Static methods obtain a reference to the class, whereas nonstatic methods obtain a reference to the implicit `this` argument object.

Now we access the `salary` field of the implicit argument. In the "raw" Java-to-C binding of Java 1.0, this was easy—a programmer could directly access object data fields. However, direct access requires all virtual machines to expose their internal data layout. For that reason, the JNI requires programmers to get and set the values of data fields by calling special JNI functions.

In our case, we need to use the `GetDoubleField` and `SetDoubleField` functions because the type of `salary` is a `double`. There are other functions—`GetIntField`/`SetIntField`, `GetObjectField`/`SetObjectField`, and so on—for other field types. The general syntax is:

```
x = (*env)->GetXxxField(env, class, fieldID);
(*env)->GetXxxField(env, class, fieldID, x);
```

Here, `class` is a value that represents a Java object of type `Class`, and `fieldID` is a value of a special type, `jfieldID`, that identifies a field in a structure and *Xxx* represents a Java data type (`Object`, `Boolean`, `Byte`, and so on). There are two

ways for obtaining the `class` object. The `GetObjectClass` function returns the class of any object. For example:

```
jclass class_Employee = (*env)->GetObjectClass(env, obj_this);
```

The `FindClass` function lets you specify the class name as a string (curiously, with / instead of periods as package name separators).

```
jclass class_String
   = (*env)->FindClass(env, "java/lang/String");
```

Use the `GetFieldID` function to obtain the `fieldID`. You must supply the name of the field and its *signature,* an encoding of its type. For example, here is the code to obtain the field ID of the `salary` field.

```
jfieldID id_salary
   = (*env)->GetFieldID(env, class_Employee, "salary", "D");
```

The string `"D"` denotes the type `double`. You will learn the complete rules for encoding signatures in the next section.

You may be thinking that accessing a data field seems quite convoluted. However, since the designers of the JNI did not want to expose the data fields directly, they had to supply functions for getting and setting field values. To minimize the cost of these functions, computing the field ID from the field name—which is the most expensive step—is factored out into a separate step. That is, if you repeatedly get and set the value of a particular field, you incur only once the cost of computing the field identifier.

Let us put all the pieces together. The following code reimplements the `raiseSalary` method as a native method.

```
JNIEXPORT void JNICALL Java_Employee_raiseSalary
  (JNIEnv* env, jobject obj_this, jdouble byPercent)
{  /* get the class */
   jclass class_Employee = (*env)->GetObjectClass(env,
      obj_this);

   /* get the field ID */
   jfieldID id_salary = (*env)->GetFieldID(env, class_Employee,
      "salary", "D");

   /* get the field value */
   jdouble salary = (*env)->GetDoubleField(env, obj_this,
      id_salary);

   salary *= 1 + byPercent / 100;

   /* set the field value */
   (*env)->SetDoubleField(env, obj_this, id_salary, salary);
}
```

CAUTION: Class references are only valid until the native method returns. Thus, you cannot cache the return values of `GetObjectClass` in your code. Do *not* store away a class reference for reuse in a later method call. You need to call `GetObjectClass` every time the native method executes. If this is intolerable, you can lock the reference with a call to `NewGlobalRef`:

```
static jclass class_X = 0;
static jfieldID id_a;
. . .
if (class_X == 0)
{  jclass cx = (*env)->GetObjectClass(env, obj);
   class_X = (*env)->NewGlobalRef(env, cx);
   id_a = (*env)->GetFieldID(env, cls, "a", ". . .");
}
```

Now you can use the class reference and field IDs in subsequent calls. When you are done using the class, make sure to call

```
(*env)->DeleteGlobalRef(env, class_X);
```

Examples 11–11 and 11–12 show the Java code for a test program and the `Employee` class. Example 11–13 contains the C code for the native `raiseSalary` method.

Accessing Static Fields

Accessing static fields is similar to accessing nonstatic fields. You use the `GetStaticFieldID` and `GetStatic`*`Xxx`*`Field`/`SetStatic`*`Xxx`*`Field` functions. They work almost identically to their nonstatic counterpart. There are only two differences.

- Since you have no object, you must use `FindClass` instead of `GetObjectClass` to obtain the class reference.
- You supply the class, not the instance object, when accessing the field.

For example, here is how you can get a reference to `System.out`.

```
/* get the class */
jclass class_System = (*env)->FindClass(env,
   "java/lang/System");

/* get the field ID */
jfieldID id_out = (*env)->GetStaticFieldID(env,
   class_System, "out", "Ljava/io/PrintStream;");

/* get the field value */
jobject obj_out = (*env)->GetStaticObjectField(env,
   class_System, id_out);
```

Example 11–11: EmployeeTest.java

```
public class EmployeeTest
{  public static void main(String[] args)
   {  Employee[] staff = new Employee[3];
```

```
        staff[0] = new Employee("Harry Hacker", 35000));
        staff[1] = new Employee("Carl Cracker", 75000));
        staff[2] = new Employee("Tony Tester", 38000));

        int i;
        for (i = 0; i < 3; i++) staff[i].raiseSalary(5);
        for (i = 0; i < 3; i++) staff[i].print();
    }
}
```

Example 11–12: Employee.java

```
public class Employee
{  public Employee(String n, double s)
   {  name = n;
      salary = s;
   }

   public native void raiseSalary(double byPercent);

   public void print()
   {  System.out.println(name + " " + salary);
   }

   private String name;
   private double salary;

   static
   {  System.loadLibrary("Employee");
   }
}
```

Example 11–13: Employee.c

```
#include "Employee.h"

#include <stdio.h>

JNIEXPORT void JNICALL Java_Employee_raiseSalary
  (JNIEnv* env, jobject obj_this, jdouble byPercent)
{  /* get the class */
   jclass class_Employee = (*env)->GetObjectClass(env,
      obj_this);

   /* get the field ID */
   jfieldID id_salary = (*env)->GetFieldID(env,
      class_Employee, "salary", "D");

   /* get the field value */
   jdouble salary = (*env)->GetDoubleField(env, obj_this,
      id_salary);
```

```
    salary *= 1 + byPercent / 100;

    /* set the field value */
    (*env)->SetDoubleField(env, obj_this, id_salary, salary);
}
```

Accessing object fields

- `jfieldID GetFieldID(JNIEnv *env, jclass cl, const char name[], const char sig[])`
  returns the identifier of a field in a class.

Parameters:	`env`	the JNI interface pointer
	`cl`	the class object
	`name`	the field name
	`sig`	the encoded field signature

- *Xxx* `Get`*Xxx*`Field(JNIEnv *env, jobject obj, jfieldID id)`
  returns the value of a field. The field type *Xxx* is one of `Object`, `Boolean`, `Byte`, `Char`, `Short`, `Int`, `Long`, `Float`, or `Double`.

Parameters:	`env`	the JNI interface pointer
	`obj`	the object whose field is being returned
	`id`	the field identifier

- `void Set`*Xxx*`Field(JNIEnv *env, jobject obj, jfieldID id,` *Xxx* `value)`
  sets a field to a new value. The field type *Xxx* is one of `Object`, `Boolean`, `Byte`, `Char`, `Short`, `Int`, `Long`, `Float`, or `Double`.

Parameters:	`env`	the JNI interface pointer
	`obj`	the object whose field is being set
	`id`	the field identifier
	`value`	the new field value

- `jfieldID GetStaticFieldID(JNIEnv *env, jclass cl, const char name[], const char sig[])`
  returns the identifier of a static field in a class.

Parameters:	`env`	the JNI interface pointer
	`cl`	the class object
	`name`	the field name
	`sig`	the encoded field signature

- `Xxx GetStaticXxxField(JNIEnv *env, jclass cl, jfieldID id)`
  returns the value of a static field. The field type *Xxx* is one of `Object`, `Boolean`, `Byte`, `Char`, `Short`, `Int`, `Long`, `Float`, or `Double`.

Parameters:	`env`	the JNI interface pointer
	`cl`	the class object whose static field is being set
	`id`	the field identifier

- `void SetStaticXxxField(JNIEnv *env, jclass cl, jfieldID id, Xxx value)`
  sets a static field to a new value. The field type *Xxx* is one of `Object`, `Boolean`, `Byte`, `Char`, `Short`, `Int`, `Long`, `Float`, or `Double`.

Parameters:	`env`	the JNI interface pointer
	`cl`	the class object whose static field is being set
	`id`	the field identifier
	`value`	the new field value

Signatures

To access object fields and call methods that are defined in the Java programming language, you need to learn the rules for "mangling" the names of data types and method signatures. (A method signature describes the parameters and return type of the method.) Here is the encoding scheme:

`B`	`byte`
`C`	`char`
`D`	`double`
`F`	`float`
`I`	`int`
`J`	`long`
`L`*`classname`*`;`	a class type
`S`	`short`
`V`	`void`
`Z`	`boolean`

Note that the semicolon at the end of the L expression is the terminator of the type expression, not a separator between parameters. For example, the constructor

```
Employee(java.lang.String, double, java.util.Date)
```

has a signature

```
"(Ljava/lang/String;DLjava/util/Date;)V"
```

As you can see, there is no separator between the `D` and `Ljava/util/Date;`.

Also note that in this encoding scheme, you must use `/` instead of `.` to separate the package and class names.

To describe an array type, use a `[`. For example, an array of strings is

```
[Ljava/lang/String;
```

A `float[][]` is mangled into

```
[[F
```

For the complete signature of a method, you list the parameter types inside a pair of parentheses and then list the return type. For example, a method receiving two integers and returning an integer is encoded as

```
(II)I
```

The print method that we used in the preceding example has a mangled signature of

```
(Ljava/lang/String;)V
```

That is, the method receives a string and returns `void`.

TIP: You can use the `javap` command with option `-s` to generate the field signatures from class files. For example, run:

```
javap -s -private Classname
```

You get the following output, displaying the signatures of all fields and methods.

```
public synchronized class Employee extends java.lang.Object
    /* ACC_SUPER bit set */
{
    private java.lang.String name;
        /*   Ljava/lang/String;   */
    private double salary;
        /*   D   */
    private java.util.Date hireDay;
        /*   Ljava/util/Date;   */
    public Employee(java.lang.String,double,java.util.Date);
        /*   (Ljava/lang/String;DLjava/util/Date;)V   */
    public void print();
        /*   ()V   */
    public void raiseSalary(double);
        /*   (D)V   */
    public int hireYear();
        /*   ()I   */
}
```

NOTE: There is no rational reason why programmers are forced to use this mangling scheme for describing signatures. The designers of the native calling could have just as easily written a function that reads signatures in the Java programming language style, such as `void(int,java.lang.String)`, and encodes them into whatever internal representation they prefer. Then again, using the mangled signatures lets you partake in the mystique of programming close to the virtual machine.

Calling Java Methods

Of course, Java programming language functions can call C functions—that is what native methods are for. Can we go the other way? Why would we want to do this anyway? The answer is that it often happens that a native method needs to request a service from an object that was passed to it. We first show you how to do it for nonstatic methods, and then we show you how to do it for static methods.

Nonstatic Methods

As an example of calling a Java method from native code, let's enhance the `Printf` class and add a member function that works similarly to the C function `fprintf`. That is, it should be able to print a string on an arbitrary `PrintWriter` object.

```
class Printf3
{  public native static void fprint(PrintWriter out,
      String s, double x);
      . . .
}
```

We first assemble the string to be printed into a `String` object `str`, as in the `sprint` method that we already implemented. Then, we call the `print` method of the `PrintWriter` class from the C function that implements the native method.

You can call any Java method from C by using the function call

```
(*env)->CallXxxMethod(env, implicit parameter, methodID,
   explicit parameters)
```

Replace *Xxx* with `Void`, `Int`, `Object`, etc., depending on the return type of the method. Just as you need a `fieldID` to access a field of an object, you need a method ID to call a method. You obtain a method ID by calling the JNI function `GetMethodID` and supplying the class, the name of the method, and the method signature.

In our example, we want to obtain the ID of the `print` method of the `PrintWriter` class. As you saw in Chapter 1, the `PrintWriter` class has nine different methods, all called `print`. For that reason, you must also supply a string describing the parameters and return value of the specific function that you want to use. For example, we want to use `void print(java.lang.String)`. As described in the preceding section, we must now "mangle" the signature into the string `"(Ljava/lang/string;)V"`.

Here is the complete code to make the method call, by:

1. Obtaining the class of the implicit parameter;
2. Obtaining the method ID;
3. Making the call.

```
/* get the class */
class_PrintWriter = (*env)->GetObjectClass(env, out);

/* get the method ID */
id_print = (*env)->GetMethodID(env, class_PrintWriter,
   "print", "(Ljava/lang/String;)V");

/* call the method */
(*env)->CallVoidMethod(env, out, id_print, str);
```

Examples 11–14 and 11–15 show the Java code for a test program and the `Printf3` class. Example 11–16 contains the C code for the native `fprint` method.

NOTE: The numerical method IDs and field IDs are conceptually similar to `Method` and `Field` objects in the reflection API. You can convert between them with the following functions:

```
jobject ToReflectedMethod(JNIEnv* env, jclass class,
   jmethodID methodID); // returns Method object
methodID FromReflectedMethod(JNIEnv* env, jobject method);
jobject ToReflectedField(JNIEnv* env, jclass class,
   jfieldID fieldID); // returns Field object
fieldID FromReflectedField(JNIEnv* env, jobject field);
```

Static Methods

Calling static methods from native methods is similar to calling nonstatic methods. There are two differences.

- You use the `GetStaticMethodID` and `CallStatic`*`Xxx`*`Method` functions.
- You supply a class object, not an implicit parameter object, when invoking the method.

As an example of this, let's make the call to the static method

```
System.getProperty("java.class.path")
```

from a native method. The return value of this call is a string that gives the current class path.

First, we need to find the class to use. Since we have no object of the class `System` readily available, we use `FindClass` rather than `GetObjectClass`.

```
jclass class_System = (*env)->FindClass(env, "java/lang/System");
```

Next, we need the ID of the static `getProperty` method. The encoded signature of that method is

```
"(Ljava/lang/String;)Ljava/lang/String;"
```

since both the parameter and the return value are a string. Hence, we obtain the method ID as follows:

```
jmethodID id_getProperty = (*env)->GetStaticMethodID(env,
   class_System, "getProperty",
   "(Ljava/lang/String;)Ljava/lang/String;");
```

Finally, we can make the call. Note that the class object is passed to the `CallStaticObjectMethod` function.

```
jobject obj_ret = (*env)->CallStaticObjectMethod(env,
   class_System, id_getProperty,
   (*env)->NewStringUTF(env, "java.class.path"));
```

The return value of this method is of type `jobject`. If we want to manipulate it as a string, we must cast it to `jstring`:

```
jstring str_ret = (jstring)obj_ret;
```

C++ NOTE: In C, the types `jstring`, `jclass`, as well as the array types that will be introduced later, are all type equivalent to `jobject`. The cast of the preceding example is therefore not strictly necessary in C. But in C++, these types are defined as pointers to "dummy classes" that have the correct inheritance hierarchy. For example, the assignment of a `jstring` to a `jobject` is legal without a cast in C++, but the assignment from a `jobject` to a `jstring` requires a cast.

Constructors

A native method can create a new Java object by invoking its constructor. You invoke the constructor by calling the `NewObject` function.

```
jobject obj_new = (*env)->NewObject(env, class, methodID,
   construction parameters);
```

You obtain the method ID needed for this call from the `GetMethodID` function by specifying the method name as `"<init>"` and the encoded signature of the constructor (with return type `void`). For example, here is how a native method can create a `FileOutputStream` object.

```
const char[] fileName = ". . .";
jstring str_fileName = (*env)->NewStringUTF(env, fileName);
jclass class_FileOutputStream = (*env)->FindClass(env,
   "java/io/FileOutputStream");
jmethodID id_FileOutputStream = (*env)->GetMethodID(env,
   class_FileOutputStream, "<init>", "(Ljava/lang/String;)V");
jobject obj_stream = (*env)->NewObject(env,
   class_FileOutputStream, id_FileOutputStream, str_fileName);
```

Note that the signature of the constructor takes a parameter of type `java.lang.String` and has a return type of `void`.

Alternative Method Invocations

There are several variants of the JNI functions for calling a Java method from native code. These are not as important as the functions that we already discussed, but they are occasionally useful.

The CallNonvirtual*Xxx*Method functions receive an implicit argument, a method ID, a class object (which must correspond to a superclass of the implicit argument), and explicit arguments. The function calls the version of the method in the specified class, bypassing the normal dynamic dispatch mechanism.

All call functions have versions with suffixes "A" and "V" that receive the explicit parameters in an array or a va_list (as defined in the C header stdarg.h).

Example 11–14: Printf3Test.java

```
import java.io.*;

class Printf3Test
{  public static void main(String[] args)
   {  double price = 44.95;
      double tax = 7.75;
      double amountDue = price * (1 + tax / 100);
      PrintWriter out = new PrintWriter(System.out);
      Printf3.fprint(out,
         "Amount due = %8.2f\n", amountDue);
      out.flush();
   }
}
```

Example 11–15: Printf3.java

```
import java.io.*;

class Printf3
{  public static native void fprint(PrintWriter out,
      String format, double x);
   static
   {  System.loadLibrary("Printf3");
   }
}
```

Example 11–16: Printf3.c

```
#include "Printf3.h"
#include <string.h>
#include <stdlib.h>
#include <float.h>

char* find_format(const char format[])
/**
 * @param format a string containing a printf format specifier
 * (such as "%8.2f"). Substrings "%%" are skipped.
 * @return a pointer to the format specifier (skipping the '%')
 * or NULL if there wasn't a unique format specifier
 */
{  char* p;
   char* q;
```

```
   size_t n;

   p = strchr(format, '%');
   while (p != NULL && *(p + 1) == '%') /* skip %% */
      p = strchr(p + 2, '%');
   if (p == NULL) return NULL;
   /* now check that % is unique */
   p++;
   q = strchr(p, '%');
   while (q != NULL && *(q + 1) == '%') /* skip %% */
      q = strchr(q + 2, '%');
   if (q != NULL) return NULL; /* % not unique */
   q = p + strspn(p, " -0+#"); /* skip past flags */
   q += strspn(q, "0123456789"); /* skip past field width */
   if (*q == '.') { q++; q += strspn(q, "0123456789"); }
      /* skip past precision */
   if (strchr("eEfFgG", *q) == NULL) return NULL;
      /* not a floating point format */
   return p;
}

JNIEXPORT void JNICALL Java_Printf3_fprint
   (JNIEnv* env, jclass cl, jobject out, jstring format,
   jdouble x)
{  const char* cformat;
   char* fmt;
   jstring str;
   jclass class_PrintWriter;
   jmethodID id_print;

   cformat = (*env)->GetStringUTFChars(env, format, NULL);
   fmt = find_format(cformat);
   if (fmt == NULL)
      str = format;
   else
   {  char* cstr;
      int width = atoi(fmt);
      if (width == 0) width = DBL_DIG + 10;
      cstr = (char*)malloc(strlen(cformat) + width);
      sprintf(cstr, cformat, x);
      str = (*env)->NewStringUTF(env, cstr);
      free(cstr);
   }
   (*env)->ReleaseStringUTFChars(env, format, cformat);

   /* now call ps.print(str) */

   /* get the class */
   class_PrintWriter = (*env)->GetObjectClass(env, out);

   /* get the method ID */
   id_print = (*env)->GetMethodID(env, class_PrintWriter,
```

```
        "print", "(Ljava/lang/String;)V");

    /* call the method */
    (*env)->CallVoidMethod(env, out, id_print, str);
}
```

Executing Java methods from C code

- `jmethodID GetMethodID(JNIEnv *env, jclass cl, const char name[], const char sig[])`

  returns the identifier of a method in a class.

  Parameters:

	`env`	the JNI interface pointer
	`cl`	the class object
	`name`	the method name
	`sig`	the encoded method signature

- `void Call`*`Xxx`*`Method(JNIEnv *env, jobject obj, jmethodID id, args)`
- `void Call`*`Xxx`*`MethodA(JNIEnv *env, jobject obj, jmethodID id, jvalue args[])`
- `void Call`*`Xxx`*`MethodV(JNIEnv *env, jobject obj, jmethodID id, va_list args)`

  These functions call a method. The return type *Xxx* is one of `Object`, `Boolean`, `Byte`, `Char`, `Short`, `Int`, `Long`, `Float`, or `Double`. The first function has a variable number of arguments—simply append the method parameters after the method ID. The second function receives the method arguments in an array of `jvalue`, where `jvalue` is a union defined as

  ```
  typedef union jvalue
  { jboolean z;
    jbyte b;
    jchar c;
    jshort s;
    jint i;
    jlong j;
    jfloat f;
    jdouble d;
    jobject l;
  } jvalue;
  ```

  The third function receives the method parameters in a `va_list`, as defined in the C header `stdarg.h`.

  Parameters:

	`env`	the JNI interface pointer
	`obj`	the implicit argument of the method
	`id`	the method identifier
	`args`	the method arguments

- `void CallNonvirtualXxxMethod(JNIEnv *env, jobject obj, jclass cl, jmethodID id, args)`
- `void CallNonvirtualXxxMethodA(JNIEnv *env, jobject obj, jclass cl, jmethodID id, jvalue args[])`
- `void CallNonvirtualXxxMethodV(JNIEnv *env, jobject obj, jclass cl, jmethodID id, va_list args)`

  These functions call a method, bypassing dynamic dispatch. The return type *Xxx* is one of `Object`, `Boolean`, `Byte`, `Char`, `Short`, `Int`, `Long`, `Float`, or `Double`. The first function has a variable number of arguments—simply append the method parameters after the method ID. The second function receives the method arguments in an array of `jvalue`. The third function receives the method parameters in a `va_list`, as defined in the C header `stdarg.h`.

Parameters:	`env`	the JNI interface pointer
	`obj`	the implicit argument of the method
	`cl`	the class whose implementation of the method is to be called
	`id`	the method identifier
	`args`	the method arguments

- `jmethodID GetStaticMethodID(JNIEnv *env, jclass cl, const char name[], const char sig[])`

  returns the identifier of a static method in a class.

Parameters:	`env`	the JNI interface pointer
	`cl`	the class object
	`name`	the method name
	`sig`	the encoded method signature

- `void CallStaticXxxMethod(JNIEnv *env, jclass cl, jmethodID id, args)`
- `void CallStaticXxxMethodA(JNIEnv *env, jclass cl, jmethodID id, jvalue args[])`
- `void CallStaticXxxMethodV(JNIEnv *env, jclass cl, jmethodID id, va_list args)`

  These functions call a static method. The return type *Xxx* is one of `Object`, `Boolean`, `Byte`, `Char`, `Short`, `Int`, `Long`, `Float`, or `Double`. The first function has a variable number of arguments—simply append the method parameters after the method ID. The second function receives the method arguments in an array of `jvalue`. The third function receives the method parameters in a `va_list`, as defined in the C header `stdarg.h`.

Parameters:	`env`	the JNI interface pointer
	`cl`	the class of the static method

	`id`	the method identifier
	`args`	the method arguments

- `jobject NewObject(JNIEnv *env, jclass cl, jmethodID id, args)`
- `jobject NewObjectA(JNIEnv *env, jclass cl, jmethodID id, jvalue args[])`
- `jobject NewObjectV(JNIEnv *env, jclass cl, jmethodID id, va_list args)`

These functions call a constructor. The method ID is obtained from `GetMethodID` with a method name of `"<init>"` and a return type of `void`. The first function has a variable number of arguments—simply append the method parameters after the method ID. The second function receives the method arguments in an array of `jvalue`. The third function receives the method parameters in a `va_list`, as defined in the C header `stdarg.h`.

Parameters:	`env`	the JNI interface pointer
	`cl`	the class to be instantiated
	`id`	the constructor method identifier
	`args`	the constructor arguments

Arrays

All array types of the Java programming language have corresponding C types, as shown in Table 11–2.

Table 11–2: Correspondence between Java array types and C types

Java type	C type
`boolean[]`	`jbooleanArray`
`byte[]`	`jbyteArray`
`char[]`	`jcharArray`
`int[]`	`jintArray`
`short[]`	`jshortArray`
`long[]`	`jlongArray`
`float[]`	`jfloatArray`
`double[]`	`jdoubleArray`
`Object[]`	`jobjectArray`

The type `jarray` denotes a generic array.

C++ NOTE: In C, all these array types are actually type synonyms of `jobject`. In C++, however, they are arranged in the inheritance hierarchy shown in Figure 11–2.

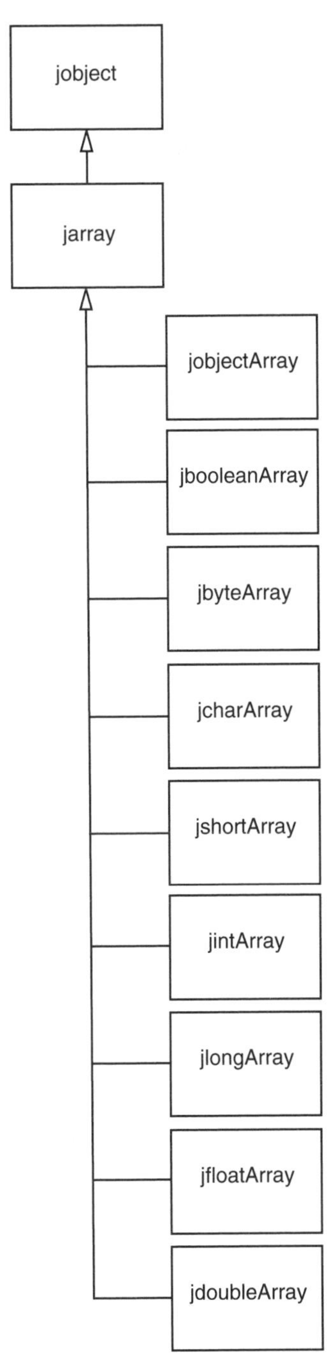

Figure 11–2: Inheritance hierarchy of array types

The `GetArrayLength` function returns the length of an array.

```
jarray array = ...;
jsize length = (*env)->GetArrayLength(env, array);
```

How you access elements in the array depends on whether the array stores objects or a primitive type (`bool`, `char`, or a numeric type). You access elements in an object array with the `GetObjectArrayElement` and `SetObjectArrayElement` methods.

```
jobjectArray array = ...;
int i, j;
jobject x = (*env)->GetObjectArray(env, array, i);
(*env)->SetObjectArray(env, array, j, x);
```

While simple, this approach is also clearly inefficient; you want to be able to access array elements directly, especially when doing vector and matrix computations.

The `Get`*`Xxx`*`ArrayElements` function returns a C pointer to the starting element of the array. As with ordinary strings, you must remember to call the corresponding `Release`*`Xxx`*`ArrayElements` function to tell the virtual machine when you no longer need that pointer. Here, the type *`Xxx`* must be a primitive type, that is, not `Object`. You can then read and write the array elements directly. However, since the pointer *may point to a copy,* any changes that you make are guaranteed to be reflected in the original array only when you call the corresponding `Release`*`Xxx`*`ArrayElements` function!

NOTE: You can find out if an array is a copy by passing a pointer to a `jboolean` variable as the third parameter to a `Get`*`Xxx`*`ArrayElements` method. The variable is filled with `JNI_TRUE` if the array is a copy. If you aren't interested in that information, just pass a `NULL` pointer.

Here is a code sample that multiplies all elements in an array of `double` values by a constant. We obtain a C pointer `a` into the Java array and then access individual elements as `a[i]`.

```
jdoubleArray array_a = ...;
double scaleFactor = ...;
double* a = (*env)->GetDoubleArrayElements(env, array_a, NULL);
for (i = 0; i < (*env)->GetArrayLength(env, array_a); i++)
   a[i] = a[i] * scaleFactor;
(*env)->ReleaseDoubleArrayElements(env, array_a, 0);
```

Whether the virtual machine actually copies the array depends on how it allocates arrays and does its garbage collection. Some "copying" garbage collectors routinely move objects around and update object references. That strategy is not compatible with "pinning" an array to a particular location because the collector cannot update the pointer values in native code. However, the garbage collector in the current virtual machine supplied with the JDK is not a copying collector, which means that currently arrays are pinned.

NOTE: In the Sun JVM implementation, `boolean` arrays are represented as packed arrays, and the `GetBooleanArrayElements` method copies them into unpacked arrays of `jboolean` values.

If you want to access a few elements of a large array, use the `Get`*`Xxx`*`ArrayRegion` and `Set`*`Xxx`*`ArrayRegion` methods that copy a range of elements from the Java array into a C array and back.

You can create new Java arrays in native methods with the `New`*`Xxx`*`Array` function. To create a new array of objects, you specify the length, the type of the array elements, and an initial element for all entries (typically, `NULL`). Here is an example.

```
jclass class_Employee = (*env)->FindClass(env, "Employee");
jobjectArray array_e = (*env)->NewObjectArray(env, 100,
   class_Employee, NULL);
```

Arrays of primitive types are simpler. You just supply the length of the array.

```
jdoubleArray array_d = (*env)->NewDoubleArray(env, 100);
```

The array is then filled with zeroes.

Manipulating Java Arrays in C code

- `jsize GetArrayLength(JNIEnv *env, jarray array)`
  returns the number of elements in the array.

Parameters:	`env`	the JNI interface pointer
	`array`	the array object

- `jobject GetObjectArrayElement(JNIEnv *env, jobjectArray array, jsize index)`
  returns the value of an array element.

Parameters:	`env`	the JNI interface pointer
	`array`	the array object
	`index`	the array offset

- `void SetObjectArrayElement(JNIEnv *env, jobjectArray array, jsize index, jobject value)`
  sets an array element to a new value.

Parameters:	`env`	the JNI interface pointer
	`array`	the array object
	`index`	the array offset
	`value`	the new value

- `Xxx* GetXxxArrayElements(JNIEnv *env, jarray array, jboolean* isCopy)`

  yields a C pointer to the elements of a Java array. The field type *Xxx* is one of `Boolean`, `Byte`, `Char`, `Short`, `Int`, `Long`, `Float`, or `Double`. The pointer must be passed to `Release`*Xxx*`ArrayElements` when it is no longer needed.

Parameters:		
	`env`	the JNI interface pointer
	`array`	the array object
	`isCopy`	is either `NULL` or points to a `jboolean` that is filled with `JNI_TRUE` if a copy is made; with `JNI_FALSE` otherwise

- `void Release`*Xxx*`ArrayElements(JNIEnv *env, jarray array, `*Xxx*` elems[], jint mode)`

  notifies the virtual machine that a pointer obtained by `Get`*Xxx*`ArrayElements` is no longer needed.

Parameters:		
	`env`	the JNI interface pointer
	`array`	the array object
	`elems`	the pointer to the array elements that is no longer needed
	`mode`	`0` = free the `elems` buffer after updating the array elements
		`JNI_COMMIT` = do not free the `elems` buffer after updating the array elements
		`JNI_ABORT` = free the `elems` buffer without updating the array elements

- `void Get`*Xxx*`ArrayRegion(JNIEnv *env, jarray array, jint start, jint length, `*Xxx*` elems[])`

  copies elements from a Java array to a C array. The field type *Xxx* is one of `Boolean`, `Byte`, `Char`, `Short`, `Int`, `Long`, `Float`, or `Double`.

Parameters:		
	`env`	the JNI interface pointer
	`array`	the array object
	`start`	the starting index
	`length`	the number of elements to copy
	`elems`	the C array that holds the elements

- `void Set`*Xxx*`ArrayRegion(JNIEnv *env, jarray array, jint start, jint length, `*Xxx*` elems[])`

copies elements from a C array to a Java array. The field type *Xxx* is one of Boolean, Byte, Char, Short, Int, Long, Float, or Double.

Parameters:	env	the JNI interface pointer
	array	the array object
	start	the starting index
	length	the number of elements to copy
	elems	the C array that holds the elements

Error Handling

Native methods are a significant security risk to programs in the Java programming language. The C runtime system has no protection against array bounds errors, indirection through bad pointers, and so on. It is particularly important that programmers of native methods handle all error conditions in order to preserve the integrity of the Java platform. In particular, when your native method diagnoses a problem that it cannot handle, then it should report this problem to the Java virtual machine. Then, you would naturally throw an exception in this situation. However, C has no exceptions. Instead, you must call the Throw or ThrowNew function to create a new exception object. When the native method exits, the Java virtual machine will throw that exception.

To use the Throw function, call NewObject to create an object of a subtype of Throwable. For example, here we allocate an EOFException object and throw it.

```
jclass class_EOFException = (*env)->FindClass(env,
   "java/io/EOFException");
jmethodID id_EOFException = (*env)->GetMethodID(env,
   class_EOFException,
   "<init>", "()V"); /* ID of default constructor */
jthrowable obj_exc = (*env)->NewObject(env, class_EOFException,
   id_EOFException);
(*env)->Throw(env, obj_exc);
```

It is usually more convenient to call ThrowNew, which constructs an exception object, given a class and an UTF string.

```
(*env)->ThrowNew(env, (*env)->FindClass(env,
   "java/io/EOFException"),
   "Unexpected end of file");
```

Both Throw and ThrowNew merely *post* the exception; they do not interrupt the control flow of the native method. Only when the method returns does the Java virtual machine throw the exception. Therefore, every call to Throw and ThrowNew should always immediately be followed by a return statement.

C++ NOTE: If you implement native methods in C++, you cannot currently throw a Java exception object in your C++ code. In a C++ binding, it would be possible to implement a translation between exceptions in the C++ and Java programming languages—however, this is not currently implemented. You need to use `Throw` or `ThrowNew` to throw a Java exception in a native C++ method, and you need to make sure that your native methods throw no C++ exceptions.

Normally, native code need not be concerned with catching Java exceptions. However, when a native method calls a Java method, that method might throw an exception. Moreover, a number of the JNI functions throw exceptions as well. For example, `SetObjectArrayElement` throws an `ArrayIndexOutOfBoundsException` if the index is out of bounds and an `ArrayStoreException` if the class of the stored object is not a subclass of the element class of the array. In situations like these, a native method should call the `ExceptionOccurred` method to determine whether an exception has been thrown. The call

```
jthrowable obj_exc = (*env)->ExceptionOccurred(env);
```

returns `NULL` if no exception is pending, or it returns a reference to the current exception object. If you just want to check whether an exception has been thrown, without obtaining a reference to the exception object, use

```
jbool occurred = (*env)->ExceptionCheck(env);
```

Normally, a native method should simply return when an exception has occurred so that the virtual machine can propagate it to the Java code. However, a native method *may* analyze the exception object to determine if it can handle the exception. If it can, then the function

```
(*env)->ExceptionClear(env);
```

must be called to turn off the exception.

In our next example, we implement the `fprint` native method with the paranoia that is appropriate for a native method. Here are the exceptions that we throw:

- A `NullPointerException` if the format string is `NULL`;
- An `IllegalArgumentException` if the format string doesn't contain a `%` specifier that is appropriate for printing a `double`;
- An `OutOfMemoryError` if the call to `malloc` fails.

Finally, to demonstrate how to check for an exception when calling a Java method from a native method, we send the string to the stream, a character at a time, and call `ExceptionOccurred` after each call. Example 11–17 shows the code for the native method, and Example 11–18 contains the definition of the class containing the native method. Notice that the native method does not immediately terminate when an exception occurs in the call to `PrintWriter.print`—it first frees the `cstr` buffer. When the native method returns, the virtual machine again raises

the exception. The test program in Example 11–19 demonstrates how the native method throws an exception when the formatting string is not valid.

Example 11–17: Printf4.c

```
#include "Printf4.h"
#include <string.h>
#include <stdlib.h>
#include <float.h>

char* find_format(const char format[])
/**
 * @param format a string containing a printf format specifier
 * (such as "%8.2f"). Substrings "%%" are skipped.
 * @return a pointer to the format specifier (skipping the '%')
 * or NULL if there wasn't a unique format specifier
 */
{  char* p;
   char* q;

   p = strchr(format, '%');
   while (p != NULL && *(p + 1) == '%') /* skip %% */
      p = strchr(p + 2, '%');
   if (p == NULL) return NULL;
   /* now check that % is unique */
   p++;
   q = strchr(p, '%');
   while (q != NULL && *(q + 1) == '%') /* skip %% */
      q = strchr(q + 2, '%');
   if (q != NULL) return NULL; /* % not unique */
   q = p + strspn(p, " -0+#"); /* skip past flags */
   q += strspn(q, "0123456789"); /* skip past field width */
   if (*q == '.') { q++; q += strspn(q, "0123456789"); }
      /* skip past precision */
   if (strchr("eEfFgG", *q) == NULL) return NULL;
      /* not a floating point format */
   return p;
}

JNIEXPORT void JNICALL Java_Printf4_fprint
   (JNIEnv* env, jclass cl, jobject out, jstring format,
   jdouble x)
{  const char* cformat;
   char* fmt;
   jclass class_PrintWriter;
   jmethodID id_print;
   char* cstr;
   int width;
   int i;

   if (format == NULL)
   {  (*env)->ThrowNew(env,
         (*env)->FindClass(env,
```

```
         "java/lang/NullPointerException"),
         "Printf4.fprint: format is null");
      return;
   }

   cformat = (*env)->GetStringUTFChars(env, format, NULL);
   fmt = find_format(cformat);

   if (fmt == NULL)
   {  (*env)->ThrowNew(env,
         (*env)->FindClass(env,
         "java/lang/IllegalArgumentException"),
         "Printf4.fprint: format is invalid");
      return;
   }

   width = atoi(fmt);
   if (width == 0) width = DBL_DIG + 10;
   cstr = (char*)malloc(strlen(cformat) + width);

   if (cstr == NULL)
   {  (*env)->ThrowNew(env,
         (*env)->FindClass(env, "java/lang/OutOfMemoryError"),
         "Printf4.fprint: malloc failed");
      return;
   }

   sprintf(cstr, cformat, x);

   (*env)->ReleaseStringUTFChars(env, format, cformat);

   /* now call ps.print(str) */

   /* get the class */
   class_PrintWriter = (*env)->GetObjectClass(env, out);

   /* get the method ID */
   id_print = (*env)->GetMethodID(env, class_PrintWriter,
      "print", "(C)V");

   /* call the method */
   for (i = 0; cstr[i] != 0 && !(*env)->ExceptionOccurred(env);
         i++)
      (*env)->CallVoidMethod(env, out, id_print, cstr[i]);

   free(cstr);
}
```

Example 11–18: Printf4.java

```
import java.io.*;

class Printf4
{  public static native void fprint(PrintWriter ps,
```

```
      String format, double x);
   static
   {  System.loadLibrary("Printf4");
   }
}
```

Example 11–19: Printf4Test.java

```
import java.io.*;

class Printf4Test
{  public static void main(String[] args)
   {  double price = 44.95;
      double tax = 7.75;
      double amountDue = price * (1 + tax / 100);
      PrintWriter out = new PrintWriter(System.out);
      Printf4.fprint(out, "Amount due = %%8.2f\n", amountDue);
      out.flush();
   }
}
```

Error handling in C code

- `jint Throw(JNIEnv *env, jthrowable obj)`
  prepares an exception to be thrown upon exiting from the native code. Returns 0 on success, a negative value on failure.

Parameters:	`env`	the JNI interface pointer
	`obj`	the exception object to throw

- `jint ThrowNew(JNIEnv *env, jclass clazz, const char msg[])`
  prepares an exception to be thrown upon exiting from the native code. Returns 0 on success, a negative value on failure.

Parameters:	`env`	the JNI interface pointer
	`cl`	the class of the exception object to throw
	`msg`	an UTF string denoting the `String` construction argument of the exception object

- `jthrowable ExceptionOccurred(JNIEnv *env)`
  returns the exception object if an exception is pending, or `NULL` otherwise.

Parameters:	`env`	the JNI interface pointer

- `jboolean ExceptionCheck(JNIEnv *env)`
  returns `true` if an exception is pending.

Parameters:	`env`	the JNI interface pointer

- `void ExceptionClear(JNIEnv *env)`
  clears any pending exceptions.

Parameters:	`env`	the JNI interface pointer

The Invocation API

Up to now, we have considered programs in the Java programming language that made a few C calls, presumably because C was faster or allowed access to functionality that was inaccessible from the Java platform. Suppose you are in the opposite situation. You have a C or C++ program and would like to make a few calls to Java code, perhaps because the Java code is easier to program. Of course, you know how to call the Java methods. But you still need to add the Java virtual machine to your program so that the Java code can be interpreted. The so-called *invocation API* is used to embed the Java virtual machine into a C or C++ program. Here is the minimal code that you need to initialize a virtual machine.

```
JavaVMOption options[1];
JavaVMInitArgs vm_args;
JavaVM *jvm;
JNIEnv *env;

options[0].optionString = "-Djava.class.path=.";

memset(&vm_args, 0, sizeof(vm_args));
vm_args.version = JNI_VERSION_1_2;
vm_args.nOptions = 1;
vm_args.options = options;

JNI_CreateJavaVM(&jvm, (void**)&env, &vm_args);
```

The call to `JNI_CreateJavaVM` creates the virtual machine and fills in a pointer `jvm` to the virtual machine and a pointer `env` to the execution environment.

You can supply any number of options to the virtual machine. Simply increase the size of the `options` array and the value of `vm_args.nOptions`. For example,

```
options[i].optionString = "-Djava.compiler=NONE";
```

deactivates the just-in-time compiler.

TIP: When you run into trouble and your program crashes, refuses to initialize the JVM, or can't load your classes, then turn on the JNI debugging mode. Set an option to

```
options[i].optionString = "-verbose:jni";
```

You will see a flurry of messages that indicate the progress in initializing the JVM. If you don't see your classes loaded, check both your path and your class path settings.

Once you have set up the virtual machine, you can call Java methods in the way described in the preceding sections: simply use the `env` pointer in the usual way. You need the `jvm` pointer only to call other functions in the invocation API. Currently, there are only four such functions. The most important one is the function to terminate the virtual machine:

```
(*jvm)->DestroyJavaVM(jvm);
```

The C program in Example 11–20 sets up a virtual machine and then calls the `main` method of the `Welcome` class, which was discussed in Chapter 2 of Volume 1.

CAUTION: Under Windows, the JVM code is in the library `\jdk\jre\bin\classic\jvm.dll` or `\jdk\jre\bin\hotspot\jvm.dll`. You must set your path to include that directory. If you don't, then Windows complains about a missing `jvm.dll` file.

If you deploy a Java application by using a Windows launcher, then you may not trust your users to set the path to the `jvm.dll` file. You can help your users and load the DLL manually. (The `javac` and `java` programs do just that.) For sample code, see the file `launcher\java_md.c` in the `src.jar` file that is a part of the JDK.

Example 11–20: InvocationTest.c

```
#include <jni.h>
#include <stdlib.h>

int main()
{  JavaVMOption options[1];
   JavaVMInitArgs vm_args;
   JavaVM *jvm;
   JNIEnv *env;
   long status;

   jclass class_Welcome;
   jclass class_String;
   jobjectArray args;
   jmethodID id_main;

   options[0].optionString = "-Djava.class.path=.";

   memset(&vm_args, 0, sizeof(vm_args));
   vm_args.version = JNI_VERSION_1_2;
   vm_args.nOptions = 1;
   vm_args.options = options;

   status = JNI_CreateJavaVM(&jvm, (void**)&env, &vm_args);
   if (status == JNI_ERR)
   {  printf("Error creating VM\n");
      return 1;
   }

   class_Welcome = (*env)->FindClass(env, "Welcome");
   id_main = (*env)->GetStaticMethodID(env, class_Welcome,
      "main", "([Ljava/lang/String;)V");

   class_String = (*env)->FindClass(env, "java/lang/String");
   args = (*env)->NewObjectArray(env, 0, class_String, NULL);

   (*env)->CallStaticVoidMethod(env, class_Welcome,
```

```
        id_main, args);

    (*jvm)->DestroyJavaVM(jvm);

    return 0;
}
```

To compile this program under Windows, you use the command line

```
cl -Ic:\jdk\include -Ic:\jdk\include\win32 InvocationTest.c
c:\jdk\lib\jvm.lib
```

Suppose you want to deliver this program to your customers. You need to supply the following items:

- Your executable program (`InvocationTest.exe`);
- The class files of your Java code (`Welcome.class`);
- The Java Runtime Environment (JRE).

Invocation API functions

- `jint JNI_CreateJavaVM(JavaVM** p_jvm, void** p_env, JavaVMInitArgs* vm_args)`
  initializes the Java virtual machine. The function returns 0 if successful, `JNI_ERR` on failure.

Parameters:	`p_jvm`	filled with a pointer to the invocation API function table
	`p_env`	filled with a pointer to the JNI function table
	`vm_args`	the virtual machine arguments

- `jint DestroyJavaVM(JavaVM* jvm)`
  destroys the virtual machine. Returns 0 on success, a negative number on failure. This function must be called through a virtual machine pointer, i.e., `(*jvm)->DestroyJavaVM(jvm)`.

Parameters:	`jvm`	the virtual machine pointer

A Complete Example: Accessing the Windows Registry

In this section, we describe a full, working example that covers everything we discussed in this chapter: using native methods with strings, arrays, objects, constructor calls, and error handling. What we show you is how to put a Java platform wrapper around a subset of the ordinary C-based API used to work with the Windows registry. Of course, being a Windows-specific feature, a program using the Windows registry is inherently nonportable. For that reason, the standard Java library has no support for the registry, and it makes sense to use native methods to gain access to it.

An Overview of the Windows Registry

For those who are not familiar with the Windows registry: It is a data depository that is accessed by the Windows 95 and NT operating systems and that is available as a storage area for application programs. (A good book is *Inside the Windows 95 Registry* by Ron Petrusha [O'Reilly 1996]) In older versions of Windows, the operating system as well as applications used so-called INI files to store configuration parameters. Windows 95 and NT programs are supposed to use the registry instead. The registry has a number of advantages.

- INI files store data as strings; the registry supports other data types such as integers and byte arrays.
- INI file sections cannot have subsections; the registry supports a complete tree structure.
- Configuration parameters were distributed over many INI files; placing them into the registry provides a single point for administration and backup.

Admittedly, the registry is also a single point of failure—if you mess up the registry, your computer may malfunction or even fail to boot! The sample program that we present in this section is safe, but if you plan to make any modifications to it, you should learn how to back up the registry before proceeding. See the book by Petrusha for information on how to back up the Windows registry. (Also, programs like Norton Utilities come with user-friendly programs for registry backup.)

The principal tool for inspecting the registry is the *registry editor*. Because of the potential for error by naive but enthusiastic users, there is no icon for launching the registry editor. Instead, start a DOS shell (or open the Start | Run box) and type `regedit`. Figure 11–3 shows the registry editor in action.

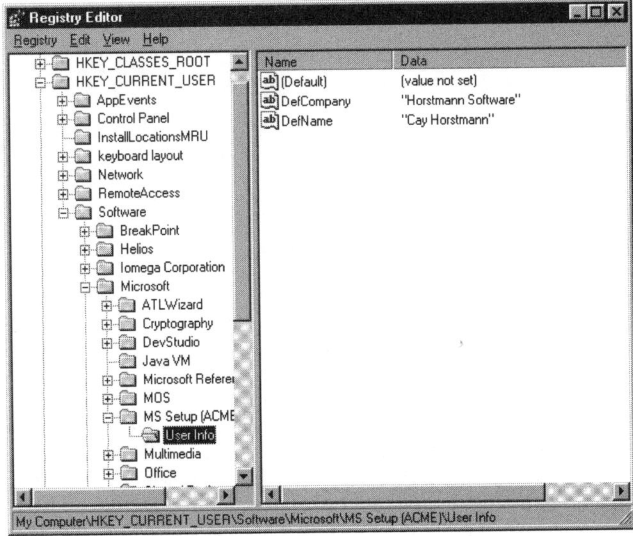

Figure 11–3: The registry editor

The left-hand side shows the keys, which are arranged in a tree structure. Note that each key starts with one of the `HKEY` nodes like

```
HKEY_CLASSES_ROOT
HKEY_CURRENT_USER
HKEY_LOCAL_MACHINE
. . .
```

The right-hand side shows the name/value pairs that are associated with a particular key. For example, the key

```
HKEY_CURRENT_USER\Software\Microsoft\MS Setup (ACME)\User Info
```

has two name/value pairs, namely,

```
DefCompany="your organization"
DefName="your name"
```

In this case, the values are strings. The values can also be integers or arrays of bytes.

A Java Platform Interface for Accessing the Registry

We will implement a simple interface to access the registry from Java code and then implement this interface with native code. Our interface allows only a few registry operations; to keep the code size down, we omitted other important operations such as adding, deleting, and enumerating keys. (Following our model and the information supplied in Petrusha's book, it would be easy to add the remaining registry API functions.)

Even with the limited subset that we supply, you can

- Enumerate all names stored in a key;
- Read the value stored with a name;
- Set the value stored with a name.

Here is the Java platform class that encapsulates a registry key.

```
public class Win32RegKey
{  public Win32RegKey(int theRoot, String thePath) { . . . }
   public Enumeration names() { . . . }
   public native Object getValue(String name);
   public native void setValue(String name, Object value);

   public static final int HKEY_CLASSES_ROOT = 0x80000000;
   public static final int HKEY_CURRENT_USER = 0x80000001;
   public static final int HKEY_LOCAL_MACHINE = 0x80000002;
   . . .
}
```

The `names` method returns an enumeration that holds all the names stored with the key. You can get at them with the familiar `hasMoreElements`/`nextElement` methods. The `getValue` method returns an object that is either a string, an

Integer object, or a byte array. The value parameter of the setValue method must also be of one of these three types.

Here is a simple function that lists the strings that are stored with the key.

```
HKEY_CURRENT_USER\Software\Microsoft\MS Setup (ACME)\User Info
public static void main(String[] args)
{  Win32RegKey key = new Win32RegKey(
      Win32RegKey.HKEY_CURRENT_USER,
      "Software\\Microsoft\\MS Setup (ACME)\\User Info");

   Enumeration enum = key.names();

   while (enum.hasMoreElements())
   {  String name = (String)enum.nextElement();
      System.out.println(name + " = " + key.getValue(name));
   }
}
```

A typical output of this program is as follows:

```
DefCompany = Horstmann Software
DefUser = Cay Horstmann
```

Implementing the Registry Access Functions as Native Methods

We need to implement three actions:

- Get the value of a key;
- Set the value of a key;
- Iterate through the names of a key.

Fortunately, you have seen essentially all the tools that are required, such as the conversion between Java strings and arrays and those of C. And you saw how to raise a Java exception in case something goes wrong.

Two issues make these native methods more complex than the preceding examples. The getValue and setValue methods deal with the type Object, which can be one of String, Integer, or byte[]. And the enumeration object needs to *store* the *state* between successive calls to hasMoreElements/nextElement.

Let us first look at the getValue method. The code (which is shown in Example 11–22) goes through the following steps.

1. Open the registry key. To read their values, the registry API requires that keys be open.
2. Query the type and size of the value that is associated with the name.
3. Read the data into a buffer.
4. If the type is REG_SZ (a string), then call NewStringUTF to create a new string with the value data.
5. If the type is REG_DWORD (a 32-bit integer), then invoke the Integer constructor.

6. If the type is REG_BINARY, then call NewByteArray to create a new byte array and SetByteArrayRegion to copy the value data into the byte array.
7. If the type is none of these or if there was an error when calling an API function, throw an exception and carefully release all resources that had been acquired up to that point.
8. Close the key and return the object (String, Integer, or byte[]) that had been created.

As you can see, this example illustrates quite nicely how to generate Java objects of different types.

In this native method, it was not difficult to cope with the generic return type. The jstring, jobject, or jarray reference was simply returned as a jobject. However, the setValue method receives a reference to an Object, and it must determine its exact type so it can save it as either a string, integer, or byte array. We can make this determination by querying the class of the value object, finding the class references for java.lang.String, java.lang.Integer, and byte[], and comparing them with the IsAssignableFrom function.

If class1 and class2 are two class references, then the call

```
(*env)->IsAssignableFrom(env, class1, class2)
```

returns JNI_TRUE when class1 and class2 are the same class or class1 is a subclass of class2. In either case, references to objects of class1 can be cast to class2. For example, when

```
(*env)->IsAssignableFrom(env,
   (*env)->GetObjectClass(env, value)
   (*env)->FindClass(env, "[B"))
```

is true, then we know that value is a byte array.

Here is an overview of the code of the setValue method.

1. Open the registry key for writing.
2. Find the type of the value to write.
3. If the type is String, call GetStringUTFChars to get a pointer to the characters. Also, obtain the string length.
4. If the type is Integer, call the intValue method to get the integer stored in the wrapper object.
5. If the type is byte[], call GetByteArrayElements to get a pointer to the bytes. Also, obtain the string length.
6. Pass the data and length to the registry.
7. Close the key. If the type is String or byte[], then also release the pointer to the characters or bytes.

Finally, let us turn to the native methods that enumerate keys. These are methods of the Win32RegKeyNameEnumeration class (see Example 11–21). When the

enumeration process starts, we must open the key. For the duration of the enumeration, we must retain the key handle. That is, the key handle must be stored with the enumeration object. The key handle is of type `DWORD`, a 32-bit quantity, and, hence, can be stored in a Java integer. It is stored in the `hkey` field of the enumeration class. When the enumeration starts, the field is initialized with `SetIntField`. Subsequent calls read the value with `GetIntField`.

TIP: As this example shows, using a Java object field to store native-state data is very useful for implementing native methods.

In this example, we store three other data items with the enumeration object. When the enumeration first starts, we can query the registry for the count of name/value pairs and the length of the longest name, which we need so we can allocate C character arrays to hold the names. These values are stored in the `count` and `maxsize` fields of the enumeration object. Finally, the `index` field is initialized with −1 to indicate the start of the enumeration, is set to 0 once the other object fields are initialized, and is incremented after every enumeration step.

Here, we walk through the native methods that support the enumeration. The `hasMoreElements` method is simple.

1. Retrieve the `index` and `count` fields.
2. If the index is −1, call the `startNameEnumeration` function, which opens the key, queries the count and maximum length, and initializes the `hkey`, `count`, `maxsize`, and `index` fields.
3. Return `JNI_TRUE` if `index` is less than `count`; `JNI_FALSE` otherwise.

The `nextElement` method needs to work a little harder.

1. Retrieve the `index` and `count` fields.
2. If the index is −1, call the `startNameEnumeration` function, which opens the key, queries the count and maximum length, and initializes the `hkey`, `count`, `maxsize`, and `index` fields.
3. If `index` equals `count`, throw a `NoSuchElementException`.
4. Read the next name from the registry.
5. Increment `index`.
6. If `index` equals `count`, close the key.

To compile the program, you must link in the `advapi32.lib` library. Before compiling, remember to run `javah` on both `Win32RegKey` and `Win32RegKeyNameEnumeration`. The complete command line is

```
cl -Ic:\jdk\include -Ic:\jdk\include\win32 -LD
   Win32RegKey.c advapi32.lib -FeWin32RegKey.dll
```

Example 11–23 shows a program to test our new registry functions. We add three name/value pairs, a string, an integer, and a byte array to the key.

```
HKEY_CURRENT_USER\Software\Microsoft\MS Setup (ACME)\User Info
```

We then enumerate all names of that key and retrieve their values. The program should print out

```
DefName = Cay Horstmann
DefCompany = Horstmann Software
Default user = Bozo the clown
Lucky number = 13
Small primes = 2 3 5 7 11 13
```

Although adding these name/value pairs to that key probably does no harm, you may want to use the registry editor to remove them after running this program.

Example 11–21: Win32RegKey.java

```
import java.util.*;

public class Win32RegKey
{  public Win32RegKey(int theRoot, String thePath)
   {  root = theRoot;
      path = thePath;
   }
   public Enumeration names()
   {  return new Win32RegKeyNameEnumeration(root, path);
   }
   public native Object getValue(String name);
   public native void setValue(String name, Object value);

   public static final int HKEY_CLASSES_ROOT = 0x80000000;
   public static final int HKEY_CURRENT_USER = 0x80000001;
   public static final int HKEY_LOCAL_MACHINE = 0x80000002;
   public static final int HKEY_USERS = 0x80000003;
   public static final int HKEY_CURRENT_CONFIG = 0x80000005;
   public static final int HKEY_DYN_DATA = 0x80000006;

   private int root;
   private String path;

   static
   {  System.loadLibrary("Win32RegKey");
   }
}

class Win32RegKeyNameEnumeration implements Enumeration
{  Win32RegKeyNameEnumeration(int theRoot, String thePath)
   {  root = theRoot;
      path = thePath;
   }

   public native Object nextElement();
```

```
   public native boolean hasMoreElements();

   private int root;
   private String path;
   private int index = -1;
   private int hkey = 0;
   private int maxsize;
   private int count;
}

class Win32RegKeyException extends RuntimeException
{  public Win32RegKeyException() {}
   public Win32RegKeyException(String why)
   {  super(why);
   }
}
```

Example 11–22: Win32RegKey.c

```
#include "Win32RegKey.h"
#include "Win32RegKeyNameEnumeration.h"
#include <string.h>
#include <stdlib.h>
#include <windows.h>

JNIEXPORT jobject JNICALL Java_Win32RegKey_getValue
  (JNIEnv* env, jobject this_obj, jstring name)
{  const char* cname;
   jstring path;
   const char* cpath;
   HKEY hkey;
   DWORD type;
   DWORD size;
   jclass this_class;
   jfieldID id_root;
   jfieldID id_path;
   HKEY root;
   jobject ret;
   char* cret;

   /* get the class */
   this_class = (*env)->GetObjectClass(env, this_obj);

   /* get the field IDs */
   id_root = (*env)->GetFieldID(env, this_class, "root", "I");
   id_path = (*env)->GetFieldID(env, this_class, "path",
      "Ljava/lang/String;");

   /* get the fields */
   root = (HKEY)(*env)->GetIntField(env, this_obj, id_root);
   path = (jstring)(*env)->GetObjectField(env, this_obj,
      id_path);
```

```
cpath = (*env)->GetStringUTFChars(env, path, NULL);

/* open the registry key */
if (RegOpenKeyEx(root, cpath, 0, KEY_READ, &hkey)
   != ERROR_SUCCESS)
{  (*env)->ThrowNew(env,
      (*env)->FindClass(env, "Win32RegKeyException"),
      "Open key failed");
   (*env)->ReleaseStringUTFChars(env, path, cpath);
   return NULL;
}

(*env)->ReleaseStringUTFChars(env, path, cpath);
cname = (*env)->GetStringUTFChars(env, name, NULL);

/* find the type and size of the value */
if (RegQueryValueEx(hkey, cname, NULL, &type, NULL, &size) !=
   ERROR_SUCCESS)
{  (*env)->ThrowNew(env,
      (*env)->FindClass(env, "Win32RegKeyException"),
      "Query value key failed");
   RegCloseKey(hkey);
   (*env)->ReleaseStringUTFChars(env, name, cname);
   return NULL;
}

/* get memory to hold the value */
cret = (char*)malloc(size);

/* read the value */
if (RegQueryValueEx(hkey, cname, NULL, &type, cret, &size) !=
   ERROR_SUCCESS)
{  (*env)->ThrowNew(env,
      (*env)->FindClass(env, "Win32RegKeyException"),
      "Query value key failed");
   free(cret);
   RegCloseKey(hkey);
   (*env)->ReleaseStringUTFChars(env, name, cname);
   return NULL;
}

/* depending on the type, store the value in a string,
   integer or byte array */
if (type == REG_SZ)
{  ret = (*env)->NewStringUTF(env, cret);
}
else if (type == REG_DWORD)
{  jclass class_Integer = (*env)->FindClass(env,
      "java/lang/Integer");
   /* get the method ID of the constructor */
   jmethodID id_Integer = (*env)->GetMethodID(env,
      class_Integer, "<init>", "(I)V");
```

```
      int value = *(int*)cret;
      /* invoke the constructor */
      ret = (*env)->NewObject(env, class_Integer, id_Integer,
         value);
   }
   else if (type == REG_BINARY)
   {  ret = (*env)->NewByteArray(env, size);
      (*env)->SetByteArrayRegion(env, (jarray)ret, 0, size,
         cret);
   }
   else
   {  (*env)->ThrowNew(env,
         (*env)->FindClass(env, "Win32RegKeyException"),
         "Unsupported value type");
      ret = NULL;
   }

   free(cret);
   RegCloseKey(hkey);
   (*env)->ReleaseStringUTFChars(env, name, cname);

   return ret;
}

JNIEXPORT void JNICALL Java_Win32RegKey_setValue
  (JNIEnv* env, jobject this_obj, jstring name, jobject value)
{  const char* cname;
   jstring path;
   const char* cpath;
   HKEY hkey;
   DWORD type;
   DWORD size;
   jclass this_class;
   jclass class_value;
   jclass class_Integer;
   jfieldID id_root;
   jfieldID id_path;
   HKEY root;
   const char* cvalue;
   int ivalue;

   /* get the class */
   this_class = (*env)->GetObjectClass(env, this_obj);

   /* get the field IDs */
   id_root = (*env)->GetFieldID(env, this_class, "root", "I");
   id_path = (*env)->GetFieldID(env, this_class, "path",
      "Ljava/lang/String;");

   /* get the fields */
   root = (HKEY)(*env)->GetIntField(env, this_obj, id_root);
   path = (jstring)(*env)->GetObjectField(env, this_obj,
```

```
   id_path);
cpath = (*env)->GetStringUTFChars(env, path, NULL);

/* open the registry key */
if (RegOpenKeyEx(root, cpath, 0, KEY_WRITE, &hkey)
   != ERROR_SUCCESS)
{  (*env)->ThrowNew(env,
      (*env)->FindClass(env, "Win32RegKeyException"),
      "Open key failed");
   (*env)->ReleaseStringUTFChars(env, path, cpath);
   return;
}

(*env)->ReleaseStringUTFChars(env, path, cpath);
cname = (*env)->GetStringUTFChars(env, name, NULL);

class_value = (*env)->GetObjectClass(env, value);
class_Integer = (*env)->FindClass(env, "java/lang/Integer");
/* determine the type of the value object */
if ((*env)->IsAssignableFrom(env, class_value,
   (*env)->FindClass(env, "java/lang/String")))
{  /* it is a string--get a pointer to the characters */
   cvalue = (*env)->GetStringUTFChars(env, (jstring)value,
      NULL);
   type = REG_SZ;
   size = (*env)->GetStringLength(env, (jstring)value) + 1;
}
else if ((*env)->IsAssignableFrom(env, class_value,
   class_Integer))
{  /* it is an integer--call intValue to get the value */
   jmethodID id_intValue = (*env)->GetMethodID(env,
      class_Integer, "intValue", "()I");
   ivalue = (*env)->CallIntMethod(env, value, id_intValue);
   type = REG_DWORD;
   cvalue = (char*)&ivalue;
   size = 4;
}
else if ((*env)->IsAssignableFrom(env, class_value,
   (*env)->FindClass(env, "[B")))
{  /* it is a byte array--get a pointer to the bytes */
   type = REG_BINARY;
   cvalue = (char*)(*env)->GetByteArrayElements(env,
      (jarray)value, NULL);
   size = (*env)->GetArrayLength(env, (jarray)value);
}
else
{  /* we don't know how to handle this type */
   (*env)->ThrowNew(env,
      (*env)->FindClass(env, "Win32RegKeyException"),
      "Unsupported value type");
   RegCloseKey(hkey);
   (*env)->ReleaseStringUTFChars(env, name, cname);
```

```
      return;
   }

   /* set the value */
   if (RegSetValueEx(hkey, cname, 0, type, cvalue, size)
      != ERROR_SUCCESS)
   {  (*env)->ThrowNew(env,
         (*env)->FindClass(env, "Win32RegKeyException"),
         "Query value key failed");
   }

   RegCloseKey(hkey);
   (*env)->ReleaseStringUTFChars(env, name, cname);

   /* if the value was a string or byte array, release the
      pointer */
   if (type == REG_SZ)
   {  (*env)->ReleaseStringUTFChars(env, (jstring)value,
         cvalue);
   }
   else if (type == REG_BINARY)
   {  (*env)->ReleaseByteArrayElements(env, (jarray)value,
         (byte*)cvalue, 0);
   }
}

static int startNameEnumeration(JNIEnv* env, jobject this_obj,
   jclass this_class)
/* helper function to start enumeration of names
*/
{  jfieldID id_index;
   jfieldID id_count;
   jfieldID id_root;
   jfieldID id_path;
   jfieldID id_hkey;
   jfieldID id_maxsize;

   HKEY root;
   jstring path;
   const char* cpath;
   HKEY hkey;
   int maxsize = 0;
   int count = 0;

   /* get the field IDs */
   id_root = (*env)->GetFieldID(env, this_class, "root", "I");
   id_path = (*env)->GetFieldID(env, this_class, "path",
      "Ljava/lang/String;");
   id_hkey = (*env)->GetFieldID(env, this_class, "hkey", "I");
   id_maxsize = (*env)->GetFieldID(env, this_class, "maxsize",
      "I");
   id_index = (*env)->GetFieldID(env, this_class, "index",
```

```
         "I");
      id_count = (*env)->GetFieldID(env, this_class, "count",
         "I");

      /* get the field values */
      root = (HKEY)(*env)->GetIntField(env, this_obj, id_root);
      path = (jstring)(*env)->GetObjectField(env, this_obj,
         id_path);
      cpath = (*env)->GetStringUTFChars(env, path, NULL);

      /* open the registry key */
      if (RegOpenKeyEx(root, cpath, 0, KEY_READ, &hkey)
         != ERROR_SUCCESS)
      {  (*env)->ThrowNew(env,
            (*env)->FindClass(env, "Win32RegKeyException"),
             "Open key failed");
         (*env)->ReleaseStringUTFChars(env, path, cpath);
         return -1;
      }
      (*env)->ReleaseStringUTFChars(env, path, cpath);

      /* query count and max length of names */
      if (RegQueryInfoKey(hkey, NULL, NULL, NULL, NULL,
         NULL, NULL, &count, &maxsize, NULL, NULL, NULL)
         != ERROR_SUCCESS)
      {  (*env)->ThrowNew(env,
            (*env)->FindClass(env, "Win32RegKeyException"),
             "Query info key failed");
         return -1;
      }

      /* set the field values */
      (*env)->SetIntField(env, this_obj, id_hkey, (DWORD)hkey);
      (*env)->SetIntField(env, this_obj, id_maxsize, maxsize + 1);
      (*env)->SetIntField(env, this_obj, id_index, 0);
      (*env)->SetIntField(env, this_obj, id_count, count);
      return count;
   }

   JNIEXPORT jboolean JNICALL
      Java_Win32RegKeyNameEnumeration_hasMoreElements
      (JNIEnv* env, jobject this_obj)
   {  jclass this_class;
      jfieldID id_index;
      jfieldID id_count;
      int index;
      int count;
      /* get the class */
      this_class = (*env)->GetObjectClass(env, this_obj);

      /* get the field IDs */
      id_index = (*env)->GetFieldID(env, this_class, "index",
```

```
      "I");
   id_count = (*env)->GetFieldID(env, this_class, "count",
      "I");

   index = (*env)->GetIntField(env, this_obj, id_index);
   if (index == -1) /* first time */
   {  count = startNameEnumeration(env, this_obj, this_class);
      index = 0;
   }
   else
      count = (*env)->GetIntField(env, this_obj, id_count);
   return index < count;
}

JNIEXPORT jobject JNICALL
   Java_Win32RegKeyNameEnumeration_nextElement
   (JNIEnv* env, jobject this_obj)
{  jclass this_class;
   jfieldID id_index;
   jfieldID id_hkey;
   jfieldID id_count;
   jfieldID id_maxsize;

   HKEY hkey;
   int index;
   int count;
   int maxsize;

   char* cret;
   jstring ret;

  /* get the class */
   this_class = (*env)->GetObjectClass(env, this_obj);

   /* get the field IDs */
   id_index = (*env)->GetFieldID(env, this_class, "index",
      "I");
   id_count = (*env)->GetFieldID(env, this_class, "count",
      "I");
   id_hkey = (*env)->GetFieldID(env, this_class, "hkey", "I");
   id_maxsize = (*env)->GetFieldID(env, this_class, "maxsize",
      "I");

   index = (*env)->GetIntField(env, this_obj, id_index);
   if (index == -1) /* first time */
   {  count = startNameEnumeration(env, this_obj, this_class);
      index = 0;
   }
   else
      count = (*env)->GetIntField(env, this_obj, id_count);

   if (index >= count) /* already at end */
```

```
    {  (*env)->ThrowNew(env,
          (*env)->FindClass(env,
          "java/util/NoSuchElementException"),
          "past end of enumeration");
       return NULL;
    }

    maxsize = (*env)->GetIntField(env, this_obj, id_maxsize);
    hkey = (HKEY)(*env)->GetIntField(env, this_obj, id_hkey);
    cret = (char*)malloc(maxsize);

    /* find the next name */
    if (RegEnumValue(hkey, index, cret, &maxsize, NULL, NULL,
       NULL, NULL) != ERROR_SUCCESS)
    {  (*env)->ThrowNew(env,
          (*env)->FindClass(env, "Win32RegKeyException"),
          "Enum value failed");
       free(cret);
       RegCloseKey(hkey);
       (*env)->SetIntField(env, this_obj, id_index, count);
       return NULL;
    }

    ret = (*env)->NewStringUTF(env, cret);
    free(cret);

    /* increment index */
    index++;
    (*env)->SetIntField(env, this_obj, id_index, index);

    if (index == count) /* at end */
    {  RegCloseKey(hkey);
    }

    return ret;
}
```

Example 11–23: Win32RegKeyTest.java

```
import java.util.*;

public class Win32RegKeyTest
{  public static void main(String[] args)
   {  Win32RegKey key = new Win32RegKey(
         Win32RegKey.HKEY_CURRENT_USER,
         "Software\\Microsoft\\MS Setup (ACME)\\User Info");

      key.setValue("Default user", "Bozo the clown");
      key.setValue("Lucky number", new Integer(13));
      key.setValue("Small primes", new byte[]
```

```
         { 2, 3, 5, 7, 11 });

      Enumeration enum = key.names();

      while (enum.hasMoreElements())
      {  String name = (String)enum.nextElement();
         System.out.print(name + " = ");

         Object value = key.getValue(name);

         if (value instanceof byte[])
         {  byte[] bvalue = (byte[])value;
            for (int i = 0; i < bvalue.length; i++)
               System.out.print((bvalue[i] & 0xFF) + " ");
         }
         else System.out.print(value);

         System.out.println();
      }
   }
}
```

Type inquiry functions

- `jboolean IsAssignableFrom(JNIEnv *env, jclass cl1, jclass cl2)`
  returns `JNI_TRUE` if objects of the first class can be assigned to objects of the second class; `JNI_FALSE` otherwise. This is the case when the classes are the same, `cl1` is a subclass of `cl2`, or `cl2` represents an interface that is implemented by `cl1` or one of its superclasses.

Parameters:	`env`	the JNI interface pointer
	`cl1,cl2`	class references

- `jclass GetSuperClass(JNIEnv *env, jclass cl)`
  returns the superclass of a class. If `cl` represents the class `Object` or an interface, returns `NULL`.

Parameters:	`env`	the JNI interface pointer
	`cl`	a class reference

Index

A

903

D

E

F

G

H

I

J

K

L

M

N

O

P

Q

R

S

917

T

U

V

W

Sun Microsystems, Inc.

Binary Code License Agreement

READ THE TERMS OF THIS AGREEMENT AND ANY PROVIDED SUPPLEMENTAL LICENSE TERMS (COLLECTIVELY "AGREEMENT") CAREFULLY BEFORE OPENING THE SOFTWARE MEDIA PACKAGE. BY OPENING THE SOFTWARE MEDIA PACKAGE, YOU AGREE TO THE TERMS OF THIS AGREEMENT. IF YOU ARE ACCESSING THE SOFTWARE ELECTRONICALLY INDICATE YOUR ACCEPTANCE OF THESE TERMS BY SELECTING THE "ACCEPT" BUTTON AT THE END OF THIS AGREEMENT. IF YOU DO NOT AGREE TO ALL OF THESE TERMS, PROMPTLY RETURN THE UNUSED SOFTWARE TO YOUR PLACE OF PURCHASE FOR A REFUND OR, IF THE SOFTWARE IS ACCESSED ELECTRONICALLY, SELECT THE "DECLINE" BUTTON AT THE END OF THIS AGREEMENT.

1. **License to Use.** Sun grants to you a non-exclusive and non-transferable license for the internal use only of the accompanying software and documentation and any error corrections provided by Sun (collectively "Software"), by the number of users and the class of computer hardware for which the corresponding fee has been paid.

2. **Restrictions**. Software is confidential and copyrighted. Title to Software and all associated intellectual property rights is retained by Sun and/or its licensors. Except as specifically authorized in any Supplemental License Terms, you may not make copies of Software, other than a single copy of Software for archival purposes. Unless enforcement is prohibited by applicable law, you may not modify, decompile, disassemble, or otherwise reverse engineer Software. Software is not designed or licensed for use in on-line control of aircraft, air traffic, aircraft or navigation or aircraft communications; or in the design, construction, operation or maintenance of any nuclear facility. You warrant that you will not use Software for these purposes. You may not publish or provide the results of any benchmark or comparison tests run on Software to any third party without the prior written consent of Sun. No right, title or interest in or to any trademark, service mark, logo, or trade name of Sun or its licensors is granted under this Agreement.

3. **Limited Warranty.** Sun warrants to you that for a period of ninety (90) days from the date of purchase, as evidenced by a copy of the receipt, the media on which Software is furnished (if any) will be free of defects in materials and workmanship under normal use. Except for the foregoing, Software is provided "AS IS". Your exclusive remedy and Sun's entire liability under this limited warranty will be at Sun's option to replace Software media or refund the fee paid for Software.

4. **Disclaimer of Warranty.** UNLESS SPECIFIED IN THIS AGREEMENT, ALL EXPRESS OR IMPLIED CONDITIONS, REPRESENTATIONS AND WARRANTIES, INCLUDING ANY IMPLIED WARRANTY OF MERCHANTABILITY, FITNESS FOR A PARTICULAR PURPOSE, OR NON-INFRINGEMENT, ARE DISCLAIMED, EXCEPT TO THE EXTENT THAT THESE DISCLAIMERS ARE HELD TO BE LEGALLY INVALID.

5. **Limitation of Liability.** TO THE EXTENT NOT PROHIBITED BY APPLICABLE LAW, IN NO EVENT WILL SUN OR ITS LICENSORS BE LIABLE FOR ANY LOST REVENUE, PROFIT OR DATA, OR FOR SPECIAL, INDIRECT, CONSEQUENTIAL, INCIDENTAL OR PUNITIVE DAMAGES, HOWEVER CAUSED AND REGARDLESS OF THE THEORY OF LIABILITY, ARISING OUT OF OR RELATED TO THE USE OF OR INABILITY TO USE SOFTWARE, EVEN IF SUN HAS BEEN ADVISED OF THE POSSIBILITY OF SUCH DAMAGES. In no event will Sun's liability to you, whether in contract, tort (including negligence), or otherwise, exceed the amount paid by you for Software under this Agreement. The foregoing limitations will apply even if the above stated warranty fails of its essential purpose.

6. **Termination.** This Agreement is effective until terminated. You may terminate this Agreement at any time by destroying all copies of Software. This Agreement will terminate immediately without notice from Sun if you fail to comply with any provision of this Agreement. Upon termination, you must destroy all copies of Software.

7. **Export Regulations.** All Software and technical data delivered under this Agreement are subject to U.S. export control laws and may be subject to export or import regulations in other countries. You agree to comply strictly with all such laws and regulations and acknowledge that you have the responsibility to obtain such licenses to export, re-export, or import as may be required after delivery to you.

8. **U.S. Government Restricted Rights.** Use, duplication, or disclosure by the U.S. Government is subject to restrictions set forth in this Agreement and as provided in DFARS 227.7202-1(a) and 227.7202-3(a) (1995), DFARS 252.227-7013(c)(1)(ii) (Oct 1988), FAR 12.212(a)(1995), FAR 52.227-19 (June 1987), or FAR 52.227-14 (ALT III) (June 1987), as applicable.

9. **Governing Law.** Any action related to this Agreement will be governed by California law and controlling U.S. federal law. No choice of law rules of any jurisdiction will apply.

10. **Severability.** If any provision of this Agreement is held to be unenforceable, this Agreement will remain in effect with the provision omitted, unless omission of the provision would frustrate the intent of the parties, in which case this Agreement will immediately terminate.

11. **Integration.** This Agreement is the entire agreement between you and Sun relating to its subject matter. It supersedes all prior or contemporaneous oral or written communications, proposals, representations and warranties and prevails over any conflicting or additional terms of any quote, order, acknowledgment, or other communication between the parties relating to its subject matter during the term of this Agreement. No modification of this Agreement will be binding, unless in writing and signed by an authorized representative of each party.

For inquiries please contact: Sun Microsystems, Inc., 901 San Antonio Road, Palo Alto, California 94303

JAVA™ DEVELOPMENT KIT VERSION 1.2
SUPPLEMENTAL LICENSE TERMS

These supplemental terms ("Supplement") add to the terms of the Binary Code License Agreement ("Agreement"). Capitalized terms not defined herein shall have the same meanings ascribed to them in the Agreement. The Supplement terms shall supersede any inconsistent or conflicting terms in the Agreement.

1. Limited License Grant. Sun grants to you a non-exclusive, non-transferable limited license to use the Software without fee for evaluation of the Software and for development of Java™ applets and applications provided that you: (i) may not re-distribute the Software in whole or in part, either separately or included with a product. (ii) may not create, or authorize your licensees to create additional classes, interfaces, or subpackages that are contained in the "java" or "sun" packages or similar as specified by Sun in any class file naming convention; and (iii) agree to the extent Programs are developed which utilize the Windows 95/98 style graphical user interface or components contained therein, such applets or applications may only be developed to run on a Windows 95/98 or Windows NT platform. Refer to the Java Runtime Environment Version 1.2 binary code license (http://java.sun.com/products/JDK/1.2/index.html) for the availability of runtime code which may be distributed with Java applets and applications.

2. Java Platform Interface. In the event that Licensee creates an additional API(s) which: (i) extends the functionality of a Java Environment; and, (ii) is exposed to third party software developers for the purpose of developing additional software which invokes such additional API, Licensee must promptly publish broadly an accurate specification for such API for free use by all developers.

3. Trademarks and Logos. This Agreement does not authorize Licensee to use any Sun name, trademark or logo. Licensee acknowledges as between it and Sun that Sun owns the Java trademark and all Java-related trademarks, logos and icons including the Coffee Cup and Duke ("Java Marks") and agrees to comply with the Java Trademark Guidelines at http://java.sun.com/trademarks.html.

4. High Risk Activities. Notwithstanding Section 2, with respect to high risk activities, the following language shall apply: the Software is not designed or intended for use in on-line control of aircraft, air traffic, aircraft navigation or aircraft communications; or in the design, construction, operation or maintenance of any nuclear facility. Sun disclaims any express or implied warranty of fitness for such uses.

5. Source Code. Software may contain source code that is provided solely for reference purposes pursuant to the terms of this Agreement.

Installing the Core Java Example Files

The CD-ROM contains the source code for all example programs in the book. All files are packed inside a single ZIP archive, `corejava.zip`.

If you have a ZIP utility such as WinZip (which is supplied on the CD-ROM), you can use it to unzip the files. Otherwise, you need to first install the Java 2 SDK. Then use the `jar` program to unzip the file:

- Make sure the SDK is installed.
- Make a directory `CoreJavaBook`.
- Copy the `corejava.zip` file to that directory.
- Change to that directory.
- Execute the command
  ```
  jar xvf corejava.zip
  ```

Updates and Bug Fixes

The CD-ROM contains well over a hundred sample programs, and some of them are bound to have minor glitches and inconsistencies. We keep a list of frequently asked questions, a list of typographical errors, and bug fixes on the *Core Java* Web page at `http://www.horstmann.com/corejava.html`. We very much welcome any reports of typographical errors, example program bugs, and suggestions for improvement.

Before contacting us, please consider the following:

1. Please check the FAQ and list of bug reports on the *Core Java* Web page before mailing us. We get many duplicate queries and bug reports.
2. Please, no requests for handholding. Many readers have successfully compiled and executed the programs on the CD-ROM. If you have problems, there is an overwhelming likelihood that the problem is on your end, not because of a flaw with the CD-ROM contents. On the other hand, if we goofed and there is a serious problem with the CD-ROM, then there is an overwhelming chance that hundreds of readers complained to us already and that you will find a resolution on the FAQ.
3. We want to support and improve the *Core Java* book and example files, but we cannot help you with problems with your development environment or the free programs on the CD-ROM. Please contact the product vendor for assistance in those cases.
4. Finally, when contacting us, please use e-mail only. Please don't be disappointed if we don't answer every query or if we don't get back to you immediately. We do read all e-mail and consider your input to make future editions of this book clearer and more informative.

Technical Support

Prentice Hall does not offer technical support for the software on this CD-ROM. However, if there is a problem with the media, you may obtain a replacement copy by e-mailing us with your problem at: `disc_exchange@prenhall.com`.

Installing the CD-ROM

Contents of the CD-ROM

The CD-ROM has the following directory structure:

```
corejava
hxwrkshp
jdk
oracle
pointbas
textpad
winzip
```

The `corejava` directory contains the example files for this volume of *Core Java*. The `jdk` directory contains the Java™2 SDK Standard Edition, v. 1.2, for Windows 95/NT and for the Solaris™ Operating Environment. The `pointbas` directory contains an evaluation version of the PointBase Mobile Edition database. The `oracle` directory contains JDBC drivers for the Oracle 8.1 database.

NOTE: If you do not have a CD-ROM drive, you can download the materials from the Internet. Look for them at the following URLs:

Core Java files	`www.phptr.com/corejava`
Hex Workshop	`www.bpsoft.com`
Java 2 SDK	`java.sun.com/jdk`
Oracle	`www.oracle.com`
PointBase	`www.pointbase.com`
TextPad	`www.textpad.com`
Winzip	`www.winzip.com`

TIP: Sun Microsystems frequently releases updates to the Java 2 SDK. You should check the Java web site `http://java.sun.com/jdk` to see whether a newer version is available. In that case, we recommend that you download and install the SDK from the Web instead of the CD-ROM.

(continued on previous page)